THE ROUGH GUIDE TO

Sardinia

written and researched by

Robert Andrews

ROUGH GUIDES

roughguides.com

Contents

Introduction to
Sardinia

Undeniably and exuberantly Italian, yet expressing a unique regional identity, Sardinia presents a distinctive take on the Mediterranean island experience. Its position midway between the Italian mainland and the North African coast, and the traces left by the many invaders and settlers who shaped its history, have together forged a hybrid, fragmented character – "lost between Europe and Africa", as D.H. Lawrence put it, "and belonging to nowhere". In fact the Sard people reject the need to "belong" anywhere. While accepting their shared Italian culture, they are also passionately loyal to their island home in all its diversity, from the rocky headlands and secluded beaches on the coast to the forested mountains and pungent expanses of wilderness in the interior.

Together with these physical differences go deep cultural contrasts, often corresponding to the mosaic of smaller territories that make up the island. From Gallura and Logudoro in the north to Sulcis and Sarrabus in the south, each has its own traditions, dialects and historical roots. At a still more local level, each village celebrates its individuality at the many flamboyant **festivals** that take place throughout the year, ranging from rowdy medieval pageants to dignified religious processions, all helping to keep tradition alive in an island where the past is inescapable.

And yet, while Sardinia is big enough to accommodate this range of diverse faces – it's the Mediterranean's second-biggest island after Sicily (though with less than a third of Sicily's population) – it's small and manageable enough to allow you to travel from the sleek yachts and glistening beaches of the fabled Costa Smeralda to the granite *stazzi*, or farm dwellings, of the mountainous interior in less than an hour.

ABOVE COASTAL WATCHTOWER, SANTA MARIA NAVARRESE

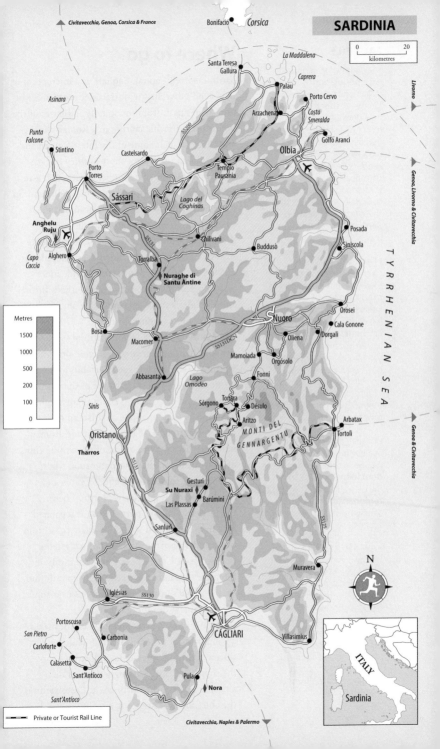

FACT FILE

• Sardinia (Sardegna in Italian) has a **population** of 1.66 million, and nearly twice that number of **sheep**. The flocks have diminished significantly in recent years, but the Italian mainland's cartoon caricature of the Sards perpetuates the image of the wily shepherd, be-capped and in brown corduroys, or else swathed in hairy sheepskins. The local sheep's cheese, **Pecorino Sardo**, is one of Italy's most flavoursome cheeses.

• Sardinia's position on the chief Mediterranean trade routes has ensured that it has rarely been free of foreign intervention – though this has endowed the island with a rich **heritage** of archeological and artistic monuments. The most truly Sardinian remains, however, are prehistoric, notably the "fairy houses", "giants' tombs" and seven thousand-odd *nuraghi* (stone towers) dotted around.

• Despite the centuries of occupation, Sardinia has retained a fiercely **independent identity**. Since 1948 the island has had a degree of **regional autonomy**, but only a minority of the population supports the separatist cause.

• The official **Sardinian flag** is known as the Quattro Mori, for the four Moors depicted on a white background. Until 1999, the four were blindfolded and facing west – towards Spain, the former colonial ruler – but the flag was altered to show the heads unblindfolded and looking east: liberated, enlightened and gazing steadily across to the Italian mainland.

Where to go

Sardinia's lively capital, **Cágliari**, is a microcosm of the island's diversity, with traces of every phase of the island's past, from the spindly statuettes of the prehistoric nuraghic culture to a Roman theatre and Pisan citadel. Some of the finest Roman and Carthaginian ruins are a short journey outside town at **Nora**, one of a number of sites that attest to Sardinia's former prominence in Mediterranean trade. Many of the powers that occupied the island were drawn to its mines, still visible throughout the regions of **Sulcis** and **Iglesiente**, west of Cágliari. Off the Sulcis coast, the islands of **Sant'Antíoco** and **San Pietro** provide more archeological remains, while the southern littoral and the Iglesiente's **Costa Verde** are among Sardinia's most scenic coastlines.

La Marmilla, a hilly region north of Cágliari, contains Sardinia's greatest nuraghic site, **Su Nuraxi**, while the rugged **Sarrabus** area east of the capital is fringed by some of the island's most spectacular beaches. Halfway up Sardinia's western side, the province of **Oristano** holds numerous nuraghic, Carthaginian and Roman remains, the most important of which, the ruins of **Tharros**, lie on the **Sinis peninsula**, whose lagoons and coasts attract aquatic birds and beach pilgrims respectively. North of here, the picturesque river port of **Bosa** is separated by a long, unspoiled stretch of rocky coast from the popular resort of **Alghero**, which retains its distinctive Catalan character, the result of intensive settlement five centuries ago. **Stintino**, on the island's northwestern tip, lies near some beaches of jaw-dropping beauty.

Inland, Sardinia's second city, **Sássari**, makes a good base for touring the Pisan churches scattered throughout the Logudoro area to the south and east. Strikingly situated on a promontory of the north coast, **Castelsardo** is the chief town of **Anglona**, a region indelibly

RIGHT THARROS, SINIS PENINSULA

associated with the Doria family of Genoa – one of the Mediterranean's leading mercantile powers in the Middle Ages. Bordering it, **Gallura**'s jagged-peaked interior makes a dramatic backdrop to its famously beautiful granite coastline, where the **Costa Smeralda** remains an exclusive enclave for celebs and tycoons. This and other areas of the northeast coast hold some enticing stretches of rocky or sandy shore, with some of the best beaches clustered around **Palau**, embarkation point for trips to the beautiful **Maddalena archipelago**, and **Santa Teresa Gallura** on Sardinia's northern tip, the chief port for connections with Corsica.

Below **Olbia** – the main entry point from the mainland – most of Sardinia's eastern coast is largely inaccessible, the sheer cliff walls punctuated by a few developed holiday spots such as **Cala Gonone** and **Santa Maria Navarrese**. The provinces of **Nuoro** and **Ogliastra** occupy most of the mountainous interior of this coast, and are the best places to encounter the last authentic remnants of the island's rural culture, particularly its costumes and village festivals. This is especially true in the central area known as **Barbagia**, where the sparse population is concentrated in small, insulated villages that provide an excellent opportunity to view the quiet life of the interior at

SARDINIA'S TOP 10 BEACHES

Sardinia has some of the Mediterranean's most gorgeous **beaches**. On the whole, they're clean and pollution-free, and many have facilities operating from June to September – a bar or two, sunloungers and parasols to rent, and often activities available such as windsurfing and pedalo and canoe rental. Otherwise, seek out more remote sections without any of the paraphernalia, and bring your own shade.

Liscia Ruja, Costa Smeralda (see p.245)
Chia, south coast (see p.86)
Rena Bianca, Santa Teresa Gallura (see p.257)
Capo Carbonara, southeast coast (see p.129)
Cala Sinzias, Costa Rei (see p.131)

Piscinas, Costa Verde (see p.108)
Cala Corsara, Spargi, La Maddalena (see p.257)
Sa Mesa Lunga, Sinis peninsula (see p.155)
La Pelosa, northwest (see p.199)
Spiaggia Cartoe, east coast (see p.300)

first hand, and make useful bases for mountain rambles. If your image of Sardinia is all shaggy sheep and offbeat folklore – the kind of place depicted in films like *Padre Padrone* – then these mountain slopes will probably fit the bill.

When to go

The best advice is to avoid the month of **August** if at all possible. Travelling at this time is by no means impossible, but the negative factors include sweltering heat, crowds, increased prices, frayed tempers and scarce accommodation. June, July and September can also be oppressively hot, but there is nothing like the kind of holiday

ABOVE SU GIUDEU BEACH, CHIA **RIGHT FROM TOP** SANT'EFISIO FESTIVAL, CÁGLIARI; NIGHTLIFE IN CÁGLIARI

SARDINIA'S PISAN CHURCHES

Visitors to Sardinia who have spent any time in Tuscany may be surprised to discover a whole string of **Romanesque churches** scattered throughout the island which would look more at home in that mainland region. The odd juxtaposition is due to the close association of **Pisa** with Sardinia between the eleventh and fourteenth centuries. Religious orders were introduced and architects imported, leading to the construction of churches all over the island, with a particular concentration in the Logudoro and Anglona areas of northern Sardinia. You'll encounter the characteristic black-and-white pattern in the unlikeliest of places, sometimes in remote countryside, such as the marooned-looking **Santíssima Trinità di Saccargia**. Two of the most monumental examples, **San Gavino** and **San Símplicio**, seem lost among the quiet backstreets of Porto Torres and Olbia respectively. Most of the surviving specimens are in a good state of repair, but the interiors have little in the way of decoration – which helps to preserve their murky medieval atmosphere intact.

frenzy of the peak weeks. You can count on **swimming** fairly comfortably at any time between May and October, and you won't be considered excessively eccentric if you take dips during the winter months. There's much to be said for travelling in Sardinia in **winter** – the weather can be warm and clear and the tourist presence is refreshingly low-key, though the diminished daylight hours can limit your freedom of movement, and you may find many facilities (including most campsites) closed. Some of the **best festivals** take place in **spring**, and this is also the ideal period for walking, when the countryside is at its most vibrant, the air limpid and the wildlife abundant. **Autumn** is also an inspiring time for being outdoors, especially for the gradations of colour on the forested slopes of the interior.

AVERAGE DAILY TEMPERATURES AND MONTHLY RAINFALL

	Jan	Feb	Mar	Apr	May	Jun	Jul	Aug	Sep	Oct	Nov	Dec
CÁGLIARI (SEA LEVEL)												
Av temp (°C)	10	11	12.5	14.5	18	24	25	25.5	23	18.5	14	12
Av temp (°F)	50	52	54.5	58	64.5	75	77	78	73.5	65.5	57	53.5
Rainfall (mm)	4.4	4	3.9	3.5	3.5	0.8	0.5	0.8	3	5	6	7
NUORO (ALT 550M/1804FT)												
Av temp (°C)	4	5	7	10	14	19	23	22	19	15	9	6
Av temp (°F)	39	41	44.5	50	57	66	73.5	71.5	66	59	48	43
Rainfall (mm)	15.5	15	14	11.5	10	3.5	1.5	1.5	6	10.5	15	18

ABOVE SANTÍSSIMA TRINITÀ DI SACCARGIA, NEAR SÁSSARI

Author picks

Sardinia is a place that constantly throws up new discoveries and experiences not always appearing in the tourist brochures. Here's a selection of personal favourites:

Church treasures You don't have to visit galleries to see great art in Sardinia – some of the smallest, most unprepossessing churches preserve some real gems of medieval art; the magnificent altarpiece in San Pietro Apostolo, Tuili (p.124), is well worth a detour.

Rides and drives The landscape of Sardinia is itself one of its greatest pleasures, best appreciated on long, meandering journeys through the mountainous interior. Favourite routes include the roads running through Gerrei (p.128), south of Dorgali (p.298) and west of Aggius (p.266).

Isles of wonder The island has its own subgroups of islands, the most dramatic of which is the archipelago of La Maddalena, off the northeastern coast; you can explore the pristine beaches and silky waters on boat trips – join a group or rent your own motor-dinghy (p.252).

Ancient towers *Nuraghe*-spotting is one of the classic pastimes when travelling through the island. Some of these prehistoric monuments are well restored and can only be visited with a ticket; others are mossy ruins in fields, free to enter. One of the most satisfying is the Nuraghe Mannu outside Cala Gonone (p.300).

Culinary pursuits You'll enjoy exquisite sea- and land-based dishes in restaurants throughout the island, but some of the best places, combining tasteful decor, friendly service and outstanding, reasonably priced food, are off the tourist track, in such inland centres as Sássari (p.212) and Nuoro (p.279).

On the beach Even the pickiest of beach aficionados will be sated with the choice of swimming spots around Sardinia's coasts. From perennial favourites to scrubby hideaways in secluded coves or wild, dune-backed strands stretching to the horizon, there's something for everyone. We've listed our top spots on p.8.

> Our author recommendations don't end here. We've flagged up our favourite places – a perfectly sited hotel, an atmospheric café, a special restaurant – throughout the guide, highlighted with the ★ symbol.

FROM TOP MORTORIO, AN ISLAND OFF THE COSTA SMERALDA; A PANEL FROM THE RETABLO DI SAN PIETRO, SAN PIETRO APOSTOLO

17

things not to miss

It's not possible to see everything Sardinia has to offer in one trip – and we don't suggest you try. What follows is a selective taste of the island's highlights: historic monuments, dramatic landscapes and great beaches. All highlights are colour-coded by chapter and have a page reference to take you straight into the Guide, where you can find out more.

1

1 THARROS, SINIS PENINSULA
Founded by the Phoenicians on a promontory jutting into the sea, this historic site retains extensive evidence of the Punic and Roman settlers who followed.

2 S'ARDIA, SÉDILO
This manic horse race at dawn has ancient origins – it was originally held in honour of the emperor Constantine. Swathed in clouds of dust and soot, the riders tear around the church of the local saint with reckless abandon.

3 SEAFOOD IN ALGHERO
Alghero's restaurants are renowned for their fresh seafood platters, with ingredients straight off the boat.

4 BOSA
Explore the atmospheric lanes of this quiet riverside town overlooked by a hilltop castle, dine at its excellent restaurants and enjoy the enticing beaches nearby. Lobster is the local speciality.

5 WALK TO TÍSCALI
The climb to this nuraghic village – cunningly hidden within a huge cave in the Lanaittu valley east of Nuoro – makes a fabulous half-day hike.

6 ETHNOGRAPHIC MUSEUM, NUORO
A visit to this extensive collection – crammed with masks, costumes, craftwork and musical instruments – offers intriguing insights into the local culture.

7 INLAND GALLURA
Interspersed with thick groves of cork oaks, the granite rockscape of this scarcely populated mountainous zone offers unforgettable panoramas.

8 EASTER CELEBRATIONS
Costumes, processions and intense drama are the main ingredients of Sardinia's various *feste* commemorating Easter.

9 NORA
An important Phoenician, Carthaginian and Roman centre for more than a thousand years, Nora's splendid seaside position and fragmentary ruins still evoke its former glory.

10 CASTELSARDO OLD TOWN
With historic churches buried among its steep lanes, and a castle/museum at its summit affording distant coastal views, this old Doria stronghold repays the uphill slog.

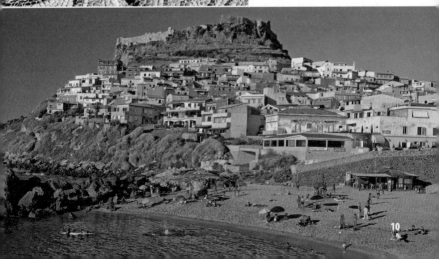

11 LA PELOSA
The beaches and rocky backdrop of this beauty spot are postcard-perfect, with aquamarine water and mesmerizing views.

12 NURAGHE SANTU ANTINE
One of the island's most imposing *nuraghi*, on the plains southeast of Sássari amid a cluster of these prehistoric monuments.

13 SA SARTIGLIA, ORISTANO
Costumed high jinks and equestrian showmanship recall the medieval roots of this boisterous festival.

14 SÁSSARI'S OLD TOWN
The compact old quarter of Sardinia's second city makes for an atmospheric wander through its medieval lanes.

15 NEPTUNE'S GROTTO, ALGHERO
Stalactites, stalagmites and eccentric rock formations are the highlights of a tour through the Grotta di Nettuno, a cave complex set in towering cliffs by the sea.

16 MUSEO ARCHEOLOGICO, CÁGLIARI
Sardinia's premier archeological collection includes grinning deities, nuraghic figurines and ancient Phoenician inscriptions.

17 BASTIONE SAINT REMY, CÁGLIARI
Part of the formidable city walls surrounding the old citadel, this offers stupendous views of the city and coast – especially recommended at sunset.

14

15

16

17

Itineraries

The following itineraries suggest a framework for enjoying the best that Sardinia has to offer. They dip into the island's historical treasures as well as allowing you to leg-stretch amid some of Sardinia's finest scenery.

ON THE CASTLE TRAIL

Whether they are prestige projects for bored aristocrats, eccentric family mansions or grim reminders of past oppression, Sardinia's castles come in all shapes and sizes. Often, however, they occupy lofty sites with unrivalled views over the landscape.

❶ Siliqua Probably built by the notorious Ugolino della Gherardesca in the thirteenth century, the lofty, ruined Castello di Acquafredda later became a prison for Ugolino's son. **See p.103**

❷ Sanluri The compact Castello di Eleonora di Arborea is named after Sardinia's medieval warrior queen and holds an entertaining array of military and historical mementos. **See p.117**

❸ Bosa The shell of Castello Malaspina crowns this riverside town with 360-degree views. The walls are all that's left of the thirteenth-century construction, within which stands a frescoed medieval church. **See p.192**

❹ Burgos Completed in the fourteenth century, La Reggia dominates the Tirso valley from its high vantage point, and contains an exhibition on Sardinian castle-building. **See p.281**

❺ Castelsardo This Doria stronghold overlooking the sea was at the centre of political and military power struggles for centuries; these days, by contrast, it houses an innocuous museum of basketwork. **See p.220**

❻ Palau There's nothing dainty or self-effacing about the brutally functional fortress overlooking Palau and the Maddalena archipelago, dating from the nineteenth century – but it's still a fabulously panoramic spot. **See p.250**

❼ Posada At the top of this old village, the Castello della Fava stands sentinel over the coast, an atmospheric watchtower with superb views to reward your climb up ladders and through trapdoors to the parapet. **See p.295**

MOUNTAINS AND NATURE

Although most famous for its beaches, Sardinia is essentially a place of mountains and forests, the perfect terrain for cycling, hiking and getting up close to its natural marvels.

❶ Monte Arcosu Home to deer, wildcats and birds of prey, this remote, thickly forested wildlife reserve is crisscrossed with paths and trails. **See p.83**

❷ Sette Fratelli The "Seven Brothers" are easily accessible from Cágliari, but it's one of the island's least-known ranges, sparsely populated and cut through by splashing streams. **See p.132**

❸ Giara di Gésturi Not exactly a mountain, this high plateau is nonetheless a secluded, uncontaminated area of forest and swampy meadows, where miniature wild horses, boars, migrating birds and goats are among the creatures to look out for. **See p.125**

ABOVE CASTELLO MALASPINA, BOSA

❹ Gennargentu Sardinia's central Gennargentu mountains hold the island's highest peaks and remotest tracts. Largely covered with chestnut and oak forests, the area is rich with hiking possibilities and peppered with traditional communities – generally regarded as representing the "real Sardinia". **See p.288**

❺ Montes This high tableland south of Nuoro is empty and desolate but has a scenic splendour – ideal for relatively unstrenuous walking, biking and horseriding. **See p.284**

❻ Supramonte Rising dramatically above Sardinia's east coast, this massif includes two of the island's most renowned hiking trails, leading through the Gorropu gorge and to the nuraghic eyrie of Tíscali, both best explored on organized expeditions. **See p.281**

❼ Monte Limbara The granite peaks of Gallura are perhaps the most breathtaking of Sardinia's highlands, a landscape of boulder-strewn slopes, tranquil lakes, cork forests and distant views to the sea. **See p.264**

NURAGHIC INVESTIGATIONS

From top to bottom, Sardinia is filled with the enigmatic remains of its nuraghic civilization, flourishing between around 1800 BC and 900 BC. The tapering, broad-stoned towers are in various states of dilapidation, and they're usually well worth checking out, but be careful – nuraghe-hunting can become an obsession.

❶ Arzachena Far in spirit from the nearby Costa Smeralda, this inland town has a rich concentration of nuraghi, "giants' tombs" (burial sites), shrines and stone circles within easy reach. **See p.246**

❷ Nuraghe Maiore Outside Tempio Pausania in Gallura, this nuraghe rises grandly above the cork woods and hosts a breeding colony of Lesser Horseshoe bats. There are wonderful views from the top. **See pp.263–264**

❸ Santu Antine Probably a royal palace at one time, with walls nearly 18m high, this stands in an area dubbed "La Valle dei Nuraghi" for its profusion of these monuments. **See p.226**

ON THE CASTLE TRAIL
MOUNTAINS AND NATURE
NURAGHIC INVESTIGATIONS

❹ Losa This mighty example of the nuraghic genre is perhaps the most aesthetically pleasing of all, with clean lines, neat stonework and a vivid growth of orange, yellow and green lichen adorning its sides. **See p.162**

❺ Su Nuraxi The granddaddy of all nuraghi, UNESCO-listed and the one that attracts most visitors, this is the greatest and most sophisticated of all the island's nuraghic complexes – an essential stop. **See p.122**

❻ Arrubiu Unique for its five-towered construction, this rust-red complex sits in isolated majesty in a forsaken tract of country. Sign up for one of the atmospheric night tours to experience it by torchlight. **See p.128**

SARDINIAN CHEESE FOR SALE IN PORTO TORRES

Basics

Getting there

Of the two ways to reach Sardinia – by air or by sea – flying is obviously the quicker, and prices compare well with the long rail/ferry option. Even so, arriving by sea has much to recommend it, helping to give a sense of Sardinia as an island, as well as being more fuel-efficient. Note, however, that the ferries can get uncomfortably congested in high season.

Most direct **flights** from the UK are seasonal, confined to the May–September period; some other services are routed via the Italian mainland. Airfares usually depend on the **season**, with the highest being around July and August; prices drop during the "shoulder" seasons – April to June and September to October – and are cheapest from November to March (excluding Christmas and New Year). The price ranges quoted here assume midweek travel during the high (but not peak) season. The main Sardinian **airports** are outside the towns of Cágliari, Olbia and Alghero.

You might also consider a **package deal** from a tour operator (see pp.22–26). Although Sardinia is not a particularly cheap package holiday destination, many operators offer rates as competitively as you could find on your own and also provide specialized tours, on themes such as hiking or archeology.

Flights from the UK and Ireland

Direct flights from the UK take two to three hours. The **budget airlines** Ryanair (London Stansted and London Luton to Alghero), easyJet (London Stansted to Cágliari and London Gatwick to Olbia) and Thomson (London Gatwick and Manchester to Alghero) usually offer the cheapest fares, with flight-only deals starting at around £40 one-way; some routes are operated between May and September only.

It may also be worth looking at cheap flights to **other Italian destinations** if your preferred dates are unavailable or if you want to combine Sardinia with a visit to somewhere else in Italy, making onward connections by air. We've provided a summary of flights from the Italian mainland (see p.22) and ferries from the Italian mainland and France (see pp.24–25).

Apart from a Ryanair connection between Dublin and Alghero, there are no **direct flights from Ireland** to Sardinia. Aer Lingus and Ryanair fly from Dublin to Rome and Milan; Ryanair also flies to Bologna, Turin, Pisa and Palermo and Aer Lingus flies to Milan, Bologna, Naples and Catania. Flights to Rome (around 3hr) and Milan (2hr 30min) are once or twice daily in summer, less frequent in other periods. Prices can be wildly erratic. Return fares from Dublin to Rome or Milan might cost around €200, according to availability.

Price-wise, it sometimes pays to get to London on one of the numerous daily flights and catch a Sardinia-bound plane from there.

Flights from the US and Canada

Although there are no direct flights **from North America** to Sardinia, you can fly to the Italian mainland from a number of cities. The main point of entry is Rome, though Alitalia, Delta and United also fly direct to Milan. There are plenty of connecting flights from both airports to Sardinia. You could also take advantage of well-priced routes available from all over North America to other **European cities** for onward flights to Sardinia.

Alitalia, the Italian national airline, offers the widest choice of routes between the US and Italy, flying direct from New York, Boston, Chicago, Miami and Los Angeles to Rome and Milan. The **US airlines** Delta Airlines, American Airlines and United also fly to Rome and Milan from New York, taking around 8 hours 30 minutes; for the **connection to Sardinia** add another hour or two, depending on the service, plus any time spent waiting for the connection itself.

Basic round-trip **fares to Italy** vary little between airlines, though it's always worth asking about special promotions. Generally, the cheapest round-trip fare travelling from New York midweek in high season starts at around US$1500.

From Canada, Alitalia flies daily from Toronto to Rome, and Air Canada and Air Transat fly to Rome

A BETTER KIND OF TRAVEL

At Rough Guides we are passionately committed to travel. We believe it helps us understand the world we live in and the people we share it with – and of course tourism is vital to many developing economies. But the scale of modern tourism has also damaged some places irreparably, and climate change is accelerated by most forms of transport, especially flying. All Rough Guides' flights are carbon-offset, and every year we donate money to a variety of environmental charities.

from Toronto and Montréal, all taking 8 to 9 hours. Air Transat also flies to Venice from the same cities. The return fare costs from around Can$1000, to which you should add the fares for the onward flights.

Flights from Australia, New Zealand and South Africa

There are no direct flights **from Australia** and **New Zealand** to Italy or Sardinia, although many airlines fly from Hong Kong, Singapore, Beijing, Shanghai or a Middle Eastern hub to Rome or Milan, from where it's easy to pick up a connecting flight. Reckon on paying Aus$1300–2500 return. The best deals **from New Zealand** work out at around NZ$2200 return, and may involve changes at Los Angeles, Sydney or Hong Kong. With stops, flights to Europe from Australia or New Zealand may take 22 to 35 hours.

From South Africa, flights from Johannesburg or Cape Town to Rome or Milan usually involve a transfer at a European hub such as Amsterdam, Frankfurt, Zürich or Paris, or at Istanbul, Dubai or Abu Dhabi. Journey time is 14 to 20 hours including stops, and the high-season price starts at around ZAR5230 return.

Flights from the Italian mainland

There are plentiful flights to Sardinia **from the Italian mainland** connecting all three of Sardinia's airports with major Italian cities. The most frequent flights are between Rome and **Cágliari** (at least 10 daily; 1hr 10min), and Cágliari also has one or two flights daily from Bologna, Milan, Naples, Pisa, Turin, Venice and Verona. There are one to three flights daily from Rome (45min) and five to seven daily from Milan to **Olbia** (1hr 25min), and four weekly from Naples (1hr 15min); **Alghero** has two to five daily from Rome and one to three from Milan (both 1hr 5min).

The main **carriers** are Volotea, Meridiana, Alitalia and Ryanair. Fares vary seasonally and according to

how far in advance you book: the cheapest fares are between Rome and Olbia, from €70 one-way.

Overland from the UK and Ireland

The **overland route** to one of the embarkation ports for Sardinia may prove quite an endurance test, whether you do it by coach, train or your own transport. Obviously, you can choose to make the journey at a more leisurely pace, with numerous stops en route, but this will add to the expense.

By rail from the UK and Ireland

Travelling **by train** to Sardinia isn't usually cheaper than flying, but it is more climate-friendly, and in some ways less stressful. If you timed it well, you could hop onto a ferry within an hour of arriving at your port of embarkation for Sardinia (allowing 30min–1hr for a taxi or métro ride across Paris to change stations).

From London, the fastest journey across the Channel (using Eurostar) and through France to the nearest port of Marseille, including at least one change of trains, will take 7 to 10 hours, usually costing £200–300 return, while the journey time to Genoa, the nearest Italian port, is around fifteen hours (with two changes, usually Paris and Turin) and costs from £300 return. **Fares** vary according to availability and how far in advance you book (bookings may be made up to three months in advance); discounts apply to under-26s. The total fare sometimes works out cheaper if you buy each leg of the journey separately.

Eurostar trains go from St Pancras in London via the Channel Tunnel to Lille (about 1hr 30min) or Paris (about 2hr 20min), where passengers must change stations for onward travel. In Paris, this will necessitate a métro or taxi journey from the Gare du Nord to the Gare de Lyon. You can get through-ticketing – including the tube journey to St Pancras – from Eurostar (see p.26), from most travel agents or from mainline train stations in Britain.

PACKAGE HOLIDAYS

If you don't want to move around much, it's worth looking at travel-plus-accommodation **package holidays**. The major package destinations are Alghero and Stintino in the northwest, Santa Teresa Gallura and the Costa Smeralda in the northeast, Santa Margherita di Pula in the southwest and the area around Villasimius in the southeast. It's obviously cheapest to go out of season – something to be recommended anyway, as the resorts and sights are much less crowded, and the sea is often warm enough to bathe in as early as Easter and as late as October. Should you want to rent a car, check with the package company before you leave, as some **fly-drive deals** work out very cheaply.

Rail passes

If you're planning to make Sardinia part of a longer European trip, it might be worth investing in a **rail pass** – InterRail and Eurail passes offer unlimited rail travel in European countries within a given period, and must be bought before leaving home. None of the passes available is likely to pay for itself if you're planning to stick to Sardinia or even just Italy, however. **W** voyages-sncf.com is the main company for European rail journeys (tickets can be purchased from here or from one of the other agents listed on p.26). The comprehensive website The Man in Seat 61 (see p.26) is an invaluable source of information on which passes are available and current prices, as well as rail routes.

The **InterRail** pass is only available to European residents, and you'll be asked to provide proof of residency of at least six months in order to buy one. Passes cover 28 European countries (including Turkey) and are available as either one-country passes (for example Italy) or global passes, covering all countries. An **Italy pass** in standard class costs from £89 for three days in a month to £180 for eight days in a month. **Global passes** can be for either flexible or continuous periods: for five days in ten the cost in standard class is £169, for ten days in 22 it's £240, for 22 continuous days it's £310, and for

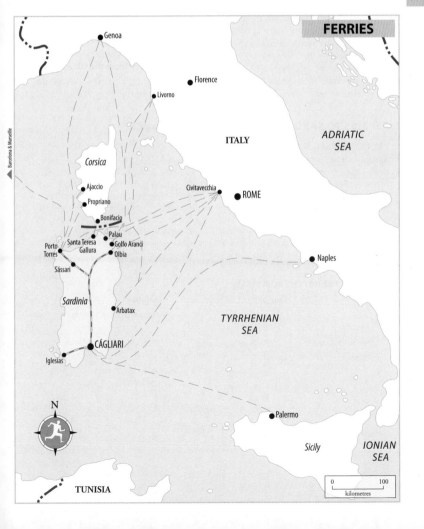

FERRIES

Genoa

Florence

Livorno

ITALY

ADRIATIC SEA

Corsica

Ajaccio

Propriano

Bonifacio

Civitavecchia

ROME

Palau

Santa Teresa Gallura

Golfo Aranci

Porto Torres

Olbia

Sássari

Naples

Sardinia

Arbatax

TYRRHENIAN SEA

CÁGLIARI

Iglesias

N

Palermo

Sicily

IONIAN SEA

0   100
kilometres

TUNISIA

Barcelona & Marseille

one month it's £400. There are significant reductions for travellers aged 12–25. Although InterRail passes do not include travel between Britain and the Continent, pass-holders for zones covering England, Ireland, France or Belgium are eligible for a discount on some ferry services.

A **Eurail** pass, only available to non-European residents, allows unlimited free first-class train travel in Italy and 27 other countries and is available for continuous periods of fifteen days (€580), 21 days (€746), one month (€917), two months (€1291) and three months (€1592), and for flexible periods of any ten or fifteen days within two months (€682 and €894 respectively). Eurail also offers a Regional Pass allowing travel in two bordering European countries, and a **Select Pass** allowing travel in four bordering European countries – both available for four to ten days within a two-month period – and a **one-country pass** for three to eight days within one month. There are reductions for under-26s travelling in standard class and for two or more people travelling together.

The national rail companies of many European countries also offer their own passes, most of which can be bought direct from the national rail company.

By bus from the UK and Ireland

There are currently no direct **bus services** from the UK or Ireland to the French or Italian ports, though **Eurolines** operates a daily service from London's Victoria Coach Station to Paris, from where you can board a bus for Marseille (the nearest ferry port for Sardinia), taking around 22 hours for the whole journey (return trip from London around £125), and to Milan (£115 return), taking about 24 hours, from where there are frequent connections to Genoa and Livorno. Buses use the Channel ferry crossing, which is included in the price.

By car and ferry from the UK and Ireland

If you're travelling with your **own vehicle**, the best cross-Channel options for most drivers will

---

FERRIES TO SARDINIA FROM ITALY AND FRANCE

FROM THE ITALIAN MAINLAND

Tirrenia run most of the services to Sardinia from the Italian mainland and from Palermo in Sicily. Daytime crossings take the shortest time, but may cost more. Nearly all companies operate a **flexible-fare system**, worked out according to demand and availability. In general, the further ahead you book, the lower the cost. The most expensive fares are usually at weekends in August, when demand is highest. The prices given below are the approximate price you might expect to pay for a one-way fare for deck class in high season – typically July or September. Promotional discounts and special deals may also be available. Reclining seats add at least €4 more, berths in shared cabins another €10–50. The car fares given are for vehicles less than 4m in length; reckon on another €10–20 for cars longer than this.

FERRIES (TRAGHETTI) FROM ITALY

Route	Company	Frequency	Length of crossing	Single passenger	Car fare
Civitavecchia–Arbatax	Tirrenia	2 weekly	10hr	€50	€100
Civitavecchia–Cágliari	Tirrenia	1 daily	13–15hr	€45	€65
Civitavecchia–Olbia	Moby	4–9 weekly (June–Sept)	5–8hr	€45	€30
Civitavecchia–Olbia	Tirrenia	1 daily (April–Sept)	6hr–7hr 30min	€38	€42
Genoa–Arbatax	Tirrenia	2 weekly (July & Aug)	15hr 30min–16hr 30min	€70	€120
Genoa–Olbia	Moby	1–2 daily (late May to early Oct)	11hr 30min	€45	€50
Genoa–Olbia	Tirrenia	3–5 weekly	10hr–12hr 15min	€60	€90

be via the Channel Tunnel or on the standard ferry/hovercraft links between Dover and Calais/ Ostend or Newhaven and Dieppe. Crossing using the Channel Tunnel (24hr service, departures every 15min at peak periods) will speed up the initial part of the journey. From England's southwest, you can cut driving time by using the more expensive Portsmouth–Caen/Cherbourg routes operated by Brittany Ferries.

Bear in mind when calculating driving costs that **motorway tolls** can add around €80 per car driving through France from Calais to Marseille (tolls are also charged on Italian autostradas).

By ferry from the Italian mainland and France

Ferries run year-round from **ports in mainland Italy** and **Sicily**, and there are also direct ferries from Marseille and (occasionally) Toulon in France. From the Italian mainland, the shortest ferry **crossing to Sardinia** is from Civitavecchia (near Rome) to Olbia.

There are also numerous connections to Sardinia **from Corsica**. You can reach Bastia, in northern Corsica, from Italy on Corsica Ferries from Savona and Livorno, and on Moby Lines from Genoa and Livorno. Bastia lies 178km from the southern port of Bonifacio, from where it's a short hop to Santa Teresa Gallura in Sardinia. From France, Marseille, Toulon and Nice have regular connections with all the Corsican ports on SNCM, La Meridionale and Corsica Ferries.

You can look up schedules and make advance bookings (essential in high season if you're driving) on such websites as Ⓦaferry .co.uk and Ⓦdirectferries.co.uk, or via the companies' own websites. We've provided a basic summary of all the routes (see box below). For the lowest prices, book ahead and watch out for **special offers** that apply on certain dates, usually available when you're buying a return ticket on your outward journey and when you're travelling with a car.

Route	Company	Frequency	Length of crossing	Single passenger	Car fare
Genoa–Porto Torres	Grandi Navi Veloci	4 weekly (late May to early Oct)	13hr 30min	€50	€65
Genoa–Porto Torres	Tirrenia	1 daily	11hr 30min	€40	€65
Livorno–Golfo Aranci	Sardinia Ferries	7–14 weekly	6hr 30min–10hr	€40	€40
Livorno–Olbia	Moby	1–2 daily (Feb–Oct)	6hr 30min–10hr	€40	€45
Naples Cágliari	Tirrenia	2 weekly	13hr 30min	€50	€100
Palermo–Cágliari	Tirrenia	1–2 weekly	12hr	€50	€100

FROM THE FRENCH MAINLAND AND CORSICA

There are numerous connections from mainland France and Corsica to Sardinia. The main departure point on Corsica is Bonifacio, on the island's southern tip, just an hour across the straits from Santa Teresa Gallura. SNCM and La Meridionale also sail from Propriano to Porto Torres.

Route	Company	Frequency	Length of crossing	Single passenger	Car fare
Bonifacio (Corsica)– Santa Teresa Gallura	Moby	4 daily (April–Sept)	50min	€25	€35
Bonifacio (Corsica)– Santa Teresa Gallura	Saremar	2–3 daily	1hr	€18	€31
Marseille–Porto Torres	SNCM/ La Meridionale	1–2 weekly (May–Oct)	17hr 30min	€108	€155
Propriano (Corsica)– Porto Torres	SNCM/ La Meridionale	1–2 weekly (May–Oct)	4hr	€40	€45

AGENTS AND OPERATORS

Citalia UK ☎ 01293 731464, ⓦ citalia.com. Package holidays based in some of Sardinia's smartest resorts, including the Costa Smeralda and around Chia. Look for the regular special offers.

CIT World Travel Australia ☎ 1300 380 992, ⓦ cit.com.au. Italy specialists offering packages to hotels in the Villasimius area, plus car rental and rail passes.

Flight Centre UK ☎ 0800 587 0058, ⓦ flightcentre.co.uk; US ☎ 855 984 9388, ⓦ flightcenter.com; Canada ☎ 1 877 967 5302, ⓦ flightcentre.ca; Australia ☎ 133 133, ⓦ flightcentre.com.au; New Zealand ☎ 0800 243 544; ⓦ flightcentre.co.nz. Discount international airfares and holiday packages.

Headwater UK ☎ 01606 828 289, ⓦ headwater.com. Guided walking holidays in the Barbagia region and around Golfo di Orosei.

Just Sardinia UK ☎ 01202 484 858, ⓦ justsardinia.co.uk. Sardinian specialists offering tailor-made holidays and tours throughout the island, with various accommodation options, flights and car rental.

North South Travel UK ☎ 01245 608 291, ⓦ northsouthtravel .co.uk. Friendly travel agency offering discounted fares worldwide. Profits are used to support projects in the developing world, especially the promotion of sustainable tourism.

Sardatur UK ☎ 020 8973 2292, ⓦ sardatur-holidays.co.uk. Hotels and self-catering villas and apartments on the southwest coast, Villasimius, the Costa Smeralda, Santa Teresa Gallura, Oristano and Cala Gonone.

Sardinian Experiences ☎ 0843 886 4567, ⓦ sardinianexperiences .com. Group and tailor-made packages for culture and activity holidays, based in Bosa and run by a *Rough Guides* author.

STA Travel UK ☎ 0333 321 0099, US ☎ 800 781 4040, Australia ☎ 134 782, New Zealand ☎ 0800 474 400, South Africa ☎ 0861 781 781; ⓦ statravel.com. Worldwide specialists in independent travel; also student IDs, travel insurance, car rental, rail passes and more. Good discounts for students and under-26s.

Student Flights US ☎ 1 800 255 8000 or ☎ 480 951 1177, ⓦ usa.isecard.com. Student/youth fares, student IDs and passes.

Tabona & Walford UK ☎ 020 8767 6789, ⓦ tabonaandwalford .co.uk. Eight-day coastal and mountain walking trips around Oliena and Cala Gonone and in Sarrabus, taking in Cágliari, Nuoro and Su Nuraxi. Also bespoke tours.

Thomson UK ⓦ thomson.co.uk. Charter flights and accommodation in large and glitzy hotels, mainly in Alghero and on the northern coast.

Trailfinders UK ☎ 020 7938 1200, Ireland ☎ 01 677 7888; ⓦ trailfinders.com. One of the best-informed and most efficient agents for independent travellers, offering flights, hotels, insurance and car rental.

Travel Cuts Canada ☎ 1 800 667 2887, ⓦ travelcuts.com. Canadian student-travel firm for flights, rail travel, tours, accommodation and student cards.

USIT Ireland ☎ 01 602 1906, ⓦ usit.ie. Ireland's main student and youth specialists for transport, tours, passes and insurance.

RAIL CONTACTS

CIT World Travel Australia ☎ 1300 380 992, ⓦ cit.com.au.

etrains4u UK ☎ 020 7619 1083, ⓦ etrains4u.com.

Eurail ⓦ eurail.com.

Eurostar UK ☎ 0343 218 6186, ⓦ eurostar.com.

The Man in Seat 61 ⓦ seat61.com. Comprehensive information and advice for rail travel in Europe.

Railcc ⓦ rail.cc. International train tickets and passes.

Rail Europe US ☎ 1 800 622 8600, Canada ☎ 1 800 361 7245; ⓦ raileurope.com.

Rail Plus Australia ☎ 03 9642 8644 or ☎ 1300 555 003, ⓦ railplus.com.au; New Zealand ☎ 09 377 5415; ⓦ railplus.co.nz.

STA Travel See Agents and Operators (above).

Trenitalia (Italian State Railways or FS) Italy ☎ 892 021, ⓦ trenitalia.com.

BUS CONTACTS

Eurolines ☎ 0871 781 8177, ⓦ eurolines.co.uk.

FERRY OPERATORS AND UK AGENTS

Corsica Ferries ⓦ corsica-ferries.co.uk, in UK c/o Viamare ☎ 020 8206 3420, ⓦ viamare.com.

Enermar ⓦ enermar.it.

Grandi Navi Veloci ⓦ gnv.it, in UK c/o Viamare (see above).

Grimaldi ⓦ www.grimaldi-lines.com, in UK c/o Viamare (see above).

La Meridionale ⓦ lameridionale.com, in UK c/o Viamare (see above).

Moby Lines ⓦ moby.com, in UK c/o Viamare (see above).

Sardinia Ferries ⓦ sardiniaferries.com, in UK c/o Viamare (see above).

SNCM ⓦ sncm.fr, c/o Southern Ferries in UK ☎ 0844 815 7785, ⓦ southernferries.co.uk.

Tirrenia Line ⓦ tirrenia.it, c/o SMS Travel & Tourism, in UK ☎ 020 7370 6293.

Getting around

Touring Sardinia by car is the most hassle-free option, though also the most expensive. Getting around by public transport is cheap and allows you to enjoy the landscape, but it's not always easy: the rail system is slow, few buses run on Sunday, and route information can be frustratingly difficult to obtain.

Travelling **by train** is an efficient way to journey between major towns, but isn't always the best way to see the island. Some stations are kilometres away from the towns or villages they serve, while much of the east and centre of Sardinia is accessible only by bus or car. In the event of strikes, a small number of essential transport services are guaranteed to run (though these can get packed).

As for the **roads**, drivers, bikers and pedestrians alike are advised to keep their wits about them at all times. Driving in Sardinia is not the competitive sport that it can be in Rome, Naples or Sicily, but neither is slow or indecisive behaviour at the wheel or when crossing roads much tolerated. Nonethe-

DISTANCES IN KILOMETRES

	Cágliari	Oristano	Alghero	Olbia
Cágliari	–	93	227	276
Oristano	93	–	135	184
Alghero	227	135	–	136
Olbia	276	184	136	–

less, anyone used to negotiating mainland Italy's roads will find Sardinia a doddle, and pedestrians accustomed to being treated as human skittles will be pleasantly surprised to find that drivers actually stop at pedestrian crossings and respect red lights. Local pedestrians also respect signals, and especially in Cágliari and Sássari, where traffic is heavy and constant, it is sensible to do likewise.

If you're in a hurry, you can always travel around Sardinia **by plane**; flights are frequent and it's usually possible to purchase your ticket at the airport and jump on the first flight (though prior booking is recommended).

By rail

Sardinia's **train network** connects all the major towns. The main lines are operated by Italian State

MAIN PUBLIC TRANSPORT OPERATORS IN SARDINIA

ARST ☎ 800 865 042, ⓦ arst.sardegna.it. The main regional bus company, also running a few train routes including the Trenino Verde tourist service.

Deplano ☎ 0784 295 030, ⓦ deplanobus.it. Private bus company operating between Nuoro and Olbia airport.

Digitur ☎ 079 262 039, ⓦ digitur.it. Private bus company operating a year-round service between Porto Torres, Bosa and Cúglieri, and a summer service between Alghero airport and Santa Teresa Gallura via Porto Torres and Castelsardo.

Redentours ☎ 0784 30 325, ⓦ redentours.com. Private bus company operating between Nuoro and Alghero's airport.

Sardabus ☎ 079 262 039, ⓦ sardabus.it. Private bus company serving Castelsardo, Stintino, Santa Teresa Gallura and Tempio Pausania.

Saremar ☎ 199 118 877, or ☎ 02 3959 5016 from outside Italy, ⓦ saremar.it. Ferry company for crossings to San Pietro and La Maddalena.

Trenitalia (Italian State Railways, or FS) ☎ 892 021, ⓦ trenitalia.it. State railways.

Turmo ☎ 0789 21 487, ⓦ gruppoturmotravel.com. Private bus company operating services linking Olbia with Santa Teresa Gallura, Nuoro, Sássari and Cágliari.

Railways, **Trenitalia**, also known as Ferrovie dello Stato (**FS**), while a few local routes are run by the independent company, **ARST**, which also runs most of the buses. Trenitalia is responsible for services between Cágliari, Iglésias, Carbónia, Oristano, Sássari, Porto Torres and Olbia, while ARST operates routes between Cágliari and Mandas, Sássari and Alghero, and Nuoro and Macomer. ARST also runs a few very limited internal routes in summer (including the Trenino Verde), between Mandas and Arbatax, Ísili and Sórgono, and Tempio Pausania and Palau. These are usually diesel-powered, noisy and slow, though they run through some spectacular countryside.

Generally, trains leave punctually and arrive within ten minutes or so of the scheduled time. All trains can get quite full at certain times – for example, the school runs in the morning and at lunchtime – and smoking is not permitted. **Tickets** can be bought from any train station, by telephone or through the Trenitalia website (see p.26), and from some travel agents. Fares are very reasonable, calculated according to the distance travelled; the longest trip you can make on the island, the 300km journey between Olbia and Cágliari, costs around €17 for a second-class ticket. Note that all tickets must be validated – punched in machines scattered around the station and platforms – within six hours for distances of less than 200km, or 24 hours for distances of more than 200km. Failure to do this can land you with an on-the-spot fine. If you don't have time to buy a ticket, you can simply board your train and pay the conductor, though you'll be charged a *supplemento*.

A **rail pass** is worth considering if you plan to travel extensively around Italy or Europe, though it's not actually a lot of help once you've arrived in Sardinia, with its limited rail network. The Europe-wide InterRail and Eurail passes (see p.23) give unlimited travel on the FS network, though you'll be liable for (small) supplements on the faster trains.

Timetables

Train **timetables** can be consulted on boards displayed at train stations, online at the Trenitalia website (see above) and in daily newspapers.

"Departures" are *Partenze*, "Arrivals" *Arrivi*, "Delayed" *In Ritardo*, "On time" *In Orario*. Pay close attention to the timetable notes, which may specify the dates between which some services run (*Si effetua dal… al….*), or whether a service is limited or seasonal (*periódico*), denoted by a vertical squiggle; *feriale* is the term for the Monday to Saturday service, symbolized by two crossed hammers, *festivo* means that a train runs only on Sundays and holidays, with a Christian cross as its symbol.

By bus

Sardinia is served by an extensive network of **buses** (*autobus* or *pullman*) covering every town, most villages and a good number of beaches too, though schedules can be sketchy and are much reduced on Sundays. Prices are marginally more expensive than trains, with a Cágliari to Sássari trip, for example, costing around €19 and taking 3hr 40min, as opposed to €16 by train with a journey time of 3hr to 3hr 30min.

The main regional bus company, **ARST** (*Azienda Regionale Sarda Trasporti*), covers local and long-distance routes from the main cities of Cágliari, Oristano, Sássari, Nuoro and Olbia. Smaller companies such as Digitur, Deplano and Turmo run services connecting the island's airports and tourist resorts to various towns and cities, mainly in summer. Note that some ARST services covering beach areas only operate during the summer, while others are linked to work/school/market requirements – sometimes meaning a frighteningly early start, and last departures as early as 1 or 2pm. Occasionally there are no buses at all during school holidays. **Schedules** are summarized in the Guide, but the companies' websites (see box, p.27) have fuller information. Timetables are rarely available to be given out, but are usually displayed at bus stops and stations, and local tourist offices can usually help out too.

City **bus terminals** are all very central, and most buses make stops at the local train station – if you want the bus station, ask for the autostazione. Wherever possible, you should buy **tickets** before boarding, from ticket offices and local bars and *tabacchi*, though if everywhere is closed you can buy tickets on board (for which a small supplement is usually charged). For longer hauls (and if you want to be sure of a place), it's worth buying them in advance. Bus stops are often quite difficult to track down; if you want directions, ask: *Dov'è la fermata dei pullman?* ("Where's the bus stop?"). If you want to get off a bus, ask *posso scéndere*? ("Can I get off?"); "the next stop" is "*la próssima fermata*".

City buses, usually charging a flat fare of €1, valid for ninety minutes, are good for quick rides across town. It's best to purchase tickets before boarding from bars and shops that display the bus company sticker, or from the kiosks and vendors at bus terminals and stops, but, again, you can buy them directly from the driver for which you'll generally be charged a €0.50 supplement. Once aboard, you must punch the tickets in the machine or they're invalid; checks are occasionally made by inspectors, who can charge spot fines. Smoking is strictly prohibited.

By car

Car travel across the island can be very quick as long as you follow the main roads. Minor roads can be narrow, very bendy and often confusing, though they can also be the most spectacular routes. The island has no motorways or autostradas, and therefore no tolls; instead, good dual carriageways, or **superstradas**, run for most of the way between Cágliari, Oristano, Olbia, Sássari and Nuoro. The straightest and fastest is the **SS131**, aka the **Carlo Felice highway**, named after the king who commissioned it. Extending the length of the island, from Cágliari via Oristano and Sássari as far as Porto Torres, it is rarely congested, though occasionally poorly lit and surfaced; beware of tricky junctions. Other superstradas branch off east to Nuoro and Olbia, and link Cágliari with Iglésias, Carbónia and Sant'Antíoco.

Sardinia's **secondary roads** are the most rewarding to explore, though these may increase your journey time, and you'll need to exercise maximum caution in negotiating their twists and turns. The going can be especially slow along the coasts in summer.

At all times while driving in **rural areas**, be prepared for the sudden appearance of a flock of sheep, wild pigs or a panniered horse on the road. In remoter parts, there are *strade bianche*, or "white roads" – little more than rough tracks which can continue for hours, seemingly going nowhere; these can become very rocky, and should not be attempted with a low axle. Signposting on these lanes is nonexistent, and it's easy to lose one's direction. Nonetheless, they're perfect for spontaneous detours, and can lead to excellent spots for a walk or picnic, not to mention the splendid beaches often lying at the end of them.

Fuel

Italy is one of the most expensive countries in Europe in which to buy **fuel**: it's currently around

€1.60 per litre for unleaded (*senza piombo*), €1.45 per litre for diesel (*gasolio*), though gas (*PLG*) is more reasonable at about €0.60 per litre. Fuel stations are spaced at fairly regular intervals along the superstradas, and there are pumps in most towns and villages. Although most are closed 12.30pm to 3.30pm and after 7.30pm, and often on Sunday or one other day of the week, the majority have self-service dispensers which take euro notes and credit cards. Make sure your notes aren't dog-eared, or the machines won't accept them. If your tank is filled before all your prepaid fuel is dispensed, you can punch a button for a receipt and ask for a refund when the station opens. All stations accept major credit cards.

Legal requirements

As for **documentation**, you need a valid driving licence and, if you are a non-EU licence holder, an international driving permit. It's compulsory to carry your car documents and passport while you're driving in Italy, and you'll be required to present them if stopped by the police. You are also required to carry a portable triangular danger sign and a fluorescent jacket in case of an accident or breakdown, supplied in rented vehicles and available in most car accessory shops (for other local regulations, consult ⓦtheaa.com). If bringing your own car, you should contact your insurance company prior to departure to request cover for outside your home country.

Rules of the road

The **rules of the road** are straightforward: drive on the right; at junctions, where there's any ambiguity, give precedence to vehicles coming from the right; and observe the speed limits (50km/h/30mph in built-up areas, 90km/h/55mph on country roads or 110km/h/70mph on dual carriageways). Note that some road customs are markedly different from what you may be used to: flashing headlights, for example, mean: "Get out of my way!"

Traffic restrictions

In towns, keep your eyes peeled for signs indicating a **ZTL** (*Zona di Tráffico Limitato*), where restrictions are in force for parking or even passing through. The red-rimmed signs give details of which restrictions are in force and when. Where there are no *vigili* (local policemen) visible, there will usually be a camera recording number plates, and fines will invariably find their way to you (car rental agencies will take the sum using your credit card details and impose a hefty admin charge on top).

Parking

Parking can be a real headache in Sardinia. The task of finding a space is easier in the early afternoon, when towns are quiet, or at night. At all other times, strictly enforced restrictions operate, allowing you to leave your vehicle only in designated areas – usually between blue lines. Seek out the parking attendant and buy a ticket for as long as you think you'll be parked; it's not expensive, usually around €0.50–1 for the first hour, €1–2 for every subsequent hour. If you park in a *zona di rimozione*, your car will most likely be towed away; and if you've chosen a street that turns into a market by day, you'll be stuck until it closes down.

Breakdown

If you break down, dial ☎116 and tell the operator where you are, the type of car and your registration number. The nearest office of the **Automobile Club d'Italia** (ACI) will send someone out to fix your car, though it's not a free service, and you'll pay a further hefty bill if you need a tow. Temporary membership of ACI (☎803 116, ⓦaci.it) gives free or discounted tows and repairs; alternatively, arrange cover with a motoring organization in your country before you leave. Any ACI office in Sardinia can tell you where to get **spare parts** for your particular car.

Security

Although **car crime** is rarer than in most of mainland Italy, it's prudent not to leave anything visible in the car when you park it, including the radio. If you're taking your own vehicle, consider installing a detachable car radio, and always depress your aerial and tuck in your wing mirrors. The main cities and ports have **garages** where you can leave your car, a safe enough option. The car itself is unlikely to be stolen if it's got a right-hand drive and a foreign number-plate: they're too conspicuous to be of much use to thieves.

Car rental

Car rental (*autonoleggio*) in Sardinia can be expensive, from around €70 to €140 per week for a Fiat 500 or similar when booked in advance from one of the major international firms, usually more from local companies (contact details are given in the city listings). Under-25s may face additional charges. Some rental deals cost less per day, but involve an additional charge for every kilometre driven over, say, 100km. You can arrange car rental in conjunction with your flight/holiday, though this does not always turn out to be the cheapest solution. The major **rental companies** have offices at each of the main airports.

You can also check local and national companies on the website ⓦ autonoleggi.sardegna.it. Note that, apart from its fuel efficiency, choosing a smaller car is preferable both for negotiating narrow alleys and for easier parking. Most rental companies offer **GPS** (Sat Nav) equipment for a supplement of €10–15 per day.

CAR RENTAL AGENCIES

Auto Europe ⓦ autoeurope.com.
Avis ⓦ avis.com.
Europcar ⓦ europcar.com.
Hertz ⓦ hertz.com.
Holiday Autos ⓦ holidayautos.co.uk.
Maggiore ⓦ maggiore.it.
Sardinya ⓦ autonoleggiosardinya.it.
Sixt ⓦ sixt.com.
Thrifty ⓦ thrifty.com.

Hitchhiking

Hitchhiking (*autostop*) is not widely practised in Sardinia and is not recommended as a means of getting around. Women hitching should travel in pairs and always ask where the car is headed before accepting a lift ("*Dov'è diretto?*"). If you want to get out, say: "*Mi fa scéndere?*".

By ferry

You'll use **ferries** to get to the inhabited offshore islands: from Palau for La Maddalena, and Calasetta or Portovesme for San Pietro. The main company is Saremar. Departures are at least hourly, with more in high season, and there's a night-time service every two hours or so. All take vehicles, and if you are transporting yours it makes sense to get to the port early to be sure of a place (things can get quite congested, especially in August); some offices are only open twenty minutes before departure.

Frequencies are listed in the Guide. Saremar and Moby Lines also operate daily services between Santa Teresa Gallura and Bonifacio in Corsica, while most seaside holiday centres offer boat tours of the coast and islands.

Accommodation

On the whole, accommodation in Sardinia is cheaper than in the rest of Italy. The main problem is lack of availability, as the various options can be fully booked in summer. Even outside the high season, it's advisable to book as early as you can.

As well as hotels, there are hostels, B&Bs, *agriturismi* (rural accommodation), self-catering villas and apartments, and campsites with bungalows or caravans to rent. Several of the general websites (see pp.50–51) have links to accommodation options with online booking, as have the dedicated accommodation sites (see opposite).

Nearly all hotels and B&Bs include **breakfast** in the price, whether you want it or not. Cheaper places may have shared bathrooms, though many also have a few en-suite rooms. Increasingly, the owners and staff of most establishments have a smattering of English, otherwise the phrases provided in our Language section (see p.325) should help you overcome the linguistic barriers.

Hotels

There's a vast range of **hotel** accommodation in Sardinia, officially graded from one to five stars, and taking in everything from small, family-run places to large, impersonal establishments with

---

ACCOMMODATION PRICES

The **prices** of all serviced accommodation should be listed in the local booklets provided by the tourist office, and all the lodgings listed in the Guide have been given an approximate rate, representing the **cheapest** available option for two people sharing a room or pitch in high season – typically July, as opposed to peak season (Aug) – or for single dormitory beds in hostels. Outside high season, you'll usually pay much less; in peak season you'll pay the top whack. Be prepared to treat all prices as flexible – even the rates provided by the establishment itself are fluid, varying according to demand. It's always worth trying to negotiate a lower price than the "official" rate, especially in low season, and always if you're staying more than a couple of nights (ask: *c'è uno sconto per tre/quattro/cinque notti?*). Campsite and hostel rates, however, are more rigid. Note that all operators of hotels, B&Bs, apartments and campsites will also collect a local *tassa di soggiorno* (tourist tax) of €0.25–0.50 per person per night, which is usually doubled in the summer months (each *comune* sets its own rate). The tax may be absorbed in the cost of your stay, however, and does not apply to children.

sports facilities, private parking and restaurants on the premises.

Prices vary according to grading, location, season and availability. When demand is high, many establishments require that you take **half or full board**, and there may also be a **minimum stay** of three nights or a week. In practice, if you call on spec, you'll often be given a room for just a night or two if there's availability. In all cases, always ask to see the room before you agree to stay: *posso vedere?* ("May I see?").

There are few **single rooms** available, and these are often occupied during the week by workers and commercial travellers. In high season especially, lone travellers will often pay most (if not all) the price of a double. Three or more people sharing a room should expect to pay around 35 percent on top of the price of a double room.

B&Bs and agriturismi

Recent years have seen a huge growth in **B&Bs** in Sardinia, mostly in towns. These can vary a lot, but are generally clean and comfortable, and set apart from the host family's living quarters. Increasingly, rooms have private **bathrooms**, either en suite or close by. Some places can be fairly luxurious, with all the facilities you might expect in a three-star hotel, but with better breakfasts. The quality of the accommodation isn't always reflected in the price; most charge €30–45 per person per night, depending on the season and location. Ask at the local tourist office for a list of B&Bs; alternatively, consult the websites of B&B associations (see below), and watch for "B&B" or "*câmere*" (rooms) signs. An *affittacâmere* (rented room) is simply a bureaucratic name for a B&B with more than three rooms – otherwise there's little difference between the two categories.

Outside towns, you might consider a night or two in an **agriturismo**, a cottage or farmhouse offering informal dinner, bed and breakfast. Many also have various activities available, such as escorted walks and excursions, horseriding, hunting and mountain-biking. Some of these places are relatively remote, but if you want to get close to nature, or to isolated beaches, they're ideal. Although some *agriturismi* have expanded and standardized their facilities, detracting from one of the main reasons to stay in them in the first place, others retain a homely feel, and often offer more authentic country cooking than most restaurants – indeed, some are renowned for their cuisine. They tend to be pricier than B&Bs, charging around €70–100 for a double room, and another €25–30 a head for a three-course dinner. Some *agriturismi* are

detailed in the Guide, and local tourist offices can tell you of all the suitable places in the area. *Agriturismo* associations, from which you can get details of properties and book online, are listed below.

B&B ASSOCIATIONS

Airbnb Ⓦ airbnb.com.
BB Planet Ⓦ bbplanet.com.
Bed and Breakfast Ⓦ bed-and-breakfast.it.
Domus Amigas Ⓦ domusamigas.it.
SardegnaBB Ⓦ sardegnabb.eu.
Sardegna B&B Ⓦ sardegnabb.it.

AGRITURISMO ASSOCIATIONS

Agriturismo di Sardegna Ⓦ agriturismodisardegna.it.
Agriturismo Online Ⓦ agriturismo-on-line.com.
Agriturismo.com Ⓦ agriturismo.com.
Agriturismo.it Ⓦ agriturismo.it.
Agriturismo.net Ⓦ agriturismo.net.

Rented apartments and villas

For longer-term stays in resorts, you might consider renting a **villa** or **apartment**. This can be horrendously expensive in high summer – €800–1000 a week for a one-bedroom place in Alghero, for example – but there are real bargains to be had in May, June and September, not to mention the winter months; ask in the local tourist office or estate agency (*agenzia immobiliare*), and keep an eye out for local advertisements.

APARTMENT AND VILLA RENTALS

Affitto.it Ⓦ affitto.it.
casa.it Italy Ⓦ casa.it.
Interhome UK ☏ 01483 863 500, Ⓦ interhome.co.uk.
My Villa in Sardinia Ⓦ myvillainsardinia.it.
Owners Direct Ⓦ ownersdirect.co.uk.
Rent Sardinia Italy ☏ 070 684 545, Ⓦ rentsardinia.com.
Rural Journey Ⓦ ruraljourney.com.
Sardinian Places UK ☏ 01489 866 959, Ⓦ sardinianplaces.co.uk.

Hostels

Sardinia has five official Hostelling International (HI) **youth hostels**: two in the north of the island – in Fertilia (near Alghero) and Lu Bagnu (near Castelsardo) – one at Lanusei (near Arbatax), one in the southeast, at San Priamo (near Muravera) and one in Cágliari. There are also unofficial hostels, for example at Oristano (see p.146) and Bosa (see p.194). For the official ones, you need to have HI membership, and booking in advance is essential, either over the phone or on the websites of AIG (the Italian Youth Hostel Association; ⓦ aighostels .com), or Hostelling International (ⓦ hihostels.com). Availability is limited at all times, and in the summer months hostels are almost permanently full. **Charges** for HI or AIG members are around €20 for a dormitory bed, €12 for an evening meal and €2 for breakfast (if this is not included in the overnight rate). AIG membership costs €2, valid for a year, and comes with a few perks such as discounts on car rental, student cards and travel insurance. For HI membership, contact your home hostelling organization (see below).

YOUTH HOSTEL ASSOCIATIONS

UK and Ireland

Youth Hostel Association (YHA) England and Wales ☎ 0800 019 1700, ⓦ yha.org.uk.
Hostelling Scotland ☎ 0345 293 7373, ⓦ syha.org.uk.
An Óige (Irish Youth Hostel Association) ☎ 01 830 4555, ⓦ anoige.ie.
Hostelling International Northern Ireland ☎ 028 9032 4733, ⓦ hini.org.uk.

US and Canada

Hostelling International USA ☎ 240 650 2100, ⓦ hiusa.org.
Hostelling International Canada ☎ 613 237 7884, ⓦ hihostels.ca.

Australia and New Zealand

YHA Australia ⓦ yha.com.au.
YHA New Zealand ☎ 0800 278 299, ⓦ yha.co.nz.

Camping

Sardinia has about ninety officially graded **campsites** dotted around its coasts and the islands, but there are no official sites in Sardinia's interior apart from the occasional field attached to a hotel or *agriturismo*. Facilities range from very rudimentary to the full gamut of shops, disco, pool and diving tuition. Campers can expect to pay €15–35 per pitch in high season, sometimes with an extra charge per person, and a car may cost an extra €5 per day or so, a campervan €10–15. Many sites also offer **bungalows**, **caravans** or **cabins** with cooking facilities at reasonable rates – €30–80 a night for a bungalow or caravan for two people in high season. Electricity and gas are included in the price; extras may include bed linen (around €10) and final cleaning (€20–30).

Months of opening are detailed in the Guide – though these periods are very flexible, and campsites generally open or close whenever they want, depending on business. Only a handful of campsites stay open between October and April. Don't assume there will always be availability in

summer: the better sites fill up quickly (particularly in August), so always phone first. More details of Sardinia's campsites and reviews can be found on the websites ⓦ easycamping.it, ⓦ camping.it and ⓦ campeggi.com.

By and large, **camping rough** is a nonstarter: it's frowned upon in the tourist areas and regarded with outright suspicion in the interior (locals are especially wary of the danger of forest fires).

Food and drink

Eating and drinking are refreshingly good value in Sardinia, and the quality is usually high. Often, even the most out-of-the-way village will boast somewhere you can get a decent lunch, while towns like Cágliari and Alghero can keep foodies happy for days. A full meal with local wine averages at around €30 a head, though there are often much cheaper set-price menus available.

The summary below and the food glossary in the Language section (see pp.327–331) will help you find your way around supermarkets and menus, and point out some of the specialities that are found in nearly every restaurant.

Sardinian cuisine

Historically, the twin pivots of traditional **Sardinian cuisine** have been land- and sea-based local produce, and this continues to be the principal distinction today. Mutton, beef, game, boar, horsemeat and donkeymeat are the staples of the cooking in the interior, while the coasts rely on fish – tuna, sea bass and sardines all figure heavily. Add to these the essential components of Italian gastronomy – pasta, tomato sauce, olives and fresh vegetables – and a choice of seasonal fruit and sheep's cheese. Some of the most famous Italian wines hail from Sardinia – wine was already being made on the island at the time of the Phoenicians – and a meal is often rounded off with traditional biscuits of almonds and honey.

The mild winters and long summers mean that **fruit** and **vegetables** have longer seasons than in northern Europe, and are much bigger and generally tastier: strawberries appear in April, oranges are available right through the year, and even bananas are grown on a small scale. Unusual and unexpected foods are a bonus too, such as prickly pears (introduced from Mexico by the

Spanish), wild asparagus and wafer bread (*pane carasau*), while foreign elements have been introduced to specific areas – couscous on the island of San Pietro, and Catalan dishes in Alghero.

Breakfasts and snacks

Most Sardinians start the day in a bar, their **breakfast** (*prima colazione*) consisting of an espresso and the ubiquitous *cornetto* – a croissant, either plain or filled with jam, custard or chocolate, which you usually help yourself to from the counter; bigger bars and patisseries (*pasticcerie*) will have more choice. Hotel breakfasts may be limp, forgettable affairs, but you'll often find a truly impressive spread at B&Bs and *agriturismi*, including home-made jams, fruit and yoghurt.

At other times of the day, **rolls** (*panini*) can be pretty substantial, packed with any number of fillings. Numerous bars sell these, though you may find fresher fare by going into an *alimentari* (grocer's shop) or supermarket and asking them to make you one from whatever's on offer, for which you'll pay €1.50–3.50, depending on what and how much you choose for the filling. Bars may also offer *tramezzini*, ready-made sliced white bread sandwiches with mixed fillings – lighter and less appetizing than your average *panino*. Toasted sandwiches (*toste*) are common too: in a sandwich bar you can get whatever you like put inside them; in bars which have a sandwich toaster you're more likely to be limited to cheese with ham or tomato.

Apart from sandwiches, other takeaway food is pretty thin on the ground. You'll get small pizzas, portions of prepared pasta, chips, even full hot meals, in a **távola calda**, a snack bar that's at its best in the morning when everything is fresh. The bigger towns have them, often combined with normal bars.

You'll get more adventurous ingredients in **markets** – good bread, fruit, pizza slices and picnic food, such as cheese, salami, olives, tomatoes and

NO SMOKING
Note that, unless you're sitting outside, **smoking** is not permitted in Italian bars or restaurants.

salads. Some markets sell traditional takeaway food from stalls, such as boiled artichokes, cooked octopus, sea urchins, mussels, and *focacce* – oven-baked pastry snacks either topped with cheese and tomato, or filled with spinach, fried offal or meat. For picnics, look out for sweet peppers (*peperoni*), baby squid (*calamari*), seafood salad (*insalata di mare*) and dry-roast tomatoes or aubergines in oil, all of which can also be found in the **supermarkets** present in most towns and larger villages.

Pizza

As elsewhere in Italy, **pizza** in Sardinia comes flat and not deep-pan, and the choice of toppings is fairly traditional. It's still common to find pizza cooked in wood-fired ovens (*forno a legna*), rather than squeaky-clean electric ones, so that the pizza arrives blasted and bubbling on the surface, with a distinctive charcoal taste. However, because of the time it takes to set up and light the wood-fired ovens (and the sweltering heat they generate), these pizzas are usually only served at night, except in some resorts in summer.

When served at table, a basic cheese and tomato pizza costs around €6, something a bit fancier between €7 and €10. It's quite acceptable to cut it into segments and eat with your hands, washing it down with a beer or Coke rather than wine. Most sit-down outlets are hybrid pizzeria-*ristoranti*, which serve full meals too, and most places will also sell pizzas to **take away** (*pizza d'asporto*). Check our list of pizzas (see p.327) for what you get on top of your dough.

ICE CREAM
You'll probably end up with an **ice cream** (*gelato*) at some point during your stay: many people eat a dollop of ice-cream in a brioche for breakfast, and in summer, a cone (*un cono*) is an indispensable accessory to the evening *passeggiata*. Many bars have a fairly good selection, but for real choice go to a **gelateria** (ice cream parlour) where the range is a tribute to the Italian imagination and flair for display. If they make their own on the premises, there'll be a sign saying *produzione propria*. As for **flavours** (*gusti*), you'll have to go by appearance rather than attempt to decipher their exotic names, many of which don't mean much even to Italians; you'll find it's often the basics – chocolate (*cioccolato*), lemon (*limone*), strawberry (*frágola*) and coffee (*café*) – that are best. There's no trouble in identifying the finest gelateria in town: it's the one that draws the crowds.

Full meals: lunch and dinner

Full meals can be elaborate affairs. These are generally served in a trattoria or a ristorante, though these days there's often a fine line between the two: traditionally, a **trattoria** is cheaper and more basic, offering home cooking (*cucina casalinga*), while a **ristorante** is more upmarket (tablecloths and waiters). There may not be a written menu in a trattoria, in which case the waiter will simply reel off a list of what's on that day. There will almost always be a proper menu in a ristorante, and you'll find more choice. In either, a plate of pasta, a meat or fish course, fruit and a drink should cost €20–40 (though seafood usually pushes up the price). Watch out for signs saying *menu turístico, pranzo turístico, pranzo completo* or *prezzo fisso* – a limited set menu with or without wine, which can cost as little as €15, but is usually more in the region of €20–25 (less at lunchtime). Classier *ristoranti* will charge around €40–80 per head, including quality wine. Many of these are worth blowing the budget and going out of your way for.

Other eateries usually found in tourist resorts include the hybrid trattoria-ristorante-pizzeria; the *spaghetteria*, which specializes in pasta dishes; and the *birreria* – a pub with snacks and music, often the haunt of the local youth. Lastly, if you ever tire of the Sardinian diet you might try out one of the many **Chinese**, **North African** and **Indian restaurants** that have sprouted in the bigger towns in recent years – they're mostly as good as or better than the ones at home, and significantly cheaper than most Italian restaurants. Many eating places close for three or four weeks in November or February.

Traditionally, a **meal** (lunch is *pranzo*, dinner is *cena*) starts with an **antipasto** (literally "before the meal"), at its best when you circle around a table and pick from a selection of cold dishes, main items including stuffed artichoke hearts, olives, salami, anchovies, seafood salad, aubergine in various guises, sardines and mixed rice. A plateful will cost around €10. If you're moving on to pasta and a main course, however, you'll need to pace yourself.

The main **menu** starts with **primi**: soup, pasta or rice, usually costing €7–12. **Secondi**, meat or fish dishes costing roughly €12–18, are generally served alone except for perhaps a wedge of lemon or a tomato. **Side dishes** (*contorni*) and **salads** (*insalate*) are ordered and served separately, and often there won't be much choice: potatoes will usually come as chips (*patatine fritte*), but you can also find them boiled (*lesse*) or roast (*arroste*), while salads are simply green (*verde*) or mixed (*mista*), usually with tomato. **Bread** (*pane*), which in Sardinia comes in a variety of forms – though rarely brown (*integrale*) – will be served with your meal. Used in ceremonies as well as for everyday needs, Sardinian bread can be thin and crispy or soft, floury and delicately shaped, and differs from place to place.

If there's no menu, the verbal list of what's available can be a bit bewildering, but if you don't hear anything you recognize just ask for what you want: everywhere should have pasta with tomato sauce (*pomodoro*) or meat sauce (*al ragù*). When **ordering fish**, bear in mind that it is usually priced by weight (usually per 100g, *all'etto*) – if you don't want the biggest one they've got, ask to see what you're going to eat and check the price first.

Afterwards, you'll usually get a choice of **fruit** (*frutta*) or other **desserts** (*dolci*). Sardinia is renowned for its almond-based sweets, though they're not always available; most restaurants will only have fresh fruit salad (*macedonia*) and fresh or packaged ice cream and desserts – in common with the rest of Italy, Sardinia has embraced mass-produced, packaged sweets such as *tiramisù*, *tartufo* and *zuppa inglese*; some of them aren't bad, but they're a poor substitute for local desserts.

It's useful to know that you don't have to order a full meal in trattorias and restaurants. Asking for just pasta and a salad, or the main course on its own, won't outrage the waiter. Equally, asking for a dish listed as a first course as a second course, or having pasta followed by pizza (or vice versa), won't be frowned upon.

Special diets

Vegetarians may find their food principles stretched to the limit in Sardinia. If you're a borderline case, the abundance of excellent fish and shellfish and the knowledge that most meat is free range might just push you over the edge. On the whole, though, it's not that difficult if you're committed. Most pasta sauces are based on tomatoes or dairy products, and it's easy to pick a pizza that is meat- (and fish-) free. Note, however, that even "vegetarian" minestrone and risotto are cooked with meat or fish stock. To be sure, state clearly your position ("I am vegetarian" – *sono vegetariano/a*) and ask whether the dish has meat in it (*c'è carne dentro?*). The majority of places can be persuaded to cook egg dishes or provide you with a big mixed salad.

If you're a **vegan**, you'll be in for a hard time, though pizza without cheese is a good standby, and the fruit is excellent. **Coeliacs** and others on a

gluten-free diet will find similar difficulties, though gluten-free options are increasingly common on menus. The best solution may be to stock up with food items to prepare yourself: many bigger stores and independent shops in the main towns will have vegan-friendly and gluten-free products as well as other foods suitable for special diets.

The bill

At the end of the meal, ask for **the bill** (*il conto*). In many trattorias this doesn't amount to much more than an illegible scrap of paper, and if you want to be sure you're not being diddled, ask to have an official receipt (*una ricevuta*), something they're legally obliged to give you anyway. Nearly everywhere, you'll pay cover (*pane e coperto*), which amounts to €1–2.50 per person. **Service** (*servizio*) will be included as well in some restaurants, which adds another ten percent – and up to fifteen percent or even twenty percent in some places. If service is included, you won't be expected to **tip**; otherwise leave 10–15 percent, though bear in mind that the smaller places – pizzerias and trattorias – won't expect this.

Drinks

Although Sard children are brought up on wine, there's not the same emphasis on dedicated **drinking** here as there is in some other countries. You'll rarely see drunks in public, young people don't make a night out of getting wasted, and women especially are frowned upon if they're seen to indulge. Nonetheless, there's a wide choice of alcoholic drinks available in Sardinia, at low prices; soft drinks come in multifarious hues, thanks to the abundance of fresh fruit and there's also mineral water and crushed ice drinks.

Coffee, tea and soft drinks

One of the most distinctive smells in a Sardinian street is the aroma of fresh **coffee** wafting out of a bar (many trattorias and pizzerias don't serve hot drinks). It's usually excellent: the basic choice is either small, black and very strong (espresso, or just *caffè*), or white and frothy (cappuccino), but there are other varieties, too. A caffelatte is an espresso in a big cup filled up to the top with hot milk. If you want your espresso watered down, ask for a *caffè lungo*; with a shot of alcohol – and you can ask for just about anything in your coffee – is *caffè corretto*; with a drop of milk is *caffè macchiato* ("stained"). If you want to be sure of a coffee without sugar, ask for *caffè senza zúcchero*, though in most bars you help yourself to sugar. Most places also sell decaffeinated coffee (ask for Hag, even when it isn't). In summer you may prefer your coffee cold (*caffè freddo*). In some holiday centres, you'll find *granita di caffè* in summer – cold coffee with crushed ice and topped with whipped cream (*senza panna* if you prefer it without).

Tea is available in all bars, and is especially popular in summer, when you can drink it iced (*tè freddo*) – usually sweet and mixed with lemon (it's also available in tins with lemon or peach), it's an excellent thirst-quencher. Hot tea (*tè caldo*) comes with lemon (*con limone*) unless you ask for milk (*con latte*). **Milk** itself is drunk hot as often as cold, or you can get it with a dash of coffee (*latte macchiato*), and in a variety of flavoured drinks (*frappé*) too.

Alternatively, there are various **soft drinks** (*analcóliche*) to choose from. A **spremuta** is a fresh fruit juice, squeezed at the bar, usually orange, occasionally also lemon and grapefruit. You might need to add sugar to a lemon juice (*spremuta di limone*), but orange juice (*spremuta di arancia*) is usually sweet enough on its own, especially the crimson-red variety, made from blood oranges. You can also have orange and lemon mixed (*mischiato*). A **frullato** is a fresh fruit shake, often made with more than one type of fruit. A **granita** (a crushed-ice drink) comes in several flavours including coffee. Otherwise, there's the usual range of fizzy drinks and bottled juices; Coke is prevalent, but the home-grown Italian alternative, Chinotto, is less sweet – good with ice and a slice of lemon. As for **water**, mineral water (*acqua minerale*) is the usual choice in bars and restaurants, either still (*senza gas* or *naturale*) or fizzy (*con gas*, *gassata* or *frizzante*). Tap water (*acqua normale*) is drinkable almost everywhere and you won't pay for it in a bar. Water is especially prized when it comes from mountain springs, of which you'll see a great many as you travel around the island. Avoid water wherever you see a sign saying "*acqua non potabile*" (unsafe for drinking), and always ask a local if you're unsure about the water in a public fountain.

Beer and spirits

Beer (*birra*) is usually a lager-type brew which comes in a third of a litre (*píccola*) or two thirds of a litre (*grande*) bottles: commonest (and cheapest) are the Italian brand, Peroni, and the Sardinian Ichnusa (brewed in Assémini, near Cágliari). A small (33cl) bottle of Ichnusa beer costs about €4 in a bar or restaurant, a larger (66cl) bottle €6; if this is what you want, ask for *birra nazionale*, otherwise you'll be given the more expensive imported beers, like Carlsberg and Becks. In some bars and bigger restaurants and in all *birrerias* (pubs) you also have a choice of draught lager (*birra alla spina*), sold in units of 25cl (*píccola*) and 50cl (*media*), measure for measure more expensive than the bottled variety. In some places you might find so-called "dark beers" (*birra nera*, *birra rossa* or *birra scura*), which have a slightly maltier taste, and in appearance resemble stout or bitter. These are the most expensive of the draught beers, though not necessarily the strongest. As in the rest of Italy, Sardinia is enjoying a revival of interest in quality, locally produced craft beers (*birra artigianale*, or "artisan beer") – a couple of places specializing in these are noted in the Guide (see p.94 & p.214).

All the usual **spirits** are on sale and known mostly by their generic names – except **brandy**, which you should call *cognac* or ask for by name. The best Italian brandies are Stock and Vecchia Romagna; for all other spirits, if you want the cheaper Italian stuff, again, ask for *nazionale*. A generous shot costs around €3–5. Among the **liqueurs**, favourite in Sardinia is *mirto*, made from the leaves and berries of wild myrtle, which you should drink chilled; the more common red is rated more highly than the white. There's also the standard selection of **amari** (literally "bitters"), an after-dinner drink served with (or instead of) coffee. It's supposed to aid digestion, and is often not bitter at all, but can taste remarkably medicinal. Favourite brands include Averna and Ramazzotti, but there are dozens of different kinds.

Other **strong drinks** available are *grappa di mirto*, almost pure alcohol, from distilled myrtle husks; *Filè Ferru*, a fiery grappa-like concoction brewed in the interior; and, though not especially Sardinian, *sambuca* – a sticky-sweet, aniseed liqueur, traditionally served with one or more coffee beans in it and set on fire (though only tourists are likely to experience this these days).

Wine

With just about every meal you'll be offered **wine** (*vino*), either red (*rosso*) or white (*bianco*), labelled or local. If you want the local stuff, ask for *vino locale* or *sfuso*; on the whole it's fine, often served straight from the barrel in jugs and costing as little as €6 a litre (a *caraffa*, or carafe, is a litre, a *mezza caraffa* a half-litre).

Bottled wine is much more expensive, though still good value; expect to pay from around €8 for a mid-quality wine in a restaurant, more like €12–18 in places like Alghero.

SOME CLASSIC SARDINIAN WINES

Rich and fruity, cool and refreshing, Sard wines rank among Italy's finest. The following are ones to look out for.

Cannonau Robust, ruby-coloured red, quite dry, and ubiquitous in Sardinia. Nepente di Oliena and Cannonau di Jerzu are two of the best.

Carignano Full-bodied red largely from Sulcis in the southwest, good with starters, meat and cheese.

Malvasia From Bosa or Cágliari, a delicious golden aperitif or dessert wine.

Mandrolisai Fruity dry red or rosé, produced around Sórgono.

Monica Light, slightly cherry-ish red, mainly from the southern half of the island.

Moscato Velvety, sweet white, drunk with desserts.

Nasco Fashionable among aficionados, a dry or sweet amber-coloured white from around Cágliari.

Nuragus A light white from the Cágliari area, whose origin dates back to pre-Roman times. Great with seafood.

Torbato Cool and dry white wine from Alghero.

Vermentino A dry, light, white wine from Gallura or Alghero – good with fish or as an aperitif.

Vernaccia From Oristano, a strong, sherry-like dry white, often drunk as an aperitif, and a perfect accompaniment to *dolci*.

Sardinia also produces delicious **dessert wines**, the most famous being **Vernaccia**, sweet or dry, honey-coloured, with a bitter-almond taste, from the Tirso river area around Oristano. If you're heading to Bosa, watch out for mellow **Malvasia**, also served as a table wine, and also produced around Cágliari. Sweet white **Moscato** comes from Cágliari, Sorso-Sénnori and Tempio Pausánia, while the Alghero territory produces **Anghelu Ruju**, one of the strongest and best dessert wines, a sweet red with cherry and cinnamon aromas.

Fortified wines are fairly popular too: Martini (red or white) and Cinzano are nearly always available; Cynar (an artichoke-based sherry) and Punt'e Mes are other common aperitifs. If you ask for a Campari-Soda you'll get a ready-mixed version in a little bottle; if you want the barman to mix you one, ask for a Campari bitter. A slice of lemon is *uno spicchio di limone*; ice is *ghiaccio*.

Where to drink

Bars in Sardinia are either functional refuelling stops – good for a coffee in the morning, a quick beer or a cup of tea – or social centres, which have tables and a greater range of snacks, and are conducive to whiling away part of a morning or afternoon, reading or people-watching. Many bars don't stay open much after 9pm, though this varies from place to place, and hours are extended in summer, sometimes to midnight or 1am. As in bars throughout the Mediterranean, there are no set licensing hours and children have free access. All have toilets, and most won't object to you using their facilities even if you're not drinking there.

If you're just having a drink at a stand-up bar, pay first at the cash till (*la cassa*), present your receipt (*scontrino*) to the bar person and give your order. If there's no cashier, pay either before or after being served. If you're sitting down, wait for someone to take your order, and there'll usually be a 25–35-percent service charge (shown on the price list as *tàvola*); you're often expected to pay the bill on being served. If you don't know how much a drink will cost, there should be a list of prices (*listino prezzi*) behind the bar or *cassa*. When you present your receipt, it's customary to leave an extra €0.50 or so on the counter – though no one will object if you don't.

For more serious drinking, you can repair to a pub or **birreria**, where people go just to drink and socialize, though often these places sell snack food too. You'll usually find a younger crowd here, and there's often a music soundtrack. Other places to get a drink are an **enoteca**, a rudimentary wine

bar selling cheap local wine by the glass; a **bar-pasticceria**, which sells wonderful cakes and pastries too; and a **tàvola calda**, which, in a train station, always has a bar.

Note that, as with restaurants, bars are **nonsmoking** (in rare cases there is a separate smoking room), but you can still smoke at tables outside.

The media

Sards are among Italy's most avid readers of newspapers and magazines, which are readily available on every shopping street and in train stations. Foreign-language publications are sold in the same outlets in all the main centres, though at a considerable mark-up (so it is cheaper to read them online).

Television and **radio** are provided in most hotel and some B&B rooms. You'll need the internet or your own short-wave receiver to pick up non-Italian radio stations. To keep in touch with Italian news in English go to Ⓦ lifeinitaly.com.

Newspapers and magazines

You'll find the main **national newspapers** on any newsstand: *La Repubblica* (Ⓦ repubblica.it), centre-left, with a lot of cultural coverage; *Il Corriere della Sera* (Ⓦ corriere.it), authoritative and rather conservative; *L'Unità* (Ⓦ unita.tv), the former Communist Party organ, also strong on culture; *Il Manifesto* (Ⓦ ilmanifesto.info), a more radical and readable left-wing daily; and the pink *Gazzetta dello Sport* (Ⓦ gazzetta.it), essential reading for the serious sports fan.

Most people, however, prefer Sardinian **local papers**, which offer non-Sards good insights into local concerns as well as being useful for transport timetables, entertainment listings, festival announcements and local chemists, hospitals, internet cafés, etc. There are two main ones: *L'Unione Sarda* (Ⓦ unionesarda.it), most read in Cágliari and the south of the island, and *La Nuova Sardegna* (Ⓦ lanuovasardegna.it), also called "La Nuova", favoured in Sássari and the north. There's little to tell between them in terms of content, and each has local editions for the island's main towns. Note that Monday editions of all national and regional newspapers are almost exclusively devoted to sport, with very slim coverage of any other news.

English-language and other foreign-language newspapers can be found at some kiosks and newsagents in Cágliari, Sássari, Oristano, Nuoro, Olbia, Porto Cervo and Alghero, usually available the same day in thinned-down editions, though costing more than at home.

Television

Surprisingly, for such an outdoor society, Italians are among the most dedicated TV-watchers in the world. The three state-run channels, RAI 1, 2 and 3, have got their backs against the wall in the face of the domination of the numerous private channels by Silvio Berlusconi's Mediaset corporation, which includes Rete 4, Canale 5 and Italia 1 – three of the biggest in the **independent sector**. On the whole, the output is fairly bland, with a heavy helping of soaps, sitcoms, cabaret shows and films, though the **RAI channels** have less advertising and mix some good reporting in among the dross. RAI 3 has the most intelligent coverage, and broadcasts Sardinian news programmes. Of the **local channels**, Videolina is most popular in Cágliari, Sardegna Uno in the north, TeleSardegna around Nuoro and Tele Regione transmits everywhere; advertising is constant on all of these. **Satellite TV** is increasingly available in hotels.

Radio

The situation in **radio** is even more anarchic than the TV scene, with the FM waves crowded to the extent that you can pick up a new station just by walking down the corridor. The myriad of **commercial stations** broadcast virtually undiluted chart music. Again, the RAI stations are generally more sober, with far less advertising: **RAI 1** and **RAI 2** include serious news programmes among the phone-ins and pop, while for higher-brow culture, including literature and classical and jazz music, tune into **RAI 3**, which might devote a couple of hours to themes such as Brazilian or Celtic music. Frequencies vary according to where you are, so be prepared for regular retuning.

With a mobile device or a short-wave radio, you can also pick up programmes of the **BBC World Service** (Ⓦbbc.co.uk/worldserviceradio) and **Voice of America** (Ⓦvoanews.com).

Festivals

Sardinia's festivals – *feste* and *sagre* – are high points of the island's cultural life, and excellent opportunities to view traditional costumes and dancing and to hear local music. While many are religious in origin – mostly feast days for saints having a special role for a particular locality – others are purely secular, celebrating harvest or some other event, or simply perpetuating ancient games and competitions. These are still basically unchanged in the smaller towns and villages, though some have evolved into much larger affairs spread over three or four days, while others have been developed with an eye to tourism.

In all, **masks** and **costumes** play a prominent role, emblems of local identity representing a variety of functions and traditions, and injecting an eerie theatricality into the proceedings. **Horses**, too, are often present, and may be the main protagonists. Many *feste* attract groups of singers and dancers from surrounding villages, and special food and sweets are available from stalls. Local people spend months preparing for the occasion, and they're well worth scheduling into your visit.

Carnival

Traditionally, the **Carnival** season starts with Sant'Antonio's day on January 17, but in practice most of the action takes place over three days climaxing on Shrove Tuesday, usually in February. Although the occasion is intended as a prelude to the abstinence of Lent, most Carnival celebrations smack of paganism. Children wear fancy dress, and impressive masks are commonly worn, producing a somewhat sinister effect.

In Mamoiada, south of Nuoro, the three-day festival features music, dancing and the distribution of wine and sweets, climaxing in the ritual procession of the *issohadores* and *mamuthones* representing respectively hunters and hunted. The latter are clad in shaggy sheepskin jerkins, their faces covered in chilling black wooden masks, their backs hidden beneath dozens of sheep-bells with which they create a jangling, discordant clamour. Meanwhile the "hunters" lasso bystanders who are supposed to appease them with gifts of wine (but rarely do).

Oristano's **Sa Sartiglia** is wildly different, a medieval pageant involving much horseback racing and a jousting competition in which masked and mounted "knights" attempt to ram their swords through a hanging ring, called *sartija* – a Spanish word which gives its name to the festival.

Various other strange goings-on take place during this period: a six-day festival at Bonorva, between Oristano and Sássari, includes masked processions, dances and ritual burnings of puppets; Bosa, south of Alghero, holds another six-day event, with theatrical funeral processions and costumed searches for the *Giolzi*, spirit of Carnival and sexuality; the normally taciturn mountain town of Tempio Pausania, in Gallura, bursts into life with masks and floats as another symbolic puppet is incinerated; while frenetic horse races are held at Santu Lussurgiu, in the mountains north of Oristano.

Ferragosto

August is the month when tourists flood into the island, emigrés return for the summer and all the resorts devote every last euro to entertainment. The high point comes in the middle of the month with **Ferragosto**, officially the Feast of the Assumption, or *Assunta*, though in practice stripped of its religious aspects by most people. The national holiday is celebrated all over Italy more exuberantly than Christmas, with towns and villages erupting with dazzling fireworks displays. Some of Sardinia's Ferragosto celebrations are coupled with another festival, as in Sássari's spectacular **I Candelieri**. This event – which had its origin in the fifteenth century when plague was apparently averted by divine intervention – starts on August 14, and takes its name from the huge candles carried through thronged streets amid delirious dancing.

A similar festa is held in the nearby village of Nulvi, also starting on August 14, but with just three candles (here representing shepherds, farmers and craftsmen), which are preceded by twelve monks – representing the apostles – singing medieval hymns. The Madonna herself is wheeled around town on August 15, and there follows some sort of religious ceremony every day until August 22.

Religious festivals

The vast majority of Sardinia's festivals are related to religion, though sometimes in the loosest possible way. The saints' days, of course, always have a religious element, but the most dramatic scenes are usually to be seen at Easter. Most towns and villages feature events on **Good Friday**, when silent processions carrying a statue of Jesus on the cross file through the streets and into the main church, where the image may be ritually taken down from the cross before being laid in a coffin. On **Easter**

Sunday, the image is again paraded through the streets, to meet a statue of the Madonna in a symbolic encounter known as *Su Incontru*, amid much celebration and gunfire. One of the most dramatic Easter celebrations takes place in Iglésias, where there are almost daily processions for a week, beginning on the Tuesday of Easter week and culminating in a re-enactment of the Passion, with all the local guilds represented.

On the first Sunday after Easter, more religious processions and musical events take place in Alghero and Valledoria (near Castelsardo).

Fifty days after Easter, **Pentecost** sees a prolonged series of events at Suelli, north of Cágliari. In fact, the festival kicks off the Friday before, when the entire population exits from the village and spends the night in the fields gathering wood, singing songs and dancing. The wood collected is brought into the town, and a bonfire is lit on Pentecost Sunday, amid costumed processions and games. In Porto Torres, statues of the local martyrs are borne ceremonially to the basilica of San Gavino, and on the following day transported to the sea. There's a boat race, a costumed parade and a huge fish fry-up.

Sardinia has a number of *chiese novene*, remote churches open only for nine days a year when **pilgrimages** take place. The best-known of these are Sant'Antine, outside Sédilo, and San Salvatore, on the Sinis peninsula, where pilgrims gather at the beginning of July and the beginning of September respectively – both places are in Oristano province.

Cultural events

Aside from the festivals, there's a range of **cultural events** throughout the year. Concerts and dramatic performances are sometimes held at outdoor venues in summer, and films, too, can be enjoyed under the stars. Any of the provincial tourist offices can tell you about forthcoming events; see also Ⓦ sardegnacultura.it and Ⓦ sardegnaturismo.it.

A festival calendar

Festivals marked ★ are especially worth checking out.

JANUARY

Festa di Sant'Efisio Jan 14–15. The martyrdom of Sant'Efisio is remembered in Pula and Nora by costumed processions of marching bands, praying women and traditional musicians, followed by fireworks.
Festa di Sant'Antonio Jan 16–17. St Anthony's day is celebrated in dozens of Sardinian villages, usually with bonfires, since the saint is supposed, Prometheus-like, to have given the gift of fire to men after he stole it from hell. The liveliest celebrations are at the villages of

Abbasanta, near Oristano, and Mamoiada, Bitti, Lodè, Orosei and Lula, all located around Nuoro.

Festa di San Sebastiano Jan 19–20. Among the villages commemorating this day are Turri and Ussana, both in Cágliari province, and Bulzi, inland from Castelsardo. Again, bonfires, processions and hymns are the order of the day, usually ending up with wine and food all round.

FEBRUARY

Su Sessineddu Feb 3. San Biagio's day in Gergei (north of Cágliari) is the occasion of this bucolic event, which is named after the reed frames that are hung with sweets, fruits and flowers and attached to the horns of oxen. This is primarily a children's festival, which involves seeing who can scoff the most goodies before staggering home.

★ **Carnival** Weekend preceding Shrove Tues. Processions, fancy dress and festivities just about everywhere, with especially theatrical events in Bonorva, Bosa, Mamoiada (see p.286), Oristano, where Sa Sartiglia is the big draw (see p.147), Santu Lussurgiu (see p.163) and Tempio Pausania (see p.265).

MARCH

★ **Sagra degli Agrumi** March is traditionally bereft of merry-making on account of Lent, though Muravera (on the coast east of Cágliari) enthusiastically marks the citrus fruit (*agrumi*) harvest. Traditional Sardinian dances are performed as peasant carts trundle through town (see p.134). It's always held on a Sunday, though the date varies, and may occur in April.

APRIL

Festa di San Giorgio April 23. Several villages on the island celebrate St George's day: Bonnanaro, southeast of Sássari, is the scene of religious processions and prayers conducted entirely in Sard; Bitti, a mountain village north of Nuoro, has a horseback procession in traditional costume and renditions of mournful shepherds' songs; and Onifai, near Orosei, holds horseback processions, dances and poetry competitions.

Sagra del Cus Cus Last weekend of April. Couscous, in all its myriad forms, is the star at this festival on the island of San Pietro, southwest Sardinia. Apart from the cooking and eating, there are concerts, dance and cabaret.

★ **Easter** The most significant religious festival of the year sees holy processions and events throughout the island. Some of the most distinctive rites can be seen at Alghero, Castelsardo, Iglésias (see p.104), Sássari, Oliena (near Nuoro), Santu Lussurgiu (north of Oristano) and Valledoria (near Castelsardo).

Festa di Sant'Antíoco Second Sun after Easter. Festivities commemorating this North African-born saint are most exuberant in the town named after him (see p.94), where events take place over nine days, but St Antiochus is also remembered in Dolianova (outside Cágliari), Gavoi, in the Barbagia region southwest of Nuoro Mogoro (south of Oristano), Ulassai, south of Lanusei on the east coast, and Villasor (northwest of Cágliari).

MAY

★ **Festa di Sant'Efisio** May 1–4. Cágliari's feast day in honour of the Roman martyr St Efisius is the city's biggest event (see p.67),

commemorating the saint's delivery of the city from plague in 1656. Costumed delegations from dozens of the island's towns and villages participate, making the opening and closing ceremonies excellent opportunities to view Sardinia's diverse costumes.

Festa dei Mártiri Turritani May 3. The first part of Porto Torres' major festival sees an impressive procession accompanying plaster images of the town's martyred saints from the Pisan basilica of San Gavino to the clifftop church of Balai, where they remain until Pentecost.

Festa di San Símplicio May 15. Olbia's yearly extravaganza commemorates its patron saint, and consists of fireworks, the distribution of sweets and wine, and various games and water competitions.

La Cavalcata Penultimate Sun. Costumed revelry takes over Sássari for this pageant (see p.209), which, as its name suggests, has a distinctly horsey flavour to it, culminating in grand equestrian stunts in the afternoon.

Festa di San Bachisio May 29. In the countryside outside Onanì, northeast of Nuoro, traditional Sardinian dances take place for three consecutive days and nights.

Pentecost Fifty days after Easter. Celebrations at Suelli, north of Cágliari, and Porto Torres, with costumed processions and games.

JUNE

Girotonno ⓦ girotonno.org; first week. Carloforte, on the isle of San Pietro, celebrates the annual tuna catch with four days of eating, drinking, concerts and dance performances (see box, p.96).

Fiera di San Leonardo ⓦ cavallinfiera.it; June 2–3. The island's most important horse fair takes place around the Romanesque church of San Leonardo di Siete Fuentes, near Santu Lussurgiu, north of Oristano.

Festa della Beata Vérgine dei Mártiri Second Sun. Fonni, south of Nuoro, hosts a festival devoted to the "Blessed Virgin of the Martyrs", featuring costumes and processions on horseback.

Festa di San Vito June 15. The village of San Vito, outside Muravera (on the coast east of Cágliari), honours its saint with three days of spirited feasting.

Festa di San Giovanni Battista June 24. A pre-Christian feast day marking the summer solstice coincides with St John the Baptist's day, and is celebrated in more than fifty villages all over Sardinia, with processions, dances, songs and poetry competitions. Among the villages are Bonorva (between Oristano and Sássari), Buddusò (in the Galluran mountains between Olbia and Nuoro), Escalaplano (a mountain village between Cágliari and Lanusei), Fonni and Gavoi (both near Nuoro).

Festa di San Pietro e San Paolo June 29. Saints Peter and Paul are commemorated in a score of Sardinian villages, notably Ollolai and Orgósolo (both south of Nuoro), Terralba (south of Oristano) and Villa San Pietro (on the coast south of Cágliari). On the island of San Pietro, there's music, dancing, a procession of boats and spectacular fireworks.

JULY

★ **S'Ardia di Costantino** July 6–8. Locals at Sédilo, between Oristano and Nuoro, indulge their passion for horses with characteristic gusto in this three-day event (see p.161), in honour of the Roman emperor (and saint) Constantine. The reckless horse racing guarantees plenty of thrills and spills and attracts thousands of fans.

Gara di Poesia July 25. Orosei, on the coast east of Nuoro, stages one of the most important of the island's many poetry competitions, in which contestants recite or sing verses in *sardo*.

Narcao Blues Last weekend. The village of Narcao, in Sulcis, southwest Sardinia, hosts the island's main festival for blues music, attracting national and international musicians over four days (🔖 narcaoblues.it).

Festa di Sant'Ignazio Nearest Sun to July 31. Three days of merriment – with all the usual festival paraphernalia – take place at Musei, just off the Iglésias–Cágliari road, in honour of the founder of the Jesuit order, St Ignatius of Loyola.

AUGUST

Festa di Santa Maria del Mare First Sun. Bosa hosts various events in honour of its patron saint, with an emphasis on water, including a river procession and various watersports.

Ferragosto Aug 15. This mid-summer jamboree to mark the festival of the Madonna is celebrated with displays of dazzling fireworks. In Sássari, the event is combined with the rough and tumble of I Candelieri (see p.209). Other places worth mentioning are Dorgali, near Nuoro, Golfo Aranci, north of Olbia, Guasila, north of Cágliari, Nulvi, near Sássari, and Orgósolo, also in the Nuoro region.

Sagra del Redentore Last ten days. The most colourful event in Sardinia's mountainous Barbagia region, Nuoro's famous festival (see p.279) includes traditional music and the most important of the island's costume competitions. The second, religious part features a procession up to the statue of Christ the Redeemer on top of nearby Monte Ortobene.

Festa di San Giovanni Battista Aug 29. St John the Baptist has a second holy day, celebrated in several villages, notably Orotelli, west of Nuoro, and San Giovanni di Sinis, west of Oristano.

SEPTEMBER

★ **La Corsa degli Scalzi** First Sun. The lagoon town of Cabras, near Oristano, re-enacts the rescue of its statue of San Salvatore from raiders in the sixteenth century: an army of barefoot young men dressed in white sprint the 8km from the saint's sanctuary into town with the saint borne aloft (see p.152).

Sagra Campestre di Santa Maria de Sauccu Sept 7–17. Two separate processions take off from Bortigali, near Macomer, to Santa Maria de Sauccu, a sanctuary 10km away in the mountains, the venue for dances, picnics and poetic competitions over the next nine days.

Festa di Santa Maria Sept 8. The Madonna is venerated in Ales, a village southeast of Oristano, when her statue is brought out amid much fanfare no fewer than six times in three days.

Festa di Nostra Signora di Regnos Altos Second Sun. Not for the first time in the year, banners and bunting are strung across the narrow lanes of Bosa's old centre. Once the religious formalities are out of the way, tables are laid, food is guzzled and drink quaffed.

Festa di Santa Greca Last Sun. More than a hundred thousand devotees every year come to pay their tributes to Santa Greca, in five days of festivities at Decimomannu, outside Cágliari.

OCTOBER

Festa di San Francesco Oct 4. Nestled in the mountains between Nuoro and Olbia, the village of Alà dei Sardi takes to the fields and spends two days

attending open-air Masses, eating and feasting in honour of St Francis.

Sagra delle Castagne Last Sun. This chestnut fair is held at Aritzo in the heart of the Barbagia mountains (see p.291). The smell of the cooking nuts permeates the air for days.

NOVEMBER

Tuttisanti (or Ognissanti) Nov 1–2. All Saints' Day is a public holiday and is followed by I Morti, the Day of the Dead, a time of mourning observed all over the Catholic world. Families troop en masse to the local cemetery where loved ones are buried; in parts of Sardinia, the table is laid and the favourite dishes of the deceased are served up and left overnight – apparently, just the odours are enough to satisfy them.

DECEMBER

Christmas Dec 24–25. Not the big commercial hoo-ha it is in some countries, Christmas is primarily a family event. Fish is normally eaten on Christmas Eve, and lamb is the traditional fare on Christmas Day, followed by *panettone*, a dry, sweet cake.

Culture and etiquette

Broadly speaking, Sardinia shares many of the cultural characteristics you'll be familiar with if you've travelled elsewhere in Italy. Sards are a mainly Catholic, family-centred, food-loving people who largely share the Italian devotion to sun, style and good living. There are also, however, differences that become apparent to anyone who has spent time both here and on the Italian mainland.

As an island with its own separate language, Sardinia has a slightly less accessible feel, the people are marginally more standoffish, their traditions more esoteric. Perhaps because of the island's comparatively low density of population, personal space is more valued here – Sards have a subtle sense of dignity in themselves and their relations with others. As a result the island can sometimes have a distinctly muted feel in comparison with some of Italy's more buzzing hot spots – less extrovert and less showy.

Most Sards are polite and approachable. Even in obscure rural spots, where suspicion of outsiders is ingrained, basic decorum is always observed. The **Church** may not wield as much influence as in former times, but the institution remains at the centre of community life and commands respect locally. The rules for **visiting churches** are much as they are all over the Mediterranean: dress modestly (which usually means no vests, shorts or short skirts, and covered shoulders), and avoid wandering around during a service.

Sardinia's attitudes on **gender issues** show few traces of the prejudices prevailing in much of the Italian south, perhaps due to the greater tolerance required to deal with the regular flow of tourists. The importance placed on good manners alone will mean that abuse and discrimination are rarely encountered. The sexual harassment of **women** for which Italy was once well known is a rare event nowadays, and while women can expect to attract occasional unwelcome attention in bars, restaurants and on the beach, such intrusion is increasingly frowned upon. If you are pestered, however, it can usually be stopped with a loud "*Lasciátemi in pace!*" ("Leave me alone!"), though stronger language is not advised. And in a place where the sanctity of the family is still paramount, the best protection of all is to flaunt a wedding ring.

Sports and outdoor activities

In spite of the traditional stereotype of a holiday in Sardinia as a passive, beach-lounging affair, the island is becoming increasingly popular for hiking, biking, riding and watersports. There is also growing interest in such pursuits as free climbing, caving and kayaking. The island has one ski run, in the Gennargentu mountains near Fonni (see p.289), with a season extending from December to March. There are public tennis courts in most towns and attached to hotels, with racquets sometimes available for rent.

Biking

Increasing numbers of people in Sardinia are using **bicycles**, either for long-distance pedalling or for getting around locally. Most big towns have rental facilities, as do seaside resorts like Alghero and Santa Teresa Gallura and some of the offshore islands, and bikes are also available at some hotels. Outlets are given in the Guide; the charge is usually €12–15 per day, less in low season. If you use a bike, take care to make yourself conspicuous, especially outside towns, where the relative rarity of cyclists means people won't be expecting you. Prepare too for some arduous uphill pedalling.

The roads are perfect for petrol-assisted cruising, however, and have become a favourite touring ground for squads of bikers from Germany and Switzerland. **Motorbike** rental is rare, though most places that rent out bicycles also rent out scooters. If you opt for one of these, remember that the smaller models are not suitable for any kind of long-distance travel, though they're ideal for buzzing around towns and beaches; expect to pay from €40 a day in high season. Helmets are compulsory.

BIKE INFORMATION, TOURS AND ITINERARIES

Dolce Vita Bike Tours ☎ 070 920 9885, ⓦ dolcevitabiketours .com. Group and self-guided biking tours all over the island, including an eight-day trip from Olbia in the north to Pula in the south. Accommodation, food and luggage transport arranged.

Federazione Ciclistica Italiana ⓦ federciclismo.it. Italy's main cycling organization.

IchnusaBike ☎ 070 773 8424, ⓦ ichnusabike.it. Various organized tours, including week-long trips on the Transardinia route between Cágliari and Olbia, with accommodation, food and luggage transport arranged. Bike rental too, with delivery and collection anywhere on the island.

Sardinia Mountain Bike ⓦ sardiniamountainbike.com. Events, itineraries and excursions, mainly in central and southern Sardinia.

Climbing

Sardinia offers some of the best year-round **climbing** terrain in Europe. With peaks inland and sea-cliffs on every coast, it's becoming increasingly known, attracting sports climbers and boulderers to the areas around Ísili and Domusnovas in the south, and Dorgali, Baunei, Jerzu and Cala Gonone on the eastern coast. See ⓦclimb-europe.com/RockClimbingSardinia.html for areas, routes and local accommodation, and ⓦ sardiniaclimb.com for popular climbs and climbing news. Local tourist offices can put you in touch with climbing clubs, some offering courses, while *The Lemon House* guesthouse (ⓦpeteranne.it) is a well-known reference point for climbers – as well as bikers, walkers and kayakers – in Lotzorai, in the Ogliastra region. See also Books.

Hiking

Hiking was until recently a fairly rare phenomenon in Sardinia, and there are no long-distance paths and few marked and maintained routes (though the situation is improving). Nonetheless, the island can boast some of the most magnificent walking country in Europe, including the Gorropu canyon (see p.299); Supramonte, south of Nuoro (see pp.281–283); and the Gennargentu mountains of the interior (see pp.288–292). In fact almost every part of Sardinia offers scope for serious or casual hikes, and there are scores of hiking cooperatives that will supply **guides** for walks of all levels of diffi-culty. Phone numbers for some of these are given in the Guide; others may be contacted through local tourist offices, such as that at Oliena (see p.282), which can also supply itineraries and rough maps, or else through the Sardinian branch of the Asso-ciazione Italiana Guide Ambientali Escursionis tiche (AIGE ☎070 307 385, Ⓦaigae.org), which has a database listing eighty guides on the island.

We've outlined in the Guide some of the island's most memorable hikes (see p.133, p.282 & p.299). Remember to bring suitable footwear, a sun hat (for some stretches, a helmet is advised) and a good supply of water. Always inform somebody (for example, the hotel or local tourist office) where you're heading. Longer hikes are inadvisable without an experienced guide. We've recommended a few maps for general use (see p.48), though large-scale hiking maps are thin on the ground.

Riding

Horses and Sardinia have been an item for centuries, and Sards have long been acknowledged as among Italy's finest riders. There's ample evidence of this on display in the festivals featuring equestrian skills, notably in Oristano province, and in the **riding courses** and **excursions** available throughout the island. The largest of the riding operations is outside Arborea, south of Oristano (see p.157); it organizes courses and a range of treks through pinewoods and on the nearby beaches, and can provide infor-mation on riding activities over the whole island. The Barbagia, too, provides myriad possibilities for riding in the hills, for example from Su Gologone, near Oliena and Nuoro (see p.281). Rates depend on the length of the excursion and whether or not you're part of a group.

Watersports

You'll find a full range of **watersports** available on most coasts from Easter onwards. Apart from the dedicated operators, facilities are often offered at the bigger hotels, even for non-residents, and from some campsites. **Waterskiing** has largely been supplanted by **windsurfing**, for which the favourite spot is Porto Pollo, near Palau (see p.252) – the place for **kitesurfing**, too. **Surfers** tend to congre-

gate on and around the Sinis peninsula, near Oristano, especially at Capo Mannu (see p.155).

Sailing is another favourite summer pastime, particularly around Alghero, the Costa del Sud, the Costa Smeralda and the Maddalena archipelago. This is a high-spending pursuit in Sardinia, however, and most enthusiasts will have to make do with joining a group with a full crew to do the actual sailing. Ask at tourist offices in Alghero, Olbia, Palau and La Maddalena about companies offering these expeditions. Alternatively, individual outfits, such as Amfibie Treks (☎0039 346 320 9311, Ⓦamfibietreks .co.uk), based on the east coast south of Olbia, offer sailing and windsurfing courses with accommoda-tion in campsites.

Sardinia is one of the Mediterranean's best locations for **diving**. The best sites are around Alghero, Stintino, Santa Teresa Gallura, the Maddalena archipelago, Cala Gonone and Muravera; local outfits operate in all of these places, offering tuition and excursions with full equipment provided. Contact details are given in the Guide.

Shopping

Sardinia has no shortage of temptations for shoppers and souvenir-hunters. The island is renowned for its local craftwork, which includes basketware and ceramics in Castelsardo, cork objects in Gallura, carpets in the Barbagia and masks and shepherd's knives just about every-where, though most famously in the mountains around Nuoro.

Every large village and town has at least one weekly **market**, and though these are usually geared towards household goods, they can be useful for picking up cheap clothing and items for the beach. These are the places where you can exercise your **haggling** skills – indeed, it's virtually *de rigueur* to negotiate when dealing with craft items and the like – ask for *uno sconto* ("a discount"). Bargaining is not practised for food, however, or in most shops, unless for quite costly items (a rug or antique, for example).

Often even cheaper than markets are the **Chinese shops**, which can be found in every middling Sardinian town. Usually marked by a red lampshade hanging outside, they sell a vast range of household goods, gadgets, clothes, suitcases and computer items.

Supermarkets are ubiquitous and good for food and day-to-day merchandise, including basic clothing. Sardinia's larger towns have branches of many of the well-known Italian **chains** for shoes, handbags and other fashion items, while smart **boutiques** proliferate in Cágliari, Sássari, Alghero, Olbia and Porto Cervo.

Tabacchi, or tobacco shops – recognizable by a sign displaying a white "T" on a black or blue background – also sell sweets, postcards, stationery, stamps and sometimes bus tickets and toiletries.

Note that shops, bars and restaurants are all legally obliged to provide you with a **receipt** (*una ricevuta* or *uno scontrino*). Don't be surprised when it's thrust upon you, as they – and indeed you – can be fined if you don't take it.

Travelling with children

Children are adored in Sardinia, and will be welcomed and catered for in bars and restaurants (all now smoke-free). Hotels normally charge around thirty percent extra to put a bed or cot in your room, though kids pay less on trains and enter museums and other tourist sites for free. Many coastal hotels and most campsites are well equipped for family holidays, and lay on a range of entertainments and activities for kids and parents.

Parents of **babies** and **toddlers** will find everything they need for their day-to-day requirements in pharmacies and supermarkets – nappies, baby food, medication, milk, etc. However, it's rare to find highchairs in cafés or restaurants, or changing facilities in public places, and breast-feeding in public is unusual.

Although there are few **attractions** designed specifically for kids, the island's beaches provide all the entertainment most kids would want, while prehistoric *nuraghi*, numerous castles and some archeological sites provide plenty of outdoor fun inland. Some attractions, such as the aquarium and "tourist train" in Alghero and Sardegna in Miniatura near Barúmini, have a universal appeal.

The main **hazards** when travelling with children in Sardinia are the heat and sun in summer. Sunblock can be bought at any pharmacy, and bonnets or straw hats in most markets. Other risks include the possibility of stepping on sea urchins or brushing against jellyfish (see p.46).

Take advantage of the less intense periods – mornings and evenings – for travelling, and use siesta time to recover flagging energy. The rhythms of the southern climate soon modify established patterns,

and you'll find it more natural carrying on later into the night, past normal bedtimes. In summer, it's not unusual to see Sardinian children out at midnight, and not looking much the worse for it.

Travel essentials

Costs

While Sardinia isn't particularly cheap compared with some other Mediterranean holiday spots, it's still noticeably less expensive than mainland Italy. You'll find that transport, food and accommodation are good value, but items such as fuel and car rental are quite pricey by southern European standards. Prices rise considerably from July to September.

With a tight rein on your budget – camping or hostelling, buying some of your own food in the shops and markets – you could get by on €40–67 per day; a more realistic **average daily budget** is around €67–121 a day, including meals in restaurants, hotel accommo-dation and some travel costs; while on €121–202 a day you could be living pretty comfortably. Most basic things are fairly inexpensive: a pizza and a beer cost around €11 just about everywhere, a full meal with wine around €20–40, less at lunchtime; buses and trains are relatively cheap, and distances between towns small; and accommodation in hotels or B&Bs starts at around €60 a double. It's the snacks and drinks that add up: ice creams, soft drinks and coffee all cost around the same price as at home (if not more). And if you sit down for any of these, it'll usually cost around thirty percent more.

Of course, these prices are subject to where and when you go. Accommodation and food in the Costa Smeralda are notoriously expensive, and you might eat much better at a fraction of the price in an unpretentious trattoria in a small village. On the whole, the coastal resorts are more costly, while places in the interior are relatively cheap (though don't expect much choice of places to stay and eat). In holiday areas, you'll pay more in summer for accommodation, but you can find some fantastic bargains out of season, when nearly all establishments drop their prices. You'll often get a "special price" for rooms if you're staying a few days, but note that for single accommodation, which can be hard to come by, you may find yourself paying most of the price of a double room.

There are few benefits for **students** in Sardinia, though the various official and quasi-official youth/student ID cards may be useful for discounts for some performances and other entry tickets. Under-18s and over-65s, on the other hand, get into museums and archeological sites free. All full-time students are eligible for the **International Student ID Card** (ISIC, ⓦisic.org), which costs £12.

You only have to be under 31 to qualify for the **International Youth Travel Card**, while **teachers** qualify for the **International Teacher Card**; both carry the same benefits, and cost the same as the ISIC card. All these cards are available in the Republic of Ireland from USIT, in the US and the UK from STA, and in North America from Travel Cuts (see p.26).

Several other travel organizations and accommodation groups also sell their own cards, good for various discounts. A university photo ID might open some doors, but is not as easily recognizable as ISIC cards.

Crime and personal safety

Mention **crime** in Sardinia to most people and they think of bandits in the hills. The abduction of rich industrialists or members of their families has been the most high-profile felony practised on the island since it was found to be more lucrative than sheep-rustling, though kidnapping is now a comparatively rare event, and should not affect tourists at all. In the interior, road signs peppered with gunshot are more an indication of bored youth than anything more menacing, and the feuds which occasionally erupt between families are always "domestic" affairs, and now rarely violent.

In fact, Sardinia is one of Italy's safest regions, with a remarkably low level of violence, drunken-ness and delinquency. Most **petty juvenile crime** is connected with drug addiction in the cities of Cágliari and Sássari. You can minimize the risk of falling victim to muggings or pickpockets by being discreet: don't flash anything of value, keep a firm hand on your camera and carry shoulder bags, as you'll see many Sardinian women do, slung across your body. You might consider entrusting money, credit cards and valuables to hotel managers, rather than leave them in your room, and it's wise to avoid badly lit or deserted areas at night. Confronted with a robber, your best bet is to submit meekly – panic can lead to violence, though very few tourists see anything of this.

If the worst happens, you'll be forced to have some dealings with the **police**. In Sardinia, as in the rest of Italy, they come in many forms. The most innocuous are the **Polizia Urbana** or **Polizia Municipale** (town police), mainly concerned with directing the traffic and punishing parking offences. The **Guardia di**

EMERGENCIES
ⓞ **112** for the police (Polizia or Carabinieri)
ⓞ **113** for any emergency (*emergenza*) service
ⓞ **115** for the fire brigade (Vígili del Fuoco)
ⓞ **116** for road assistance (Soccorso Stradale)
ⓞ **118** for ambulance (Pronto Soccorso)

Finanza, often heavily armed and racing ostentatiously through the cities in their cars, are responsible for investigating smuggling, tax evasion and other similar crimes. Most conspicuous are the **Carabinieri** and **Polizia Statale**; no one knows what distinguishes their roles, apart from the fact that the Carabinieri – usually in black uniforms – are organized along military lines and are a branch of the armed forces.

Hopefully, you won't need to get entangled with either, but in the event of theft you'll need to report it at the headquarters of the Polizia Statale, the **Questura**; you'll find their address in the local telephone directory. If you're staying for any length of time, the Questura is also where you obtain a *permesso di soggiorno* (residence permit) or visa extension.

In any brush with the authorities, your experience will depend on the individuals you're dealing with, though most Sard police officers – male and female – are unfailingly polite. Apart from **topless bathing** (tolerated in appropriate surroundings, but don't try anything more daring) and **camping rough**, don't expect a soft touch if you've been picked up for any offence, especially if it's drug-related. **Drugs** are generally frowned upon, the judicial process is disgracefully slow and labyrinthine in Italy, and any possibility of getting caught up in it should be avoided. **Foreign consulates** (see below) are unlikely to be very sympathetic or do anything more than put you in touch with a lawyer.

EMBASSIES AND CONSULATES IN ITALY

Apart from a UK Honorary Consul in Cágliari (which cannot be contacted directly), all the following consular agencies are located in Rome:

Australia ⓞ 06 852 721, ⓦ italy.embassy.gov.au.
Canada ⓞ 06 854 442 911, ⓦ international.gc.ca.
Ireland ⓞ 06 585 2381, ⓦ ambasciata-irlanda.it.
New Zealand ⓞ 06 853 7501, ⓦ nzembassy.com/italy.
South Africa ⓞ 06 852 541, ⓦ sudafrica.it.
UK ⓞ 06 4220 0001, ⓦ ukinitaly.fco.gov.uk.
USA ⓞ 06 46 741, ⓦ italy.usembassy.gov.

Electricity

The supply is 220V, though anything requiring 240V will work. Most plugs have two round pins, but some have three: a travel plug is useful.

Entry requirements

British, Irish and other EU citizens can enter Sardinia and stay as long as they like on production of a valid **passport**. Citizens of the United States, Canada, Australia, New Zealand and South Africa also need only a valid **passport**, but are limited to stays of three months. All other nationals should consult the relevant embassies about **visa** requirements.

Legally, you're required to **register** with the police within three days of entering Italy, though if you're staying at a hotel this will be done for you. Although the police in some towns have become more punctilious about this, most would still be amazed at any attempts to register yourself down at the local police station while on holiday. If you're going to be living here for a while, you'd be advised to obtain the necessary *permesso di soggiorno* (permit), usually available from the local Questura.

ITALIAN EMBASSIES AND CONSULATES ABROAD

Australia ☎ 02 6273 3333, ⓦ www.ambcanberra.esteri.it. Consulates in Melbourne (☎ 03 9867 5744), Sydney (☎ 02 9392 7900), Adelaide (☎ 08 8337 0777), Brisbane (☎ 07 3229 9844) and Perth (☎ 08 9322 4500).

Canada ☎ 613 232 2401, ⓦ www.ambottawa.esteri.it. Consulates in Montréal (☎ 514 849 8351), Toronto (☎ 416 977 1566) and Vancouver (☎ 604 684 7288).

Ireland ☎ 01 660 1744, ⓦ www.ambdublino.esteri.it.

New Zealand ☎ 04 473 5339, ⓦ ambwellington.esteri.it.

South Africa ☎ 012 423 0000, ⓦ www.ambpretoria.esteri.it.

UK ☎ 020 7312 2200, ⓦ www.amblondra.esteri.it. Consulate in Edinburgh (☎ 0131 220 3695).

US ☎ 202 612 4400, ⓦ www.ambwashingtondc.esteri.it. Consulates in Chicago (☎ 312 467 1550), New York (☎ 212 737 9100) and Los Angeles (☎ 310 820 0622).

Gay and lesbian travellers

Sardinia's **gay** and **lesbian** scene is slowly emerging from the clubs, bars and beaches to which it has long been confined. However, while physical contact is fairly common – on the level of linking arms and kissing cheeks at greetings and farewells – overt displays of strong affection between members of the same sex may meet with disapproval. Gays and lesbians will certainly find a more sympathetic atmosphere in the cities of Cágliari and Sássari, and in the trendy hots pots of the Costa Smeralda. For general information on the **LGBT scene**, contact Arcigay (☎ 051 095 7241, ⓦ arcigay.it) or Arcilesbica (ⓦ arcilesbica.it). The website ⓦ gay.it also has a wealth of information for gays and lesbians in Italy.

Health

Citizens of all European Economic Area countries (EU plus Switzerland, Norway, Iceland and Lichtenstein) are entitled to **emergency medical care** under the same terms as the residents of the country, as well as reduced-cost or free medical treatment. For British citizens, this means presenting a **European Health Insurance Card** (EHIC), valid for up to five years. This can be applied for, free of charge, by calling ☎ 0300 330 1350 or online at ⓦ gov.uk, or ⓦ hse.ie in Ireland.

The Australian Medicare system also has a reciprocal healthcare arrangement with Italy. However, it's advisable for any non-EU citizen to take out ordinary travel insurance (see p.47).

On the whole, Sardinia doesn't present any more health worries than anywhere else in southern Europe – the worst that's likely to happen is suffering from the extreme heat in summer or from an upset stomach – shellfish or sunstroke are the usual culprits. Mosquitoes can also be a problem, especially wherever there is vegetation near the coast or a river. In the water, beware of sea urchins (*ricci*), black or brown spiky balls that lurk on rocks and can be extremely painful when stepped on – if this happens, ask advice on how to remove the spines. Jellyfish (*meduse*) are an occasional hazard at sea, according to the current. If stung, you should brush an ammonia stick (available from pharmacies) or your own pee on the affected area, and, if necessary, scrape off the sting (a credit card would do), being careful not to take off the skin.

Staff at an Italian **pharmacy** (*farmacia*) are well qualified to give you advice on minor ailments, and to dispense prescriptions. There's generally one open all night in the bigger towns; they work on a rota system, and you should find the address of the one currently open on any *farmacia* door or listed in the local paper. Condoms (*profilático*) are available over the counter from all pharmacists and some supermarkets; the contraceptive pill (*la píllola*) is available on prescription only.

If you need further treatment, your first port of call should be the local **doctor** (*médico*): ask at a pharmacy, or consult the local *Págine Gialle* (Yellow

Pages) under *Azienda Unità Sanitaria Locale* or *Unità Sanitaria Locale*, or *Pronto Soccorso*. The *Págine Gialle* also list some specialist practitioners in fields such as acupuncture and homeopathy, the latter quite common in Italy. If you're eligible, take your EHIC with you to the doctor's: this should enable you to get free treatment and prescriptions for medicines at the local rate – about ten percent of the price of the medicine. For repeat medication, take any empty bottles or capsules with you to the doctor's – the brand names often differ.

The **Guardia Médica**, available in most towns, operates a service when doctors are not available (weekends, holidays and night-time). The local clinic is usually signposted and, though sometimes minimally equipped, is generally a useful first point of call. There may be a charge per visit of around €15 for anyone who is not a local resident.

If you get taken seriously ill, or are involved in an accident, head for the nearest **hospital** and go to the *Pronto Soccorso* (casualty) section, or phone ☎118 and ask for "*ospedale*" or "*ambulanza*". Small places without a fulll-blown hospital may still have a 118 emergency service with an ambulance and small drop-in clinic. Hospital standards don't differ significantly from other clinics in Western Europe. Don't expect medical and other hospital staff to speak fluent English, however. Throughout the Guide, you'll find listings for pharmacies, hospitals and emergency services in all the major cities.

Incidentally, try to avoid going to the **dentist** (*dentista*) while you're in Sardinia. These aren't covered by the health service, and for the smallest problem they'll make you pay through the teeth. Take local advice, or consult the local *Yellow Pages*.

If you don't have a spare pair of **glasses** or **contact lenses**, take a copy of your prescription with you; an optician (*óttico*) will be able to make you up a new pair should you lose or damage them.

Insurance

Even though EU healthcare privileges apply in Italy, you'd do well to take out an **insurance** policy before travelling to cover against theft, loss and illness or injury. Before paying for a new policy, however, it's worth checking whether you're already covered: some all-risks home insurance policies may cover your possessions when overseas, and many private medical schemes include cover when abroad. In Canada, provincial health plans usually provide partial cover for medical mishaps overseas, while holders of official student/teacher/youth cards in Canada and the US are entitled to meagre accident coverage and hospital in-patient benefits. Students will often find that their student health coverage extends during the vacations and for one term beyond the date of last enrolment.

If not already covered, you might want to contact a specialist travel insurance company, or consider the travel insurance deal we offer (see box below). A typical travel insurance policy usually provides cover for the loss of baggage, tickets and – up to a certain limit – cash or cheques, as well as cancellation or curtailment of your journey. Most of them exclude so-called **dangerous sports** unless an extra premium is paid: in Sardinia this can mean scuba diving, windsurfing and trekking, though probably not kayaking or jeep safaris. Many policies can be chopped and changed to exclude coverage you don't need – for example, sickness and accident benefits can often be excluded or included at will. If you do take medical coverage, ascertain whether benefits will be paid as treatment proceeds or only after you return home, and whether there is a 24-hour **medical emergency number**. When securing baggage cover, make sure that the per-article limit – typically under £500 – will cover your most valuable possession. If you need to make a claim, you should keep receipts for medicines and medical treatment, and in the event you have anything stolen, you must obtain an official statement from the police (Polizia or Carabinieri).

ROUGH GUIDES TRAVEL INSURANCE

Rough Guides has teamed up with WorldNomads.com to offer great **travel insurance** deals. Policies are available to residents of over 150 countries, with cover for a wide range of **adventure sports**, 24hr emergency assistance, high levels of medical and evacuation cover and a stream of **travel safety information**. Roughguides.com users can take advantage of their policies online 24/7, from anywhere in the world – even if you're already travelling. And since plans often change when you're on the road, you can extend your policy and even claim online. Roughguides.com users who buy travel insurance with WorldNomads.com can also leave a positive footprint and donate to a community development project. For more information go to ⓦ**roughguides.com/shop**.

Internet

Almost all types of accommodation and many bars now have a free wi-fi facility, which you'll need the code to access. In addition, most towns in Sardinia have an **internet point** (which we list in the Guide), where printing is also available, and someone can usually point out a bar or office in smaller places that provides this service. The usual cost is around €1 for twenty to thirty minutes.

Laundry

Coin-operated laundries are listed in the Guide for Oristano, Sássari, Alghero and Cala Gonone; the alternative is a **service wash** in a *lavanderia*, where items are individually charged – say €4 for a shirt, €5 for a skirt or trousers – to be collected a day or two later, immaculately ironed. Although you can usually get away with it, washing clothes in your hotel room is disapproved of, and the water supply itself may be limited in summer.

Mail

Post office opening hours are usually Monday to Friday 8.20am to 7.05pm, Saturday 8.20am to 12.35pm (smaller towns and villages won't have a service on weekday afternoons and/or on Sat morning). If you want stamps (*francobolli*), you can buy them in *tabacchi* too, as well as in some gift shops in the tourist resorts.

Letters can be sent **poste restante** to any main post office in Sardinia, by addressing them "Fermo Posta", followed by the name of the town. When collecting something, take your passport, and if your name doesn't turn up make sure they check under middle names and initials.

Maps

The best large-scale **road maps** of Sardinia are published by the Touring Club Italiano, Marco Polo (both 1:200,000), Automobile Club d'Italia (1:275,000) and Michelin (1:350,000), all sold from bookshops and tourist outlets. Otherwise, state and local tourist offices in Sardinia may have maps of varying quality to give away.

For **hiking**, you'll need at least a scale 1:100,000 map (ideally 1:50,000), though there's not much around; those that are available can be from online specialists, or check with the Club Alpino Italiano (**☎**02 205 7231, **Ⓦ**cai.it). For specific towns, the maps in the Guide should be fine for most

purposes, though local tourist offices also often hand out reasonable town plans.

Online, look up Ⓦsardegnageoportale.it, Ⓦmappe.virgilio.it or Ⓦviamichelin.com, which also has a route planner.

Money

In common with most other European Union countries, Italy's currency is the **euro** (€), which is split into 100 cents. **Notes** come in denominations of 500, 200, 100, 50, 20, 10 and 5 euros, and eight different **coin** denominations, including 1 and 2 euros, then 50, 20, 10, 5, 2 and 1 cents (*centésimi*). It's a good idea to have some cash in euros with you when you arrive in Sardinia, if only for the bus or taxi fare into town, though airports and ports will usually have banks with ATMs. In any case it's worth bringing enough euros with you to tide you over should your other financial arrangements for some reason fail to work immediately. The **exchange rate** at the time of writing is €1 = £0.72 or US$1.13; £1 = €1.39 and US$1 = €0.91.

Most small towns in Sardinia are supplied with at least one **bank**, usually with an ATM. Banking **hours** vary slightly from town to town, but generally banks are open Monday to Friday from 8.30am to 1.15pm and 3pm to 4.15pm. Outside these times you can change cash at most post offices and some large hotels, and at exchange shops in the resorts.

Credit cards are widely accepted everywhere, including most petrol stations, stores and super-markets, but excluding the majority of B&Bs. MasterCard and Visa are most common, American Express much less so. Cash withdrawals can be made from ATMs, though remember that these are treated as loans, with interest accruing daily from the date of withdrawal, and there's usually a transaction fee on top of this. Make sure you have a personal identification number (PIN) that's designed to work overseas, and always inform your bank or credit card supplier that you will be using your card abroad, to avoid it being blocked. The best option is usually to bring a prepaid debit card, which works with a PIN for all transactions in places that take Visa cards, and in most ATMs.

Opening hours and public holidays

Basic **opening hours** for most shops and businesses in Sardinia are Monday to Saturday from 8 or 9am to

PUBLIC HOLIDAYS

January 1 New Year's Day
January 6 Epiphany
Good Friday
Easter Monday
April 25 Liberation Day
May 1 Labour Day
August 15 Ferragosto; Assumption of the Blessed Virgin Mary
November 1 Ognissanti, or Tutti i Santi (All Saints)
December 8 Immaculate Conception of the Blessed Virgin Mary
December 25 Christmas Day
December 26 St Stephen's Day

around 1pm, and from around 4pm to 7 or 8pm, though some offices work to a more standard European 9am to 5pm day. Everything, except museums, bars and restaurants, closes on Sunday, though you might find *pasticcerie*, and fish shops in some coastal towns, open until Sunday lunchtime.

Occasionally you'll come across museums, churches and other monuments **closed for restoration** (*chiuso per restauro*). Some of these are long-term closures, though you might be able to persuade a workman or curator/priest to give you a peek, even if there's scaffolding everywhere.

Other disrupting factors are national holidays (see box above) – when you can expect shops and offices to be closed and a Sunday transport service – and strikes. Local religious holidays don't generally close down shops and businesses, but accommodation space may be tight.

Most **churches** open around 7 or 8am for Mass and close around 11am or noon, opening up again at 4 to 5pm, and closing at 7 or 8pm; smaller ones will only open for early morning and evening services; some only open on Sunday and on religious holidays.

Museums are generally open either all day or from 9am to 1pm and 4pm to 8pm, 3pm to 7pm in winter. Those that aren't open daily are most likely to be closed on Monday. **Archeological sites** are usually open daily from 9am until an hour before sunset, in practice until around 5pm in winter, 8pm in summer. The most important *nuraghi* (Sardinia's famous prehistoric towers) share these hours, though most of the smaller ones are either open to anyone at all hours, or open only on request, or closed permanently. If you need to cross private land to reach them, it's best to ask first. In summer, some museums and other attractions stay open until midnight, though such decisions are usually made at the last minute, and late closing times have not been detailed in the Guide.

Phones

Public **telephones** come in various forms, usually with clear instructions in English. For the most common type, you'll need a **phone card** (*scheda telefónica*), available for €5 from *tabacchi* or newsstands; the perforated corner must be torn off before the card can be used. Some kiosks still accept coins, though these are being phased out, and some take credit cards. Note that you need to insert your card or a coin (which will be refunded) even when dialling toll-free numbers. Alternatively you could find a call centre (see p.50) or phone from a hotel, where you'll normally be charged 25 percent more.

Mobile phones work on the GSM European standard. You'll hardly see an Italian without one; if you plan to join them, make sure you make the necessary arrangements with your mobile phone company before you leave. After arrival, your phone should lock onto one of the Italian frequencies – Vodafone, Wind, 3 or Tim, and you'll be texted the **tariffs** applicable; they're usually quite expensive, and you're also charged for part of the cost of incoming calls. Accessing your message centre can also be pricey, and you'll need to check with your company that this service will be available to you,

INTERNATIONAL TELEPHONE CODES

Note that the initial zero is omitted from the area code when dialling the UK, Ireland, Australia, New Zealand and South Africa from abroad.
UK international access code + 44 + city code.
Republic of Ireland international access code + 353 + city code.
USA and Canada international access code + 1 + area code.
Australia international access code + 61 + city code.
New Zealand international access code + 64 + city code.
South Africa international access code + 27 + city code.

and the relevant access number. The alternative, cheaper option is to acquire an Italian SIM card from one of the local providers (see above), for which you'll need to present your passport.

When **making calls** to Italian landlines, you must always dial the local area code with the number wherever you are (in Italy or abroad). All telephone numbers listed in the Guide include the entire number, including the relevant area code. Numbers beginning ❶800 are free, while those beginning ❶199 and ❶848 are charged at the national rate. To look up a number, call your service provider or consult ⓦtuttinumeri.it or ⓦelencosi.it.

For **calling Sardinia** from your home country, dial the international access code; then 39 (for Italy); then the area code including the first zero (mobile numbers do not start with zero); and then the subscriber number.

The cheapest way of **phoning home** from Sardinia (see box, p.49) is to have a **Skype** account, enabling you to call for free from a laptop or an internet café. Alternatively, you might consider an **international phone card** (*carta telefónica internazionale*) available in various denominations from post offices, tobacconists and some other shops. All phones accept them, but before each call you need to dial the special access and PIN printed on the back of the card. The most reliable are those issued by **Edicard**, available from bars and tobacconists with a Sisal (lottery) terminal, in denominations of €5.

A third option for making international calls is to seek out a **cheap-call centre,** an increasing number of which can be found in the island's main towns, often doubling as internet/fax points.

To make a **collect/reverse charge** call (*cárico al destinatario*), dial ❶170 and follow the instructions.

Time

Sardinia (along with the rest of Italy) is one hour ahead of Britain. Italy is seven hours ahead of Eastern Standard Time and ten hours ahead of Pacific Time.

Toilets

Public **toilets** are a rare thing in Sardinia. However, every bar has a toilet (*gabinetto, toeletta* or *bagno*) which you'll generally be allowed to use whether you're drinking or not – but ask first. Most places are fairly clean, though it's advisable to carry some toilet paper in your bag.

Tourist information

Outside Italy, the **Italian State Tourist Office** (ⓦenit.it) can usually provide maps, brochures, accommodation booklets and a list of pending cultural events – though much of this information can easily be picked up later in Sardinia.

Most Sardinian towns and the three principal airports have a **tourist office**: either one covering the province or one for the town, or both. Some places have a **Pro Loco** office, run by the town hall or by volunteers, which may have much the same kind of information, though these generally keep much shorter hours. All offices vary in usefulness, but you should at least be able to pick up a free town plan, accommodation list and information on local events. In the larger places, most of the staff will speak English, and some offices will reserve you a room and sell tickets for performances and seats at *feste*. You will also see unofficial **independent tourist offices** in some places, offering a host of other services such as car rental, apartment rental, excursions etc, as well as dispensing free information.

Summer **opening hours** are usually Monday to Friday 9am to 1pm and 4pm to 7pm, Saturday 9am to 1pm, but check the Guide for individual variations.

ITALIAN STATE TOURIST OFFICES

The website ⓦ enit.it has information for all the following offices.

Australia Ground Floor, 140 William St, East Sydney, NSW 2011 ❶ 02 9357 2561.

Canada 110 Yonge St, Suite 503, Toronto, ON M5C 1T4 ❶ 416 925 4882.

UK 1 Princes St, London W1B 2AY ❶ 020 7408 1254.

US 686 Park Ave, New York, NY 10065 ❶ 212 245 5618; 500 North Michigan Ave, Suite 506, Chicago, IL 60611 ❶ 312 644 0996; 10850 Wilshire Blvd, Suite 575, Los Angeles, CA 90024 ❶ 310 820 1898.

SARDINIAN WEBSITES

ⓦ **paginegialle.it** Italian *Yellow Pages* online (Italian only).

ⓦ **paradisola.it** All-purpose Sardinian site, with articles on local dialects, fauna and flora, as well as recipes, festivals, activities, beaches and info on accommodation, museums and archeological sites. There are also discussion forums (Italian only).

ⓦ **sardegnacultura.it** Reams of information on Sardinian art, cinema, festivals, language and literature (Italian only).

ⓦ **sardegnainblog.it** Excellent site for festivals, topical news, transport, beaches and other areas of insider knowledge (Italian only).

ⓦ **sardegnaturismo.it** Official regional tourism site, giving copious, wide-ranging background and specific information on the whole island in five languages, including what's on and examples of Sard music, with links to websites for all Sardinia's provinces.

Ⓦ **sardinialifestyle.com** A good resource for festivals and events (Italian only).

Ⓦ **sardinia.net** Accommodation-booking site, with information on hotels and campsites, plus itineraries and articles on culture, cuisine and history (English and Italian).

Ⓦ **sardiniapoint.it** Pages of useful information on the island, taking in everything from accommodation options and car rental to descriptions of local food, history and beaches (Italian only).

Ⓦ **sarnow.com** Good all-round introduction to Sardinia, in Italian and English, including features on food and wine, festivals, music and various localities, with photos.

Travellers with disabilities

Although most Sardinians are helpful enough if presented with a specific problem, the island is hardly geared towards accommodating **travellers with disabilities**. Things are (slowly) improving, but many sites and monuments may pose significant obstacles for anyone with restricted mobility, while few budget or mid-range hotels have lifts, let alone ones capable of taking a wheelchair (higher-grade hotels may have some rooms adapted for use by disabled visitors).

In the medieval city centres and old villages, narrow cobbled streets, steep inclines and chaotic driving and parking are hardly conducive to a stress-free holiday either, while crossing the street in Cágliari is a trial at the best of times. That said, Sardinia presents a much less frenetic level of bustle than other areas in Italy's south, while Alghero, the most popular resort, has a highly user-friendly grid of traffic-free streets.

However, there are measures you can take to make your visit to Sardinia easier. Contacting one of the organizations listed below puts you in touch with a wide range of facilities and information that may prove useful. **Organized tours** may be more expensive than planning your own trip, but accommodation is usually in higher-category hotels that should have experience of and facilities for disabled travellers; you'll also have someone on hand who speaks Italian to smooth the way. It's also worth consulting a specialist Sardinian tour operator (see p.26) for an assessment of specific resorts and destinations.

CONTACTS FOR TRAVELLERS WITH DISABILITIES

In Italy

Accessible Italian Holiday ☎ 333 119 1809,
Ⓦ accessibleitalianholiday.com. Accommodation, transport, tours and carers can be arranged, though currently only in Alghero.

In the UK and Ireland

Irish Wheelchair Association ☎ 01 818 6400, Ⓦ iwa.ie. Information and listings for wheelchair-users travelling abroad.

Tourism for All ☎ 0845 124 9971, Ⓦ tourismforall.org.uk. Free lists of accessible accommodation abroad, and information on financial help for holidays.

In the US

Mobility International USA ☎ 541 343 1284, Ⓦ miusa.org. Information and referral services, access guides, tours and exchange programmes.

Society for Accessible Travel and Hospitality (SATH) ☎ 212 447 7284, Ⓦ sath.org. Nonprofit educational organization that has actively represented travellers with disabilities since 1976. Articles and advice for travellers available online.

In Australia

National Disability Services ☎ 02 6283 3200, Ⓦ nds.org.au. Provides lists of travel agencies and tour operators for people with disabilities, mostly for members only.

Cágliari

CÁGLIARI

1

Cágliari

Situated at the centre of the broad curve of the Golfo di Cágliari, backed by lagoons and surmounted by an imposing ring of medieval walls, Cágliari is visually the most impressive of Sardinia's cities. Viewing it from the sea at the start of his Sardinian sojourn in 1921, D.H. Lawrence compared it to Jerusalem: "strange and rather wonderful, not a bit like Italy". Cágliari – or Casteddu ("Castle") in the local dialect – retains a very distinctive identity, offering both chic sophistication and medieval charm in the raggle-taggle of narrow lanes crammed into its high citadel and port area.

As the island's capital since Roman times at least, Cágliari is also strewn with the relics of two thousand years of history, and has a splendid and diverse collection of museums, archeological remains and historic churches. The city's old core is small and compact enough to explore on foot, with almost all its attractions encompassed within the four oldest quarters of the city: Castello, Marina, Stampace and Villanova. You will probably do most of your sightseeing in the old citadel, **Castello**, location of the city's flamboyant cathedral and its finest museums, and the best place to take in the superb vistas. Beneath the citadel walls, the seafront **Marina** quarter holds most of the shops, restaurants, banks and hotels, as well as a couple of absorbing historical remains. Bounding the area to the north, pedestrianized **Via Manno** – home to some of the city's smartest boutiques as well as one of Sardinia's most elegant evening promenades – drops down to **Piazza Yenne**, a favourite venue for sitting with an ice cream or a beer, while arcaded **Via Roma** is another popular spot for a coffee and pastry, looking straight across to the port.

West of Largo Carlo Felice, the **Stampace** district contains some of Cágliari's oldest churches, and lies within a short walk of a grand Roman amphitheatre and a residential complex from the imperial era. **Villanova**, the area extending east of Castello and Marina, is less picturesque, but it does contain two of Sardinia's most important religious monuments, the ancient church of **San Saturnino** and the **santuario di Bonaria**. If you succumb to sightseeing fatigue, you can unwind on the enormous sandy beach at nearby **Poetto**.

With Sardinia's best choice of hotels and some of its cheapest restaurants, Cágliari makes an ideal base for excursions farther afield, and is within easy reach of places in the southwest of the island (see p.80) and the south and southeast (see p.112).

Brief history

Probably founded by the **Phoenicians** in the seventh century BC, Cágliari went on to pass through many hands – from the Romans to the Catalans – before becoming part of modern Italy in the nineteenth century.

From the Roman era to the thirteenth century

Karalis – as it was then known – was a **Carthaginian** colony until its capture by the **Romans** in 238 BC. As an important and flourishing *municipium*, it became one of the major trading ports in the Mediterranean, but declined with the demise of Roman power, eventually falling to the Vandals and Goths in 455 AD. Following a brief period of Byzantine rule, Cágliari was repeatedly plundered by the **Saracens**, the threat becoming so great that, in the tenth century, during the era of the *giudicati* (see p.309) the site of

The Scuola di Stampace p.66   Cágliari's festivals p.76
Festa di Sant'Efisio p.67

FESTA DI SANT'EFISIO

Highlights

❶ Sunset from the Bastione di Saint Remy
The majestic views over city, sea and mountain
from this wide terrace in the old citadel are at
their best at sunset. **See p.57**

❷ Museo Archeologico Set aside several
hours for the island's most important
archeological collection, whose treasures
include nuraghic figurines, 6000-year-old
female deities and Phoenician jewellery.
See p.62

❸ Museo delle Cere Anatomiche A
strangely beautiful waxworks collection,
created in the nineteenth century for anatomy

students, this is one of Cágliari's more offbeat
attractions. **See p.63**

❹ Festa di Sant'Efisio Sardinia's biggest festival
is a great opportunity to experience the island's
traditional costumes, dances and songs. **See p.67**

❺ A day on the beach at Poetto Cágliari's
seaside satellite has 6km of silky sand, with bars
and parasols on hand for shelter and
refreshment. **See p.71**

❻ Bar-hopping in Castello The old citadel
has some of the island's most congenial
bars, best appreciated from the late evening
onwards. **See p.75**

HIGHLIGHTS ARE MARKED ON THE MAP ON P.56

1

Santa Igia, on a lagoon to the west of the city, was preferred as a more defensible base.

Cágliari's fortunes only revived in the middle of the thirteenth century after the local *giudichessa* granted the hill behind her capital to the **Pisans**. They walled and populated it, creating the citadel now known as Castello, which soon became the principal Pisan base in Sardinia, the fortifications later extended to encompass the city's lower quarters.

Rule by Spain and the House of Savoy

The formal cession of Sardinia to the **Aragonese** by Pope Boniface VIII in 1297 and a two-year siege of Cágliari by Alfonso d'Aragona led to the Pisans withdrawing from the city in 1326. Cágliari, however, retained its position under the Aragonese as Sardinia's capital, and Philip III opened the island's first university here in the early seventeenth century. Even so, absorption into the ramshackle Spanish empire proved a mixed blessing for Cágliari – in 1700, the city's population stood at a mere fifteen thousand, fewer than when the Spanish first arrived more than three centuries earlier.

In 1708, during the War of the Spanish Succession, the city was bombarded by an Anglo-Dutch fleet and occupied by an English regiment in the name of Austria; twelve years later, along with the rest of the island, it came under the rule of the Piemontese **House of Savoy**. During the eighteenth century, the city first began to emerge from its protective walls, which were dismantled in the quarters of Stampace, Marina and Villanova, to be replaced by the broad boulevards along which the traffic rumbles today.

From independence to modern times

Although Cágliari repulsed an attack by French forces in 1793, the ideas of the French Revolution were infiltrating the island in other ways. The following year, the so-called "Sardinian Revolution" broke out in Cágliari against the centralizing tendencies of the Savoyard government, and was brutally suppressed. However, the city benefited over the following decades from the social and institutional reforms that filtered through under the Savoy dynasty, and, in common with the rest of the island, welcomed being integrated into the new kingdom of Italy in 1861.

During **World War II**, heavy aerial bombardment destroyed nearly half the city in February and May 1943. Much of the bomb damage has only recently been made good, but today Cágliari presents itself as a brisk, confident city, with a population of nearly 150,000, rising to around 425,000 for the whole metropolitan area. True, it's saddled with Sardinia's densest traffic, but Cágliari also has the island's most engaging museums and monuments, and the most progressive cultural scene.

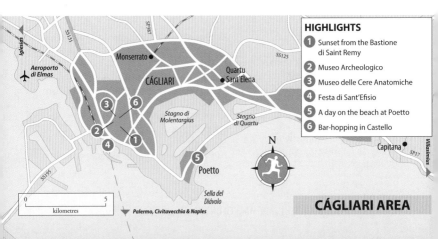

HIGHLIGHTS

1. Sunset from the Bastione di Saint Remy
2. Museo Archeologico
3. Museo delle Cere Anatomiche
4. Festa di Sant'Efisio
5. A day on the beach at Poetto
6. Bar-hopping in Castello

CÁGLIARI AREA

Castello

Served by bus #7 every 30min from Piazza Yenne, with a stop in Piazza Indipendenza; there are also lifts up from the lower town – from behind Santa Chiara (above Piazza Yenne) on Castello's western side, and from Via Fossario and Piazzetta Mundula on the eastern side

Secure on its hill, Cágliari's **Castello** district was traditionally the seat of Sardinia's administration, aristocracy and highest ecclesiastical offices. The intricate knot of alleys visible today, accessed from various points in its thick girdle of walls, has altered little in appearance since the Middle Ages, though most of the dwellings date from much later. Draped with washing strung across the balconies, many of the high blocks are run down and don't admit much light, though the lack of fuss or traffic makes for an agreeable stroll through the long alleys during the day, when there's a steady murmur of low-level activity in the antiques shops, restorers' workshops and artists' studios. At night, the area can get pretty ghostly, though there are signs of a gradual revitalization with the recent influx of a few chic bars – particularly on the western and southern edges – catering to summer tourists and the local student population. The nucleus of the district is **Piazza Palazzo**, an elongated area lined with historic monuments.

Bastione di Saint Remy

The most evocative entry to the Castello district is from the monumental **Bastione di Saint Remy**, rising above Piazza Costituzione. Constructed in white limestone, this southern spur of the defensive walls was remodelled to create its current appearance between 1899 and 1902. It's worth the haul up the grandiose double flight of steps to the broad terrace above, Terrazza Umberto I, which offers fabulous vistas over the port and the lagoons and mountains beyond. You can catch some of the best views at sunset, though it makes a good place for a pause at any time, with shady benches conducive to picnics or siestas, and a couple of good bars. A flea market, *il mercatino del Bastione*, sets up here most Sunday mornings (currently suspended while work on the Bastione is underway).

From the bastion, you can wander off in any direction to enter the tangled maze of Castello's alleys and steps. Leading off to the northwest, Via Università curves round the lower perimeter of the walls past the main **university** building and the old **Seminario Tridentino**, both built in the eighteenth century.

Note that parts of the Bastione are closed for renovation work until 2017.

Torre dell'Elefante

Via Santa Croce • Tues–Sun: May–Sept 10am–7pm; Oct–April 10am–5pm • €3; no under-7s • ☎ 366 256 2826

Hastily erected by Pisa as one of the main bulwarks of Cágliari's defences against the Aragonese threat, and tested in the siege of the city twelve years later, the **Torre dell'Elefante** – a twin of the Torre San Pancrazio farther up the hill (see p.61) – is considered a masterpiece of military engineering, designed by famed local architect Giovanni Capula. The Elephant Tower, named after a small carving of an elephant on a plinth to one side, dates from 1307, a little later than its sister tower; its sheer, unbattlemented walls are constructed of great blocks of off-white granite. Like other Pisan towers, it has the inward-facing side completely open, giving it a half-finished look. If you want to climb only one of Cágliari's towers, this is the better choice, as it has access to the top terrace. At the bottom, notice the surviving gate mechanism and the spiked gate itself, menacingly poised over the entrance.

Cattedrale di Santa Maria del Castello

Piazza Palazzo • Mon–Sat 8am–8pm, Sun 8am–1pm & 4.30–8.30pm • ☎ 070 663 837, 🖲 duomodicagliari.it

The buildings that line Piazza Palazzo are mostly eighteenth century, though the **Cattedrale di Santa Maria del Castello** has a longer history. Originally built in the

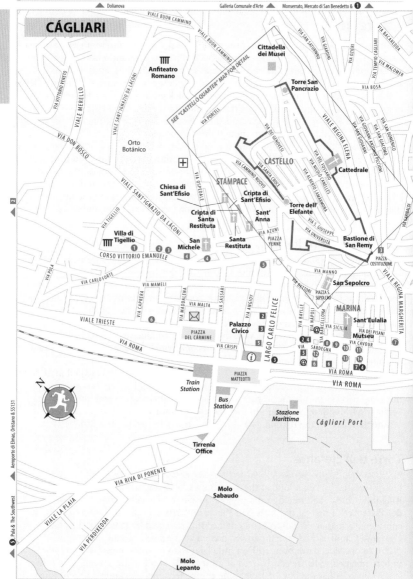

CÁGLIARI

thirteenth century, it later, as D.H. Lawrence put it, went through "the mincing machine of the ages, and oozed out Baroque and sausagey". Nothing of this is visible in the present frontage – Lawrence's sausages went back into the mincer in 1933, to be replaced by the present tidy pastiche of a typical Pisan Romanesque arcaded facade.

The interior

The cathedral's **interior** is a mixture of Gothic and Baroque, the ornate painted ceiling rising to a trim cupola. The nave is lined with shallow side chapels, the third on the

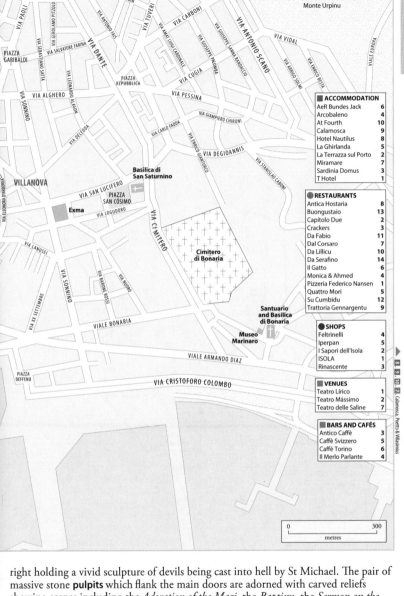

Monte Urpinu

VIA LUIGI CHERUBIN
VIA PAOLI
VIA GERÓLAMO PITZOLO
VIA TUVERI
VIA ANTONIO PACS
VIA CARBONI
VIA GIUSEPPE SANNA BANDACCIO
VIA AMAT LUIGI CARDINALE
VIA GIUSEPPE PALOMBA
VIA ANTONIO SCANO
VIA VIDAL
VIA ENRICO BESTA
VIA ARRIGO SOLMI
VIALE EUROPA
VIA SEBASTIANO SATTA
VIA SALVATORE FARINA
VIA DANTE
PIAZZA GARIBALDI
PIAZZA REPUBBLICA
VIA CUGIA
VIA LEONARDO ALAGON
VIA PESSINA
VIA ALGHERO
VIA SONNINO
VIA GIAMPIERO CHIRONI
VIA DELEDDA
VIA CARLO FADDA
VIA ENRICO GNIFETRICO
VIA DEGIOANNIS
VIA STANISLAO CABONI

ACCOMMODATION
AeR Bundes Jack	6
Arcobaleno	4
At Fourth	10
Calamosca	9
Hotel Nautilus	8
La Ghirlanda	5
La Terrazza sul Porto	2
Miramare	7
Sardinia Domus	3
T Hotel	1

VILLANOVA
VIA ELEONORA D'ARBOREA
VIA SAN LUCIFERO
PIAZZA SAN CÓSIMO
Basilica di San Saturnino
Exma
VIA LOGUDORO
VIA CIMITERO
RESTAURANTS
Antica Hostaria	8
Buongustaio	13
Capitolo Due	2
Crackers	3
Da Fabio	11
Dal Corsaro	7
Da Lillicu	10
Da Serafino	14
Il Gatto	6
Monica & Ahmed	4
Pizzeria Federico Nansen	1
Quattro Mori	5
Su Cumbidu	12
Trattoria Gennargentu	9

VIA LANUSEI
Cimitero di Bonaria
VIA SONNINO
VIA MARONE ROSSI
VIA NUORO
VIA XX SETTEMBRE
VIALE BONARIA
Santuario and Basilica di Bonaria

SHOPS
Feltrinelli	4
Iperpan	5
I Sapori dell'Isola	2
ISOLA	1
Rinascente	3

Museo Marinaro
VIALE ARMANDO DIAZ
PIAZZA DEFFENU
VIA CRISTOFORO COLOMBO

VENUES
Teatro Lírico	4
Teatro Mássimo	2
Teatro delle Saline	7

▶ **8, 9, 10, 7, Calamosca, Poetto & Villasimius**

BARS AND CAFÉS
Antico Caffè	3
Caffè Svizzero	5
Caffè Torino	6
Il Merlo Parlante	4

0 — 300
metres

right holding a vivid sculpture of devils being cast into hell by St Michael. The pair of massive stone **pulpits** which flank the main doors are adorned with carved reliefs showing scenes including the *Adoration of the Magi*, the *Baptism*, the *Sermon on the Mount* and the *Last Supper*. They were crafted around 1160 by Guglielmo da Innsbruck (also called Guglielmo da Pisa) as a single piece, which graced Pisa's cathedral for a century and a half before being presented to Cágliari, where it was divided in the seventeenth century. Four lions by the same sculptor adorn the steps leading up to the altar.

1

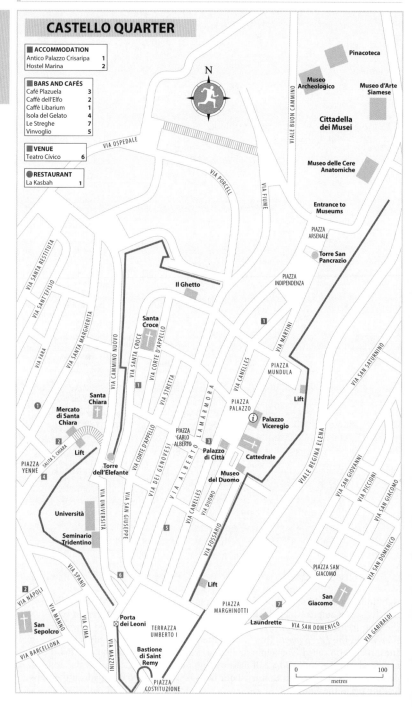

CASTELLO QUARTER

ACCOMMODATION
Antico Palazzo Crisaripa 1
Hostel Marina 2

BARS AND CAFÉS
Café Plazuela 3
Caffè dell'Elfo 2
Caffè Libarium 1
Isola del Gelato 4
Le Streghe 7
Vinvoglio 5

VENUE
Teatro Cívico 6

RESTAURANT
La Kasbah 1

N

Pinacoteca

Museo
Archeologico

Museo d'Arte
Siamese

VIALE BUON CAMMINO

Cittadella
dei Musei

VIA OSPEDALE

Museo delle Cere
Anatomiche

VIA PORCELL

VIA FIUME

Entrance to
Museums

PIAZZA
ARSENALE

VIA SANTA RESTITUTA

VIA SANT'EFISIO

Torre San
Pancrazio

Il Ghetto

PIAZZA
INDIPENDENZA

VIA FARA

VIA SANTA MARGHERITA

VIA CAMMINO NUOVO

Santa
Croce

VIA SANTA CROCE

VIA CORTE D'APPELLO

VIA MARTINI

VIA SAN SATURNINO

VIA STRETTA

PIAZZA
MUNDULA

VIA CANELLES

Santa
Chiara

Mercato
di Santa
Chiara

Lift

VIA ALBERTO LAMARMORA

PIAZZA
PALAZZO

Lift

Palazzo
Viceregio

VIA REGINA ELENA

PIAZZA
YENNE

SALITA S. CHIARA

Torre
dell'Elefante

VIA CORTE D'APPELLO

VIA DEI GENOVESI

PIAZZA
CARLO
ALBERTO

Palazzo
di Città

Cattedrale

Museo
del Duomo

VIA DUOMO

VIA SAN GIOVANNI

VIA PICCIONI

VIA SAN GIACOMO

Università

VIA UNIVERSITÀ

VIA SAN GIUSEPPE

VIA CANELLES

VIA FOSSARIO

PIAZZA SAN
GIACOMO

VIA SAN DOMENICO

Seminario
Tridentino

VIA SPANO

Lift

San
Giacomo

VIA NÁPOLI

VIA MANNO

VIA CIMA

San
Sepolcro

Porta
dei Leoni

TERRAZZA
UMBERTO I

PIAZZA
MARGHINOTTI

Laundrette

VIA SAN DOMENICO

VIA GARIBALDI

VIA BARCELLONA

VIA MAZZINI

Bastione
di Saint
Remy

PIAZZA
COSTITUZIONE

0   100
metres

Of the numerous tombs crammed into the cathedral, the most important is the incredibly elaborate fifteenth-century sepulchre of Martin II of Aragon in the left transept, and those of the Savoyard royal family in the densely adorned subterranean **crypt** beneath the altar. Little of the walls and ceiling of this low, vaulted chamber hewn directly out of the rock has been left undecorated; the carvings include work by Sicilian artists of Sardinian saints whose ashes were said to have been found under the basilica of San Saturnino (see p.69) in 1617.

Museo del Duomo

Via del Fossario 5 • Tues–Fri 4.30–7.30pm, Sat & Sun 10am–1pm & 4.30–7.30pm • €4 • ☎ 070 680 244, ⓦ museoduomodicagliari.it

Behind the cathedral, the **Museo del Duomo** is primarily worth visiting to see two religious artworks. One, the fifteenth-century *Tríttico di Clemente VII*, is probably the work of more than one Flemish artist at various periods, and may itself be a copy of a lost painting by Rogier van der Weyden. The triptych shows the wan figure of the dead Christ with the Madonna in the central panel, flanked by Sts Anne and Margaret, the latter holding a dragon. The work once formed part of a collection of precious items stolen from the private apartments of Pope Clement VII during the sack of Rome in 1527. It was brought to Cágliari by Catalan sailors, who, having been caught up in a fierce storm during the crossing from the mainland, confessed their guilt. The treasure was handed in to the archbishop of Cágliari, and the painting was subsequently presented to the cathedral by Pope Clement. The museum's second masterpiece is the powerful *Retablo della Crocefissione*, a six-panelled polyptych attributed to Michele Cavaro (1517–84) or, more probably, to his workshop.

Palazzo di Città

Piazza Palazzo • Tues–Sun: mid–June to mid–Sept 10am–9pm; mid-Sept to mid-June 10am–6pm • €4; €8 with Museo d' Arte Siamese and Galleria Comunale d' Arte • ☎ 070 677 6482, ⓦ museicivicicagliari.it

Next to the cathedral, Cágliari's old town hall, the **Palazzo di Città**, has been restored to house an excellent gallery of local and regional art and crafts. You'll see lacework, embroidered fabrics, ceramics and paintings on the first floor, sacred art on the top floor and temporary exhibitions in the basement, which also reveals traces of the building's original fourteenth-century construction.

Palazzo Viceregio

Piazza Palazzo • Tues–Sun 10am–6.30pm • Free • ☎ 070 409 2000

Just up from the cathedral, the **Palazzo Viceregio** was built in the eighteenth century for Sardinia's governors and viceroys under the Piemontese, and is now used for meetings of the provincial assembly. The porticoed Neoclassical facade sports a dedication to Carolus Emanuel III (Carlo Emanuele III), duke of Savoy and king of Sardinia. Inside, the stately staircase leads up to sumptuous reception rooms hung with the portraits of be-wigged Piemontese viceroys and adorned with low chandeliers, gilt mirrors and painted ceilings. Some rooms are used for temporary **exhibitions**, while the impressive **Sala Consiliare** (council chamber) hosts assembly meetings beneath huge paintings depicting heroic events in the island's history.

Torre San Pancrazio

Piazza Indipendenza • Daily: May–Sept 10am–7pm; Oct–April 9am–5pm • €3; no under-7s • ☎ 366 256 2826

Via Martini leads up from Piazza Palazzo to the smaller Piazza Indipendenza, overlooked by the best-restored of Cágliari's fortified towers, the **Torre San Pancrazio**. Very similar in design to the Torre dell'Elefante (see p.57), and also open at one side, the tower repays

1

the climb up four levels with magnificent views over the old town and port, extending south as far as the refinery at Sarroch and the sliver of land holding the remains of Nora. The tower, which rises to 36m, dates from 1305, and was the work of the renowned Giovanni Capula. It subsequently became a prison and later an observatory, when Alberto di Lamármora, Sardinia's greatest all-round scientist in the nineteenth century, installed stargazing and cartographic instruments on its top in 1835.

The tower stands above the Porta di San Pancrazio gateway, usually busy with cars passing through Piazza dell'Arsenale, where a plaque records the brief visit made to Cágliari in 1573 by the Spanish author of *Don Quixote*, Miguel de Cervantes, shortly before his capture and imprisonment by Moorish pirates.

Cittadella dei Musei

A fortified arched gateway at the top of Piazza dell'Arsenale gives access to the **Cittadella dei Musei**, a museum and study complex erected on the site of the former royal arsenal. The modern concrete structure, softened by greenery, incorporates parts of the older building. The most essential collection here is the **archeological museum**, but the other, wildly contrasting displays are all worth exploring.

Museo Archeologico

Cittadella dei Musei • Tues–Sun 9am–8pm, last entry at 7.15pm • €5 • ☎ 070 655 911, ⓦ archeocaor.beniculturali.it

The island's most important prehistoric, Phoenician, Carthaginian and Roman finds are gathered in the **Museo Archeologico**, including jewellery, coins, busts and statues of gods and muses, as well as funerary items from the sites of Nora, Tharros and Sant'Antíoco. Some of the museum's earliest exhibits are from the island's Bonu Ighinu culture (c. 4000–3500 BC), including, on the ground floor, striking sculptures of rotund **female deities**, with broad, inscrutable smiles. Elsewhere, a Phoenician bronze **statue of Hercules** highlights the strong trading links that stretched across the Mediterranean to Italy in the fourth century BC, and to Etruria and Greece before then.

Upstairs, look out for the **Stele di Nora**, a stone tablet showing, in Phoenician characters, what may be the first recorded occurrence of the name "Sardinia". The ninth- or eighth-century-BC stele, unearthed near Nora in 1773, is the most ancient Phoenician inscription to be found in the western Mediterranean, and appears to commemorate the building of a temple erected on the arrival of the first Phoenician settlers on the island.

The nuraghic bronzetti

The museum's most absorbing pieces come from Sardinia's nuraghic culture (see pp.307–308), notably a series of **bronze statuettes**, or *bronzetti*, ranging from about 30cm to 90cm in height, spindly and highly stylized but packed with invention and quirky humour. Representing warriors and hunters, athletes, shepherds, nursing mothers, bulls, stags and other wild animals, these figurines constitute the main source of information about this obscure phase of the island's history. Most were probably votive offerings, made to decorate the interiors of temples and later buried to protect them from the hands of invaders. You can recognize the chieftain by his cloak and raised right arm, and the warriors by their extravagantly horned helmets.

Other nuraghic items here have a more primitive look: fragments of pots, axe-heads, jewellery and various domestic implements.

Pinacoteca

Cittadella dei Musei • Tues–Sun 9am–7.15pm • €5 • ☎ 070 662 496, ⓦ pinacoteca.cagliari.beniculturali.it

Adjacent to the archeological museum, the **Pinacoteca** art gallery holds an excellent collection of primarily Catalan and Italian religious art from the fifteenth and sixteenth centuries. The well-displayed paintings have mostly been brought here from local churches and include wooden altarpieces by the foremost Sard painters of the time,

1

Pietro Cavaro and Antioco Mainas, as well as Flemish work and a Sienese *Madonna* that ended up in Cágliari on account of a mistaken attribution. Other works to look out for include a *Giudizio Universale* (Last Judgement), showing distinct African elements, by the Sard Mastro di Olzai, and, next to each other on the top level, a trio of large, multi-panelled altarpieces: the *Retablo di San Bernardino* by Joan Figuera and Rafael Thomas, an *Annunciation* by Joan Mates and a *Visitation* by Joan Barcelo.

The lowest floor displays a collection of traditional **Sardinian jewellery** – amulets, necklaces, earrings and rosaries – worked in silver and gold, mostly dating from the nineteenth century. You can pick up a free catalogue with English translation on the way in.

Museo d'Arte Siamese

Cittadella dei Musei • Tues–Sun: mid-June to mid-Sept 10am–8pm; mid-Sept to mid-June 10am–6pm • €2; €8 with Palazzo di Città and Galleria Comunale d'Arte • ☎ 070 651 888, ⓦ museicivicicagliari.it

Displaying items collected by Stefano Cardu, a local engineer who spent twenty years in what is now Thailand, the **Museo d'Arte Siamese** is a cultural leap away from the Cittadella's other museums. Chinese bowls and boxes sit alongside Japanese statuettes and a fearsome array of weaponry, but most of the work is from Siam, including vases, silk paintings and ink drawings featuring vivid portrayals of Hindu and Buddhist legends, mainly from the period 1400–1800.

Museo delle Cere Anatomiche

Cittadella dei Musei • Tues–Sun 9am–1pm & 4–7pm • €1.50 • ☎ 070 675 7624

The smallest and most surprising of the Cittadella's museums is the **Museo delle Cere Anatomiche**, displaying 23 somewhat gruesome wax models of anatomical sections made in the early nineteenth century by the Florentine Clemente Susini. Items include cutaways of a head and neck, showing the intricate network of nerves and blood vessels linking the brain and facial organs, and one of a pregnant woman displaying the foetus within the womb. Each display has explanatory diagrams in Italian and English.

Galleria Comunale d'Arte

Giardini Púbblici, Viale Regina Elena • Mon & Wed–Sun: mid-June to mid-Sept 10am–9pm; mid-Sept to mid-June 10am–6pm • €6; €8 with Palazzo di Città and Museo d'Arte Siamese • ☎ 070 677 7598, ⓦ museicivicicagliari.it

A short walk from the Porta di San Pancrazio – or take the lift on Piazzetta Mundula – a brief area of flat greenery below the walls of Castello constitutes Cágliari's **Giardini Púbblici**. At the far end, Cágliari's **Galleria Comunale d'Arte** offers a more contemporary slant on Sardinia and its people than the city's Pinacoteca. Exhibitions of Sard artists take place alongside a permanent collection of some of the island's best modern artworks. Among the most notable of these is a moving sculpture by the Nuorese Francesco Ciusa (1883–1949), *Madre dell'Ucciso* ("Mother of the killed man"), depicting a barefooted crone swathed in a shawl, whose bony face is a poignant display of grief. Presented at the Biennale at Venice in 1907, the work helped to establish Ciusa's national reputation.

Other local artists are represented here by portraits of islanders and island landscapes, illustrating aspects of the Sard experience and often focusing on Sardinia's interactions – and simmering tensions – with the outside world. The rest of the gallery is occupied by the **Ingrao collection**, a bequest of modern Italian art that includes drawings and pallid still lifes by the Bologna artist **Giorgio Morandi**.

Marina

Like Castello, the lanes of the **Marina** quarter are narrow and tightly packed, but unlike those in the upper town, these streets are always animated, busy with the comings and

1

goings from the city's main concentration of restaurants and hotels. Marina's proximity to the docks meant that it was heavily bombed during World War II. The damage is still visible in places; elsewhere, the bombed-out buildings have been replaced by new constructions, sometimes startlingly at odds with the neighbourhood's predominantly medieval flavour.

Palazzo Civico

Piazza Matteotti • Free • ☎ 070 6771

The neo-Gothic **Palazzo Civico** (or *Palazzo Comunale*) – a white, pinnacled concoction from 1907, combining Catalan-Gothic with Art Nouveau motifs – was one of the victims of World War II bombing, but was rebuilt to match its prewar appearance, complete with bronze eagles and heraldic devices. Cágliari's tourist office is housed within.

Museo del Tesoro e Area Archeologica di Sant'Eulalia

Piazza Sant'Eulalia • Tues–Sun 10am–1pm & 4–7pm • €5 • ☎ 070 663 724, ⊕ mutseu.org

Attached to the church of **Sant'Eulalia** is the museum and archeological area together known as the **Museo del Tesoro e Area Archeologica di Sant'Eulalia**, or MUTSEU. In the subterranean complex lying directly beneath the church's altar, a fragment of the Roman city dating from the first century AD has been unearthed, which you can see from a raised walkway. The broad limestone slabs were unlikely to have been a main thoroughfare, judging by the absence of wheel-ruts, but more likely a pedestrian avenue giving access to a major temple. Another route leading down towards the port is visible, and there are also a couple of wells and even a public urinal. Most of the walls here belong to the medieval city built on the ruins of the Roman one, which was abandoned some time between the sixth and eighth centuries.

Upstairs, the **Treasury** displays priestly mantles and fine silverware, as well as a couple of interesting paintings: one, a fourteenth-century *Madonna and Child*, Tuscan in style, with additions by a Sard artist of the sixteenth century; the other, a Flemish *Ecce Homo* of the seventeenth century, painted on both sides, the rear of the canvas giving a close-up of Christ's gorily flayed back.

San Sepolcro

Piazza San Sepolcro • Daily 9.30am–noon & 4.30–7pm • ☎ 070 663 724

One of Marina's most eye-catching churches is **San Sepolcro**, off Via Dettori, with a surprisingly spacious and painstakingly restored interior. Its treasures have also been cleaned up, most notably an eye-poppingly huge gilded altarpiece covering one entire wall, created in the seventeenth century to hold a Madonna revered by the wife of one of the Spanish viceroys after a supposed miracle. The viceroy had to drastically change the church's fifteenth-century structure to hold the outsize wooden altarpiece, which he did by knocking through two chapels built into the rock, accounting for the church's unorthodox shape. At the same time, the **crypt** below it was hacked out of a natural hollow in the rock, comprising two large, bare rooms devoid of decoration except for some images of Death on the walls and ceilings, one of them bearing the words *Nemini parco* ("I spare nobody") on his scythe.

Back in the nave of the church, the sacristy to the right of the altar gives access to a much older relic of the building's long history: a large-scale paleo-Christian **baptismal font**, thought to date back to the fourth century. Set into the ground, the wide, circular basin in which converts were completely immersed was unearthed during routine maintenance work in 2000.

FROM TOP CASTELLO QUARTER (P.57); POETTO BEACH (P.71) >

1

Stampace

Lying to the west of Largo Carlo Felice, the quarter of **Stampace** has given its name to Sardinia's most influential school of art (see box below), and five hundred years later it still retains an active – if low-key – working population of artists and craftsmen. To the north of the Corso, a scattering of **churches** are worth a brief visit, though you may find the crypts and caverns over which these were built of more immediate interest. Running off the top of Piazza Yenne, and parallel to Corso Vittorio Emanuele, Via Azuni gives access to four of Stampace's historic churches.

Piazza Yenne

At the top of Largo Carlo Felice, **Piazza Yenne** was the site of the old Porta Stampace gateway before the destruction of the quarter's walls. The cobbled square that now forms a pedestrianized enclave to one side of the bustling traffic marks the start of the Carlo Felice highway, Sardinia's main north–south artery (now the SS131). A pair of monuments recall the building of this: a bronze statue of its instigator, King Carlo Felice, dressed in Roman garb and for some reason gesturing away from the road, and, across the street, a strange arrangement of a ball topped by an elongated pyramid above a simple stone column. From here, the highway starts its journey up Corso Vittorio Emanuele, today a narrow thoroughfare cutting through Stampace.

Sant'Anna

Via Azuni • Tues–Sun 7.30am–noon & 5–8pm • ☎ 070 653 839

With its monumental white Neoclassical facade atop a grand flight of steps, and sporting a double tier of Corinthian columns and pilasters, the church of **Sant'Anna** was begun during the Savoy era in 1785 on the site of an earlier Pisan church, though not completely finished until the 1930s. Faithfully reconstructed after serious damage during the bombing raids of 1943, the late Baroque design is marked by strong Piemontese features, notably its tall twin belltowers and octagonal cupola. The airy interior holds a fourteenth-century wooden crucifix and a painting by Giovanni Marghinotti, *Christ the Saviour*.

Cripta di Santa Restituta

Via Sant'Efisio 14 • Tues–Sun 10am–1pm • Free • ☎ 366 256 2826

To the left of Sant'Anna, the narrow Via Sant'Efisio leads north past the mainly sixteenth-century church of **Santa Restituta** to a doorway that gives entry to the **Cripta di Santa Restituta**. Originally a place of pagan rites linked to the water collected here, this subterranean cavern was subsequently dedicated to Restituta, a victim of Diocletian's persecution, and provided a home for African refugees during the fifth century, and later for a Greek Orthodox community. Later still it served as a prison, while the scribbled signatures faintly visible on the walls of the crypt belong to locals who sheltered here

---

THE SCUOLA DI STAMPACE

Founded by Stampace resident Pietro Cavaro (d. 1537), Cágliari's **Scuola di Stampace** influenced painting throughout Sardinia in the sixteenth century. It included artists such as Antioco Mainas and Pietro's son Michele Cavaro, and drew much of its inspiration from Spain, blending the influence of Raphael with late Gothic elements. Major works by members of the school can be seen in Cágliari's Pinacoteca (see pp.62–63) and Oristano's Antiquarium Arborense (see p.145); few examples remain in Stampace itself, though the district's churches are still redolent of the tightknit community that gave birth to the school.

1

FESTA DI SANT'EFISIO

Popularly represented as a flamboyant knight with a plumed helmet, **Sant'Efisio** (St Efisins) was born in Elia, Asia Minor, and served as a soldier in the Roman army during the reign of the emperor Diocletian (283–310 AD). According to tradition, he was sent to Sardinia to combat the tribes of the Barbagia in the interior. Having refused to renounce his Christian faith, he was imprisoned in the hypogeum that is now the crypt of the Stampace church of Sant'Efisio, then taken to Nora where he was beheaded in 303. A cult soon grew up around the saint, increasing over the centuries with the attribution of various **miracles** to him – notably the rescue of the city from a plague in 1652 and the repulsion of the French attack on Cágliari in 1792–93.

Since saving the city from plague, the saint has been commemorated annually at the beginning of May in Sardinia's biggest religious festival, the **Festa di Sant'Efisio**. Setting forth from **Sant'Efisio church** on the morning of May 1, a solemn procession embarks on the long walk to **Nora**, 40km south along the coast (see p.83), bearing the holy statue of the saint that at other times is kept in the church. As the procession makes its way through Cágliari, it is preceded by a long column of costumed participants from every part of the island, sometimes mounted, often accompanied by **traditional singing** and the playing of drums and instruments such as the *launeddas* (shepherd's pipes). The costumed part of the procession soon melts away, however, while the holy statue continues with a small retinue, joined for part of its way by villagers and bands in the places it passes through, before arriving at Nora on the evening of the following day. After religious services have taken place, the statue departs from the church at Nora on the evening of May 3, entering Cágliari the next evening to a much more muted reception.

The festa is a spectacular affair, and a great chance to view a panoply of traditional **costumes** from the villages, as well as to hear authentic Sard music. If you can't be present for the whole four-day event, the May 1 festivities are the highlight, for which you might consider a ticket for the stadium-like seats (*tribune*) around Piazza Matteotti and surrounding streets on the route. These give a high, unimpeded view of the proceedings and cost around €25. Contact the Box Office agency (☎070 657 428, ⊛boxofficesardegna.it) to purchase tickets, which normally go on sale in early April and quickly sell out.

during air raids in 1943. The interior is mostly bare, but for an altar and a statue of the saint in the main chamber, which has niches and murky corridors running off it.

Sant'Efisio

Via Sant'Efisio • Daily 9am–12.30pm & 4–8pm • ☎ 070 652 130

Dating from the eighteenth century, the small church of **Sant'Efisio** is intimately connected with the eponymous martyr and with the large-scale festa dedicated to him, which kicks off from here (see box above). Inside, the second chapel on the right holds the jaunty effigy of the saint that provides the focal point of the procession, with various offerings – medals, rosaries and the like – fastened to the wall alongside. A cross carried at Easter is in the third chapel on the right. At the back of the church, look out for the cannonballs embedded in the wall, originally fired by the French fleet during their attack on Cágliari in 1793 – the rout of the fleet was another miracle attributed to Sant'Efisio.

Cripta di Sant'Efisio

Via Sant'Efisio • Daily 9am–1pm • Donations welcomed • ☎ 349 340 5509

Below the church of Sant'Efisio, one of the oldest of Cágliari's cavernous crypts, the **Cripta di Sant'Efisio**, once served as a hypogeum or cistern of the Punic-Roman city of Karalis. According to tradition, the Roman soldier, Efisius, was imprisoned here for his Christian beliefs before being taken to Nora to be decapitated. You can see the column to which he was supposedly bound, an object of veneration for local believers. There is evidence of a church in existence here as far back as the fifth century; more recently, the crypt served as an air-raid shelter and rubbish dump. If the entrance is closed (which it often is), there may be someone in the church to show you around – otherwise call to arrange a visit.

Anyone interested in further exploring Cágliari's subterranean sites can contact L'Isola Che Vorrei (see p.73), which offers tours to the crypts of Santa Restituta, Sant'Efisio and San Sepolcro (see p.64), as well as the Galleria dei Salesiani, a nineteenth-century tunnel used as an air-raid shelter during World War II.

San Michele

Via Azuni • Mon–Sat 8–11am & 6.30–8.30pm, Sun 9am–noon & 7–9pm • ☎ 070 658 626

Just up from Corso Vittorio Emanuele, the triple-arched facade of the church of **San Michele** beautifully frames the western end of Via Azuni. Consecrated by the Jesuits in 1738, the highly ornamented building is one of Sardinia's most opulent examples of the Baroque. The striking porticoed facade gives a foretaste of the majestic interior, a densely stuccoed and painted octagonal space, sumptuously marbled and topped by a frescoed cupola. On the steps outside, a richly decorated **pulpit** – said to have been used by Charles V before setting off on his expedition against Tunis in 1535 – stands on four Corinthian columns.

Anfiteatro Romano

Via Sant'Ignazio da Láconi • Fri–Sun 9am–6pm • €5 • ☎ 070 231 0022, ⓦ anfiteatroromano.it

Though access to Cágliari's **Anfiteatro Romano** may be restricted, you can still appreciate its scale and structure from the outside. The amphitheatre was cut out of solid rock in the second century AD, when it could hold the city's entire population of about ten thousand. Despite its state of decay (much of the site was cannibalized to build churches in the Middle Ages) and the intrusion of scaffolding, you can make out the network of underground passages and chambers cut out of the rock, including cages and trenches for the animals.

Orto Botánico

Via Sant'Ignazio da Láconi • Mon–Fri: April–Oct 9am–6pm; Nov–March 9am–1pm • €4 • ☎ 070 675 3522

Downhill from the amphitheatre, the **Orto Botánico** is one of Italy's most famous botanical gardens, with around two thousand species of Mediterranean and tropical plants, including examples of local carob trees, lentisks and holm oaks, as well as exotic yuccas, palms, papyrus, cacti and some carnivorous species. The collection was initiated in the seventeenth century and transferred to this site in the second half of the nineteenth century (the mother of the writer Italo Calvino later became director of the gardens). You don't need to be a plant enthusiast to enjoy this quiet and shady retreat, especially on a sizzling afternoon. On the northwest side of the garden, you can also find a spring located at the base of a limestone cliff, a pool swarming with turtles and Carthaginian and Roman remains, including four cisterns.

Villa di Tigellio

Via Tigellio • Daily: April–Oct 10am–2pm & 3–7pm; Nov–March 9am–5pm • €2 • ☎ 366 256 2826, ⓦ beniculturalicagliari.it

Close to Corso Vittorio Emanuele, a fenced enclosure holds one of the remnants of Cágliari's Roman era, the **Villa di Tigellio**. The ruins were supposedly once the house of Tigellius, a Sardinian poet whose singing and versifying were appreciated by the Roman emperor Augustus but loathed by perhaps better judges such as Horace and Cicero.

Excavations have also brought to light a later villa of the second and third centuries, quite a substantial complex arranged on either side of a narrow lane. On one side, a set of thermal baths is identifiable by the raised floor of the hypocaust, while three buildings from the imperial era with tetrastyle porticos stand opposite. The first, the atrium, where guests were received, has two Ionic columns and a *tablinum* (a room giving onto an atrium) with mosaic decorations, and is paved with black-and-white mosaics; the second – the "stuccoed house" – has remnants of patterned decoration on the walls; few traces remain of the third. Excavations continue, sometimes revealing oddments like the lapidary monuments from nearby tombs currently displayed here.

Villanova

Much of the quarter of **Villanova** is modern and traffic-thronged, but the streets to the east of Viale Regina Margherita hold two important religious sites of historical significance, the **Basilica di San Saturnino** and the **Santuario di Bonaria**.

Basilica di San Saturnino

Piazza San Cósimo • Tues–Sat 9am–1pm • Free • ☎ 070 20 101

Just off the busy Via Dante, the fifth-century **Basilica di San Saturnino** is an important surviving example of early Christian architecture in the western Mediterranean. The basilica was erected on the spot where the Christian martyr Saturninus met his fate during the reign of Diocletian (283–310 AD), and is claimed to be one of Sardinia's two oldest churches, the other being San Giovanni di Sinis near Oristano (see p.153). The building sustained severe damage in World War II, and today the weathered stone of the tall, domed structure is offset by the modernistic darkened glass which makes up most of three sides. Despite this, the church retains an unmistakeable Middle Eastern flavour, with its palm trees and cupola.

The monument is entered through an open atrium, within which a palm is surrounded by various remnants from the past: shattered pillars, fragments of Roman sarcophagi, slabs of stone carved with Latin inscriptions and a small collection of cannonballs. The church's stark **interior**, of ponderous dimensions, is empty of any decoration or distraction, though the glass walls allow you to see an excavated paleo-Christian **necropolis**, the tombs clearly visible on either side of the nave.

Exma

Via San Lucífero 71 • Tues–Sun: mid-July to mid-Sept 10am–9pm; mid-Sept to mid-July 9am–8pm • Free; charge for exhibitions • ☎ 070 666 399, ⓦ camuweb.it

A former *mattatoio* (slaughterhouse), **Exma** has been converted into one of the city's most venerable cultural centres. The galleries host regular **exhibitions**, mainly featuring the work of Sard artists, while the spacious courtyard is the occasional venue for jazz and classical concerts in summer – the bar also hosts regular DJ nights (Thurs–Sat until late).

Bonaria

Rising to the southeast of the city, the hill of **Bonaria** holds the **Cimitero Monumentale di Bonaria** – site of numerous grandiose tombs and mausoleums – and affords commanding views out to sea. Valued for its clean air ("*buon'aria*") and for its distance from Cágliari's pestilential conditions, this was an important military base for the Aragonese during their efforts to prise the Pisans out of Cágliari. The fortifications quickly evolved into a significant city and port with a population of six thousand, and

1

it was only when the Catalans were persuaded to transfer to Cágliari's castle in 1336, ten years after the Pisans were finally expelled from there, that Bonaria's fortifications were abandoned. A few decades later they were in ruins.

Santuario di Bonaria

Piazza Bonaria • Daily 6.30am–noon & 4.30–7.30pm, or 4–7pm in winter • ☎ 070 301 747, ⓦ bonaria.eu • Take any bus to Poetto or the #5 (Sun #5/11) from Piazza Matteotti and Via Roma (every 10–20min; 15min)

Built by the Aragonese in 1325, the **Santuario di Bonaria** is said to be the first example of the Gothic-Catalan style in Sardinia. The church is now most famous for the legendary image of Our Lady of Bonaria housed within. When a Spanish trading vessel was caught in a storm on the way to Italy in 1370, its crew jettisoned everything on board in their efforts to save themselves, including one chest that refused to sink, and which allegedly had a miraculously becalming effect on the waters. The chest washed ashore, at a spot now marked by a column, and was found to contain an image of the Madonna holding the infant Jesus in one hand, a lit candle in the other. The church soon became a place of pilgrimage, of special significance to all sailors who have traditionally invoked the Madonna di Bonaria as protectress; viceroys, bishops and popes have all paid their respects.

Conserved on the high altar in the Gothic apse, the statue of the Madonna and Child, both crowned, is fashioned from a single piece of locust-tree wood, finely carved and painted. The first chapel on the right has an even more ancient and much venerated statue, the **Madonna del Mirácolo**, which has stood here since the church's construction. The sanctuary's original Aragonese belltower is visible from the park at the back of the church.

Basilica di Bonaria

Piazza Bonaria • Daily 6.30am–noon & 4.30–7.30pm, or 4–7pm in winter • ☎ 070 301 747, ⓦ bonaria.eu

Adjoining the Santuario di Bonaria, the imposing Neoclassical **Basilica di Bonaria** almost overwhelms the plain lines of the older building. The basilica was constructed in 1704, but had all of its frescoes, stuccos and precious decoration devastated by a bomb in World War II. Its marbled interior has been carefully restored, and today it plays an integral role in the ceremonies next door.

Museo Marinaro

Piazza Bonaria • Tues–Sun erratic hours, usually 10am–noon • ☎ 070 301 747, ⓦ bonaria.eu

Adjoining the far side of the Santuario, the **Museo Marinaro** occupies the floor above the monastery's cloister. It's an eclectic and entertaining collection, much of it consisting of a hoard of ex-voto model ships, mostly dating from the eighteenth century and later. Among the silver galleons, clippers, steamers, warships, Arab dhows and assorted fishing boats (some in bottles), there are several French, US and British ships reproduced, including an *Ark Royal* which burned in 1587 (reconstructed in matches), a *Bounty* and a couple of *Cutty Sarks*. There are also eighteenth- and nineteenth-century paintings of dramatic shipwreck scenes. The donors range from liberated slaves to nobles and sovereigns – items include weapons donated by soldiers, a golden crown presented in 1816 by King Vittorio Emanuele I and Queen Maria Teresa, and a silver anchor given by Queen Margherita di Savoia on the safe return of an expedition to the North Pole in 1899, led by her son.

The museum holds a miscellany of other objects of local interest, including finds from the excavation immediately to the west of Bonaria's sanctuary: nuraghic odds and ends (obsidian blades and ceramics), Punic coins, clay figurines and fragments of sarcophagi, amphorae and cinerary urns from the third century BC to the first century AD. You'll also see a cistern from the fourteenth-century Aragonese castle and one unexpectedly gruesome display: the mummified bodies of four members of the noble Alagon family, who died of plague in 1604, the three adults and child still fully clothed.

Monte Urpinu

Bus #10 from Piazza Yenne (every 15min; 15min)

When you need a break from the city centre, head for the lofty heights of **Monte Urpinu**, which affords breathtaking views of the city, the lagoons and the coast. The rocky elevation forms part of the city's most extensive public gardens, and is a favourite haunt of keep-fitters – though you'll find plenty of peaceful nooks to enjoy a picnic and a nap. There are ducks and peacocks, and a kids' playground too. The main entrance is on Via Pietro Leo; other access points are on Viale Europa and Via Vidal.

Stagno di Molentargius

Entrances on Via Don Giordi in Quartu Sant'Elena, and Via la Palma on the Cágliari side • Daily: April to mid-Oct 6.30am–9pm; mid-Oct to March 7am–6pm • Free • ☎ 070 3791 9201, ⓦ parcomolentargius.it • Bus #10 from Piazza Yenne (every 15min; 15min)

The 360-degree vista from the top of Monte Urpino takes in the grey expanse of the **Stagno di Molentargius**, the saltwater lagoon that separates the sprawling city of Quartu Sant'Elena from the saltpans and beaches of Poetto. Designated a national park on account of its importance as a wetland area, it's often crowded with graceful flamingos, especially between the months of April and July when they congregate here by the thousand to breed and nest. Close up, other wading species can also be spotted, as well as rare amphibians, reptiles and endangered plants.

The park organizes **wildlife-watching tours**, on land and by boat, otherwise you can wander around the wetlands or rent bikes.

Poetto

Buses PF, PQ or Poetto Express from Piazza Matteotti (every 15–20min; 15min)

For swimming, sunbathing and beach-lounging, Cágliari's suburb of **Poetto** ticks all the boxes: a 6km-long continuum of fine sandy beach (the Spiaggia di Quartu), with bars, activities and shower facilities all conveniently to hand.

The liveliest of Poetto's beaches is at the westernmost end, where the tidy **Marina Píccola** provides an anchorage for boats and a popular promenading area in summer. Other spots along this beach strip can get fairly raucous throughout the summer. PQ buses run along the whole length, while PF and Poetto Express buses cover most of it, allowing you to take your pick of the various stretches of sand, though there's little to distinguish between them. The private **lidos** lining the beach charge around €5 for entry and use of showers and toilets, plus €10 for a parasol and €10 for sunloungers per day, and it's usually also possible to rent pedalos, canoes and surf-bikes. **Windsurfing** courses are available too (see p.73).

ARRIVAL AND DEPARTURE   CÁGLIARI

BY PLANE

Cágliari airport (☎ 070 211 211, ⓦ sogaer.it) sits beside the city's largest *stagno* (lagoon), 6km northwest of the centre. Facilities include banks with ATMs and an information desk (daily 9am–9pm; ☎ 070 2112 1281). A train service to the station at Piazza Matteotti in the town centre runs every 15–20min and takes less than 10min (tickets €1.25 from the ticket machine); a taxi costs €15–20.

BY FERRY

Cágliari's port lies in the heart of the town, adjacent to Via Roma, the main thoroughfare; the Stazione Maríttima here

has a left-luggage office. The main ferry company operating from Cágliari is Tirrenia (☎ 892 123, ⓦ tirrenia .it), whose ticket office is on Via Riva di Ponente opposite the Molo Sabaudo (Mon–Sat 8.30am–12.20pm & 4–7pm, Sun 5–7pm; ☎ 070 666 065).

Destinations Civitavécchia (1 daily; 13–15hr); Naples (2 weekly; 13hr 30min); Palermo (1–2 weekly; 12hr).

BY TRAIN

Cágliari's main station is centrally located on Piazza Matteotti, served by Trenitalia (FS) trains (☎ 892 021, ⓦ ferroviedellostato.it). Gottardo station, for ARST trains

1

(☎ 800 865 042 or ☎ 070 579 301, ⊕ arst.sardegna.it) to Dolianova and Mandas, is in Monserrato, north of the centre, reachable on bus #8 (not Sun) or #M from Piazza Matteotti, or by tram from Piazza Republica). Services listed below are FS unless otherwise indicated.

Destinations Carbónia (Mon–Sat hourly, Sun 8 daily, some change at Villamassárgia; 1hr 5min); Dolianova (ARST; Mon–Sat 8 daily, some change at Settimo; 25min); Iglésias (6 daily, some change at Decimomannu or Villamassárgia; 55min); Macomer (6–9 daily, some change at Oristano; 1hr 45min–2hr 15min); Mandas (ARST; Mon–Sat 1 daily with change at Settimo; 1hr 15min); Olbia (5 daily, some change at Oristano or Ozieri-Chilivani; 3hr 45min); Oristano (every 30min–1hr; 1hr 10min); Sássari (5–6 daily, some change at Ozieri-Chilivani; 3hr–3hr 45min).

BY BUS

All buses, including the ARST airport bus, use the bus station on Piazza Matteotti. The main bus company is ARST (☎ 800 865 042 or ☎ 070 732 2244, ⊕ arst.sardegna.it); Turmo also operates a limited service to and from Olbia and Santa Teresa Gallura (☎ 0789 21 487, ⊕ gruppoturmotravel.com).

Services listed here are ARST unless otherwise indicated.

Destinations Barúmini (Mon–Sat 2 daily; 1hr 30min); Burcei (Mon–Sat 6–9 daily; 1hr 20min); Calasetta (Mon–Sat 2 daily; 2hr 20min); Capitana (mid-June to mid-Sept Mon–Sat every 30min–1hr, Sun 6 daily; mid-Sept to mid-June Mon–Sat 6 daily, Sun 2 daily; 45min); Carbónia (Mon–Sat 3–4 daily, Sun 1 daily; 1hr 25min–2hr 50min); Chia (Mon–Sat every 30min–1hr, Sun 5–8 daily; 1hr 15min); Costa Rei (mid-June to mid-Sept Mon–Sat 9 daily, Sun 6 daily; mid-Sept to mid-June 2–3 daily; 2hr 10min); Dolianova (Mon–Sat 6 daily, Sun 2–3 daily; 45min); Ísili (3–4 daily; 1hr 40min–2hr); Mandas (3–4 daily; 1hr 30min); Muravera (Mon–Sat every 30min–1hr, Sun 1–3 daily; 1hr 45min–3hr 15min); Nuoro (2 daily; 2hr 40min); Olbia (Turmo; Mon–Sat 1–2 daily; 4hr 15min–5hr); Oristano (ARST & Turmo; Mon–Sat 3 daily, Sun 1 daily; 1hr 20min–2hr); Pula (Mon–Sat every 30min–1hr, Sun 3–7 daily; 50min); Sanluri (Mon–Sat every 30min–1hr, Sun 2 daily; 1hr); Sant'Antíoco (Mon–Sat 2 daily; 2hr); Santa Teresa Gallura (Turmo; 1 daily; 6hr 20min); Sássari (1 daily; 3hr 40min); Villasimius (Mon–Sat 6 daily, Sun 2–6 daily; 1hr 30min).

GETTING AROUND

You can easily **walk** between the main points of interest in Cágliari, though there are plenty of alternatives. For public transport-users and drivers alike, the bilingual website ⊕ muovetevi.it is a useful resource for getting round the city and its environs.

BY CAR

Cágliari is not much fun to drive around, with heavy traffic, narrow or one-way streets and pedestrian areas. Don't even attempt to enter the Castello quarter by car – it's a ZTL (*Zona di Tráffico Limitato*), with access restricted to residents; you'll be picked up by camera surveillance and fines will follow.

Parking You'll need to pay for parking almost everywhere in the central area during peak hours (Mon–Sat 9am–1pm & 4–8pm). Look out for the payment board to indicate parking fees, as they vary (usually either €0.50 for the first hr and €1 for every subsequent hr, or €0.30 for 15min, €0.50 for 30min, €1 for 1hr, €2 for every subsequent hr); if there are no meters within sight, there's usually a parking attendant in the vicinity, or you can buy parking tickets from some newspaper kiosks or *tabacchi*. For all-day parking, it's best to find a car park (for example at the train station) or a garage (there's one on Viale Regina Margherita) where you'll pay €5–10/day.

Car rental Most agencies have offices at the airport, including Hertz (☎ 070 240 037, ⊕ hertz.it), which also has an office at Piazza Matteotti 8 (☎ 070 651 078), Ruvioli (☎ 070 240 323, ⊕ ruvioli.it) and Sixt (☎ 070 212 045, ⊕ sixt.it).

BY BUS

Piazza Matteotti is the terminus for most city buses.

Services and routes The most useful services are the circular #7 from Piazza Yenne to the Castello quarter and #8

(Sun #8A) from Piazza Matteotti to Viale Buon Cammino for the Botanical Gardens and Roman amphitheatre. Buses #1, #9 and #9P run from Piazza Matteotti to Viale Sant'Avendrace, taking in Via Roma and Piazza Yenne, while #5 (Sun #5/11) goes to Bonaria to the east of the centre. For all routes and schedules, call ☎ 800 078 870 or ☎ 070 20 911 (Mon, Wed & Fri 9am–1.15pm, Tues & Thurs 9am–1.15pm & 3.30–5.30pm) or see ⊕ ctmcagliari.it.

Tickets Tickets cost €1.20, valid for unlimited rides for 1hr 30min from when you punch the ticket on board for your first journey; €2, valid for 2hr; and €3, valid for one day (*biglietto giornaliero*). Buy them in advance from the kiosk on Piazza Matteotti and from some *tabacchi* and news kiosks, or on board (except for the *biglietto giornaliero*) for €0.50 supplement.

BY BIKE OR SCOOTER

Cágliari is too hilly and traffic-swamped to be traversed easily on two wheels, but rides to Poetto or destinations outside town are more feasible. A bike rental scheme, Bicincittà, is in operation, with a dozen bike stations scattered around the centre (including Piazza Matteotti and Piazza Arsenale). Sign up at the tourist office (see p.73) for a range of subscriptions, starting at €8, which allows up to 4hr use within a 24hr period. The first half-hour's rental is free; then for all-mechanical bikes €0.50 for 30min, €1.50 for the second hr, €2/hr for subsequent hours, or double these rates for electric bikes. Otherwise, Rentacar, behind the bus station at Via Molo Sant'Agostino 13 (☎ 070 656 503, ⓦ ciarent.it), has bikes for €15/day, €35/three days, and scooters of 150cc or more for €35–50/day.

BY TAXI
There are taxi ranks at the airport and Piazza Matteotti; Coop Radio Taxi 4 Mori (☎ 070 400 101) and Rossoblu (☎ 070 6655) both operate 24hr.

INFORMATION

City tourist info The main office is in the Palazzo Civico on Piazza Matteotti (daily: April–Oct 9am–8pm; Nov–March 9am–5pm; ☎ 070 677 7397 or ☎ 338 649 8498, ⓦ cagliariturismo.it). In summer, when a cruise ship is docked at the port, there may also be an information kiosk open outside the Stazione Maríttima.

Provincial tourist info For information on Cágliari province, there's an office conveniently sited in the Palazzo Viceregio on Piazza Palazzo (daily 10am–7pm, reduced hours in winter; ☎ 070 409 2306, ⓦ turismo.provincia.cagliari.it). The office in the Palazzo Civico may also be able to provide an accommodation booklet covering the province.

TOURS AND ACTIVITIES

Cágliari Segway and bike tours ☎ 347 053 3196, ⓦ newwaysardinia.com. Escorted rides around town between mid-March and Dec, either on Segways or bikes. Tickets for Segway tours around the centre cost €32 for 1hr 30min, €50 for 2hr 30min, or to Stagno Molentargius to view the flamingos €55 for 3hr, all including an audioguide and refreshments. Bike tours around the centre cost €20 for 2hr. Tickets should be booked at the departure point at Via Sardegna 91 (10.30am–4.30pm).

City Tour ☎ 800 422 850, ⓦ citytourcagliari.com. Operates hour-long open-top bus tours of Cágliari, taking in Castello and extending as far as Poetto and Monte Urpino (daily 9am–7.30pm; €10, including multilingual audioguide); board at Piazza Yenne.

L'Isola Che Vorrei ☎ 328 276 1164, ⓦ sardinia magicexperience.com. Themed walking tours around the city and its environs with commentary in various languages. Prices vary – tours of Cágliari's crypts are €18/person, for example (minimum two people).

Sailing excursions Marina Píccola, Poetto ☎ 340 007 8543, ✉ cvmarinapiccola@gmail.it. You can explore the coast around the Sella del Diávolo on a sailing expedition, available for 2hr (€25), 4hr (€35–40) or 8hr (€50–60) from the Centro Velico sailing club. Sailings are dependent on weather conditions.

Windsurfing Club Marina Píccola, Poetto ☎ 070 372 694, ⓦ windsurfingclubcagliari.it. Tuition costs €100 for three 1hr lessons.

ACCOMMODATION

Most of Cágliari's **hotels** and **B&Bs** are in or around the **Marina** district, near the port and bus and train stations. Availability may be restricted in high season, and single rooms are at a premium at all times (though easiest to find at weekends). If you want to stay near a beach, head for the *Calamosca* hotel, *Hotel Nautilus* or *At Fourth* B&B in Poetto. All the places listed below offer free wi-fi.

★ **AeR Bundes Jack** Via Roma 75 ☎ 070 667 970, ⓦ hotelbjvittoria.it; map pp.58–59. Right across from the port, on the second floor (there's a lift), this *pensione* has spotless a/c rooms, mostly en suite, with solid wood furnishings and antique tiled floors. Larger rooms facing the front have great views and cost extra, but can be noisy. The host family is friendly, and there's a ten-percent discount on presentation of this book. **€92**

★ **Antico Palazzo Crisaripa** Via Canelles 104 ☎ 347 923 0287, ⓦ crisaripa.it; map p.60. Offering a rare opportunity to stay in Cágliari's Castello quarter, this B&B in a tastefully renovated seventeenth-century building (though parts date from much earlier) has three spacious en-suite rooms, a friendly owner and quirky details, such as the ancient cistern in the basement *cantina*. Breakfasts are self-service in your room. No credit cards. Closed Nov & Dec. **€75**

Arcobaleno Via Sardegna 38 ☎ 070 684 8325, ⓦ affittacamerearcobalenocagliari.com; map pp.58–59. A decent, functional choice for a short stay in the heart

of Marina. The clean, modern and mostly spacious en-suite rooms are in a renovated apartment with exposed brickwork, a/c and fridges. Try to see the rooms first – some don't have windows, while street-facing ones can be noisy. Breakfast is very basic, served in your room. **€80**

★ **At Fourth** Via Ísola Strómboli 3, Poetto ☎ 388 320 9394, ⓦ atfourthbb.com; map pp.58–59. A brief hop from the beach at Poetto and easily reached by buses from the centre, this B&B has two rooms with private but separate bathrooms and a/c, and a back garden planted with citrus trees where breakfast is taken (including home-made cakes and jams). Closed Dec & Jan. **€90**

Calamosca Viale Calamosca ☎ 070 371 628, ⓦ hotelcalamosca.it; map pp.58–59. Right on the sea, this is an excellent choice for avoiding Cágliari's noisy centre, 2km away. The terrace overlooks a secluded cove near the lighthouse on Capo Sant'Elia, where there's a small beach. You can also swim off rocks from the hotel garden. There's a restaurant and a good pizzeria next door.

1

The far preferable sea-facing rooms cost slightly extra. The hotel's about 20min from the centre on any Poetto-bound bus from Piazza Matteotti, changing to #11 (summer only) at Stadio Amsicora. €90

Hostel Marina Piazza San Sepolcro ☎070 670 818, Ⓦaighostels.it; map p.60. Modern hostel in the heart of the Marina quarter, with dorms sleeping from three to six, family rooms and doubles. Nonmembers must pay for temporary membership (€2), but all prices include breakfast. There's no kitchen or restaurant. Dorms €26; doubles €62

Hotel Nautilus Via Lungomare Poetto, Poetto ☎070 370 091, Ⓦhotelnautiluspoetto.com; map pp.58–59. Facing the beach at Poetto, this modern holiday hotel with cool blue and white decor is an ideal base for a seaside sojurn. The best rooms, costing extra, have balconies. Look out for good-value last-minute deals. €149

★**La Ghirlanda** Via Baylle 7 ☎070 204 0610 or ☎339 889 2648, Ⓦlaghirlandacagliari.it; map pp.58–59. Smart and central B&B in a late nineteenth-century building with painted ceilings and welcoming hosts. The five large rooms are equipped with TV, a/c, fridges and bathrooms; breakfast is at a bar on Via Roma. €80

La Terrazza sul Porto Largo Carlo Felice 36 ☎070 658 997 or ☎339 876 0155, Ⓦlaterrazzasulporto.com; map pp.58–59. Funky, brightly painted rooms with TVs and CD players are available in this easygoing B&B, which has shared or private bathrooms, self-service breakfasts, a washing machine and a communal, panoramic roof terrace. A small apartment is also available. No credit cards. €50

Miramare Via Roma 59 ☎070 664 021, Ⓦhotel miramarecagliari.it; map pp.58–59. Arty, small hotel, centrally located, with a range of boldly coloured rooms on two floors, each individually designed and fully equipped. There's a comfortable lounge with sofas and books, and a mini-courtyard with ferns and orchids. Note that the cheaper rates don't include breakfast, which is a jaw-dropping €28/person. €170

Sardinia Domus Largo Carlo Felice 26 ☎070 659 783, Ⓦsardiniadomus.it; map pp.58–59. Pleasant, professionally run *affittacámere* with clean and spacious rooms, all en suite (rooms for three and four are also available). It's up a flight of stairs, with no lift. Breakfast is taken at a nearby bar. €89

T Hotel Via dei Giudicati 66 ☎070 47 400, Ⓦthotel.it; map pp.58–59. Large, swish and contemporary hotel that's chiefly geared towards a well-heeled business clientele, with fully equipped rooms, a fitness centre and a good courtyard restaurant. It's some distance from the old centre, connected by bus #1 or #M from Piazza Matteotti. €130

CAMPSITE

Camping Pini e Mare Capitana ☎070 803 103, Ⓦpiniemare.com. The nearest campsite to Cágliari is by the sea (but separated by a road), and close to some choice beaches, some 20km east of the capital (about 40min on any Villasimius-bound bus from Piazza Matteotti). Bungalows are available for €75. Closed Oct–Easter. Pitches €90

EATING

Cágliari has the best range of **restaurants** on the island, many of them clustered around Via Sardegna in the Marina quarter. The best ones fill up quickly, so pass by earlier or telephone ahead to make a booking to be sure of a table. You'll find a similar choice of food everywhere, almost invariably Italian standards augmented by traditional Sard recipes, with a strong emphasis on seafood. For **takeaway food**, try one of the *salumerie* (delicatessens) on Via Sardegna and Via Baylle, in Marina.

MARINA

Antica Hostaria Via Cavour 60 ☎070 665 870; map pp.58–59. Upmarket though not over-formal restaurant, with antique trimmings. Meat and fish are given equal billing, and are usually excellent. There's a lunchtime fixed-price menu for €15–18, otherwise you'll spend around €40 a head, excluding drinks. Mon–Sat 1–3pm & 8–11pm.

Buongustaio Via Concezione 7 ☎070 668 124; map pp.58–59. Close to the port, this casually smart restaurant is a notch up from the other cheapies in the neighbourhood, and popular with locals. Prices are comparatively low (€6–12 for starters, €8–14 for mains) and there are fixed-price menus (€18–25). Mon & Tues 1–3.30pm, Wed–Sun 1–3.30pm & 7.30–11.30pm.

Da Fabio Via Sardegna 90 ☎070 682 140; map pp.58–59. Easygoing trattoria with the usual choice of meat and fish dishes plus pizza in the evening, and an English-speaking boss. You'll share dining space with the artfully incorporated remains of a Roman wall and cistern, or sit outside in summer. Prices are low, and there's an €18 tourist menu. Tues–Sun noon–3pm & 7.15–11pm; closed two weeks Nov.

★**Dal Corsaro** Viale Regina Margherita 28 ☎070 664 318; map pp.58–59. At this venerable institution – one of Cágliari's oldest and best restaurants – the dominant tone is hushed elegance. Modern versions of classic fish and meat dishes are truly memorable, and there's a long wine list. It'll make a serious dent in your budget though, with main courses at €20–30 and tasting menus for €65 and €75. Tues–Sun 12.30–2.30pm & 8–10.30pm; closed two weeks Jan.

★**Da Lillicu** Via Sardegna 78 ☎070 652 970; map pp.58–59. This Cágliari institution with marble tables serves sensational *antipasti*, spaghetti and a limited menu of mainly fishy Sard specialities (mostly €12–20). Booking advised. Daily 1–3pm & 8.30–11pm.

Da Serafino Via Sardegna 109 & Via Lepanto 6; map pp.58–59. No-frills trattoria that's popular with locals, offering great value for its simple but well-prepared Sard staples (around €7 for first courses and mains), with large portions and friendly service. Tourist menus are €15–25. Daily except Thurs noon–2.30pm & 7.30–11pm.

★**Su Cumbidu** Via Napoli 11 ☎070 660 017; map pp.58–59. This casual, wood-beamed restaurant serves heaving plates of *antipasti*, pasta and (mainly) meaty Sardinian specialities. Service is friendly, and there are tables outside. Set-price menus range from €13–25. Daily noon–3pm & 7–11.30pm.

Trattoria Gennargentu Via Sardegna 60c; map pp.58–59. Straight-talking Sard trattoria with plain, narrow rooms, where Sardinian staples are served at reasonable prices (€7–10 for all dishes, or a €20 tourist menu). Sample tasty *gnocchetti sardi alla Gennargentu*, made with ham, bacon, olives and tomatoes, or *spigola alla Vernaccia* (sea bass cooked in wine). Daily except Wed 12.30–3pm & 8–11pm.

STAMPACE

★**Capítolo Due** Corso Vittorio Emanuele 199 ☎070 451 0719; map pp.58–59. For a change from Sard cuisine, drop into this stylish "multiethnic" restaurant with atmospheric brick vaulting and a range of sushi, sashimi, tempura and other Japanese dishes, as well as Thai, Indian and Mexican specialities. There's a €30 tasting menu. Mon 8.30–11pm, Tues–Sat 1–3pm & 8.30–11pm.

Crackers Corso Vittorio Emanuele 195 ☎070 653 912; map pp.58–59. This restaurant specializes in Piemontese cuisine, including a great choice of risottos cooked with asparagus, wild mushrooms or truffles for around €9; mains are €8–16. Daily except Wed noon–3pm & 8.30–10.30pm.

Il Gatto Viale Trieste 15 ☎070 663 596; map pp.58–59. Spacious, vaulted restaurant and pizzeria outside the main dining zone, off Piazza del Cármine. It's a little more innovative than most, offering expertly prepared seafood or meat dishes (€9–11 for pastas, €12–15 for mains, or a fixed-price menu at €18), plus a huge range of pizzas as well as wines and imported bottled beer. Daily 1–3pm & 7.45pm–midnight.

La Kasbah Via Santa Margherita 10 ☎070 654 267; map p.60. This restaurant off Piazza Yenne serves North African street food: couscous, tagines, kebabs, "Arab pizzas" and *panini*, all €4–10. There are outdoor tables and a takeaway service. Mon–Sat 7am–3pm & 7pm–1am, Sun 7.30pm–1am.

Monica & Ahmed Corso Vittorio Emanuele 119 ☎070 640 2045; map pp.58–59. This place is known for its traditional seafood subtly enhanced by North African touches. These are most evident in the *antipasti*, and dishes such as *seppie allo yoghurt* (cuttlefish cooked in yoghurt). There's a good range of grappas too. Set-price menus are €20–30. Mon 8–10.30pm, Tues–Sun 1–3pm & 8–10.30pm.

Pizzeria Federico Nansen Corso Vittorio Emanuele 269 ☎070 667 0335; map pp.58–59. Small, stripped-down pizza joint that's renowned for its thick but light Roman-style pizzas, to take away or eat in at one of the few tables. Simply choose from the pizzas available, indicating quantities – everything is straight from the oven. Beers and soft drinks are available too. Two people can sup royally for around €10. Tues–Sun 11.30am–2.30pm & 6.30–11.30pm; closed every alternate Sun.

Quattro Mori Via Angioy 93 ☎070 650 269; map pp.58–59. This place off Corso Vittorio Emanuele is renowned for its Bacchanalian abundance of *antipasti*. The accent is on seafood and traditional Sard dishes (€20–30/ head for a full meal). It's a small space and booking is essential. Mon–Sat 1–2.30pm & 8.30–11pm.

DRINKING AND NIGHTLIFE

Cágliari is well endowed with places to drink, starting with the **cafés** under the arcades of Via Roma, most of which add fifty to eighty percent to the bill for table service. For a morning coffee or evening drink, **Piazza Yenne** is a pleasant spot to sit out away from the traffic, though it gets quite boisterous at *passeggiata* time. The **Castello** quarter is worth exploring after dark for the new **bars** and **birrerias** that are opening up all the time. In summer, **Poetto** is gaudier; a blitz of bars, pizzerias, fairground stalls and ice cream kiosks by the sea provide an evening's entertainment. Note that the last bus from here leaves at around midnight.

CASTELLO

Antico Caffè Piazza Costituzione ☎070 658 206; map pp.58–59. Dating from 1855, and the one-time haunt of illustrious artists and writers, this café next to the Bastione di Saint Remy makes an agreeable spot for a midday pause, and serves good snack lunches and dinners too. There are outdoor tables, though the traffic can be oppressive. Daily 7am–2am.

Café Plazuela Piazza Carlo Alberto ☎070 655 345; map p.60. This quiet bar with outdoor seating below the

cathedral makes an atmospheric spot for a *piadina* (filled flatbread) and/or a beer or *aperitivo*. Daily 8am–10pm.

Caffè Libarium Via Santa Croce 33 ☎346 522 0212; map p.60. With tables and divans outside on the old city walls, affording marvellous views, this is an excellent nook for a drink and a snack. Service can be offhand though. June–Oct daily 7.30am–2am; Nov–May closed Mon.

Vinvoglio Via Lamármora 45–47 ☎070 204 2094; map p.60. Squeezed into a tiny space in Castello, this "wine jazz

1

CÁGLIARI'S FESTIVALS

As well as the Festa di Sant'Efisio (see box, p.67), Cágliari has several other **festivals** and events that are full of drama and spectacle. Usually in February or March, **Carnevale** is a rowdy affair, kicking off with a carousal through the streets of Castello on the first official day of the season – a long procession with dancing and extravagantly costumed celebrations, all accompanied by *sa ratantina*, a deafening drum tattoo. **Easter** is taken seriously in Cágliari, with a procession from the church of Sant'Efisio up to the Cattedrale taking place on the morning of Easter Monday, and cowled columns trailing through town on Good Friday and Easter Sunday.

bar" has a cool, late-night ambience, with a soundtrack ranging from French ballads to funk, as well as live jazz most nights. There's a great selection of wines, beers and whiskies, and you can eat here, too (booking recommended). Tues–Sat 7pm–3am.

MARINA
Caffè Svizzero Largo Carlo Felice 6–8 ☎070 653 784; map pp.58–59. Antique café with a high vaulted ceiling, a genteel ambience and a choice of breakfast snacks, including fresh juices, *cornetti* with honey, and bread and jam. There are tables inside and on the busy Largo. Mon–Sat 7am–9pm.
Caffè Torino Via Roma 121 ☎070 664 765; map pp.58–59. A cut above the other bars lining Via Roma, because it has its own bakery in the basement, producing wonderful pastries and cakes. Daily 4am–10.30pm.

STAMPACE
Caffè dell'Elfo Salita Santa Chiara 4–6 ☎070 682 399; map p.60. Intimate bar just up from Piazza Yenne, with exposed-brick walls and a great evening atmosphere. It's open during the day for coffees, salads and *panini*, and there are tables outside. Mid–June to Sept daily

8am–1pm & 3pm–late; Oct to mid June closed Mon & Sun.
Il Merlo Parlante Via Portascalas ☎333 977 4573; map pp.58–59. Tucked up an alley off Corso Vittorio Emanuele, this cramped, studenty *birreria* offers two hundred types of bottled beer and twelve draught *birre artigianali* artisan beers. There are excellent *panini* and a lively vibe. Daily 8pm–late; winter from 7pm.
★**Isola del Gelato** Piazza Yenne 35 ☎070 659 824; map p.60. This gelateria offers a range of lip-smacking ice cream concoctions – including vegan and gluten-free varieties – as well as yoghurt with granola or fresh fruit, making this a good breakfast stop too. Daily 6am–midnight; closed Jan.

VILLANOVA
★**Le Streghe** Via Piccioni 12 ☎070 673 174; map p.60. Just above the elegant Piazza San Giácomo, this boho bar has an interior that resembles an outdoor pavement café, with streetlamps, a "cobbled" floor and a water fountain. As well as serving excellent wine, cocktails and snacks, *Le Streghe* hosts cultural evenings, including live music, films and theatre from about 10pm. Daily except Tues noon–3pm & 7.30pm–late.

ENTERTAINMENT

In summer, music, dance and other entertainments are staged in the piazzas of Marina and Castello and on Poetto's beach. Pick up details of all events from Cágliari's tourist office and their website, or from a local newspaper (*L'Unione Sarda* is best).

Teatro Civico Via Marco de Candia, Castello ☎070 677 7660 or ☎338 362 3596; map p.60. Partly open-air, this historic theatre stages classical, rock and jazz concerts in summer, as well as drama productions.
Teatro Lírico Via Sant'Alenixedda ☎070 408 2230, ⊛teatroliricodicagliari.it; map pp.58–59. Also known as the Teatro Comunale, this brutalist structure north of Castello is Cágliari's main venue for classical concerts, ballet and opera, in a season stretching between Oct and June. Tickets for most events range in price from €10–75.

Teatro Mássimo Via De Magistris 12 ☎070 677 8121, ⊛teatrostabiledellasardegna.it; map pp.58–59. Off Viale Trento, this is one of the city's major theatre venues, with two stages.
Teatro delle Saline Piazzetta Sechi ☎070 341 322, ⊛teatrodellesaline.it; map pp.58–59. On the eastern side of town towards Poetto, this theatre stages works by the resident Akròama company, from Shakespeare to contemporary drama.

SHOPPING

Via Manno, ascending to the Bastione di Saint Remy from Piazza Yenne, is the place to find **boutiques** and **fashion shops**. Running northeast from the Bastione, Via Garibaldi has more run-of-the-mill clothes outlets with cheaper prices. In Castello, Via Lamármora, below the cathedral, has a cluster of **galleries** and **antiques shops**. Sardinian **craftwork** is sold in numerous shops in the Marina district – to a lesser extent in Castello. Marina also has dozens of Asian and African shops for clothes and **jewellery**, and there are a couple of stores selling army surplus and equipment for campers and travellers in Via Sardegna. Largo Carlo Felice and Via Roma are popular spots for Asian and African street traders hawking everything from leather **handbags** and Senegalese **masks** to lighters and nail clippers. Via Roma's newspaper kiosks sell **foreign newspapers** and **magazines**, including same-day UK titles.

SHOPS

Feltrinelli Via Roma 51 ☎ 070 650 256; map pp.58–59. This central bookshop has a good range of English-language publications and books on Sardinia. Mon–Sat 9am–8.30pm, Sun 10am–1pm & 5–8.30pm.

Iperpan Viale La Plaia ☎ 070 658 264; map pp.58–59. Find everything you'll ever need at this huge supermarket in the shopping centre on the road west out of town, behind the train station. Daily 8.30am–9pm.

I Sapori dell'Isola Via Sardegna 50 ☎ 070 669 479; map pp.58–59. This is Marina's best *alimentari* for simple DIY lunches using quality ingredients. They also sell Sardinian specialities, from honey and cheese to *pane carasau* – the island's wafer bread. Mon–Sat 8am–1.30pm & 4.30–8.30pm.

ISOLA Via Bacaredda 176 ☎ 070 492 756; map pp.58–59. This government-sponsored store north of the centre is a great showcase for quality Sardinian handicrafts – bags, scarves, rugs, ceramics, jewellery (including coral) – though prices are steep. Mon–Fri 9.30am–1pm & 4.30–8pm, Sat 9.30am–1pm.

Rinascente Via Roma 143 ☎ 070 653 271; map pp.58–59. Well-stocked department store with a good range of quality items from bags to blouses. The Food Hall on the top floor has gourmet food products as well as two restaurants and a bar with panoramic views. Mon–Sat 9am–9pm, Sun 10am–9pm.

MARKETS

Antiques and curios Piazza del Cármine becomes the scene of low-level haggling on Sundays (except the third Sun of the month, and July & Aug), as does Piazza Carlo Alberto (in front of the cathedral) on the second and fourth Sundays, and the Bastione di Saint Remy on most Sundays (except Aug) after the renovation work is complete; all close down by lunchtime. ViviCastello is an arts, crafts and collector's market above the Anfiteatro Romano on Viale Buon Cammino (July to mid-Sept Fri–Sun 5pm–midnight; mid-Sept to June Sun mornings).

Food The most central of Cágliari's *mercati civici* is also the oldest and smallest: the Mercato di Santa Chiara on Scaletta Santa Chiara. You'll find plenty more choice at the vivacious Mercato di San Benedetto, a brief walk north of Castello at Via Cocco Ortu, Cágliari's main market for foodstuffs of every description, with stalls on two levels – the fish section on the lower floor is especially worth delving into. There's a third indoor market south of the centre, in front of the Stadio Sant'Elia on Via Raspi, and an outdoor one on the seafront nearby on Via dei Navigatori. The latter is the only market to open on Sunday; all the others open Mon–Sat 7am–2pm.

DIRECTORY

Banks and exchange There's a cluster of banks on or around Largo Carlo Felice, all with ATMs and generally open Mon–Fri 8.20am–1.20pm & 3–4.30pm.

Consulates Denmark and Norway ☎ 070 668 208; Germany ☎ 070 307 229; Netherlands and Sweden ☎ 070 670 830; UK ☎ 06 4420 2431, ⊛ ukinitaly.fco.gov.it; US ☎ 06 46 741, ⊛ italy.usembassy.gov.

Hospital Ospedale San Giovanni di Dio, Via Ospedale 54 (☎ 070 6091).

Internet and telephone services Western Union, Via Napoli 8 (daily except Sat 9am–1pm & 4–8pm; internet €2/30min); printing, photocopying and fax services also available. Lamarì is a more relaxed internet café: Via Napoli 43 (Mon–Sat 8am–9pm; €3/hr).

Laundry Lavanderia San Giacomo, Via Piccioni 4 (€5/11kg; dryer €2/16min; daily 8am–9pm).

Left luggage Bus station, Piazza Matteotti (€1/bag/hr; 7am–7pm).

Pharmacy Farmacia Scanu, Largo Carlo Felice 46 (Mon–Sat 8.30am–1.30pm & 4.30–8pm). When closed, consult the list of open pharmacies by the door.

Post office Piazza del Cármine (Mon–Fri 8.20am–7.05pm, Sat 8.20am–12.35pm).

Travel agents CTS, Via Balbo 12 (☎ 070 488 260, ⊛ associazione.cts.it); Viaggi Orrù, Via Pola 41 (☎ 070 658 458, ⊛ viaggiorru.com).

The southwest

TÉMPIO DI ANTAS

The southwest

Predominantly mountainous, Sardinia's southwest corner is a complex area of diverse identities, where you'll encounter superb beaches, thick forest, long swathes of undeveloped coast and a scattering of mountain villages, modern resorts and workaday towns. The region's eventful history is reflected in numerous remains of settlements, temples and fortifications, including towns that were founded by Phoenicians, colonized by Carthaginians and occupied by Rome. To the south and west of the region, Sulcis is the name given to the area most heavily settled by the Carthaginians, for whom the mountains provided valuable ores and minerals, as they have done for successive rulers almost until the present day. Traces of the mining industry are most evident in the Iglesiente region, to the north, a sparsely populated area whose cliff-hung coast punctuated by beaches benefits from the lack of development, though the tourist industry is beginning to wake up to its charms.

The most famous of the region's ancient settlements can be seen at **Nora**, 35km south of Cágliari on the SS195: a Carthaginian and Roman city whose ruins are picturesquely spread out over a promontory in the Golfo di Cágliari. Inland, the lively town of **Pula** is the main holiday centre for this area, though for swimming you'd do better to continue to **Chia** and beyond, where broad, dune-backed beaches stretch south as far as Capo Spartivento. The craggy, undeveloped **Costa del Sud** runs west from here, a spectacular string of tranquil creeks and coves studded with Pisan and Spanish watchtowers.

The western side of this region, **Sulcis**, was known as Solki to the Phoenicians and Carthaginians who established their main base on the island of **Sant'Antíoco**. The eponymous town here is packed with interest, not least its Punic remains and Christian catacombs. Sant'Antíoco and the neighbouring isle of **San Pietro** are among the area's most appealing destinations, bustling in summer, serene at any other time, and supplied with excellent restaurants.

Back on the mainland, just below another ancient Carthaginian settlement on **Monte Sirai**, the inland mining town of **Carbónia** was founded by Mussolini in his drive for Italian self-sufficiency, and today holds three excellent museums. To the north, **Iglésias**, which retains an attractive old core, is the chief town of the **Iglesiente** territory, whose mountainous terrain shows ample evidence of the mineworkings that underpinned the region's economy, often in a poignant state of abandon. A short distance north of here, the Roman **Témpio di Antas** owes its fine state of preservation to its remote valley location, while some of Sardinia's choicest **beaches** lie to the west on the highly scenic **Golfo di Gonnesa**, where the **Pan di Zúcchero** outcrop sprouts dramatically out of the sea. Apart from the occasional

Highlights

❶ Drive or cycle the Costa del Sud This stunning coastline, rugged and undeveloped, offers photo opportunities at every turn – perfect for a leisurely drive or bike ride. **See p.87**

❷ Museo Archeologico, Sant'Antíoco Don't miss this outstanding display of finds from the island's rich history, packed with Carthaginian and Roman artefacts. **See p.91**

❸ Tuna on the island of San Pietro Feast on the fish for which San Pietro is famous, best between April and July; it's on every restaurant menu. **See p.96**

❹ Easter at Iglésias The town draws on its Spanish traditions to commemorate Easter, one of the island's most dramatic and atmospheric events. **See p.104**

❺ Témpio di Antas Occupying a lovely rural spot in the mountains, this temple mixes Carthaginian, Roman and Sard religious elements – and makes a great backdrop for a picnic. **See p.105**

❻ Swim off the Costa Verde Some of the island's most pristine beaches are located on this western coast of the Iglesiente, offering a real back-to-nature experience. **See p.108**

HIGHLIGHTS ARE MARKED ON THE MAP ON P.82

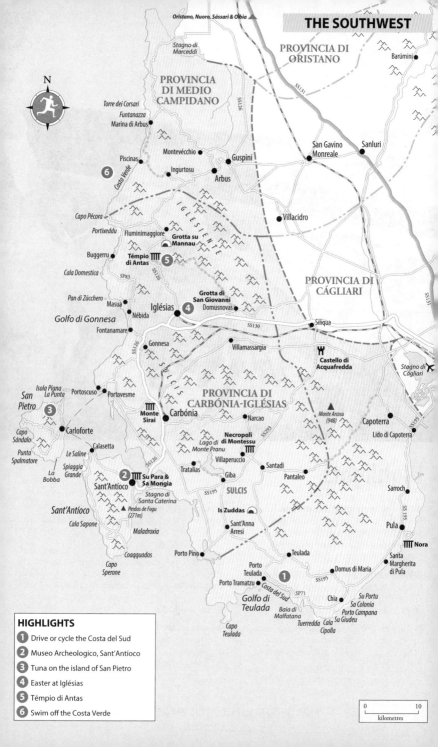

THE SOUTHWEST

PROVINCIA DI ORISTANO

PROVINCIA DI MEDIO CAMPIDANO

IGLESIENTE

PROVINCIA DI CÁGLIARI

SULCIS

PROVINCIA DI CARBÓNIA-IGLÉSIAS

SULCIS

Oristano, Nuoro, Sássari & Olbia

Stagno di Marceddi

Barúmini

N

SS131

Torre dei Corsari
Funtanazza
Marina di Arbus

Montevécchio
Piscinas
Costa Verde
Ingurtosu
Arbus
Guspini

San Gavino Monreale
Sanluri

Capo Pécora
Portixeddu
Fluminimaggiore
Grotta su Mannau
Buggerru
Témpio di Antas
Cala Domestica
SP83
SS126
Villacidro

Pan di Zúcchero
Masua
Nébida
Iglésias
Grotta di San Giovanni
Domusnovas
Golfo di Gonnesa
Fontanamare
SS126
Gonnesa
Villamassargia
SS130
Siliqua

SS131

Isola Piana
La Punta
San Pietro
Portoscuso
Portovesme
Monte Sirai
Carbónia
Narcao
Monte Arcosu (948)
Castello di Acquafredda
Stagno di Cágliari
Capoterra
Lido di Capoterra

Capo Sándalo
Carloforte
Le Saline
Calasetta
SS126
Necropoli di Montessu
Lago di Monte Pranu
Villaperuccio
Santadi
Pantaleo
Sarroch
SS195

Punta Spalmatore
La Bobba
Spiaggia Grande
Su Para & Sa Mongia
Sant'Antíoco
Stagno di Santa Caterina
Tratalias
Giba
Is Zuddas
Pula
Nora

Sant'Antíoco
Cala Sapone
Perdas de Fogu (271m)
Maladroxia
SS195
Sant'Anna Arresi
Santa Margherita di Pula

Coaqquados
Capo Sperone
Porto Pino
Porto Teulada
Porto Tramatzu
Teulada
Costa del Sud
SP71
Domus de Maria
Chia
Su Portu
Sa Colonia
Porto Campana
Su Giudeu

Golfo di Teulada
Baia di Malfatana
Tuerredda
Cala Cipolla
SS195

Capo Teulada

HIGHLIGHTS

1. Drive or cycle the Costa del Sud
2. Museo Archeologico, Sant'Antíoco
3. Tuna on the island of San Pietro
4. Easter at Iglésias
5. Témpio di Antas
6. Swim off the Costa Verde

0 10
kilometres

INTO THE MOUNTAINS

Following the SS195 south of Cágliari, the first place you'll reach is the **Lido di Capoterra**, whose renowned seafood restaurant, *Sa Cardiga e Su Schironi* (☏ 070 71 652, ⓦ sacardigaesuschironi.it), is well worth a visit. Five kilometres inland from the Lido, the village of **Capoterra** is the starting point for a very minor road running some 40km through the mountains to Santadi (see p.88). It's a laborious drive, much of it on a stony surface, but it allows you to glimpse the wildest and remotest part of the **Sulcis mountains**, forested with holm oaks and thick with Mediterranean *macchia* (scrub). A lane branching off the Santadi road leads a few kilometres to the protected wildlife zone of **Monte Arcosu**, a rugged terrain sheltering *cervo sardo* (deer), martens, wildcats and boars, kestrels, buzzards, hawks and even golden eagles. There's a network of waymarked paths – contact Cooperativa Il Caprifoglio (☏ 347 346 3546, ⓦ ilcaprifoglio.it) for walking advice and guided **excursions**.

2

presence of old mines, the coast maintains an almost pristine feel, nowhere more so than on the **Costa Verde** – acres of untrammelled sand backed by an impressive system of dunes and lapped by uncontaminated waters.

GETTING AROUND   THE SOUTHWEST

By train FS trains (☏ 892 021, ⓦ trenitalia.it) run to Carbónia and Iglésias; apart from the Iglésias–Cágliari line, almost all train journeys involve a change at Villamassárgia.

By bus ARST buses (☏ 800 865 042, ⓦ arst.sardegna.it) cover Pula (for Nora) and the southern coast, and provide a regular service to Iglésias, Carbónia and Sant'Antíoco, running as far as Calasetta and Portovesme, both embarkation points for San Pietro.

By bike Cycling is an excellent way to explore the southern coast and its islands: you can rent bikes at Pula, Sant'Antíoco and Carloforte.

Pula and around

South of Cágliari, the large inland village of **PULA** has mushroomed as a holiday centre and a convenient bolthole for weekenders from Cágliari. Apart from its hotels and restaurants, the village is best known for its proximity to the seaside archeological site at **Nora**, and is home to a useful museum for visitors to the site.

Museo Patroni

Corso Vittorio Emanuele 69 • Closed at the time of writing • ☏ 070 920 9610, ⓦ coptur.net

Pula's **Museo Patroni** is mostly dedicated to Phoenician, Iberian, Greek, Gallic and Punic cups, glassware and pottery fragments fished out from the sea around Nora. Although the display is small – the most significant finds are in Cágliari's archeological museum – the background information, plans of the site and the model of its theatre as it would have appeared in the first century AD help put it all into context. The museum is closed indefinitely at time of writing while works to expand the exhibition space are underway – call or ask at the archeological site at Nora for the latest news.

Nora

Thanks to its strategic position, dominating the Gulf of Cágliari, **Nora**, 4km south of Pula on the Capo di Pula promontory, flourished for over a thousand years under successive waves of invaders. These days it requires an imaginative leap to grasp the city's former scale, but its position on the tip of a peninsula gives it plenty of atmosphere, overlooked by a defensive tower built by the Spanish in the sixteenth century.

Brief history

The site of Nora was already a Sard settlement when the Phoenicians founded a colony here in the ninth century BC. It was ruled from Carthage from the sixth century BC and taken by the Romans in 238 BC, under whom it became the provincial capital for the whole island. However, the gradual incursion of the sea meant that the site became increasingly precarious, and it was abandoned after the third century AD.

The archeological site

Località Nora • Daily: mid-Feb to March 10am–6pm; April–Sept 10am–8pm; Oct 10am–6.30pm; Nov to mid-Feb 10am–5.30pm; last entry 1hr before closing • €7.50 • ☎ 070 920 9138, ⓦ coptur.net

Although a good part of the **site** is submerged beneath the sea, and little has survived intact above ground level, crashed arches and walls give some idea of the original size of Nora's buildings. Evidence of the long Carthaginian dominion is scant, despite the intense commercial activity suggested by the foundations of warehouses and the contents of tombs, though a slight elevation holds the ruins of a temple dedicated to Tanit, goddess of fertility. Other pre-Roman remnants, among them a Phoenician inscription featuring the first recorded use of the name "Sardinia", are displayed in Cágliari's archeological museum (see p.62). Most of the remainder belongs to the Roman period, including a temple, with a single column still standing, and a small theatre – much reconstructed, but splendidly sited, and still used for concerts and plays.

Farther on, four upright columns mark a patrician's villa, surrounded by one- and two-room dwellings. The villa's well-preserved black, white and ochre-coloured **mosaic floors** are among Nora's most arresting sights. Along with the town's four sets of baths and good network of roads with their drainage system still intact, the opulence of these simple but splendid designs suggests something of the importance of this Roman outpost.

Visitors to the site must be accompanied – **tours** (mostly in Italian) take place every half-hour or so. The entry ticket also admits you to the **Torre del Coltellazzo**, a sixteenth-/seventeenth-century Spanish watchtower at a commanding height.

Nora's beaches

Immediately north of the archeological site, the exquisite sandy bay of **Spiaggia di Nora** is lapped by crystal-clear water, though at peak season this can rapidly transform into day-tripper hell. Following the bay north for about 500m, you'll come to another attractive beach, **Su Gunventeddu**, which is usually less congested.

Sant'Efisio

Località Nora • Sat 4–8pm, Sun 10am–noon & 4–8pm; winter Sun 10am–noon & 3–6pm • ☎ 340 485 1860

Standing rather incongruously behind Nora's beach, the undistinguished-looking **church of Sant'Efisio** is actually one of Sardinia's most famous Christian monuments. It

---

LA NOTTE DEI POETI

One memorable way to experience the site of Nora is to attend one of the **evening performances** in the Roman theatre. The season, entitled **La Notte dei Poeti** (ⓦ lanottedeipoeti.it), usually extends from early July to early August and features poetry readings, theatre, cinema, exhibitions, dance, jazz concerts and other musical events. The archeological site isn't the only venue: others might include Nora's church of Sant'Efisio; the Ex-Municipio at Via Nora 195 in Pula; Casa Frau, off Piazza del Pópolo, and the main piazza itself. Tickets cost €20 at the Roman theatre or €5–10 at other venues, and can be bought at the gate on performance days; at Pula's information kiosk; in Cágliari at the Box Office agency at Viale Regina Margherita 43 (☎ 070 657 428), and online at ⓦ vivaticket.it. On performance evenings, a *navetta* **bus service** operated by Follesa (☎ 070 920 9026, ⓦ follesa.com) ferries festivalgoers from Cágliari's Piazza Giovanni XXIII at 6.30pm (with a stop at Piazza Matteotti), returning to Cágliari at the end of the evening (tickets €7 return). Most events start at 8pm.

was built by Vittorini monks in the eleventh century on the site of the martyrdom of St Efisius, a Roman soldier of the third century who converted to Christianity and was later credited with stemming an outbreak of plague in 1656. Since then the church has been the ultimate destination of Cágliari's May Day procession (see box, p.67). The rendered facade robs the front of the church of much of its character, but the interior is more pleasing: a dark, narrow nave lined with thick pillars and round arches.

Laguna di Nora

Località Nora • Daily: June–Aug 10am–8pm, tours at 11.30am & 6.30pm; Sept 10am–7pm, tours at 11.30am & 5.30pm • €8; canoe & snorkelling excursions €25/3hr including entry ticket • ☎ 070 920 9544, ⓦ lagunadinora.it

South of the archeological site (to the right of the entrance), a placid circle of water, the **Laguna di Nora**, forms part of a small nature reserve. A learning centre with an **aquarium** stands on a rocky causeway built onto the lagoon, where individuals and groups are guided on ninety-minute tours of exhibitions of the local ecology. The Laguna is also a monitoring centre for dolphins, whales and turtles out at sea; you can visit the Centro Recupero on the same ticket, where the injured and young are tended. Supervised snorkelling and canoe trips on the lagoon are also available, with the primary aim of exploring local ecosystems. There's a nice restaurant too, on a terrace with sea views.

ARRIVAL AND DEPARTURE
PULA AND AROUND

By bus ARST buses connect Cágliari with Pula roughly hourly. If you want to go straight to the site of Nora, get off the bus at Pula's Piazza del Pópolo or Via Corinaldi, from where there are 5–9 local bus services daily (Oct–May daily except Sun; tickets on board).

Destinations Cágliari (Mon–Sat every 30min–1hr, Sun 3–9 daily; 50min); Chia (Mon–Sat every 30min–1hr, Sun 5–7 daily; 25min); Santa Margherita di Pula (Mon–Sat every 30min–1hr, Sun 5–8 daily; 10min); Teulada (6–8 daily; 1hr).

GETTING AROUND

By bus Follesa (☎ 070 920 9026, ⓦ follesa.com) operates a year-round minibus service between Pula and Nora (up to 9 daily), and a separate service to Santa Margherita di Pula between mid-June and mid-Sept (10 daily). In Pula there are stops at Piazza Municipio and Via Corinaldi. One-way tickets on board cost €1.

By bike ProBike, Corso Vittorio Emanuele 118 (☎ 070 920 8077, ⓦ probikeinresort.com) rents out bikes (€15/day) and organizes cycling excursions.
By taxi Call ☎ 339 786 5493, ☎ 347 618 0731 or ☎ 347 614 0027.

INFORMATION

Tourist office A kiosk on Piazza Municipio provides local information (June–Sept daily 9am–1pm & 6–10pm; Oct–May Mon–Fri 10am–noon & 4–6pm; ☎ 070 920 9333, ⓦ visitpula.info).

ACCOMMODATION

There are a couple of decent **hotels** in **Pula** for those who want to be close to a choice of bars and restaurants, otherwise there are good options nearer the sea at **Nora** or 4km down the coast in **Santa Margherita di Pula**, a dispersed area of luxury golf courses and pinewoods sheltering campsites and swanky hotels that cater largely to groups and families. Santa Margherita is accessible from the main SS195 coast road and on ARST and town buses.

Quattro Mori Via Cágliari 10, Pula ☎ 070 920 9124. Flower-bedecked *pensione* near the centre of Pula offering good-value, very simple rooms with shared facilities (some singles have private bathrooms) – perfectly adequate for a night or two. No wi-fi, no credit cards. €40
Su Gunventeddu Località Su Gunventeddu ☎ 070 920 9092, ⓦ sugunventeddu.com. Just 100m from the beach, surrounded by greenery, this modern *pensione* has

spacious and quiet rooms and a good restaurant. It's 1km from Nora; local buses stop outside. €93
Villa Madau Via Nora 84, Pula ☎ 070 924 9033, ⓦ villamadau.it. This is the kind of place you could chill out for a few days, with colourful modern decor, a courtyard and a relaxed, indoor/outdoor café-restaurant. There's a computer available for guests. Breakfasts are mediocre. Ask for a room away from the road to minimize noise intrusion. €135

2

PULA'S SUMMER ENTERTAINMENTS

In summer, Pula's social hub, Piazza del Pópolo – the site of snack bars, cafés and pizzerias with tables outside – becomes the venue of **free concerts** and traditional **dancing** staged almost nightly. Entertainments are also organized at Nora's Roman theatre as part of the Notte dei Poeti festival (see box, p.84).

CAMPSITES

Cala d'Ostia Santa Margherita di Pula ☎ 070 921 470, ⓦ campingcaladostia.com. The coast 3km south of Pula holds two seaside campsites sheltered by pinewoods. They're very similar, though this one has slightly better facilities and has access to a wilder beach. Caravans cost €55

for two in high season. Closed late Oct to March. Pitches €32
Flumendosa Santa Margherita di Pula ☎ 070 461 5332, ⓦ campingflumendosa.com. Behind a popular stretch of beach, this site's a bit closer to Pula than *Cala d'Ostia*, and also has caravans (€70) and a minibus connection to Pula. Closed mid-Nov to mid-Feb. Pitches €30

EATING AND DRINKING

DiVino Wine Bistro Piazza del Pópolo ☎ 342 773 0666. Casual but stylish wine bar with tables inside and on a terrace overlooking the main square. The land and sea menus are chalked up inside – you can have a whole set menu (€35 and €40 respectively) or select individual courses (around €14 for starters, €18 for mains), all beautifully presented. There's a great selection of wines, too. Feb–Oct daily 8am–3pm & 6pm–2am.
Madrigal Via XXIV Maggio 9 ☎ 070 920 8128. This "Irish" pub with outdoor tables has bottled Danish and Belgian beers as well as Irish and Italian draught beers, and also serves *bruschette*, crêpes and grilled meat, all with musical accompaniment. Daily except Wed 7pm–2am.
★ **Su Furriadroxu** Via XXIV Maggio 11 ☎ 070 924

6148. With tables in an arcaded courtyard, this place specializes in dishes with unpronounceable names from the Campidano area (the waiters will advise). Try the ravioli stuffed with ricotta and saffron, cooked in butter and orange, or a mixed meat grill. Pastas and soups are €7, mains €10–13. Booking advised. Daily except Wed 8–10.45pm.
Su Gunventeddu Località Su Gunventeddu ☎ 070 920 9092. The restaurant of this small hotel serves tasty local dishes at moderate prices, with tables outside in summer. Recommended starters include *spaghetti con bottarga* (with fish roe) or *fregola con arselle* (semolina pasta with clams). Reckon on €25–35 for a full meal excluding drinks. Mon & Wed–Sun 12.30–2.30pm & 8–11pm.

Chia and around

Eighteen kilometres south of Pula, **CHIA** is a scattered locality worth visiting mainly for its **beach**, a perfect sandy arc with a small lagoon behind, overlooked by a Pisan watchtower. Around the tower are the scant remains of the fourth-century-BC Phoenician and Carthaginian town of **Bythia**, and from the top of it are marvellous views south down the coast, taking in the range of beaches that count among Sardinia's finest, extending all the way down to the southern cape, **Capo Spartivento**.

Chia's beaches

Chia's **beaches** are roughly divided into five: from north to south Su Portu, Sa Colonia, Porto Campana, Su Giudeu and Cala Cipolla, each with its own character. The immense **Sa Colonia**, one of the busiest of the beaches, is furnished with bars and windsurf and canoe rental, while **Su Portu** and **Cala Cipolla** are more intimate and more spartan. **Su Giudeu** is probably the most scenic – like Sa Colonia it's backed by a lagoon where flamingos can often be seen. Su Portu and Cala Cipolla are more sheltered, but don't count on finding much refuge from either the sun or the wind that often buffets this coast. In summer, you can rent a parasol and two loungers for €18–30 per day at most places, while **car parks** charge €5–10 per day between May and September.

ARRIVAL AND INFORMATION

By bus ARST buses running roughly hourly connect Chia with Cágliari, Pula and Teulada (less frequent on Sun and in winter).

CHIA AND AROUND

Tourist office A kiosk behind Chia's main beach is open in summer (late June to mid-Sept daily 10.30am–12.30pm & 4–7.30pm).

ACCOMMODATION AND EATING

Al Nuraghe Chia Via Carducci, Chia ☎333 135 1415, ⓦalnuraghechia.com. This luxurious, modern B&B with a lawned garden is in Chia village, a few minutes' drive inland from the beach. The three rooms, including one with a balcony, have fridges and a/c. Breakfast with fresh cakes and biscuits is served on the terrace in summer. Guests have use of a separate kitchen for snacks. No credit cards. €70

Sa Colonia Località Chia ☎070 923 0001, ⓦsacoloniachia.it. Signposted on a side road 150m away from the beach, this *pensione* offers six traditionally styled rooms with en-suite bathrooms and a/c. There's a good pizzeria/ristorante, serving fresh seafood – for example *fregola con arselle* (€12) – and excellent pizzas. March–Oct

daily 12.30–3pm & 7.30–10.30pm. €90

Su Giudeu Località Capo Spartivento ☎070 923 0002, ⓦhotelsugiudeu.it. One of the few hotels around the southern cape, this peaceful spot is surrounded by gardens and lies 500m from the broad expanse of Su Giudeu beach. There's a decent restaurant here too; half board is €85/person. €120

Torre Chia Località Chia ☎070 923 0054, ⓦcampeggiotorrechia.it. Conveniently located just behind Su Portu beach, this well-equipped campsite has shady pitches, small bungalows for up to four people, a tennis court and bike rental. Closed late Oct to April. Pitches €23; bungalows €115

The Costa del Sud

West of Capo Spartivento, the SP71 climbs and swoops for some 20km along the largely deserted **Costa del Sud**, one of Sardinia's most scenic drives. To the north, groves of olive and eucalyptus give way to a backdrop of bare mountains, while the jagged coast of the **Golfo di Teulada** presents a procession of indented bays overlooked by lonely Spanish watchtowers. It makes a highly rewarding cycle ride, though hikers would need to follow most of the route by road.

The sea is often difficult or unfeasible to reach, too, though swimming is possible from rocks or the few isolated **beaches** along the way. One popular bathing spot lies about 4km west of the cape at **Tuerredda**, with silky white sand. Further west, the deep **Baia di Malfatano** provides shelter for boats and has a few scraps of beach, while at **Porto Teulada** you can go diving and rent dinghies, canoes or pedalos. Just beyond Porto Teulada, **Portu Tramatzu** has more alluring – and popular – beaches, with parasols and loungers to rent.

Teulada and around

The main SS195 meanders inland to the small town of **TEULADA**, whose usually drowsy air is enlivened by odd pieces of **sculpture** dotted around its streets and squares. Sculptors come from all over the world to compete in the town's annual exhibition, **Scultura e Pietra**; they're given a block of local marble, granite or trachyte in June, when the theme – usually locally inspired – is announced. The pieces are finished by September, and then placed around the village. Other than sculpture, Teulada is distinguished for its **handicrafts**, available in various shops, in particular embroidery, tapestries, carpets, cork objects and terracotta pipes.

West of Teulada, the SS195 loops inland of the cliffy coast and Sardinia's southernmost tip, **Capo Teulada**, a regular venue for military exercises and effectively inaccessible. A right turn at the village of **Sant'Anna Arresi** (the last stop on the bus route from Cágliari) brings you to the pinewoods, dunes and lagoons of **Porto Pino**, a favourite place for day-trippers for its shady picnic spots and dazzling sand beaches.

Is Zuddas

Località Is Zuddas · March noon–4pm; April–June tours at 11am, 12.15pm, 3pm, 4.15pm & 5.30pm; July–Sept 10am–noon & 2.30–6pm; Oct tours at noon & 4pm · €10 · ☎ 0781 955 741, ⓦ grotteiszuddas.com

Twelve kilometres northwest of Teulada on the minor SP70, you can explore the dramatic **Is Zuddas** grottoes on hour-long guided tours. The five main chambers of the cave system reveal stalagmites resembling frozen cascades, organ pipes and Walt Disney characters, and marvellous formations of delicate white spiky aragonite. The cool temperatures here (16°C) make a welcome respite from a baking sun.

ARRIVAL AND DEPARTURE

TEULADA AND AROUND

ARST **buses** run to Teulada from Cágliari (5–7 daily; 1hr 50min), and there's a summer service connecting Teulada

with the local beaches, operating up to five times daily.

ACCOMMODATION

Portu Tramatzu Località Portu Tramatzu ☎ 070 928 3027, ⓦ campingportutramatzu.it. Popular campsite with direct access to the beach, a bar-restaurant and a

shop. Self-catering caravans are available to rent (€50 for two). Closed Nov–March. Pitches **€26**

Santadi

Twenty-one kilometres north of Teulada on the SP70, the nondescript agricultural centre of **SANTADI** on the banks of the Rio Mannu is famous for its **Matrimonio Mauritano**, a re-enactment of a Mauretanian wedding on the first Sunday of August, said to derive from an African colony here during the Roman era. The village is also renowned for its **Carignano wine**, which you can sample at the winery on Via Cágliari 78 (ⓦ cantinadisantadi.it), and has a couple of small museums worth a glance.

Museo Etnográfico Sa Domu Antiga and Museo Archeologico

Via Mazzini 37 · Tues–Sun: April, May & Sept–Nov 9am–1pm & 4–6pm; June–Aug 9am–1pm & 5–7pm; Dec–March 9am–1pm & 3–5pm · €2.60 · ☎ 0781 954 203

An engaging collection of rural and domestic bric-a-brac is on show at Santadi's **Museo Etnográfico Sa Domu Antiga** – a grand name for a typical peasant dwelling of the Sulcis region. The four rooms and garden are filled with an assortment of traditional items, including a loom, bread-making equipment and agricultural tools. The same ticket allows you into the local **Museo Archeologico** on nearby Via Umberto, consisting of little more than one large room displaying fragments of pottery dug up in the area.

Montessu

Daily: April–Sept 9am–7pm; Oct–March 9am–5pm; last tour 1hr 30min before closing · €5 · ☎ 0781 806 077, ⓦ mediterraneacoop.it

West of Santadi and 3km north of the village of Villaperuccio (off the SP293 Giba–Siliqua road), the necropolis of **Montessu** is one of Sardinia's most important pre-nuraghic burial sites. Hewn out of a natural amphitheatre of trachyte rock by people of the Ozieri culture of the fourth and third millennia BC, the forty-odd tombs – popularly called *domus de janas*, or "fairy houses" – have diverse forms. The square openings in either the top or sides were originally sealed with stone doors (one is still in place); four have wide canopies, behind which circular areas are marked out by stones, probably used for funerary rites. Niches and small annexes in several of the clean-cut chambers are pointed out on the hour-long guided tour: look out for the sacred symbols cut into the walls – graffiti, reliefs and incisions linked to earth cults, mostly representing the mother goddess and bull god. The best are visible in the **Tomba delle Spirali**, showing a cluster of alien-looking spirals, possibly the "eyes" of the goddess, and the **Tomba delle Corna**, with multiple horn shapes.

Linked to the same complex is a group of **menhirs** up to 5m tall situated in the open country about 1km south of Villaperuccio, in the **Terrazzu** district. Associated with obscure fertility rites, the stark monoliths are conspicuous landmarks amid the flat cultivated fields.

2

Tratalias

A short diversion from the SS195 heading west brings you to **TRATALIAS**, whose fine Romanesque church of **Santa Maria** was consecrated in 1213 as the cathedral for the entire Sulcis region, a status it retained for two hundred years. The transfer of the diocese from Sant'Antíoco was part of a general move inland from exposed coastal sites throughout this period. The original nucleus of Tratalias was the quarter now known as **Vecchio Borgo**, abandoned by its inhabitants when the creation of the nearby Lago di Monte Pranu in 1951 led to infiltration of water into the foundations of the houses, forcing the townsfolk to relocate to the modern town a little way north. Along with the church, one or two *palazzi* in Vecchio Borgo preserve their medieval lines, but most of the historic buildings have disappeared.

Santa Maria

Vecchio Borgo • March, April & mid- to end Oct Tues–Sun 9am–1pm & 3–5pm; May, June & early to end Sept Tues & Thurs 9am–1pm, Wed & Fri–Sun 9am–1pm & 4–7pm; July to early Sept Tues 9am–1pm, Wed, Fri & Sat 9am–1pm & 5–8pm, Thurs & Sun 9am–1pm & 8pm–midnight; early to mid-Oct Tues & Thurs 9am–1pm, Wed & Fri–Sun 9am–1pm & 4–6pm; mid-Oct to Feb Wed–Sun 9am–1pm & 3–5pm • €2.50 • ☎ 0781 688 046

Excellently preserved, the Romanesque church of **Santa Maria** fuses Pisan and French styles, with a small rose window and a section of an external staircase at the top of its simple square facade – a Byzantine motif symbolizing the ascent to heaven. There's more of the staircase visible within, where the thick columns and plain bricks are topped by a wooden roof, though all the finery has long since disappeared. Tickets are available from the small **Museo del Territorio Trataliese** across the piazza, which has a few displays on the locality and can also supply local information.

EATING   **TRATALIAS**

Il Gallo Nero Vecchio Borgo ☎ 0781 697 003. Handy trattoria across from Santa Maria where local Sard dishes are served, such as *zuppa di cozze*, *culurgiones* with fresh pecorino and beetroot, and *pasta con bottarga* with fish roe. Starters are €7–12, mains €8–16; there are good pizzas too. July–Sept Tues–Sun 12.30–2pm & 8–11pm; Oct–June Fri 7.30–10.30pm, Sat & Sun 12.30–2pm & 7.30–10.30pm.

★**Locanda Monserrat** Vecchio Borgo ☎ 0781 688 376, ⊛ locandamonserrat.it. Perfectly positioned in front of the church, this swanky restaurant offers a gastronomic treat, with a menu strong on seafood and challenging on the wallet – expect to pay €35–45 a head excluding drinks. You can dine inside or in the romantic garden. Easter–June & late Sept Tues–Sun 12.30–2.30pm & 7.30–11.30pm; July to mid-Sept daily 7.30–11.30pm.

Sant'Antíoco

The island of **Sant'Antíoco** is joined to the Sardinian mainland by a 3km-long isthmus that meets the coast 8km west of Tratalias. This causeway has existed since Carthaginian times, though the last section now runs over a modern bridge, dwarfing the remains of its Roman predecessor. The waters of the **Stagno di Santa Caterina** on the left are the occasional habitat of flamingos, cormorants and herons.

2

SANT'ANTÍOCO

Carbónia, Iglesias & Cágliari ▼

Some 16km in length, Sant'Antíoco has an agreeable, off-the-beaten-track appeal, with a cluster of historical **remains** (as well as the majority of the island's hotels and restaurants) concentrated in its main town, also called Sant'Antíoco. Elsewhere, the undeveloped rocky coast shelters some first-class **beaches**, most of them along the northwest and southeast littorals. The SS126 continues northwest from Sant'Antíoco town as far as Calasetta, embarkation point for the neighbouring isle of San Pietro. To reach the island's southern zone, turn left soon after the bridge (signposted *spiagge*). The road south follows the coast past bays and beaches before swinging over to the island's rocky western shore; only primitive tracks cross the hilly interior.

Brief history

Settled by Phoenicians as early as the ninth century BC, Sant'Antíoco was the main base of operations for the territory of **Sulcis** – or Solki as it was then known – forming an important link in their network of trade routes which extended to France and the Iberian peninsula. The area was also a valuable source of minerals, extracted with the help of the enslaved local population. Carthaginians and Romans followed in the wake of the Phoenicians, all keen to exploit the lucrative mines, though the importance of Sant'Antíoco itself declined, as Nora and Kalaris (Cágliari) became more dominant.

Sant'Antíoco town

Sant'Antíoco town centres on the long axis of Via Nazionale – a right turn after the bridge – which becomes Via Roma, Corso Vittorio Emanuele and Via Regina Margherita, interspersed by piazzas Repubblica, Italia and Umberto. Tree-lined Corso Vittorio Emanuele is pedestrianized in the evening, when it's filled with promenaders.

Basilica di Sant'Antíoco

Piazza Parrochia • Basilica daily 8am–1pm & 3.30–8pm; catacombs Mon–Sat 9.30am–12.30pm & 3.30–5.30pm (also 7–8pm in summer), Sun 3.30–5.30pm (also 7–8pm in summer) • Catacombs €5 • ☎ 0781 83 044

At the top of Via Regina Margherita, the **Basilica di Sant'Antíoco** makes a good place to start a tour of the old town. Part-hidden behind the old town hall, the Romanesque construction dates from the twelfth century, and was built over Christian catacombs. In the southern aisle, look out for what are taken to be the remains of Saint Antiochus himself – a skull and miscellaneous bones – in a display case. The saint's mortal remains were discovered in the **catacombs** in 1615, which can be accessed from the right transept. These were enlarged by early Christians in the sixth century from five existing Carthaginian hypogea (underground vaults). Guides are on hand for tours of the dark and dingy corridors, pitted with numerous low-ceilinged mini-chambers and graves in which skeletons are displayed – the remains of Christians buried in the eighth century – along with reproductions of ceramic objects unearthed during excavation, some of them of Byzantine origin. You'll also see the remains of a rare Byzantine tomb, and fragments of primitive frescoes.

The zona archeologica and around

Various combinations of ticket are available; one that includes all the sites below costs €13, available from any of the major sites • ☎ 0781 82 105, ⓦ archeotur.it

The earliest traces of Solki, dating from the eighth century BC, are visible in and around Sant'Antíoco's extensive **zona archeologica**, occupying a hillside at the north end of town. The main entrance and ticket office are at the museum at the bottom of the hill towards the sea, reachable from Lungomare Cristóforo Colombo or from the basilica, signposted up Via Castello. Other sites are scattered around the residential streets at the top of the hill, west of the archeological zone.

Museo Archeologico

Zona archeologica • Daily 9am–7pm • €6 • ☎ 0781 82 105, ⓦ archeotur.it

The region's most important collection of archeological finds is vividly displayed in the modern **Museo Archeologico**, featuring a good sample of finds from the Punic acropolis. These include inscribed stelae and a plethora of amphoras, plates, ceramics and jewellery, including bracelets, earrings and necklaces made of bronze, amber, glass, gold and silver. The items actually represent a tiny fraction of what is claimed to be one of the largest collections of Carthaginian ware outside the site of Carthage itself. You'll also see a model of how the port of Solki would have appeared in Carthaginian times, eye-catching Roman artefacts, including sculptures of human figures and bulls' heads, and some impressive mosaics, notably one in a North African style showing panthers apparently drinking from a plant pot (second to third century AD).

The Punic tophet and acropolis

Zona archeologica • Daily 9am–7pm • €4 • ☎ 0781 82 105, ⓦ archeotur.it

Spread over the highest part of the *zona archeologica*, the extensive **Punic tophet**, or burial site, forms the most prominent part of the excavations here. The ruined walls of the sanctuary originally dedicated to the supreme Phoenician god, Baal-Hammon, and the fertility goddess Tanit are surrounded by a scattering of funerary urns (mostly modern reproductions). The original urns were long held to contain the ashes of the sacrificed first-born children of Phoenician and Carthaginian aristocrats, but this is now thought to have been Roman propaganda: the ashes, it seems, were the cremated remains of children stillborn or dead from natural causes, and of animals. At the summit of the site stand the massive square blocks of a Punic temple, commanding far-reaching views of the sea and Sardinian mainland.

Five hundred metres south stand the meagre remains of the **Punic acropolis**, little more than a few truncated columns and the surviving blocks of what once must have been massive walls. Audioguides available at the entrance identify and explain different parts of the area.

Villaggio ipogeo

Via Necrópoli • Daily: April–Sept 9am–8pm; early Oct 9am–1pm & 3.30–8pm; mid-Oct to March 9.30am–1pm & 3–6pm • €2.50 • ☎ 0781 82 105, ⓦ archeotur.it

Outside the archeological zone, flights of steps carved out of the rock along Via Necrópoli lead between modern houses to the narrow chambers that make up the

villaggio ipogeo, or Punic necropolis. Many of these were taken over and inhabited by townsfolk in later centuries but all lie empty now. Near one of the entrances, look out for the cannons dredged up from the sea and relocated here, belonging to a French man-of-war sunk in local waters in 1793.

Museo Etnográfico

Via Necrópoli • Daily: April–Sept 9am–8pm; early Oct 9am–1pm & 3.30–8pm; mid-Oct to March 9.30am–1pm & 3–6pm • €3 • ☏ 0781 82 105, Ⓦ archeotur.it

There's quite a different tone in the last museum on the circuit, the small but engrossing **Museo Etnográfico**, consisting of one capacious room crammed to the rafters with examples of rural culture – tools, agricultural implements, craftwork, bread- and pasta-making equipment, most of them only recently superseded by modern machinery. There are also examples of the famous local embroidery using *bisso*, or "sea silk" – an almost extinct tradition. A few more items are displayed in a yard at the back.

Forte Su Pisu

Via Castello • Daily: April–Sept 9am–8pm; early Oct 9am–1pm & 3.30–8pm; mid-Oct to March 9.30am–1pm & 3–6pm • €2.50 • ☏ 0781 82 105, Ⓦ archeotur.it

The **Forte Su Pisu** – also called the *Fortino Sabaudo*, or just *Castello* – is a Piemontese stronghold built in 1812, incorporating parts of pre-existing nuraghic and Punic fortifications. Its garrison was massacred three years later by corsairs. There's little to see within, but there are good views to be enjoyed from the walls.

ARRIVAL AND INFORMATION   SANT'ANTÍOCO TOWN

By bus ARST buses stop on Via Nazionale and Piazza Repubblica, in the lower town, before continuing on to Calasetta. For Cágliari, it's best to catch a bus to Carbónia or Iglésias and take a bus or train from there.
Destinations Cágliari (Mon–Sat 1 daily; 2hr); Carbónia (Mon–Sat every 30min–1hr, Sun 4 daily; 30min); Iglésias

(4–5 daily; 1hr 20min).
Tourist office Pro Loco, Piazza Repubblica (erratic hours; ☏ 0781 82 031, Ⓦ comune.santantioco.ca.it).
Banks Banks with ATMs are on Piazza Umberto and Via Roma, just off Piazza Italia.

GETTING AROUND

By local bus Piazza Repubblica is a stop for the local minibuses operated by Senis (Ⓦ autoservizisenis.it), connecting the centre of town with the *zona archeologica* (7–9 daily; 10min) and in summer with the beaches south of town at Maladroxia and Coaquaddus, and with Cala

Sapone on the west coast (mid-June to mid-Sept 5 daily; 10min); buy tickets on board (€1.20–2.50).
By bike, scooter or car Euromoto, Via Nazionale 57 (☏ 0781 840 907) has bikes to rent (€10–15/day), as well as scooters (€30–40/day) and cars (€40–50/day).

ACCOMMODATION

You won't find a particularly inspiring range of accommodation in **Sant'Antíoco town**, and prices tend to be high. Hotel choices **elsewhere on the island**, within a shortish drive or bus ride from the town, are covered later in this chapter (see pp.95–96).

Eden Piazza Parrocchia ☏ 0781 840 768, Ⓦ edenhotel .com. In the upper town, just behind the basilica and convenient for the museums and archeological zone, this hotel is very dated, but adequate for a night. Ask to see the hotel's own Punic hypogea, or necropolis, later transformed into Christian catacombs very similar to those at the nearby basilica. **€80**
Hotel del Corso Corso Vittorio Emanuele 32 ☏ 0781 800 265, Ⓦ hoteldelcorso.it. On the town's main promenading route, this rather old-fashioned three-star

above a bar has fairly standard but spacious rooms with fridges and modern bathrooms (avoid street-facing rooms for a quieter experience). Breakfast features fresh pastries and fruit juice. **€80**
Il Nido Via Nazionale 110 ☏ 0781 841 046 or ☏ 349 730 1923, Ⓦ ilnidobeb.it. Near Piazza Repubblica, this B&B run by a young couple has small but pretty attic rooms with wooden ceilings. They also offer separate self-catering apartments nearby and rural accommodation. No credit cards. **€55**

FROM TOP THE PUNIC TOPHET, SANT'ANTÍOCO (P.91); GOLFO DI GONNESA, THE IGLESIENTE COAST (P.107) >

2

SANT'ANTÍOCO'S FESTIVITIES

Said to be Sardinia's oldest religious festival, the **Festa di Sant'Antíoco** takes place around the second Sunday after Easter, with nine days of costumed processions, traditional songs and dancing, poetry recitations and rock concerts. On the preceding Saturday, **Is Coccois** is one of the highlights, named after the decorated loaves that are carried in procession, while the culmination of the festival features another religious procession followed by music, dancing and fireworks. Summer sees a full programme of evening entertainments, including free concerts and open-air films in the piazzas.

★ **La Jacaranda** Via Risorgimento 22 ☎ 0781 82 008, ⓦ lajacaranda.it. In a quiet lane a short walk from Piazza Garibaldi and the port, this B&B has helpful hosts and spacious rooms with fridges and a/c. Breakfasts (featuring home-made jam) and dinners (€25) are served in the garden in summer. €80

Moderno Via Nazionale 82 ☎ 0781 83 105, ⓦ hotel -moderno-sant-antioco.it. This renovated hotel a few minutes' walk from the centre offers spacious, simply furnished rooms, friendly management and a highly rated restaurant (see below). €95

Solki Piazzale Pertini ☎ 0781 800 521, ⓦ hotelsolki.it. Near the portside, but with only five rooms looking towards the sea, this modern hotel is spacious, quiet, well equipped and well run, but fairly dull. €100

EATING AND DRINKING

Sant'Antíoco's streets are abuzz most evenings with amblers and scooters, the rich selection of **restaurants** here making up for their scarcity elsewhere on the island. **Snacks** and **ice creams** are available from bars on Piazza Italia and along Corso Vittorio Emanuele, the course of the evening promenade.

Da Achille Via Nazionale 82 ☎ 0781 83 105. Part of the *Moderno* hotel, this restaurant in an unusual, hangar-like space is popular with locals and tourists alike for its sophisticated takes on local cuisine and its artistic presentation. Seafood is the main event: try *polpo arrostito* (roast octopus) or a tuna steak. It's pricey though: first courses are around €15, mains €22, and there are fixed-price menus for €40–60. June–Oct Mon–Sat 8–10pm.

La Fenicia Viale Trieste 41 ☎ 342 044 5672. Intimate trattoria where you can sample grilled fish and local wines at reasonable prices – *antipasti* at €5–10, pastas €10–12 and mains €12–16. The *spaghetti con vongole* (with clams) and steamed tuna are recommended, and there are also pizzas. Daily except Wed 12.30–2.30pm & 7.30–11.30pm; also Wed in Aug.

★ **La Sulcitana** Lungomare Colombo 66 ☎ 329 196 7803. Run by a fishermen's cooperative, this no-frills self-service *friggitoria* dispenses simple but delicious seafood dishes using whatever the boats have brought in. Whether it's *spaghetti ai ricci* (with sea urchins) or *frittura calamari e gamberi* (battered squid and prawns), all dishes are €5–8. Set your own table in the blue-tiled interior or outside facing the seafront. Mon 8.30–11pm, Tues–Sun 12.30–2.30pm & 8.30–11pm.

★ **Rubiu** Via Bologna ☎ 346 723 4605, ⓦ rubiubirra.it. Well off the beaten track, this industrial-style place specializes in *birre artigianali* – artisan beers – brewed here or elsewhere in Italy. Try Flavia, a fruity, full-bodied and much-awarded light-coloured ale. The beers are served with *taglieri* (wooden boards) of cold meats and seafood, salads, *focaccia* (€3–7) and the island's best pizzas (€6–10). Gets packed, so worth booking. Daily 7pm–1am.

South of Sant'Antíoco town

Outside town, the island of Sant'Antíoco mainly consists of *macchia*-covered slopes, with a few white houses dotted among the vineyards and scrub. Most of the **beaches** lie on the southern and eastern shores, accessible from the road running south out of town. One of the best is at **Maladroxia**, a sheltered bay reached via a turn-off 5km down the road, with a narrow arc of sand.

The main road south curls round the island's highest point, **Perdas de Fogu** (271m), from where hikers can enjoy sweeping views across to the Sardinian mainland. A left turn leads to another fine beach, **Coaquaddus**, equipped with deckchairs, parasols and a couple of bars. Much of the coastline around here is high and rocky, especially at the southern tip of the island at **Capo Sperone**, occupied by a solitary watchtower with a sandy beach below.

Bathing spots on the remoter **western side** of the island are harder to find: the best is **Cala Sapone**, a small, sheltered inlet with swimming mainly from rocks, sunloungers, canoes and pedalos to rent, and a bar with food.

ACCOMMODATION   SOUTH OF SANT'ANTÍOCO TOWN

Hotel Maladroxia Località Maladroxia ☎ 0781 817 012, ⓦ hotelmaladroxia.it. Tranquil, 1970s-style holiday hotel 150m from the beach, with spacious rooms, seven of them facing the sea and three with a balcony. There's a veranda restaurant, also with good views. Closed Nov–Easter. **€90**
★Mala Blu Località Maladroxia ☎ 348 100 8468, ⓦ malablu.it. Twenty metres from the beach, this B&B run by a young couple has three bright en-suite rooms with a/c. In summer, the self-service breakfasts, which include home-made jam and cakes, are taken on the terrace. Sunloungers and parasols are available for the beach. No credit cards. Closed mid-Jan to mid-March. **€60**
Tonnara Cala Sapone ☎ 0781 809 058, ⓦ camping tonnara.it. On the western side of the island, with a pool and direct access to the sheltered Cala Sapone beach. There's a restaurant and shop, and caravans and bungalows are available to rent (€90). Closed early Oct to mid-April. Pitches **€35**

Calasetta

At the island's northern extremity, Sant'Antíoco's second town, **CALASETTA**, lies 10km from the main town. Many visitors come only for the ferry service from here to San Pietro, but it makes a great holiday destination in its own right, close to some of the island's best **beaches** and with almost nightly music in summer. With its low white buildings on a regular grid of lanes, it has an almost Middle Eastern feel.

A ten-minute walk west of the port will bring you to **Sotto Torre** beach, small but perfect for a quick dip; further southwest, the beautiful, dune-backed, fine-sand beach of **Le Saline** has clean, shallow water ideal for families. A couple of kilometres farther south, there's the long, narrow **Spiaggia Grande**. At Le Saline and Spiaggia Grande, umbrellas, deckchairs and boats are available to rent and bars serve refreshments.

Museo d'Arte Contemporanea

Via Savoia 2 · July–Sept Tues–Fri 6–9pm, Sat & Sun 11am–1pm & 6–9pm; Oct–June Fri–Sun 10am–noon & 4–6pm · €3 · ☎ 0781 887 219, ⓦ fondazionemacc.it

Calasetta's right-angled grid of lanes holds one unexpected item of interest: the **Museo d'Arte Contemporanea**, an outpost of abstract art of the twentieth century. Occupying two large, white-walled rooms once used as an abattoir, the collection displays works by around a hundred European artists from the 1930s to the 1970s, and there are regular exhibitions.

ARRIVAL AND DEPARTURE   CALASETTA

By ferry Saremar (☎ 0781 854 005, ⓦ saremar.it) and Delcomar (☎ 0781 857 123, ⓦ delcomar.it) operate ferry services between Calasetta and Carloforte, on the island of San Pietro (roughly every 1hr 30min; 30min). Tickets cost around €5.50/person, €10–12 for a medium-sized car, depending on period and day (winter weekends are cheapest). At peak periods, drivers should arrive at the ferry port in good time, as queues develop. Keep an eye on times of last departures, and book as early as possible; if you get stuck, however, note that Delcomar ferries make night-time crossings every 1hr 30min (tickets on board).
By bus ARST buses to and from Sant'Antíoco town and Cágliari pull up at the port.
Destinations Cágliari (Mon–Sat 1 daily; 2hr 20min); Carbónia (every 30min–1hr; 1hr); Iglésias (5 daily; 1hr 45min); Sant'Antíoco (every 30min–1hr; 25–30min).

ACCOMMODATION AND EATING

Most places in Calasetta require **half or full board** in August.

Cala di Seta Via Regina Margherita 61 ☎ 0781 88 304, ⓦ hotelcaladiseta.it. This central hotel has modern, well-equipped rooms and friendly management. Those at the top, costing extra, are wood-beamed and have great harbour views, and some have a balcony; the cheapest rooms are small and look onto a courtyard. **€110**
FJBY Via Solferino 83 ☎ 0781 88 444, ⓦ hotelfjby.it. Run by three brothers, this functional, 1960s-style

2

two-star hotel with a panoramic terrace is the nearest accommodation to the port. Rooms have a/c and some enjoy good views. **€80**
Le Saline Località Le Saline ☎0781 88 615, ⓦcamping lesaline.com. Well-managed campsite 2km southwest of town, right next to the beach of the same name. It has clean and modern facilities, a pizzeria and self-service restaurant, a

tennis court and bungalows to rent (from €100). Pitches **€32**
Nord Oveste Via Barcellona 14 ☎349 177 4949. You can dig into first-class and gigantic pizzas, tuna cutlets and seafood fry-ups at this casual place near the harbour, with pirate-themed decor and a veranda. You'll spend around €12 for a pizza, €20 for a fish dish. May–Oct daily noon–3pm & 7.30pm–midnight.

San Pietro

The island of **San Pietro** has a more intimate and insular feel than neighbouring Sant'Antíoco, preserving a carefree, laidback air despite the boatloads of holiday-makers disembarking every summer. Most visitors confine themselves to the only town, **Carloforte** (named after the Savoy king, Carlo Emanuele), but the rest of the island is well worth exploring. Although the **eastern seaboard** is not exactly enhanced by the prospect of Portovesme's smoky industrial works on the Sardinian mainland, the few beaches on the **southern coast** are pleasantly secluded, while the high western shore vaunts some exquisite panoramas as well as one or two great places for swimming and snorkelling. The **west coast**'s cliffy terrain also provides sanctuary for a protected species of falcon. Dotted with white villas, most of the island's **interior** is covered with *macchia* that gives way to bare craggy or round peaks, the slopes rising to a height of about 200m. A car is not essential: an infrequent bus service covers most of the island (see opposite), though a bike would give you most independence (see opposite).

Almost all of San Pietro's facilities are located in Carloforte. Virtually all the island's restaurants feature **tuna** on their menus, a local speciality due to the rich harvest of tuna fished here every year. The annual slaughter of the tuna fish, **La Mattanza**, takes place in May and June (see box below).

Brief history

In former times San Pietro was known as Enosim by the Carthaginians and Accipitrum by the Romans, both names referring to the numbers of sparrowhawks that once dwelt here. Its present name derives from a legend according to which St Peter washed up on the island after being shipwrecked (a claim made by dozens of other Mediterranean islands), subsequently teaching the locals new fishing techniques. In fact the methods

---

LA MATTANZA: SAN PIETRO'S TUNA BLOODBATH

Though the annual tuna massacre is also enacted on Sant'Antíoco (at Punta Maggiore, southwest of Calasetta), San Pietro's age-old rite of **La Mattanza** is a much bigger, bloodier affair. Nets are laid down as early as March, but the killing mainly takes place in May and June, when the tuna pass through the northern straits on their way to their mating grounds in the eastern Mediterranean. Channelled through a series of nets culminating in the **camera della morte**, or death chamber, the fish are bludgeoned to death as the net is slowly raised.

The *Mattanza* – the word is from Spanish roots ("the killing") – has mixed **origins**. The methods are identical to those used at other places where the Ligurians settled, such as the Égadi islands off Sicily's western tip, but there's also a strong Arab influence evident in the use of titles such as *Raís* (Arab for chief), referring to the coordinator of the operation. Although deplored by many for its brutality, the practice attracts crowds of spectators every season, and has given rise to a **festival** that highlights the tuna's central role in the island's economy, culture and cuisine: the **Girotonno**, taking place in late May/early June (see box, p.98). Even so, the gory details of the *Mattanza* are understandably played down in San Pietro's numerous restaurants that serve the fish, the island's top speciality. You can learn about the customs and methods of the *Mattanza* – and see graphic photos – in Carloforte's Museo Cívico (see opposite).

used in the tuna fishing for which San Pietro is best known were probably bequeathed by a colony of Ligurians who were invited to settle here by Carlo Emanuele III in 1738.

Originally from the town of Pegli, west of Genoa, the immigrants arrived from the island of Tabarka, near Tunisia, where they had scraped a precarious living as merchants and coral-gatherers since settling there in 1541. The newcomers were not left in peace for long, however: in 1793, San Pietro was occupied by French forces, and five years later it was the target of one of the last great corsair raids, when nearly a thousand of the Ligurians were abducted and taken back to Tunisia, enslaved. The islanders eventually returned to San Pietro in 1803 on payment of a hefty ransom by Vittorio Emanuele I. Still today, the local dialect is an antiquated version of Genoan, Ligurian elements remain in the local cuisine and dialect, and some of the buildings hark back to Genoan styles of architecture.

2

ARRIVAL AND DEPARTURE   SAN PIETRO

By ferry Carloforte is connected to Calasetta on Sant'Antíoco and Portovesme on the mainland by Saremar (☎0781 854 005, ✆saremar.it) and Delcomar (Calasetta only; ☎0781 857 123, ✆delcomar.it), with tickets around €5.50/person, €10–12 for a car, depending on season and day. In Carloforte, the Saremar ticket office is on Piazza Carlo Emanuele; buy Delcomar tickets from a kiosk on the quayside or on board the ferry. You should arrive at the embarkation point in good time in Aug and other peak periods, and be aware of last departure times to and from the island. There's a night-time service run by Delcomar on the Calasetta route only.

Destinations Calasetta (every 1–2hr; 40min); Portovesme (hourly; 30min).

GETTING AROUND

By bus A bus service links Carloforte with La Punta, Capo Sándalo and La Caletta, leaving from the stop on Piazza Carlo Emanuele every 1–2hr (tickets €2.50 return, available from *tabacchini* on Via Roma).

By bike or scooter Autonoleggio Melis, Piazza Carlo Emanuele (☎0781 856 397 or ☎393 978 9030) rents pedal cycles (€10/day), electric bikes (€15/day) and scooters (€35/day).

By taxi Capriata (☎0781 855 746 or ☎338 723 4495); Peloso Viaggi (☎348 659 7137); Poma Tours (☎393 754 0126).

Carloforte

With its old town made up of a web of *carruggi*, or narrow lanes, **CARLOFORTE** centres on the broad and animated **Piazza Carlo Emanuele**. Planted with palms, the square opens onto the port, where water-polo matches take place in cordoned-off sections in summer. From here, **Corso Battellieri** runs south along the seafront to a placid lagoon, the occasional home of pink flamingos. An observatory sits between the lagoon and the sea, located on the exact line of the 39th parallel.

Museo Cívico

Via Cisterna del Re • Tues 10am–12.30pm, Wed & Fri 5–7.30pm, Sat 10am–12.30pm & 5–7.30pm, Sun 10am–12.30pm • €2 • ☎0781 855 880

Carloforte's only specific sight of any interest is its small **Museo Cívico**, housed in an eighteenth-century guardhouse at the entrance to the old citadel (follow signs from Piazza Repubblica). The items are displayed in five small rooms, each dedicated to a specific aspect of the island's history and culture. The Sala dei Galanzieri evokes local life in the nineteenth century, while the Sala della Tonnara has photos and diagrams illustrating how tuna are caught in the island's annual *Mattanza*, with examples of nets and the hooks used. Other rooms hold fossils, molluscs and historical documents.

In front of the museum stands the **Cisterna del Re**, a curious domed archway marking the site of a cistern dating back to the town's construction in the eighteenth century.

INFORMATION   CARLOFORTE

Tourist office Piazza Carlo Emanuele (April–Oct daily 10am–1pm & 5–8pm; ☎0781 854 009, ✆www .prolococarloforte.it). In summer, a kiosk on the quayside, mainly concerned with selling services, can also provide some information.

Websites As well as the tourist office's own website, it's

2

worth looking at ⓦcarloforte.net and ⓦwww.carloforte.it, both packed with practical tips for walkers, wildlife enthusiasts and divers, as well as providing overviews of San Pietro's history, cuisine and culture.

Internet Trycomp, Via Segni 68 (Mon–Fri 9.30am–1pm & 5.30–8.30pm, Sat 9.30am–1pm; €1/15min).

TOURS AND ACTIVITIES

Boat tours Tickets for boat tours around San Pietro's coast are sold from kiosks on the quayside (€20–30/person). Most excursions depart from the port every morning and afternoon between June and mid-Sept, visiting all the most important grottoes and some secluded beaches, taking around 3hr.

Diving Carloforte Tonnare Diving Center (☎349 690 4969, ⓦcarlofortediving.org) organizes dives and snorkelling expeditions from the Tonnare fishery, Località La Punta.

ACCOMMODATION

Hieracon Corso Cavour 62 ☎0781 854 028, ⓦhotelhieracon.com. At the quiet end of the seafront, this four-star hotel is an ornate Art Nouveau concoction with period furnishings, a restaurant on two levels and an internal garden. Some rooms overlook the harbour; cheaper ones are loft conversions and viewless. €100

★**Hotel California** Via Cavallera 15 ☎0781 854 470, ⓦhotelcaliforniacarloforte.com. About a 10min walk south of the port, near the lagoon, this friendly, family-run place has simple rooms with minibars, a/c, bathrooms and balconies. The owners also have rooms and apartments to rent. €70

Hotel Paola La Punta Tonnare ☎0781 850 098, ⓦhotelpaolacarloforte.it. Signposted off the road to La Punta, 3km north of Carloforte and about a 10min walk from the sea, this three-star hotel enjoys fantastic views and an air of deep tranquillity. There's a good terrace restaurant, too. Closed Nov–March. €80

★**Il Ghiro** Piazza Repubblica 7 ☎338 205 0553, ⓦcarlofortebedandbreakfast.it. Ecofriendly B&B in a converted townhouse from the 1790s overlooking Carloforte's liveliest square (so not for light sleepers in summer). The two smallish, wood-beamed rooms have arty decor and organic breakfasts. No credit cards. €65

Villa Pimpina Via Genova 62 ☎0781 854 180, ⓦvillapimpina.it. In a narrow alley in the upper part of the old town, this contemporary hotel – a renovation of a much older building – has airy, individually furnished rooms with balconies, views and tasteful Sard-inspired decor. There's no restaurant. €90

EATING AND DRINKING

A Galaia Via Segni 36 ☎0781 854 081. Relaxed back-street trattoria offering land- and sea-based dishes in attractive surroundings and with some tables outside. First courses are around €12, mains are €10–15, and there's a €20 fixed-price lunch menu. Tues–Sun 12.15–2.30pm & 7.30–11pm; daily July & Aug; closed Nov.

★**Al Tonno di Corsa** Via Marconi 47 ☎0781 855 106. With two rooms adorned with paintings and old photos, and terraces with views over the town, this seafood restaurant is dedicated to the local *cucina tabarkina* in general, and tuna dishes in particular, though numerous other choices are also available. There are tasting menus for €25 and €35, otherwise you'll pay €40–50 for a full meal excluding drinks. The alley is most easily reached from the Lungomare via the steps at the top of Via Caprera. Tues–Sun 12.30–2.30pm & 8–10.30pm; Aug daily; closed mid-Jan to Feb.

Barone Rosso Via Venti Settembre 26 ☎334 757 3504. By day, this tiny bar with a few tables outside makes an ideal spot for a sit down, and provides *paninis*, toasties,

---

SAN PIETRO'S FESTIVALS

A full programme of festivities punctuates the spring and summer in San Pietro. Two foodie extravaganzas kick off the season: the **Sagra del Cus Cus** on the last weekend in April, dedicated to couscous in all its manifestations but with other diversions on hand, and the **Girotonno** festival (ⓦgirotonno.org), spread over four days in late May/early June in the wake of the *Mattanza* (see box, p.96). The latter is the event most associated with the island, celebrating the annual tuna catch and involving much eating and drinking from stalls, along with concerts and dance performances in Piazza Repubblica and on the seafront. The biggest religious festival of the year is the **Festa di San Pietro** on June 29, which features music, dancing, fireworks and a procession of boats. Lastly, **Posidonia** (ⓦposidoniafestival.com), over three days in June or July, is dedicated to art, the environment and sustainable development, with free workshops, concerts and debates. Book accommodation ahead if you're planning to stay during these times.

hamburgers and salads (€5–15). In the evening it's a modish hangout with some forty types of bottled and draught beers as well as Sardinian grappas. daily except Tues April–Oct noon–4pm & 7pm–2am, mid-July to mid-Sept daily; Dec–Feb daily except Tues 7pm–midnight.

Da Nicolo Corso Cavour 32 ☎0781 854 048. One of Carloforte's finest restaurants, just up from Piazza Carlo Emanuele, with tables outside. The menu features local dishes such as *cuscus carlofortino*, *maccheroni con pesto*

and, of course, tuna. There's a good-value two-course lunch menu for €25, otherwise starters are €15–18, mains around €20. Mid-May to mid-Sept Tues–Sun 12.45–3pm & 8–11pm July & Aug, daily.

★ **Pizzeria Lo Scugnizzo** Via Garibaldi 8 ☎0781 186 3102. With old photos on the walls and tables outside, this little place has the best pizzas and *calzoni* on the island. They come in two sizes (€2–3.50 and €4–7) and include wholemeal and gluten-free varieties. Tues–Sun 5–11pm.

The western and southern shores

From Carloforte, a twisty road leads across to the island's western shore at **Capo Sándalo**, a rugged beauty spot on the western tip with memorable views along the coast. Most of this coast is inaccessible without a boat, though you can reach **La Caletta**, the island's widest beach, in the Spalmatore district, along the road running south out of Carloforte and winding round the southern tip. Here, you'll find a cluster of houses and pristine sands amid trees and thick vegetation.

More rough strips of beach lie sheltered in a series of inlets on the island's southeastern edge, for example **La Bobba**, where the twin rock formations known as *Le Colonne* spring abruptly out of the sea.

North of Carloforte

North of Carloforte, a six-kilometre road ends up at **La Punta**, a bracing spot on San Pietro's exposed northern corner, looking towards the offshore **Isola Piana**. This is the venue for the annual tuna slaughter, but you can see the old *tonnare*, or tuna fisheries, at any time.

Portovesme and Portoscuso

On the mainland coast facing San Pietro, the smoking stacks of **PORTOVESME** are the biggest blot on the otherwise undeveloped west coast of Sulcis. Built as an aluminium extraction plant after coal exports dried up following World War II, it is the embarkation point for ferries to Carloforte, and connected to Cágliari by regular buses.

A couple of kilometres north, the low-key fishing port of **PORTOSCUSO** is usually overlooked by island-hoppers, but it still gets quite lively in summer. It has a few old tuna fisheries, a Spanish watchtower and a good beach close by (Portupaleddu), as well as banks, bars and hotels.

ARRIVAL AND DEPARTURE   PORTOVESME AND PORTOSCUSO

By bus ARST buses pull up in Via Palermo in Portoscuso, and at Portovesme's port. There are services from both places to Carbónia (6–8 daily; 25min) and Iglésias (6–8 daily; 50min), which both offer onward services to Cágliari.
By ferry Saremar (☎0781 854 005, ⊚saremar.it)

operates ferries between Portovesme and Carloforte (San Pietro) all year. The 30min crossing runs roughly hourly from 5am, with last departures from Portovesme at midnight in summer, 10.20pm in winter, and from Carloforte at 11.10pm in summer, 9.10pm in winter.

ACCOMMODATION

Panorama Via Giúlio Césare, Portoscuso ☎0781 508 077, ⊚cortehotelpanorama.com. This smart, fairly modern hotel on the portside offers excellent value – go

online for the best deals (rooms overlooking the port cost slightly more). **€60**

Carbónia

Mussolini's push for self-sufficiency in the 1930s led to a series of initiatives to boost Sardinia's economy, the most ambitious of which was the founding of **CARBÓNIA** as a coal-mining centre in 1938. With the dwindling of mining operations since the 1950s, mainly due to the costs of extraction and the poor quality of "Sulcis coal", the town has lost much of its *raison d'être*, but it's still worth a visit to sense Il Duce's presence in the orderly streets of regimented workers' houses and to see a trio of first-rate museums.

Carbónia now has a high level of unemployment, which gives the place a somewhat somnolent air. At the centre of town, idiosyncratic **Piazza Roma** is dominated by the mud-brown tower of San Ponziano (a copy of the campanile of the cathedral of Aquileia) and the stout, four-square Municipio. Most of the town's activity, however, is concentrated on Viale Gramsci, a modern shopping street leading off from the top of the piazza – though any vitality that this might possess is soon dissipated as it gives way to anonymous, right-angled residential quarters.

Museo Archeologico

Villa Sulcis, Via Nápoli • Tues–Sun: April–Sept 10am–7pm; Oct–March 10am–5pm • €6, or €10 with Museo PAS and Monte Sirai • ☎ 0781 63 512, ⓦ mediterraneacoop.it

Sited within Carbónia's Giardino Púbblico, the **Museo Archeologico** consists mainly of finds from Monte Sirai (see opposite). The most noteworthy exhibits are from the tombs found in the necropolis there: bone, silver and gold ornaments from the sixth century BC, an iron dagger and a necklace made of bone and shells. In one corner of the museum, a computer gives a good overview of the excavations, allowing you to view the site as it must have once appeared and home in on details, with full explanations. There are also objects from farther afield, including a smattering of pre-nuraghic items from the Bonnanaro culture – necklaces and domestic implements – and Phoenician and Carthaginian amphorae from Sant'Antíoco.

Museo PAS (Museo dei Paleoambienti Sulcitani)

Località Serbariu • Tues–Sun: April–Sept 10am–2pm & 3–7pm; Oct–March 10am–2pm & 3–5pm • €6, or €10 with Museo Archeologico and Monte Sirai • ☎ 0781 662 199, ⓦ mediterraneacoop.it

Across town, signposted off the SS126 to the west of Carbónia, the ex-mining centre of Serbariu hosts the **Museo dei Paleoambienti Sulcitani**, packed with a surprisingly engaging collection of rock specimens, fossils and caving bric-a-brac. The Sulcis area holds the oldest fossils anywhere in Italy and the display is augmented by non-Italian material donated from around the world. The paleontological section progresses in chronological order, from trilobites from 590–225 million years ago, to ammonites from the Mesozoic era (225–65 million years ago), followed by corals, fish, fossilized wood and even four ants set in amber. From the Quaternary period (about a million years ago) a fossilized tree trunk, a skeletal reconstruction of the *Prolagus sardus* rodent unique to Sardinia (a sort of tailless rabbit extinct for the last thousand years) and the jaws and tusk of a dwarf elephant from the Palermo area take us up to the present era. The speleological collection consists mainly of photos and diagrams of local cave complexes, with glass cases displaying caving equipment.

Museo del Carbone

Località Serbariu • Late June to late Sept daily 10am–7pm; late Sept to late June Tues–Sun 10am–6pm; last entry 1hr before closing • €8 • ☎ 0781 62 727, ⓦ museodelcarbone.it

You can delve into the area's industrial history at the **Museo del Carbone**, or museum of coal, housed within the Serbariu mine itself, where various subterranean chambers and tunnels can be explored on a guided tour (English spoken). Modern installations illustrate the history of mining in the area, and photographs and films vividly bring to life the pitiful working conditions endured by the miners until the mine's closure in the 1960s.

ARRIVAL AND DEPARTURE
CARBÓNIA

By train The train station, Carbónia Serbariu, lies a couple of kilometres west of Piazza Roma, to which it's connected by buses (Mon–Sat every 30min).
Destinations Cágliari (every 1–2hr, some with change at Villamassargia-Domusnovas; 1hr 5min); Iglésias (every 1–2hr, with change at Villamassargia-Domusnovas; 35min).

By bus All out-of-town buses stop in Piazza Roma.
Destinations Cágliari (1–2 daily; 1hr 25min–3hr); Iglésias (Mon–Sat every 30mins–1hr, Sun 8 daily; 50min); Portovesme (Mon–Sat every 30mins–1hr, Sun 4–7 daily; 35min–1hr); Sant'Antíoco (Mon–Sat every 30mins–1hr, Sun 7 daily; 25–40min).

ACCOMMODATION AND EATING

★**Aquarius** Via Sardegna 3 ☎0781 662 143, ⓦ aquariushotel.it. A brief walk from the centre, this *pensione* with friendly management is marked out by its sky-blue exterior and well-equipped rooms. There's a decent restaurant, too, in a conservatory-style space, with moderate prices, open to all and offering a lunchtime menu for €10 and pizzas in the evening (a full dinner will cost around €20). Tues–Sun 12.30–2pm & 8–10.30pm. **€80**

Tanit Località Sirai ☎0781 673 793, ⓦ tanit.tv. Outside town on the Portovesme road, 1km from Monte Sirai, this good-value hotel complex displays a collection of rural and agricultural tools and artefacts. There's a pool and two restaurants, including one outdoors for barbecues. Daily noon–3pm & 7–11pm. **€80**

Monte Sirai

Four kilometres northwest of Carbónia off the SS126 Iglésias road, a signposted turning leads up to the high, flat top of **Monte Sirai**. Phoenicians occupied the site in around the eighth century BC, having ejected a pre-existent nuraghic settlement, and they were displaced in turn by Carthaginians at the end of the sixth century BC, who made this their principal military base on the island. The Romans then occupied the site, but abandoned it at the end of the second century AD for reasons that have never been identified.

The strategic advantages of the location are immediately obvious: from a height of nearly 200m, it dominates the surrounding tracts of sea and land for an immense distance, taking in the islands of Sant'Antíoco and San Pietro – come at sunset for the most exquisite panorama.

Archeological site

Località Sirai • Tues–Sun: April–Sept 10am–7pm; Oct–March 10am–5pm • €6, or €10 with Museo Archeologico and Museo PAS in Carbónia • ☎0781 64 040 or ☎320 571 8454, ⓦ mediterraneacoop.it

In a lofty location, with dwarf palms and olive trees bent almost double by the force of the *maestrale* wind, the **archeological site** of Monte Sirai was first excavated by a Tunisian team in 1966. Three streets of terraced houses were unearthed, of which only the foundations are now visible, everything else, made of mud and straw, having long since disappeared. More recently, the **tombs** of two substantial necropolises have come to light, many marked with the symbols of Tanit, the Phoenician goddess: a circle, horizontal line and triangle, looking something like a character from *Charlie Brown*. Some of the tombs can be entered, and you can see Tanit's symbol – for some reason upside down – in tomb number five. Apart from the red rubble of the crumbled walls, little else remains of the Phoenician/ Carthaginian settlement, as the major finds are now on display in Carbónia's archeological museum. Guided **tours** in English or Italian lasting an hour or more are available, which will point out and explain some of the most interesting features of the site.

Iglésias

Surrounded by mineshafts and quarries gouged out of the red rock, the principal city of the Iglesiente region, **IGLÉSIAS**, makes an appealing stop, its Spanish-tinged atmosphere especially evident during its flamboyant Easter festivities. Though it lacks much tourist infrastructure, the inland town is the biggest and liveliest in the area, with a handful of medieval churches worth visiting and the impressive ruins of a huge mine on the outskirts. The town is also a viable base for exploring the clutch of beach resorts a short drive away, as these have little in the way of accommodation.

The focus of the action in the modern town is the central **Piazza Sella**, lively by day and a noisy rendezvous every evening. At the top end of the square, what's left of the ruined Aragonese (originally Pisan) **Castello Salvaterra** crowns a knoll, its impact softened by landscaped flowerbeds. The castle is usually closed except for occasional performances and exhibitions.

The old town's labyrinth of traffic-free lanes and squares runs off Piazza Sella's western side. The main Corso Matteotti threads through the heart of the *città vecchia* almost as far as **Piazza Municipio**, site of the town hall and cathedral, and one of the few really classic Italian piazzas in this part of the island. It's a harmonious composition, with the town hall taking up one entire side, opposite the cathedral and bishop's palace, which are joined by an elegant enclosed bridge.

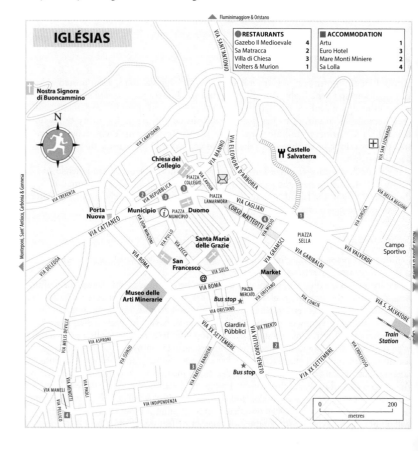

IGLÉSIAS

● RESTAURANTS		■ ACCOMMODATION	
Gazebo Il Medioevale	4	Artu	1
Sa Matracca	2	Euro Hotel	3
Villa di Chiesa	3	Mare Monti Miniere	2
Volters & Murion	1	Sa Lolla	4

UGOLINO DELLA GHERARDESCA

Iglésias enjoyed its greatest prosperity under the rule of the **Gherardesca family**, one of the foremost Tuscan dynasties, based in or around Pisa. At the beginning of the thirteenth century, they led the pro-imperial Ghibelline party of the Pisan republic against the pro-papal Guelf party led by the Visconti family of Milan, but **Ugolino della Gherardesca** (d. 1289) became the most reviled member of the family by switching allegiance from the Ghibellines to the Guelfs. Having assumed control of Pisa, he soon alienated his allies and was eventually accused of treason in 1288 by the archbishop Ruggieri degli Ubaldini, who wanted to revive the republican order. Imprisoned in the tower of Gualandi along with two of his sons and two of his grandsons, Ugolino was said to have eaten his own children before himself dying of starvation, an event depicted in numerous works of art, most famously in Dante's *Divina Commedia*, in which the poet encounters the tyrant frozen in the ice of the ninth circle of hell (*Inferno*, canto 33); Archbishop Ruggieri is also there.

Ugolino is remembered with more affection in Iglésias, where, for the purposes of exploiting the area's mineral resources, he introduced Tuscan methods of planning and political organization. The resulting **statutory code** of local rights was enshrined in a *Breve*, or law book, a meticulously drafted volume which can be viewed on application in the town's Archivio Stórico, in Via delle Cárceri, near the church of Santa Maria delle Grázie (Mon 9am–1pm, Tues–Fri 9am–1pm & 3.30–5.30pm; ☎0781 24 850). Ugolino's son, Guelfo, was imprisoned in the **Castello di Acquafredda**, a thirteenth-century fortress on a jagged elevation 4km south of Siliqua, off the SS130.

The more down-to-earth side of Iglésias is represented by its Art Nouveau-style mining institute on Via Roma, home to a mining museum, and by the Monteponi works outside town (see box, p.106). In summer, **outdoor concerts** take place in Piazza Municipio, Piazza Sella, the castle and other points of the old town – the tourist office has a full list of events.

Brief history

Iglésias owes both its present name and its former name of Villa di Chiesa to its numerous churches, of which a good number survive. Its livelihood has depended more on **mining** operations, however. The town was founded in the thirteenth century by the notorious Pisan Count Ugolino della Gherardesca (see box above), who reopened the old Roman mines. Gold, silver, iron, zinc and lead have all been extracted from the surrounding hills at different times, making Iglésias the chief mining centre of Sardinia, despite bearing little resemblance to the stereotyped image of a grimy mining town.

The Duomo

Piazza Municipio • Daily 9am–12.30pm & 4–8pm

Iglésias' **Duomo** shows a mixture of Pisan and Aragonese styles, reflecting the two dominant (and warring) powers in the region during the Middle Ages. The bell in the squat tower was cast by the great Tuscan sculptor Andrea Pisano in 1337. The main interest in the low-vaulted interior is the spectacular gilded altarpiece in the left transept, carved in the seventeenth century to hold the relics of St Antiochus, which had been removed from the church at Sant'Antíoco during a spate of pirate raids and brought here for safekeeping. However, the bones – which were kept behind the curtain in the middle panel – were forcibly reclaimed in the nineteenth century after the clerics of Iglésias refused to return them. An image of the saint adorns the front of the sculpture, his hands blackened, according to legend, from the barrel of pitch in which he had been forced to hide to escape persecution; he appears again in the painting behind the altar in the bottom left corner, opposite St Clare.

San Francesco

Piazza San Francesco • Daily 8am–noon & 4–8pm

Across the piazza from the Duomo, take Via Pullo to reach the church of **San Francesco**, a predominantly Catalan-Gothic structure built between the fourteenth and sixteenth centuries. Behind a minimalist facade of pinkish trachyte stone, perforated by three circular windows, the nave has a wooden ceiling and seven chapels on either side, each framed by an ogival arch. The first chapel on the left shows a recently restored *retablo della vergine*, a lovely sixteenth-century triptych of the Madonna with saints by Antioco Mainas.

Santa Maria delle Grazie

Piazza Manzoni • Daily 7.30am–noon & 4–8pm

Squeezed between houses off Via Zecca, the tiny church of **Santa Maria delle Grazie** has a medieval stone facade incongruously topped by a pink Baroque upper portion. There's an ornate, antique-looking painted wooden panel inside depicting the Madonna enthroned with archangels, though this is in fact modern. To the right is a painting of San Saturnino of Cágliari, to whom the church was originally dedicated. Since 1925 the church has been run by Capuchin monks based in the annexed convent.

ARRIVAL AND INFORMATION   IGLÉSIAS

By car Parking is not always easy to find, but should be available fairly centrally in blue-line spaces, for which tickets from parking attendants, meters and some *tabacchini* cost €0.30 for the first hour, then €1/hr subsequently.

By train The train station is on Via San Salvatore, a short walk southeast of the centre. You need to change at Villamassargia-Domusnovas for some trains to and from Cágliari, and for all trains to and from Carbónia.

Destinations Cágliari (every 1–2hr; 55min); Carbónia (every 30min–1hr; 30min).

By bus Most out-of-town buses stop at Piazza Mercato, a 5min walk from Piazza Sella; tickets and timetables are available from the bar on the corner of Piazza Mercato and

Via Oristano. Buses to and from Cágliari stop nearby on Via XX Settembre (on the southern side of the Giardini Púbblici), as well as at the train station.

Destinations Buggerru (Mon–Sat 6–10 daily, Sun 2–4 daily; 1hr 15min); Cágliari (Mon–Sat 2 daily; 1hr 15min); Carbónia (Mon–Sat every 30min–1hr, Sun 3 daily; 45min); Fontanamare (3–4 daily; 25min); Masua (Mon–Sat 8 daily, Sun 4 daily; 30min); Nébida (Mon–Sat 8 daily, Sun 4 daily; 25min); Portoscuso/Portovesme (Mon–Sat every 30min– 1hr, Sun 5–7 daily; 35min–1hr 5min); Sant'Antíoco (Mon– Sat 3 daily, Sun 1 daily; 1hr 15min).

Tourist office Piazza Municipio (April–Oct Mon–Sat 10am–noon & 4–8pm; may close in winter; ☎0781 274 507, ⓦ visitiglesias.it).

ACCOMMODATION

None of the lodgings in **central Iglésias** is ideal, but the town has a few options that are fine for a night or two. Alternatively, there are good options in and around **Gonnesa**, 7km south (see p.107).

IGLÉSIAS FESTIVALS

Iglésias comes into its own during its famous **Easter festivities**, when processions weave solemnly between the churches of the old town in a tradition dating back to the seventeenth century. Marching to the rhythm of traditional instruments, the white-robed, sometimes cowled, cortege (the dress is known as *baballotti*) performs this ritual during the whole of Easter week, though the highlight is the second procession, Christ's funeral, on Good Friday evening. Another traditional ceremony, **I Candelieri**, takes place on or around August 15. As in the better-known festa at Sássari that occurs on the same day (see box, p.209), seven (sometimes eight) huge candles, one for each section of the city, are borne through the streets in the evening, from the chiesa del Collegio to the cathedral, to be returned eight days later. If you're thinking of visiting Iglésias at either of these times, book your accommodation first.

Artu Piazza Sella 15 ☎ 0781 22 546, ✆ hotelartuiglesias .it. In a premium location in the centre of town, this family-run hotel has small, clean and functional rooms, friendly staff and a small garage (€3.50/night). It's desperately old-fashioned and breakfasts are paltry, but there's a bar and a decent restaurant. **€78**

Euro Hotel Via Fratelli Bandiera 34 ☎ 0781 22 643, ✆ eurohoteliglesias.it. Completely over-the-top period hotel, dripping with chandeliers, Rococo furniture and kitsch art. It's certainly luxurious, though, with spacious rooms, and prices drop in low season. Parking available. **€80**

Mare Monti Miniere Via Trento 10 ☎ 0781 41 765 or ☎ 348 331 0585, ✆ maremontiminiere-bb.it. Close to the bus stops and just outside the *centro stórico*, this B&B has three spacious, modern rooms, but with traditional Sard trimmings. Copious breakfasts may include local pastries made by the genial hostess. **€48**

Sa Lolla Via Mameli 2–4 ☎ 0781 251 120, ✉ wcontu @libero.it. This plain B&B a few minutes' walk south of the centre has small but modern rooms equipped with a/c and minibars. Excursions in the Iglesiente can be arranged, and two bikes are available to guests. The same family runs the *Le Due Anfore* B&B on the top floor, with more basic accommodation (€50). No credit cards. **€60**

EATING AND DRINKING

Iglésias has no outstanding **restaurants**, but there are several places where you can eat reasonably well and cheaply. For picnic ingredients, there's an indoor **market** open Monday to Saturday mornings just up from Piazza Sella on Via Gramsci.

Gazebo Il Medioevale Via Musio 21 ☎ 0781 30 871. Full of medieval atmosphere, this brick-vaulted hall off Corso Matteotti offers such local specialities as *trofie alla tabarchina* (pasta with prawns, tomato, garlic, basil and white wine) and some innovative fish dishes. The bill should be €25–35 each. Mon–Sat noon–3pm & 8–10.45pm; open daily in Aug.

★**Sa Matracca** Via Repubblica 46 ☎ 0781 877 242. Intimate *osteria* with exposed stone walls (surviving from the Roman, Pisan and Aragonese eras), wooden ceilings and an ancient well. You can eat outside in summer. Regional specialities include tasty *gnocchetti alla campidanese* and a mixed meat grill; pizzas are available too. Mains are around €15, the set-price lunch is €10. Mon–Sat noon–2pm & 7.30pm–midnight.

Villa di Chiesa Piazza Municipio 2 ☎ 0781 31 641. This restaurant enjoys the best location in town, especially in summer when you can dine in the square. The menu includes fresh pasta, pizzas and a selection of fish and meat dishes. Prices are reasonable: €9–12 for starters, €12–20 for mains. July–Sept Mon 7–11pm, Tues–Sun noon–3pm & 7–11pm; Oct–June closed Mon.

Volters & Murion Piazza Collegio ☎ 0781 33 788. Pub and restaurant with outdoor seating, offering simple snacks, including excellent pizzas, pastas and meat dishes (fixed-price menus €10 and €15). Also a nice place to drop by for a late-night drink. July & Aug daily, 10am–3pm & 6pm–1am; Sept–June closed Mon; food served noon–2.30pm & 7pm–midnight.

North of Iglésias

North of Iglésias, the slow and twisty SS126 heads north through forested mountains to Fluminimaggiore, a scenic ride with a couple of important sights en route that warrant a visit.

Témpio di Antas

Località Antas • April, May & Oct daily 9.30am–5.30pm; June daily 9.30am–6.30pm; July–Sept daily 9.30am–7.30pm; Nov–March Tues–Sun 9.30am–4.30pm • €4, or €5 with Museo Mulino • ☎ 0781 580 990 or ☎ 347 817 4989, ✆ startuno.it • Take any bus running between Iglésias and Fluminimaggiore, then walk 2km from the main road

Fifteen kilometres north of Iglésias, a right turn off the SS126 wanders down a valley to the remote **Témpio di Antas**, a heavily restored Roman temple built on the site of a nuraghic and later Carthaginian sanctuary. Its Punic origins are thought to date back to around 500 BC, but it probably assumed its final form in the third century AD. As an inscription records, the Romans dedicated the temple to Sardus Pater Babai, a local deity worshipped as the father of the Sards in the kind of synthesis of imperial and local cults that was practised throughout the Roman Empire. The Ionic-style columns are still standing, topped by a simple pediment, and you can see inside the remains of the sacred

2

MINING THE IGLESIENTE

Travellers in the Iglesiente region can't fail to notice the numerous **mineworks** dramatically pitting the landscape, though there's plenty more that's out of sight – all testament to the mineral wealth excavated from the mountains since earliest times. If you're intrigued by the industrial archeology of the area, you can view some excellent museums and visit many of the old works on guided tours. We give details of some of the best below; combined tickets are sometimes available for those planning to see more than one. The websites ⓦ parcogeominerario.eu and ⓦ minieredisardegna.it have **information** on mining and mines throughout Sardinia.

Ecomuseo Miniere Rosas Località Rosas, near Narcao ☎ 0781 185 5139, ⓦ ecomuseominiererosas .it. Lead, zinc and iron were worked at this site in the mountains some 25km east of Carbónia, which now has a museum with guided tours of the mine and nearby filtering plant (€6; 1hr 30min). You can even rent an ex-miners' cottage for the night (€50) and dine in the old post office. Daily June–Sept 9am–7.30pm; Oct–May 9am–1pm & 2–6pm.

Galleria Henry Buggerru. Dating from 1860, this site provides insights into the life of the thriving community that worked here until the mine's closure in 1991. Guided tours should be booked ahead (☎ 347 145 4459; €8).

Ingurtosu Ghostly remains of an old mining settlement located off the SS126 southwest of Gúspini (see p.108).

Monteponi Iglésias Evocative site outside town, a vast, desolate area of mineworkings abandoned in 1992. Contact the tourist office in Iglésias for guided tours of the Galleria Villamarina (€10).

Montevécchio ☎ 070 973 173, ⓦ miniera montevecchio.it. This mine, 8km west of Gúspini, is one of Sardinia's oldest, and was Italy's most important source of lead ore in the 1860s. Tours (€14) last 3hr: consult website for days and opening times. Usually mid-July to Sept Tues–Sun 10am–1pm, sometimes also 3.30–6.30pm; Oct to mid-July weekends only; visits at other times can be booked.

Museo del Carbone Carbónia. Essential stop for an all-round view of Sardinia's coal industry (see p.100).

Museo dell'Arte Mineraria Via Roma 47, Iglésias ☎ 328 809 4091, ⓦ museoartemineraria.it. Displays mining machinery, models, photos and reconstructions of the pit-face as well as a collection of minerals dug out of the local rock. June–Sept Sat & Sun 6.30–8.30pm; call to visit at other periods; €4, or €11 with Porto Flavia, Masua (see below).

Porto Flavia Masua. This mine right over the sea dates from 1924. Contact Iglésias tourist office (see p.104) for guided tours (€10).

chambers, while rooms and houses used by the priests and other members of the ethnically mixed population are faintly visible behind. It's an idyllic spot, the air full of the aromas of *macchia* and the jangle of distant goat bells, spoilt only by the pylons and cables strung across the valley.

A combined ticket allows entry to the **Museo Mulino** (Tues–Sun 10am–1pm & 5–8pm, 4–7pm in winter; €3 museum alone) in Fluminimaggiore, located within and around an eighteenth-century watermill over the River Mannu off Via Vittorio Emanuele 225, where you can view a miscellany of items relating to rural customs and culture.

Grotta Su Mannau

Località Mannau • Daily: Easter–June 9.30am–5.30pm; July–Oct 9.30am–6.30pm • €10 • ☎ 0781 580 411 or ☎ 347 541 3624, ⓦ sumannau.it • Take any bus running between Iglésias and Fluminimaggiore, then walk 1km from the main road

Five kilometres north of the Témpio di Antas, the **Grotta Su Mannau** is one of the most accessible of the many grottoes scattered throughout this area. A tourist trail penetrates for 800m, enough to see some spectacular rock formations, brilliantly illuminated, while cavers can go on for as far again inside the mountain. Hour-long tours leave every half-hour or so; in winter, groups can visit by booking ahead. Many visitors choose to walk between the grotto and the Témpio di Antas – it's only about 3km but, involving a steep ascent, takes up to an hour and a quarter; ask the staff to point out the path.

The Iglesiente coast

West of Iglésias, the remote villages and beaches on the **coast** have few transport links with the outside world, but are easily accessible under your own steam. The villages and resorts here are hardly the attraction: the real appeal is the refreshing emptiness of the coast, either cliff-hung tracts or wildernesses of bare dunes.

Gonnesa and around

2

GONNESA, 9km southwest of Iglésias, is a fairly unremarkable inland village in and around which are some good accommodation options for visitors to Iglésias and the nearby coast. From the SS126, a road branches 4km west to the long sandy beach at **Fontanamare**, a popular bathing spot with bars and a pizzeria open in summer, but quiet the rest of the time.

ACCOMMODATION AND EATING   GONNESA AND AROUND

Frau Via della Pace, Gonnesa ☏ 0781 45 104. In the village centre, this small B&B offers modest but clean accommodation at rock-bottom prices. It's run by a friendly *signora* who can rustle up a meal at short notice. Rooms are plain and share bathrooms; breakfast is extra. No credit cards. **€40**

★ **Lo Sperone** Località S'Ortu de Coccu ☏ 0781 36 247, ⟁ agriturismolosperonegonnesa.it. This relaxed *agriturismo*, clearly signposted on the SS126 (opposite the Masua turn-off), is convenient for the Fontanamare beach (see above). Six rooms are available, all en suite; in July and Aug half or full board is preferred (€50/person for half board). There are also two apartments for weekly rent and riding is available at the stables. The food is authentic Sardinian country cuisine, with set-price meals for €25 – non-guests can dine here with prior notice. No credit cards. **€60**

Nébida and around

The coastal route continues north from Gonnesa along the mainly high and cliffy littoral of the **Golfo di Gonnesa**, one of Sardinia's most scenic stretches of sea and mountain. **NÉBIDA** is the first village you'll meet, perched above the water 3km north of Fontanamare. Next to a public garden and sports ground on the southern approach, a path rounding a cliffy promontory gives access to a **belvedere** offering the area's best views of the sheer coast on either side, as far as the Pan di Zúcchero *scoglio* to the north (see below). Below the path, at the bottom of a four-hundred-step descent, you'll see the ramshackle **Laveria La Mármora**, built in 1897 for the filtering and washing of mine products but now abandoned. At the north end of the village, a small lane dives steeply down to the tiny sandy cove of **Porto Banda**, where two large *faraglioni* – needle-shaped stacks of rock – poke up from the sea.

EATING AND DRINKING   NÉBIDA

906 Operaio Belvedere di Nébida ☏ 338 916 5388. With its covered terrace, this bar-pizzeria built into a grotto on the cliff path makes the perfect venue for taking in the wonderful sea views – not least at sunset. The light and crusty pizzas are superb; count on about €17 for a pizza and a draught beer. No credit cards. Easter–Oct daily 8am–midnight.

Masua and around

North of Nébida, the mountain road winds 3–4km on to **MASUA**, where there are bars and a pizzeria, and a lovely but restricted **beach** backed by shade-giving rocks and ruined walls. The seascape is dominated by the colossal outcrop known as the **Pan di Zúcchero** (Sugarloaf), whose prodigious white hulk is depicted on countless postcards. Owing its name to its unique shape and colour, it's said to be the oldest such *scoglio*, or rock formation, in Italy, with a height of over 133m.

More huge **mineworks** dominate the knot of houses at Masua, dedicated to extracting zinc and lead, the two main products of this region. One of the old mines and a mining museum can be visited on guided tours (see box, p.106).

Buggerru and around

From Masua, a tortuous road climbs 10km north to reach **BUGGERRU**, a fishing port and tourist resort superimposed on another old mining centre. Once accessible only by sea, Buggerru was largely self-sufficient during its mining days; it was the first place in Sardinia to have a regular electrical system, and the miners enjoyed health and recreational facilities long before such practices were introduced by other companies. As in Masua, you can tour one of the old mines here (see box, p.106).

Away from the regimented marina packed with small pleasure boats, there are some superb **beaches** in the vicinity, including the solitary **Cala Domestica**, a deep, sheltered and sandy inlet 4.5km south of Buggerru. Much of Derek Jarman's 1976 film, *Sebastiane*, was shot here. There's a seasonal bar for refreshments; parking costs €5 per day, and you can rent a parasol and deckchairs for around €10 per half-day.

Alternatively, head north to the much wider **Portixeddu**, a sweeping swathe of sand with little or no construction nearby. The road ends a little farther north at **Capo Pécora**, a wild, deserted spot with a small stony beach.

ACCOMMODATION	BUGGERRU AND AROUND
Ortus de Mari Località Portixeddu ☎0781 54 964, ✉ortusdemari@virgilio.it. Less than a kilometre inland of Portixeddu beach, this is the only campsite on this	stretch of coast, offering very minimal facilities: showers, a bar, wi-fi and shady trees. Closed Oct to late May. No credit cards. Pitches €30

The Costa Verde

There is little that's "green" about the **Costa Verde**, stretching north from Capo Pécora, most of it consisting of arid rock, scrub and sand. Access is from the SS126, either from the village of Gúspini, from where a road twists for 25km to the desolate coast, or, 13km farther south, via the dirt road threading westwards from the deserted mining town of **Ingurtosu**. If your vehicle can stand it, this is the preferable route; it's shorter, and allows a stop at the ghostly ruins of this once vibrant community.

Piscinas

Seven kilometres below Ingurtosu, the road emerges on the coast at **Piscinas**, a barren spot, about as remote as it gets in Sardinia, with superb swimming. Apart from a few traces of nineteenth-century mineworks, there's nothing here but immense sand dunes and an upmarket hotel (see below), though in summer you'll find fast-food kiosks in the vicinity. If you don't want to pay to stay, camping rough is feasible in this out-of-the-way area.

ACCOMMODATION AND EATING	PISCINAS
★ **Hotel Le Dune** Piscinas di Ingurtosu ☎070 977 130, ⓦledunepiscinas.it. This chic, secluded and highly expensive retreat is a fabulous place to hole up for a few days if it's in your price range. Its restaurant (daily 1–2.15pm & 8–9.45pm), open to anyone, has tables	outside right by the beach – a memorable place to dine at sunset. Alternatively, you can use the bar, which serves *panini*. The hotel has a spa, and yoga sessions are held on the beach. Rates plummet in low season. Closed Oct to mid-April. €360

Marina di Arbus and around

From Piscinas, a dirt road follows the coast north, passing more dune-backed sands and perfect seas, until it meets civilization among the shops, restaurants and holiday homes of **MARINA DI ARBUS**. There are more good beaches here and a couple of kilometres north at **Funtanazza**, lying below and out of sight of an eyesore of a ruined 1950s holiday complex, and reached along a private road that is barred at night but otherwise open to anyone.

From the junction beyond, a winding but scenic road threads inland towards the villages of Gúspini and Arbus, passing through what was once a productive mining area centred on **Montevécchio** (see box, p.106). Ten kilometres east of Montevécchio, **GÚSPINI** has a bank, fuel station and a couple of trattorias to meet all immediate requirements. Continuing east from here, the road crests the ridge of mountains to give long views over the plain of Campidano (see p.112).

Alternatively, heading about 10km north up the coast from Funtanazza, you'll reach a superb, broad sand beach backed by high dunes at **Torre dei Corsari**. The towering cliffs beyond, ending at **Capo Frasca**, are inaccessible by land. Curling eastwards, the road gives access to a causeway/bridge running across the Stagno di Marceddi and into Oristano province (see p.157).

2

Campidano, La Marmilla and Sarrabus

CAPO CARBONARA

Campidano, La Marmilla and Sarrabus

The regions to the north and east of Cágliari are remarkably diverse in both tone and physical appearance, and include some essential stops as well as several worthwhile places well off the beaten track. To the northwest of Cágliari, Campidano has Sardinia's most extensive plain and comprises its richest agricultural region, nourished by numerous rivers and benefiting from past drainage and antimalaria schemes. North and east of here, the flat uniformity of Campidano gives way to the hill country of La Marmilla, location of some of the island's most important nuraghic remains. In Sarrabus, the region occupying Sardinia's southeastern corner, the farmlands give way to the inhospitable, jagged peaks of the Sette Fratelli mountains, much of the range too desolate even for shepherds, but with abundant wildlife and excellent hiking. The emptiness and desolation of this inland rugged wilderness are far removed from the holiday ambience of the coast, whose rocky indentations shelter some of Sardinia's finest beaches.

Much of this disparate territory could be explored on excursions from Cágliari, or on brief detours on your way farther afield. The main route north of the capital, for example, the SS131 – still known as the Carlo Felice highway after the king who commissioned it in the 1820s – brings you right past **Sanluri**, home to the well-preserved but rather diminutive medieval castle that houses what must be Sardinia's quirkiest museum collection. Farther up the SS131, you could pause at the villages of **Sárdara** and **Villanovaforru** for their diverse historical remnants. From here it's an easy ride through La Marmilla to the extensive complex of **Su Nuraxi**, the largest and most famous of all Sardinia's nuraghic sites. North of here, La Marmilla ends at the high plateau of **Giara di Gésturi**, a protected area of woods and scrubland that shelters a variety of birdlife and other fauna and flora, most famously a breed of miniature wild pony.

On the eastern edge of Campidano, due north of Cágliari, the agricultural centre of **Dolianova** is worth visiting chiefly for its Romanesque ex-cathedral. Again, this would make an easy stop on the road north into the mountainous **Gerrei** region, a magnificently rugged and empty stretch of country that holds the **Nuraghe Arrubiu**, another of the island's most impressive prehistoric monuments. The mountains dominating the interior of Sarrabus can be admired from the SS125, the twisty road linking Cágliari to the island's eastern seaboard, but they are best appreciated from close up, preferably on a hike. Development is sporadic along the Sarrabus coast, but gets more intense around the main resort here, **Villasimius**, as well as farther north on the popular **Costa Rei** and around the inland town of Muravera. In between the pockets of construction lies some of the island's most alluring coastline, and outside July and August you'll have the beaches pretty much to yourself.

The Trenino Verde p.128
A walk in the Monte dei Sette Fratelli p.133

Muravera's festivals p.134

Highlights

❶ **Chiesa di Santa Maria, Uta** Slightly off the beaten track, this perfectly preserved medieval church is southern Sardinia's Romanesque gem. **See p.116**

❷ **Castello di Eleonora d'Arborea, Sanluri** The delightfully eclectic collection of historical and military bric-a-brac in this well-preserved medieval castle provides a thoroughly entertaining couple of hours. **See p.117**

❸ **Su Nuraxi** The largest and most intriguing of Sardinia's ancient nuraghic complexes is an essential stop on any island tour. **See p.122**

❹ **La Giara di Gésturi** This distinctive high basalt plateau rising above La Marmilla is teeming with wildlife, from rare orchids to miniature wild horses – perfect for a breather. **See p.125**

❺ **Costa Rei beaches** It's a modern, somewhat pricey holiday zone, but you'll enjoy some superlative swimming from flawless, sandy beaches on this coast, as well as secluded coves. **See p.131**

❻ **Sette Fratelli mountains** Stretch your legs in one of Sardinia's great scenic wildernesses, easily accessible by road. **See p.132**

HIGHLIGHTS ARE MARKED ON THE MAP ON PP.114–115

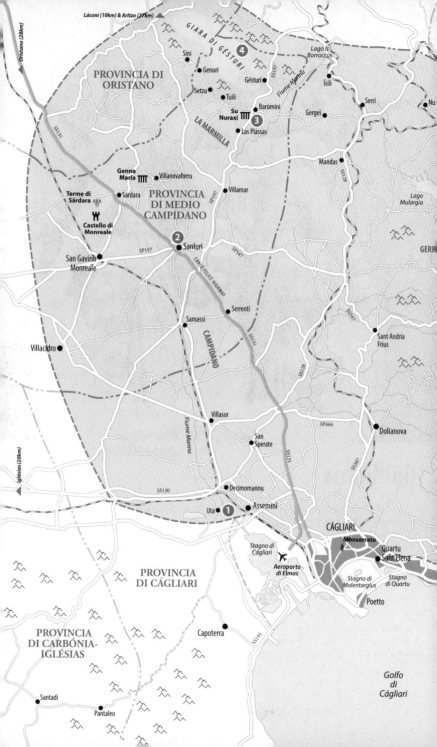

HIGHLIGHTS

1. Chiesa di Santa Maria, Uta
2. Castello di Eleonora d'Arborea, Sanluri
3. Su Nuraxi
4. Giara di Gésturi
5. Costa Rei beaches
6. Sette Fratelli mountains

0 — 10
kilometres

Plateau area

PROVINCIA DI OGLIASTRA

PROVINCIA DI CÁGLIARI

Tortolì

Tertenia

Perdasdefogu

Escalaplano

Ballao

San Nicolo Gerrei

Flumendosa

San Vito

Villaputzu

Muravera

Porto Corallo

Nuraghe Asoru

S'a Picocca

San Giovanni

Torre Salinas

Colostrai

Feraxi

SARRABUS

Burcei

MONTE DEI SETTE FRATELLI

Capo Ferrato

Castiadas

Costa Rei

Cala Sinzias

FORESTA DI MINNIMINNI

Serpentara

Torre delle Stelle

Solanas

Villasimius

Golfo di Carbonara

Simius
Stagno di Notteri
Capo Carbonara
Isola dei Cávoli

Spiaggia Del Riso

N

Quirra

SS125

SS387

CAMPIDANO, LA MARMILLA & SARRABUS

By car The dual carriageway SS131, Sardinia's main north to south artery, is fast and convenient for Campidano and La Marmilla, while the SS125 links Cágliari to Muravera and the eastern coast. For Villasimius take the slow but scenic SP17 coast road from Cágliari, or the faster inland route SS125/SS554bis/SS125var before joining the SP17. A car is best for Giara di Gésturi and to view the *nuraghi* of Genna Maria and Arrubiu.

By train From Cágliari's Gottardo (Monserrato) station, there's a frequent service to Dolianova and once-daily trains run to Mandas (not Sun). For more info, consult ARST on ☎ 800 865 042 or ⊛ arst.sardegna.it.

By bus ARST (see above) runs frequent services from Cágliari to Uta, San Sperate, Sanluri, Dolianova, Villasimius and Muravera, plus a very infrequent service to Barúmini (for Su Nuraxi).

Uta

Campidano lacks scenic drama, but compensates with its range of cultural and historical sites, not least what is arguably the loveliest Romanesque church in southern Sardinia, located outside the agricultural centre of **UTA**, 15km northwest of Cágliari. Unless you're here during the last week of August, when the **Festa di Santa Lucia** is celebrated with a procession to the church of peasant carts, or *traccas*, there's little else to detain you here.

Chiesa di Santa Maria

Via Santa Maria · Usually daily 8.30am–noon & 2.30–6pm, otherwise call to arrange access · ☎ 347 876 1173

Built by Vittorini monks from Marseille around 1140, the **Chiesa di Santa Maria** stands in the country outside the eastern end of the village, at the centre of a landscaped area that was formerly a cemetery. Its light stonework is embellished with arcading running round under the roof, at the base of which human heads, rams, dogs, stags, calves and various abstract devices are chiselled. This florid Provençal style is fused with Pisan elements, apparent in the portals and the bare interior, where two columns of perfect round arches have well-restored capitals. The grey stone interior is in keeping with the outside – unadorned, with arches supported by columns from the Roman era.

By bus ARST buses to and from Cágliari (Mon–Sat every 30mins–1hr, Sun 4 daily; 30–50min) stop in Piazza Santa Giusta, in Uta's centre.

By train On the main line between Cágliari, Carbónia and Iglésias, Stazione di Villaspeciosa-Uta lies around 2km north of the centre.

Destinations Cágliari (Mon–Sat hourly, Sun every 1–2hr; 25min); Carbónia (Mon–Sat hourly, Sun every 1–2hr, some with change at Villamassargia; 40min); Iglésias (Mon–Sat hourly, Sun every 1–2hr; 35min).

Tourist information See ⊛ prolocouta.it.

San Sperate

Ten kilometres northeast of Uta, the village of **SAN SPERATE** is famous for its **murals** and **sculptures**. Dating from the late 1960s and executed by local artists in a variety of styles, including trompe l'oeil, four hundred or so murals depict domestic and rural scenes that evoke an older, simpler and more parochial society. The tradition was probably initiated by **Pinuccio Sciola**, Sardinia's best-known contemporary sculptor, born in San Sperate in 1942. Several open-air sculptures by him are also on show, almost exclusively carved from local trachyte – its mutating, seasoned textures are particularly appropriate for Sciola's grand pieces, which resemble menhirs or even nuraghic Giants' Tombs burial stones.

By bus There's a good ARST service to and from Cágliari (Mon–Sat every 30mins–1hr, Sun 6 daily; 30min). Change

at Decimomannu for connections to or from Uta.
Tourist information See ⓦ turismosansperate.com.

EATING

Ada Via Cágliari 21 ☎ 070 960 0972. An excellent spot to sample traditional *campidanese* cooking, offering a rich assortment of dishes using strictly seasonal local produce, for example ravioli stuffed with goat's meat and artichokes.

Pizzas and a huge range of craft beers are also available. There's a fixed-price menu at lunchtime (€12) – otherwise count on around €30 for a full meal without drinks. Mon–Sat 12.30–2.30pm & 7.30–10.30pm.

Sanluri

Occupying a commanding position in the hinterland between the old *giudicati* of Arborea and Cágliari, Campidano's biggest town, **SANLURI**, 45km northwest of the capital, grew up around the thirteenth-century castle that is named after Eleonora, the warrior queen who spent a lifetime in arms against the Aragonese (see box, p.143) and who briefly resided here.

While you're here, call in at any Sanluri bakery for a loaf of the local **bread**, *civraxiu* – huge and flavoursome, it's renowned throughout Campidano.

Castello di Eleonora d'Arborea

Via Generale Villa Santa • Daily 9.30am–1pm & 4–7.30pm • €5 • ☎ 070 930 7184, ⓦ castellodisanluri.it

A high, square keep surrounded by fir trees off the main road slicing through the centre of Sanluri, the **Castello di Eleonora d'Arborea** was a linchpin of the Sard-Aragonese conflict that embroiled the island in the fourteenth and fifteenth centuries. The castle was the venue for a peace treaty signed by the Aragonese king, Pedro IV, and Mariano IV, father of Eleonora d'Arborea – though this turned out to be merely a breathing space. In 1409, following Eleonora's death, Pedro's son, Martino, won a definitive victory at Sanluri against forces commanded by the new *giudice*, a defeat that marked the end of Arborea's resistance and was followed by the swift occupation of almost the whole island by Aragonese forces. The castle later became home to the noble Villa Santa family, who amassed a motley collection of military and historical memorabilia as well as various works of art.

The ground floor

Modern artillery pieces and copies of antique catapults arranged outside the castle give some hint of what lies within. In fact, although one of the castle's collections is named the **Museo Risorgimentale**, there is little here that relates to the Risorgimento – Italy's struggle for independence in the nineteenth century – notwithstanding the strong military flavour to most of the items on display on the ground floor. This is most conspicuous in the **Salone delle Milizie**, once the stables of the castle, where a fascinating collection of curios, portraits and trophies was assembled by the local count, Generale Nino Villa Santa, and augmented by the donations of various enthusiasts in the 1920s. Museum guides will point out idiosyncratic mementos and relate details of the lives of the soldiers who fought in the Brigata Sássari, a renowned infantry brigade that suffered massive casualties in the long Alpine campaign of 1918. War-torn banners, yellowed photographs and newspapers and even a primitive bicycle are jumbled together, jostling for space with a veritable arsenal of weaponry. Other items are from the little-known Italian-Turkish war of 1911–12, from Mussolini's Ethiopian campaign of 1936 and from World War II, including, surprisingly, a batch of English postcards of the period.

3

The first floor and roof

Upstairs, the rest of the castle proves as absorbing as the military exhibits. Reached by a fine staircase, the succession of beamed **rooms** are richly furnished with rugs, tables, dressers and paintings, mainly from the eighteenth and nineteenth centuries, and including such items as an iron bed from the 1700s belonging to the Genoan Doria dynasty. In the study you can see fragments of writings by controversial Italian man of letters and swashbuckling patriot, Gabriele d'Annunzio, while an adjoining room displays a sabre belonging to Joachim Murat, Napoleon's brother-in-law, and drinking glasses used by Josephine (marked "J"). The next room has a collection of around 350 **wax figurines**, some dating as far back as the sixteenth century, and some by the master in the field Clemente Susini, whose ingenious creations can also be seen in Cágliari (see p.63). The most arresting waxwork, however, is by Gaetano Zumbo (1656–1701), La Putrefazione – a horrifically graphic study of a plague victim, half-consumed by rats and worms.

Before leaving, climb up to the castle's **roof** for a good view of the town and countryside (you may need to ask one of the museum staff).

3

ARRIVAL AND DEPARTURE   **SANLURI**

By bus Sanluri is easy to reach on the frequent buses travelling through this region.
Destinations Barúmini (Mon–Sat 3–5 daily; 30–45min); Cágliari (Mon–Sat every 30mins–1hr, Sun 4 daily;

50min–1hr 50min); Oristano (Mon–Sat 2 daily; 1hr 15min); Sárdara (Mon–Sat 13 daily, Sun 3 daily; 15min); Tuili (Mon–Sat 5–7 daily; 35min–1hr).

ACCOMMODATION AND EATING

Free Time's Pub Piazza Porta Nuova 13 ☎340 951 9941. Whether you're after a sandwich, a pasta, seafood or steak dish, or just a late drink, this Irish-style pub is the right place. There are cocktails and Belgian beers (among others), and a veranda for sitting outside (with a ten percent supplement to pay). All dishes are €7–12, and there's a €12 tourist menu. DJs provide musical

accompaniment in the evening. Daily 6pm–3am.
Mirage Via Carlo Felice ☎070 930 7100, ⓦ hotelmirage.biz. At the northern entry into town, this functional business hotel is the area's only accommodation option, with modern rooms but patchy wi-fi and mean breakfasts. Avoid rooms near the nightclub below when it's open. **€80**

Sárdara and around

Nine kilometres northwest of Sanluri on the SS131, the otherwise unexceptional village of **SÁRDARA** and its environs hold a handful of relics connected to the local therapeutic waters from the nuraghic, Roman and medieval periods. The fourteenth-century church of **San Gregorio** presents a striking sight, its tall, narrow facade with a fine rose window is a graceful blend of Romanesque and Gothic, while late-Gothic workmanship dominates in the fifteenth-century church of **Sant'Anastasia,** at Sárdara's highest point.

Two kilometres south, the squat ruins of the **Castello di Monreale** crown a hillock overlooking the surrounding plain – an evocative backdrop, though the sparse remains don't merit closer exploration.

Témpio Nurágico

Piazza Anastasia • Tues–Sun: June–Sept 9am–1pm & 5–8pm; Oct–May 9am–1pm & 4–7pm • €2.60, €4.50 with Museo Cívico • ☎ 070 938 6011

Surrounding Sárdara's church of Sant'Anastasia is a much more ancient centre of worship, the **Témpio Nurágico**. Constructed in basalt and calcareous bricks, the site dates from around the eighth century BC and centres on a sacred well, known locally as Funtana de Is Dolus, or "Fountain of Pains", a reference to the various ailments its waters were supposed to cure. The remains of several nuraghic buildings clustered around the well have yielded some notable finds, including ornate water jugs, some of them displayed in the town's museum.

Museo Cívico

Piazza Libertà • Tues–Sun: June–Sept 9am–1pm & 5–8pm; Oct–May 9am–1pm & 4–7pm • €2.60, €4.50 with Témpio Nurágico • ☎ 070 938 7304

Eight rooms in Sárdara's ex-town hall hold various items unearthed in the town and at other local archeological sites. The cream of the crop has been transferred to Cágliari, but some of the more eye-catching finds have been copied for display here, including a handsome pair of nuraghic bronze archers.

Santa Maria Is Acquas

Località Santa Maria Is Acquas, 2km west of Sárdara • Open only for services

The late-Gothic church of **Santa Maria Is Acquas**, a pretty, pale stone building surrounded by trees, is the venue for a **festival** deriving from the pagan water cult, taking place around the penultimate Monday of September when a holy image is carried here in procession from its normal home in Sárdara's church of L'Assunta, culminating in singing and dancing.

Terme di Sárdara

Località Santa Maria Is Acquas, 2km west of Sárdara • Thermal pools €20 for half-day; treatments extra • ☎ 070 938 7200, ☯ termedisardara.it

Sardinia's prehistoric people weren't the only ones to value the waters around Sárdara: the Romans built the now-vanished Aquae Neapolitanae here, while today a modern spa hotel complex, the **Terme di Sárdara**, uses the sodium-rich waters issuing from the five hot springs to treat liver and digestive complaints. The complex has two outdoor **thermal pools** and a fitness centre that are open to all, and a range of therapies is available.

ARRIVAL AND ACCOMMODATION	**SÁRDARA**

By bus The village is served by buses from Cágliari (Mon–Sat 10 daily, Sun 4 daily; 1hr 10min–1hr 45min) and Sanluri (Mon–Sat 13 daily, Sun 3 daily; 15min).

Terme di Sárdara Località Santa Maria Is Acquas ☎ 070 938 7200, ☯ termedisardara.it. The village has a couple of budget hotels, but the spa hotel 2km outside offers a much fancier experience. Rates include access to all the facilities for guests on half or full board, otherwise you'll pay separately for these. Between Jan and April/May, it's open at weekends only. **€93**

Villanovaforru and around

Roads trail north and east from Sanluri and Sárdara into the hills of **La Marmilla**, on the confines of the provinces of Medio Campidano, Oristano and Nuoro. At its southern fringes, the quiet and tidy village of **VILLANOVAFORRU**, founded by the Spanish in the seventeenth century, was historically an important grain market for the surrounding area. Apart from its museum, however, the slow-moving village has little else to detain you.

Museo Archeologico

Piazza Costituzione • Tues–Sun: April–Sept 9.30am–1pm & 3.30–7pm; Oct–March 9.30am–1pm & 3.30–6pm • €3.50, €5 with Genna Maria • ☎ 070 930 0050, ☯ gennamaria.it

In Villanovaforru's centre, a sympathetically restored grain store holds the **Museo Archeologico**, exhibiting some of the earliest evidence of local Bronze and Iron Age civilizations. The well-lit displays mostly consist of the contents of tombs: a procession of ritual vases, oil lamps (some boat-shaped), jewellery and assorted ceramics, sometimes painted with complex geometric patterns. Many of the metal items are distinctively polished, an effect attained using specially crafted bones. Finds from Su Nuraxi (see p.122) are well represented, while one section upstairs is entirely devoted to Carthaginian and Roman objects, including coins, the clay contents of a Punic tomb found at Villamar and part of a Roman millstone. The importance of water to the local communities is reflected in the abundance of containers found, often with elegantly curving designs.

Though stripped of its original furnishings, the grain store's interior retains its beamed ceilings, arched walls and a central well on the ground floor. A separate entrance beside the museum gives access to the small **Sala Mostre**, hosting occasional exhibitions.

Nuraghe di Genna Maria

Località Genna Maria • Tues–Sun: April–Sept 9.30am–1pm & 3.30–7pm; Feb, March & Oct 9.30am–1pm & 3.30–6pm; Nov–Jan 9.30am–1pm & 2.30–5pm • €2.50; €5 including Museo Archeologico • ☏ 070 930 0050, ⓦ gennamaria.it

A kilometre west of Villanovaforru, a left turn off the Collinas road leads to the **Nuraghe di Genna Maria**, occupying the summit of Marmilla's highest hill (408m) and commanding far-reaching views. From the car park it's a short but fairly steep climb to the site itself, which covers an extensive area dominated by a central ruined tower surrounded by the circular structures of a village. The remains are in worse condition than some of Sardinia's other nuraghic monuments, partly a result of the use of local sandstone as a building material, but this still ranks among the island's most important sites, not least for the quantity of finds it has yielded. First excavated between 1951 and 1954 by the renowned Sardinian archeologist Giovanni Lilliu, but only fully revealed in 1977, the site is still the subject of digs. A raised walkway above the walls, in parts 3m high, allows you to look down on the chambers and passages of the main building, as well as the lower walls encircling the small rooms pressed up against it.

The construction

The difficulties of building on this elevated site are shown in the many successive **stages of construction**. The central keep (*mastio*) was erected during the first phase, possibly as early as the fifteenth century BC, while the quadrilobate bastion and part of the curtain wall (*antemurale*) certainly go back to the thirteenth century BC. A new phase extended over the thirteenth and twelfth centuries BC, while the village dwellings were built between the twelfth and ninth centuries BC, the beginning of Sardinia's Iron Age. Finally, the curtain wall was completed during the ninth and eighth centuries BC. The village, some of whose buildings have a central courtyard, was also inhabited in Carthaginian and Roman periods until the third century AD.

To one side of the site, you can see diagrams illustrating how the complex might once have looked, while a map shows how densely the Marmilla is filled with other nuraghic settlements. From this high, windy vantage point, you can spot many of the hills and areas identified on the map, the most significant landmark being the high, flat Giara di Gésturi, to the north (see p.125).

ARRIVAL AND DEPARTURE   VILLANOVAFORRU AND AROUND

By bus ARST buses stop in Villanovaforru's centre off Piazza Costituzione from Mon to Sat.

Destinations Cágliari (Mon–Sat 2 daily; 1hr 40min–2hr);

Sanluri (Mon–Sat 2–3 daily; 30min); Sárdara (Mon–Sat 5–8 daily; 15min); Tuili (Mon–Sat 2 daily; 25min).

ACCOMMODATION AND EATING

Funtana Noa Via Vittorio Emanuele III ☏ 070 933 1020, ⓦ hotelfuntananoa.it. This large, convent-like hotel and restaurant has rooms with tiled floors, beamed ceilings, a/c and a courtyard. The restaurant menu features local dishes such as *pasta fresca con sugo di cinghiale* (with boar sauce). Starters are around €9 and fixed-price tourist menus are €15 and €20. Daily except Wed 1–3pm & 8–10.30pm. **€65**

★**Sa Muredda** Vico San Sebastiano ☏ 070 933 1142, ⓦ samuredda.it. Centrally located but tucked away off the main Via Vittorio Emanuele, this B&B in a renovated nineteenth-century building has four spacious, traditionally furnished rooms with modern bathrooms. The owner also prepares excellent meals using fresh, local ingredients – well worth booking. **€68**

FROM TOP PORTO GIUNCO BAY, VILLASIMIUS (P.128); SU NURAXI (P.122) >

Su Nuraxi and around

East of Villanovaforru stretches a varied landscape of cultivated fields interspersed with some pasturage, overlooked by a horizon of knobbly brown peaks. The most prominent feature for many kilometres around is the extraordinary conical hill of **Las Plassas** (274m), on whose round pinnacle fragments of the twelfth-century **Castello di Marmilla** stick up like broken teeth. The hill is a perfect example of the bosomy bumps characteristic of the Marmilla region.

Sardinia's best-known nuraghic site, **Su Nuraxi**, lies 3km north of Las Plassas outside **BARÚMINI**. It's a draw for coachloads of visitors year round, spawning a cluster of other local attractions to capitalize on its fame, making this essentially run-of-the-mill village a hive of activity. Apart from the *nuraghe*-related sights, the only other item of interest in Barúmini itself is the bijou, seventeenth-century church of **Santa Tecla** (daily 8am–noon & 3–6pm), by the crossroads at the centre of the village, distinguished by its swirling rose window and battlements.

The site

Viale Su Nuraxi • Daily: March, Oct & Nov 9am–5.30pm; April–June 9am–8pm; July & Aug 9am–8.30pm; Sept 9am–7.30pm; Dec–Feb 9am–5pm; last tour 1hr before closing • €10 with Casa Zapata and Centro Lilliu • ☎ 070 936 8128, ⓦ fondazionebarumini.it • 10min west of Barúmini on foot

The largest nuraghic complex on the island, as well as one of the oldest (dating from around 1500 BC), the site of Su Nuraxi has been continuously excavated since 1949 and was listed as a UNESCO World Heritage Site in 1997. There's plenty to take in, and all visits to the site are escorted by guides who provide a knowledgeable commentary (in various languages) – as well as warning you to keep off the walls, which would otherwise invite much clambering over.

Note that the dialect name of Su Nuraxi means simply "the *nuraghes*"; Sardinian x's are pronounced either with a "sh" sound, or like the French "j". "Su Nuraxi" is thus pronounced "Su Nurashi" or "Su Nuraji".

Brief history

Despite all the research, the origins of Su Nuraxi remain largely obscure, though it seems likely that it was a palace complex at the very least, possibly even a capital city. The first traces of human settlement on the site date from the middle Bronze Age (sixteenth to thirteenth centuries BC); the place was destroyed in the seventh century BC, then rebuilt and resettled until the Roman period. In between, the complex was constantly expanded, with towers added to the central bastion, which were joined by a stone wall. The whole area is thought to have been covered with earth by Sards and Carthaginians at the time of the Roman conquest, accounting for its good state of preservation.

You'll find more on Sardinia's nuraghic culture in Contexts (see p.307).

The central tower

The imposing **central tower**, built of dark grey basalt blocks, lies at the centre of a tight mesh of walled dwellings separated by a web of lanes. The tower originally reached 21m (now shrunk to about 14.5m), and contained three chambers, one above the other, of which two remain. At the end of a corridor, the tholos-type lower chamber has alcoves once lined with cork, and an opening halfway up the walls suggesting the existence of a wooden flight of stairs to reach the next storey. To reach this room now you have to backtrack along the elaborate network of passageways and rugged steps connecting the various inner chambers. Most of the topmost storey is missing, but still provides good views over the whole site.

Next to the tower on ground level, a deep, crescent-shaped **courtyard** holds a well that still contains water.

The outer defences

The courtyard gives access to three of the four external towers that form the corners of the quadrilobate **outer defences**, part of a second phase of construction, probably dating from the thirteenth or twelfth centuries BC. The height of the enclosing walls was raised at a later period, an alteration clearly visible in the contrast between the more regular masonry of the later work and the rougher-hewn stones of the lower parts. The outer walls were strengthened between the twelfth and tenth centuries BC, and encompassed within them a further line of defence: a polygonal **curtain wall** studded with (now roofless) round towers.

The nuraghic village

The same period saw the expansion of the settlement, though most of the **nuraghic village** dates from later, between the tenth and sixth centuries BC, when the nucleus of the settlement was already in a state of decay. Scattered around the curtain walls, it's a dense, untidy outgrowth of more than two hundred circular and horseshoe-shaped buildings, all now roofless, but many reconstructed to a height of about 2m. In appearance, these huts must have resembled the small stone-roofed shepherds' *pinneddas* still used today in some parts of Sardinia (see p.159).

Centro Giovanni Lilliu

Viale Su Nuraxi • Daily: March & Nov 10am–5.30pm; April & Sept 10am–7pm; May–Aug 10am–8pm; Oct 10am–6.30pm; Dec–Feb 10am–5pm • €10 with Su Nuraxi and Casa Zapata; free when there is no exhibition • ☎ 070 936 1041, ⓦ fondazionebarumini.it

A modern, bunker-like construction opposite Su Nuraxi holds the **Centro Giovanni Lilliu**, named after Sardinia's greatest archeologist, the first to excavate the site of Su Nuraxi. There are a few permanent displays here – primarily photographs of the excavations taken by Lilliu himself and items of local craftwork, including masks – but the space is normally used for temporary exhibitions. As entry to the exhibitions costs little more than the price of the Su Nuraxi/Casa Zapata ticket, it's usually worth a glance inside.

Casa Zapata

Via Roma, Barúmini • Daily: March & Nov 10am–5.30pm; April & Sept 10am–7pm; May–Aug 10am–8pm; Oct 10am–6.30pm; Dec–Feb 10am–5pm • €10 with Su Nuraxi and Centro Lilliu • ☎ 070 936 8476, ⓦ fondazionebarumini.it

Finds from Su Nuraxi are displayed in Barúmini's **Casa Zapata**, the former residence of a Spanish family granted the fiefdom of La Marmilla in 1541. The palace was actually constructed over another nuraghic site, only discovered during renovations in 1990, and the remains are now revealed to form part of the museum, viewable from a walkway installed above. Among the displays, look out in particular for the diminutive *bétilo*, a 1.5cm-tall model of a nuraghic tower found in the *capanna delle riunioni*, or assembly chamber, in the nuraghic village – similar items, thought to have a totemic significance, have been found at several other nuraghic sites.

As well as the archeological material, the museum has an ethnographic section, including an impressive collection of *launeddas* (Sardinian pipes), and rooms devoted to the Zapata dynasty.

Sardegna in Miniatura

Località Lardi, 1.5km west of Barúmini • Daily: Easter–Sept 9am–8pm; Oct–Easter consult website or call for times • €10, plus €4 for astronomy museum and planetarium, and €3 each for Charles Darwin exhibition and Biosphere, or €15 combined ticket • ☎ 070 936 1004, ⓦ sardegnainminiatura.it

Outside Barúmini, off the road to Tuili, **Sardegna in Miniatura** provides excellent family entertainment for whatever time you have left after visiting the area's main sights. The centrepiece is a (mainly) 1:25 scale version of Sardinia's most famous monuments and sights arranged on a miniature Sardinia-shaped island, from Cágliari's cathedral in the south to the beaches of the Costa Smeralda in the north, taking in Pisan churches and various archeological sites – including Su Nuraxi itself – en route. You can tour the model reconstructions by boat and get an overview of it from a wooden tower.

The park also holds a near life-size version of huts in a **nuraghic village**, complete with bearded mannequins and explanatory commentaries in Italian and English. Other attractions, for which separate tickets are available, include a **museum of astronomy**, a **planetarium**, an exhibition devoted to **Charles Darwin** and a **Biosphere**, in which you can view tropical fauna and flora within a 15m-diameter transparent dome. There's a restaurant and picnic area.

ARRIVAL AND DEPARTURE

By bus Buses to Barúmini (none on Sun) stop in the centre of the village, from where it's a 10min walk to Su Nuraxi. Note that both departures to Cágliari are early in the morning.

SU NURAXI

Destinations Cágliari (Mon–Sat 2 daily; 1hr 30min); Gésturi (Mon–Sat 4–6 daily; 7min); Ísili (Mon–Sat 2–3 daily; 30min); Láconi (Mon–Sat 2–3 daily; 35min); Tuili (4–6 daily; 5min).

ACCOMMODATION AND EATING

Casa Piras Traversa Seconda Principessa Maria 13, Barúmini ☎070 936 8372 or ☎349 883 7015, ⊛web .tiscali.it/casapiras. Modern B&B with three simple rooms and two separate private bathrooms. There's a *salone* with a fridge for guests' use, and a small garden. The house is tricky to find – look for signs off Corso Umberto and Via Roma. No credit cards. **€50**
Sa Lolla Via Cavour, Barúmini ☎070 936 8419,

✉salollarist@libero.it. This small, rustic-style *pensione* has only seven spacious and minimally decorated rooms, some overlooking the garden. The restaurant – open to non-guests – has outdoor seating under a vine and concentrates on *campidanese* specialities; a full meal will cost around €30 (pizzas are also served). Tues–Sun 12.30–3pm & 8–10.30pm; open Mon in Aug, restaurant closed Mon–Fri in winter. **€70**

Tuili and around

Three kilometres west of Barúmini, **TUILI** is the most interesting of the villages circling the Giara di Gésturi. Its church of **San Pietro Apostolo** – marked out by a neat, round-topped belltower – contains a real treasure. Occupying the whole of a chapel at the back of the right-hand aisle, the vividly coloured polyptych, the **retablo di San Pietro**, was painted by the artist known only as the **Maestro di Castelsardo**, and is in fact the only one of his works that is dateable – to 1500, according to a legal document specifying his fee. Its style is predominantly Gothic, with few signs of the impact of the Renaissance. Against richly detailed landscapes, the central panels show Christ crucified and the Madonna with saints; on the left, St Michael (slaying the devil) and St Peter are depicted; on the right are St James and St Paul, respectively above and below. Considered by some to be Sardinia's finest work of medieval art, it's a solemn and absorbing study, the facial expressions and garments superbly rendered. To view it properly in the church's dim interior, make sure the lights are turned on (the switch is behind the painting on the left). The rest of the building is also richly painted – there's another *retablo* on the corresponding chapel across the nave, dated 1534, painted by another anonymous artist.

Five kilometres north of Barúmini, the village of **GÉSTURI** is dominated by the campanile of the church of **Santa Teresa d'Ávila**, reckoned to be Sardinia's very latest example of the Catalan-Gothic style, dating from 1674.

ARRIVAL AND DEPARTURE

By bus ARST buses stop in Tuili's centre; note that there are no Sun services.

Destinations Barúmini (Mon–Sat 4–5 daily; 5min);

TUILI

Cágliari (Mon–Sat 1 daily; 2hr); Sanluri (Mon–Sat 5 daily; 35–55min); Sárdara (Mon–Sat 1 daily; 40min).

La Giara di Gésturi

North of Barúmini and Tuili, the high tableland of the **Giara di Gésturi**, or *Sa Jara*, dominates the landscape. Roughly 12km long, covering some 42 square kilometres at a maximum height of 560m, it is the largest of a series of basalt plateaux thrown up in ancient eruptions. Protected as a nature reserve, the area is controlled by rangers and has no roads. There are, however, surfaced tracks winding up from the villages at its base, leading to places where you can leave your vehicle. The Giara ("plateau") is fairly bare on its lower flanks, but as you climb you'll come across thicker brushwood and groves of ancient cork trees.

On the flat summit, the impervious basalt rock has created *paulis*, or depressions, which fill up with rainwater to create swampy ponds; these, together with the thick vegetation, help to provide a perfect terrain for a variety of **wildfowl**, from buzzards to bee-eaters. Spring is the best season to visit, when the area is at its greenest and a magnet for migrating birds.

The plateau has also become home to goats and wild boars, though the most rarely seen beasts are those that appear most frequently on the tourist literature – packs of **wild ponies**, or *cavallini* (known as *quaddedus* in dialect). At the last count there were around five hundred of these diminutive creatures, which measure less than 130cm at shoulder height; a smaller number live in Le Prigionette protected zone at Porto Conte, near Alghero (see p.186). Their origins are unknown, but they are thought to have links with oriental breeds, possibly introduced by the Phoenicians three thousand years ago. Though free to roam at will, the ponies are either privately owned or the property of the local community. The best time to see them is after foaling at the end of March.

You're allowed to wander where you please over the rough terrain (you'll need stout shoes), though you might also consider using an experienced **guide**. Ask one of the forest rangers, normally stationed in shacks near the car parks, or contact Jara Escursioni (☎070 936 4277 or ☎348 292 4983, ⓦparcodellagiara.it), which conducts expeditions on foot (around €50 for 2hr).

ARRIVAL AND DEPARTURE   **LA GIARA DI GÉSTURI**

By car The only way to reach the plateau is by car. The nearest villages are Génuri, Setzu, Tuili and Gésturi, which all have tracks leading to parking areas at the top (unmissably signed "Altopiano della Giara"). Note that none of these villages has much in the way of tourist facilities.

Ísili and around

Like many of Sardinia's inland centres, **ÍSILI**, an 18km drive east of Gésturi, makes little visual impact, but it has a handful of attractions and some striking country worth exploring in the vicinity. In recent years it has been a popular base for free climbers, attracted to the sheer rock faces of the surroundings, though the village has a longer-established fame as a centre of *artigianato*, particularly copperware, which is readily available in the shops in and around the central Corso Vittorio Emanuele III.

It's the area around Ísili that commands most interest, however, studded as it is with prehistoric remains. Least compelling but nearest to hand are two **domus de janas** – so-called "fairy houses", actually pre-nuraghic tombs – which are easily visited on foot from the western end of the Corso. A sign points the way along a cul-de-sac on the edge of town, from where a path leads to square-cut openings giving onto low-roofed chambers.

Farther afield, you can explore the **Lago di Is Barroccus**, a dammed lake visible from the village's western side and overlooked by the ruins of a church. Three or four kilometres west of town, the canyon of **Is Barroccus**, carved out by the Mannu river, is one of the rare nesting sites in Sardinia of Bonelli's eagle.

Museo per l'Arte del Rame e del Tessuto

Piazza San Giuseppe • Tues–Sun 10am–1pm & 4.30–7.30pm (4–7pm in winter) • €3.50; €6 with Is Paras • ☎ 0782 802 641

You can see the best examples of local craftsmanship in the **Museo per l'Arte del Rame e del Tessuto**, dedicated to copper and textiles and housed in a seventeenth-century convent. The copperware consists mainly of an array of domestic items, while the art of weaving – another enduring tradition in the area – is illustrated by rugs and tapestries.

Is Paras

Località Is Paras • Tues–Sun: April, May & Oct 10am–1pm & 2.30pm–dusk; June–Sept 10am–1pm & 3.30pm–dusk; Nov–March call to visit • €3; €6 with museum • ☎ 380 455 3856

Splendidly sited on a bare hillock on Ísili's northern outskirts (unmissable from the SS128 from Láconi or from the train), the **nuraghe of Is Paras** constitutes one of Sardinia's most impressive single-towered nuraghic monuments. Its smooth-walled "tholos" interior is also, at 12m, the highest on the island. Inside you'll find a small chamber in front of the main entrance and a niche for a sentry on its right-hand side.

Santuario Nurágico di Santa Vittoria

Località Santa Vittoria • Daily 9am–1hr before sunset • €4 • ☎ 346 066 9068, ⚑ santuarionuragicoserri.it

A significant nuraghic site lies south of Ísili, reached from the village of **Serri**, 8km down the SS128, from where it's signposted another 4km northwest. Scattered around the country church of Santa Vittoria, the extensive ruins of the **Santuario Nurágico di Santa Vittoria**, dating from the end of the second millennium BC, have thrown up a rich assortment of nuraghic finds, including some of the most eye-catching *bronzetti* on display in Cágliari's archeological museum (see p.62).

The settlement was built around a sacred well and a temple, and the various remains strewn across the area include a circular assembly room, a grand oval festival area (*recinto delle feste*) and numerous habitations. The sacred well (*pozzo*) is the most complete survival; its thirteen basalt steps making a precisely carved descent to the spring. Regular pilgrimages and gatherings are thought to have taken place here, a tradition perpetuated by the two-day harvest **festival** that nowadays centres on the church of Santa Vittoria around September 11.

ARRIVAL AND DEPARTURE   ÍSILI

By train Ísili's train station is at the southern end of town (there's another station to the north), served by infrequent ARST-run services. Some or all journeys on the regular train service to Mandas, Dolianova and Cágliari may be replaced as far as Mandas or Dolianova by a bus service leaving from the train station. The Sun service to Mandas, Láconi, Belvì-Aritzo and Sórgono is on the seasonal Trenino Verde heritage line (⚑ treninoverde.com).
Destinations Belvì-Aritzo (late June to mid-Sept; Sun only; 2hr 35min); Cágliari Gottardo (Mon–Sat 3 daily; 1hr

40min); Dolianova (Mon–Sat 3 daily; 1hr 20min); Láconi (late June to mid-Sept; Sun only; 1hr); Mandas (Mon–Sat 3 daily; 20min); Sórgono (late June to mid-Sept; Sun only; 3hr 20min).
By bus Most ARST buses stop on Corso Vittorio Emanuele; some of those for Mandas stop at Ísili's train station.
Destinations Barúmini (2–3 daily; 30min); Cágliari (1–3 daily; 1hr 30min–2hr); Dolianova (Sun 1–2 daily; 1hr 15min); Láconi (Mon–Sat 5–6 daily, Sun 2 daily; 20–35min); Mandas (3–4 daily; 20–35min).

ACCOMMODATION AND EATING

Del Sole Corso Vittorio Emanuele 124 ☎ 0782 802 024. The most convenient of Ísili's hotels is this two-star at the western end of town near the museum, with simple, modern rooms. Sharing the same premises but independent of the hotel, the ristorante-pizzeria here

(☎ 0782 802 371) is a great spot for a bite, with – unusual so far inland – a good choice of seafood at moderate prices, including a superb *antipasto di mare* (€13). Tues–Sat 12.30–3pm & 8–10.30pm, Sun 8–10.30pm. **€45**

Dolianova

Fifteen kilometres north of Cágliari, off the SS387, the market town of **DOLIANOVA** is the main centre of a region renowned for its olives and olive oil, and for its wines, which include Nuragus, Moscato and Malvasia. A workaday place with a few handsome nineteenth-century *palazzi*, Dolianova does have one outstanding relic in the form of its ex-cathedral, signposted at the northern end of town.

Chiesa di San Pantaleo

Via Vescovado · Daily 8am–noon & 3.30–7pm

Occupying one side of a small piazza and topped by a short belltower, the **Chiesa di San Pantaleo** – formerly the town's cathedral – sports blind arcading running right round the walls, adorned with eroded stone carvings of animals, plants, moons and some human forms. Started between 1150 and 1160 by a team which had previously worked on the church of Santa Giusta, outside Oristano (see p.156), the pale stone exterior was completed by Arab architects a century later, accounting for its *mudéjar* style, which mixes Romanesque, Gothic and Arab elements. Next to the side entrance, a Roman sarcophagus suspended on slender columns protrudes incongruously from the main body of the church.

The interior

The church's **interior** is decorated with an impressive array of murals, one of them depicting Christ crucified on what looks like the tree of life; in fact it is an *álbero genealógico*, or family tree, a favourite theme in medieval art showing Abraham and the prophets (a quarter of it is missing). Next to this, an oriental-looking *ancona*, or six-panelled altarpiece, shows the martyrdom of San Pantaleo, probably the work of an unknown Spanish painter in the sixteenth century. There's a horribly immolated Christ on the same wall of the church, and at the back of the church a stone *baldacchino* (canopy) is crudely carved with figures of animals, angels and humans. Some of the capitals of the wonky columns of the nave display more figures, including one near the *baldacchino* carved with a man and woman embracing, and there are more murals behind the altar.

ARRIVAL AND DEPARTURE   DOLIANOVA

By train Trains operated by ARST run to Dolianova's station at the west end of town, a 15min walk from the centre. Some services to Mandas and Ísili may be replaced by a bus service.
Destinations Cágliari Gottardo (Mon–Sat 10 daily; 20min);

Ísili (Mon–Sat 1–2 daily; 1hr 10min); Mandas (Mon–Sat 8 daily; 50min).
By bus ARST buses connect Dolianova with Cágliari (Mon–Sat 9–13 daily, Sun 3–5 daily; 45min) and San Nicolò Gerrei (Mon–Sat 4 daily, Sun 1 daily; 1hr).

EATING AND DRINKING

New Burger Time Piazza Brigata Sássari 3 ☎ 070 743 144. The name is misleading: this is nothing like a fast-food burger dive, but a friendly bar-restaurant in the town's main square with a good seafood menu. Menu items include *pasta con frutti di mare* (with seafood), *zuppa di*

cozze (mussel soup) and *grigliata di pesce* (seafood grill). Prices are low – *primi* are up to €8, *secondi* around €12, and there's a €12 lunchtime tourist menu. Tasty pizzas are also served in the evening. Tues–Sun 8am–10.30pm.

Gerrei

The main reason for heading north from Dolianova into the bleak, sparsely inhabited highlands of the **Gerrei** region is to visit one of Sardinia's most important nuraghic sites, standing alone on a high, windblown plain. There's no easy way to

> ### THE TRENINO VERDE
>
> The otherwise unremarkable village of Mandas, some 60km north of Cágliari, is a starting point for expeditions into Sardinia's interior on the small-gauge trains of the ARST-run **Trenino Verde**. The ride is strictly for leisure, and only runs in the summer months. If you're in a hurry, take one of the more efficient bus services to reach your destination; otherwise sit back and enjoy the ride through some of Sardinia's most remote and scenic countryside.
>
> From Mandas, the Trenino Verde weaves a meandering, often tortuous journey through the beautiful highlands of the Sarcidano and Barbagia Seulo as far as **Arbatax**, the port on Sardinia's eastern coast (see p.303). The service operates between mid-June and mid-September once daily (except Tues), currently leaving Mandas at 8.40am. It's usually necessary to change at Gairo, though this may involve a long wait at Gairo: the Mandas train currently arrives there at noon, and the train for Arbatax leaves at 6.35pm, arriving at 8.35pm.
>
> **From Cágliari** you can reach Mandas by ARST bus from Piazza Repubblica (3–4 daily; 1hr 20min) or by train (Mon–Sat 8 daily; 1hr 30min) from the Gottardo station in **Monserrato**, around 5km northeast of the centre (connected by Metropolitana trams every 10min from Piazza Repubblica, a 20min ride). To reach Mandas on the same day as the Trenino Verde's departure, you'd need to take the 6.55am bus from Piazza Repubblica or the 7am train from Gottardo; see ⓦarst.sardegna.it for full schedules for both. For Trenino Verde timetables, call ⓣ070 265 7612 or see ⓦtreninoverde.com.

reach it, but the tortuous mountain road from Dolianova to **San Nicolò Gerrei**, without a building to be seen along its whole 33km length, will allow you to savour this little-visited area. At **Ballao**, 11km north of San Nicolò Gerrei, the minor SP10 continues north to the *nuraghe*, midway between the nondescript villages of **Escalaplano** and **Orroli**.

Nuraghe Arrubiu

SP10 • Daily 9.30am to 1hr before sunset • €4 • ⓣ0782 847 269

Thought to have been built between 1400 and 900 BC, **Nuraghe Arrubiu** – sometimes called Orrubiu – is the only five-towered nuraghic complex in existence, and one of the biggest, with a central tower which may once have reached a height of 27m, now reduced to 16m. Seven towers remain on the outer walls, and there are the remnants of five more, survivors of the 21 towers that, according to archeologists, originally stood here. The formidable ruin, which takes its name ("red") from the reddish basalt stone and the orange lichen covering it, was opened in 1996. Curiously, no nuraghic finds have so far been unearthed, only Punic, Roman and even Mycenaean artefacts, though future excavations are expected to throw up more valuable material. The Roman finds, which include mills, basins and stone tools used for pressing olives and grapes, are displayed in a separate walled area near the site's entrance.

Visitors are guided round the murky chambers and corridors on hour-long tours, usually in Italian (no tours 1–3pm). If you're in the area on a summer night, you can sign up for one of the atmospheric illuminated **night tours** (€3 per person, with a minimum of 25 people). **Refreshments** are available from a bar at the entrance.

Villasimius and around

South and east of Gerrei, the equally wild and sparsely populated **Sarrabus** region is dominated by the Sette Fratelli ("Seven Brothers") mountains, but fringed by pockets of development along the beach-studded coast. The biggest of the holiday centres, **VILLASIMIUS**, was little more than a small and unassuming village not so long ago, but has assumed the typical dual identity of a resort town – in summer fizzing with bars, boutiques, pizzerias and almost nightly entertainments, the rest of the time practically deserted, with most facilities closed between October and April.

Although it's located a kilometre or two inland, Villasimius is within easy reach of some enticing coastline and a choice of fantastic beaches. Past the central Piazza Gramsci and the smaller, adjacent Piazza Generale Incani, the main Via Umberto forks left to the nearest stretch of sand at **Simius**, 1.5km east of town, and right to **Marina di Villasimius** (or the Porto Turistico), from where you can take **boat tours** in summer. The tourist port lies in the **Golfo di Carbonara**, named after the charcoal produced in the nearby forests, a by-product of which was the black powder added to gunpowder for damp-proofing (favoured by Nelson among others). Just south of the port is the **Fortezza Vecchia**, a square fortification probably dating from the fourteenth century, now used for exhibitions.

Museo Archeologico

Via Frau • Tues–Sun: mid-June to mid-Sept 10am–1pm & 6–9pm; mid-Sept to mid-June 9am–1pm & 4–6pm • €3 • ☎ 070 793 0290

The only essential sight in Villasimius itself is the town's **Museo Archeologico**, off the main Via Umberto. It's a surprisingly large and well-planned collection, with exhibits arranged in four zones, accompanied by panels in Italian and English, and videos in various languages explaining the local archeological heritage. Most of the museum is dedicated to finds from the Phoenician, Carthaginian and Roman periods, including amphorae, statues and coins, with a particular focus on **Is Kokkureddus**, one of Sardinia's main Phoenician settlements that was subsequently rebuilt by the Carthaginians and then the Romans. Leaping a thousand years, the last room displays items recovered from a fifteenth-century Spanish shipwreck, most strikingly a collection of **azulejos**, blue-painted tiles from Manises, Valencia, that were possibly intended for the decoration of a noble's palace in Sicily or Campania.

The beaches

To reach the town's nearest beach, **Simius**, you only have to follow the main drag east to where an arc of pale gold sands backed by luxury hotels faces the offshore isles of **Serpentara**, a long strip of bare rock, and the more southerly **Isola dei Cávoli**. You'll find less developed bathing spots heading south towards **Capo Carbonara**, where the eastern shore of the thin peninsula is backed by the calm **Stagno di Notteri** lagoon, a stopover for flamingos in winter.

East of Capo Carbonara and north of Marina di Villasimius lies another prize beach, **Spiaggia del Riso**, adjacent to a campsite (see p.130), beyond which are the smaller beaches of **Campulongu** and **Campus**, with turquoise and aquamarine waters. There are more scraps of sandy beaches west of Capo Boi, in the **Golfo di Cágliari**, sometimes visible from the tortuous coast road that winds west towards Cágliari, as at **Cala Regina**, **Torre delle Stelle** and – the prettiest village on this stretch – **Solanas**, next to one of the numerous sentinel towers dotting the Gulf's coast. Less picturesque are the uniform rows of peach-coloured villas that intrude upon the scene.

ARRIVAL AND INFORMATION   VILLASIMIUS AND AROUND

By bus The frequent buses that connect Cágliari and Villasimius can drop you at any of the beaches en route between the two. In Villasimius, ARST buses stop on Via Roma near *La Lanterna* restaurant; buy tickets from the *alimentari* Market Patrizia, Via del Mare 115.
Destinations Cágliari (Mon–Sat 6–12 daily, Sun 2–8 daily; 1hr 30min); Castiadas (Mon–Sat 2 daily; 40min); Costa Rei (Mon–Sat 3–9 daily, Sun 2–6 daily; 40min); Muravera

(Mon–Sat 4–5 daily; 1hr 20min–1hr 50min).
By taxi Travel Tour, Via Vittorio Emanuele 114 (☎ 070 791 726) offers transfers to and from Cágliari airport for €95 (more after 10pm).

Tourist office Piazza Giovanni XXIII, next to the church off Piazza Gramsci (June–Oct daily 10am–11pm; ☎ 070 793 0271, ✆ villasimiusweb.com).

GETTING AROUND

By bus Between June and Sept, a daily shuttle bus service (*navetta*) connects Villasimius with Marina di Villasimius, Simius, Capo Boi, Capo Carbonara and all the beaches hourly until 11pm. Buy tickets (€2 one-way or €5/day) on board or from the tourist office.

By car, bike or scooter Car, bike and scooter rental is available at La Via del Mare, Via Umberto 122 (☎070 791 009, ⓦ laviadelmare.com). A small car costs €70–85/day, scooters are from €39/day and bikes €10/day. Note that between June and Sept the centre of Villasimius is closed to traffic from 7.15pm, presenting numerous challenges to drivers.

By taxi Travel Tour (☎070 791 726 or ☎338 369 3219); Zanda Viaggi (☎338 496 9496).

ACCOMMODATION

Prices rise steeply if you want to stay near the sea, though low-season rates are more reasonable. The Via del Mare agency, Via Umberto 122 (☎070 791 009, ⓦ laviadelmare.com), deals with weekly **apartment rentals** in the area.

Belvir Hotel Via Umberto I 99 ☎070 451 9620, ⓦ hotelbelvir.it. At the less busy end of the main drag, this elegant, modern place has nine clean, well-equipped rooms, some with balconies from which there are mountain views. There's also a sun terrace and a courtyard. Breakfast includes a choice of pastries. Closed Nov to early April. **€120**

Fiore di Maggio Località Campulongu ☎070 797 382, ⓦ fioredimaggio.com. Smaller and more personal than most of the hotels hereabouts, this family-friendly place lies 2km from town and 80m from the beach of Campulongu. Overlooking a citrus grove, the rooms have Sardinian decor, and there's a pool and restaurant. During the summer months there's a three-day or one-week minimum stay, and half or full board may be required too. Closed late Oct to early April. **€200**

★**Il Patio** Via Giardini 7 ☎070 791 207 or ☎340 965 1403, ⓦ bedandbreakfastilpatio.it. The four rooms in this friendly B&B are fresh and modern, arranged around a peaceful courtyard that gives the place a secluded air despite its central location. No credit cards. **€90**

Spiaggia del Riso ☎070 791 052, ⓦ villaggio spiaggiadelriso.it. If you want to stay near the sea without paying high hotel prices, try this clean and well-equipped campsite with access to two beaches. Non-campers can rent four-bed bungalows or stay in (rather pricey) B&B rooms. There's a twenty-day minimum stay in peak season. Closed Nov to late April. Pitches **€26**; rooms and bungalows **€130**

Stella d'Oro Via Vittorio Emanuele 25 ☎070 791 255, ⓦ villaggiospiaggiadelriso.it. This family-run hotel is centrally located off Piazza Incani, but quiet and relaxed. The en-suite rooms are fine, most of them looking onto a large courtyard. There's parking (a big plus in Villasimius) and a good restaurant (see below). **€90**

EATING AND DRINKING

Acquarius Via Umberto 41 ☎070 790 276. A good central choice for thin, crispy pizzas at reasonable prices (mostly €4–8). There's a good choice of toppings and *antipasti* on the menu, fast and efficient service, and Ichnusa beer on draught. Booking recommended in peak season. June–Sept daily except Wed 12.30–2.30pm & 7.30pm–midnight; Oct–May closed Wed.

Carbonara Via Umberto 60 ☎070 791 270. Sober seafood restaurant with local art on the walls and a traditional feel. Among the *primi* (mostly €8–12) are *linguine alla spada* (pasta with swordfish), while mains (mostly €13–18) include *pesce alla griglia* (grilled) and *alla vernaccia* (cooked in wine). Feb to mid-July & mid-Sept to Dec daily except Wed 12.30–2.45pm & 7.30–11pm; mid-July to mid-Sept daily, same hours.

La Mora Bianca Via Roma 14 ☎331 399 5999. If you can stomach the lounge-style background music, this elegant place makes an excellent venue for dinner, both for its tranquil courtyard setting and its adventurous cuisine. Alongside the original range of pizzas (€7–10) are some choice meat and seafood dishes, including shrimps on skewers and grills. Most starters are €10, mains are €15, and there's a €28 tourist menu. In summer, there's live music on Tues and Fri evenings. May–Oct Mon–Sat 7–11pm, Sun noon–2.30pm & 7–11pm.

Stella d'Oro Via Vittorio Emanuele 25 ☎070 791 255. The inner courtyard of this hotel (see above) gets packed with diners in the evening, tucking into excellent local dishes and a good selection of Sardinian wines. A house speciality is *malfatti* – literally "badly made" spinach and ricotta balls in tomato sauce. Starters are €9–14, most mains around €15. May–Oct daily 7–11pm.

DIRECTORY

Internet Log on at Internet Point, Via Umberto 62 (Mon–Sat 9.30am–1pm & 5.30–8pm; June–Sept 5.30–11pm); €3/30min). Printing and photocopy service also available.

Market A food, clothing and craft market takes place on Sat mornings in Via Donatello, next to the Carabinieri barracks.

Post office Via del Mare 72 (Mon–Fri 8.20am–1.35pm, Sat 8.20am–12.35pm).

The Costa Rei

The long ribbon of beaches that makes up the **Costa Rei**, famous for its shimmering expanses of fine white sand lapped by crystal waters, begins 18km north of Villasimius, reached via a circuitous coastal road. Here, **Cala Sinzias** is a broad swathe of sand cupped within a beautiful small bay, though the area's hinterland is rapidly being developed. Most of the new construction is concentrated in the central section of the bay, where the beach is backed by villas, promenades and bars, and a range of watersports is available in summer (you'll pay €10–15 per day for sunbeds and parasols). Even if you're here between June and September, you can always avoid the crowds by moving on to the top end of this bay, towards the pine-clad **Capo Ferrato**, where dirt tracks running off the road lead to remoter scraps of sandy beach. Around the cape, the asphalt degenerates into a dusty track that winds behind Capo Ferrato to the next bay, and more dazzling beaches.

ARRIVAL AND INFORMATION THE COSTA REI

By bus ARST buses provide services to and from Costa Rei, though these are much reduced in winter.
Destinations Cágliari (Mon–Sat 4–10 daily, Sun 1–6 daily; 2hr 10min–2hr 30min); Muravera (Mon–Sat 3–5 daily; 45min–1hr); Villasimius (Mon–Sat 4–10 daily, Sun 1–6

daily; 35–55min).
Tourist office There's a seasonal tourist office on Piazza Bonaria (May to early Oct Mon–Sat 9am–1pm & 4–8pm; ☎ 347 139 2266, ⓦ visitmuravera.it).

ACCOMMODATION AND EATING

★**Albaruja** Via C. Colombo ☎ 070 991 557, ⓦalbaruja.it. Almost all the accommodation on the Costa Rei is in villas rented out by the week, though there are a couple of expensive hotels, including this well-maintained place 150m from the beach. Spacious, modern rooms and mini-apartments are grouped around a quiet garden and pool, with access to a tennis court. Rooms have either a small patio or a balcony, and there's a good bistro on the premises. Closed early Oct to late April. €178

Capo Ferrato Monte Nai ☎ 070 991 012, ⓦ camping capoferrato.it. This centrally located campsite is shaded by

mimosa and eucalyptus and has bungalows available; it's right by a broad sweep of sand, though perhaps too close to the ranks of holiday villas for comfort. There are shops, plus windsurfing and canoeing facilities, nearby. Closed Nov–March. Pitches €38; bungalows €102

Su Nuraxi Via Ichnusa 47 ☎ 070 991 9020. With plenty of space for dining alfresco, this is the best choice in town for pizzas and standout dishes such as *risotto alla pescatora* (seafood risotto) and grilled meat. A pizza and beer will be less than €15, pasta dishes are €10–15 and there's a €30 tourist menu. Booking necessary in Aug. Feb–Oct daily 12.30–3pm & 7–11.30pm.

Castiadas and around

Inland of the Costa Rei, the land is largely flat and verdant. The main settlement here, up a slight ascent 7km west, is **CASTIADAS**, centred on a straggle of buildings around the pink walls of an ex-penal colony set up in the nineteenth century, now part-occupied by a museum. There's not much else here, but Castiadas makes a convenient starting point for exploring the Monte dei Sette Fratelli to the north (see p.132), and the Foresta di Minniminni, a couple of kilometres south.

Museo del Territorio di Castiadas

Via Centrale • Daily: June–Sept 9.30am–12.30pm & 5–11.30pm; early Oct 9.30am–12.30pm & 5–8.30pm; last entry 1hr 15min before closing • €3 • ☎ 070 9945 0307

The offices of Castiadas' former penal colony have been smartly restored to house the **Museo del Territorio di Castiadas**, dedicated to the inmates of the prison during its existence from 1875 to 1956. The men – mostly from the mainland – were kept busy clearing the surrounding forest and cultivating the land at a time when malaria was rife, claiming the lives of many of the workers. The hour-long guided tours take in holding cells, photographs of the colony and background information on the history and geography of the area, as well as two fifteen-minute documentary films (one from 1954). It's all in Italian but you get the gist. Some rooms also hold examples of local art and handicrafts.

Foresta di Minniminni

A protected area of holm oak and thick *macchia*, the **Foresta di Minniminni** is only passable on foot, donkey or, to an extent, in 4WD vehicles. As well as the ubiquitous arbutus, juniper and cyclamen of the *macchia*, the area holds two plantations of pine trees left by the inmates of the Castiadas penal colony, one from 1875, when they arrived, the second from when the colony was closed down in 1956. Waymarked trails wind through the forest to the summit of Monte Minniminni, only 723m high but affording wonderful views over the surrounding coast.

ARRIVAL AND DEPARTURE	**CASTIADAS**

By bus ARST buses connect Castiadas with Cágliari (Mon–Sat 3 daily; 2hr 10min), Muravera (Mon–Sat 2 daily; 45min–1hr 10min) and Villasimius (Mon–Sat 3–4 daily; 40min). The stop is right outside the old prison.

EATING

Le Vecchie Carceri Via Centrale ☎ 070 994 7171. Grab a snack or a meal at this simple trattoria with tables inside and outside. The menu includes some great seafood dishes as well as local specialities such as *salsiccia alla griglia* (sausages), horse and donkey. There are also pizzas. Prices are reasonable, with lunchtime menus from €18. April–Sept daily 12.30–2pm & 7.30–11pm; Oct–March Fri–Sun 12.30–2pm & 7.30–10pm.

Monte dei Sette Fratelli

Linking Cágliari with Muravera, the tortuous and highly scenic SS125 cuts through the heart of Sarrabus, where the dramatic **Monte dei Sette Fratelli** ("Seven Brothers") range reaches a height of about 1020m. If you want to strike out on foot, there are plenty of opportunities to stop along the way (see box, p.133). For more ambitious climbs, however, you'll need expert guidance; the tourist office at Villasimius (see p.129) has details of guides. The steep, granite slopes are either *macchia*-covered or forested with cork oak and holm oak, and provide a habitat for the rare cervo sardo, the diminutive Sardinian deer for which this is a protected zone; about 750 are estimated to exist in the region.

The only significant settlement in these parts is **BURCEI**, a small village at a height of 648m, famed for its cherry trees which come into full, flamboyant blossom in May.

Nuraghe Asoru

At the eastern end of the Sette Fratelli range, at the bottom of the desolate gorge of the River Picocca, littered with monolithic boulders, you'll pass the **Nuraghe Asoru** (also called Nuraghe S'Oro), unmissable by the side of road. It was constructed between the tenth and eighth centuries BC in a dominating position over the surrounding plain and the inland approaches and is the only *nuraghe* worthy of note in these parts, which evidently proved too barren even for the hardy locals. There's a small internal courtyard, and a hole in the coarse masonry of the wall reveals a bench running all around its interior.

A WALK IN THE MONTE DEI SETTE FRATELLI

This moderately easy **hike** in the Sette Fratelli takes you into the heart of the range, along paths strewn with wild clematis and fennel. Climbing skills are not required, but bring stout shoes, at least one litre of water per person and some sun protection; also, let other people know where you're bound (there's a Forestry Corps station near the beginning of the walk). The entire walk should take less than four hours, not counting breaks.

You can reach the **start of the route** on public transport along the SS125 from Cágliari or Muravera. Coming from Cágliari, soon after the junction for Burcei on the left, look out for a bridge over a small river (signposted Rio Campuomo), on the far side of which there is a clearing on the right where drivers can park, immediately before a Corpo Forestale station. The path begins here, signposted "Sentiero Italia, Campuomo, Castiadas". The route is waymarked with the symbol of a white diamond with a red stripe across.

Follow the level track for about ten minutes until you reach a fork, where you should bear left (uphill); there's no symbol here, but you'll see them again soon. It gets a little steeper up the rough path before it emerges onto a good unasphalted road, where there's a signpost: follow "Conventu" to the left. A few minutes later, there's an unsignposted second fork – take the right-hand path, slightly descending before levelling out and climbing again. About 45 minutes after setting out, you'll reach the ruins of a former monastery, the **Conventu de Sette Fradi** (also called Convento dei Sette Fratelli), in a shady clearing (600m). The name of the range might derive from the erstwhile inhabitants of this establishment, or it may refer to the peaks themselves. Travellers on the route between Burcei and Castiadas would lodge here for the night.

Proceed past the monastery; after five minutes or so, take a right-hand fork onto a rough mule track, which descends through woods to a river, the **Riu Guventu**. If there's water here, you can cross on stepping stones, before climbing steeply up the far side (following the symbols) along a smaller riverbed. The trail soon diverges to the left, continuing up through dense woods, where the symbols are fairly sparse. The path continues uphill in a similar vein, with occasional clearings affording good views on the way, until, less than an hour after leaving the convent, you'll reach the bare summits of the Sette Fratelli. The path dives in and out of the woods as far as the highest peak, **Punta Sa Ceraxa** (1015m). From here, the trail continues towards Castiadas. From Sa Ceraxa, your return journey should take another 1hr 30min or so.

ARRIVAL AND DEPARTURE   MONTE DEI SETTE FRATELLI

By bus Buses between Cágliari and Burcei and those on the inland route between Cágliari and Muravera stop along the SS125 running through the range (Mon–Sat every 30min–1hr, Sun 3 daily).

Muravera and around

The River Picocca flows into a flat, fertile area, with thick groves of citrus and lesser growths of almonds and other fruit and nut trees. Having accompanied the river as far as its outlet on the coast, the SS125 swings north, passing close to some choice beaches before heading inland again to enter **MURAVERA**. The only centre between Villasimius and Tortolì, it's a thriving agricultural town, known as the island's **citrus** capital, and with the neighbouring villages of Villaputzu and San Vito renowned for the authenticity of such local produce as honey, wine and *dolci*. Muravera doesn't invite much lingering; its main Via Roma is a constant stream of traffic with pedestrians squeezed onto minuscule pavements. Among the first-class **beaches** in the vicinity, the nearest is **San Giovanni**, 2km south, beyond which the fine sands of **Torre Salinas**, **Colostrai** and **Feraxi** are backed by lagoons where you can see a range of aquatic birdlife.

From San Vito, the SS387 curls inland along the course of the River Flumendosa and into the hilly Gerrei region (see p.127), a panoramic route into the interior. North of Muravera, the SS125 follows the course of the **River Quirra**, separated from the coast by a wall of mountains. It's a fertile area, with scattered nut trees that burst into blossom in early spring. After about 20km, the road crosses the Cágliari–Ogliastra provincial boundary, continuing north to the villages of Tertenia and Lanusei (see p.305).

Porto Corallo

East of Villaputzu, the river joins the sea near **Porto Corallo** where, on the approximate site of a long-disappeared Phoenician port, a small harbour has been re-created, this time for pleasure craft. Overlooked by a Spanish watchtower, Porto Corallo was the scene of one of the last battles against North African pirates, when the locals succeeded in driving back their attackers in 1812. South of the river mouth, the broad beach is backed by eucalyptus woods, and there are picnic tables, a bar/pizzeria and a gelateria close at hand.

ARRIVAL AND INFORMATION   MURAVERA AND AROUND

By bus ARST buses to and from Muravera stop at various points along Via Roma, including the central Piazza Europa. If you're leaving town, buy tickets at any of the bars showing the ARST sticker.
Destinations Cágliari (Mon–Sat 9–12 daily, Sun 2–8 daily; 2hr 45min–3hr 45min); Castiadas (Mon–Sat 3–4 daily; 40min–1hr 20min); Costa Rei (Mon–Sat 4 daily;

35min–1hr); Porto Corallo (July & Aug 3 daily; 20min); Villasimius (Mon–Sat 5 daily; 1hr 15min–2hr).
Tourist office Muravera has a summer-only tourist office on Piazza Ricchi, almost opposite the *Corallo* hotel off Via Roma (May to early Oct Mon–Sat 9am–1pm & 4–7.30pm; ☎ 070 991 350 or ☎ 347 139 2266).

ACCOMMODATION

Green Gallery Piazza Libertà ☎ 070 993 1652, ⊛ greengalleryhotel.com. At the southern end of Via Roma, this hotel with young, friendly staff has simple, clean and functional rooms with a/c. There's also parking and a good outdoor ristorante/pizzeria (see p.135). **€85**
Ostello San Priamo Via Rio Cannas 16, San Priamo ☎ 333 711 9728, ⊛ ostellosanpriamo.it. Ten kilometres south of Muravera and 4km south of Torre Salinas, this hostel is set in a verdant part of the coast, 4km from the beach and 200m from the ARST bus stop. Accommodation is in dormitories for three to four people and doubles – all with en-suite bathrooms – or in mini-apartments with cooking facilities and a/c (€75/night; one week min stay in high season). Prices include breakfast, and dinners cost €15. Closed mid-Sept to May. Dorms **€25**; doubles **€59**
★**Su Pasiu** Via Speranza 8 ☎ 377 323 7518, ⊛ locandasupasiu.it. Signposted off Via Roma, this relaxed B&B managed by a young couple is set around a traditional courtyard. Rooms are cool, spacious and

beautifully decorated, with a/c and large showers. There's an honesty bar, abundant breakfasts and bikes to rent. **€90**

CAMPSITES

Quattro Mori Località Is Perdigonis ☎ 070 999 110, ⊛ 4mori.it. The nearest campsite to town (5km south), this provides everything for a self-contained holiday right by the beach, with four-star, family-friendly facilities including a pool and self-catering four-bed mini-apartments to rent (from €91/night). Closed early Oct to late May. Pitches **€39**
Torre Salinas Località Torre Salinas ☎ 070 999 032, ⊛ campingvillagetorresalinas.it. Very close to a good beach 8km south of Muravera, this eucalyptus-shaded, German-run campsite has bungalows and caravans available (from €45/night), and you can also rent tents (€41 for two). There's a bar and ristorante/pizzeria, and bikes available to rent. Closed mid-Oct to March. Pitches **€25.50**

EATING AND NIGHTLIFE

Restaurants are easy to find in the summer season, less so in winter. Piazza Europa, off Via Roma, is the venue for nightly **concerts** and other entertainments in summer. Head to **Porto Corallo** for the lively summer bar scene until the small hours.

Domus Aurea Via Roma 138 ☎ 345 419 7657. This pub has a good range of Sard beers and wines, and an outdoor eating area for its *panini*, salads and other snacks. A large craft beer, *bruschette* and a tray of local cheeses and salamis should set you back around €15. The bar hosts music and themed events on summer evenings. Daily 8am–2am.

Green Gallery Piazza Libertà ☎ 070 993 1652. Part of the hotel of the same name, this has a lively atmosphere and a wide-ranging menu that includes meat and fish dishes plus filling pizzas. There's a terrace for alfresco dining. Daily 12.30–2.30pm & 7.30–11.30pm.

★ **Su Nuraxi** Via Roma 257 ☎ 070 993 0991. At the northern end of the main drag, this is the best choice in town for pizzas and such dishes as *pesce spada agli agrumi* (swordfish with citrus dressing). Starters are €6–9 and mains €10–15. Feb–Dec daily 12.30–3pm & 7.30–11pm.

3

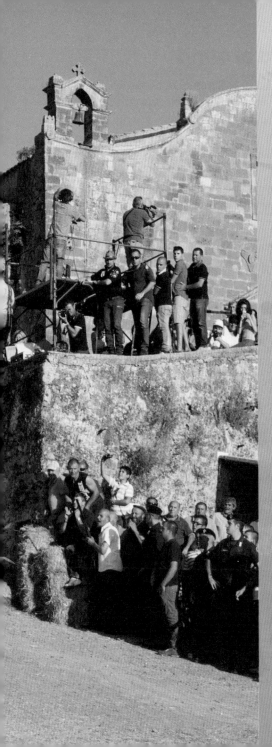

Oristano and around

S'ARDIA HORSE RACE

Oristano and around

The province of Oristano roughly corresponds to the much older entity of Arborea, the medieval *giudicato* which championed the Sardinian cause in the struggle against the Spaniards. Then as now, the city of Oristano was the region's main town, and today it retains more than a hint of medieval atmosphere, mixed with equal measures of burgeoning youth culture and prim parochialism. The small-town, pedestrian-friendly tone makes this an undemanding stop – an attractive base for exploring the surrounding area – and it also possesses one of Sardinia's best museums, the Antiquarium Arborense.

West of Oristano, the **Sinis Peninsula** is a flat, largely empty wedge of land, with good beaches and some important historical sites. You can still occasionally spot the traditional rush-constructed boats, or *fassonis*, on the peninsula's **lagoons**, used for fishing, hunting and racing. There's a museum dedicated to the lagoons' past inhabitants in **Cabras**, the only town hereabouts, with the best choice of accommodation locally. There's a lot more zip in the nearby summer resort of **Marina di Torre Grande**, though this too reverts to a more lethargic pace out of season.

Farther west along the peninsula, the church of **San Salvatore**, destination of an annual barefoot race from Cabras, is built over an ancient pagan sanctuary. Almost Middle Eastern in appearance, the much older church of **San Giovanni di Sinis** stands on the southern tip of the peninsula, very close to **Tharros** – one of the best-preserved classical sites on the island. Comparable to Nora (see p.83) in scale and location, the extensive remains of this venerable Punic-Roman town lie on a prong of land jutting from the coast. Elsewhere on Sinis, the watery terrain is a magnet for all kinds of birdlife, while the dune systems backing the coast are a protected zone – helping to preserve the choice **beaches** around here from excessive development.

On the southern outskirts of Oristano, don't miss the basilica of **Santa Giusta**, one of the earliest of Sardinia's Pisan-Romanesque churches. In the 1920s the fertile land south of here was drained and farmed by settlers from the mainland, who recreated a little corner of their native northern Italy in the town of **Arborea**, which still exudes the orderly virtues of Fascist town planning. There are traces of Roman occupation a short way inland at **Fordongianus**, where a system of baths occupies a scenic spot on the banks of the River Tirso. Just off the main route north of Oristano lie a couple of important nuraghic sites: **Santa Cristina**, where a pleasantly ramshackle *nuraghe* and an impressive sacred well are nestled within an ancient olive grove, and the monumental complex of **Losa**. Just east of Losa, **Ghilarza** has a museum devoted to the great political theorist Antonio Gramsci, who grew up here. Near the coast, **Cornus** was the scene of a historic Roman victory and displays a few archeological remnants in a remote-feeling but easily accessible spot. The prize beaches flanking the resort of **Santa Caterina di Pittinuri** are just a brief hop away.

Accommodation is scattered rather thinly throughout the region, with the best selection in Oristano itself. Apart from hotels and a few campsites (which are all on the coast), there are also several B&Bs both here and in the smaller centres.

ANTIQUARIUM ARBORENSE, ORISTANO

Highlights

❶ **Antiquarium Arborense** Oristano's superb collection of art and archeology is a richly rewarding introduction to the region, from Roman glassware to Renaissance canvases, with copious material on nearby Tharros. **See p.145**

❷ **Sa Sartiglia festival** Costumed pageantry and thrilling equestrian prowess make this one of Sardinia's most flamboyant events. **See p.147**

❸ **Cycling around Sinis** The flat landscape of this compact peninsula west of Oristano is ideal for touring by bike, with a choice of inviting beaches for cooling off. **See pp.150–156**

❹ **Tharros** The ruins of this Carthaginian and Roman city occupy a magnificent spot on the very tip of the Sinis peninsula. **See p.154**

❺ **Santa Cristina** In the midst of an olive grove, the sacred well and other monuments from the nuraghic era exude a powerfully pagan atmosphere. **See p.160**

❻ **Casa di Antonio Gramsci, Ghilarza** Dedicated to one of the architects of Communism in Europe, this small museum staffed by enthusiastic volunteers draws devotees from far and wide, but will also appeal to anyone interested in twentieth-century history. **See p.161**

HIGHLIGHTS ARE MARKED ON THE MAP ON P.140

Brief history

In prehistoric times, the area that subsequently became Oristano province was the cradle of a flourishing **nuraghic culture**, of which the complexes of Nuraghe Losa and Santa Cristina are only the most visible remnants – in fact the area around Paulilátino has the highest concentration of *nuraghi* anywhere on the island. The arrival of the **Phoenicians** in the second half of the eighth century halted the growth of the nuraghic culture, though the two peoples lived mainly in harmony. The Phoenicians' chief base was at Tharros, which was to remain the centre of commercial and political activity for the best part of the next two millennia.

Carthage and Rome

Phoenicians and Sards joined forces against **Carthaginian incursions** during the sixth century BC, and both suffered as a result of the Punic triumph. As the island passed under the direct control of Carthage following the treaty with Rome of 509 BC, North African colonies were established at Neapolis, on the southern coast of the Golfo di Oristano, and at Cornus, near present-day Cúglieri. It was at Cornus that a combined

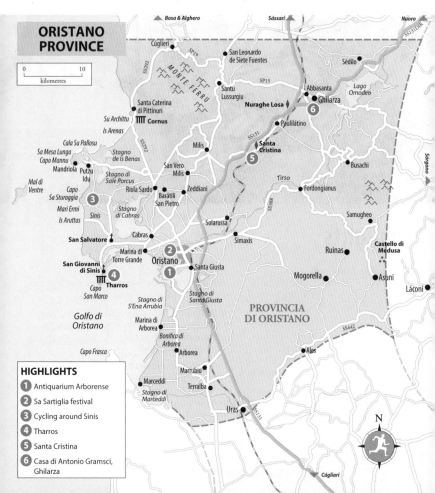

LOCAL FESTIVALS

The province has some of the island's most compelling **annual festivals**, mostly with a horsey theme: Oristano's medieval **Sa Sartiglia** at Carnival time is the most famous, and well worth going out of your way for, but there are smaller, less trumpeted affairs at **Sédilo**, northeast of Abbasanta, and **Santu Lussurgiu**, in the wooded folds of Monte Ferru.

force of Sards and Carthaginians suffered a decisive defeat by the **Romans** in 216 BC, an event which helped to bring about the total occupation of Sardinia by Rome. The Oristano region was thoroughly penetrated by the new rulers, as evidenced by the thermal baths of Forum Traiani, now Fordongianus. Tharros was revitalized, and it remained the local capital until its decline and eventual evacuation in the face of Arab assaults during the second half of the first millennium.

The Middle Ages

Most of the inhabitants of Tharros resettled inland at Oristano, which became the principal power base during the **Middle Ages**, and the capital of one of Sardinia's four *giudicati* (autonomous territories) in the tenth century. In common with the other three, the **Giudicato of Arborea** depended for its authority on the endless power shifts and temporary alliances between Pisa, Genoa and Aragon. Arborea reached its zenith during the thirteenth and fourteenth centuries, first under **Mariano II** (d.1298), and later at the forefront of the island's resistance to the Aragonese. **Eleonora d'Arborea** (see box, p.143) emerged as the champion of independence in the few areas of the island that remained free of Aragonese domination. Her fortitude and success ensured that she would become one of the greatest figures in Sardinia's history, though her near-legendary fame is also due to the **Carta de Logu**, a body of laws she introduced in 1392, which formed the basis of Sardinia's legislative structure until 1817.

The Spanish and modern periods

After Eleonora's death in 1404, anti-Aragonese resistance collapsed, and her realms joined the rest of the island under Aragonese – and subsequently Spanish – colonial rule. Arborea itself disappeared, while Oristano sank into provincial oblivion, languishing in neglect until Sardinia was taken on by the **Piemontese** in the eighteenth century. The linking of Oristano to the Carlo Felice highway (now the SS131) in the 1820s gave the town a much-needed boost, and programmes of social reform were attempted, but other problems – principally the increasingly encroaching malarial marshland – were not addressed until **Mussolini**'s initiatives got under way after 1924. His land-reclamation scheme south of Oristano was sustained by colonies of settlers from northern Italy, centred on the new town he originally called "Mussolinia" – later renamed Arborea. The whole territory became a **province** in 1974.

GETTING AROUND   ORISTANO PROVINCE

By car A car provides the best means for exploring the region and is particularly useful for the Sinis peninsula. Neither of the area's main nuraghic sites is much more than a 20min drive northeast from Oristano on the SS131; Santa Caterina is about the same distance up the SS292, running inland of Sinis, while the Roman baths at Fordongianus are slightly farther on the smaller SS388 eastbound.

By train Oristano itself is on the main north to south rail line; for train info consult ☎ 892 021 or ⓦ trenitalia.com.

By bus Public transport isn't much use to reach some of the remoter historic sites, but you can rely on buses from Oristano to Sinis in summer, and there are regular year-round services to Cabras, Santa Giusta, Fordongianus and Santa Caterina di Pittinuri. The main operator is ARST (☎ 800 865 042, ⓦ arst.sardegna.it).

By taxi For destinations that aren't served by buses, nondrivers should be able to negotiate a reasonable taxi fare from Oristano, especially if there are three or four of you.

Oristano

The city of **ORISTANO**, 100km northwest of Cágliari, is a flat, unprepossessing place, its old walls mostly replaced by busy traffic arteries. The quiet centre has a relaxed yet purposeful ambience, however, with quiet nooks and unexpected pleasures. Though it lies just 4km from the sea and is surrounded by lagoons, irrigation systems and the River Tirso, the city has an inland air, the prosperous centre of a richly productive agricultural zone.

At its heart, Oristano's **Duomo** is as old as anything in town, dating from the early thirteenth century, though a seventeenth-century refashioning has given it an overlay of Baroque opulence. The medieval stamp is more evident in the central Piazza Roma, where the **Torre di Mariano II** has been a sturdy survivor of the city's chequered fortunes since its erection in the thirteenth century; another, much smaller remnant of the old defences, the **Portixedda**, lies a short walk away. But the old town's most essential attraction is the marvellous repository of prehistoric and classical finds and medieval works of art at the local museum, the **Antiquarium Arborense**.

The best time to be in Oristano is for the colourful medieval **Sa Sartiglia**, a vivid, highly ritualized horseback competition at Carnival (see box, p.147). Advance bookings are essential for **accommodation** during that time; indeed, they're a good idea at any period, as hotel space is scarce. There are, however, plenty of **restaurants** and **bars**, and local cuisine makes good use of the area's agricultural produce and seafood.

ELEONORA D'ARBOREA

As the last of Sardinia's medieval rulers to enjoy any significant success against the island's aggressors, **Eleonora of Arborea** (c.1340–1404) is venerated throughout the island. Occupying a sort of Joan of Arc role in the popular imagination, she also made a significant contribution to the evolution of **civil rights** in Sardinia with her promulgation of a book of law that eventually became the benchmark of local freedoms for the whole island.

When Eleonora's father, the *giudice* Mariano IV (reigned 1346–76) – himself a Catalan – was required by the Aragonese King Pedro IV to have his two daughters betrothed to Spanish princes, he matched one, Beatrice, with Amerigo VI of Narbonne, but allowed Eleonora to be wedded instead, in 1366 or 1367, to the Genoan **Brancaleone Doria**, scion of Spain's main rivals in Sardinia at that time (though they were nominally Aragon's vassals). Eleonora spent most of the following fifteen years in Castelsardo (then called Castelgenovese) and Genoa, where she ingratiated herself with the doge and laid the foundations of a future anti-Aragonese alliance.

Following the assassination of her brother, Eleonora became **regent of Arborea** in 1383. As the wife of a vassal of Aragon, she managed to maintain a delicate balance of power and negotiate a degree of independence, enabling her to concentrate on the concerns of her subjects. In a short time she had acquainted herself with the entire *giudicato*, her tours round the territory greeted with enthusiastic acclaim. Her popular appeal was no doubt enhanced by the ten years of **tax exemptions** she granted to the downtrodden population, exhausted by the economic hardship induced by the long period of war.

The struggle against Aragon simmered on, however. Eleonora's intransigence finally paid off in 1388, with the signing of a **treaty** that guaranteed Arborean independence in return for restoring to Aragon the cities occupied by the *giudicato*. From her new position of strength, Eleonora forged a tactical alliance with the Genoans and launched a new offensive against Spain, as a result of which Brancaleone, with Genoan help, even managed to occupy Sássari on her behalf.

Of more lasting benefit was Eleonora's formulation around 1392 of a legal code, or **Carta de Logu**, for Arborea. Although her statue in the centre of Oristano represents this as a brief scroll, in fact the document comprised 198 chapters, addressing rural, civil and penal issues and attempting to define the legal status and rights of people at every level of society – including children, slaves and (in particular detail) women. First mooted by her father, Mariano IV, the code was far ahead of its time in its scope and application, and it remains the most enduring legacy of Eleonora's rule. It was adopted by the Aragonese in 1421, and later extended throughout the island, remaining in force until the enactment of the Carlo Felice code by the Piemontese in 1817. As the eighteenth-century English lawyer and traveller John Tyndale put it: "The framing of a body of laws so far in advance of those of other countries, where greater civilization existed, must ever be the brightest ornament in the diadem of the Giudichessa."

Eleonora's military achievements, however, did not long survive her death from plague in 1404, following which the Aragonese were quickly able to occupy Arborea and its territories. Her rule marked the end of Sardinian independence, and her brief triumph was all the more poignant in light of the obstacles she faced on every side – not just her severely circumscribed role as regent for infant male heirs, but above all her status as a woman in a feudal, male-dominated society.

Piazza Eleonora d'Arborea

The heart of Oristano, pedestrianized **Piazza Eleonora d'Arborea** holds the Neoclassical town hall and one of the town's most important churches, and is the main arena for Oristano's annual Sa Sartiglia festivities (see box, p.147). Presiding over all is the marble **statue of Eleonora**, sculpted in 1881, showing the *giudichessa* with the scroll bearing the famous *Carta de Logu* with which she is associated, while inset panels depict her various victories (see box above).

San Francesco
Piazza Eleonora d'Arborea • Daily 7.30–11.30am & 5–7pm, 4.30–6pm in winter

At the western end of the elongated piazza, four stout Ionic columns front the nineteenth-century church of **San Francesco**. Designed by the eminent Cágliari architect Gaetano Cima, the building incorporates the remains of a much older construction, traces of which – Gothic arches and Corinthian columns – are visible on the right-hand side. The most compelling item within the church's octagonal domed interior is the so-called *Crocifisso di Nicodemo*, housed in a Neoclassical marble altar on the left side. Carved in the fourteenth century by an unknown Catalan, the crucifix is considered one of the most precious and influential wooden sculptures on the whole island; the emaciated, sunken-eyed Christ, his skin scored by cuts and raw abrasions, is drenched with emotion.

If there's someone around, ask them to admit you to the **sacristy** to see the central panel of Pietro Cavaro's polyptych of St Francis receiving the stigmata, the rest of which is now in the Antiquarium Arborense (see p.145). Opposite is a small sculpture of St Basil by Nino Pisano.

Torre di Mariano II
Piazza Roma

Narrow, pedestrianized Corso Umberto links Piazza Eleonora with Piazza Roma, where pavement bars cluster around the base of the crenellated **Torre di Mariano II**. Also known as the Torre di San Cristóforo, the tower was erected by one of Oristano's greatest rulers, the *giudice* Mariano II, in 1290, and has a height of 28m. The bastion originally formed the centrepiece of Oristano's medieval fortifications. The walls to which it was joined were demolished at the end of the nineteenth century; the gateway through it, the Porta Mariano or Porta Manna, was the city's northern gate. The tower is occasionally open for exhibitions in summer and during festivals, when you can climb the three levels to view the huge bell at the top and, on a clear day, vistas of the sea.

Portixedda
Via Mazzini • Ask at Antiquarium Arborense for access • Free

Besides the more imposing Torre di Mariano II, the only survivor of the city's defences is the squat **Portixedda** ("little gate"), off Via Garibaldi – one of two towers protecting the eastern approaches into town. These days it holds small temporary exhibitions and you can climb to the top for rather limited views around town.

Santa Chiara
Via Garibaldi • Open only for services, currently Mon–Sat 7.15am & Sun 8.30am • ☎ 0783 78 093

The fourteenth-century church of **Santa Chiara** was long thought to hold the burial place of Eleonora d'Arborea, but the tomb here is in fact that of her aunt, Costanza di Saluzzo. The church is part of a convent, making access difficult unless you drop in during the daily Mass or make a request to the resident Clarisse sisters.

The Duomo
Piazza Duomo • Daily: April–Oct 8.30am–7pm; Nov–March 8.30am–6pm

With its detached octagonal, onion-roofed belltower dating from the fifteenth century, and the next-door seminary from 1712, Oristano's **Duomo** forms part of an atmospheric ensemble. The present building is mostly the result of a Baroque-era renovation, with only sections of the apses surviving from the original thirteenth-century construction.

The Duomo's spacious but fussy **interior** has three ornate chapels on either side of the nave. The first on the right has a painted wooden statue of the *Annunziata*, thought to be by **Nino Pisano** (c.1315–68). Full of expression, the statue is surrounded by a majolica and gilt altar busy with *putti* (cherubim). The two **marble panels** in front were carved by an anonymous Catalan in the fourteenth or fifteenth century. Far more interesting, however, are the other sides of the slabs, carved three hundred years earlier: eleventh- and twelfth-century Byzantine work, illustrating biblical scenes, including a portrayal of Daniel in the lions' den.

Antiquarium Arborense

Piazzetta Corrias • Mon–Fri 9am–8pm, Sat & Sun 9am–2pm & 3–8pm • €5 • ☎ 0783 791 262

A handsome sixteenth-century merchant's house holds one of Sardinia's most absorbing museums – Oristano's **Antiquarium Arborense**. As well as rotating exhibitions of nuraghic, Phoenician, Roman and Greek artefacts, the museum gives permanent space to Tharros and its occupants, and includes a good gallery of late medieval art.

Ground floor

The Antiquarium's **ground floor** displays pre-nuraghic and nuraghic finds, including Neolithic blades, axeheads and spearheads – many of obsidian or flint – from the Sinis peninsula, and a small collection of jewellery, bone hairpins and other personal items recovered from tombs. More gripping are the finds from Carthaginian Tharros, much of it from burial sites, including masks to ward off the evil eye, elegantly shaped *askoi* (curved vessels) and terracotta figurines, mostly from the fifth century BC and often Ionic Greek in inspiration. There are equally numerous exhibits from the Roman period in Tharros: pins, plates, ceramic objects, bottles and myriad other glass containers including first-century AD cinerary urns from northern Italy and Gaul. One display case is devoted to items of foreign manufacture found in tombs at Tharros, including Cretan, Etruscan and mainland Greek ceramics.

First floor

Up on the **first floor** you'll find an imaginative reconstruction of Roman Tharros as it might have appeared at the height of its power in the fourth century AD. Around it, texts in Italian explain the various buildings and monuments: the port, baths, amphitheatre, the tetrastyle Doric temple, the houses, roads, aqueduct and excavated tombs. Display cases on the balcony above hold funerary items from a Phoenician necropolis excavated at San Giovanni di Sinis (see p.153), and Roman and Byzantine objects from Tharros and Cabras.

The Pinacoteca

The air-conditioned **Pinacoteca** houses a small but rich collection of medieval and Renaissance art. The chief exhibits come from the studio of Renaissance Cágliari artist Pietro Cavaro. His most outstanding work, the five-panelled *Retablo del Santo Cristo* (1533), from Oristano's church of San Francesco, depicts with great subtlety and sensitivity the martyrdom of Franciscans in Morocco. The central panel, showing St Francis receiving the stigmata, remains in the sacristy of San Francesco (see p.144).

There are two other famous *retabli* (paintings on wood) here: the *Madonna dei Consiglieri* by sixteenth-century artist Antioco Mainas (also from Cágliari), showing five bearded town councillors kneeling around the Madonna and baby Jesus, with Sts Andrew and John the Baptist, and the much earlier *Retablo di San Martino*, two parts of a triptych by an anonymous early fifteenth-century Catalan. The central panel shows the Madonna surrounded by angels playing medieval instruments; the right panel has St Martin cutting off part of his cloak to give to a beggar.

ARRIVAL AND DEPARTURE   ORISTANO

By train Oristano's train station is in Piazza Ungheria at the eastern end of town, a 20min walk from the centre. Local buses connect it with the centre every 20–35min; buy tickets (€1, or €1.50 on board; valid 1hr 30min) from authorized bars – there's one outside the station (the bus stop is across the road). Train information can be accessed at ☎ 892 021 and ⓦ trenitalia.com.

Destinations Abbasanta (6–8 daily; 30min); Cágliari (10–14 daily; 1hr 10min); Macomer (6–9 daily; 50min); Olbia (5 daily, some change at Ozieri-Chilivani; 2hr 35min); Sássari (5–6 daily, some change at Ozieri-Chilivani; 2hr–2hr 30min).

By bus All ARST buses pull in at Oristano's bus station, centrally located off Via Cágliari, with pedestrian access also from Via Episcopio, off Via Vittorio Emanuele; some buses also make a stop at the train station. For information, call ☎ 0783 355 808 or toll-free ☎ 800 865 042, or check ⓦ arst.sardegna.it.

Destinations Abbasanta (Mon–Sat 10 daily; 1–2hr); Arborea (Mon–Sat every 30min–1hr; 25min); Bosa (Mon–Sat 5 daily; 2hr); Cabras (Mon–Sat every 30min–1hr; Sun 5–10 daily; 15min); Cágliari (Mon–Sat 2 daily; 2hr); Cúglieri (Mon–Sat 5 daily, plus July & Aug Sun 2 daily; 1hr); Fordongianus (Mon–Sat 5 daily; 40min); Is Aruttas (July & Aug 5 daily; 50min); Marina di Torre Grande (Mon–Sat 11–12 daily, Sun 5–6 daily; 25min); Putzu Idu (Mon–Sat 2–7 daily, July & Aug also Sun 4 daily; 35–50mins); Samugheo (Mon–Sat 5–6 daily; 40min–1hr 10min); San Giovanni di Sinis (July & Aug 5 daily; 35min); Santa Caterina di Pittinuri (Mon–Sat 5 daily, July & Aug also Sun 2 daily; 40min); Santa Giusta (Mon–Sat every 30min–1hr; 10min); Santu Lussurgiu (Mon–Sat 6 daily; 50min–1hr 10min); Sássari (Mon–Sat 2 daily; 2hr 5min); Tharros (July & Aug 5 daily; 35min).

GETTING AROUND

By car Much of Oristano's centre is pedestrianized or barred to non-resident drivers. Parking restrictions are in force (for parking between the blue lines) Mon–Fri 9am–1pm and 4–8pm, Sat 9am–1pm; tickets from machines cost €0.50 for the first 30min, €0.80 for the first hour, €1.20 for the second hour, then €1.50/hr. Car rental is available at Avis, Via Liguria 17 (☎ 0783 310 638, ⓦ avis .com); Maggiore, Vico Bruxelles, 2km south of town in Zona Industriale Nord (☎ 0783 350 028, ⓦ maggiore.it) and Sardinya, Via Cágliari 436 (☎ 0783 779 106, ⓦ auto noleggiosardinya.it).

By bus Lines #3 and #7 are the most useful services, connecting the train station at Piazza Ungheria with the centre at Piazza Mariano (#3 also goes to Piazza Roma) every 25min or so (except Sun). Buses #8 (in winter) and #9 and #10 (in summer) head out from the train station to Marina di Torre Grande daily until 8pm (8.35pm in winter); the summer-only #11 runs there from Via Tirso

until 1.45am. It's always worth mentioning your intended destination to the driver who will indicate the most convenient stop. Tickets valid for 1hr 30min (€1 from authorized outlets or €1.50 on board) or for one day (€2.50 or €3 on board) must be machine-punched on first use. For detailed timetable information, call ☎ 0783 355 808 or toll-free ☎ 800 865 042, or consult ⓦ arst.sardegna.it.

By taxi You'll find taxi stands outside the train station in Piazza Ungheria (☎ 0783 74 328) and in Piazza Roma (☎ 0783 70 280); the fare should be around €5 for most destinations in town.

By bike or scooter Bikes can be rented at Dore, Via Tirso 138 (☎ 0783 212 172); rates are €7/5hr, €12/day. There's another rental outfit on the Sinis peninsula (see p.150). Alternatively, rent scooters from Marco Moto, Via Cágliari 99 (☎ 0783 310 040); 125cc scooters cost €40/day, €180/ five days.

INFORMATION

Tourist office Information on the whole province is dispensed at Piazza Eleonora 19 (April–Sept Mon–Thurs 8.30am–1pm & 3–6pm, Fri 8.30am–1pm & 3.30–7.30pm, Sat & Sun 10am–2pm; Oct–March Mon–Thurs 8.30am–1pm & 3–6pm, Fri 8.30am–1pm, Sat 9.30am–1.30pm & 4–8pm,

Sun 9.30am–1.30pm; ☎ 0783 368 3210, ⓦ gooristano.com).

Pro Loco The volunteer-run office at Via Ciutadella de Menorca 14 has information on the city but keeps erratic hours (Mon–Fri 9am–1pm plus some afternoons; ☎ 0783 70 621).

ACCOMMODATION

Oristano has a small selection of **hotels** and **B&Bs** scattered around town. During the Sa Sartiglia festivities in particular, you'll need to book way ahead. The nearest **campsite** is 6km away at Marina di Torre Grande (see p.152).

Eleonora B&B Piazza Eleonora d'Arborea12 ☎ 0783 70 435 or ☎ 347 481 7976, ⓦ eleonora-bed-and-breakfast .com. Dead central, this B&B is in a medieval palazzo and has five large rooms, including a four-bed suite. The four rooms overlooking the garden are quietest. **€80**

Hostel Rodia Viale Repubblica ☎ 0783 251 881, ⓦ hostelrodia.it. Around a 15min walk from the old centre, this modern complex houses both a hostel and a hotel, though as hostel accommodation is in en-suite doubles, twins

and family suites, there's little to distinguish these from the hotel rooms, except the latter have minibars and TVs. Breakfast costs €2–7, meals are €15–18, and there are bikes to rent (book ahead). Beds in shared rooms €25; doubles €80

★ **Hotel Regina d'Arborea** Piazza Eleonora d'Arborea 4 ☎ 0783 302 101, ⓦ hotelreginadarborea.com. Right on Oristano's central (pedestrianized) piazza, this hotel is a theatrical evocation of nineteenth-century splendour, with ceiling frescoes, period furnishings and antiques aplenty.

There are just seven rooms, four facing the piazza, the others overlooking an internal garden. Breakfasts are equally sumptuous. **€120**

★**Iride Guest House** Via Bellini 29 ☎ 347 481 7976, ⓦ guesthouseiride.com. Six contemporary, colour-themed apartments a short walk from the old centre. They provide stylish accommodation, including kitchen facilities, but no breakfast. Modern art by local artists adorns the walls. **€80**

L'Arco Vico Ammirato 12 ☎ 335 690 4240, ⓦ arco bedandbreakfast.it. Centrally located off Piazza Martiri, this spotless, wood-beamed and relaxed B&B with friendly

hosts has two good-sized rooms, simply but elegantly furnished, with a/c and a shared modern bathroom. There's a small terrace, too. No credit cards. **€60**

Villa delle Rose Piazza Italia 5 ☎ 0783 310 101, ⓦ hotelvilladellerose.com. Originally a Carabinieri barracks, this hotel is located on a quiet piazza off Via Lombardia, a 10min walk from Piazza Roma. Rooms are solidly furnished, each with a spacious bathroom, and the staff are kind and friendly. There's a restaurant, parking and a bus stop close by for connections with Piazza Mariano and the train station. **€70**

SA SARTIGLIA

Oristano's flamboyant **Sa Sartiglia** festival is the biggest date in the town's calendar. The three-day event, which features jousting and various horseback stunts, along with traditional costumes, music and dancing, takes place between the last Sunday of Carnival period and Shrove Tuesday.

The **arcane rituals** of the festival perhaps originated with knights on the Second Crusade, who may have brought the trappings of Saracen tournaments to Sardinia in the twelfth century, or it could be a Spanish import – a similar annual festival, *La Sortilla*, is held on the island of Menorca in June. Whatever the case, under Spanish rule, similarly lavish feasts were held for Oristano's knights at regular intervals throughout the year; in time, these celebrations took on a more theatrical aspect, finally merging with the annual Carnival revelries. With all participants masked and costumed, the whole affair exudes a theatrical spirit unrivalled by Sardinia's other festivals.

The main events take place on the first and third days, staged by the guilds of San Giovanni (representing the farmers) and San Giuseppe (the carpenters) respectively. Each event is presided over by a white-masked arbiter known as **Su Componidori**, chosen for his riding prowess. The *Componidori* represents the continuation of the *giudice*'s role, and is decked out in a bizarre pastiche of medieval garb, complete with mask, ribbons and top hat. The *Componidori* initiates the proceedings, riding up and down the sanded track on Via Duomo, blessing the track, contenders and audience alike with a bouquet of violets. The **joust** itself consists of mounted charges with an extended rapier, with the aim of lancing a star-shaped ring – *stella* or *sartiglia* – suspended 3m above the ground. Each charge is heralded by a fanfare of drums and trumpets, and followed by groans of disappointment or wild cheering according to whether the ring is speared or missed; traditionally, more hits represent a better chance of a good harvest and thus good luck for the townspeople.

After the *corse alla stella*, the afternoon is given over to **Le Pariglie** – hair-raising **horseback stunts** (for example several riders balancing on steeds tied together at full gallop), usually taking place on a sanded track along Via Mazzini, with prizes given to the greatest equestrian feats. The whole rigmarole is repeated two days later for the *gremio* (guild) of San Giuseppe, while on the second day, a relatively recent addition, the **Sartigliedda**, is dedicated to younger riders mounted on the miniature horses of the Giara di Gésturi (see p.125).

Other highlights of the festa include the *vestizione*, or formal dressing of the *componidori*, which generally takes place in Via Aristana for the San Giovanni *sartiglia*, and in the church of Sant'Efisio for San Giuseppe's, and the equally elaborate *svestizione*, or disrobing, at the end of each day; the proclamation to announce the opening of each day's proceedings, read out by a mounted herald accompanied by a phalanx of drummers and trumpeters (normally around 10am in Piazza Roma and Piazza Eleonora); and the **songs** and traditional **dances** in Piazza Eleonora on the eve of the festivities and at the end of them.

Although the festival draws big **crowds** of both locals and tourists, it's usually possible to get a view of the events. The best vantage, however, is from the **grandstand seats** on Via Duomo and Via Mazzini, for which **tickets** cost €10–40, available a few days before the event from the **Fondazione Sa Sartiglia** office at Via Eleonora 15 or online at ⓦ sartiglia.info. If you don't want to attend the whole three-day event, Tuesday is the best day to be here, when the crowds are smaller.

4

EATING

You can eat well and cheaply in Oristano without straying from the centre. You might precede or finish your meal with a glass of Vernaccia, the celebrated local wine drunk both as an *aperitivo* and with dessert.

Cocco & Dessi Via Tirso 31 ☎ 0783 252 648. In former hotel premises, this idiosyncratic but elegant place retains a retro feel, and has five eating areas, including a gazebo and a balcony. The menu is strong on seafood (mains are €11–15), and there are pizzas in the evening. Daily 12.30–2.30pm & 7.30–11.30pm.

Da Salvatore Via Pietro Ricci 16 ☎ 0783 357 134. The plain white walls and high, arched ceiling lend an austerely elegant air to this place, but it's actually a family-run neighbourhood trattoria with a strong emphasis on seafood (the *risotto alla pescatora* is divine). Prices are reasonable – a couple of courses for €20–25 – and desserts should not be missed. Mon–Sat noon–3pm & 7.30–10.30pm, Sun 12.30–3pm.

La Torre Piazza Roma ☎ 0783 301 494. For down-to-earth and authentic pizzas, head for *La Torre*; their speciality is *pizza ai funghi porcini* (with mushrooms). Pizzas are around €7, other dishes cost €6–8 for pastas, €10–17 for meat and fish mains. Tues–Sun noon–3pm & 7–11pm; in Aug open daily.

★**Osteria del Vícolo** Via Episcopio 14 ☎ 0783 300 138. An enticing array of dishes taking in traditional Sardinian, North African and even Thai elements are offered at this slightly offbeat place with some outdoor seating near the bus station. You can either order from the menu (starters around €8, mains €8–15), or fill a plate (€5 or €8) from the buffet. Vegetarians and vegans will also be well satisfied here. June–Sept Mon–Sat noon–3pm & 7pm–midnight; Oct–May closes 11pm.

Ristorante Craf Via De Castro 34 ☎ 0783 70 669. This intimate, brick-vaulted restaurant specializes in local meat dishes (all €10–15), including horse and donkey. The *antipasti* are worth dipping into, vegetarian dishes include the delicious *risotto alla bonarcadese* (with mushrooms) and there's a good range of Sardinian wines. The atmosphere is smart but not over-formal. Mon–Sat 12.30–3pm & 7.30–10pm, Sun 7.30–10pm (June–Sept) or 12.30–3pm (Oct–May).

★**Trattoria Gino** Via Tirso 13 ☎ 0783 71 428. This straightforward, reliable little eatery features traditional Sardinian dishes such as *gnocchi sardi* and *sebadas* (warm, cheese-filled pastry cases topped with honey). Everything is well prepared, and service is polite and friendly. Pasta dishes are €8–10, mains €9–13. Arrive early or book – there are only ten tables. Mon–Sat 12.30–3pm & 8–11pm.

DRINKING AND NIGHTLIFE

Oristano has plenty of congenial **bars** to while away an afternoon or evening, many of them staying open late. On summer nights, locals converge on the bars and clubs in Marina di Torre Grande (see p.152).

Bar Eleonora Piazza Eleonora d'Arborea ☎ 0783 71 454. A great breakfast bar or coffee stop at any time, with *cornetti*, pastries and *pizzette*, and a few tables on the piazza. Mon–Fri 7.15am–8.30pm, Sat 7.15am–2pm & 4–8.30pm.

★**Friends Old Town Pub** Vico Antonio Garau ☎ 0783 462 237. Lively *birreria* where you can sit in booths inside or in the small garden. There's food (grills, *panini*, salads), Guinness (among other beers), and music in the winter months (live bands, DJs and karaoke). Tues–Sun 7.30pm–2am; may close Aug.

La Dolce Vita Via De Castro 13 ☎ 0783 71 209. Traditional and civilized brick-vaulted café with chandeliers, a good central spot for a sit-down. You can order *cornetti*, pastries and good coffee, as well as *panini* and plates of pasta and risotto. Mon–Sat 7am–10pm, Sun 7am–2pm & 6–10pm.

★**Lolamundo** Piazzetta Corrias ☎ 0783 301 284. For daytime snacks or an evening drink, this contemporary café in a quiet piazza next to the Antiquarium has a cool vibe and tables outside in summer. It's also good for snack lunches and has wi-fi. Mon–Sat 7am–1am; closes 11pm in winter.

SHOPPING

Canu Via De Castro 20 ☎ 0783 78 723. Stocks a good range of guides as well as some English-language books. Mon–Fri 8am–1pm & 4–8pm, Sat 8am–1pm & 5–8pm.

Eurospar/OVS Via Diaz 53 ☎ 0783 78 191. Useful store for a range of food, drink and reasonably priced clothes and accessories. Mon–Sat 8.30am–9pm, Sun 8.30am–1.30pm & 4.30–9pm.

MARKETS

Antiques and curios Piazza Eleanora hosts an antiques and curios market on the first Sat morning of the month.

Food, clothes and household goods The main food market is between Via Mazzini and Via Mariano IV (accessible from either), Mon–Sat mornings. Clothes, household goods, fruit and vegetables are traded on Via Aristana, near the train station, Tues–Sat mornings.

FROM TOP SANTA CRISTINA (P.160); SA SARTIGLIA FESTIVAL, ORISTANO (P.147) >

DIRECTORY

Hospital Ospedale San Martino, Via Rockefeller (☎ 0783 3171).

Internet Genius Point, Via Pietro Riccio 4, off Via De Castro (Mon–Sat 8.30am–1pm & 4.15–8pm; €4/hr).

Laundry Coin-operated machines at Lava Più, Via Campanelli 13, west of Via Cágliari (daily 8.30am–10pm; €4 for 7kg, €1.50 for a dryer).

Pharmacy Farmacia Sanna, Piazza Roma (Mon–Fri 8.30am–1.30pm & 4.30–8.30pm, Sat 8.30am–1.30pm & 5–8.30pm). See rota posted on pharmacy doors for current late-night opening.

Post office Via Mariano IV (Mon–Fri 8.20am–7.05pm, Sat 8.20am–12.35pm). You can change cash and travellers' cheques here.

Travel agencies Alerica Viaggi, Via Pietro Riccio 8 (☎ 0783 300 203), can arrange tickets for air and sea journeys.

The Sinis peninsula

For many visitors, Oristano is just a stop en route to the **Sinis peninsula**, the low-lying promontory at the northern end of the Golfo di Oristano. Fringed with beaches and dotted with lagoons where reserves protect the birds that nest here for part of the year, Sinis is unlike anywhere else in Sardinia, and merits unhurried exploration, ideally by bike. The peninsula also holds some of Sardinia's most important archeological sites, most notably the ruined Phoenician, Punic and Roman city of **Tharros**, superbly situated by the sea 20km west of Oristano. Other parts of the area have also yielded some significant finds, and ongoing work promises much more to come. A museum in the peninsula's main town of **Cabras** displays some of the finds and gives a good overview of the ancient history of the peninsula, though there is little other reason to hang about here unless for the shops, hotels and restaurants.

Teeming with fish, the marshes and lagoons of Sinis provide a livelihood for locals, not least for the highly prized *bottarga di múggine*, or mullet roe. In the past, fishermen perfected the art of negotiating the watery terrain on reed-built craft, or **fassonis** – coracle-like, flat-bottomed boats resembling truncated canoes, for which the peninsula is famous, and which can be assembled by experts in a matter of minutes. There is evidence of these in use since prehistoric times, and though they are now mainly taken out for ceremonial occasions, you may still see the flimsy-looking vessels on remote backwaters, usually being punted along from a standing position.

Accommodation and restaurants in Sinis are pretty sparse, with a few options in Cabras and **Marina di Torre Grande**, Oristano's beach resort.

GETTING AROUND AND INFORMATION   **THE SINIS PENINSULA**

By car Drivers will be able to access the whole peninsula relatively easily, though cars may need robust suspension to reach some of the beaches, such as Is Arenas. The better-known beaches have staffed car parks where you pay between mid-June and mid-Sept (around €4.50/4hr).

By bus Tharros, Is Aruttas, Putzu Idu, Mandriola and Su Pallosu are connected to Oristano by 4–6 ARST buses daily in July and Aug, and there are good year-round services to Cabras and Marina di Torre Grande.

By bike The cooperative running the tourist office Pratza de Is Ballus rents out bikes (€3/hr or €10/6hr) and offers bike tours (€20/2–3hr) between April and Oct. They also organize walking, diving and boat excursions on the peninsula and rent out dinghies.

Tourist office The independent tourist office in Pratza de Is Ballus, near Tharros and San Giovanni di Sinis church (see p.153), covers the whole Sinis peninsula (April, May & Oct Sat & Sun 10am–6pm; June–Sept daily 9am–7pm; ☎ 0783 371 006 or ☎ 349 530 3029, ⓦ cultour .sardegna.it). There's also a luggage deposit here.

Cabras

Spread along the eastern shore of the **Stagno di Cabras** lagoon, the site of **CABRAS** has been settled since Sardinia's earliest prehistory, as shown by the abundance of archeological finds in the area. Today Cabras is a low-key, low-built town, probably best known for its **Corsa degli Scalzi**, a race to the church of San Salvatore during the

THE GIANTS OF MONT'E PRAMA

Archeological digs begun in the 1970s at **Mont'e Prama**, a low hill in the centre of the Sinis peninsula, have brought to light a stunning haul of nuraghic sculptures which have only recently been cleaned up, painstakingly restored and displayed to the public. Excavated from an extensive funerary complex dating from some time between the ninth and eleventh centuries BC, most of the five-thousand-odd fragments were from thirty to fifty large statues that today constitute the only stone sculptures to be recovered from this era, the so-called Giganti di Mont'e Prama. Some 25 of them, thought to represent archers, warriors and boxers, have been reassembled, and these form the highlights of the collection: formidable and highly stylized figures up to 2.5m tall, some with hypnotic, concentric eyes (or masks) that may have indicated some sort of magical power. Other fragments represent models of nuraghic constructions. At the time of writing, the collection is shared between the Museo Cívico, Cabras (see below) and Cágliari's Museo Archeologico (see p.62), but it is eventually intended to be brought together in a new extension to the existing museum at Cabras.

first weekend of September (see box, p.152). You won't find much in the way of commotion or excitement at other times, and as it lacks a central piazza or other focal point, the town has rather an aimless air. Despite its small size, it's a labyrinth where it's easy to get lost. With the lagoon mostly out of view, the bulky, domed profile of the seventeenth-century parish church of **Santa Maria** is the town's only distinctive feature, behind which you might pick out the scanty traces of a castle belonging to the *giudici* of Arborea that once stood here.

It does however boast a good museum and has a couple of excellent eating and accommodation options. The local lagoons or *stagni* are abundant sources of fish, especially eels and mullet, the basis of one of Sardinia's oldest-known dishes: *sa merca*, salted mullet cooked in herbs (the dialect name suggests a Phoenician ancestry).

Museo Cívico

Via Tharros 121 • April–Oct Mon–Sat 9am–1pm & 4–8pm, Sun 9am–1pm & 3–8pm; Nov–March Tues–Sun 9am–1pm & 3–7pm • €5; €8 including Tharros • ☎ 0783 290 636, ⓦ museocabras.it

On the banks of the lagoon near the southwest entrance to town, the **Museo Cívico** is well worth a look for its rich trawl of nuraghic and pre-nuraghic items excavated throughout the Sinis peninsula. The museum's arrangement will change once the promised extension to house the Mont'e Prama statues is complete, but the modern purpose-built block is currently arranged in five sections. Only one of these displays finds from Tharros – the most important material on view at Cágliari's archeological museum (see p.62) – including stelae, needles, amphorae and a Roman milestone. More unique are the objects from **Cúccuru is Arrius**, a site at the mouth of the Stagno di Cabras lagoon 3 or 4km south of Cabras, where excavations have revealed a huge shrine and necropolis going back to the Bonu Ighinu culture of the fourth millennium BC. Exhibits include obsidian arrowheads, ceramic urns, vases, necklaces and tiny statuettes.

Apart from a section showing fragments from and the contents of a Roman cargo ship sunk near the island of Mal di Ventre, most of the rest of the museum is devoted to nuraghic culture, notably two rooms holding items relating to the **Mont'e Prama** site (see box above). When you've had your fill, take a breather along the eucalyptus-fringed, lagoonside park behind the museum.

ARRIVAL AND DEPARTURE   CABRAS

By bus ARST buses (ⓦ arst.sardegna.it) stop in the centre and near the museum.
Destinations Is Aruttas (July & Aug 5 daily; 35min); Marina di Torre Grande (Mon–Sat 11 daily, Sun 5 daily; 5min); Oristano (Mon–Sat every 30min–1hr, Sun 5–10 daily; 15min); San Giovanni di Sinis (July & Aug 5 daily; 20min).

ACCOMMODATION AND EATING

I Giganti Via Tharros 78 ☎0783 024 663. The modest exterior and plain interior give no inkling of the quality of the fresh seafood on offer here. Try the *burrida* (local fish stew) or anything with *bottarga* (mullet roe). There are delicious land-based dishes too, such as *gnocchetti alla campidanese*. A three-course blow-out should cost under €30. Booking advised at weekends. Daily except Tues 1–2.30pm & 8–11pm.

★**Il Caminetto** Via Cesare Battisti 8 ☎0783 391 139. This is a good choice for sampling local dishes sourced from the lagoons or the open sea around Cabras. Such specialities as pasta with *bottarga di múggine* (mullet roe) and grilled eels are always on the menu. Look out for *risotto all'inferno* (black rice with cuttlefish) too. Most mains are €12–16. Tues–Sun 12.40–2.40pm

& 8–10.15pm; Aug open daily.

Sa Cottilla Via Quattro Mori 19 ☎333 229 5405, ⓦsacottilla.it. This secluded and colourful B&B is in a modern villa in a quiet street in the centre of Cabras. All rooms have private bathrooms, breakfast is served on the veranda gving onto the garden, and bike rental can be arranged. No credit cards. **€75**

Villa Canu Via Firenze 9 ☎0783 290 155, ⓦhotelvillacanu.com. Under the same ownership as *Il Caminetto* restaurant, this restored country house with traditional Sardinian trimmings in the centre of town is the most appealing of the local hotels. Most rooms have access to an internal patio, and there's a small pool. Closed Nov–Feb. **€100**

Marina di Torre Grande

The main seaside resort for both Oristano and Cabras, **MARINA DI TORRE GRANDE**, 8km west of the provincial capital, is centred on the solid cylindrical Aragonese watchtower for which it is named. From here, Lungomare Eleonora d'Arborea runs for about a kilometre along the seafront, lined with ranks of holiday homes and dwarf palms, and with twinkling views across the gulf to Tharros. With its broad beach and a bay ideal for **windsurfing**, Torre Grande makes a lively place to visit in summer, abuzz with the bikes and blaring radios of Oristano's youth and offering a choice of animated bars and pizzerias. The nightlife kicks off with a vivacious evening *passeggiata* up and down the Lungomare.

ARRIVAL AND DEPARTURE

MARINA DI TORRE GRANDE

By bus Apart from the regular ARST bus services from Oristano and Cabras, daily local buses #8 (winter), #9 and #10 (both summer) connect Oristano's train station and centre with the resort every 30min–1hr; the #11 night

service also runs in July and Aug.

Destinations Cabras (Mon–Sat 11 daily, Sun 5 daily; 5min); Oristano (Mon–Sat 12 daily, Sun 5 daily; 25min).

ACCOMMODATION AND EATING

La Pineta Via della Pineta 36 ☎349 442 5414. Small pizzeria that serves enormous pizzas, thin and richly garnished using quality ingredients including *frutti di mare*, local mushrooms and asparagus, as well as *múggine* (mullet) from the lagoon at Cabras. Prices are average but service is a bit hit-and-miss. It's located near the entrance to the resort; seating is inside or at tables on the street. Tues–Sun 7.30pm–midnight; closes earlier in winter.

Spinnaker Strada Torre Grande ☎0783 22 074, ⓦspinnakervacanze.com. Less than 1km east of Torre Grande and the nearest campsite to Oristano, this well-equipped complex set in pinewoods has its own private beach, a pool and basic huts (€39), and bungalows (€89) to rent. The *Alfred* restaurant here offers good meals for €35. In summer, frequent Oristano city buses stop right outside. Closed Oct to mid-May. Pitches **€26**

LA CORSA DEGLI SCALZI

Run between Cabras and San Salvatore on the first weekend of September, the **Corsa degli Scalzi** is a re-enactment of a frantic rescue mission undertaken four centuries ago to save the statue of San Salvatore from Moorish attackers. Departing from Cabras, 8km away, the first part of the race is run on Saturday at dawn by the town's boys, all barefoot and clad only in white shirts and shorts. The following day, the boys return, bearing aloft the holy statue from its sanctuary to safe custody in Cabras. It's a spirited caper, infused with rowdy enthusiasm.

ACTIVITIES

Windsurfing Eolo, which operates from the beach in summer, offers windsurfing and kitesurfing courses and equipment rental (☎ 329 613 6461, ⊛ eolowindsurf.com).

Eolo also organizes various beach sports, runs a beach bar and rents out loungers and parasols.

San Salvatore

Six kilometres west of Marina di Torre Grande (signposted off the Tharros road), **San Salvatore** is one of Sardinia's *chiese novenari* – churches open for just nine days a year, when devotees stay in nearby *cumbessias*, or pilgrims' lodgings. The *novena* of San Salvatore takes place between August and September, culminating in the **Corsa degli Scalzi** (see box, p.152). The rest of the time the place is eerily deserted, the sixteenth-century church surrounded on all sides by shuttered pilgrims' shacks. Indeed, the scene recalls nothing so much as an adobe-built ghost town, and if it all looks vaguely familiar, it may be because the place was used as a set for various spaghetti Westerns in the 1960s and 1970s.

The pagan sanctuary

Ipogeo di San Salvatore • April–Oct Mon–Sat 9.30am–1pm & 3.30–6pm, Sun 9.30am–12.30pm; Nov–March 9.30am–1pm only (call first) • Free, but donation appreciated • ☎ 347 818 4069

Belying its unexceptional appearance, the church of San Salvatore reveals a fascinating past, since it was erected on top of an ancient **pagan sanctuary**, connected in nuraghic times with a water cult and later dedicated to Mars and Venus. When the building is open, a guide will accompany you down into the fourth-century subterranean chambers, where you can just make out some faded frescoes of Venus, Cupid and Hercules.

In addition to these, there are black-inked drawings and graffiti from a number of sources, most intriguingly a repeated "RF". This may be a Carthaginian prayer for healing (*Rufu* in their Semitic language), but the use of the Latin alphabet suggests that a degree of Punic culture survived later into the Roman era than was previously thought. Greek and Arabic writing adds to the cultural mix, which can be explained by the fact that the holy site lay close to Tharros, then an important port. The pictures of boats – including a Sard *fassoni* and a Spanish galleon – were possibly votive drawings, while an image of a person in a cage could well be a prisoner's doodle from when the chambers were used as a gaol during the Spanish period.

4

ACCOMMODATION AND EATING   **SAN SALVATORE**

Abraxas Località San Salvatore di Sinis ☎ 347 132 5254. This bar at the entrance to the huddle of *cumbessias* is decked out in the style of a Western saloon – appropriately, given the spaghetti Westerns that were filmed here. It has pasta dishes (€7–9), salads (€8), grilled meat (€15) and beers; tourist menus are €20 and €25. Daily 9am–9pm; winter closed Mon.

Sa Pedrera Strada per Cabras ☎ 0783 370 018, ⊛ sapedrera.it. Reminiscent of a Mexican hacienda, this friendly hotel 2km outside San Salvatore has large, clean rooms arranged around a garden area and an excellent restaurant with a veranda. Wonderful beaches are just a short distance away, but you need a vehicle. Bikes are available for free and bike tours are offered. Rates plummet out of season. Closed mid-Nov to mid-March. **€125**

San Giovanni di Sinis

Località San Giovanni di Sinis • Daily 9am–1hr before sunset

The sixth-century church of **San Giovanni di Sinis**, 4km south of San Salvatore, vies with Cágliari's San Saturnino (see p.69) for the title of Sardinia's oldest church. Standing on the roadside at the base of the limb of land on which Tharros sits, the paleo-Christian church presents a rather oriental – or Byzantine – appearance, with its red dome, irregular stonework and roof slung low over an asymmetrical facade. That it should still be standing at all after its long years of exposure to pirate raids is largely thanks to the French Vittorini monks who took it over in the eleventh century.

Thoroughly and sympathetically renovated, the interior is pleasingly dim and bare, stripped clean of all decoration.

Near the seashore behind the church, look out for the thatched huts, or *domus di cruccuri*, once used by local fishermen, now converted into unobtrusive holiday homes. Opposite the church, bars, pizzerias and restaurants cater to the stream of coach parties visiting Tharros. The comings and goings of these, combined with the bustle of people attracted to the arc of beach a few hundred metres further up the road, make for a fair amount of activity around here in high summer.

Tharros

Località San Giovanni di Sinis • April, May & Oct daily 9am–6pm; June, July & Sept daily 9am–7pm; Aug daily 9am–8pm; Nov–March Tues–Sun 9am–5pm • €5; €8 including museum at Cabras • ☎ 0783 370 019, ⓦ tharros.sardegna.it • Tharros is linked to Oristano by a summer bus service operated by ARST (July & Aug 5 daily; 35min)

The spit of land ending at **Capo San Marco** protrudes like a knobbly finger into the Golfo di Oristano, with a sturdy Spanish watchtower dominating its highest point. The peninsula also holds the atmospheric ruins of the Punic-Roman town of **Tharros**, one of Sardinia's most significant sites from this era.

Brief history

Providing safe anchorage on either side according to the direction of the wind, the peninsula has been settled since earliest times. Inevitably, given its strategic advantages, Phoenicians established a base here as early as 800 BC, and Tharros subsequently flourished under the Carthaginians and Romans – the latter built the baths and streets seen today. The town was already in decline by the imperial era, however; with the demise of the *Pax Romana*, it fell prey to Moorish raids, and was abandoned around 1070 in favour of the more secure Oristano, though there are traces of habitation here from the thirteenth century.

The site

You can tour the **site** alone, but it makes more sense to use a guide for at least part of the way. There is generally one available who speaks English, though you may have to wait for a sizeable group to form (note that guides are usually not available between 1 and 4pm).

For the most part, the site consists of Punic and Roman houses arranged on a grid of streets, of which the broad-slabbed **Decumanus Maximus** and **Cardo Maximus** are the most impressive, the latter with a deep open sewer visible down the centre, now partly covered over. This was probably the main shopping street – a large number of coins have been found along it, along with other clues such as a slab of stone with a groove for a sliding door. At the top of the Cardo Maximus, a basalt Roman wall stands near the remains of a **tophet** (burial ground) from the earlier Punic settlement, and the hill is crowned by the former Carthaginian acropolis, with a wide ditch alongside which was used for defence by the Carthaginians and as a burial site by the Romans, as evident from the tubular-shaped tombs dug up here.

The site's most prominent remains are the two strikingly white **Corinthian columns** on the site of a first-century-BC Roman temple, though these are in fact largely composite reconstructions, incorporating much modern concrete. Alongside lies the site's best-preserved Carthaginian structure, a **cistern** walled with large rectangular blocks. Towards the sea, east of here, are the remains of a bathhouse from the end of the second century AD, though these are not as large or impressive as the **thermal complex** on the southern edge of the site, which dates from a century later. The sheltered site to the north of the earlier baths, overlooking the sea, was probably used as a theatre by the Romans; seating has been provided for the performances that take place in summer. The Romans also built a minuscule **amphitheatre**; its remains are still visible on the hill near the Punic tophet. Tharros has much more waiting to be revealed, submerged underwater as a result of subsidence, and marine archeologists periodically return to fish out more valuable traces. You can get a good view of the whole area from the top of the **Torre Spagnola**, the old Spanish watchtower.

The Sinis coast

Outside the peak holiday season, an air of profound calm lies over the peninsula's western coast. Straight roads branch westwards over the Sinis peninsula to a string of undeveloped **beaches** (there is no coast road). Though certain parts get crowded in summer, you can always find unoccupied stretches of sand if you're prepared to walk a little. The Sinis coast and the island of Mal di Ventre form part of a protected marine zone (Ⓦareamarinasinis.it), which restricts most watersports and the lighting of fires.

Is Aruttas

One of the best beaches, **Is Aruttas** consists of a long white strand of fine quartz, lent interest by rocky outcrops to the north and south, beyond which more beaches extend in both directions. Occasional rollers attract surf enthusiasts, and can also bring pungent heaps of seaweed ashore. There's a bar open in season, and pedalos and windsurf boards are available for rent. The beach is easily reached in summer by bus (see p.150).

Mari Ermi and around

Three kilometres north of Is Aruttas (drivers have to backtrack inland, then head north and west again), the beach at **Mari Ermi** presents a similar picture, with bar and beach facilities, but here the sands back onto a small lagoon, and there's a high headland a brief distance north, **Capo Sa Sturaggia**.

   North again, there's a much larger lagoon, the elongated **Stagno di Sale Porcus**, which usually hosts a colony of pink flamingos, though it sometimes dries out completely in summer.

Putzu Idu and around

There are signs of civilization – bars and ugly holiday homes – around **Putzu Idu**, where there's a sheltered beach, and adjoining **Mandriola**. The bulbous promontory to the north, **Capo Mannu**, attracts surf enthusiasts in search of what are reputed to be the biggest breakers in the Mediterranean – however, the sea can be very flat too. In summer, you'll find various outfits with equipment to rent as well as surfing, kitesurfing and windsurfing courses.

   You'll also find excellent bathing spots beyond Capo Mannu – **Sa Mesa Lunga** is idyllic – and on the north side of the peninsula, at **Su Pallosu** and the endless, dune-backed **Is Arenas**. You can reach Sa Mesa Lunga and Su Pallosu with your own transport, but for Is Arenas you need a 4WD or you can walk from Cala Su Pallosu or Santa Caterina di Pittinuri (see p.165).

Mal di Ventre

Apart from passing ships, the only feature punctuating the horizon from the Sinis coast is a small island 10km out, the oddly named **Mal di Ventre** ("stomach ache"). The origin of the name is uncertain, but, in view of the fast winds that can make for rocky sailing conditions hereabouts, it may either refer to seasickness or be a corruption of *Malu Entu*, dialect for bad wind (of the gusty sort). The island is uninhabited and is now a marine reserve, though boats call here daily in summer. The remains of a double-towered *nuraghe* testify to the island's occupation in prehistoric times.

Is Aruttas Località Marina Is Aruttas ☎ 0783 192 5461, ⓦ campingisaruttas.it. Near the beach of the same name, this campsite has caravans (€92; three–seven nights minimum) and tents to rent (€41), plus a pizzeria and shop. Bike rental and internet access are also available. Closed Oct–March. Pitches €27

ACTIVITIES

Boat tours Excursions to Mal di Ventre leave daily in summer from Mandriola and Putzu Idu (around €25 for trips of 4–6hr). Among the operators, try Capo Mannu at Mandriola (☎ 329 612 0372, ⓦ capomannu.it), which also offers trekking on the island and snorkelling stops.
Windsurfing Capo Mannu Windsurf School, Lungomare Putzu Idu (☎ 347 688 1793, ⓦ capomannuwindsurf.it) offers courses (€35/1hr) and board rental (€15–20/hr).

Santa Giusta

Once the Punic town of Othoca, **SANTA GIUSTA** is now little more than a suburb of Oristano, 3km north. As such, it only merits a stop for its celebrated **basilica**, though the lagoon immediately west of town, the **Stagno di Santa Giusta**, makes a pleasant venue for picnics shaded by the encircling eucalyptus woods. Birdwatchers are also attracted by the itinerant population of aquatic wildfowl that continues to feed on the lagoon, despite the passing traffic and the industry along its western shore. On the first Sunday of August a **regatta** is held here, using the *fassonis* (see p.150).

4 Basilica di Santa Giusta

Via Manzoni • Daily 8.30am–12.30pm & 4.30–6.30pm • ARST buses leaving Oristano for Arborea and Cágliari stop by the basilica (Mon–Sat every 30min–1hr; 10min)

The austere Romanesque **Basilica di Santa Giusta** was one of the earliest of the string of Tuscan-style churches built in the eleventh to fourteenth centuries across central and northern Sardinia. This one, whose severe lines suggest Lombard influence, dates from around 1135 and was elevated to cathedral status in the sixteenth century; prominently sited in the centre of town at the top of a flight of steps behind a public garden. The church's facade displays a black basalt cross and a triple-mullioned window, topped by a typically Pisan recessed rhomboid motif in the tympanum. Below the cross, the tall portal is flanked by two truncated columns and a pair of stone lions. Three rusting cannons lie within a railed area to the right, while the main entrance is on the left side of the building.

Inside, a wooden-beamed ceiling covers the **nave**, which is illuminated by slit windows cut into the walls and apses, and lined with a motley array of marble and granite columns, some of them scavenged from the ruined city of Tharros, though the first two columns on the left and the second on the right show evidence of Arab workmanship. Round arches give access to brick-vaulted aisles and a series of lateral chapels, the first of which on the right has a painted altar and ceiling and a wooden crucifix. Otherwise, there is little concession to ornament. Round the back of the church, the square, rather graceless belltower dates from 1908, a poor replacement for the original. The basilica is the venue for four days of celebration around its saint's day on May 14, featuring a large bonfire in the piazza.

Arborea and around

Five kilometres south of the Stagno di Santa Giusta, a smaller lagoon, the **Stagno di S'Ena Arrubia**, has a greater variety of birdlife, including sandpipers, herons and rare white-headed ducks. Although this area has been left a protected site, the land south of here, the **Bonifica di Arborea**, was the subject of a large-scale land-reclamation scheme in 1919. What was formerly a malarial swamp was transformed by drainage, canalization and irrigation into a richly fertile zone, and the area is still famous for its fruit and vegetables, tobacco and beetroot. The land also supports herds of cows that account for most of the island's milk production, while the country surrounding **Terralba** to the south is famous for its wine.

The area's main town is **ARBOREA**, a quiet, rural, twentieth-century settlement whose name is a conscious throwback to the old *giudicato*. Founded in 1928 during the campaign to maximize Sardinia's domestic production, the town was originally called "Mussolinia", and was intended to house the rural colonies introduced into the area from the Veneto, Friuli and Emilia-Romagna regions to which the town owes its incongruous northern Italian appearance. This is most noticeable in the main square, **Piazza Maria Ausiliatrice**, where a formal garden with neat flowerbeds and palm trees is overlooked by a red-brick parish church and town hall, all surrounded by right-angled, tree-lined streets.

The whole place exudes the cardinal Fascist values of planning and orderliness, and the neo-Gothic church, **Cristo Redentore**, even sports a tidy grotto carved into the left side, with a Madonna presiding. On nearby Corso Italia, a renovated mill houses a museum dedicated to the *bonifica* (reclaimed land), but it's been closed for years with no sign of reopening.

The Arborea coast

Much of the **coast** hereabouts is fringed by a dense pine forest, with sandy beaches looking across the Golfo di Oristano to Tharros. The main settlement is **MARINA DI ARBOREA**, little more than a handful of houses behind the shore, but there's more interest 11km south of Arborea off the SP69, where the placid **Stagno di Marceddì** lagoon, with picnic tables and benches under the pines, forms a natural frontier between Oristano's cultivated plains and the rugged hills of Medio Campidano province. Near the mouth of the lagoon, the sleepy village of **MARCEDDÌ** has a low-key port, or *porticciolo*, with a small selection of bars and restaurants. A narrow causeway runs south across the lagoon to Sant'Antonio di Santadi and the Costa Verde (see p.109).

4

ARRIVAL AND DEPARTURE   ARBOREA AND AROUND

ARST **buses** running almost hourly connect Arborea with Santa Giusta (15min) and Oristano (25min).

ACCOMMODATION AND EATING

★ **Da Lucio** Via Lungomare 40, Marceddì ☎ 0783 867 130. Steps from the seafront, this is an excellent end-of-the-road spot to sample the local seafood accompanied by a glass of Terralba wine. The menu features the freshest fish grilled, poached or roasted, plus *anguille* (eels) and sea urchins; main courses are around €14 and there's a tourist menu for €31 (including wine). The upstairs terrace is open at weekends for pizzas. June & Sept daily except Thurs 12.30–2.45pm & 8.30–10.45pm; July & Aug daily, same hours.

Gallo Bianco Piazza Ausiliatrice, Arborea ☎ 0783 800 241, ⓦ locandadelgallobianco.it. Endearingly old-fashioned hotel on Arborea's central square, whose boxy Mussolini-era rooms cannot be modernized due to their historic character. The restaurant (open to all) offers Sard and Italian dishes (including polenta), mostly €8–12, and there's a fixed-price menu for €18. Daily 12.45–3.30pm & 8–11pm. €56

Horse Country Strada a Mare 24 ☎ 0783 80 500, ⓦ horsecountry.it. This grand hotel complex on the coast (signposted from the main road north of Arborea) is great for families, with a pool and fitness centre, and the beach just a few steps away beyond the curtain of pinewoods. The main attraction, though, is the riding facilities; they are among the best in Sardinia. All ages and levels are catered for, and excursions are organized along the coast, through the woods and inland. Look out for good online deals and discounts for families and for longer stays. Half board may be required in summer. €125

Il Canneto Marina di Arborea ☎ 0783 800 027, ⓦ ilcannetoarborea.it.gg. Right on the sandy beach, this *pensione* has ten simple, en-suite rooms that fill quickly in summer. The ristorante-pizzeria below specializes in grilled fish and is open to all – a couple of courses will cost €20–25 (half-board is €55/person). May–Oct daily noon–2.30pm & 7–10.30pm. €50

Fordongianus

East of Oristano, 28km up the River Tirso from Oristano, **FORDONGIANUS** was a Roman spa town founded at the end of the first century AD under the emperor Trajan; the present name is a corruption of Forum Traiani. A Roman bridge still spans the river, on whose banks you can visit the old **baths**, which still remain in fairly good condition.

The town has several examples of public **sculpture** carved out of local red trachyte. Some are entries for – or past winners of – an international competition held annually in Fordongianus, **Il Simposio Internazionale di Scultura**; if you're here in late July and August, you'll see the sculptors chiselling away in the streets.

Casa Aragonese

Via Traiano • Tues–Sun: April, May & Oct 9.30am–1pm & 3.30–6.30pm; June & Sept 9.30am–1pm & 3.30–7.30pm; July & Aug 9.30am–1pm & 3.30–8pm; Nov–March 9.30am–1pm & 3–5pm • €4, with Terme Romane • ☎ 0783 60 157, ⓦ forumtraiani.it

Signposted left near the western entrance to Fordongianus, **Casa Aragonese** is constructed from the distinctive red stone typical of the locality, and marked out by its pillared portico. The dwelling is thought to have been built for a noble Catalan family at the end of the sixteenth or beginning of the seventeenth century. The mostly bare rooms show few signs of life, but you'll see Gothic decorated windows and doors, and the window seats where the ladies of the household would sit and sew. The building hosts regular exhibitions, and there are more of the town's trachyte sculptures outside and in the back garden.

Terme Romane

Località Cadda • Daily: April, May & Oct 9.30am–1pm & 3.30–6.30pm; June & Sept 9.30am–1pm & 3.30–7pm; July & Aug 9.30am–8pm; Nov–March 9.30am–1pm & 3–5pm • €4 with Casa Aragonese • ☎ 0783 60 157, ⓦ forumtraiani.it

The **Terme Romane** (Roman baths) stand on the banks of the River Tirso at the lower end of town. The baths retain much of their original structure, the oldest sections including the main pool, while the frigidarium, tepidarium and calidarium date from a third-century expansion. Behind the main building, part of a **forum** still stands, from which a stairway leads to what is thought to be either an ancient hotel or butcher's shop, partly frescoed. Half the pleasure here, though, is the evocative riverside site, the thermal water steaming as it gushes into the river at a temperature of 54°C (the scene is especially striking in the early morning). Until relatively recently, local women used the hot spring water to scrub their laundry as they had done for millennia.

Is Bangius Bagni Termali

Località Cadda • Daily: April, May & Oct 9.30am–12.30pm & 3.30–6.30pm; June & Sept 9.30am–12.30pm & 3.30–7.30pm; July & Aug 9.30am–12.30pm & 3.30–8pm; Nov–March 9.30am–12.30pm & 3–5pm • €4, €5 on Sun • ☎ 0783 60 157, ⓦ forumtraiani.it

If you fancy a washdown in the healthy mineral waters, seek out **Is Bangius** (Bagni Termali), the renovated nineteenth-century bathhouses tucked away below the road by the river, 250m from the Roman baths. The thermal waters filter up into the individual baths; sessions last half an hour, though ten minutes under the waters is enough for some. Bring a swimming costume and sandals; you can rent a towel and bathing cap at the ticket office.

Chiesa di San Lussório

SS388 • Aug daily 10am–1pm & 3.30–8pm; rest of year Sun only 10am–1pm & 4–7pm (or 3–5pm in winter), call to visit on other days • €2.50 • ☎ 0783 60 157, ⓦ forumtraiani.it

A kilometre or so west of Fordongianus on the Oristano road, the church of **San Lussório** stands within a walled enclosure, its wonky red trachyte facade looking rough and unadorned at first glance. Closer inspection in fact reveals a very eroded relief around the base of the doorway, and another on one of the columns around the apse, where excavations of a paleo-Christian necropolis are currently under way. The interior is bare but atmospheric.

ARRIVAL AND DEPARTURE   FORDONGIANUS

By bus ARST buses connect Fordongianus with Oristano (Mon–Sat 9–10 daily, Sun in July & Aug 1 daily; 35min) and Samugheo (Mon–Sat 7–8 daily, Sun in July & Aug 1 daily; 30min).

ACCOMMODATION AND EATING

Sardegna Grand Hotel Terme SP23 ☎0783 605 016, ⓦtermesardegna.it. You can sample the therapeutic effects of the local water in the rather institutional surroundings of this modern thermal complex on the north bank of the river. Accommodation is in balconied a/c rooms, with free use of the two naturally heated pools, and you can choose between a range of treatments from massages to mudpacks (book ahead to ensure availability). Closed July. **€150**

Su Montigu Via Carlo Alberto Dalla Chiesa ☎0783 60 018. A modern building housing a traditional country restaurant which offers tasty and moderately priced dishes (€20–30 for a full meal including drinks). Lamb, boar and local mushrooms are among the top choices. In the evenings it opens for bookings only, so call first. No credit cards. Tues–Sun noon–2.30pm & 7.45–10.30pm.

Samugheo and around   4

A right turn off the SS388 east of Fordongianus leads south to Allai (this is a much shorter route than the zigzagging SP33 going directly there from Fordongianus) and **SAMUGHEO**, a large village of the Mandrolisai region, famous for its textiles (*tessile*). You can take in a good sample of these at the **Museo Regionale Arte Tessile Sarda** on Via Bologna (Wed–Sun 10am–1pm & 5–8pm or 4–7pm in winter; €2.50; ☎0783 631 052, ⓦmurats.it), which is also the main venue for the **Mostra dell'Artigianato Sardo**, a craft exhibition and fair between early August and early September, when you'll find piles of rugs, blankets, tapestries and furniture for sale in the shops and stalls.

Castello di Medusa

Three or four kilometres south of Samugheo on the SP38 Asuni road, a dirt track – indicated by a yellow signpost on the left – leads off towards the **Castello di Medusa**, a ruined redoubt in the Araxisi gorge, which makes a rewarding trip either on foot or with your own transport. On the way you'll pass several *pinneddas*, igloo-type constructions used by the local shepherds; they resemble miniature *nuraghi* at first glance, but are made of much lighter, smaller stones. As you follow the high ridge with steep drops below, look out for glimpses of the distant peaks of the Gennargentu mountains to the east. The castle itself is about 5km along the track: for orientation, aim for the orange church on the horizon. The ruins appear below the track on the left, isolated above a gorge.

Little is known of the origins of the castle, though it's thought that it was an outpost of Fordongianus during the Roman occupation and rebuilt under the Byzantines. The fortified site was later used by Arborea's *giudicati*. The straggling ruins give little idea of how it might have appeared intact, but it's a grand spot nonetheless, overlooking high pastoral country crossed by dry-stone walls and dotted with herds of goats and sheep.

ARRIVAL AND DEPARTURE   SAMUGHEO

By bus Samugheo has bus connections with Fordongianus (Mon–Sat 4–5 daily, Sun in July & Aug 1 daily; 30min) and Oristano (Mon–Sat 4–5 daily, Sun in July & Aug 1 daily; 1hr 5min).

ACCOMMODATION AND EATING

A Ruota Libera Via Vittorio Emanuele 38 ☎0783 649 206, ⓦaruotaliberasamugheo.it. It looks like a simple bar from the outside but you'll find tables inside and in an interior garden. Local specialities such as *fregola con agnello* (semolina pasta with lamb) are recommended and in the evening there are pizzas – reckon on around €35 for a full meal for two. B&B is also available in three clean, modern rooms with shared bathrooms. Daily except Wed 8am–midnight. €50

Santa Cristina and around

Travelling up the main SS131 from Oristano, you'll soon pass through the so-called "**Vernaccia triangle**", an area bounded by the villages of Zeddiani, Barátili San Pietro and Solarussa that forms the core of the Vernaccia wine-producing region. The villagers of Barátili San Pietro are also famous for their skills in making and navigating the reed-built *fassonis*. Farther on, you might stop to buy a kilo or two of what are reputed to be Sardinia's best oranges, grown around **Milis**; the season extends over ten months of the year.

Santa Cristina

SS131 • Daily 8.30am–1hr before sunset • €5 with Museo Etnográfico • ☎0785 55 438, ⓦarcheotour.net

Twenty-five kilometres north of Oristano, look out for the signposted exit from the superstrada to the nuraghic complex of **Santa Cristina**, dispersed within a shady grove of olive trees, and comprising a *nuraghe*, a sacred well and other nuraghic buildings, some of them dating back to 1800 BC. The *nuraghe*'s main tower, about 15m high, has an egg-shaped "tholos"-type interior, hewn with niches and alcoves. From the top, the views over the green, wooded surroundings take in other fragments of this extensive site, including dwellings and assembly rooms of the surrounding nuraghic village and various **capanne** – long, stone-built structures of unknown function and uncertain age, though some have yielded Roman finds from the third century BC. But the most impressive part of the complex is a short walk away, a **sacred well** and underground shrine reached via a narrow-walled flight of perfectly smooth steps. Back on the surface, a round meeting room stands nearby, among several more nuraghic remains in varying states of preservation.

It's an impressive grouping, the overall effect enhanced by the mossy green ambience and ancient olive trees, one of which is said to be over a thousand years old. The entry ticket includes a guided tour of the site in Italian (no tours 1–3pm), and also includes entry into the Museo Archeologico-Etnográfico in the centre of **Paulilátino**, 5km northwest (see below).

Museo Archeologico-Etnográfico

Via Nazionale 127, Paulilátino • Tues–Sun 9.30am–1pm & 4.30–7pm (3–5.30pm in winter) • €5 with Santa Cristina • ☎0785 55 438, ⓦarcheotour.net

Housed in the handsomely restored seventeenth-century Palazzo Atzori in the centre of **Paulilátino**, 5km northwest of Santa Cristina, the **Museo Archeologico-Etnográfico** includes finds from Santa Cristina alongside items of social history – local photographs, traditional furnishings, tools and other exhibits of folkloric interest. It's an engaging collection, with enthusiastic staff who can provide details and context. In summer, temporary exhibitions are laid out on the roof and in the courtyard.

Ghilarza and around

Merging into the sister town of Abbasanta, 8km northeast of Paulilátino, small, run-of-the-mill **GHILARZA** has achieved worldwide fame as the hometown of the great

ANTONIO GRAMSCI

Italy's most influential political theorist of the Left, **Antonio Gramsci** (1891–1937) was born in the village of Ales, southeast of Oristano, but grew up in Ghilarza, where his father worked with the land registry. Never physically strong, Antonio suffered from rickets as a child, a condition aggravated by poverty after his father was jailed for "administrative irregularities". Despite such obstacles, the young Gramsci doggedly pursued his education, and by the time he was 20, Antonio had enrolled to study letters at the University of Turin. Here, he was drawn into working-class politics, and in 1921 became one of the founders of the **Italian Communist Party**. In 1924 he was elected to the Chamber of Deputies, where he became one of the most effective and articulate **opponents of Fascism**. Inexorably, the regime closed in. Gramsci was arrested in November 1926; he was 35, and would spend the rest of his life in jail, dying of tuberculosis in 1937.

As it turned out, Gramsci's imprisonment allowed him to develop his ideas untainted by Stalinism, and his **Prison Notebooks**, when they were published immediately after World War II, helped to revitalize the discredited Left during the 1950s and 1960s. The alternative theoretical framework that he provided was a decisive factor not just in the evolution of the Italian Communist Party but in the development of the "Eurocommunism" that underlay the electoral successes of Sard Enrico Berlinguer in the 1970s.

political theorist **Antonio Gramsci**. Although he was born near Oristano, Gramsci spent most of his youth in this unassuming place, in a house that is now devoted to his life and works.

Casa di Antonio Gramsci

Corso Umberto 57 • May–Sept daily except Tues 10am–1pm & 4–7pm; Oct–April Wed 4–7pm, Sat & Sun 10am–1pm & 4–7pm • Donations appreciated • ☎ 0785 54 164, ⓦ casagramscighilarza.org

The modest house where Gramsci and his family lived, near the church on the town's narrow main street, has been converted into the **Casa di Antonio Gramsci**, a study centre and museum dedicated to Gramsci's life and writings. Much of the small building is taken up by a meeting hall and library, where taped reminiscences by people who knew him are stored alongside shelves of books and documents. Items on display are a mix of the personal – letters to his mother, boyhood photographs, toys – and writings relating to his academic and political development. Photos of and objects from the prison cell outside Bari where he spent five years for anti-Fascist activities can be seen upstairs, and there's a 35-minute film (in Italian) narrating his life and achievements. T-shirts and posters are available for sale.

ARRIVAL AND DEPARTURE   GHILARZA

By train There's a mainline train station at neighbouring Abbasanta, with frequent connections to Oristano (6–8 daily; 20–40min) and, for services to Sássari and Olbia, Ozieri-Chilivani (5 daily; 1hr). From Abbasanta station, it's a 30min walk to Ghilarza, or you could take a taxi or catch a bus (Mon–Sat roughly hourly).

By bus ARST services stop close to the main Corso Umberto.
Destinations Fordongianus (Mon–Sat 3 daily; 25min–1hr 15min); Oristano (Mon–Sat 2 daily; 1hr 10min–1hr 50min); Santu Lussurgiu (Mon–Sat 2 daily; 25min).

Sédilo

Just north of Lago Omodeo, the town of **SÉDILO** hosts the annual **S'Ardia** horse race, held in honour of the Roman emperor Constantine in his saintly guise of San Costantino. The race takes place at dawn on July 6 and 7, at breakneck speed and over a danger-strewn course around the church of **Sant'Antine di Sédilo**. It's an attractive, woody spot outside the village and within sight of the lake, though tranquillity is notably absent during the S'Ardia itself. The risks to participants and spectators alike are increased by people whose sole job is to harass the horses and their riders, to the extent of shooting dud bullets at them. It's a thrilling spectacle, full of hot tempers, commotion and displays of virility. Folk concerts take place in the evenings, and there's a race on foot on the following weekend.

The church of **Sant'Antine** – a *novena* church, open for nine days a year – deserves a look for the copious ex-votive graffiti scribbled on its walls.

ARRIVAL AND DEPARTURE **SÉDILO**

ARST **buses** run to Sédilo from Ghilarza (Mon–Sat 4 daily; 15–30min). There are no direct connections with Oristano.

Nuraghe Losa

Località Nuraghe Losa, SS131 (3km from Abbasanta train station) • Daily 9am–1hr before sunset • €5 • ☎ 0785 52 302, ⊛ nuraghelosa.net

Standing alone in bare, flat country just west of the SS131, the **Nuraghe Losa** makes an easy stop for anyone following Sardinia's main north–south highway in either direction (look out for the exit signs). Dating from the Middle Bronze Age (the second millennium BC), the flat, grassy site is encompassed within a prodigious perimeter wall, giving a better idea of the extent of a nuraghic settlement than other similar structures in Sardinia.

What most commands attention, however, is the massive sheer-walled trilobate (three-cornered) *nuraghe* – the compact, fortified structure growing in impact as you approach. Composed of regular basalt stones half-covered with striking orange lichen, the tapering walls of the truncated **central tower** are smoother than those of most other *nuraghi*, and reach a height of nearly 13m. The design and arrangement of the various parts of the complex are, as ever, baffling. Directly in front of the *nuraghe*'s main entrance, a circular meeting chamber leaves little room for coming and going, and there are equally cramped spaces on the *nuraghe*'s western side, where an inner rampart forms an additional protective wall, enclosing a courtyard accessible through a lintelled door. Two minor **defensive towers** – now topless – are incorporated into the rampart, furnished with narrow slits for viewing the surrounding area and for archers to fire through. Cradled within the rampart at the northern end are more remains of stone buildings, and an entrance – again tiny – for access to the northern tower of the trilobate.

The central tower

The **central tower** – the oldest part of the structure – is entered through a narrow corridor with a large recess hacked out of the right-hand wall, possibly for a sentry. To the left, a flight of stone steps curls up to a second-floor chamber, continuing on to the open terrace from which, on a clear day, you can see the peaks of the Gennargentu mountains to the east. Back on ground level, the main corridor also has lateral passages leading to the bare windowless chambers within the bastion's two southern towers. The main central tower has a tall conical interior, dimly lit by electric lighting, with alcoves and niches gouged out of the walls. The overall complex shows continuous occupation from around 1500 BC to the seventh century AD, while most of the village to the northeast and southwest of the bastion has yet to be uncovered.

The perimeter wall

Either before or after visiting the *nuraghe* itself, take a bit of time to follow the **perimeter wall** round for new angles on the central structure, and to explore the three shattered **external towers**, which provided secondary entrances to the complex. The wall encloses the scanty remains of a **prehistoric village** and, just inside the site's main entrance, the remains of a first- to second-century-AD cemetery from the settlement's post-nuraghic phase, showing exposed cinerary urns.

The museum

The site holds a small **museum** of very fragmentary local finds: needles and vases from the nuraghic period; pottery with zigzag designs from the fifth and sixth centuries AD; and photos of other *nuraghi* in the area from which some of the finds originate. The best stuff, however, is on view or in store in Cágliari's museum (see p.62). You can read more on Sardinia's nuraghic culture in Contexts (see p.307).

Santu Lussurgiu and around

The large village of **SANTU LUSSURGIU** sits in the crater of an extinct volcano some 35km north of Oristano and 15km west of Abbasanta on the SP15. The surrounding landscape of bare craggy hills and woods of olives and chestnut was once a highly volatile seismic zone, though nowadays the atmosphere is one of utter serenity. In the village itself, not even cars can enter the tight web of steep cobbled lanes that make up the old centre, which harbours several handsome churches. One of the finest is the heavily buttressed, late fifteenth-century **Santa Maria degli Ángeli** above the public gardens, containing a wooden altar from the eighteenth century.

4

Museo della Tecnologia Contadina

Via Deodato Meloni • No fixed opening hours – call at least a day in advance to make an appointment • €3 • ☎ 349 686 8600,
Ⓦ museotecnologiacontadina.it

Below the public gardens, the **Museo della Tecnologia Contadina** gathers together everyday items from different eras and areas of Sardinia. The eleven rooms are dedicated to various aspects of rural culture, starting with agricultural tools and taking in weaving, bread-making, winemaking, children's toys, craftwork and archeology. Rat traps, coffee grinders and flax-combs are among some of the more unexpected items here.

ARRIVAL AND DEPARTURE   SANTU LUSSURGIU

By bus Santu Lussurgiu is served by buses to and from Abbasanta/Ghilarza (Mon–Sat 2 daily; 25min) and Oristano (Mon–Sat 7–8 daily; 50min–1hr 10min).

ACCOMMODATION AND EATING

★**Antica Dimora del Gruccione** Via Michele Obinu 31 ☎0783 552 035, Ⓦanticadimora.com. Based in a renovated eighteenth-century villa, this is one of three *alberghi diffusi* (with rooms in various buildings) in Santu Lussurgiu. The rooms are all different, with modern or period furnishings. The gourmet restaurant concentrates

---

HORSING AROUND – SANTU LUSSURGIU'S FESTIVALS

Rearing and riding horses is in the blood in Santu Lussurgiu, and at no time is this more apparent than in the village's annual party, a horse race spread over three days during **Carnival** (usually Sunday, Monday and Shrove Tuesday). As in Oristano, riders gallop hard through the narrow streets of the old town, though there are few or no costumed theatrics here – this is serious bareback riding, and highly exciting to watch. The village's saint's day, around **August 21**, is also an excuse to saddle up for horseback competitions during four days of festivities. The horses take a break at **Easter**, however, which Santu Lussurgiu marks with choral singing, but the equine theme is ever present in the local craftwork for sale in the village shops.

on local meat products and charges €35 for a five-course meal (reservation advised if you're not staying). In summer you can eat in the courtyard garden. Hotel open mid-Feb to Dec; restaurant daily 8.30pm–late, but only Fri–Sun or with prior notice in winter. **€90**

★**Sas Benas** Via Cambosu 4 ☎0783 550 379, ⓦsasbenas.it. Rather tricky to find, this *albergo diffuso*

– with rooms in three locations in the village – has exposed-stone walls, arches and richly atmospheric rooms (with modern bathrooms). Its superb restaurant offers local and seasonal specialities, with an endless selection of *antipasti* and set menus at €25 and €35. Breakfast is abundant and delicious too. Tues–Sun 1–2.15pm & 8–9.30pm. **€90**

San Leonardo de Siete Fuentes

North of Santu Lussurgiu, weekend picnickers head up the minor road towards Macomer (see p.196) for the wooded area around the hamlet of **SAN LEONARDO DE SIETE FUENTES**. The village's Spanish name ("Seven Fountains") is a reference to its highly prized mineral waters, which attract droves of connoisseurs. The crumbly old Romanesque church is the burial place of Guelfo, son of Count Ugolino della Gherardesca, who died in 1292 (see box, p.103). San Leonardo is also the scene of a **horse fair** held every June 2 – one of Sardinia's most important markets of this kind. A much smaller-scale market of everyday items also sets up here on Sundays in summer.

Monte Ferru

West of Santu Lussurgiu looms the mainly forested **Monte Ferru** – or Montiferru, the name a reminder of the iron once mined here – which reaches a height of more than 1000m. This former volcanic zone is now endowed with an abundance of rivers and springs which nourish its thick forests of oak, elm and chestnut. Mouflons and deer inhabit certain parts, such as the **Sa Pabarile** area.

If you're tempted to get a closer look, take the twisty and highly scenic SP19 heading north and west of Santu Lussurgiu, which offers opportunities to explore on foot – Sa Pabarile can be reached from the lane on the left leading up to the RAI TV transmitter, 8km from the village. A further 10km or so along the SP19, you'll spot the ruined **Castello di Monte Ferru** (in Sard: "Casteddu Etzu"), a formidable twelfth-century hilltop fortification subjected to over-zealous restoration, reachable via a side road.

Cúglieri

The silver dome of the basilica at the top of the village of **CÚGLIERI** makes a prominent landmark for many kilometres around. There are superb panoramic views over the coast from here, but the church itself is a disappointment, its broad brown exterior only feebly enlivened by two marble carvings on either side of the portal and with a run-of-the-mill interior. The rest of Cúglieri doesn't inspire much interest either, though there are a couple of excellent restaurants.

ARRIVAL AND DEPARTURE

CÚGLIERI

By bus Cúglieri is a stop on the ARST bus route between Bosa and Oristano and for Digitur buses (☎079 262 039, ⓦdigitur.it) to and from Porto Torres and Sássari. Destinations Bosa (Mon–Sat 9 daily, Sun 1 daily; 1hr);

Oristano (Mon–Sat 5–8 daily, Sun in July & Aug 2 daily; 1hr); Santa Caterina (Mon–Sat 5–8 daily, Sun June–Sept 2–3 daily; 20min).

ACCOMMODATION AND EATING

★**Desogos** Vico Cugia, off Via Cugia ☎0785 39 660. The women who run this authentic backstreet trattoria are carrying on a 75-year family tradition. The fixed-price menus (€25 and €30 including drinks) are geared to carnivores

– lamb or boar cooked with olives, and hare or donkey stew. Call ahead in winter. Daily 1–2.30pm & 8–10.30pm.
★**S'Imbiligu** Località Sentis, Sennariolo ☎347 528 0382, ⓦfattoriasimbiligu.it. It may prove a challenge to

find this remote *agriturismo* deep in the countryside – 5km north of Cúglieri between Sennariolo and Scano di Montiferro (look for signs on the SS192) – but it's worth persevering. The secluded setting provides a peaceful ambience for simple, spacious accommodation and a restaurant where you can dine royally for €25. There's no menu; instead you're presented with a succession of tasty local dishes, prepared from recipes that go back generations. Daily 7.30–10pm; always book ahead. Closed Dec–Feb. **€48**

Santa Caterina and around

From Cúglieri, the SP292 heads rapidly downhill and south along the western flank of Monte Ferru to the main resort on this stretch of coast, **SANTA CATERINA DI PITTINURI**, a busy summer holiday centre. In winter, the local economy relies on olive production – the area is famed for its olive groves and is one of the island's major sources of olives and olive oil. The **beaches** hereabouts are also renowned, a mixture of sand and rocks sheltered within pretty inlets. The most photogenic are at **Su Archittu**, a couple of kilometres south of town, where a ruined watchtower stands on a point above the natural rock arch it is named after, which you can swim through and climb above. South of here, the long, dune-backed strand **Is Arenas** extends for 6km (see p.155). Santa Caterina itself, however, almost overwhelmed by holiday homes, has little of interest.

Cornus

Località Cornus, off SP292 • Always open • Free

A kilometre or so south and inland of Su Archittu, a signposted dirt road leads 2–3km to the site of **Cornus**, an ancient settlement that was the focus for an alliance of Carthaginian and Sard forces, led by a local chieftain, **Ampsicora**, opposed to the growing power of Rome. The rebellion was swiftly crushed by Roman forces in 216 BC, Ampsicora took his own life, and with the Carthaginian threat banished for ever, the way was clear for Rome's domination of the island.

The battlefield itself is a little farther inland on a hill, though there's nothing to mark the exact spot. The main site of Cornus, however, reveals the interesting remains of an early Christian centre of worship established here in the third and fourth centuries AD. The outlines of a double-apsed **basilica** are clearly visible, with tombs jammed into every available space, even the apses. A **baptistry** is marked out by a well-preserved cruciform font. It's a serene, deserted spot, within sight of the sea, ideal for a quiet picnic.

ARRIVAL AND DEPARTURE | SANTA CATERINA

By bus Services between Bosa, Cúglieri and Oristano stop along Santa Caterina's main street.
Destinations Bosa (Mon–Sat 6–7 daily, Sun June–Sept 1 daily; 1hr); Cúglieri (Mon–Sat 6 daily, Sun June–Sept 2–3 daily; 20min); Oristano (Mon–Sat 5–6 daily, Sun in July & Aug 2 daily; 40min).

ACCOMMODATION AND EATING

Is Arenas Località Is Arenas ⊕ 0783 52 103, ⓦ villaggio isarenas.com. The smaller of two adjacent campsites shaded by thick pinewoods with direct access to the beach at Is Arenas. This has a shop, restaurant and bungalows for rent (€70). Closed Oct–March. Pitches **€23**
La Baja SP292 ⊕ 0785 389 149, ⓦ coopsinis.it. Comfortable if somewhat isolated lodgings are available at this tidy four-star signposted off the SP292 north of Santa Caterina. Its clifftop location affords marvellous sea views, and there are steps down to the beach (there's a pool too). Half board comes to €176 for two. **€126**
La Scogliera Corso Alagon ⊕ 0785 38 231. The best thing about this trattoria near the beach is the veranda with its entrancing views. Seafood dishes (mostly €12–14) include *seppiette alla griglia* (grilled cuttlefish), and pizzas are available. April–May & Oct–Dec daily except Wed 1–2.30pm & 8–11pm, June–Sept daily, same hours.

4

Alghero and the northwest coast

GROTTA DI NETTUNO

5

Alghero and the northwest coast

Sardinia's northwest coast shelters a trio of the most attractive seaside resorts on the island, separated by some of its most spectacular coastline. The biggest and busiest of the towns, Alghero, has long been a tourist hot spot, its old centre a tight web of narrow lanes packed with boutiques, bars and restaurants. It is the most "Italian" of Sardinia's holiday towns, and though it may lack the glamorous sheen of mainland resorts like Sorrento or San Remo, it's also refreshingly free of their cynical hard sell. At the same time, Alghero retains a distinctive Catalan character – the result of intense Spanish colonization in the fourteenth century – that sets it apart from anywhere else in Italy. Nearby, you'll find enticing beaches and fascinating archeological sites, not to mention the famous Grotta di Nettuno (Neptune's Grotto) on the point at Capo Caccia.

North of Alghero, the ghost town of **Argentiera** and Sardinia's only natural lake, **Lago di Baratz**, make diverting half-day trips, while the resort of **Stintino**, at Sardinia's northwestern tip, merits a more prolonged exploration, not least for the largely undeveloped coastline on either side. The pick of the beaches here are the once-seen, never-forgotten sands around the point at **La Pelosa**, where calm, turquoise waters extend to rocky offshore isles. Boat excursions from Stintino call at the biggest of these islands, **Asinara**, a nature reserve with yet more exquisite beaches.

The unspoiled rocky coast south of Alghero has a wild grandeur, and is one of the last habitats in Sardinia of the griffon vulture. The stretch of coast ends at the River Temo, where a ruined castle presides over the medieval port of **Bosa** and its compact warren of streets. Despite being a stop for coach parties, Bosa preserves a quiet, low-key charm that is perfectly in tune with the slow rhythms of the local community. Its seaside satellite, **Bosa Marina**, keeps beach aficionados happy, while inland, **Macomer** has some intriguing nuraghic sites, but should otherwise detain you only as a transport junction.

Accommodation options are rather limited in Stintino and Bosa, but plentiful in Alghero, which also has most of the **campsites**. There are **hostels** at Fertilia (near Alghero) and Bosa. However, availability can be very scarce throughout the region in summer, and many places are closed altogether between October and April.

GETTING AROUND   **THE NORTHWEST COAST**

Although **public transport** services are adequate for travelling between the main towns and villages, a **bike** or **car** offers more freedom to explore. There's plenty of scope for **walkers** too, with few strenuous tracts and mostly traffic-free roads.

Alghero

The predominant flavour in **ALGHERO** is Catalan, owing to the wholesale Hispanicization that followed the overthrow of the Doria family by Pedro IV of Aragon in 1353 – a

SEAFOOD IN ALGHERO

Highlights

❶ Walk along Alghero's sea walls The formidable old walls of the port offer great views across to Capo Caccia by day, and a cooling breeze on summer nights. **See p.176**

❷ Seafood in Alghero Feast on lobster and other seafood treats in one of the town's renowned fish restaurants. **See p.179**

❸ Cycle along the Alghero–Bosa coast This wild stretch of coast warrants a leisurely ride, with stops at secluded beaches. See p.188

❹ Castello Malaspina, Bosa Once you've recovered your breath, take in the wonderful views from this lofty vantage point, and admire the medieval frescoes in the small church. See p.192

❺ La Pelosa One of Sardinia's premier beaches – sandy, shallow, and surrounded by alluring waters and magnificent scenery. **See p.199**

❻ Boat trip to Asinara Off-limits for centuries, the island's wildlife and pristine beaches can be visited on boat tours from Stintino. **See p.199**

HIGHLIGHTS ARE MARKED ON THE MAP ON P.170

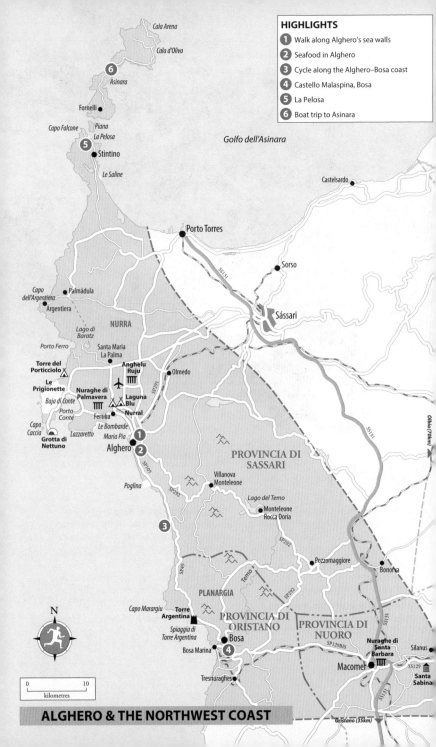

HIGHLIGHTS

1. Walk along Alghero's sea walls
2. Seafood in Alghero
3. Cycle along the Alghero–Bosa coast
4. Castello Malaspina, Bosa
5. La Pelosa
6. Boat trip to Asinara

Golfo dell'Asinara

Cala Arena
Cala d'Oliva
6
Asinara
Fornelli
Capo Falcone
Piana
La Pelosa
5 Stintino
Le Saline

Castelsardo

Porto Torres

Sorso

Capo
dell'Argentiera
Palmádula
Argentiera
NURRA
Lago di Baratz
Porto Ferro
Santa Maria La Palma
Anghelu Ruju
Olmedo
Sássari
SS131

Torre del Porticciolo
Le Prigionette
Nuraghe di Palmavera
Laguna Blu
Baja di Conte
Porto Conte
Fertilia
Nurral
Capo Caccia
Grotta di Nettuno
Lazzaretto
Le Bombarde
Maria Pia
1 Alghero
2

SS291

Poglina
SP105

PROVINCIA DI SASSARI

Villanova Monteleone
SP292

Lago del Temo
Monteleone Rocca Doria

SP293

Pozzomaggiore

Bonorva

SS131

Olbia (70km)

SP49

PLANARGIA

Temo

Capo Marargiu
Torre Argentina
Spiaggia di Torre Argentina
Bosa
4
Bosa Marina

PROVINCIA DI ORISTANO

PROVINCIA DI NUORO

SP129BIS

Nuraghe di Santa Barbara
Macomer
Silanus
SS129
Santa Sabina

SS131

Tresnuraghes

Oristano (35km)

N

0 — 10
kilometres

ALGHERO & THE NORTHWEST COAST

5

process so thorough that the town (Alguer in Catalan) became known as "Barcelonetta". A walk around the intricate mesh of car-free lanes that make up the atmospheric **old town** reveals Catalan street names (*carrer*, *plaça*, *iglesia* and *palau* for "via", "piazza", "chiesa" and "palazzo"), handsome sixteenth-century architecture in a congenial Catalan-Gothic style, and Catalan dishes such as *paella* on restaurant menus. It's this mixed heritage that sets Alghero apart from other Sardinian towns, and has helped make it one of Sardinia's most favoured tourist destinations. Thankfully, however, the resort has escaped the fate of many other Mediterranean hot spots and stood firm against both tweeness and commercial hype. Instead, it remains a sophisticated and easy-going place with a sharp but good-humoured population, who like nothing better than a good night out in a trattoria.

Brief history

While archeological finds in the area around Alghero suggest a degree of social organization as early as 6000 BC, the history of the modern town really begins in the first half of the twelfth century with the fortification of an obscure fishing port by the Doria family of **Genoa**. The town successfully defended itself from assaults by the Pisans and Aragonese until 1353, when, after the conquest of Cágliari and Sássari, a large **Spanish fleet**, supported by the Venetians, routed the Genoans at the nearby bay of Porto Conte and took possession of Alghero. Following an uprising in which the Spanish garrison was massacred, the town was subjected to a thorough "ethnic cleansing", in which waves of **Catalan settlers** displaced the locals, forcing them to settle at Villanova, a mountain village 25km to the south. Laws were passed limiting the number of native Sards who could enter, and compelling them to leave town at the sound of a trumpet signal.

A Catalan colony

Because of its geographic and strategic importance on Sardinia's northwestern coast, Alghero quickly became the foremost **port** for traffic between Sardinia and Catalonia. From the fourteenth to the sixteenth century, its defences were massively strengthened; most of the ramparts and towers still standing today date from this period, when they sheltered a substantial garrison and fleet, providing a powerful bulwark against seaborne raids on Sássari and the whole western interior.

The town suffered a downturn in its economic fortunes following the expulsion in 1492 of its substantial **Jewish community**, or *Aljama*. This forced the Aragonese to reopen Alghero to foreign and Sard traders – though the core of the town remained stoutly Catalan in character and culture. Links with Spain were bolstered in 1541, when the emperor **Charles V** made a historic visit to the town, accompanied by his admiral Andrea Doria – the most eminent member of the Genoan dynasty, formerly in the vanguard of the emperor's enemies before becoming his staunch ally. The two were en route to flush out the corsair **Hassan Aga** from his lair in Algiers, for which they had assembled one of the biggest fleets ever seen. (The pirate chief was himself a Sard: born of shepherds, he was abducted as a slave, forcibly converted and castrated for harem service, and swiftly rose to become right-hand man to the feared Khair al-Din, or Barbarossa.)

THE CATALAN DIALECT

The most obvious index of Alghero's distinctive culture, the *catalano* or *algherese* **dialect**, has largely lost the battle against uniformity. While older townsfolk – many of whom still regard themselves as primarily Catalan – are attached to it, few of the post-1960s generations are at all adept, and the existence of evening classes for locals to learn or perfect their knowledge of *catalano* is a gauge of its present precarious state. The best way to hear the *algherese/catalano* dialect today is to drop in on one of the church services conducted in the local vernacular at the church of San Francesco (see p.175).

5

Modern times

After Sardinia was taken over by the **House of Savoy** in 1720, Alghero became increasingly marginalized. The destruction of its landward-facing walls in the nineteenth century was unable to arrest its steady decline, a process that was only halted in the 1960s, with the flow of new money into the town in the wake of its discovery and development as a package **tourist resort**. The last fifty years have seen the establishment of Sardinia's greatest concentration of hotels and restaurants in Alghero, with a string of new developments along the coast north of the centre. However, the town's remoteness from the mainland has enabled it to escape total mass-market annihilation, while its well-established port has ensured the continuation of the key role of fishing in the local economy.

Giardini Púbblici

Via Catalogna

Near the port, Alghero's **Giardini Púbblici** (Public Gardens) are the location of the tourist office and main bus stop, and are an obvious starting place for any exploration of the *centro stórico*. The shady and well-tended gardens are always busy with families, off-duty taxi drivers and chatting pensioners. A remnant of the old town's defensive structure lies at the bottom of the gardens, towards the port, where the huge hollow shell of the **Bastione della Maddalena** holds a tower embedded within the crumbling ruins, and is now a venue for open-air entertainment in summer, chiefly films, music and dance.

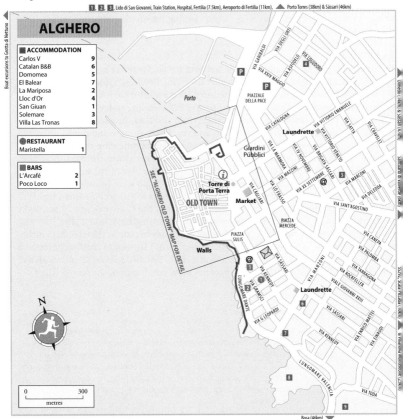

Torre di Porta Terra

Piazza Porta Terra • July & Aug Mon–Sat 9am–1pm & 4–11pm/midnight, Sun 10.30–1pm & 5–11pm; Sept–June Mon–Sat only: closes 8pm • Free • ☎ 079 973 4045, 🌐 smuovi.com

Any walkabout around the old town should take in the series of seven towers dominating Alghero's centre. One of the towers, the **Torre di Porta Terra**, stands at the top of the public gardens, originally intended to guard one of the two gates into the walled town. Also known as the Torre del Portal, it has been identified by some as the medieval *Torre dels Ebreus*, erected by Alghero's Jewish community. Today, the tower has an incongruous Art Deco-style war memorial, and a tourist bookshop has been installed inside, from which you can gain access to the roof for a good view over Alghero's rooftops.

Piazza Cívica

The main square of the old town, **Piazza Cívica**, is a traffic-free but bustling arena of locals and tourists, lined with bars and boutiques. The elongated piazza provides access to the port through the **Porta a Mare**, one of the two main gateways of the old city. The opposite side of the square holds the Gothic **Palazzo d'Albis** (*Palau Albis*), the former governor's palace with mullioned Gothic and Renaissance windows, from which the emperor Charles V addressed the crowds in 1541 before embarking for Algiers on his campaign against the Turks. He is said to have uttered the words, long cherished in local lore as granting instant nobility to the assembled throng, "*Estade todos caballeros*" ("You are all knights"). The palazzo now contains private apartments.

The Cattedrale

Piazza Duomo • **Interior** Daily 7am–7.30pm • Guided tours (free) Feb–Oct Mon–Fri 10am–noon & 4–6pm • **Campanile** Via Príncipe Umberto • May, June & Sept Mon & Fri 11am–1pm & 5–8pm, Tues–Thurs & Sat 11am–1pm; Oct–April by arrangement; may close in bad weather • €3; €5 with Museo Diocesano • ☎ 079 973 3041

From Piazza Cívico, Via Manno leads to the four tall, fluted columns that dominate the white Neoclassical facade of Alghero's **Cattedrale**, a grandiose entry somewhat out of keeping with the sixteenth-century edifice. Founded in 1510, seven years after Alghero was promoted to city status, the cathedral was not fully completed or consecrated until 1730, though it had long since been established as the customary place for Spanish viceroys to take a preliminary oath before assuming office in Cágliari.

The interior

The **interior** is a bit of a hotchpotch: the alternating pillars and columns on either side of the lofty nave survive from the original construction, the impressive dome and creamy marble central altar date from the eighteenth century, and the lateral chapels are predominantly Neoclassical or Baroque. Behind the altar, an ambulatory said to derive architecturally from the Islamic mosque of the old Moorish city gives onto five radiating chapels, also part of the original building. The left transept holds the marble funerary monument of the Savoy duke of Monferrato, brother of King Carlo Felice, dated 1799.

The exterior and belltower

To see an original part of the cathedral's **Gothic exterior**, walk round to the back of the building, where there's a lovely carved portal. The doorway sits at the base of the octagonal, sixteenth-century **campanile**, which can be climbed for stunning views.

Museo Diocesano

Piazza Duomo • Early Jan to March Thurs–Sat 10.30am–1pm & 4.30–7.30pm; April–June, Sept & Oct daily except Wed 10am–1pm & 5–8pm; July & Aug Mon–Sat 10.30am–1pm & 6–9pm; Nov to late Dec open for groups by arrangement, late Dec to early Jan 11am–1pm & 4–7pm • €3.50; €5 with cathedral campanile • ☎ 079 973 3041

5

Close to the cathedral, the former church of the Rosario holds the **Museo Diocesano**, a collection of sacred treasures connected to the cathedral and other churches in town, including paintings, Catalan silverware, wooden statues and crucifixes. The old stone walls and Baroque ornament of the church make a fitting setting for the crosses and cups, whose wide-ranging provenance – from Barcelona, Palermo and even Palestine – testifies to Alghero's one-time importance at the heart of the Mediterranean world. Exhibitions are also held here.

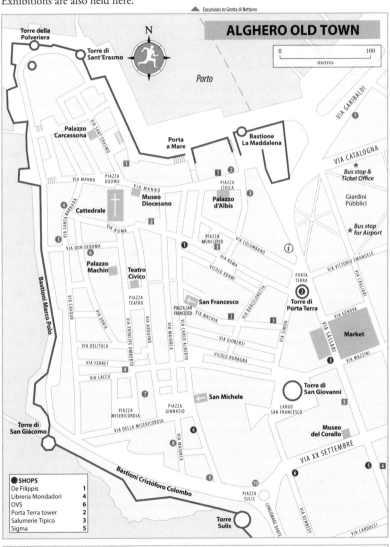

● SHOPS	
De Filippis	1
Libreria Mondadori	4
OVS	6
Porta Terra tower	2
Salumerie Tipico	3
Sigma	5

■ ACCOMMODATION		● RESTAURANTS				■ CAFÉS & BARS	
Aigua	3	Al Tuguri	8	Casablanca	7	Café Latino	1
La Margherita	4	Al Vecchio Mulino	6	Il Ghiotto	2	Diva Café	3
La Terrazza sul		Angedras	5	Il Pavone	10	Jamaica Inn	4
Porto	1	Bar Milese	1	La Lépanto	9	La Bajada	2
San Francesco	2	Bella Napoli	3	Mabrouk	4	Pasticceria Ciro	5

Palazzo Carcassona

Via Sant'Erasmo

North of Piazza Duomo along Via Sant'Erasmo, or accessible from the bastions, the elegantly austere **Palazzo Carcassona** is worth a swift detour to admire its well-restored exterior enlivened by brown-and-white patterns around the windows. The palace was probably owned by the Jewish Carcassona family before their eviction in 1492; the ground floor is now a restaurant, the rest apartments.

Via Príncipe Umberto

Of the long lanes running the length of the old town, **Via Príncipe Umberto** is one of the quietest and most attractive. Notable buildings include, on the right, the decrepit seventeenth-century **Palazzo Machin** at no. 9–11, still retaining its Catalan-Gothic windows and Renaissance portal. Farther along, Piazza Teatro holds the eighteenth-century **Teatro Cívico**, the venue for dramatic performances in winter.

Via Carlo Alberto

Stretching between Piazza Cívica and Piazza Sulis, **Via Carlo Alberto** is the busiest of old Alghero's lanes, crowded with amblers browsing among the succession of tourist shops and bars. Many of the shops are jewellery stores, specializing in the coral for which Sardinia's northwestern coast in general and Alghero in particular are famous. The street also holds a couple of the town's most important **churches**.

San Francesco

Piazza San Francesco • Mon–Sat 7.15am–12.30pm & 5–6.30pm, Sun 7.15am–10.30pm & 5–6.30pm

Halfway along Via Carlo Alberto, the fifteenth-century church of **San Francesco** is architecturally the finest of Alghero's churches. The building encompasses several different styles, its Gothic campanile and some of the lateral chapels – survivals from the original construction – blending successfully with the Renaissance ceiling, round arches and swirling carved windows. The centrepiece of the dim interior is a polychrome marble altar, though this vies for attention with a horribly emaciated (*grattugiato*) figure of Christ bound to a column to the left; it looks modern, but is in fact from the seventeenth century. Behind the statue, prayers and personal items – even jewellery – are pinned up as votive offerings.

To the left of the altar, the **presbytery**, with its happily irregular cross-vaulted Gothic ceiling, gives onto a simple **cloister** with round, rough-hewn arches originating from the beginning of the fourteenth century. In summer, the cloister is an occasional venue for alfresco classical concerts. **Services in Catalan** are held in the church on Sundays (July & Aug 8pm; Sept–June 7pm).

San Michele

Via Carlo Alberto • Open daily 30min before Mass, currently taking place Mon–Fri 10am, Sat 10am & 7pm, Sun 9am & 7pm

The majolica-tiled cupola of **San Michele** is a sparkling feature of Alghero's skyline, though the haughty interior remains true to its seventeenth-century Jesuit origins. One of the elaborately stuccoed and decorated chapels contains a sculpture of St Michael slaying the dragon; look out also for the gilt wooden choir box over the main entrance.

Piazza Sulis and around

At the southern end of Via Carlo Alberto, **Piazza Sulis** marks the end of the old town and the start of the traffic. Nonetheless, it makes an airy, pleasant space by the seashore, a meeting point for the town's youth – and their bikes. The square's main feature is the sturdy **Torre Sulis**, also called Torre dello Sperone (*Torre de l'Esperò Reial* in Catalan),

5

which once served as a place of detention and is named after its most celebrated prisoner, Vincenzo Sulis, incarcerated here for thirty years for his part in the Cágliari uprising of 1794–5.

Running northwards off Piazza Sulis, Via Kennedy extends a few metres to Largo San Francesco, site of another of Alghero's defensive towers, **Torre di San Giovanni**, the venue for occasional exhibitions.

Museo del Corallo

Via XX Settembre 8 • Tues–Sun: July & Aug 10am–1pm & 5–8pm ; Sept–June 10am–1pm & 4.30–7pm • €3 • ☎ 339 468 7754

Alghero has long been famed as a centre of the coral trade, and the **Museo del Corallo** allows you to get to grips with the subject. It's both informative – videos and illustrated panels show the growth and harvesting of the organism – and arresting, with numerous exquisite specimens, as well as examples of quartz, celestine, malachite, amber and other minerals and resins. There are also some dazzling items of coral jewellery on display, though disappointingly little on the destruction of coral reefs and the measures put in place to preserve them.

The bastioni

On its sea-facing side, the old town is encompassed by a stout girdle of protective walls, or **bastioni**, that make a serene place to escape Alghero's bustle and savour the views out to Capo Caccia – especially memorable at sunset. You'll pass three more of the town's defensive towers along the way: **Torre di San Giácomo**, **Torre della Polveriera** and **Torre di Sant'Erasmo**. There's a lot more coming and going here on summer evenings, with streams of people drifting between the bars and restaurants.

The port and seafront

Spread out below the lofty walls on the north side of Alghero's old quarter, the wide, usually thronged quays of the **port** are nudged by tourist excursion craft, fishing boats and ranks of sleek yachts. Farther north, an easy walk or bike ride from town, the sandy beaches around **Lido di San Giovanni** aren't the best in the vicinity, but they're clean and convenient; some are private lidos, where you'll pay around €10 per day for an umbrella and two sunloungers.

Otherwise, it's worth carrying on to the pinewoods and dunes of **Maria Pia**, about 2km north of Alghero, where the beach gently slopes into the shallow and sheltered bay – good for families, with shade provided by the trees and a couple of bars open in summer. A drive or a bike- or bus-ride further up the coast brings you to the area's best swimming spots (see p.185). Don't expect much elbow room in any of these places in peak season, however.

ARRIVAL AND DEPARTURE   **ALGHERO**

BY PLANE

Alghero's Aeroporto di Fertilia (☎ 079 935 282, ⓦ aeroporto dialghero.it) lies 10km north of town, outside Fertilia, and is served by Alitalia (☎ 892 010, ⓦ alitalia.com), easyJet (☎ 199 201 840, ⓦ easyJet.com) and Ryanair (☎ 899 552 589, ⓦ ryanair.com), among other companies. The terminal has banks with ATMs and a post office that can also change cash.

Transport from/to the airport Local Al.F.A buses to and from town leave hourly until 10.30pm (Alghero) or 11pm (airport), stopping in both Fertilia and at Alghero's

train and bus stations. At the airport, you can buy tickets from one of the machines in the terminal (€1), for which coins are required, or on board (€1.50). In the other direction, the buses run from Alghero's Via Cágliari at the Giardini Púbblici. Buy tickets from a *tabacchino* or from the office on Via Catalogna. The journey takes around 30min. Taxis into Alghero cost €20–25.

Long-distance services There are also departures (some of them summer-only) from the airport to other major towns and resorts operated by different companies, including ARST (☎ 800 865 042, ⓦ arst.sardegna.it),

Digitur (☎079 262 039, �🌐digitur.it), Logudoro Tours (☎079 281 728, �🌐logudorotours.it), Redentours (☎0784 30 325, �🌐redentours.com) and Sardabus (�🌐sardabus.it).
Destinations (from airport) Alghero (Al.F.A; 5.20am–11pm hourly; 30min); Bosa (ARST; Mon–Sat 3–4 daily, Sun 1–4 daily; 1hr 15min); Cágliari (Logudoro Tours; June–Oct 2 daily; 3hr 30min); Castelsardo (Digitur; June–Sept 1 daily; 1hr 15min); Nuoro (Redentours; 2 daily; 2hr 25min); Oristano (Logudoro Tours; June–Oct 2 daily; 2hr 10min); Santa Teresa Gallura (Digitur; June–Sept 1 daily; 2hr 30min); Sássari (ARST; 9 daily; 30min); Stintino (Sardabus; June–Sept 5 daily; 45min).

BY CAR

If you're driving into town, try to park before reaching the old centre as spaces here are extremely limited; the best bet is the portside car park off Via Garibaldi, just north of the centre, or across the road in Piazzale della Pace. Alternatively, park anywhere you see a space, avoiding yellow (reserved) lines; it's free to park between white lines, but between blue lines you must purchase a ticket from a meter: €0.50 for 30min and €1/hr (May–Sept daily 9am–midnight; Oct–April daily 9am–2pm & 4–8pm).

BY TRAIN

The small station for ARST services to and from Sássari (9–12 daily; 35min) lies some way north of the centre on Via Don Minzoni. It's served by frequent local buses (buy tickets from the bar inside the station): Bus Al.F.A. (hourly) runs into town from the bus stop across the road; in the opposite direction, the AF runs to Fertilia, for those heading straight to the hostel or campsite there. To get to the station from the centre of town, catch a bus at the Giardini Púbblici or on the seafront.

Train information Information on ARST trains to Sássari is available by calling ☎079 950 785 or visiting �🌐arst .sardegna.it; for FS services from Sássari, call ☎892 021 or see �🌐trenitalia.com.

BY BUS

Local and regional buses arrive at and depart from Via Catalogna, by the Giardini Púbblici. All buses are operated by ARST; tickets must be bought beforehand from the ticket office next to the bus stop at the Giardini Púbblici.
Destinations Bosa (2–5 daily; 55min); Capo Caccia (Mon–Sat 1–3 daily, Sun April–Sept 1–3 daily; 50min); Macomer (Mon–Sat 1 daily; 2hr); Porto Conte (Mon–Sat 6–10 daily, Sun 3–10 daily; 30min); Porto Ferro (2–4 daily; 35min); Porto Torres (5–7 daily; 45min–1hr); Sássari (Mon–Sat 10 daily, Sun 4 daily; 1hr); Villanova Monteleone (Mon–Sat 7–8 daily; June–Sept also Sun 3 daily; 45min).

GETTING AROUND

By bus Alghero is easily explored on foot, though you may use local buses for journeys to the train station, the local campsite, Fertilia and the local beaches – service AF (every 40min) is useful for the beaches north of the centre off Via Lido. Tickets from *tabacchi* and some bars cost €1 (valid 1hr 30min), otherwise pay €1.50 on board. ARST buses link Alghero to the beaches of Le Bombarde and Lazzaretto, to Porto Conte and Capo Caccia. Call ☎079 950 458 for all enquiries.

By bike A bike is good for short trips around the town and its environs. You can rent bikes at MTB, near the public gardens at Via Catalogna 28 (☎079 952 992; €8–20/day) and Raggi di Sardegna, Via Maiorca 119 (☎334 305 2480; €7–12/day).

By car You don't need a car to get around town, but

Alghero is a useful place to pick up a rental vehicle for exploring further afield. Most of the rental agencies have offices out at Fertilia airport, such as Avis (☎079 935 064, �🌐avis.com), Europcar (☎079 935 032, �🌐europcar.it) and Maggiore (☎079 935 045, �🌐maggiore.it). Avis also has an office at Via Garibaldi 87, Quarté Sayal (☎079 914 4557), Europcar has one at Via Vittorio Emanuele 57 (☎079 981 630) and the local firm Rent-a-Car Express – which can deliver and collect – is at Via Satta 52 (☎079 985 937, �🌐rentacarexpress.it). Rates start from around €60/day, €115/two days, with unlimited mileage – though it's worth hunting around.

By taxi Central taxi ranks are on Via Vittorio Emanuele, Giardini Púbblici, Piazza Sulis and the port. For 24hr service, call ☎079 989 2028.

INFORMATION

Tourist office Alghero's main information office (April–Sept Mon–Sat 8am–8pm, Sun 10am–1pm; Oct–March Mon–Sat 8am–8pm; ☎079 979 054, �🌐alghero-turismo .it), at the top end of the Giardini Púbblici, is probably the

most efficient on the island, with helpful, multilingual staff equipped with reams of maps, accommodation lists and sight details.

TOURS AND ACTIVITIES

Boat tours A choice of tours is advertised at booths on the port between March and Oct for €30–60. The main company, Navisarda (☎079 950 603, ⛵navisarda.it),

offers a full-day cruise along the coast with lunch and a swimming stop (€40).

Diving Adventure Diving, Via Aggius 14 (☎079 973 9039,

5

ⓦadventurediving.it); Blue Service Alghero, La Mariposa campsite, Via Lido 18 (ⓣ342 757 1434, ⓦblueservice alghero.it); Nautisub, Via Garibaldi 45 (ⓣ079 952 433 or ⓣ330 935 350, ⓦnautisub.com). One dive costs €40–65, two or three dives work out cheaper. There's another dive centre at Porto Conte (see p.186).

Il Cocchio This "horse-drawn" – actually electrically-operated – coach performs a circuit of the old centre in around 25min, leaving from the port every 30min or so. It features a taped commentary in English (March–Oct; €5, €3 for 2 to 10-year-olds; ⓣ338 372 997).

Il Tróttolo To view or reach the coast in comfort, board this open-top double-decker that follows the coast as far as Capo Caccia 3–6 times daily. It's a hop-on, hop-off service that stops at beaches en route (April–Oct; €18 valid for 24hr, €25 for 48hr, €12/€18 for children aged 6–14, €56/€70 family ticket; ⓣ329 875 5555, ⓦtrottolo.it). They also run a Sun day-trip to Bosa, leaving from Alghero's port

at 9.40am and returning at 5.40pm – book ahead (May–Sept; €20, €12 for children aged 3–12).

Trenino Catalano If you've got kids, or you're just tired, you might want to tour the old town on this miniature "train" leaving from the port (April–Oct; €5, €3 for 8 to 14-year-olds; ⓣ336 691 836).

Walking tours Cooperativa Smuovi, Torre di Porta Terra (ⓣ339 468 7754 or ⓣ329 438 5947, ⓦsmuovi.com), offers self-guided tours of Old Alghero using MP3 devices in various languages, lasting around 2hr (€7.50 for first audioguide, €5.50 for second).

Sailing excursions You can embark on sea trips from the port on 8hr cruises aboard the *Andrea Jensen*, a traditional 24m sailing ketch, with swimming and snorkelling stops (May to mid-Oct; €99, €49 for children aged 5–12; ⓣ338 970 8139, ⓦajsailing.com). Prices include food, drink and snorkelling equipment. Groups are small, and Italian, Spanish and English are spoken.

ACCOMMODATION

Alghero's choice of accommodation is extensive, though booking is essential at any time; availability can be especially scarce and **hotel** prices rocket in high summer, while most places close altogether in winter. However, the resort also has a profusion of more affordable **B&Bs**, which tend to remain open all year. Most places lie outside the historic core, either spread out along the seafront to either side or in the grid of parallel streets that make up the new town. The few places in the old centre don't have parking facilities. The local **campsite** is an easy bus ride north from the centre. There are two other sites 7km along the coast at Fertilia (see p.184) and the more remote Torre del Porticciolo (see p.186), a further 5km north. Fertilia also has a **hostel**.

Aigua Via Machin 22 ⓣ340 077 7688, ⓦaigua.it; map p.174. Six charming mini-apartments are available in two central, tastefully renovated buildings with exposed-stone walls and wooden floors and ceilings. The compact rooms come equipped with basic kitchen facilities for self-service breakfasts. Closed Jan & Feb. **€85**

Carlos V (Carlos Quinto) Lungomare Valencia 24 ⓣ079 972 0600, ⓦhotelcarlosv.it; map p.172. One of the plushest hotels in town, this five-star pampers with spacious, balconied rooms, most overlooking a good-sized saltwater pool surrounded by palm trees. Official rates are high, but you can find bargains online and in low season (it's worth paying the supplement for sea-facing rooms). **€274**

Catalan B&B Via Manzoni 41 ⓣ347 833 5230, ⓦalgherocasavacanze.it; map p.172. Modern apartment in the new town, a 10min walk from the old centre. There are three rooms – one with its own bathroom (the others have washbasins), one with a balcony, all with a/c, abundant breakfasts and limited cooking facilities. A separate apartment with a roof terrace is also available to rent. **€80**

Domomea Via Vittorio Veneto 47 ⓣ079 973 2011, ⓦhoteldomomea.com; map p.172. It's modern and business-like, but this four-star hotel in a quiet street 10min walk east of the old town has a friendly atmosphere and helpful staff. Rooms are a good size and well equipped. There's a small rooftop pool too. **€145**

El Balear Lungomare Dante 32 ⓣ079 975 229,

ⓦhotelelbalear.com; map p.172. This three-star hotel, a pleasant 15min walk south of the old centre, has an enviable position facing the sea near two (rocky) beaches, and a courtyard-patio, but some rooms are small. Lunch and dinner each cost €22, and bikes are available to rent. Closed Nov–March. **€96**

La Margherita Via Sássari 70 ⓣ079 979 006, ⓦhotellamargherita.it; map p.174. Close to the old town, this family-run hotel is old-fashioned in the best sense, while boasting spa facilities and an indoor pool in the basement, and a grand roof terrace where breakfast is served in summer. Rooms have fridges and front-facing ones have a small balcony, with the best views on the fourth floor. **€115**

La Terrazza sul Porto Piazza Cívica 19 ⓣ079 973 1054, ⓦbblaterrazzasulportoalghero.it; map p.174. Located on the old town's central piazza, this modern, fourth-floor B&B (there's a lift) has four rooms with their own balconies. There's a communal terrace where breakfast is taken in summer, with fantastic harbour views. **€120**

Lloc d'Or Via Logudoro 26 ⓣ334 289 7130, ⓦllocdor .com; map p.172. This friendly B&B a short walk from the old town consists of two large and airy rooms with private bathrooms, plus a self-contained apartment. There's a small kitchen for guests' use, and breakfasts on the patio include fresh fruit and yoghurt. No credit cards. Closed Jan & Feb. **€70**

★San Francesco Via Machin 2 ⓣ079 980 330, ⓦsan francescohotel.com; map p.174. The only hotel in the old

APARTMENT RENTALS

If you're staying in Alghero for a week or more, consider renting a **private apartment**; off-season rates are particularly favourable, but don't expect to find many bargains or availability in August unless you've booked far ahead. Agencies include Casa Vacanze Cau, Via Gaudì 8 (☎ 079 952 478, ⊛ appartamenticau.it); Florida, Via Carbónia 24 (☎ 079 950 500, ⊛ floridacasavacanze.com); and Gli Eucalipti, Via Lido 127 (☎ 079 951 187, ⊛ residenceucalipti .it) – the tourist office has a full list. **Prices** in summer are generally €450–850 per week for a one-room apartment for two. Alternatively, Solemare, near the train station at Via Iglésias 1 (☎ 340 290 9588, ⊛ algherosolemare.com) has modern studio apartments available for shorter periods from €72 per night.

town was formerly a convent attached to San Francesco church, and preserves a reclusive air. The 21 rooms are small but clean and quiet, with telephones, a/c and private bathrooms. Breakfast is eaten in the cloisters. Drivers must find their own parking space. Closed Nov & Dec. **€100**

San Giuan Via Angioy 2 ☎ 079 951 222, ⊛ hotelsangiuan .it; map p.172. A 15min walk north of the centre, this small three-star hotel doesn't have a great deal of character and some of the plain rooms suffer from traffic noise, but it has a roof terrace, lies steps away from Alghero's main beach and has reasonable rates. Some rooms have balconies. There's no restaurant. Closed Nov–March. **€110**

Villa Las Tronas Lungomare Valencia 1 ☎ 079 981 818, ⊛ hotelvillalastronas.it; map p.172. Grandly sited on a promontory a 10min walk south of the centre, this castellated former royal residence from 1884 is full of

character, still retaining a baronial air with its elegant old furnishings. There's also an excellent restaurant, a spa, a gym, indoor and outdoor pools and a rocky beach. **€350**

CAMPSITE

La Mariposa Via Lido 22 ☎ 079 950 480, ⊛ lamariposa .it; map p.172. A couple of kilometres north of the centre, this usually busy and crowded campsite has direct access to the beach, part of which is sectioned off for campers. Eucalyptus and pine trees provide shade and there's a bar, restaurant and shop, as well as a diving centre, windsurfing, canoes, bikes and scooters to rent. Bungalows, caravans and simple cabins with bunks are also available (from €32). Local bus #AF runs here from the public gardens; alternatively, walk 10min from the train station. Closed Oct–March. Pitches **€30**

EATING

The quality of Alghero's restaurants is very impressive – the presence of the fishing port ensures a regular supply of fresh **seafood** (spring and winter are the best seasons), including lobster (*aragosta*), a local speciality. The local cuisine also makes good use of Catalan culinary traditions – you might find paella, and for dessert, *crema catalana*, a sort of caramelized custard. The town is further blessed by its proximity to some of Sardinia's most famous vineyards. Note that you'll usually need to book ahead in August. For the freshest fruit and vegetables, drop in at the **market** (Mon–Sat 8am–1pm) off Via Sássari, between Via Génova and Via Mazzini.

Al Tuguri Via Maiorca 115 ☎ 079 976 772, ⊛ altuguri .it; map p.174. Minuscule restaurant – two rooms on two floors – specializing in authentic Catalan cuisine. The name is dialect meaning "old abandoned house", helping to explain the faintly rustic ambience. It's select and chic, but makes a memorable splurge. Pasta dishes are around €14, mains €20–25; alternatively, go for the five-course sampling menu (€45), which comes with a vegetarian option (€40). March– Oct Mon–Sat 12.30–2pm & 7.30–10pm.

★ **Al Vecchio Mulino** Via Don Deroma 3 ☎ 079 977 254; map p.174. The locals' choice: low-vaulted rooms in the old town, with friendly staff and a good selection of white wines. For a change from seafood, try the *spaghetti al Vecchio Mulino*, made with mushrooms, ham and cream; pizzas are also available. Most fish and meat dishes cost €12–16. Mid–June to mid–Sep daily 7pm–midnight; mid-Sept to mid-June closed Tues, also closed all Nov &

two weeks in Jan.

Angedras Via Cavour 31 and Bastioni Marco Polo 41 ☎ 079 973 5078, ⊛ angedrasrestaurant.it; map p.174. Part of a smart, modern hotel, this restaurant has a large, contemporary-looking dining room as well as space on the *bastioni* for lunching alfresco or soaking up memorable sunsets. The menu is seafood-based, including lobster and swordfish. There's a €16 lunchtime menu, otherwise starters are €10–16, mains €14–18. April–Oct daily noon–2.45pm & 7–11.30pm.

Bar Milese Via Garibaldi 11 ☎ 079 952 419; map p.174. Locals flock here for the *focacce* – enormous chunks of crusty bread filled to overflowing with cheese, olives, anchovies, aubergines or tuna, according to taste – all at €2.50. Toasts and salads are also available, and there's a full bar service and seating outside. July & Aug daily 7am– midnight; Sept–June closed Tues.

5

Bella Napoli Piazza Cívica 29 ☎ 079 983 014; map p.174. Popular Neapolitan-run ristorante/pizzeria, with generous portions, good salads and tables in the square; traces of an ancient *frantoio*, or olive-mill, are visible inside. Pizzas (€7–13) are also available at lunchtime; mains are around €16. Jan & Feb daily except Wed noon–midnight; March–Dec daily, same hours..

★**Casablanca** Via Príncipe Umberto 72 ☎ 079 983 353; map p.174. With vaulted rooms, this is a great venue for a straightforward pizza (also available at lunchtime) or pasta dish in a convivial atmosphere with good service; mains are €10–15. June–Sept Tues, Wed & Fri–Sun 12.30–2.30 & 7.30–11.30pm, Thurs 7.30–11.30; Oct–May also closed Wed.

Il Ghiotto Piazza Cívica 23 ☎ 079 974 820; map p.174. At lunchtime, this place has a *tavola calda* where pastas, meats, salads and seafood (mostly under €10) are served buffet-style – a good option for a swift snack. In the evening, it's a conventional restaurant serving grills and other dishes for around €10, and there's a fine selection of Sardinian wines. Easter–Nov daily noon–3pm & 7.30–10.30pm; closed Wed Nov–Easter & two weeks in Dec.

Il Pavone Piazza Sulis 3 ☎ 079 979 584; map p.174. An exclusive enclave to sample some of the best of *la cucina algherese*, including *antipasti*, paella and vegetarian dishes. First courses weigh in at around €15, mains at €17–25, and there's a fixed-price menu for €50. The *gelati* are astounding

– flavours include wild fennel and spicy coffee. Dine on the patio or in the two small, mirrored rooms, which are filled with antiques. Daily noon–3pm & 7.30pm–midnight.

La Lépanto Via Carlo Alberto 135 ☎ 079 979 116; map p.174. With large windows looking across Piazza Sulis and out to sea, this long-established seafood restaurant is renowned for its lobster – though it's pricey. The fresh fish is enticingly displayed, meat dishes are also excellent, and there's a delectable range of Sardinian sweets. Count on €50–60/head. June–Sept daily 12.30–3pm & 7pm–midnight; Oct–Jan & March–May closed Tues.

★**Mabrouk** Via Santa Barbara 4 ☎ 079 970 174; map p.174. This is about as near as Alghero comes to a cosy neighbourhood trattoria, where there's no written menu but a democratic €40 fixed-price dinner for everyone – including unlimited house wine and limoncello. It's all seafood: a typical meal might start with five *antipasti*, followed by three types of pasta, the catch of the day, prawns, calamari and delicious desserts. Mid-March to June, Sept & Oct Tues–Sun 8–11pm; July & Aug open daily.

Maristella Via Kennedy 9 ☎ 079 978 172; map p.172. Reasonable prices, tasty meat and fish dishes and terrific desserts at this trattoria near Piazza Sulis. It's popular with locals, so worth booking, especially if you want pavement seating. Pastas are €9–12, mains mostly €10–15. April–Sept daily 12.15–2.30pm & 7.30–10.30pm; Oct–March closed Sun eve.

DRINKING AND NIGHTLIFE

CAFÉS, BARS AND BIRRERIAS

Alghero's abundance of bars and cafés keep going into the small hours in summer, though things get pretty quiet out of season. For sunset views, opt for one of the places lining the town's ramparts. The following are some of the best choices staying open all year.

Café Latino Piazza Duomo 6 ☎ 079 976 541; map p.174. Stylish place for an evening aperitif, with outside tables beneath parasols on the walls overlooking the port. Snacks and ice creams are also served, though prices are high. June–Sept daily 9am–2am; closed Tues Oct–May.

Diva Café Piazza Municipio 1 ☎ 079 982 306; map p.174. Tucked up a side street off Piazza Cívica, this long-established locals' bar has tables outside. It serves toasties and other snacks (including pizzas and pasta dishes in summer). June–Sept daily 8.30am–2am, closed Sun Oct–May.

Jamaica Inn Via Príncipe Umberto 57 ☎ 340 256 1057; map p.174. This pub – right in the thick of things – is a fun stop for beers and cocktails until late. There's an open-air terrace across the road where burgers and chips are served, and live music Fri and Sat. June–Sept daily 7.30pm–2am; closed Tues Oct–May.

★**La Bajada** Via Roma 22 ☎ 348 275 5038; map p.174. A quiet nook just a few steps away from the bustle, this is a

cool place for a quiet drink, best at night. Snacks and meals are available, from *panini* to salads and tasty ravioli. Mon–Sat 10am–12.30am, Sun 5pm–midnight.

L'Arcafé Lungomare Dante 6 ☎ 079 982 662; map p.172. Seafront hangout with regular DJs and live music at weekends throughout the year (daily in Aug). Daily: June–Sept 8am–2am; Oct–March 10.30am–10.30pm.

Pasticceria Ciro Via Sássari 35 ☎ 079 979 960; map p.174. Treat yourself to the best pastries in town at this place beloved of locals, from *bigné* (éclairs) to *cannoli* (ricotta-filled tubes), traditional Sard biscuits and luscious fruit concoctions. Ice creams are also available and there's great coffee too. Tues–Sun 7.15am–8.30pm.

Poco Loco Via Gramsci 8 ☎ 079 983 604, ⓦ pocoloco alghero.com; map p.172. Beers, pizzas, steaks, live blues and jazz (usually Fri & Sat in winter), and general carousing are on offer in this spacious hall off Piazza Sulis. There's bowling upstairs (not Wed) too. Daily 7pm–late.

CLUBS

Clubs and discos in Alghero open in summer only (but may reopen for New Year's Eve). None is very central, with some attached to hotels and campsites. The music is predominantly commercial, house and Latin. Count on about €15 entry,

5

FESTIVALS AND ENTERTAINMENT IN ALGHERO

Alghero's Spanish inheritance is particularly manifest during its **Easter** festivities, when the rituals of the *Misteri* (representing the Passion of Christ) and *Incontru* (the symbolic meeting of the Virgin with Christ) are enacted, with statues carried through town amid solemn processions. In contrast, **Carnival** is a feisty affair, involving plenty of masked antics and the burning of the *pupazzo* (a "guy" representing a French soldier), ceremonially put on trial and burnt on the bonfire on Shrove Tuesday. May sees a steady procession of pilgrims to the sanctuary of Valverde, 6km east of town, in thanksgiving for the Madonna's intervention at times of disaster. A major milestone in the Italian year is **Ferragosto** (August 15), in which the Feast of the Assumption is celebrated with a range of musical and folkloric events, fireworks and boating competitions.

Religion and secular games are mixed at the **Festa di Sant'Agostino** day on August 28, and there are waterborne events and feasting organized as part of the **Sagra dei Pescatori**, or Fisherman's Fair, on a Saturday or Sunday in September, the precise date varying from year to year. Towards the end of September, Alghero's patron saint, St Michael, is commemorated in the four-day **Nit de Sant Miquel**, with open-air concerts and dance performances, culminating in a spectacular fireworks display over the harbour.

Less specifically, a wide-ranging programme of cultural **events** takes place from July to September in various parts of the town, including concerts, cabaret and folk dances, often free. In particular, look out for **open-air classical concerts** and other performances held at the Bastione della Maddalena and at the church of San Francesco in July and August; the tourist office has details.

which may include the first drink; subsequent drinks cost €5–15. See also *Poco Loco* (see p.180).

Il Ruscello 2km northeast of Alghero on the Olmedo road ☎ 328 958 8788. Frequented mainly by the 18–25 age group, this place features Latin and house music on two open-air dancefloors, and has occasional live bands. From midnight: June & Sept Fri, Sat & some Suns; July & Aug Thurs–Sat & some Suns.

La Siesta Località Scala Piccada, 10km southeast of town on the SS292 Villanova road ☎ 079 980 137. With a pedigree dating back to the 1960s, this club is famous for its magnificent views over the coast. It caters for a mixed audience, with four dancefloors playing different sounds. An ARST bus service there and back (15min; €1.20 one-way) operates from Via Catalogna, currently leaving at 2.10am and coming back at 5am and 6am – check with the tourist office – otherwise you'll have to depend on taxis, which may cost upwards of €30 each way. July & Aug Sat from midnight.

SHOPPING

De Filippis Via Carlo Alberto 23 ☎ 079 979 394. You'll find a huge choice of jewellery and ornaments fashioned from coral at this traditional shop, a stalwart of the local coral trade. Mon–Sat 9.30am–1pm & 5–8pm.

Libreria Mondadori Via Carlo Alberto 119 ☎ 079 980 496. A range of English books, guides and maps is sold here. July & Aug daily 9.30am–1pm & 4–midnight; Sept–June closes 9pm.

OVS Piazza Sulis ☎ 079 973 2096. Useful general store for clothes and accessories. Mon–Sat 9.30am–8.30pm, Sun 10am–1.30 & 4.30–8.30pm.

Porta Terra tower Piazza Porta Terra ☎ 079 989 7502. Tourist guides, maps and souvenirs are available here. July & Aug Mon–Sat 9am–1pm & 4–11pm/midnight, Sun 10.30–1pm & 5–11pm; Sept–June Mon–Sat only, closes 8pm.

Salumerie Tipico Via Sássari 25 ☎ 079 973 8801.

Quality cold meats, cheeses, wines and artisan breads. Mon–Sat 8am–2pm & 6–8pm.

Sigma Via Sássari 49 ☎ 079 601 0852. Supermarket with a good food hall. Mon–Sat 8.15am–1.45pm & 5–8.30pm, Sun 8.30am–1.30pm.

MARKETS

A daily food market occupies the block between Via Cágliari and Via Sássari, and Via Genova and Via Mazzini. Wed mornings see a large and lively general market along Viale Europa, near the Lido di San Giovanni, a great source of food, clothes and crafts. There's also a Sat morning general market on Via Fiume, Fertilia (see p.184). In summer, stalls selling local sweet delicacies – biscuits and pastries – among crafts and other knick-knacks, set up along Alghero's Via Garibaldi and at the port every night until late.

DIRECTORY

Hospital Ospedale Civile, Via Don Minzoni (☎ 079 995 5111). In an emergency, call ☎ 118.

Internet Mail Boxes Etc., Via XX Settembre 73 (Mon–Fri 9am–1pm & 4–7.30pm, Sat 9am–1pm; €1.50/15min),

5

offers internet access and printing services. Many bars in the centre have wi-fi.

Laundry Coin-operated laundries can be found at Via Sássari 113 (daily 9am–10.30pm) and Via Vittorio Veneto 3 (daily 9am–9.30pm). Both charge around €4/7kg.

Left luggage Valige Italia, Via Cágliari 31 (Mon 5–9pm, Tues–Sat 9am–1pm & 5–9pm; €3/half-day or €5/day/item).

Pharmacy Farmacia Cabras, at Piazza Sulis 10, is the largest central pharmacy (Mon–Sat 9am–1pm & 4–8.30pm, or 4–9pm in summer). Late-closing pharmacies are detailed on this and other pharmacy doors, with a telephone number for out-of-hours emergencies.

Post office Via Carducci, off Via Sássari (Mon–Fri 8.20am–7.05pm, Sat 8.20am–12.35pm). You can also change cash here.

Travel agency Agenzie Marittime Sarde, Via Vittorio Emanuele 27 (☎ 079 979 005).

Around Alghero

It's almost *de rigueur* for visitors to Alghero to make the trip out to the **Grotta di Nettuno**, one of Italy's most awesome cave complexes, at Capo Caccia, 15km due west of town. Most people visit on one of the frequent boats that leave from the port throughout the year. It's a thrilling ride along the coast, though it's cheaper to go the slow way by bus, and in some ways more rewarding, as you get to experience a dizzy descent down cliffs.

If you visit the grotto by boat, you'll pass the deep bay of **Porto Conte**, a beauty spot favoured by sailors, divers and windsurfers, part of which is set aside as a wildlife reserve. The land journey will take you through the low-key resort of **Fertilia**, 7km west of Alghero. Originally one of Mussolini's settlements linked to his land-reclamation programme, the town is remarkably quiet after the vivacity of Alghero, but it has some good eating and sleeping options, and is close to the region's best **beaches**.

Fertilia also lies near the area's most important nuraghic complex, **Nuraghe di Palmavera**, one of a pair of archeological sites that make a stimulating contrast to the sun-and-sea attractions of the rest of the region. The other site is **Anghelu Ruju**, set amid the endless vineyards that produce some of Sardinia's most renowned wines.

Farther afield, the undeveloped coast **south of Alghero** is a jagged and dramatic interplay of rock and sea, with a few select beaches tucked out of sight. There are no signs of habitation until you climb to the village of **Villanova Monteleone**, situated inland amid a bare mountainous terrain. In the opposite direction, the country **north of Alghero** is much flatter, but there are a couple of places worth exploring: **Lago di Baratz**, harbouring protected wildlife, and the abandoned mining centre of **Argentiera**, dominated by the eighteenth-century workings of a once flourishing industry.

Grotta di Nettuno

Capo Caccia • Daily: April & Oct 10am–6pm; May–Sept 9am–8pm; Nov–March 10am–4pm; tours (45min) depart hourly, on the hour; last tour 1hr before closing • €13 • ☎ 079 946 540

The most touted of the excursions from Alghero's port is west along the coast to the **Grotta di Nettuno**, or Neptune's Grotto, tucked below Capo Caccia, the sheer promontory visible from the town. The spectacular cliffs here are riddled by deep marine caves, including the Grotta Verde and Grotta dei Ricami – visited on some boat tours – but the most impressive is the Grotta di Nettuno itself, just west of the cape.

From the grotto's entrance, tours are led single-file by guides who provide commentaries in various languages. The long, snaking passage delves far into the rock, past fantastical, dramatically lit **stalagmites** and **stalactites** and along walls shimmering with phosphorescence. The guides relate the discovery of the cave complex by fishermen, pointing out imagined resemblances to helmeted warriors, toothy witches and popes. Less fanciful are the likenesses of organ pipes and columned cathedral interiors, after which two of the chambers are named. Signs point out that touching the rock and photography are

RIGHT BOSA (P.189) >

5

GETTING TO THE GROTTA DI NETTUNO

Boats operated by Navisarda (☎ 079 950 603, ⓦ navisarda.it) depart from Alghero hourly (June–Sept 9am–5pm, March–May & Oct 10am–3pm; call to check departure times); return tickets cost €16, excluding entry to the grotto. The boat ride takes thirty minutes, the entire visit and return trip taking about two and a half hours. Navisarda also operates hourly boat departures from Porto Conte (see p.186). Note that sailings are cancelled in bad weather. A cheaper alternative to the boat trip from Alghero is to drive, cycle or take the ARST **bus** to Capo Caccia from Via Catalogna, a fifty-minute ride (mid-June to Sept 3 daily; Oct to mid-June 1 daily; €2.50 one-way, €4.50 return). The Tróttolo open-top bus (see p.178) also runs here.

---

both forbidden, though neither injunction is strictly observed. The green colouring visible on some of the rock is mould, mostly caused by the lighting system.

Arriving via the land route, you'll have to negotiate a steep and spectacular 654-step descent down the **Escala del Cabirol** (the Catalan name means "goat's steps", presumably a reference to the only animal that could negotiate the perilous path before the construction of the stairway in 1954). The sheer cliff face and dark-blue water below are almost as impressive as the grotto interior itself. Try to time your arrival at the cave so that you don't have to wait up to an hour for the next tour: the descent takes ten to fifteen minutes. On the ascent back, you can reward yourself with a well-earned ice cream or thirst-quencher at the bar opposite the top of the steps.

Note that the grotto is closed in **rough weather** – worth checking beforehand as conditions on the cape may be dramatically different from those in town.

Fertilia

Providing a quiet contrast to bustling Alghero, **FERTILIA** appeals mostly for its curiosity value – the settlement is little changed since its creation by Mussolini in the 1930s, named to evoke the agricultural abundance that local land drainage would bring about (indeed, the rich agricultural land has produced some excellent wines, notably Torbato, a fairly sweet white). The arcaded **Via Pola** is the main avenue, connecting Piazza Venezia Giulia with the broad Piazzale San Marco next to the sea, marked by a memorial to the migrants who settled the area from the Friuli-Venezia region of northeast Italy. There's not much else in the town, and, out of season, little movement more frenetic than the slow padding of stray dogs.

Immediately east of town lies the long lagoon, **Stagno di Cálich**, collecting the outflow of two rivers. Its mouth is crossed by a medieval bridge sinking picturesquely into the water, known locally as the **Ponte Romano**, or "Roman" bridge; it has been superseded by a modern road bridge, and the old structure is now mainly used as a perch for fishermen.

ARRIVAL AND DEPARTURE   FERTILIA

On foot or by bike From Alghero, you can walk or cycle the seven flat kilometres along the seafront and past pine-fringed beaches, and there's even a protected bicycle lane running part of the way.

By bus Local AF and Al.F.A. buses leave for Fertilia from Alghero's Giardini Púbblici, seafront and train station; Il Tróttolo open-top bus (see p.178) also stops here.

ACCOMMODATION

Hostal de l'Alguer Via Parenzo, off Via Zara ☎ 079 930 478, ⓦ algherohostel.com. At the western end of town, this secluded hostel is modern and clean, if rather institutional. Dorms have four to ten beds and there are some private rooms with en-suite bathrooms. There are no cooking facilities, and evening meals are only available for groups. Non-HI-members can buy temporary membership for €2. Call first to check availability, as it's popular with groups even in low season. Dorms from €15; doubles €35

Laguna Blu SS127bis ☎ 079 930 111, ⓦ camping lagunablu.com. The larger of the area's two campsites, this has pitches idyllically located by the lagoon just outside

5

Fertilia, right across the road from the beach on the Alghero road and with a bus stop outside. It's shaded by pine and eucalyptus, and provides a shop, laundry and evening entertainment. Caravans (€85) and spacious bungalows (€120) are also available – choose one (or a pitch) away from the noisy bar/restaurant area. Closed mid-Oct to March. Pitches €30

Nurral SS291 ☎079 930 485, ⓦcampnurral.it. Much smaller than *Laguna Blu*, this site lies in pinewoods 100m further west along the Alghero–Fertilia road. It's fairly spartan and isn't so convenient for the beach, but it has friendly service and basic, clean caravans and self-catering bungalows to rent from €60/night in high season. Bike rental and free wi-fi are also available. Closed Oct to Feb. Pitches €20

EATING

Acquario Via Pola 34 ☎079 930 239. This traditional trattoria close to Piazzale San Marco has some tables outside and offers well-prepared meat and seafood dishes – try *spaghetti al cartoccio*: pasta with crab, squid and prawns cooked in the oven. Tourist menus are €20, €25 and €35, and pizzas are served in the evenings. Feb–Oct Tues–Sun 12.30–2.30pm & 7.30–10.30pm; Aug open daily.

Il Paguro Via Zara 13 ☎079 930 260. Near the hostel, this place has a covered terrace and does a good trade in grilled fish and pizzas. *Primi* (€10–15) and *secondi* (€12–20) include *spaghetti ai ricci* (with sea urchins) and grilled swordfish steak. Aug daily 12.30–2.30pm & 7.30pm–midnight; Sept–June closed Wed; may close in winter.

Nuraghe di Palmavera

SP127bis Porto Conte road • Daily: April & Oct 9am–6pm; May–Sept 9am–7pm; Nov–March 10am–2pm • €3.50, €6 with Anghelu Ruju (see p.186); audioguide €3; guided tour €2.50 • ☎329 438 5947, ⓦsmuovi.com • Served by Capo Caccia bus (not Sun in winter), leaving at 9.15am from the Giardini Púbblici, returning at about 12.30pm, and Il Tróttolo open-top bus (see p.178)

One of the largest nuraghic sites in this region, the **Nuraghe di Palmavera** lies just off the Fertilia–Porto Conte road, 10km west of Alghero. The site comprises a ruined palace dating from the fourteenth and thirteenth centuries BC, surrounded by fifty or so circular huts. It's well worth a visit, relatively well preserved and clearly laid out. The central tower is entered through a corridor with niches on either side, probably for sentries, and a trap door in the roof for extra security. The interior is of the rounded "tholos" type, with more shallow niches. An elliptical bastion and a minor tower were added to the main building in the second phase of construction, around the ninth century BC, when some of the round huts scattered outside the ramparts were also erected. Most of these were probably dwellings, but one, the **Capanna delle Riunioni**, distinguished by a low stone bench running round the circular walls, is believed to have been used for meetings and religious gatherings. The stool at the centre is a plaster copy of the original, now on display in Sássari's Museo Sanna (see p.205), along with numerous other finds from the site.

A third building phase took place a hundred or so years later, when more buildings were added, this time in limestone, as opposed to the softer sandstone of previous stages. The complex is thought to have been abandoned in the eighth or seventh century BC, possibly on account of fire. See Contexts for more on Sardinia's nuraghic culture (see p.307).

Le Bombarde and Lazzaretto beaches

Buses running to Porto Conte and Capo Caccia stop at the junctions for Le Bombarde and Lazzaretto, from where it's roughly a 10min walk down to the beaches; Il Tróttolo open-top bus (see p.178) goes right to the beaches

Side roads off the Fertilia–Porto Conte road lead to two of the area's best **beaches**, set in beautiful sandy coves facing Alghero across the bay. Both of these swimming spots can get quite busy in summer, with bars, toilets and beach equipment for rent between June and September (around €6/day for a parasol and sunlounger). Parking is charged in summer (€5 per half-day).

Two kilometres west of Fertilia, a straight, narrow track leads to the lovely crescent of **Le Bombarde**, a thin, white sandy strip with clear, clean water and a shallow seabed. **Windsurfing** courses are held here, and boards are available to rent, as well as pedalos

5

and canoes (€10 per hour each). The rocky seabed full of marine life makes it ideal for snorkelling, but beware of sharp rocks in places. The beach of **Lazzaretto**, guarded by a Spanish watchtower, lies about 700m farther west, at the end of another signposted turn-off close to Nuraghe di Palmavera (see p.185). Again, pedalos and canoes are available, and the water is crystal-clear. A string of smaller beaches lie beyond, which you can count on having pretty much to yourself on weekdays out of season.

Porto Conte and around

6–11 buses daily and Il Tróttolo open-top bus (see p.178) run here from Alghero

The lovely inlet of **Porto Conte** lies a couple of kilometres beyond Lazzaretto, about 10km west of Alghero. Romantically named Portus Nimpharum ("Port of the Nymphs") by the Romans, the intensely blue bay is a favourite anchorage for luxury yachts, which can be admired from the terraces of the clutch of top-notch hotels nestled among the trees. The road tracing the bay's eastern shore ends at a lighthouse; if you're looking for good bathing spots, follow the main road to Capo Caccia, turning left for the beach of **Baja di Conte** near the hotel of the same name. There are some scant **Roman ruins** here and **windsurfing** facilities on the beach.

Le Prigionette

Porto Conte • Daily: April–Sept 9am–7pm; Oct–March 9am–4/5pm • €3 on foot, €5 by car • ☎ 079 945 005, ⓦ parcodiportoconte.it •
Il Tróttolo open-top bus stops here (see p.178)

To the west of Porto Conte, the slopes of Monte Timidone (361m) hold **Le Prigionette**, a protected wildlife zone, roughly 12 square kilometres in size, clothed in a rich abundance of Mediterranean *macchia* (scrub). The park is home to miniature horses and asses from Asinara (see p.199), as well as assorted wild boar, deer, Barbary partridge and, around the coastal cliffs, griffon vultures and peregrine falcons. Forest trails wind through the area – you can explore the area on foot or join a **tour** lasting a couple of hours on an electric *trenino* (€20 per person; ☎ 331 340 0862, ⓦ exploralghero.it).

ARRIVAL AND ACCOMMODATION   **PORTO CONTE AND AROUND**

By bus From Alghero's Giardini Púbblici, 6–11 buses daily depart for Porto Conte (25min).

Torre del Porticciolo Santa Maria La Palma road ☎ 079 919 007, ⓦ torredelporticciolo.com. The largest campsite in the region (and the priciest), this is signposted on the west coast about 5km north of Porto Conte. It's a self-contained holiday complex, equipped with children's activities, two pools and a private beach in the round bay below, and it also organizes diving and riding holidays. Bungalows are available (from €74), with a minimum week-long stay in high season (though this could be relaxed). Closed Oct to mid-May. Pitches €33

ACTIVITIES

Boat excursions Navisarda (☎ 079 946 642, ⓦ navisarda .it) runs hourly trips to Neptune's Grotto from Cala Dragunara, an inlet on the western arm of Porto Conte, between June and Sept from 9.30am to 5.30pm (also March–May & Oct by arrangement); return tickets cost €14, excluding entry to the grotto. The boat ride takes about 10min, the entire visit and return trip is 1hr 30min. Sailings may be cancelled in bad weather.

Diving Diving Porto Conte, Porto Conte (☎ 079 942 122 or ☎ 340 753 8939, ⓦ divingportoconte.com) provides equipment and tuition at various levels. Alghero's tourist office has a full list of diving outfits in the area (see p.177).

Anghelu Ruju

SP42 Sássari road • Daily: April & Oct 9am–6pm; May–Sept 9am–7pm; Nov–March 10am–2pm • €3.50, €6 with Nuraghe di Palmavera (see p.185); audioguide €3, guided tour €2.50; ☎ 329 438 5947, ⓦ smuovi.com • By bus, take the service for San Marco (not Sun), leaving at 2.30pm from the Giardini Púbblici (inform driver of destination), returning at about 5.15pm •

The necropolis of **Anghelu Ruju**, a pre-nuraghic cave complex of some forty hypogea 10km north of Alghero, was discovered by chance in 1903, shortly after the land was purchased by the Sella e Mosca winery – now one of Sardinia's most celebrated wine producers (see below). The necropolis – which stands in the midst of the vineyards of Cannonau grapes beneath the planes roaring to and from nearby Fertilia airport – is a creation of the late Neolithic Ozieri culture dating back to about 2900 BC, though it was reused throughout the Copper Age (2900–1500 BC). Gouged out of the ground and accessed by low-lintelled doorways, the tombs constitute Sardinia's best examples of the so-called *domus de janas* (fairies' or witches' houses), of which there are scores on the island, for the most part murky chambers, or groups of them, some connected by sloping passages. The dead were embalmed within, occasionally in mass burials, sometimes half-cremated and in some cases skinned before burial.

Visitors are free to scramble around the tombs, though there is little to see: the rich contents have been removed to the archeological museums of Cágliari and Sássari. In some cases, however, you can just make out, carved on the lintels or in the depths of the darkness, symbolic shapes including bulls' horns in tombs A, XXb, XXVIII and XXX, the last of these – carved on the left wall of the "atrium" – a simple line which could also be a boat. Bring a torch, and be prepared for some serious stooping.

Museo e Tenuta Vitivinícola

Località I Piani, SP42 Sássari road • **Tours** June–Sept Mon–Sat 5.30pm, other times by appointment (1hr) • Free • **Wine shop** June–Sept Mon–Fri 9am–8pm, Sat 9am–1pm & 2–8pm in Aug; Oct–May Mon–Fri 8.30am–5.30pm, Sat 8.30am–1pm & 2–5.30pm • ☎ 079 997 700, ⊛ sellaemosca.it • By bus, take the service for San Marco (not Sun), leaving at 2.30pm from the Giardini Púbblici (inform driver of destination), returning from the winery at about 5.15pm

Vermentino, Cannonau and Torbato wines are produced at the vast Sella e Mosca estate, Sardinia's largest winery, which cultivates more than 1200 acres of vines in Alghero's hinterland and is open to tours and tastings. The entrance lies 600m north of Anghelu Ruju on the Alghero–Sássari road. The guided tours – usually in Italian – explain the various stages of winemaking, and take in the cellars and the **Museo e Tenuta Vitivinícola**. There's a short film which, with Vittorio Sella's black-and-white photographs, bring the history of the vineyard to life, and part of the museum is dedicated to Anghelu Ruju, displaying copies of some of the finds together with diagrams of the site. The tour ends with tastings accompanied by *pane carasau* (priced according to the wines sampled). The full range of the estate's wines is represented in the on-site **wine shop**.

Lago di Baratz

North from Alghero, Fertilia and Porto Conte, good roads lead across the territory of Nurra to **Lago di Baratz**, Sardinia's only natural lake. A path curves round the reeds and marshes of the perimeter, allowing a close-up of some of the protected plants and – if you're lucky – animals gathered here. Among these is a species of turtle (*Emys orbicularis*), while wildfowl include the little- and great-crested grebes as well as a multitude of mallards and coots. The *macchia* which partially encroaches on the shores is a pungent melee of rosemary, myrtle, wild lavender and various species of wild orchid.

Just over 1km west from the lake, easily walkable (there's also a road for drivers), the bay of **Porto Ferro** has a luscious long **beach** guarded by three watchtowers.

Argentiera

A drive or ride of 40km from Alghero, 5km west of the nondescript settlement of Palmádula, the old abandoned mining town of **ARGENTIERA** was once the greatest producer of silver on the island. Worked since Roman times, the seams were exhausted and extraction halted in 1963, and now the little town sits by itself at the end of a road on one of the most deserted expanses of the western coast. Its forlorn, haunted air is full of the echoes of its former industry: shafts lie abandoned, miners' quarters stare blindly out, and there is little movement at all outside July and August. However, things are

5

changing, holiday homes are increasingly evident, and a museum of mining is promised. There are some good shingle and sand **beaches** in the vicinity, one of which, **Porto Palmas**, you pass on the way into town – an unasphalted track leads to five more much smaller ones. You might also stretch your legs by heading out to **Capo dell'Argentiera**, a headland with terrific coastal views, about 3km southwest of the old mining centre.

ARRIVAL AND DEPARTURE   **ARGENTIERA**

There's a **bus** connection with Sássari (Mon–Sat 5 daily; 1hr 5min), where travellers to/from Alghero will need to change.

EATING AND DRINKING

Il Veliero Via Carbónia 1 ☎079 530 471. This bar-trattoria serves *panini*, mixed salads and some meat and

fish dishes – a *frittura mista* (fish fry-up) is €18. April–Sept daily 8am–11pm; Oct & Dec–March closed Mon.

Villanova Monteleone and around

There are two routes running **south of Alghero**, both strongly recommended, but very different from each other. As one route runs inland and the other along the coast, and each ends at Bosa (see p.189), you could cover both in a round-trip. The SP292 inland route southeast from Alghero climbs above the coast, affording magnificent views and leading, after 25km of twisting road, to **VILLANOVA MONTELEONE**, the mountain settlement to which the original *algherese* population was banished in 1354 after their town had been taken over by the Spanish. There's precious little to see or do here, except at the end of August, when the local **Festival of St John the Baptist** is celebrated with traditional processions and horseback races. The local craft speciality is linen embroidered with angular animals and other geometric designs.

A right turn out of Villanova takes you along the minor, little-used road which eventually winds up in Bosa, a 40km trawl through an empty but often inspiring wilderness of *macchia* and mountain. Alternatively, continue east another 9km on the SS292 to the dammed **Lago del Temo**, from which the eponymous river flows down to Bosa on the coast. It's a good place to mosey around, with grassy banks ideal for picnics.

ARRIVAL AND DEPARTURE   **VILLANOVA MONTELEONE**

By bus Villanova Monteleone is served by buses to Alghero (Mon–Sat 7–9 daily, Sun mid-June to mid-Sept 3 daily;

45min) and Bosa (Mon–Sat 1 daily; 1hr).

Monteleone Rocca Doria

Thirteen kilometres southeast from Villanova Monteleone, rising on a hill above the Lago del Temo, the village of **MONTELEONE ROCCA DORIA** was a Dorian foundation which endured a three-year siege by the combined forces of Aragon, Sássari, Bosa and Alghero, ending with its complete destruction in 1436. Monteleone's refugees joined Alghero's deportees in Villanova (hence that village's composite name), though the ruined Monteleone was later resettled and rebuilt. These days, with a population of 125, it's a bit of a backwater, but you'll find the traditional atmosphere a nice contrast to the holiday-orientated coast, and there's a pretty Romanesque basilica and a couple of bars on hand to supply refreshment while you watch the antics of the local dogs.

The coast road to Bosa

The SP105/SP49 **coast road** south of Alghero travels through a rugged, rocky landscape, the vistas encompassing an ever-changing succession of coves and inlets. There are few swimming spots, however, though you'll find a good beach at **Póglina**, 8km south of town and a stop on the Alghero–Bosa coastal bus route; there's a good bar and restaurant here, too (see below). Closer to Bosa, look out for dirt paths leading to rough-and-ready beaches near the ruined Spanish watchtower, **Torre Argentina**. Just north of the latter, around 12km north of Bosa, the promontory of **Capo Marargiu** achieved a brief notoriety in the 1980s when it was revealed that a secret right-wing commando group, Gladio, used the headland as a training ground.

This undeveloped tract of coast also makes one of Sardinia's great cycle rides – though the only viable route is along the road. The rocky terrain holds Sardinia's only significant colony of **griffon vultures** (a few others nest around Capo Caccia, west of Alghero). Many of these are being wiped out by the poisons left out by local farmers for foxes and stray dogs, and despite strictly enforced measures fewer than twenty breeding pairs are thought to exist here today. Visitors to the area should not approach nesting sites in July and August.

ARRIVAL AND DEPARTURE   **THE COAST ROAD TO BOSA**

By bus The road is served by buses between Alghero and Bosa (2–5 daily); be sure to take the coastal bus route, not the inland one via Villanova Monteleone.

EATING

La Speranza Poglina, 8km south of Alghero ☎ 079 957 6107. You could combine a lunch or dinner at this beachside restaurant with a swim. Fresh seafood, cooked in a variety of ways, is the main item on the menu, costing €5 or €6/100g (pasta dishes are €9–15). The main draw, however, is the fabulous location, with tables just steps from the sea. April & June–Sept: bar daily 9.30am–7pm, restaurant daily 12.30–2.30pm & 7–10.30pm; May & Oct closed Wed.

Bosa

Surrounded by mountains, huddled around the base of a hill capped by a ruined castle, **BOSA** (40km south of Alghero) has a self-contained air, cocooned from the main currents of Sardinian life in the middle of one of the island's last remaining stretches of undeveloped coast. The town makes a soothing spot to hole up for a few days, located on the banks of the placid River Temo, Sardinia's only navigable river of any length, and within easy reach of some fine beaches. It's a refreshingly uncommercial place, though increasingly aware of its tourist potential. Development is beginning to make a significant impact, particularly around **Bosa Marina**, the town's coastal offshoot 3km west, where hotels, bars and restaurants cluster around a sandy arc of beach.

Brief history

Phoenicians and Romans are known to have settled the banks of the River Temo, with the **Roman** town located near the site of the church of San Pietro, a couple of kilometres upstream from the present town. After the Romans left, Bosa fared badly and was repeatedly battered by barbarian and Moorish raids. In the twelfth century, the settlement was refounded by the **Malaspina** family, originating in the borderland between Tuscany and Liguria, around their fortress on the Serravalle hill. Many who had been living on the coast, near present-day Bosa Marina, willingly migrated to this more defensible spot, establishing the Sa Costa quarter on the slopes of Serravalle.

Bosa changed hands several times during the ensuing vicissitudes of war, at one time allying itself with the anti-Aragonese coalition headed by Eleonora d'Arborea, but eventually forged a happy working relationship with the **Spanish**, under whom it prospered. After an interlude of decay, the town achieved wealth and security in the **eighteenth and nineteenth centuries**, when it was briefly a provincial capital renowned for the working of precious metals, coral-gathering and leather-tanning. Much of Sa Piana, the lower town, dates from this era. Since 2005, Bosa has been part of the province of Oristano, though culturally it has little in common with the rest of the province.

5

The Cattedrale

Corso Vittorio Emanuele • Daily 8am–noon & 4–7pm

Surmounted by its colourful dome, Bosa's **Cattedrale** lies on the northern side of the old town bridge, its fifteenth-century origins largely obscured under an overlay of Baroque. The Rococo facade gives access to a lavish interior, a riot of grand arches and polychrome marble. A few individual items here are worth picking out: carved lions subduing dragons on the altar steps, frescoes in the apse painted by Emilio Scherer at the end of the nineteenth century and, behind the seventeenth-century altar, another fresco from the same period showing a town plan of Bosa – the town's appearance is scarcely different today.

Corso Vittorio Emanuele

From the cathedral, the main **Corso Vittorio Emanuele** extends west through the **Sa Piana** neighbourhood, its tone set by well-preserved *palazzi* on either side. At the Corso's western end, the grand **Palazzo Don Carlos**, dating from the eighteenth century, overlooks the outdoor bars on **Piazza Costituzione**. Beyond the much grander **Piazza IV Novembre** (or Piazza Monumento) lie the newer neighbourhoods of town.

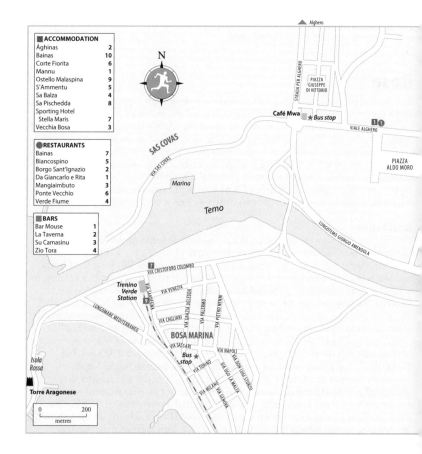

■ACCOMMODATION	
Aghinas	2
Bainas	10
Corte Fiorita	6
Mannu	1
Ostello Malaspina	9
S'Ammentu	5
Sa Balza	4
Sa Pischedda	8
Sporting Hotel Stella Maris	7
Vecchia Bosa	3

●RESTAURANTS	
Bainas	7
Biancospino	5
Borgo Sant'Ignazio	2
Da Giancarlo e Rita	1
Mangiaimbuto	3
Ponte Vecchio	6
Verde Fiume	4

■BARS	
Bar Mouse	1
La Taverna	2
Su Camasinu	3
Zio Tora	4

5

Casa Deriu

Corso Vittorio Emanuele 59 • July Mon 10.30am–1pm, Tues–Sun 10.30am–1pm & 5–8pm; Aug daily 10am–1pm, 5–8pm & 10pm–midnight; Sept–June Tues–Fri 10am–1pm & 3–5pm, Sat & Sun 10am–1pm & 3–6pm • €4.50 • ☏ 0785 377 043

Halfway along the Corso on the right, the nineteenth-century **Casa Deriu** has been restored as a museum and gallery, where you can tour a suite of rooms furnished in period style, including frescoes, ceramic floors, Art Nouveau paintings and even an Art Nouveau chandelier. Everything is a bit faded and there's a slightly dingy air about the place, but it gives a good impression of how the upper classes once lived. The third floor is devoted to local painter and ceramicist **Melkiorre Melia** (1889–1982), including local scenes and works completed when he was director of a ceramics school in Libya.

Your entry ticket also admits you to another permanent exhibition in an adjunct to the gallery across the road, where rather more arresting paintings by another local artist, **Antonio Atza** (1925–2009), are displayed, including surrealist and abstract works. A few pictures by other Sard artists are also displayed here.

Sa Costa

Take any of the lanes off the Corso to the north to penetrate the web of alleys that make up Bosa's **Sa Costa** quarter. Full of medieval gloom, corridor-like streets follow the steep contours of Serravalle, a fairly strenuous clamber of fifteen minutes or so to the brow of

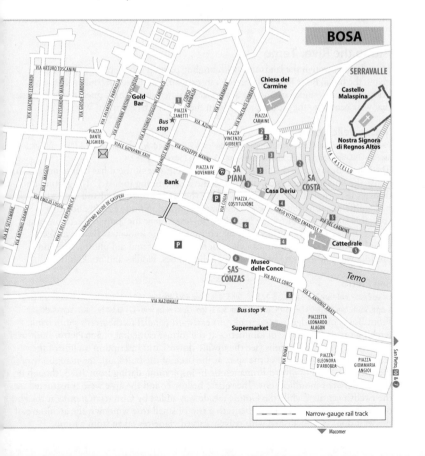

5

the hill and the castle. On the way up or down, take a look at the **Chiesa del Cármine**, on Via del Cármine, a richly decorated Baroque edifice with an elegant facade from 1779.

Castello Malaspina

Via Castello • Late March and early Nov daily 10am–1pm; April–June daily 10am–7pm; July & Aug daily 10am–7.30pm; Sept daily 10am–6pm; Oct daily 10am–5pm; mid-Nov to mid-March Sat & Sun 10am–1pm • €4 • ☎ 340 395 5048, ⓦ castellodibosa.it

Only the shell of Bosa's medieval **Castello Malaspina** survives, but its commanding position imbues it with plenty of atmosphere. Erected by the powerful Malaspina family in 1112, the walls incorporate a series of towers, notably the **torre nord**, open-sided in the fashion of other towers in Oristano and Cágliari, and the **torre maggiore**. Taller and more refined than the others, the torre maggiore is thought to have been the work of Cágliari's celebrated military architect Giovanni Capula, responsible for the Torre dell'Elefante (see p.57) and Torre di San Pancrazio (see p.61) in his home city; the pentagonal **torre ovest** is Aragonese. The bird's-eye views from the castle's red trachyte ramparts are worth savouring, giving you the chance to get to grips with the area's geography.

Within the walls, the only older construction still intact is the church of **Nostra Signora di Regnos Altos**, which contains a rare cycle of vibrant, Catalan-style frescoes from about 1300 and a couple of statues of the Madonna. Brief **guided tours** of the castle (in Italian or English) will help you to get the most of your visit, and there are leaflets indicating the main points of interest.

If you're driving, you can reach the entrance by following signs along the road skirting the back of town, leading round to the castle gate from Piazza Cármine or Piazza Dante.

Along the River Temo

Meandering through the landscape, with brightly painted fishing boats tethered to the quays, the broad **River Temo** invites closer inspection. On the south bank, near the old bridge, you can wander around the **Sas Conzas** quarter, site of the former leather tanneries that were central to the local economy from the eighteenth century to World War II.

Museo delle Conce

Via delle Conce • July Mon 10.30am–1pm, Tues–Sun 10.30am–1pm & 5–8pm; Aug daily 10am–1pm, 5–8pm & 10pm–midnight; Sept–June Tues–Fri 10am–1pm & 3–5pm, Sat & Sun 10am–1pm & 3–6pm • €3.50 • ☎ 0785 376 224

The last of Bosa's tanneries closed in the 1960s, but one of them has been renovated to house the **Museo delle Conce**, devoted to the local tanning industry. The ground floor displays the original *vasche*, or basins where the leather was soaked and washed – each had a different function in the process, most containing lime, tannin and other vegetable substances, but some including dog excrement for "purging". As one might expect, it was a smelly business, for which Bosa became known as *Bosa puzzolente* ("stinky Bosa"). Upstairs you can view more equipment and old photos. The end product was put to a variety of uses, including shoes, saddles and bookbinding.

San Pietro

Via San Pietro • April–June Tues–Sat 9.30am–12.30pm, Sun 3.30–6.30pm; July & Aug Tues–Fri 9.30am–12.30pm, Sat 9.30am–12.30pm & 4–6pm, Sun 4–7pm; Sept & Oct Tues–Sat 9.30am–12.30pm, Sun 3–5pm; call for winter visits • €2 • ☎ 340 395 5048, ⓦ castellodibosa.it

From Bosa's old bridge, a rural road runs eastward parallel to the river's south bank, fetching up after a couple of kilometres at the former cathedral of **San Pietro**. Built over an early Christian necropolis (see the upside-down Latin inscription on one of the recycled stones at the base of the apse, at the back of the building), the main body of the church is pure Lombard Romanesque in inspiration, dating from 1073, though it later underwent modifications. The square belltower and the apse were constructed in the twelfth century, while the Gothic facade was added by Cistercian monks at the end of the thirteenth century. Here, beneath a trio of small rose windows, the architrave of the west door is embellished with naively carved vignettes taken from a tomb, representing the Madonna and Child with Sts Paul, Peter and Constantinus de Castra, the church's founder (or it may represent St Constantine).

The sombre **interior** has two rows of solid, broad-stoned, rectangular columns; on the first on the right, you might just be able to make out an inscribed dedication by Bishop Constantinus de Castra. There's little else in the way of decoration, making it a silent, moody place.

Bosa Marina and around

During Bosa's long history, its inhabitants have settled on various sites along the banks of the River Temo. One of these is now **BOSA MARINA**, at the mouth of the river – a conventional minor resort with a small choice of hotels and trattorias. Here, on the main Via Cristóforo Colombo, the small station is the terminus for the **Trenino Verde**, a restored old train running seasonally on a narrow-gauge line from Macomer.

Bosa Marina's broad sandy **beach** is surveyed by a stark Spanish watchtower, while yachts and fishing boats lie at anchor in the lee of the islet of **Isola Rossa**, now linked to the mainland by a bridge. The sheltered beach is a favourite place for windsurfers, with equipment usually available to rent in summer, when the place gets thronged. The tower, or **Torre Aragonese**, is sometimes open in summer for temporary exhibitions, but is worth visiting even without these for its examples of Catalan decorative masonry work and its views encompassing two more Spanish towers along the coast.

Remoter patches of sand lie 2km south in the **Turas** district, and about the same distance north, though if you're looking for true isolation, you're best off visiting the rugged littoral north of Bosa, where you'll find rocks to swim off interspersed with patches of sandy beach.

ARRIVAL AND DEPARTURE BOSA

By car All roads in and out of town are twisty, and the centre is not conducive to driving. Park by the river or at the car park on Via Cugia to avoid tight lanes and one-way systems.

By bus ARST buses pull up at various points of the town – on Viale Alghero, Piazza Zanetti (Bosa's main bus terminal) and Via Nazionale – and some also make stops at Bosa Marina. Tickets are sold at *Gold Bar*, Via Azuni, *Café Mwa* on

Viale Alghero and at the bus depot on Via Nazionale (7am–1pm).

Destinations Alghero (Mon–Sat 4–6 daily; Sun 2–5 daily; 55min); Cúglieri (Mon–Sat 5 daily; 55min); Macomer (Mon–Sat 6 daily, Sun 3–4 daily; 50min–1hr 10min); Oristano (Mon–Sat 5 daily; 2hr); Sássari (Mon–Sat 3 daily; 2hr 15min); Villanova Monteleone (Mon–Sat 1 daily; 1hr).

GETTING AROUND

On foot Bosa's few specific sights are all easily reached on foot. A modern road bridge crosses the river farther downstream, near Bosa Marina, and between the two there's a small footbridge.

By bus or tourist train For travelling between Bosa and

Bosa Marina, you can make use of either the year-round ARST buses or, in summer, the *trenino turistico* – a tourist "train" on wheels that shuttles between the two (daily 11am–noon & 4–6pm; €5), departing from Corso Vittorio Emanuele II.

By taxi Taxi services are sparse; call ☎ 335 659 0568.

INFORMATION AND ACTIVITIES

Tourist information There's no information office in Bosa, though you'll find general – but often out-of-date – information on the town at ⊛ bosaonline.com.

Diving Excursions, supervision, instruction and equipment rental are offered at Bosa Diving Center, Via Colombo 2, Bosa Marina (☎ 335 818 9748, ⊛ bosadiving .com).

Sailing L'Altro Turismo, operating from the marina at Sas Covas, offers full-day trips aboard the *Hansiosa* yacht between April and Sept (€75; ☎ 338 322 9656, ⊛ laltroturismo.com), with lunch, drinks and swimming

stops included. Kayak and bike rental are also available for €15/day and €20/half-day respectively.

Trenino Verde Bosa Marina is a terminal for the narrow-track Trenino Verde tourist train to Macomer, 30km inland (mid-June to mid-Sept Wed & Sat; ⊛ treninoverde.com). The Wed excursion, departing at 9.30pm, includes a snack lunch, a Malvasia tasting and a visit to an ethnographic collection in Macomer, returning to Bosa by coach (€43); on Sat the train leaves Macomer at 9.30pm and returns from Bosa at 4pm (€16.50). Contact Esedra for information and bookings (☎ 0785 743 044, ⊛ esedraescursioni.it).

5

ACCOMMODATION

Most of Bosa's **hotels** stay open all year. If you want to stay near the sea, head for Bosa Marina, though none of the hotels there has much character. The modern resort also has one of Sardinia's rare youth hostels. For a longer stay, consider booking an **apartment**, either a traditional, renovated place in the old centre or a more modern property in Bosa's newer districts or at Bosa Marina.

★**Åghinas** Piazza Cármine 17 ☎ 0785 605 827, ⓦ aghinas .com. An *albergo diffuso* – with rooms in two separate buildings – this hotel in the old town has most of its rooms in a beautifully restored nineteenth-century palazzo, two others in a more modest townhouse dug out of the rock nearby in Sa Costa. All have modern fixtures and facilities, fridges and wi-fi. Breakfast is taken in *La Taverna* (see p.195). **€75**

Bainas Via San Pietro ☎ 339 209 0967 or ☎ 333 396 7819, ⓦ agriturismobainasbosa.com. A 10min walk from Bosa, this peaceful *agriturismo* is surrounded by fields and orchards which supply its excellent restaurant, where guests can dine for €25–35 (book first). The ranch-style house has spacious rooms giving onto a veranda. No credit cards. **€70**

Corte Fiorita Lungo Temo De Gásperi 45 ☎ 0785 377 058, ⓦ albergo-diffuso.it. With rooms distributed among three buildings, this hotel has its main base in a palazzo overlooking the river, combining a rustic feel – rafters, tiled floors, exposed stonework – with opulent trimmings. Check the rooms first, as each one is different: those with a balcony and river view cost extra, but ones on the side are quieter; all have satellite TV and internet connections. **€99**

Mannu Viale Alghero ☎ 0785 375 307, ⓦ mannuhotel .it. This three-star hotel, less than 1km from both Bosa and Bosa Marina, offers fairly good value for its comfortable facilities, though the location on a main road opposite a supermarket is hardly inspiring. Half or full board may be required in summer, worth considering anyway as there's a plaudit-winning restaurant (see p.195). **€90**

Ostello Malaspina Via Sardegna 1, Bosa Marina ☎ 346 236 3844, ⓦ valevacanze.com. This quiet, modern youth hostel near the beach has a relaxed atmosphere, with a veranda, meals and four-bed family rooms available. It should remain open all year, but check in winter. No credit cards. Dorms **€16**; doubles **€40**

S'Ammentu Via del Cármine 55 ☎ 346 500 4719, ⓦ samentu.com. Old-town lodging on four floors (there's a lift), with lots of character. The six en-suite rooms are small but comfortable, with a/c and TVs. Abundant breakfasts are served in a separate building nearby. **€70**

★**Sa Balza** Corso Vittorio Emanuele II 45 ☎ 349 542 6676, ⓦ sabalza.it. Right on the main street, the three rooms here are located around a courtyard with their own entrances. They don't have views but are clean, spacious and quiet, each with its own modern bathroom, a/c and fridge. There's no breakfast. The friendly and helpful owner runs the next-door SWS travel agency. **€60**

Sa Pischedda Via Roma 8 ☎ 0785 373 065, ⓦ hotel sapischedda.com. Just across the river from the centre, this fine old palazzo has a grand staircase and flashy glass lift leading up to attractive rooms with a/c, some with balcony and river views – a few are quite cramped, however. There's a classy restaurant and pizzeria, too. **€98**

Sporting Hotel Stella Maris Via Colombo 11–13, Bosa Marina ☎ 0785 375 162, ⓦ stellamarisbosa.com. Friendly three-star hotel near the river and beach, adorned with garish modern art and offering a dozen fairly ordinary en-suite rooms, some pretty small. There's a restaurant with river views, bikes are available to rent and various activities from diving to boat excursions can be arranged. Half or full board may be required in season. Closed Nov–April. **€90**

Vecchia Bosa Via Bonaria 23 ☎ 0785 377 035 or ☎ 320 172 5966, ⓦ vecchiabosa.com. In the heart of the old town, this friendly B&B has four quiet, tastefully decorated rooms in two separate buildings, all with a/c, satellite TV and private bathrooms. There's a good choice at breakfast. No credit cards. Closed Dec & Jan. **€60**

APARTMENT RENTALS

Lemon Tree House, run by an English couple (☎ 0785 374 236, ⓦ houseinbosa.co.uk), has two apartments in Sa Costa neighbourhood, one with spectacular views, the other with an internal terrace (from €425/week in July). Otherwise, check out the agency San Marco Immobiliare, Via Roma 8 (☎ 0785 375 521, ⓦ smimmobiliare.com).

EATING

Bosa has a good spread of **restaurants**, all getting quite busy in summer. Most of the places listed below are in the main town; Bosa Marina has a few more choices, mainly attached to hotels. If you want to buy your own food, try the large **supermarket**, SuperPan, over the old bridge on Via Roma (Mon–Sat 8.30am–9pm, Sun 8.30am–2pm).

Bainas Via San Pietro ☎ 339 209 0967 or ☎ 333 396 7819. This *agriturismo* outside town (see above) serves delicious, wholesome organic dishes using its own home-grown produce, but you need to call ahead. Meals cost €25–35 including drinks. No credit cards. Daily 8.30pm–late.

★**Biancospino** Corso Vittorio Emanuelle 6 ☎ 0785 374 158. Two vaulted rooms hold this smart neighbourhood trattoria serving authentic traditional dishes, local wines and craft beers. Typical choices include *pasta con ragù di coniglio* (with rabbit sauce), horse steak with cheese and courgettes, and fried conger eel. There are separate meat and seafood menus, from which one dish costs €15, two €22 and three €27. Service is on the slow side. You can sit outside in summer. Daily noon–3.30pm & 7.30–11pm.

Borgo Sant'Ignazio Via Sant'Ignazio 33 ☎0785 374 129. Rustic restaurant in an alley above the Corso offering local specialities such as *culinzones* (ravioli) and *brasato di cinghiale* (wild boar cooked in white wine). Main courses cost €12–16. July–Aug daily 12.30–2.30pm & 7.30–10.30pm; closed Mon Sept–June & eves in winter.

Da Giancarlo e Rita Viale Alghero ☎0785 375 306. Part of the *Mannu* hotel (see p.194), a kilometre or so from the centre, this sober, rather formal place has won awards for its culinary excellence. Local dishes such as spaghetti with lobster and fried mussels won't disappoint. Reckon on €30–40 for a three-course meal, though tourist menus are sometimes available. There's a good selection of island wines, too. April–Sept daily 1–2.30pm & 8–10.30pm; Oct–March closed Sun eve.

Mangiaimbuto Piazza Modoleddu ☎0785 373 736.

Well hidden on a traffic-free *piazzetta*, this restaurant with outdoor seating has an intimate air and a menu strong on fish. Try the fresh *tagliatelle con ragù di mare* (with seafood sauce) or couscous with tuna, and leave room for desserts such as *semifreddo alla Malvasia*. Mains are €12–15; service is patchy. June–Sept daily 1–3pm & 7–11pm; April, May & Oct closed Mon lunch.

Ponte Vecchio Via delle Conce ☎0785 376 140. Operated by the same family that runs the *Sa Pischedda* hotel (see p.194), this informal seafood restaurant has a perfect riverside location. The food is fine – think *fregola allo scoglio* (semolina pasta with shellfish; €12) or *spigola alla Malvasia* (sea bass in wine; €16) – but its main appeal is the site. March–Oct daily 12.30–2.30pm & 7.15–10.30pm.

Verde Fiume Via Lungotemo De Gasperi 51 ☎0785 373 482. This small riverfront trattoria – with pavement seating in summer – has a small but eclectic menu of inventively prepared dishes using fresh, local and seasonal produce. *Antipasti* and starters are around €10, mains €10–16. June–Oct daily noon–3pm & 7–11pm; Nov–May closed Mon.

DRINKING

The bars in Piazza Costituzione are good for a leisurely drink, but the service charge is high. Make sure you sample the renowned **Malvasia** wine while in Bosa; the amber-coloured, Vermouth-like drink is served at most bars and restaurants, usually as an aperitif or with dessert.

Bar Mouse Piazza Zanetti ☎339 117 4216. Cool, secluded café and wine bar with a terrace, also serving snacks – a mellow retreat on summer evenings. Mon–Sat 6am–10pm, Sun 6am–2pm.

★**La Taverna** Piazza Cármine ☎331 850 4785. This backstreet café-bar makes a quiet spot for a pause over a beer and/or an ample and delicious *panino* (around €5), inside or on the terrace. Mid–June to mid–Oct daily 7am–11pm; closes midnight in summer; mid-Oct to mid-June closed Thurs.

Su Camasinu Via del Cármine 104 ☎339 573 1677,

ⓦcamasinu.com. This cave-like *cantina* is the place to sample the best local Malvasia, accompanied by snacks. It's run by the Columbu family who produce some of the region's finest. However, it's often closed – if so, call or ask at the *Àghinas* hotel. Daily 10.30am–2pm & 5.30–8.30pm.

Zio Tora Lungo Temo De Gásperi ☎347 660 9003. Neighbourhood bar opposite the old bridge, with outdoor tables and late closing, good for people-watching. It's best in the evening – by day the passing traffic can be a turn-off. Daily 7.30am–late.

DIRECTORY

Internet Web Copy Internet Point, Via Gioberti 12 (Mon–Sat 9am–1pm & 4.30–8pm; closes later in summer).

Markets Tues is market day, with hundreds of stalls on Corso Garibaldi selling everything from hats and

BOSA'S FESTIVALS

The best **festivals** are centred on the river: the **Festa dei Santi Pietro e Paolo** on June 29 involves a regatta as far as the church of San Pietro, with local foods, while in the **Sagra di Santa Maria del Mare**, on the first Sunday of August, an image of the Madonna is transported by boat from Bosa Marina to the cathedral, returning in the afternoon for an open-air Mass and fireworks display. The **Sagra di Nostra Signora di Regnos Altos** on the second Sunday of September is a great chance to attend an open-air Mass at the castle, watch local groups perform traditional songs and dances, and enjoy local food and drink. In addition, **Carnival** in Bosa has a riotous, pagan flavour around Shrove Tuesday, and **Easter** is also enthusiastically celebrated. There's a country festival, the **Festa dei Santi Cosma e Damiano**, on September 26, accompanied by traditional singing and dancing.

5

handkerchiefs to cactus plants (mornings only). Antiques and curios are sold on Piazza Gioberti on Fri mornings.
Pharmacy Farmacia Sardu, Corso Vittorio Emanuele 51 (Mon–Sat 9am–1pm & 4.30–8pm; closed alternate Thurs & Sat). Night rotas are posted on pharmacy doors.

Post office Via Pischedda, off Viale Giovanni XXIII (Mon–Fri 8.20am–7.05pm, Sat 8.20am–12.35pm).
Travel agency SWS Viaggi, Corso Vittorio Emanuele 41 (☎0785 374 391).

Macomer and around

Thirty kilometres inland of Bosa on the SP129, **MACOMER** is not a particularly alluring destination, though you may be tempted to make a swift stop here for its *nuraghi* and Byzantine church. Called Macopissa in Roman times, when it was a major military base, the town was the site of the last serious revolt against the Aragonese by the Sards in 1478. More recently, it has become a centre of livestock, dairy farming and wool. On Sant'Antonio Abate's day, January 17, a mighty bonfire is lit outside Macomer's church of Santa Chiara for the **Festa di Su Tuva**.

Nuraghe di Santa Barbara

1km north of town • Free

Macomer's surviving *nuraghi* are the most noteworthy of an intense concentration of nuraghic sites in the area, though both lie out of the centre. The **Nuraghe di Santa Barbara**, situated outside town beside the Carlo Felice highway (SS131) and tricky to find, has a mossy central tower that reaches 15m, with primitive cupolas, minor towers and bastions tacked onto the main structure. Little more is known about the building's origins other than that it was abandoned in the ninth century BC, but used again in the Carthaginian and Roman eras as a centre of worship.

Nearby, on the other side of the highway, the ruined state of **Nuraghe Ruju** (or Ruggiu) reveals a cross section of how a nuraghic cupola was constructed. *Domus de janas* tombs are scattered about below it, their contents on view at Sássari's Museo Sanna (see p.205).

Santa Sabina

10km east of Macomer on the SS129 Nuoro road • Daily 9.30am–1.30pm & 3.30–8pm or dusk • €2.50 • ☎338 833 4859 • Take any bus to Silanus or Nuoro

In the middle of a plain outside the village of **Silanus**, look out for the charming little Romanesque chapel of **Santa Sabina** on the right (travelling eastwards), harmoniously juxtaposed with a well-preserved *nuraghe* close by. The church, possibly eleventh-century, is unlike any other of Sardinia's churches, with its Byzantine-style tiled cupolas and simple domed and arched interior. Even more bare is the basalt-built *nuraghe*, which is thought to date from around 1600BC; rough-hewn steps lead to the top for a good perspective on the church.

Try to be here for the **Festa di Santa Sabina** on the second weekend of September, a typical country festival with eating, drinking and making merry.

ARRIVAL AND DEPARTURE   MACOMER

By bus Right on the SS131 highway, Macomer is a stop on most bus routes between Oristano, Sássari and Nuoro.
Destinations Alghero (1 daily; 1hr 55min); Bosa (Mon–Sat 4–5 daily, Sun 2–4 daily; 40min); Oristano (Mon–Sat 4 daily, Sun 1 daily; 50min); Sássari (Mon–Sat 10 daily, Sun 4 daily; 1hr 10min).
By train Macomer lies on the main FS north to south train

line, and is the terminal for the rattling old narrow-gauge ARST trains (see p.277) for Nuoro. The train station is at the western end of town. For FS train services, call ☎892 021 or consult ⓦ trenitalia.com; for ARST info.
Destinations Cágliari (8 daily; 1hr 40min–2hr 15min); Nuoro (Mon–Sat 6 daily; 1hr 10min); Sássari (6 daily, some with change at Ozieri-Chilivani; 1hr 20min).

EATING

Mandiga Lestru Piazza Sant'Antonio 17 ☎346 226 4188. A useful stop for a swift lunch in the centre of town, this trattoria offers a great-value fixed-price menu for €12.50. Try the lentil soup, *risotto ragù d'agnello* (with lamb) or grilled sausages. Mon, Wed & Fri 12.30–3pm, Tues, Thurs & Sat 12.30–3pm & 7.30–10.30pm.

Stintino and around

The thin peninsula that forms the western arm of the **Golfo dell'Asinara** is an inhospitable, sparsely populated landscape of rock and *macchia*. The only town here is **STINTINO**, until a few decades ago nothing more than a remote jumble of fishermen's cottages jammed between two narrow harbours. Its discovery by the tourist industry has added conspicuous layers of concrete, new roads and kilometres of street lighting, but the tone of the place is essentially the same – small and laidback, though now furnished with a few bars, tourist facilities and a bank.

The big hotels have established themselves farther up the coast, where most of the sunning and swimming take place around the ravishing beach of **La Pelosa**. At the end of the peninsula, **Capo Falcone** overlooks the isles of **Piana** and **Asinara**, one a tiny blip, the other an ex-prison colony also known as a habitat of the miniature white ass from which gulf and island both take their name.

Stintino itself, 50km north of Alghero and 30km west of Porto Torres, is mostly modern and somewhat lacking in charm, ebullient in summer but pretty dead in winter. The compact layout is a right-angled grid of mainly residential streets spreading out from the main Via Sássari. Two harbours lie on either side of the promontory: to the north, **Portu Mannu**, also known as Porto Nuovo, caters mainly to pleasure craft, while the southern **Portu Minori**, or Porto Vecchio, is crowded with small fishing vessels. As there is no central piazza, these two inlets provide the town's main reference points. **Lungomare Colombo**, the one-way street running round the promontory, makes an easy promenade about town, taking in bars, restaurants and marvellous sea views.

Brief history

Stintino was founded little more than a century ago, when the Italian state appropriated the island of Asinara for use as a penal colony. The 45 families of the resident fishing community – specializing in the trapping and killing of tuna, once a major activity in these parts – were transferred to this sheltered spot between two natural inlets. The town today holds a permanent population of a little over 1500, but every summer tens of thousands of people flock here.

ARRIVAL AND INFORMATION
STINTINO

By bus In addition to the regular ARST services to Porto Torres and Sássari, Sardabus (🖥sardabus.it) operates a summer link to Alghero and Fertilia airport (tickets on board). All buses stop on Via Lépanto by Portu Minori. Destinations Alghero and Fertilia airport (June–Sept 5 daily; 45min–1hr); Porto Torres (Mon–Sat 5–7 daily, Sun 2–5 daily; 40min); Sássari (Mon–Sat 5–7 daily, Sun 2–5 daily; 1hr 15min).

Tourist office Via Sássari 123 (June–Sept daily 9.30am–12.30pm & 3–8pm, Aug also 10pm–midnight; Oct Mon–Sat 9.30am–12.30pm; Nov–May Mon–Sat 11am–12.30pm; ☎079 520 081, 🖥infostintino.it).

STINTINO'S FESTIVALS
Try to be in Stintino at the end of August for the **Regatta della Vela Latina**, when the waters are filled with yachts, some of them restored vintage vessels. The other major **festival** is on September 8, when a procession re-enacts the exodus of Asinara's inhabitants to their new home in Stintino.

5

DIVING AROUND STINTINO

The exceptionally clear waters around Stintino, La Pelosa and the islands offer superb opportunities for **diving** and **snorkelling**. Among the outfits based in the area in summer, try Stintino Diving Center (☎339 398 4451 or ☎339 451 5722, ⓦstintinodiving.it), at Punta Negra north of town, or, further up, Asinara Scuba Diving (☎079 527 175 or ☎389 922 9913, ⓦasinarascubadiving.com), based on the beach at Porto dell'Ancora between Stintino and La Pelosa. Both offer equipment rental and courses – one dive costs €40–50, full equipment rental is roughly €50 per day; 3hr snorkelling trips off Asinara cost around €25 excluding equipment.

GETTING AROUND

By shuttle bus Between June and Sept, a local bus (*navetta*) operated by Baraghini (☎348 697 3270, ⓦautonoleggibaraghini.it) connects Stintino with all the beaches until midnight (buy tickets on board, €1 one-way); a good option to avoid expensive car parking charges. ARST also operates a less frequent year-round service between Sássari and La Pelosa via Stintino.

By car Car rental is available at La Nassa, Via Tonnara 35 (☎079 520 060, ⓦagenzialanassa.it) for €50–80/day. They also rent bikes for €10/day.

By taxi Call ☎345 227 7744 or ☎333 266 4463.

ACCOMMODATION

Al Martin Pescatore Via Tonnara 30 ☎079 520 062, ⓦalmartinpescatore.it. A central B&B run by the owners of La Nassa agency, offering fairly basic en-suite rooms, though they're clean and spacious, with fridges. Rooms overlooking the port cost €10 extra. Breakfast is optional – if taken, it's at a nearby restaurant. **€75**

Geranio Rosso Via XXI Aprile 8 ☎079 523 292, ⓦhotelgeraniorosso.it. Small, central hotel with friendly staff and tastefully decorated rooms (including family rooms) with a/c and modern bathrooms. Some rooms are cramped, though – check first. There's an attached pizzeria/ristorante where guests can dine for €25. **€105**

Il Porto Vecchio Via Tonnara 69 ☎079 523 212 or ☎339 435 3582, ⓦbbstintino.com. This simple B&B has six mostly spacious rooms, some facing the port, with traditional Sardinian decoration. Abundant buffet breakfasts are served on the veranda in summer. **€75**

Lina Via Lepanto 30 ☎079 523 071, ⓦlinahotel.it. Overlooking the Porto Minori, this is the cheapest of the town's three hotels. There's no restaurant and therefore no half-board requirement. Half the rooms (all with a/c and private bathrooms) have balconies facing the boats; others have no view but go for the same rates. Closed Oct–March. **€80**

★**Silvestrino** Via Sássari 14 ☎079 523 007, ⓦsilvestrino.it. On the town's main street, this hotel has a touch of luxury in its rooms, some of which have their own terrace and terrific views. The restaurant is one of Stintino's best (see below). Closed Dec & Jan. **€100**

EATING AND DRINKING

Gelateria del Porto Lungomare Colombo 31 ☎079 523 268. There's usually a small crowd around this place, both for its intensively flavoured *gelati* and its traditional biscuits and pastries. Favourites include *sospiri* ("sighs", or almond sweets). Easter–Oct daily 8am–1.45pm & 4–11.30pm.

Lina Via Lépanto 30 ☎079 523 505. The best thing about this trattoria, next to the hotel of the same name (see above), is its location, with a terrace overlooking the fishing boats moored in Portu Minori. Dishes such as *gnocchetti* with saffron and lemon, and *calamari* in a pistachio sauce are tasty but expensive; set-price lunches cost €15 and €18. Easter–June & Oct daily except Wed 10am–3pm & 7.30–11pm; July–Sept daily same hours.

Opera Viva Piazza dei Quarantacinque ☎345 880 9635. Set away from the sea, this restaurant makes the best of its location on an unattractive square with a pleasant cane-covered veranda and a good seafood menu with reasonable prices. Try the excellent *antipasto*, *parmigiana di pesce spada* (baked aubergine and swordfish layers). You'll pay €40–50 a head. March–Dec daily 12.30pm–2.30pm & 7.30–11pm.

★**Silvestrino** Via Sássari 14 ☎079 523 007. Attached to the eponymous hotel (see above), this place offers first-class seafood. First courses and mains cost €10–15; tourist menus are occasionally available for €15–25. There's a deck for outdoor seating in summer. March–May and early to mid-Oct daily except Tues 12.30–2.30pm & 7.30–10.30pm; June–Sept daily same hours.

Le Saline

With most of the shore around Stintino rough and rocky, you'll have to go north or south of town to find decent beaches. About 1km to the south, near an old watchtower, a narrow road leads to the fine, *macchia*-backed beach of **Le Saline**, once site of a saltworks owned by the monks of Santa Maria di Tergu (see p.223). There are bars and facilities for renting deckchairs and parasols. A Spanish bastion stands nearby, and you might see the occasional flock of flamingos attracted to the saltpan/lagoon here.

La Pelosa

North of Stintino, tourist villages clutter the hills backing the coast almost as far as the northern tip of **Capo Falcone**, site of Torre Falcone, a Spanish watchtower. Leading up to the cape, the beach of **La Pelosa** is one of Sardinia's premier swimming spots, lapped by a shallow, turquoise sea of crystalline clarity. You won't be alone here, though – it can get horribly congested. The tiers of holiday homes spreading over the slopes are a blot on the landscape, but the perfect views over the outlying islands of Piana and the much larger Asinara are enchanting.

Asinara

In summer, regular boat tours depart from Stintino, Porto Torres and (occasionally) La Pelosa to sail round the islands' coasts and make a landing. On **Piana**, what you see is what you get: a tiny flat patch of land with a solitary watchtower standing guard. There is more on **Asinara**, 16km long, though visitors are only permitted within certain areas on organized boat tours. A prison colony from 1885 until the late 1990s, it is now a national park. The wildlife that you probably won't see – it's out of bounds – includes breeding turtles.

Called Sinuaria by the Romans on account of its indented form – making it appear from a distance like a whole archipelago of separate islands – Asinara has been sporadically inhabited in the last two millennia, even serving in 1638 as a base for French pirates. The Savoyard king sold it to the duke of Vallombrosa in 1775, but it never yielded a significant income, and was used both as a quarantine hospital for victims of cholera and a place of incarceration. At its northern end, the island's highest point (408m) is poignantly named **Punta della Scomúnica** ("Excommunication Point").

Asinara's protected status has allowed a range of **wildlife** to thrive, including the white wild donkeys for which the island is named, falcons, mouflons, pigs and goats. Both islands are still used to pasture cattle, which are walked across the shallow straits between Capo Falcone and Piana twice a year, in November and May.

TOURS TO PIANA AND ASINARA

Access to the islands of Piana and Asinara is only possible on authorized **boat excursions** from Stintino or – less frequently – Porto Torres (see p.218), normally departing between Easter and September. Once on **Asinara** (most boats sail past Piana without stopping), you can join an organized tour or set forth under your own steam to explore the various features of the coast and some of the prison buildings, or simply laze on the pristine sandy beaches of Fornelli, Cala Sabina, Cala d'Oliva and others in the north of the island. Alternatively, you can rent a bike (or bring your own), which can only be ridden on the surfaced roads. In summer a **bus service** operates, connecting Cala Reale, Cala d'Oliva and Fornelli several times daily (tickets €7, valid all day; pay on board). Bring your own food and drink, or use the bar at Cala Reale.

Excursions currently leave from Stintino's Portu Mannu at 9.30–10.30am, returning at 5–6pm. When there's sufficient demand, there may be additional departures and returns during the day. There are various options, ranging from a simple day-return ticket (€18) to a range of packages including catamaran trips to get there and tours in an off-road vehicle (€40–80).

Further information can be obtained from Asinara's website, ⓦparcoasinara.org, and you can buy tickets in Stintino, from the agency La Nassa, Via Tonnara 35 (☏079 520 060, ⓦescursioni asinara.it), or the operator Linea del Parco, Porto Mannu (☏349 260 5023, ⓦlineadelparco.it), among several others.

Sássari and around

CASTELSARDO

Sássari and around

Sardinia's second city, Sássari, is for many the island's most interesting centre, with its crowded medieval quarter and strong historical flavour. Around it, the landscape of the ancient territories of Logudoro and Anglona ranges from high tableland riven by sudden gullies to craggy peaks and valleys, with a long sandy arc edging the Golfo dell'Asinara on the northern coast. Inland and inward-looking, Sássari is less cosmopolitan than Cágliari, though there's also a high level of culture and plenty of interest in its churches and excellent archeological museum.

A short ride northwest of Sássari lies an ancient monument unique not just in Sardinia but in the whole Mediterranean basin – the "ziggurat" of **Monte d'Accoddi**, a sanctuary dating from around the third millennium BC. If you come to Sardinia by sea, you could well arrive at **Porto Torres**, to the north of Sássari, the original capital of the *giudicato* of Torres. It still holds some impressive Roman remains along with the **Basilica di San Gavino**, perhaps the island's finest example of Pisan-Romanesque architecture.

Some fine **beaches** line the Golfo dell'Asinara coast, dotted with small summer resorts and the larger town of **Castelsardo**. Capped by a fortified citadel, the town's scenic location and local handicrafts have made it a magnet for tourists, and it makes a good base for some inspiring scenic drives inland into the mountains of the **Anglona** region.

To the south and east of Sássari, the old territory of **Logudoro** is richly endowed with **medieval churches**, most of them splendidly positioned in improbably remote corners of the countryside. The medieval refinement of these buildings forms a sharp contrast to the ramshackle grandeur of the equally striking *nuraghi*. The densest concentration of them is at **Torralba**, with an outstanding museum of nuraghic culture and, a short distance outside, the majestic **Nuraghe Santu Antine**.

GETTING AROUND   **SÁSSARI AND AROUND**

Sássari is the major transport hub in northwestern Sardinia, with a good network of buses and a sketchier train service. The train station and bus stand are a 20min walk apart, though this "temporary" bus stand may have been relocated to a nearby site by the time you read this.

By train The main FS rail line heads northwest from Sássari to Porto Torres and south to Oristano and Cágliari, usually with a change at Ozieri-Chilivani for those towns and Olbia (☎ 892 021, ⌨ trenitalia.it). There are also a trio of narrow-gauge lines operated by ARST (☎ 800 865 042, ⌨ arst.sardegna.it) going to Alghero, Sorso and (summer only) Témpio Pausánia.

By bus For the most part, nondrivers wanting to explore the area around Sássari will have to rely on bus services operated by ARST (☎ 800 865 042, ⌨ arst.sardegna.it). The coast is well served, though most inland places have very limited connections, sometimes with just one or two buses on weekdays.

Sássari

First impressions of Sardinia's second city, **SÁSSARI**, do little to encourage anything more than a cursory visit; its inland location and sparse tourist facilities might seem a poor substitute for the holiday diversions of the nearby coast. But it is this very lack of glamour

Sássari's festivals p.209	**Castelsardo's festivals** p.218
Fainè p.212	**Artigianato in Castelsardo** p.220

DUOMO, SÁSSARI'S OLD QUARTER

Highlights

❶ **Sássari's old quarter** The maze-like old town retains its medieval air, with a glorious Baroque cathedral at its heart. **See p.207**

❷ **La Cavalcata, Sássari** One of the island's most flamboyant festivals, with feats of horsemanship, traditional costumes and performances of music and dance in the main piazza. **See p.209**

❸ **San Gavino, Porto Torres** Beautifully preserved, this atmospheric monument dates from the Pisan programme of church-building in the eleventh century. **See p.216**

❹ **Museo dell'Intreccio Mediterraneo, Castelsardo** The old citadel's castle, boasting far-reaching views, is an extraordinary location for this collection of the local, highly distinctive basketware. **See p.220**

❺ **Santíssima Trinità di Saccargia** With its rocket-like belltower rising abruptly above the bare countryside, this striking Romanesque church has been a landmark for nine hundred years. **See p.224**

❻ **Nuraghe Santu Antine** A fascinating relic of Sardinia's ancient culture, this venerable prehistoric palace is the most imposing of the many *nuraghi* strewn about the area. **See p.226**

HIGHLIGHTS ARE MARKED ON THE MAP ON P.204

that gives Sássari its special interest as an unpretentious – and not unattractive – working town, steeped in tradition. Sássari's historic character is most palpable in the vibrant **old quarter**'s dense network of medieval streets, old churches and *palazzi*, among them some of Sardinia's few Renaissance buildings. This atmospheric labyrinth is connected to the modern city by a sequence of squares, culminating in the stately and impressive **Piazza Italia**. Close by, **Museo Sanna** houses one of the island's top archeological collections.

As a regional transport hub, Sássari makes an invigorating alternative to a base by the sea, with an excellent range of **bars and restaurants**, a small but decent choice of **accommodation** and lower prices all round.

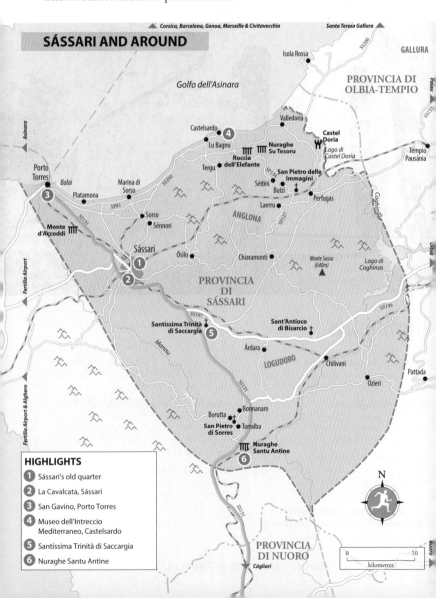

SÁSSARI AND AROUND

Corsica, Barcelona, Genoa, Marseille & Civitavecchia   Santa Teresa Gallura

GALLURA

Isola Rossa

PROVINCIA DI OLBIA-TEMPIO

Golfo dell'Asinara

Valledoria

Castelsardo **4**

Lu Bagnu

Castel Doria
Lago di Castel Doria

Nuraghe Su Tesoru

Témpio Pausánia

Roccia dell'Elefante

Tergu

San Pietro delle Immagini

Sédini

Bulzi

Perfugas

Porto Torres **3**

Balai

Platamona

Marina di Sorso

Laerru

ANGLONA

Monte d'Accoddi

Sorso

Sénnori

Sássari **1**

2

Ósilo

Chiaramonti

Monte Sassu (640m)

Lago di Coghinas

Fertília Airport

PROVINCIA DI SÁSSARI

Santíssima Trinità di Saccargia **5**

Sant'Antíoco di Bisarcio

Mannu

Árdara

LOGUDORO

Chilivani

Pattada

Ozieri

Fertília Airport & Alghero

Borutta

Bonnanaro

San Pietro di Sorres

Torralba

Nuraghe Santu Antine **6**

N

PROVINCIA DI NUORO

Cágliari

Nuoro

HIGHLIGHTS

1 Sássari's old quarter

2 La Cavalcata, Sássari

3 San Gavino, Porto Torres

4 Museo dell'Intreccio Mediterraneo, Castelsardo

5 Santíssima Trinità di Saccargia

6 Nuraghe Santu Antine

0   10
kilometres

Brief history

Built on an ancient site known as **Tatari**, or Tathari, the modern city of Sássari has roots going back to settlers from the Roman colony at what is now Porto Torres. As the port declined, so the inland town expanded; by the fourteenth century it possessed its own statute of laws and a ring of walls. Sássari was inevitably sucked into the conflict between Pisa and Genoa; then, in 1323, **James II of Aragon** established a power base here and, after a brief interlude under the control of the *giudicato* of Arborea, the city spent the next four centuries as an integral part of the Catalan-Aragonese hegemony, though that did not prevent it from being plundered several times by Moorish raiders. Ten years under Austrian rule preceded the coming of the House of Savoy in 1720. In the course of the nineteenth century, the Aragonese castle and walls were demolished, allowing the city to expand gradually.

The Spanish stamp is still evident in Sássari, not least in its churches. The city also has a strong tradition of intellectual independence; in the sixteenth century the Jesuits founded Sardinia's first **university** here, and in recent years Sássari has produced two national presidents, Antonio Segni and Francesco Cossiga, as well as long-time head of the Italian Communist Party, Enrico Berlinguer (1922–84).

Today, with just 120,000 inhabitants, Sássari presents something of a split personality – the well-to-do urbanity of Via Roma's café society contrasting with the medieval vitality of the old town, lately reinvigorated with a conspicuous immigrant population.

Piazza Italia and around

Sássari has no obvious centre, though **Piazza Italia** is its largest and grandest square and the venue for most of the city's *feste*. The imposing **Palazzo della Provincia** that occupies one side and the neo-Gothic **Palazzo Giordano** facing it (now bank offices) both date from around 1880 – surprisingly, given their very different styles. Between them, framed by palm trees in the middle of the square, a statue of King Vittorio Emanuele II lends an almost colonial flavour. The statue's inauguration in 1899 was the occasion for the revival of Sássari's main festival, La Cavalcata (see box, p.209).

The stately mood of Piazza Italia extends for a short distance up **Via Roma**, where the succession of smart cafés is abruptly terminated by the stern Fascist hulk of the **Palazzo della Giustizia**. Its ponderous presence is slyly undermined by the semi-restored Rococo villa opposite, at no. 46, sporting a cream-coloured facade adorned with whimsical *putti*. South of Piazza Italia, Via Carlo Alberto leads down to the **Giardini Púbblici**, a shady oasis of calm amid rushing traffic.

Museo Sanna

Via Roma 64 • Tues–Sun 9am–8pm • €3 • ☎ 079 272 203, ⓦ museosannasassari.beniculturali.it

The modern city's principal attraction, **Museo Sanna** is Sardinia's second-most important archeological museum (after Cágliari's), housed in a modern, well-planned block within its own garden.

Ground floor

On the **ground floor**, most of the museum's **prehistoric** items date from the period 3500–2500 BC, including pottery fragments and necklaces belonging to Sardinia's Ozieri culture and numerous slivers of smooth obsidian – the island's major export in Neolithic times, used to make arrowheads and cutting tools. One room is dedicated to the unique Copper Age ziggurat of Monte d'Accoddi (see p.217), showing a hologram of the temple as it might have appeared, while objects from the Bonnanaro culture (1800–1600 BC) include sacred skulls, each one – for reasons that remain obscure – trepanned.

The Carthaginian, Roman and classical sections display a miscellany of coins, ceramics, busts and mosaic floors. From the **Phoenician and Carthaginian period**

6

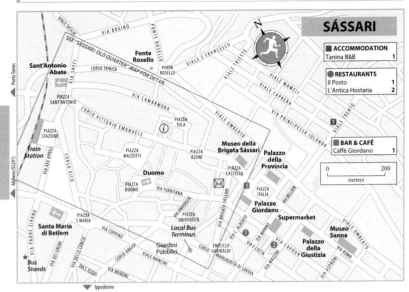

(sixth to fourth centuries BC), there are beautifully preserved articles of jewellery, terracotta masks, Greek-inspired amphorae painted with battles and sex scenes and inscribed stelae. **Roman** remains include material from Nora and Tharros: statuettes, gold rings, pendants, knives and a decree carved in stone from 69 AD commanding a group of mountain-dwellers to leave the low-lying region of the Campidano. Relating to a later period is a model of medieval Sássari, with its girdle of walls intact.

First floor

The museum's prime attraction is its **nuraghic** collection, displayed on the **first floor**. Here, fragments of pottery, jewellery and household implements are interspersed with plans and models of *nuraghi*, sacred wells and "giants' tombs", with explanations (in English and Italian) of their structure and use. Most engrossing is the display of **bronze statuettes**, including warriors with boldly stylized ox-head helmets, boats with equally extravagant prows and a shepherd holding either a dog or goat on the end of a lead. The material was unearthed at various sites throughout the province, notably the Valle dei Nuraghi (see p.226). Some of the finds – a statuette of a bearded man from the Levant, Phoenician ceramics, a necklace of Baltic amber – illustrate the strikingly far-flung trading contacts of the nuraghic civilization. One of the oldest of these items is a Mycenaean vase from around 1400 BC, excavated at Nuraghe Arrubiu (see p.128). For a sketch of Sardinia's nuraghic culture, see Contexts (see p.307).

Castello Aragonese

Piazza Castello • Tues & Sun 10am–1pm, Wed–Sat 10am–1pm & 4.30–7.30pm • €3 • ☎ 331 238 9208

Off the northwestern side of Piazza Italia, the arcades of Portici Bargone e Crispo lead onto long, sloping **Piazza Castello**, site of an Aragonese stronghold from around 1330 until its demolition in the late nineteenth century. You can explore the foundations and walls on a subterranean guided tour of the **Castello Aragonese**, which takes in gun embrasures and cells used by the Inquisition.

Museo della Brigata Sássari

Piazza Castello • Mon–Fri 8am–4.30pm, Sat 8am–1pm • Free • ☎ 079 208 5308

The army barracks that line one side of Piazza Castello contain the **Museo della Brigata Sássari**, dedicated to the renowned Sardinian regiment whose bravery and heavy losses during World War I are taught in every Italian school. Fighting mainly against Austrians in the Alps, the troops were involved in a horrific campaign of trench warfare which resulted in nearly four thousand missing or dead and more than nine thousand wounded. The story is recalled via an absorbing collection of old photos, posters and mementos, alongside a more predictable array of military uniforms, maps and documents.

6

Corso Vittorio Emanuele

Sássari's compact **old quarter** is a quirky counterpoint to the grid of the modern city. Although it is surrounded by noisy main roads, little traffic can penetrate the interior network of alleys and piazzas, making it a great place to stroll around. Effectively bisecting the old town, **Corso Vittorio Emanuele** is a long, partly cobbled ascent from Piazza Sant'Antonio, just along from the train station, to Piazza Azuni. Given its rather run-down appearance, it's easy to miss the medieval doorways, flaking *palazzi* and fragments of Gothic windows jammed in among the shops and alleys, but you should look out in particular for the fifteenth-century **Casa Farris** at no. 23, and the Catalan-Gothic **Casa di Re Enzo** from a century earlier at no. 42, distinguished by its elegantly carved mullioned windows.

Teatro Cívico

Corso Vittorio Emanuele 35 • Tours: Tues–Sat 10am–1pm & 5–8pm, Sun 10am–1pm • €3 • Performances: Sept–April; call ☎ 079 200 8072

Transformed into a theatre after 1880, the **Teatro Cívico** was built by a Piemontese architect in 1830 as the seat of the municipality, and is still the place where Sássari's mayor traditionally meets representatives of the local guilds during the Candelieri festival (see box, p.209). The facade has been elegantly restored, and you can view the grand interior at a performance or on a **guided tour**, usually in Italian, lasting twenty to thirty minutes – book at the tourist office, behind the theatre (see p.211).

The Duomo

Piazza Duomo • Mon–Sat 8.30am–noon & 4–6.45pm, Sun 8.30–11.30am & 5–6.45pm

At the core of the old town, Sássari's **Duomo** is an unexpected eruption of flamboyance amid the cramped jumble of streets. Rearing above the semicircular Piazza del Duomo, its florid seventeenth-century facade is Sardinia's most dazzling example of Baroque architecture. Statues of the *Turritani* saints Gavino, Proto and Gianuario (see p.216) are surmounted by St Nicholas. The **campanile** alongside is a survival from the original thirteenth-century building, with gargoyles and other Gothic details. Enter the church and you'll find a simpler Aragonese-Gothic structure from the fifteenth and sixteenth centuries. The eighteenth-century choir stalls, carved in walnut and much copied in other local churches, are worth seeking out.

Palazzo Ducale and Via Turritana

Palazzo Ducale Piazza del Comune • Tues–Fri 9.30am–1pm & 4.30–7.30pm, Sat 9.30am–1pm • €3 • ☎ 331 437 7156

Squeezed behind the cathedral, the imposing **Palazzo Ducale** was designed by a Piemontese architect at the end of the eighteenth century for the duke of Asinara; today, it houses the *Comune* but preserves some of the rooms and cellars of the old palace that can be visited on a guided tour. Some of the visible cisterns, sewage tanks and foundations of the building belong to a sixteenth-century construction that previously occupied the site, from which busts and majolica vases have been recovered.

6

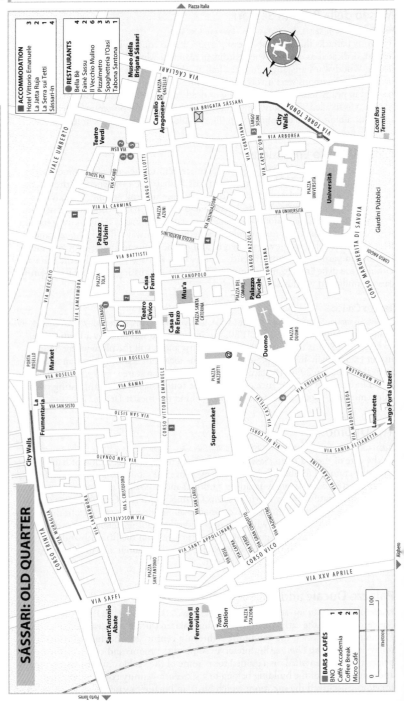

SÁSSARI: OLD QUARTER

▲ Piazza Italia

■ **ACCOMMODATION**
Hotel Vittorio Emanuele 3
La Jatta Ruja 2
La Serra sui Tetti 1
Sássari-in 4

● **RESTAURANTS**
Bella Bè 4
Fainè Sassu 2
Il Vecchio Mulino 6
Pizzalmetro 3
Spaghetteria l'Oasi 5
Tabona Santona 1

Museo della
Brigata Sássari

VIA CAGLIARI

Castello ⊠ PIAZZA
Aragonese CASTELLO

VIA BRIGATA SÁSSARI

City
Walls

VIA TORRE TONDA

Local Bus
Terminus

VIA ARBOREA

LARGO
SISINI

Teatro
Verdi

VIA TURRITANA

VIA USAI

VIA CAPO D'ORO

PIAZZA
UNIVERSITÀ

Università

VIA SEPILO

VIA SCANO

LARGO CAVALLOTTI

VIA AL CARMINE

PIAZZA
AZUNI

VIA INSINUAZIONE

VIA UNIVERSITÀ

VICOLO BERTOLISI

Palazzo
d'Usini

CORSO MARGHERITA DI SAVOIA

Giardini Pubblici

CORSO ANGIOY

VIA BATTISTI

LARGO PAZZIOLA

VIA TURRITANA

VIA MERCATO

PIAZZA
TOLA

Casa
Farris

VIA CANOPOLO

PIAZZA DEL
COMUNE

Palazzo
Ducale

VIALE UMBERTO

VIA LAMARMORA

VIA PETTENADU

Teatro
Cívico

Mus'a

PIAZZA SANTA
CATERINA

VIA SATTA

Casa di
Re Enzo

Duomo

PIAZZA
DUOMO

Market

PORTA
ROSELLO

VIA ROSELLO

VIA ROSELLO

VIA RAMAI

CORSO VITTORIO EMANUELE

PIAZZA
MAZZOTTI

@

VIA ERIGAGLIA

VIA MADDALENEDDA

Laundrette

Largo Porta Utzeri

La
Frumentaria

VIA SAN SISTO

VIA SAN SISTO

Supermarket

VIA CASTELLI

VIA DEI CORSI

VIA SANTA ELISABETTA

City Walls

VIA SAN DONATO

VIA S. CRISTOFORO

VIA MOSCATELLO

VIA SAN CARLO

CORSO TRINITÀ

VIA MURAGLIA

VIA LAMARMORA

PIAZZA
SANT'ANTONIO

VIA ROSE

VIA CAPRA

VIA VERDA

VIA GRAN CONDOTTO

VIA GAZOMETRO

CORSO VICO

VIA SANT'APPOLLINARE

VIA XXV APRILE

VIA SAFFI

Sant'Antonio
Abate

Teatro II
Ferroviario

Train
Station

PIAZZA
STAZIONE

▼ Porto Torres

▼ Alghero

■ **BARS & CAFÉS**
BNO 1
Caffè Accademia 4
Coffee Break 2
Micro Café 3

0   100
metres

Behind the palazzo extends the long **Via Turritana**, once a hive of gold- and silver-workers. The tradition is maintained today by a few watchmakers and jewellers.

Mus'a

Piazza Santa Caterina 4 • Mon & Tues 9am–1.30pm & 3–5pm; Wed–Fri 9am–1.30pm • Free • ☎ 079 231 560, ⊕ pinacotecamusa.it

Between the cathedral and the Corso, Piazza Santa Caterina holds the **Mus'a** (Museo Sássari Arte), an extensive collection of local and island art housed in an ex-Jesuit college. Arranged both thematically and chronologically on three floors, the gallery kicks off with some marvellous medieval works, a highlight of which is an exquisite fourteenth-century triptych showing three saints, probably by a Pisan or Florentine artist. Some rooms are dedicated to individuals such as the Cágliari artist Giovanni Marghinotti and Giuseppe Biasi, from Sássari, whose portraits and landscapes reflected aspects of the Sard identity in the nineteenth and twentieth centuries. Other rooms hold temporary exhibitions.

Piazza Tola and around

Sássari's old commercial centre was located on the northern side of Corso Vittorio Emanuele, at **Piazza Tola**, where a small daily market is a faint reminder of its former role. The piazza, known until the last century as *Carra Manna* (Sard for public weighing device), takes its present name from the judge and historian whose statue stands at its centre, Pasquale Tola (1800–74). Various architectural styles can be seen in the buildings facing the square – most eye-catching is the Renaissance Palazzo d'Usini, dating from 1577, once the home of the duke of Asinara and now the municipal library.

SÁSSARI'S FESTIVALS

Originally staged for the benefit of visiting Spanish kings and other dignitaries, **La Cavalcata** takes place in Sássari on the penultimate weekend of May, the highlight of a month of cultural activities. As one of Sardinia's showiest festivals, it attracts hundreds of richly costumed participants from villages throughout the province and beyond.

The festival is divided into three stages, the morning featuring a **horseback parade** and a slow **procession**, in which the embroidered and decorated costumes unique to each participating village are displayed. In the afternoon, the scene shifts to the **Ippodromo** (race track) on the southern outskirts of town, where hectic **horse races** and ever more daring equestrian feats are performed before a large crowd. Arrive early for the best views – it's about 25 minutes' walk. Saturday and Sunday evenings are devoted to traditional songs and dances in Piazza Italia, showcasing groups from all over the island – the close-harmony singing is especially impressive. A large fair takes over the centre of town during the week leading up to the Cavalcata, so expect lengthy traffic hold-ups.

A much more local affair held on the afternoon of August 14 is **I Candelieri** (or *Li Candareri*), linked to the Pisan devotion to the Madonna of the Assumption. It became a regular event when an outbreak of plague in Sássari mysteriously abated in the sixteenth or seventeenth centuries – versions differ – since when the ritual has been repeated annually on the eve of the feast of the Assumption. For all its religious intent, I Candelieri is a crowded, rumbustious occasion, involving costumed bands of **gremi**, or medieval guilds of merchants, artisans and labourers, staggering through the old town under the weight of nine gigantic wooden "candlesticks", 8m tall, weighing 200–300kg and laden with colourful ribbons and other symbols of the guilds they represent. **La Faradda** (the descent through the town) usually begins at Piazza Castello around 6pm, ending at the church of Santa Maria di Betlem, with a stop en route at the Teatro Cívico, where the representative of the farmers hails Sássari's mayor with a hearty "*A zent'anni!*" ("May you live a hundred years!"), a traditional salute to all the *sassaresi*. If you're in town on the previous afternoon, you should drop in on the **palio**, or bareback horse race, that takes place in the Ippodromo.

A short distance from Piazza Tola, **Via Rosello**, lined with jewellers, leads to the northeastern edge of the old city and the Porta Rosello gate. Opposite this, a grain store dating from around 1600 has been converted into a gallery for temporary exhibitions: **La Frumentaria** (Tues–Sun 10am–1pm & 5–8pm; €3).

Fonte Rosello

Corso Trinità • Tues–Sun: May–Aug 9am–7pm; Sept–April 9am–5pm • Free

Cross Corso Trinità from Porta Rosello to reach the city's most exquisite Renaissance relic, the graceful **Fonte Rosello**, hidden away at the bottom of a grassy flight of cobbled steps from Corso Trinità, below a flyover. The small, square monument, sculpted by Genoan stonemasons in 1606, is delicately carved with four statues representing the seasons, one on each corner, with dolphins curled around their feet.

Fed by a spring that was once one of Sássari's main sources of drinking water, the fountain was traditionally one of the busiest hubs of local life, where throngs of women would converge to scrub clothes and chat. The reconstructed washhouse alongside helps to recall its one-time role, though there's no echo of its former animation. Nonetheless, the *sassaresi* continue to regard the fountain as their greatest treasure.

The city walls

Corso Trinità holds a substantial surviving section of the medieval **city walls** that ringed Sássari until they were pulled down in the nineteenth century. Just by the fuel station, you can make out three heraldic devices bearing symbols of the alliance on which the old city depended: a tower representing Sássari, a cross for the Church and a lily for Pisa. More fragments of the old walls are scattered around the historic centre, notably along Via Torre Tonda.

Sant'Antonio Abate

Piazza Sant'Antonio • Daily 8.30am–noon & 4–6pm

At the bottom of Corso Vittorio Emanuele, the church of **Sant'Antonio Abate** is a noble Baroque structure of clean lines and elegantly proportioned arches. Inside, the star attraction is a gigantic gilded wooden **altarpiece** executed by local craftsmen to a design by Bartolomeo Augusto, a Genoan master of the seventeenth century.

Santa Maria di Betlem

Piazza Santa Maria • Daily 9am–noon & 4–7pm; not Sun during Mass

South of the train and bus stations on the edge of the old quarter, the silver-grey dome of **Santa Maria di Betlem** marks out one of the city's oldest churches and the one dearest to the local people. The building has accumulated a range of different styles during its long lifetime, much of it overlaid with heavy Baroque. Its best and oldest feature is the Romanesque facade, with its sprinkling of Gothic and even Arab styles in the zigzag cornice, rose window and French Gothic columns. The lowest part dates back to the thirteenth century, while the upper part containing the rose window was added in 1465.

The interior

Apart from its fifteenth-century Gothic vaults, the **interior** is overwhelmingly Baroque, the result of a going-over in the nineteenth century when the elliptical cupola was added. The lateral chapels are still there, though, each one dedicated to one of the local guilds which became attached to the church and convent in the thirteenth century, when this was the city's chief Franciscan centre. The best preserved is the first on the left, the Catalan-style stonemasons' chapel; others belong to builders, carpenters, tailors and so on.

Also on show here are the *candelieri*, massive wooden candles associated with the guilds, each one heavily festooned with ribbons and decoration. The items are stored in the church in readiness for their annual outings at the festival of **I Candelieri** (see box, p.209) – if they're not displayed here, you'll usually find them in the adjoining cloisters.

ARRIVAL AND DEPARTURE   SÁSSARI

By plane Fertilia airport near Alghero (see p.176) lies 30km southwest of Sássari, connected by ARST buses with Sássari's bus station (see below).

By car If you're driving, make sure you park legally: seek out a parking attendant or parking meter, and display a ticket (€0.50–€1/hr) to avoid a fine during the times when restrictions are in force (Mon–Sat 9am–1pm & 4–8pm). Free spaces can be hard to find: try around the station area or Viale Umberto.

By train Sássari is on the main FS train network (☎892 021, ⓦtrenitalia.it), with frequent departures to Porto Torres and Ozieri-Chilivani, the junction for Cágliari, Olbia and Oristano. ARST (☎800 865 042, ⓦarst.sardegna.it) also operates regular services to Alghero and Sorso on branch lines, and a summer-only, once-weekly Trenino Verde service (☎079 241 301, ⓦtreninoverde.com) to Tempio-Pausanias.

Destinations Alghero (every 30min–1hr; 35min); Cágliari (5–6 daily, some with change; 3hr 15min); Macomer (5–7 daily, some with change; 1hr 10min–1hr 35min); Olbia (6 daily, some with change; 1hr 45min); Oristano (5–6 daily, some with change; 2hr 10min); Ozieri-Chilivani (6–7 daily; 40min); Porto Torres (3–5 daily; 15min); Sorso

(Mon–Sat every 30min–1hr; 15min); Tempio-Pausanias (1 weekly, currently Sat; 3hr).

By bus The bus stands for long-distance services are on Via Padre Zirano. ARST (see p.202) operates most routes, but Digitur (☎079 262 039, ⓦdigitur.it) also runs a limited service to Bosa, Porto Torres, Castelsardo and Santa Teresa Gallura (tickets on board) and Logudoro Tours (☎079 281 728, ⓦlogudorotours.it) runs to Árdara (currently at 9am daily; tickets on board).

Destinations Alghero (4–10 daily; 45min–1hr); Alghero airport (Fertilia) (9 daily; 30min); Árdara (1 daily; 25min); Argentiera (Mon–Sat 5 daily; 1hr 5min); Bosa (Mon–Sat 3 daily; 2hr 10min); Cágliari (1 daily; 3hr 40min); Castelsardo (Mon–Sat every 30min–1hr, Sun 4–5 daily; 1hr); Chiaramonti (Mon–Sat 5–6 daily, Sun 2 daily; 45min); Monte d'Accoddi (every 30mins–1hr; 20min); Nuoro (4–6 daily; 1hr 45min–2hr 30min); Olbia (Mon–Sat 1 daily; 1hr 45min); Oristano (1 daily; 2hr); Ozieri (Mon–Sat 7–8 daily, Sun 3 daily; 1hr–1hr 30min); Porto Torres (every 30min–1hr; 30min); Santa Teresa Gallura (2–5 daily; 2hr 35min); Sédini (Mon–Sat 4 daily, Sun 1 daily; 1hr 30min); Sorso (every 30min–1hr; 30min); Stintino (Mon–Sat 5–6 daily, Sun 2–4 daily; 1hr 15min); Torralba (Mon–Sat every 30min–1hr, Sun 2 daily; 40min–1hr).

GETTING AROUND AND INFORMATION

By bus Everything of interest in Sássari is easily reached on foot, though bus route #8 is useful, plying a circular route every 12min between the train station, Corso Vittorio Emanuele, Piazza Italia and Via Roma. Buy tickets (€1.20, or €1.70 on board, valid 1hr 30min) before boarding at *tabacchi* or from the kiosk on Via Tavolara in the Giardini Púbblici (public gardens), the main city bus terminus. For more info on city buses see ⓦatpsassari.it.

By taxi There are taxi ranks on Emiciclo Garibaldi, Piazza Castello and the train station, or call ☎079 253 939 (24hr).

By car For excursions beyond town, car rental is available at Avis, Via Predda Niedda 23a (☎079 263 9011, ⓦavis.com); Maggiore, Strada 18 38, Predda Niedda (☎079 260 409, ⓦmaggiore.it); and Sardinya, Viale Caprera 8a (☎079 299 931, ⓦautonoleggiosardinya.it). Most companies also have agencies at Fertilia airport (see p.176).

Tourist office Via Sebastiano Satta 13 (Tues–Fri 9am–1.30pm & 3–6pm, Sat 9am–1.30pm; ☎079 200 8072, ⓦturismosassari.it).

ACCOMMODATION

Most of Sássari's **hotels** are geared to business travellers, though there are a few reasonably priced **B&Bs** in the centre, for which you should book ahead. Campers should head to Alghero (see p.179) or to the north coast east of Platamona (see p.215).

Hotel Vittorio Emanuele Corso Vittorio Emanuele 100 ☎079 235 538, ⓦwww.hotelvittorioemanuele.ss.it; map p.208. An old-town *palazzo* with original architectural features plus antiques and artworks scattered around. Flashily renovated to appeal to business folk, it's comfortable, reasonably priced and equipped with a good restaurant, though bedrooms

with satellite TV are a bit bland. **€70**
★**La Jatta Ruja** Via Cetti 5 ☎342 155 3634, ⓦlajattaruja.com; map p.208. Second-floor B&B off Piazza Tola with intelligent, friendly hosts and fantastic self-serve breakfasts including plenty of fresh fruit. Tastefully furnished rooms are spacious and have modern bathrooms. No credit cards. **€70**

6

La Serra sui Tetti Via al Cármine 18 ☎334 121 7623, ⓦlaserrasuitetti.it; map p.208. This slightly bohemian B&B in the old centre has loads of character, but its greatest assets are its airy top-floor lounge and its roof terrace with 360-degree views – a perfect perch for a glass of wine in the evening. No credit cards. **€70**

Sássari-In Via dell'Insinuazione 20 ☎349 139 5233, ⓦsassari-in.it; map p.208. Central, airy B&B in a quiet lane in the old quarter. The three pastel-toned, a/c rooms

are clean and attractively decorated, and there's a family room. The hosts are full of local tips and copious breakfasts include home-made cakes. **€65**

Tanina B&B Viale Trento 14 ☎346 181 2404, ⓦtaninabandb.com; map p.206. Run by a charming English-speaking host, this B&B 10min from Piazza Italia has three spacious, quiet rooms furnished with antiques. There are separate, private bathrooms, and a kitchen and terrace for guests' use. No credit cards. **€50**

EATING

Sássari's scattered **restaurants** are usually superb, with prices are among the lowest in Sardinia. In the old town, there are still a few places left that serve **fainè** (see box, p.208), and you'll often see horsemeat (*cavallo*), donkey (*asinello*) and roast snails (*lumache* or *monzette*) on the menu. In autumn, it's worth sampling the local mushrooms (*porcini* or *antunna*). Note that many places close in August. If you're **self-catering**, pick up items from the supermarkets on Piazza Matteotti or Via Cavour.

THE OLD QUARTER

Bella Bè Via Usai 8 ☎079 481 6373; map p.208. You'll find original takes on traditional Sard dishes at this restaurant with an elegant, contemporary style. Sit in the large, vaulted room adorned with photographs or in the courtyard, and tuck into *involtini di melanzane* (rolled aubergine), *risotto al cannonau*, fried ricotta with herbs, or grilled squid. Starters are around €11, mains cost €15–20, and fixed-price lunches are €8 and €14. Mon & Sun 7.30–11.30, Tues–Sat 12.30–3pm & 7.30–11.30pm.

★**Fainè Sassu** Via Usai 17 ☎079 236 402; map p.208. An unpretentious but renowned central spot for *fainè* fans (see box p.208). The menu is confined to this Ligurian and *sassarese* speciality, ideal for a snack, costing €5–8, and also available to take away. Service is brisk. Sept–May Mon, Tues & Thurs–Sun 7–11pm.

★**Il Vecchio Mulino** Via Frigaglia 5 ☎079 492 0324; map p.208. A former olive mill makes an unusual venue for this excellent restaurant, with regular music evenings and a complex of cellars where exhibitions are held. The menu focuses on traditional meat dishes, for example *bocconcini di cinghiale al Cannonau* (boar cooked in wine). All dishes cost €9–12. Mon 7.30–10.30pm, Tues–Sat 12.30–2.30 & 7.30–10.30pm, Sun 12.30–2.30pm.

Pizzalmetro Via Usai 10 ☎079 492 0837; map p.208. In this boisterous place, sizzling pizza is ordered by the

square metre – just point out how much you want (half a metre costs €6.50–11). The pizza *ai funghi*, made with a mix of local mushrooms, is luscious. You can eat alfresco in summer, or buy pizzas to take away. Summer Mon–Sat 7–11pm; winter Tues–Sun 7–11pm.

Spaghetteria l'Oasi Via Usai 7 ☎079 237 499; map p.208. This is an essential stop for pasta-lovers, offering a fantastic range of *antipasti* and pasta dishes, including creamy *penne alla carnacina* (with mushrooms, ham and cheese) and justly renowned *spaghetti ai ricci* (with sea urchins) – all around €12. Eat in the clean white interior or at a table in the alley. Mon–Sat 12.30–3pm & 7.30–10pm.

Tabona Santona Piazza Tola 22 ☎347 546 6752; map p.208. Very basic trattoria where the small choice of dishes is chalked up, available in two sizes, *assaggi* ("tasters", €4) and *piatti* (full plates, €8). It's mainly country fare, for example vegetable soups and lamb stews, and usually delicious. There are tables outside on the piazza. Mon–Sat 7.30–11pm.

THE NEW TOWN

Il Posto Via E. Costa 16 ☎079 233 528; map p.206. A casually smart trattoria in the new town, with a salmon-hued, vaulted interior hung with tasteful artworks. A good range of pizza (€5–9) and pasta (€7–11) is available, including *pennette ai quattro formaggi* (with four cheeses). Mon–Sat 7.45–11.30pm.

FAINÈ

No exploration of Sássari's cuisine would be complete without sampling **fainè** (*farinata* in Italian, meaning "floured") – a popular local dish originating in Genoa, and a legacy of that city's former close association with Sássari. This winter speciality (most *fainè* places are closed in summer) consists of *ceci* (chickpea) flour fried into a sort of thick pancake, served either plain (*normale*), or cooked up with onions (*cipolle*), sausage (*salsicce*), anchovy (*acciughe*) or some combination. Best eaten with your hands, they're normally dispatched more quickly than pizza, with second and third helpings as appetite demands; beer is the usual accompaniment. They make a great fast-food snack, costing around €7 per helping.

RIGHT SANTÍSSIMA TRINITÀ DI SACCARGIA (P.224) >

6

L'Antica Hostaria Via Cavour 55 ☎079 200 066; map p.206. In traditionally decorated rooms with pale orange walls, this refined and long-established eatery has earned a gourmet reputation for its creative versions of traditional Sard and Sicilian dishes. You can enjoy a good two-course lunch for under €20, but expect to pay €35–45 for a complete supper (excluding drinks). Mon–Sat 1–3pm & 8–11pm; closed two weeks Aug–Sept.

DRINKING

With its lively student population, Sássari has no lack of good **bars** and **cafés**, most of them packed out and open late during summer. Bars on Piazza Tola are especially animated on summer evenings.

BNO Piazza Tola 2 ☎329 166 9903; map p.208. The full name of this place – *Birreria di Nord Ovest*, or "northwest beer house" – tells you what to expect: a broad selection of craft beers, mainly from this corner of the island but also from other parts of Sardinia, Italy and Europe, served with enthusiasm. There are tables on the square; *panini* and *pizzette* are available to nibble. Daily 6.30pm–1am; closes earlier in winter.

Caffè Accademia Via Torre Tonda 11 ☎079 230 241; map p.208. Congenial spot in the university district with an enclosed veranda for sitting with an ice cream, snack lunch or *marocchino* (espresso mixed with chocolate). There's live music on Fri and Sat evenings. Mon–Sat 7.30am–10.30pm.

Caffè Giordano Piazza Italia 27 ☎079 230 635; map p.206. Ices, smoothies and meals are served at this smart place, which has tables inside, under the arcades and, in summer, on the square. Daily 7.30am–midnight; closed Sat lunch in winter.

Coffee Break Piazza Azuni 19 ☎079 200 9061; map p.208. Quiet bar for a daytime pause or a late drink with a huge range of frappés and free wi-fi. It also makes an excellent lunchtime stop on weekdays for its good-value, all-you-can-eat buffets (€8). Mon–Sat 8am–11pm.

Micro Café Largo Sisini 3 ☎328 739 4747; map p.208. As the name implies, this bar is tiny, but it's got tables in the piazzetta and a great atmosphere, making this a cool, secluded retreat for an aperitif or late-night cocktail. Mon–Sat 7am–2am.

SHOPPING

MARKETS
Food, clothes and household goods The city's main food market is off Porta Rosello (Mon–Sat mornings), and local produce is also sold on Emiciclo Garibaldi on Sat mornings. There's a much bigger open-air market of food, clothes, toys and tools on Mon mornings at Piazzale Segni, near the stadium (up Via Adua from Piazza Conte di Mariano at the southeast end of Viale Umberto). A few stalls selling household items and clothes set up in Piazza Tola every morning Mon–Sat.

Antiques and curios An antiques fair is held in Piazza Santa Caterina on the last Sun of most months (Sept–June) 8am–1pm).

SUPERMARKETS
Conad, on the corner of Via Cavour and Via Manno in the new town, has the biggest selection of food in the centre (Mon–Sat 8am–9pm, Sun 9am–1.30pm); in the old quarter, Cobec in Piazza Mazzotti has similar hours.

DIRECTORY

Hospital Ospedale Civile Santíssima Annunziata, Viale Italia (☎079 206 1000).

Internet Internet Point, Piazza Matteotti 4 (Mon–Fri 8.30am–1pm & 3–10pm, Sat & Sun 4–10pm; July & Aug closes 11.30pm); €1/20min; also long-distance calls, printing and fax service.

Laundry Lava Santa Maria, Largo Porta Utzeri (daily 9am–9pm); €4/8kg, dryer €1/8min.

Pharmacy V. Simon on Piazza Castello, open all day and night (except Mon–Fri 1–4.30pm, Sat 1–8pm, Sun 9am–8pm). When closed, a notice on the window lists open pharmacies nearby.

Post office Central Ufficio Postale is on Via Brigata Sássari. An exchange facility for cash is in the room on the left, stamps are in a separate room on the right (Mon–Fri 8.20am–7.05pm, Sat 8.20am–12.35pm).

Travel agencies Ajò Viaggi, Piazza Fiume 1, (☎079 200 222).

The Sássari Riviera

When the *sassaresi* need a break, they head 15km north to the long stretch of pine-backed beaches that make up the **Sássari Riviera**. The main resort is **PLATAMONA**, where a row of bars and pizzerias stand a stone's throw from the sea and lidos charge a few euros a day for a parasol and sunlounger, plus the use of showers and a car park. You'll find fewer crowds farther east, however, where the fine sand beaches are sheltered from the SP81 coast road by a curtain of pine, eucalyptus and juniper trees, offering numerous hideaways for a private swim or even camping rough (be extra careful not to start fires). On the other side of the SP81, you can wander around a nature reserve surrounding the **Stagno di Platamona** lagoon, a fine place for a picnic.

There's another concentration of beachside activity at **Marina di Sorso**. Five kilometres inland, the village of **SORSO** lies at the centre of the fertile **Romangia** region, whose fruit and vegetables liberally fill the shops and markets hereabouts. The local grapes go into some of Sardinia's best Cannonau, Moscato, Vermentino and Monica wines, and the place is also famed for its baskets woven with dwarf-palm leaves.

6

ARRIVAL AND DEPARTURE

THE SÁSSARI RIVIERA

By bus City buses BB (Buddi-Buddi) and MP (Marina di Platamona) leave for Platamona from Via Tavolara in Sássari's Giardini Púbblici every 40min (every 1hr 20min in winter), taking about 30min. Buy tickets before boarding from the kiosk (€1.20 valid 1hr 30min; €3 valid all day).

ACCOMMODATION

Li Nibari Località Marina di Sorso ☎079 310 303, Ⓦ campinglinibari.com. Signposted off the coast road 5km or so east of Platamona, this three-star campsite offers a bar, restaurants and a supermarket, as well as various sports facilities in summer, including two pools (one for children), while the private beach is just metres away. Two- and four-bed mobile homes and bungalows are available from €95 for two, plus extras. Closed Nov–April. Pitches **€30**

Porto Torres and around

Sixteen kilometres northwest of Sássari, the Carlo Felice highway ends its long run from Cágliari at **PORTO TORRES**, once the main Roman base on this coast and, thanks to its port, still one of the main gateways into Sardinia today. It's an unprepossessing place, with a smoky industrial zone dominating the western side of town, but it's worth pressing on to view its magnificent Romanesque **Basilica di San Gavino** and a cluster of **Roman remains** to the west of the centre, including a well-preserved, seven-arched **Roman bridge** crossing the River Mannu, almost hidden between newer bridges and thick growths of bamboo 200m west of the Antiquarium.

Most of the action in Porto Torres takes place on the main **Corso Vittorio Emanuele**, where you'll find the majority of the town's banks, travel agents and bars. The main drag ends at Piazza Colombo, overlooked by an Aragonese tower, and the **port**, which is also a hub of activity in summer. Excellent **beaches** lie east of here in the **Balai** neighbourhood, lively with bars and trattorias in season. A series of secluded rocky coves continue eastward, leading to the broad sandy beaches of Platamona (see p.214).

Brief history

There have always been settlements on this site, drawn to its natural harbour and position at the mouth of the River Mannu, one of the island's longest rivers. Most traces of the town's pre-Roman past have long been effaced, though there is considerable evidence of the Roman colony, **Turris Libyssonis**, supposedly founded by Julius Caesar in the first century BC.

Porto Torres quickly developed as an important shipping stop between the Italian mainland and the Iberian peninsula, and subsequently became the centre of a cult devoted to the *Mártiri Turritani* – three local martyrs (see p.216). By the tenth century the town had become the capital of one of Sardinia's four *giudicati*, and continued to wield commercial influence under the Pisans, though Saracen raids and Genoan assaults eventually led to its decline and a transfer of power inland to Sássari. Today,

Porto Torres is thriving once more, its economic role buoyed by the petrochemical works to the west of town as well as constant shipping traffic.

Basilica di San Gavino

Corso Vittorio Emanuele • Daily: May–Sept 9am–1pm & 3–6.45pm; Oct–April 9am–1pm & 3–5.45pm • €3, €4 with guided tour • ☎ 348 899 6823

From the port, follow the main Corso Vittorio Emanuele to find the **Basilica di San Gavino**. Originally standing in open country, its present backstreet location diminishes the monument's grandeur, though, as Sardinia's largest and – according to some – finest Romanesque structure, it still makes quite an impact. The slits of windows and blind arcading around the fine yellowy stonework contribute to its austere, fortified appearance, a reminder that it survived innumerable Saracen attacks during the Middle Ages.

Occupying the site of a Roman necropolis, there has been a church here since the sixth century, dedicated to the *Mártiri Turritani* – San Gavino, San Proto and San Gianuario, three Roman soldiers beheaded in 304. The present basilica was begun by Pisans in around 1030 and probably finished by 1080, though in the twelfth century the church was enlarged and given an unusual second apse, lending it a slightly confused, directionless look. Of the three lateral doors, the one on the north is oldest, decorated with human and animal figures; the other two are later additions, one of them, the main entrance, Catalan-Gothic from 1492.

The interior

Gloomily lit by the narrow windows, the naves and aisles of the **interior** are separated by 28 marble columns, dug up from the old Roman town. At the back of the nave, with its harmonious wooden roof, a prominent catafalque carries wooden images of the three *Mártiri Turritani*, near a dashing seventeenth-century statue of San Gavino on a horse. Across the nave, stairs lead down to the first of the basilica's two **crypts** (€1.50), a long room dating from the seventeenth century, lined with statues of saints and several Roman sarcophagi, one of them elaborately carved with figures of a seated man and woman – whose tomb this was – surrounded by Apollo and the nine Muses.

At the far end, a door gives access to the foundations of the original paleo-Christian church. From the ante-crypt, more steps lead down to a lower **crypt**, where the bones of the martyrs – placed here in the nineteenth century – are displayed in arched niches, together with more sarcophagi.

Ask at the church about visits to the paleo-Christian church of **San Gavino a Mare**, perched on the rocks above the beach at Balai, a kilometre east of the centre – supposedly the first burial place of the martyrs.

Antiquarium Turritano

Via Ponte Romano • Tues–Sat 9am–8pm, Sun 9am–2pm, or 9am–8pm first Sun of month • €2, €3 including archeological site • ☎ 079 514 433

The major archeological remains in Porto Torres lie off the seafront on the western edge of town (less than a 10min walk from the Corso, beyond Maríttima train station). Here, the poorly marked **Antiquarium Turritano** displays finds from various digs in the area of Turris Libyssonis, chiefly from the archeological site adjacent. Among the highlights is the **Maschera Maetske**, a ferocious-looking marble satyr's head, originally the mouth of a fountain, that was unearthed here in 2003. Other exhibits include ceramics and votive ornaments, a lead sarcophagus, fragments of mosaic floors and some well-preserved busts and statuettes. Labelling is practically nonexistent, however, and you'd do well to hire an **audioguide** (€3), available in various languages; alternatively you can join a **guided tour**, though groups are preferred – ask for details at the museum desk.

The archeological site

The **archeological site** holding remains of the Roman city is only accessible as part of a guided tour from the museum. Reached along flagstoned roads bordered by stumps of columns, the centrepiece is the **Terme Centrali**, a shattered baths complex dating from the third or fourth century BC, including a frigidarium and richly mosaicked floors. The structure was traditionally known as the Palazzo di Re Bárbaro ("Palace of King Barbarus"), after the semi-mythical Roman governor who presided over the martyrdom of the town's saints. A custom-built bunker shelters the **Domus di Orfeo**, holding most vivid mosaics of all, including the voluptuous **mosaico di Orfeo**, showing Orpheus strumming his lyre surrounded by birds and beasts.

6

Monte d'Accoddi

April, May, Sept & Oct Tues–Sat 9am–6pm, Sun 9am–2pm; June–Aug Tues–Sat 9am–7pm, Sun 9am–2pm; Nov–March Tues–Sun 10am–2pm • €3 • ☎ 334 807 4449 • Take any bus between Porto Torres and Sássari, stop at Ponte Secco

Six kilometres southeast of Porto Torres, a right turn off the Carlo Felice highway (SS131) brings you to **Monte d'Accoddi** where, surrounded by cereal fields, a sanctuary dating back to the Copper Age (2450–1850 BC) has been excavated. There's little visible construction remaining, but the long tapering mound, measuring 30m by 38m, and the earthen ramp ascending to a platform at its top are clearly defined. This alone sets the site apart from anything else found in Sardinia, or in the entire Mediterranean. The flat-topped pyramid seems to have more in common with Mesopotamian or Aztec temples, hence its popular name of "ziggurat" or "ziqqurat".

The outlines of various structures – including stone-walled dwellings and even a menhir – can be seen on either side of the ramp, and there's evidence that there may have been some kind of sacred spot here from as early as 3000 BC. The sanctuary was probably used for sacrifices and other ceremonial functions, though you need to make an imaginative leap to picture it as it might have once appeared – it helps to have seen the laser image in Sássari's Museo Sanna (see p.205). It's an impressive site, nonetheless, with views back to Sássari and north to the Golfo dell'Asinara.

ARRIVAL AND DEPARTURE   PORTO TORRES

BY FERRY

Ferries use either the old harbour in the centre of Porto Torres or the Porto Industriale 2km west of town, connected to the centre by a shuttle bus (*navetta*). Usually, Tirrenia (☎892 123, ⊛tirrenia.it) uses the central Porto Cívico, while Grimaldi (☎081 496 444, ⊛grimaldi-lines.it), SNCM (⊛sncm.fr) and La Meridionale (⊛lameridionale.fr) ferries dock at the Porto Industriale. The *navetta* to the Porto Industriale leaves from the Aragonese tower at the port 2hr before sailings, making a stop at the Maríttima train station.

Reservations If you're leaving Sardinia from Porto Torres, make sure you book as early as possible, especially in peak season, and particularly if you're shipping a vehicle. Buy tickets directly from the ticket offices in the Stazione Maríttima, at the bottom of Corso Vittorio Emanuele, or by phone, online or from one of the authorized travel agents in town, such as Paglietti, Corso Vittorio Emanuele 19 (☎079 514 477), the official outlet for tickets for SNCM and La Meridionale.

Destinations Barcelona, Spain (Grimaldi; April–Sept 1–5 weekly; 11hr 45min); Civitavécchia (Grimaldi; April–Sept 1–5 weekly; 7hr 15min); Genoa (Tirrenia 1 daily; 11hr 30min); Marseille, France (SNCM & La Meridionale; sporadic; 11–17hr); Propriano, Corsica (SNCM & La Meridionale; sporadic; 3hr 30min).

BY TRAIN

Porto Torres has two train stations: Porto Torres, a 10min walk south of the harbour, near the basilica, and Porto Torres Maríttima, nearer the museum and port. All services stop at both.

Destinations Cágliari (3–5 daily, most with change at Sássari and/or Ozieri-Chilivani; 3hr 35min–4hr 40min); Sássari (every 2–20min; 15min).

BY BUS

ARST (see p.202) and Digitur (for limited services to Sássari, Bosa, Castelsardo and Santa Teresa Gallura; ⊛digitur.it) buses stop at Via Mare, by the harbour.

Destinations Alghero (5–6 daily; 1hr); Bosa (1 daily; 2hr 30min); Castelsardo (June–Sept 1 daily; 45min); Monte d'Accoddi (every 30min–1hr; 10min); Santa Teresa Gallura (June–Sept; 1 daily; 2hr); Sássari (every 30min–1hr; 35min); Stintino (Mon–Sat 5–6 daily, Sun 2–4 daily; 40min).

6

INFORMATION AND ACTIVITIES

Tourist office Stazione Maríttima, Via A. Bassu (April–Sept daily 9am–1pm & 4–7pm, Oct–March Sat & Sun 9am–1pm & 3–6pm; ☎ 079 500 8711, ⓦ comune.portotorres.ss.it). The Stazione Maríttima also has an information desk for Asinara and a left-luggage office.

Tours to Asinara Boat tours to the island of Asinara (see p.199) leave from the port, taking around 1hr

30min. Delcomar (ⓦ delcomar.it) operates a public service with two departures/day (May–Sept daily; Oct–April Tues, Fri & Sun); buy tickets from the kiosk on Piazza Colombo. Ask at the tourist office or see ⓦ parcoasinara.org for a list of authorized private operators. Note that services are more frequent, shorter and cheaper from Stintino (see box, p.199).

ACCOMMODATION

Elisa Via Mare 6 ☎ 079 513 260, ⓦ hotelelisa portotorres.com. The most central hotel in town, right on the port and near the bus stop, this old-fashioned, family-run three-star is low on atmosphere, but most of its rooms overlook the boats (some have balconies) and there's a restaurant. **€80**

L'Ancora Via Cavour 65 ☎ 340 164 9541, ⓦ beblancora .it. Midway between the port and San Gavino, this B&B in an airy modern apartment offers spacious, clean rooms with fridges and efficient a/c. The owners are helpful and early breakfasts are provided for ferry-catchers. No credit cards. **€70**

EATING AND DRINKING

★**Cristallo** Piazza XX Settembre 14 ☎ 079 514 909. A portside *passeggiatta* should be accompanied by an ice cream from this locally renowned gelateria. Flavours include *torrone di Tonara* (Sardinian nougat), *cassata* and Nutella. It's a good breakfast stop too, serving coffees, snacks and pastries. Mon 6am–2pm, Tues–Sun 6am–midnight.

Il Mare Via Galilei 30 ☎ 079 502 021. On a quiet road parallel to the port, this neighbourhood ristorante serves the best seafood in Porto Torres, beautifully presented and full of flavour. The decor is elegantly simple and there's a small terrace for eating alfresco. Dishes cost €12–15 à la carte, or you could order the €35 menu. Mon–Sat 8am–1.30pm & 4.30–8pm.

La Bottega Piazza Venti Settembre 1 ☎ 079 514 834. This *alimentari* at the bottom of the Corso is the perfect stop for a do-it-yourself lunch or food for the ferry; apart from *panini* they sell a range of local cheese, salami, wines and *mirto* liqueur, yoghurt and bread. Mon–Sat 8am–1.30pm & 4.30–8pm.

Piazza Garibaldi Piazza Garibaldi ☎ 079 501 570. Occupying a prime position among the cluster of bars and restaurants in this busy piazza, this ristorante-pizzeria has won awards for its pizzas (€4–8), and the meat and fish dishes aren't bad either (€10–12), including delicious *cozze alla marinara* (mussels) and *pennette allo scoglio* (seafood pasta). Tables outside fill up quickly in summer. Daily 12.30–3pm & 8pm–midnight.

Castelsardo and around

Northeast of Sássari, the compact region of **Anglona** is a hilly landscape bound by Logudoro and Gallura to the south and east, and scattered with the remains of a prehistoric "petrified forest". The rocky northern littoral is the perfect setting for Anglona's main town, **CASTELSARDO**, picturesquely draped over a promontory overlooking the Golfo dell'Asinara, with reddish-grey houses huddled below the stout castle. The fortified citadel here was the Doria power base in Sardinia for nearly 250 years, and the historic centre preserves a pungent medieval flavour. However, while it retains a small fishing fleet, Castelsardo is first and foremost a fully fledged **holiday resort**, thanks to its photogenic setting and its pre-eminence as a centre of Sard **handicrafts**, prominently displayed in the narrow lanes of the old quarter (see box, p.220).

CASTELSARDO'S FESTIVALS

Castelsardo's **Easter festivities** are known for the dramatic torchlit procession, **Lunissanti**, a tradition predating the Spanish conquest of the town. A cortege of cowled figures threads through the old town on Easter Monday to the accompaniment of medieval chants in Latin and Sard. The town's other major festival is on August 2, when the **Madonna degli Ángeli** is celebrated with games and traditional dancing.

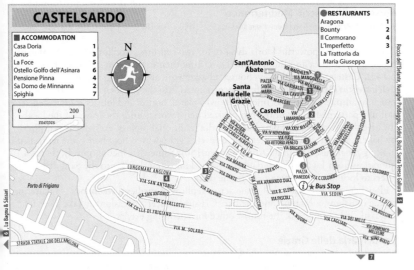

Outside the historic centre, there's little of specific interest in the newer neighbourhoods, though the rocky cove immediately below and west of the citadel is undeniably pretty, sheltering an attractive sandy beach. Farther west, the **Porto di Frigianu** fishing anchorage and yachting marina is watched over by an old defensive tower, and there are a couple of bars where you can sit and watch the low-key activity. Eastwards, there's another small beach, **La Vignaccia**, squeezed up among the rocks on the far side of town, easily reached on foot and good for a dip.

Brief history

Genoa's powerful Doria dynasty established a stronghold at Castelsardo at the start of the twelfth century, giving it the name of "Castelgenovese". Embroiled in the power clashes between Genoa, Pisa and Spain, the strategically crucial town was one of the last Genoan centres in the Torres *giudicato* to hold out against the Spaniards. When he finally took possession of the town in 1448, Alfonso V immediately changed its name to Castel Aragonese, though the locals were mollified when, in 1511, Charles V accorded the port the same rights and privileges as the rival Spanish sea base at Alghero. Supported by four thousand French troops, the Doria made a last, futile effort to recapture their home base in 1527, then virtually disappeared from the Sardinian scene altogether. The town's present, safely neutral name was given by the Savoyard kings in 1769.

The old quarter

It's a steep but rewarding ascent up the steps and alleys of Castelsardo's **old quarter**. Home-made baskets and other artefacts are displayed in doorways, brightly coloured plants are draped over walls, and time-weathered arches and crumbling doorways adorn the minute lanes. Glimpses of the rocky shore and sea below bring relief from the closed, insular air of the place, though the best views, of course, are from the top, crowned by the battlements of the heavily restored **castello**. From here, it's an uninterrupted prospect across the gulf to the isle of Asinara, off Sardinia's northwestern point; to the northeast, it's sometimes possible to sight the coast of Corsica – though for this the conditions need to be particularly good. The sunsets here are especially memorable.

6

Museo dell'Intreccio Mediterraneo
Via Marconi • Daily: April–June & Sept 10am–10pm; July & Aug 9am–1am; Oct–March 10.30am–4.30pm • €3 for castle and museum • ☎ 347 111 8547

The abode of the powerful Doria dynasty for two centuries, and for ten years home to Eleonora d'Arborea and Brancaleone Doria after their marriage in 1376 (see box, p.143), Castelsardo's **castle** now houses a basketwork and weaving museum, the **Museo dell'Intreccio Mediterraneo**, artfully incorporated into the small chambers. There's much to admire in this assortment of bowls, plates, bottles and lobster traps, often skilfully patterned, some of the most prized items woven from the leaves of the local dwarf-palm. For the most part, these are the traditional tools of everyday life, utilized by bakers, farmers and fishermen; there's even a grass-woven boat here – the truncated-looking *fassoni* used around Oristano (see p.150). Somewhat incongruously, there's a quotation from Joyce's *Ulysses* daubed onto a door – translated into the Sard dialect, it refers to local people's attachment to the land.

Elsewhere in the castle you'll come across replicas of medieval **weaponry** – a battering ram, a crossbow, a catapult and the like. Classical concerts occasionally take place in the castle in summer: ask the tourist office for upcoming events.

Santa Maria delle Grazie
Piazza Santa Maria • Daily: summer 9am–7pm; winter 9am–5.30pm

From the castle, it's a short walk to the church of **Santa Maria delle Grazie**, a misshapen building squeezed into the available space. The richly decorated church holds a special role among the townspeople, as the repository of the sacred *Critu Nieddu*, or Black Christ, a fourteenth-century crucifix kept in the sacristy. The church marks the start and end of Castelsardo's Easter Monday procession.

Sant'Antonio Ábate
Piazza del Duomo • **Church** Daily: summer 7am–1pm & 3–8pm; winter 9am–5.30pm • **Crypt** Daily: summer 10am–1pm & 3–7pm; winter 10am–1pm & 3.30–5.30pm • €4 • ☎ 348 736 6604

After the cramped lanes of most of the old centre, it's a surprise to come across the relatively large terrace that accommodates Castelsardo's cathedral, **Sant'Antonio Ábate**. Overlooking reddish boulders washed by the sea, it's an evocative spot; the octagonal campanile has a majolica-tiled cupola which adds a splash of colour. The church itself retains some evidence of the original Gothic structure, and its sixteenth-century rebuilding and Baroque accretions are not unsympathetic.

ARTIGIANATO IN CASTELSARDO

Many people come to Castelsardo purely to shop, and the lower town has plenty of outlets. The famed local **artigianato**, or handicrafts, has grown in the last twenty years from a small cottage industry to a major year-round money-spinner. Cork, coral and ceramic goods are here in abundance, as well as shelves full of African-looking Sard wooden masks, though the main craft for which Castelsardo is known is *l'intreccio*, or **basketwork**. Straw, wicker, reeds, raffia and asphodel leaves are all used to create an incredible variety of containers, trays and furniture, though the material most associated with Castelsardo is locally picked dwarf-palm leaves.

A good place to visit before shopping is the **museum of basket-weaving** in Castelsardo's castle (see above), to get an idea of what the best examples of the genre should look like. As for the emporia, don't spend too much time shopping around – you'll see the same products everywhere, with very similar price tags, and much of it is made elsewhere using synthetic materials. More satisfying is to buy directly from the weavers themselves in the old quarter – mostly women working the stuff on their doorsteps amid displays of their wares – for which you'll need to sharpen up your bargaining techniques. You can also find some good work in nearby villages such as Tergu (see p.223), where the quality is at least as decent as that in town.

Inside, the centre of the fussy marble altarpiece holds the building's main treasure, the **Madonna with Angels**, a fragment of a work by a local fifteenth-century painter known simply as the **Maestro di Castelsardo**, whose synthesis of Italian and Flemish Gothic elements was hugely influential in Sardinia. Other items worth looking out for are the painted wooden pulpit hanging off one of the piers in front of the altar, the sculpted figures of musicians and animals on the capitals of the pillars on either side of the altar and, behind this, some finely carved choir stalls.

To the left of the altar, a flight of steps leads down to the **crypt**, where, in four sombre stone chambers connected by narrow steps, there are more works of religious art, notably further sections of the Maestro di Castelsardo's *retablo*, one depicting four apostles, another – with liberal use of Byzantinesque gold – showing the Holy Trinity.

6

The Roccia dell'Elefante

SP134, 5km southwest of Castelsardo

Exiting eastwards from Castelsardo on the Sédini road (just beyond the Viddalba junction), you can't miss the **Roccia dell'Elefante**, whose elephant-shaped profile is featured on hundreds of postcards, its drooping "trunk" practically swishing the passing vehicles. Clearly the wind-eroded trachyte monolith has long held an emblematic power, for there are some pre-nuraghic *domus de janas* tombs hewn beneath it; look carefully on the wall of the right-hand chamber to make out a carving of the curling bull-horns which are such a pronounced motif on nuraghic figurines.

Nuraghe Paddaggiu

Valledoria road, 6km southwest of Castelsardo

On a grassy knoll by the roadside a kilometre or so east of the Roccia dell'Elefante, the well-preserved **Nuraghe Paddaggiu** was built during the last phase of *nuraghe* culture. Also (erroneously) called Nuraghe Su Tesoru, its correct name – "haystack" – probably refers to the use to which most farmers assigned these ancient structures. The *nuraghe* consists of a niched central chamber, with the remains of stairs leading up to a second storey that no longer survives. Traces of two lateral towers can also be seen.

Lu Bagnu

Five kilometres west of Castelsardo, the blandly functional holiday resort of **LU BAGNU** has good swimming in limpid waters off the rocks at the bottom of cliffs, an excellent hostel (see p.222) and some lively bar-life in summer that might entice you on a night out from Castelsardo.

ARRIVAL AND DEPARTURE   CASTELSARDO

By bus All buses stop at the central Piazza Pianedda, at the bottom of the old town, and there's another bus stop by the beach in the lower town. ARST runs most of the routes; Digitur (☎079 262 039, Ⱐdigitur.it) operates a fast but infrequent summer service connecting Castelsardo with Valledoria, Santa Teresa Gallura, Porto Torres and Alghero/Fertilia airport, while Sardabus (☎079 684 087, Ⱐsardabus.it) runs separate services from Castelsardo to Lu Bagnu, Tergu and Chiaramonti, and to Valledoria, Aggius and Tempio Pausania.

Destinations Bulzi (Mon–Sat 4–5 daily, Sun 1 daily; 30–40min); Porto Torres (June–Sept 1 daily; 40min); Santa Teresa Gallura (2–5 daily; 1hr 15min–1hr 40min); Sássari (Mon–Sat every 30min–1hr, Sun 4–5 daily; 1hr); Sédini

(Mon–Sat 4–5 daily, Sun 1 daily; 30min); Sorso (Mon–Sat every 30min–1hr, Sun 6–7 daily; 30min); Tempio Pausania (Mon–Sat 4–5 daily, Sun 2–4 daily; 20min); Tergu (Mon–Sat 4–5 daily, June–Sept Sun 2 daily; 20min); Valledoria (5–8 daily; 25min).

By car If you're driving, leave your vehicle around the piazza, or in the car park reached from the piazza's top-right corner. You could drive up the main Via Nazionale and take your chances parking on the road leading up to the castle, but spaces are usually limited; you can't drive into the tight web of alleys that make up the old centre, and there are summer restrictions on some roads around it (look for signs).

6

GETTING AROUND AND INFORMATION

By bus A local circular bus operates in summer linking Castelsardo with the beaches at Lu Bagnu (every 60min; 1hr 30min; €1 one-way; tickets on board). There are stops at the castle, Piazza Pianedda and Lungomare Anglona.

Tourist office The tourist office is on Piazza Pianedda (Mon–Fri 9am–noon & 4.30–6.30pm; ☎079 471 506, ⑨ castelsardoturismo.it).

ACCOMMODATION

The seafront **Lungomare Anglona** holds a string of multistorey holiday hotels, about a 1km walk from the citadel. Drivers staying in the **old town** should be prepared for lots of steps and won't be able to park nearby. In August, some hotels demand a minimum stay of three to seven nights at half or full board. There's a good hostel at the beach resort of Lu Bagnu (see p.221), where you'll also find more seasonal hotels if everywhere in town is booked up.

★**Casa Doria** Via Garibaldi 10 ☎349 355 7882, ⑨ casadoria.it. Old-town B&B with wooden ceilings, antique Sardinian furnishings and a lovely breakfast room at the top with breathtaking views. One room (costing €85) is en suite, two share facilities, and all have a/c. Closed Feb. **€60**

Janus Via Roma 85 ☎079 479 242, ⑨ janushotel.it. Just off the seafront, this hotel has plush but smallish rooms – those at the front have great views and some have balconies, but the road can be noisy in summer. Guests can use the spa facitiies and small pool in a neighbouring hotel. Closed Oct–March. **€100**

Ostello Golfo dell'Asinara Via Sardegna, Lu Bagnu ☎079 474 031, ⑨ ostellodicastelsardo.com. On the outskirts of the resort of Lu Bagnu, 5km west of Castelsardo, this spacious hostel lies amid greenery off the Tergu road, with great views from its wide terrace. Prices include breakfast, and you can eat dinner here (July & Aug only) for €10.50. No credit cards. Closed Oct–Easter. Dorms **€14**; doubles **€40**

Pensione Pinna Lungomare Anglona 7 ☎079 470 168. This old-style, family-run *pensione* is Castelsardo's cosiest option, above a popular trattoria with enchanting views over the beach and castle. The ten rooms are clean

and simply furnished. Closed Oct–Easter. **€70**

Sa Domo de Minnanna Via Mezzu Teppa 5 ☎349 367 6105, ✉ sadomodeminnanna@yahoo.it. Directly below the *centro stórico*, this simple B&B offers excellent value, with three clean and quiet rooms with private bathrooms, and great breakfasts. No credit cards. **€50**

Spighia Via Eleonora d'Arborea 77 ☎340 090 8440, ⑨ bebspighia.it. This modern B&B may not be in Castelsardo's *centro stórico*, but it has the best views of it, from its high position 400m inland. There are three rooms – one with a private bathroom. In summer, delicious breakfasts are taken on the furnished terrace, with stupendous views of the *castello*. No credit cards. **€60**

CAMPSITE

La Foce Valledoria, 15km east of Castelsardo ☎079 582 109, ⑨ foce.it. On the banks of the Coghinas river and close to acres of sandy beach, this campsite is the biggest and best equipped of the sites in the area. It offers a range of family-orientated facilities including two pools and a lagoon, across which campers are ferried to a good beach. Kayaking, sailing and windsurfing are on hand, and bungalows and caravans are available (from €90 for two in high season). Closed Oct to late April. Pitches **€33**

EATING AND DRINKING

Castelsardo has a good selection of places to **eat** and **drink**, some (in the old town) quite expensive, but many offering good-value tourist menus. There's a better choice of bars and trattorias lower down; it's worth remembering that *Pensione Pinna* (see above) has a cheerful trattoria with a terrace facing the sea.

Aragona Via Manganella ☎079 470 081. On a terrace above the sea, just along from the cathedral, this bar/restaurant run by two brothers serves drinks and light meals until late, and makes a good choice if you're looking for a view. The brothers' speciality is *spaghetti al mirto* (flavoured with myrtle; €9), and there are set-price menus for €18 and €20. If you just want a snack, you could opt for hot *panini* (€4–6) or grilled aubergines (€6.50). Mid-March to mid-Oct daily 9am–2am, meals served noon–3pm & 7pm–midnight.

★**Bounty** Via Lamármora 12 ☎079 479 043, ⑨ ristoranteilbounty.com. Among the standout dishes at

this place near the castle are excellent *zuppa di pesce* (fish soup), *risotto agli scampi*, roast pork and some of the best *seadas* you'll find anywhere. It's on two floors, a spiral staircase connecting the traditional, brick-vaulted lower floor to the more modern part above. Pasta dishes are €10–15, mains €15–20. June–Sept daily noon–2.30pm & 8–10.30pm; Oct–May closed Wed.

★**Il Cormorano** Via Colombo 5 ☎079 470 628, ⑨ ristoranteilcormorano.net. This smart, traditional restaurant below Piazza Pianedda has some of the freshest seafood dishes in town, a strong list of island wines and a veranda. Choose from the main menu (€12–15 for first courses, €23–25 for mains) or the bistro lunch menu (dishes under €10). April to mid-June & Oct Tues–Sun 12.30–2.30pm & 8–11pm; mid-June to Sept daily same times; Dec–March Sat & Sun same times.

L'Imperfetto Via Brigata Sássari 10 ☎ 344 298 1652. In a narrow lane above Piazza Pianedda, this convivial but understated seafood restaurant has exposed-granite walls, wooden tables and wooden beams. It's well worth seeking out, with wonderful *antipasti* and dishes such as *grigliata di pesce* (mixed seafood grill). Prices are average, with a tuna

steak at €18 and fixed-price menus at lunchtime (€15) and in the evening (€30). Daily 12.30–2.30pm & 7.30–10pm; reduced hours in winter.

La Trattoria da Maria Giuseppa Via Colombo 6 ☎ 079 470 661. An excellent mid-range choice round the corner from Piazza Pianedda, focusing on *cucina casalinga* – homely dishes – such as *zuppa gallurese* and roast pork or lamb. Starters cost €8–13, mains are €10–16 and pizzas €6–9. Arrive early for tables with sea views. June–Sept daily 12.30–2.30pm & 7.30–11.30pm; Oct–May closed Mon.

6

Inland from Castelsardo

With your own vehicle, you'll be able to explore the hill country **inland from Castelsardo**, stamped with the traces of Sardinia's ancient and medieval civilizations. A foray of only a few kilometres will bring you into the very heart of Anglona. Bus services, however, are limited and sporadic.

Tergu

From Lu Bagnu (see p.221), a road winds 7km inland to **TERGU**, a small village best known for its square-faced Pisan-Romanesque church of **Nostra Signora di Tergu** (also called Santa Maria; daily 9am–7.30pm), from the early thirteenth century. The facade is the most interesting feature, with blind arcading and red trachyte stone alternating with paler limestone, and there are the ruins of a once-powerful Benedictine monastery alongside. The church is unmissable at the southern end of the village.

A visit to Tergu is a good opportunity to seek out examples of local craftwork, often similar to the items on sale in Castelsardo, but cheaper.

La Rocca

Strada Statale • May–Sept Mon–Fri 10am–1pm & 3–6pm, Sat & Sun 10am–1pm; Oct–April call to visit • €2.50 • ☎ 349 844 0436 • 15km southeast of Castelsardo on SP134

On the main road in the centre of **SÉDINI** (a village preserving a number of Aragonese-Gothic buildings), a group of ancient tombs – or *domus de janas* – has been gouged out of a massive calcareous rock known as **La Rocca**. Used as a prison in the Middle Ages, and incorporated into a dwelling in the nineteenth century, the tombs now exhibit a collection of fossils, agricultural tools and other ethnographic items.

San Pietro delle Immágini

SP134, 3km south of Bulzi

Arguably the prettiest of the churches scattered around Sássari's hinterland is **San Pietro delle Immágini** (also called San Pietro di Simbranos). Marooned in a flowery meadow in a valley 3km south of **BULZI**, a village 7km east of Sédini on the SP134, the church was founded by monks from Monte Cassino in 1112, and became an important Benedictine centre during the twelfth and thirteenth centuries. It owes its excellent state of preservation today to its safe distance from coastal raiders.

The **facade** blends Romanesque and Gothic, with a brown-and-white striped pattern similar to that of the church in Tergu, and pointed blind arches surmounted by a pediment. Above the door, a lunette holds a crude relief of an abbot and two monks – the "images" from which the church takes its name. Within is a stoup formed from trunks of petrified – or, more accurately, silicified – trees, of which the surrounding area holds a considerable quantity. You'll be lucky to find the church open, though: weekends are the best bet, or be here for the Festa di San Pietro, forty days after Easter.

Laerru and Chiaramonti

If you're taking the slow but scenic route towards Sássari on the SP127, you'll pass through the village of **LAERRU**, 7km south of Bulzi, internationally reputed for the carving of tobacco pipes from briar, olivewood and juniper. Shortly before reaching the faster SS672 Sássari–Tempio road, you'll arrive at **CHIARAMONTI**, worth a stop for its intricate network of narrow streets grouped around the base of a twelfth-century Doria fortification. Though it's not particularly high (440m), there are fantastic views from the ruins over the mountains on all sides, most strikingly Monte Limbara (1359m) to the east and Monte Sassu (640m) – a notorious haunt of bandits and kidnappers – to the southeast.

South of Sássari: Logudoro

The sparsely populated country south of Sássari is the heartland of the territory historically known as **Logudoro**, whose present-day inhabitants retain the distinction of speaking the purest form of Sard, softer and more rolling than the island's other dialects. The former wealth and importance of the region is attested today by the presence of some outstanding **Pisan churches**, magnificently stranded in open countryside, while it also holds one of Sardinia's most important nuraghic complexes, the **Nuraghe Santu Antine**. The area's only town of any size, **Ozieri**, holds remnants of the Neolithic culture to which it has lent its name.

ARRIVAL AND GETTING AROUND | LOGUDORO

A **car** is needed to reach most places, though the villages of Torralba and Ozieri have good **bus** connections with Sássari.

Santíssima Trinità di Saccargia

SS597• April–Oct daily 9am–6.30pm • €3 • ☎ 347 000 7882

Sixteen kilometres southeast of Sássari, the church of **Santíssima Trinità di Saccargia** makes a striking apparition to anyone travelling on the main Sássari–Olbia road. Standing tall and solitary amid the surrounding flat country, its zebra-striped facade and belltower conspicuously mark its Pisan origins.

The church, built in 1116, supposedly owes its remote location to a divine visitation that took place while the *giudice* of Torres and his wife stopped here on the way to Porto Torres, where they intended to pray for a child at San Gavino's shrine. During the night, a celestial messenger informed the *giudice*'s wife that the pilgrimage was unnecessary since she was already pregnant, whereupon the grateful *giudice* built an abbey on this spot. The basalt and limestone facade was added some sixty years later and has survived remarkably well, although some of the carved dogs, cows and other beasts on the lovely Gothic **capitals** at the top of the entrance porch are reconstructions.

Showing elements of Lombard architecture, the stark, tall-naved **interior** is mostly unadorned but for a gilded wooden pulpit embedded in one wall and some vivid eleventh- or twelfth-century **frescoes** covering the central apse. These, illustrating scenes from the life of Christ, are attributed to a Pisan artist and are a rare example in Italy of this type of Romanesque mural. Look out, too, for the stone image at the front of the nave on the left, possibly representing Costantino I, the *giudice* supposed to have founded the church and thought to be buried here.

Santa Maria del Regno

Árdara • Daily 9am–1pm & 3–7pm

The nondescript village of **ÁRDARA**, 15km east of Santíssima Trinità di Saccargia along the SS597, shows few traces of its one-time role as Logudoro's capital, though the restored basilica of **Santa Maria del Regno** hints at its former glory. Built by Pisans around 1100, using black and brown basalt, the Romanesque church provided the model for a series of lesser churches in the region. The church was the venue for the marriage in 1239 of Enzo, son of Frederick II of Hohenstaufen, by which he came into possession of the *giudicati* of Torres and Gallura, enabling him to claim the title of king of Sardinia. Though Enzo abandoned wife and island soon afterwards, he clung onto the title, even during the last 23 years of his life in prison in Bologna.

The **interior**, which has frescoed columns, is dominated by a highly ornate sixteenth-century tableau of thirty gilded panels behind the altar, the work of various artists, depicting scenes from the lives of the Virgin Mary, Jesus and various prophets, saints and martyrs. Some of the scenes are colourfully reproduced on the frescoed columns. The church is the focus of an annual costumed **carnival** with horses on July 29.

Sant'Antíoco di Bisarcio

SS597 • Tues–Sun: April–Oct 9.30am–1pm & 3–7pm; Nov–March 9am–1pm & 2–5pm • €3 • ☎ 079 781 236

The church of **Sant-Antioco di Bisarcio** is an isolated Pisan relic visible about 10km east of Árdara along the SS597. Built in 1090 and reconstructed in 1170, it was the venue for the coronations of many of Logudoro's *giudici*. Even when closed, the building is worth a circuit to admire the French-style portico, apse, blind arcading and campanile, and for the views over the hills.

Ozieri and around

A signposted turn-off from the SS597 brings you to **OZIERI**, the main centre for this area. Arrayed along a slope that creates a natural amphitheatre, it's a wealthy-looking place, with stuccoed, sometimes faded, Neoclassical houses, though you'll also come across vividly coloured contemporary murals depicting scenes of rural life and the horrors of war. The town's best-known local products are the little almond biscuits known as **suspirus** ("sighs", also called *sospiri*, or *guelfos*), for sale in any of the town's bakeries and most bars.

The town has given its name to a whole era of Sard prehistory, the **Ozieri culture**, which prevailed mainly in the northwest of Sardinia in the fourth and third millennia BC. It is also known as the San Michele culture, after the local grotto where most of the finds identified with it were discovered.

The last Sunday of September sees Ozieri's biggest **festa**, La Sagra della Madonna del Rimédio, during which groups from all over the island participate in medieval chanting and costumed processions.

Museo Archeologico

Piazza P. Micca • Tues–Sun 9am–1pm & 4–7pm • €5; €6 with grotto • ☎ 079 785 1052

A good selection of finds relating to the Ozieri culture can be seen in the town's **Museo Archeologico**, annexed to the Convento Clarisse, signposted at the top of the town, a few minutes' walk from the main Piazza Garibaldi. Exhibits include the bone jewellery and ceramics painted with a spiral pattern that are characteristic of the culture, as well as nuraghic ornaments, Punic and Roman coins and domestic items from the Middle Ages.

Grotta di San Michele

Piazzale Ospedale • Tues–Sun 10am–1pm & 3–6pm (2–5pm in winter) • €3, €6 with museum • ☎ 079 787 638

The **Grotta di San Michele**, where many of the finds displayed in Ozieri's archeological museum were unearthed in 1914, lies a walk or brief drive from the museum along the panoramic Viale Vittorio Veneto, on the southern edge of town. The complex of caves consists of one large chamber in the limestone with connecting tunnels and passages; English-speaking guides fill out the picture with background information.

Cattedrale dell'Immacolata

Via Grixoni • Daily 8am–noon & 4–6pm

In the lower part of town, Ozieri's **Cattedrale dell'Immacolata**, an Aragonese-Gothic structure overladen with Neoclassical and Baroque, merits a brief stop. Inside there's a noteworthy polyptych, the *Madonna di Loreto*, its seven panels painted by the so-called **Maestro di Ozieri**, the foremost Sard painter of the sixteenth century.

ARRIVAL AND DEPARTURE   OZIERI AND AROUND

By bus ARST buses stopping at Piazza Garibaldi provide frequent connections to Sássari (Mon–Sat 8–9 daily, Sun 3 daily; 1hr–1hr 30min) and to the train station of Ozieri-Chilivani, 10km west towards Chilivani, a main junction for passengers between Sássari, Olbia and Cágliari.

ACCOMMODATION AND EATING

Janas Country Resort Località Baddingusti, SP63 10 ☎ 079 707 9916, ⊛ janashotel.it. There's nowhere special to stay in Ozieri itself, but this hotel-resort a 15min drive west (towards Mores) offers clean and contemporary accommodation surrounded by lawned grounds and inspiring views. Rooms have terraces, and a pool and tennis court are available. Free pick-up is offered from Ozieri-Chilivani train station. Closed mid-Nov to mid-March. **€90**

La Coccinella Via San Michele ☎ 079 770 505. Convenient for a swift lunch before or after visiting the Grotta San Michele, this bar-trattoria just around the corner should satisfy hunger pangs. Order grilled aubergines or *spaghetti ai ricci* (with sea urchins); most dishes are €8–12, and *panini* are available too. Mon–Sat 6.30am–7pm, lunch served 12.30–3pm.

Torralba and around

Thirty kilometres south of Sássari, an easy detour from the SS131 takes you to the village of **TORRALBA**, whose only point of interest is a remarkable nuraghic museum, a short distance from one of Sardinia's greatest prehistoric monuments, the **Nuraghe Santu Antine**.

Nuraghe Santu Antine

Valle dei Nuraghi • Daily: April–Oct 9am–8pm; Nov–March 9am–5.30pm • €6, including guided tour (not always in English) or audioguide, and Museo di Torralba • ☎ 079 847 481, ⊛ nuraghesantuantine.it

The **Nuraghe Santu Antine** lies just over 4km south of Torralba, in the heart of the so-called Valle dei Nuraghi, an area copiously dotted with the ancient structures. This royal palace is the biggest and most impressive of them – hence its common name *Nuraghe Majore* – and is considered to be technically the finest nuraghic structure on the island, and one of the best preserved. The oldest sections date back to the fifteenth century BC, though the site was continuously worked on and augmented, not least by the Romans. To reach the site, take the Thiesi exit from the SS131 and follow the signs.

The central complex

Built of square basalt blocks, the **central complex** consists of three external bastions, mostly crumbled, connected by a defensive wall and grouped around the original massive three-storey circular tower, with walls up to 5m thick and 17.5m high. The tower is thought to have once reached 21m, before the uppermost of its three circular rooms was demolished in the nineteenth century. Corridors and staircases link the different parts of the tower, and the grounds include a well in an internal courtyard. With its intricate network of steps, ramps, chambers and curving passages, it's a fascinating place to scramble around.

Outlying *nuraghi*

From the railed area on top, other **nuraghi** are visible among the cultivated fields – though the closest and most perfect specimen is a recent reconstruction. A scattering of circular huts lies around the walls of the main complex, the ruins of the nuraghic village onto which Carthaginian and Roman structures were added.

Museo di Torralba

Via Carlo Felice 153 • Daily: April–Oct 9am–8pm; Nov–March 9am–5.30pm • €6, including Nuraghe Santu Antine • ☎ 079 847 298, Ⓦ nuraghesantuantine.it

Easy to find in the centre of the village, the **Museo di Torralba** focuses on the nearby nuraghic complex, with a model on the ground floor, and upstairs some of the seventeen thousand shards of pottery found on the site, testifying to the continuous use of the monument and surrounding area from the twelfth century BC until the Roman era. Other items include ceramic combs, smith's tools and projectiles, while bits and pieces of Phoenician and Greek ware are evidence of extensive trading links. Also on the first floor are Roman columns and capitals, coins and pottery fragments, and there are more Roman finds in the garden, including a collection of inscribed milestones found alongside the Cágliari–Olbia road, the first one built by the Romans on the island.

ARRIVAL AND DEPARTURE   **TORRALBA AND AROUND**

By bus ARST buses, including a good connection to Sássari (Mon–Sat every 30min–1hr, Sun 2 daily; 40min), stop in the village of Torralba, but not at the archeological site.

San Pietro di Sorres

Località Borutta • Mon–Sat 9.30am–12.15pm & 3.30–6.15pm (closes 5.30pm in winter), Sun 9.30am–10.30pm & 3.30–5.15pm • €5 including tour • ☎ 334 853 7751

The hilly area north of Torralba holds one of the best preserved of Sardinia's Romanesque churches, the twelfth-century basilica of **San Pietro di Sorres**. Surmounting a bluff with sweeping views over the villages of Bonnanaro and Borutta, and still attached to a Benedictine convent housing just ten monks, the former cathedral displays more Tuscan precision than Sardinia's other Pisan churches, while its grand dimensions and ornate style also suggest French influence. The partly striped facade of white and dark grey stone has three levels of blind arcading, each embellished with coloured geometrical motifs and delicate stonework.

The slightly forbidding **interior** is a more emphatic restatement of the two-tone scheme, containing a decorated Gothic pulpit supported by four arches, and an open sarcophagus from the twelfth century, belonging to a local bishop. Guided **tours** (sometimes in English) show you around the building.

Gallura

LA MADDALENA

Gallura

Sardinia's northernmost region, Gallura, is a land of raw granite mountains and startling wind-sculpted rocks, which combine with its extraordinary coastline to imbue the area with a unique edge-of-the-wilderness appeal. The largest town in this mountainous wedge, Olbia, owes its phenomenal growth in the last half-century or so to the annual influx of tourists bound for the numerous holiday spots up and down the coast. With its wide selection of hotels, bars and restaurants, it makes a good temporary base for the region, and has a couple of first-rate sights.

7

South of Olbia, the islands of **Tavolara** and **Molara** are a stark presence looming over this stretch of coast, and can be visited by boat from the modern resort of **Porto San Paolo**. This and **San Teodoro**, farther south, typify the holiday developments hereabouts – deserted for most of the year, and buzzing in summer.

North of Olbia, the port of **Golfo Aranci** has more beaches within a short radius, but glamour-seekers should follow the tide to one of the Mediterranean's loveliest stretches of coast and premier holiday zones, the **Costa Smeralda**. The five-star development of the "Emerald Coast" in the 1960s not only transformed the local economy but also kick-started the tourist industry in the entire island, setting new standards of planned, environment-friendly tourism. On the whole, the devotion to luxury has not compromised the extraordinary natural beauty of the indented rocky coast, but you'll need a full wallet to get the most out of it.

Fortunately, the Costa Smeralda is only a tiny part of Sardinia's northeastern littoral; elsewhere on the coast, it's still possible to have fun without spending stacks of money. Near the inland centre of **Arzachena** – worth a visit for the prehistoric sites lying within a short distance – there are kilometres of shoreline still undeveloped, while offshore the **Maddalena archipelago** consists of over sixty minor islands, which you can explore on boat tours from points along the coast. From the resort of **Palau**, a daily ferry service runs to the archipelago's biggest island and eponymous main town, **La Maddalena**. Linked to this island by a road causeway, **Caprera** has an absorbing museum devoted to Giuseppe Garibaldi, the hero of Italy's independence movement, located in his former home.

West of Palau, the SS125 passes a scintillating succession of bays before reaching **Santa Teresa Gallura**, Sardinia's northernmost point. This port for ferries to Corsica is also one of the island's liveliest holiday centres, within easy reach of some of the most splendid **beaches** anywhere in Italy, cradled in coves and inlets on either side. Sailors and windsurfers have long appreciated the brisk wind conditions in the Straits of Bonifacio, and there are numerous watersports outfits around.

The ever-present backdrop to this indented shore is the jagged line of granite **mountains**. Hidden within them is a world that most tourists never discover, thickly forested with the **cork oaks** which, after tourism, provide most of Gallura's revenue.

Highlights

❶ **Arzachena's prehistoric remains** Scattered in fields and woods way off the tourist track, nuraghic and pre-nuraghic sites around Arzachena – including a pair of "giants' tombs" – make a refreshing contrast to the more sensory pleasures of the coast. **See pp.246–249**

❷ **Wind- or kitesurfing at Porto Pollo** Take advantage of the excellent conditions around this resort, which attracts windsurfers and watersports fans of all abilities. **See p.252**

❸ **Boating around the Maddalena archipelago** Swimming stops feature prominently on any boat tour of these islands off the northern coast, and the views are breathtaking. **See p.255**

❹ **Capo Testa's beaches** The dramatic granite rockscape west of Santa Teresa Gallura makes a fantastic backdrop for unforgettable swims. See p.259

❺ **Aggius** This traditional Gallura village is home to the region's two best museums: an ethnographic collection, full of unexpected curiosities, and an exhibition focusing on the banditry that flourished hereabouts in the nineteenth century. **See p.266**

HIGHLIGHTS ARE MARKED ON THE MAP ON PP.232–233

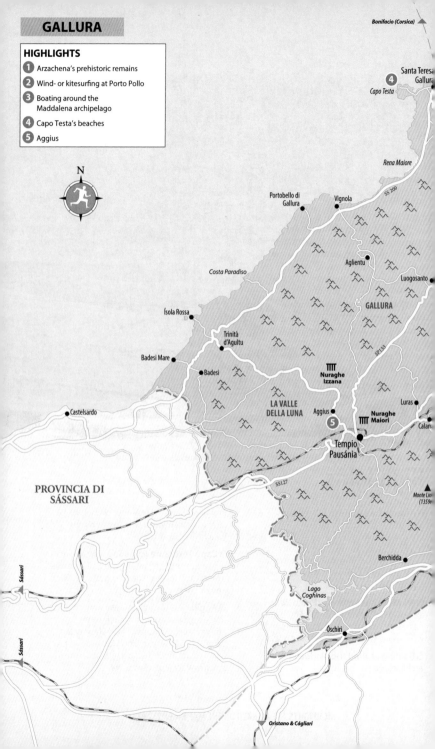

GALLURA

HIGHLIGHTS

1 Arzachena's prehistoric remains

2 Wind- or kitesurfing at Porto Pollo

3 Boating around the Maddalena archipelago

4 Capo Testa's beaches

5 Aggius

N

Bonifacio (Corsica)

Santa Teresa Gallura

4 Capo Testa

Rena Maiore

Portobello di Gallura

Vignola

SS 200

Aglientu

Luogosanto

Costa Paradiso

GALLURA

Ísola Rossa

Trinità d'Agultu

SP133

Badesi Mare

Badesi

Nuraghe Izzana

LA VALLE DELLA LUNA

Aggius 5

Nuraghe Maiori

Luras

Calan

Castelsardo

Tempio Pausánia

PROVINCIA DI SÁSSARI

SS127

Monte Lin (1359r

Berchidda

Sássari

Lago Coghinas

Sássari

Oschiri

Oristano & Cágliari

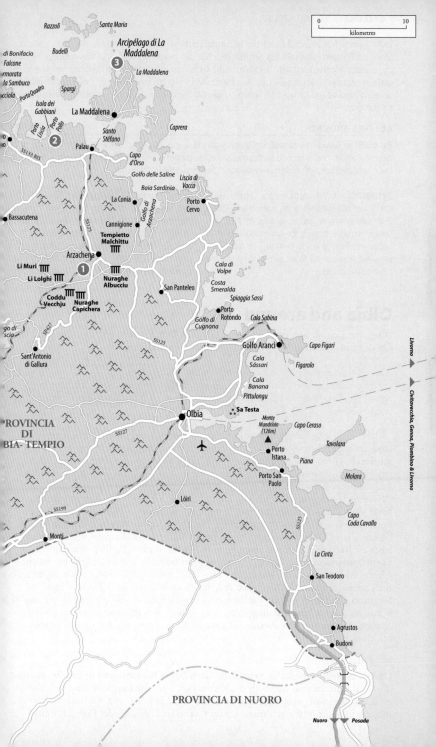

Razzoli
Santa Maria
Budelli
Arcipélago di La
Maddalena
di Bonifacio
Falcone
rmorata
la Sambuco
cciola
③
La Maddalena
Spargi
Porto Quadro
Isola dei
Gabbiani
Porto
Lisca
La Maddalena
Porto
Pollo
Santo
Stéfano
Caprera
②
Palau
Capo
d'Orso
SS133 Bis
Golfo delle Saline
Liscia di
Vacca
Baia Sardinia
La Conia
SS125
Porto
Cervo
Bassacutena
Cannigione
Golfo di
Arzachena
Tempietto
Malchittu
Cala di
Volpe
Arzachena
①
Li Muri
San Panteleo
Costa
Smeralda
Nuraghe
Albucciu
Li Lolghi
Spiaggia Sassi
Coddu
Vecchju
Nuraghe
Capichera
Porto
Rotondo
Cala Sabina
SP427
go di
scia
Golfo di
Cugnana
SS125
Sant'Antonio
di Gallura
Golfo Aranci
Capo Figari
Cala
Sássari
Figarolo
Cala
Banana
Pittulongu
Sa Testa
Olbia
PROVINCIA
DI
BIA- TEMPIO
SS127
Monte
Mandriolo
(126m)
Capo Ceraso
Tavolara
Porto
Istana
Piana
Porto San
Paolo
Molara
SS199
Lóiri
Capo
Coda Cavallo
SS125
La Cinta
Monti
San Teodoro
Agrustos
Budoni
PROVINCIA DI NUORO

Livorno
Civitavecchia, Genoa, Piombino & Livorno

0   10
kilometres

Nuoro   Posada

Now somewhat isolated from the main currents of life in the region, the grey, granite town of **Tempio Pausania** lies within sight of the pine-clad slopes of the region's highest mountain, **Monte Limbara** (1359m), and within easy reach of some of the interior's best walking routes. Excursions can also be made in the bizarre landscape of granite rubble around **Aggius**, northwest of Tempio, and in the cork forests surrounding **Calangianus** to the east.

GETTING AROUND   GALLURA

The **traffic** on Gallura's coastal roads can be unbearably slow, especially in summer when motorhomes add to the congestion already created by trucks bearing massive loads of quarried granite. **Public transport** is adequate for all the towns mentioned here, with a fuller service in summer, but is less useful for the beaches.

By train Olbia is linked to Golfo Aranci by FS trains (☎ 892 021, ⊛ trenitalia.com), while the summer-only Trenino Verde (⊛ treninoverde.com) is operated by ARST to a limited timetable through the mountainous heart of Gallura from Palau to Tempio Pausania – an appealing if somewhat laborious way to see parts of the region you might otherwise miss.

By bus Frequent bus connections link Olbia, Arzachena, Santa Teresa Gallura and Tempio Pausania with the region's other towns and villages. Most services are provided by ARST (☎ 800 865 042, ⊛ arst.sardegna.it), supplemented by Turmo buses (☎ 0789 21 487, ⊛ gruppoturmotravel.com) and, in summer, Sun Lines (☎ 0789 50 885, ⊛ sunlineseliteservice .com) and Deplano (☎ 0784 295 030, ⊛ deplanobus.it) buses.

Olbia and around

When the English barrister John Tyndale visited **OLBIA** in the 1840s, he compared its Greek name, meaning "happy", with the state he found it in:

"A more perfect misnomer, in the present condition of the town, could not be found … The whole district suffers severely from intemperie [malaria]. The wretched approach across these marshes is worthy of the town itself. The houses, none of which have an elegant or neat appearance, are built mostly of granite, and are whitewashed, as if to give a greater contrast to the filth and dirt within and around them."

Malaria has long vanished, together with the marshes and the filth, as a result of land-drainage schemes and DDT-saturation in the 1950s, as well as the income that tourism has been bringing since the 1960s. Olbia today is once more a happy place, enjoying its new-found prosperity both as the nearest Sardinian port to the mainland and the main gateway to the Costa Smeralda.

Nonetheless, few of the tourists pouring through the docks and airport stay long in town, for Olbia – perhaps the least "Sardinian" of all the island's centres – holds no more character than most transit towns. Past the unsightly ring of apartment blocks, however, is an attractive seafront and a largely traffic-free old centre, whose narrow lanes are lined with bars and restaurants busy with tourists. Partly pedestrianized **Corso Umberto** cuts through the centre of town from the seafront, at the bottom of which is the Art Nouveau **Municipio** (town hall), holding the tourist office. Apart from the impressive **Museo Archeologico** and the Pisan-Romanesque church of **San Símplicio** – the focus in May for the town's biggest festival – there's little in the way of sights, but it is at least a manageable place, with the bus terminal and train station conveniently located in the centre of town and the airport and ferry port just short bus rides away.

Brief history

Olbia was the first Sardinian town to be taken by the **Romans**, who in 259 BC expelled the Carthaginians who had been established here since the fourth century BC. The great Carthaginian general Hanno was killed in the fighting, and was buried with full military honours by the victorious Lucius Cornelius Scipio. Under Rome, the city expanded and flourished as the only natural port on Sardinia's eastern seaboard, though malaria was almost always prevalent due to the surrounding marshy lagoons.

Having survived numerous Vandal and Saracen raids in the Dark Ages, the town was completely rebuilt by Pisa after 1198. It went on to become one of the principal strongholds of the *giudicato* of Gallura, preserving its independence from Spain until the fifteenth century. Now called **Terranova Pausania** (a name which it retained until 1939), the city suffered complete destruction in 1553 at the hands of the Ottoman admiral Dragut, in alliance with France, and half its population was carried away as slaves.

Spain's shift of focus towards its Atlantic empire deprived the port of its prominent role, and Olbia languished. In 1711 the English admiral Norris briefly occupied the city, and six years later an **Austrian army** landed and took possession, intending to march on Alghero. According to the story, however, the priest they commandeered as a guide led them into a trap, and the Austrians were captured and led back to Olbia by a Sardinian force – a triumph of cunning that is still the subject of mirth among the local population.

The last century has seen the arrival of the railway, a good road connecting the port with the SS131 and the eradication of malaria, all of which have helped to restore the fortunes of the city, which today has a population of around sixty thousand.

7

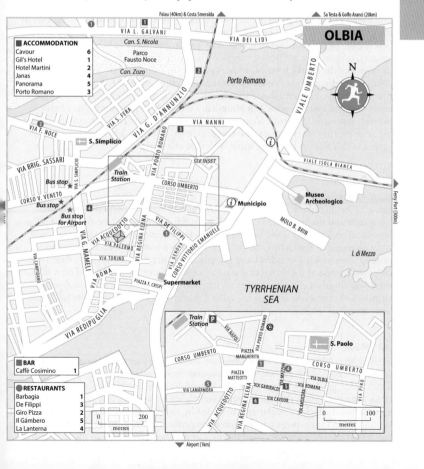

Museo Archeologico

Molo Brin • Mid-June to mid-Sept Mon & Tues 10am–1pm when cruise ships are in port, Wed–Sun 10–1pm & 5–8pm; mid–Sept to mid–June Wed–Sun only • Free • ☎ 0789 28 290

Seated on a miniature island by the portside, Olbia's **Museo Archeologico** is housed in a modernist, fortress-like construction surrounded by its own tiny moat. The museum, arranged around an atrium, is destined to hold the area's main archeological treasures, though currently only around half the rooms are used, and the only explanatory panels are in Italian. Many of the exhibits were dredged out of the old Roman port of Olbia, located on this very spot, notably the remains of cargo ships sunk during the attack on Olbia by Vandals in around 450 AD – an event that marked the passing of Roman power in Sardinia. Other displays range from Proto-Sard prehistory through to the Carthaginian, Greek and Roman eras, and include a magnificent terracotta head of Hercules wearing a lion's mane – a Roman copy of a Greek original, with a full-sized modern replica alongside, garishly painted to approximate to its original appearance. Exhibitions and evening musical performances are held regularly here – look out for posters or consult the tourist office for information.

Basilica di San Símplicio

Via S. Símplicio • Daily 8am–1pm & 4.30–7.30pm

The **Basilica di San Símplicio**, set in a piazza apart from Olbia's bustle, formed part of the great Pisan reconstruction programme of the eleventh and twelfth centuries. The best feature of the simple granite structure, the **facade**, was added in the twelfth century, capped by a mullioned window. The nave's narrow windows permit little light to penetrate the murky **interior**, whose two aisles are separated by recycled Roman columns (and note the table on the right as you enter, adapted from an ancient urn that once held cremated ashes). The church is bare but for two thirteenth-century frescoes in the apse, showing San Símplicio on the left and, on the right, a figure possibly representing Vittore Vescovo, a bishop ordained by Pope Gregory the Great in the sixth century. There are also two carved capitals, Lombard in inspiration, one carved with a human head, the other with that of a ram.

San Paolo

Piazza Civitas • Daily 8am–12.30pm & 5–7.30pm

Just off Corso Umberto, the church of **San Paolo** is easily recognizable by its tall campanile and multicoloured cupola. The church, built in 1747 on the site of a Punic temple, is typical of its time. Within the unadorned granite-faced exterior, a lovely wooden pulpit of the eighteenth-century Venetian school has inlaid panels and a canopy from which a wooden hand grasping a crucifix is thrust out. The date 1421, engraved on one of the arches of the nave, suggests San Paolo was raised on a site where there was already a church, or else that its builders utilized some material from another church. Otherwise, the interior has quite a modern appearance, its white walls splashed with murals of saints.

Sa Testa

SP82, about 5km west of Olbia towards Golfo Aranci • Always open • Free • Take any bus bound for Golfo Aranci or city bus #4 from Via S. Símplicio; drivers should turn right at the Dettori Market shopping complex before the Q8 fuel station

Set in a dry, grassy site below a modern shopping centre outside Olbia, the sacred well of **Sa Testa** dates from the late nuraghic era (eighth to sixth century BC). The well is approached through a circular area bounded by rough-hewn stones – probably a sort of waiting room for devotees who had come to perform their rites. The vestiges of a bench run round the circumference, and there's also rudimentary seating in the small paved recess at the far end, from where seventeen steps lead down to a tholos-shaped chamber holding the spring. It's one of Sardinia's cruder examples of a sacred well – you can see more sophisticated ones at Santa Cristina, near Oristano (see p.160) and Su Tempiesu, near Nuoro (see p.280) – but it makes a pleasant excursion, and a viable destination by bike from Olbia.

Pittulongu

Served by bus #4 from Via San Símplicio, Olbia

A kilometre or two beyond Sa Testa on the Golfo Aranci road, you can cool down with a swim at one of Olbia's favourite bathing spots, **Pittulongu**. The three beaches that make up the resort, La Playa, Lo Squalo and Pellicano, look across the bay to the island of Tavolara, and are lined with bars, with facilities for renting sunloungers and parasols in summer – they can get very crowded, though.

ARRIVAL AND DEPARTURE — OLBIA   7

BY PLANE

Olbia's Aeroporto di Costa Smeralda (⊚ olbiairport.it), 3km southeast of town, has frequent flights to and from the Italian mainland, Germany, France and the UK, operated by easyJet (☎ 199 201 840, ⊚ easyjet.com), Meridiana (☎ 0789 52 682, ⊚ meridiana.it) and Volotea (☎ 895 895 4404, ⊚ volotea.com), among other airlines. The airport has a tourist desk (see p.238) and banks with ATMs. Exit right from Arrivals for the bus stand and car rental offices.

Getting into town Buses #2 (not Sun) and #10 leave the airport every 10–30min until 11.40pm, taking 10min to reach Via Mameli, at the bottom of Corso Umberto (on #10 you can also get off at Piazza Margherita). Tickets cost €1 from the information desk in the terminal or €1.50 on board. Taxis into town charge about €15 (€20 on Sun). If you want to arrive at one of the coastal destinations directly by taxi from the airport, expect to pay around €60 to Arzachena, €90 to Palau (more at night or on Sun).

Long-distance buses Most long-distance services from the airport are summer-only. Other destinations can be reached from Olbia's centre.

Destinations Cala Gonone (June–Sept 4 daily; 2hr 15min); Cannigione (June–Sept 4 daily; 1hr 50min); Nuoro (3–8 daily; 1hr 45min); Porto Cervo (June–Sept 4 daily; 1hr 20min); Santa Teresa Gallura (1–6 daily; 1hr 30min).

BY FERRY

Stazione Maríttima Ferries dock at the Stazione Maríttima in Isola Bianca, 2km from the centre; it has ATMs, a left-luggage office (daily: summer 6am–10pm; winter 6.30–9.30am, 12.30–3.30pm & 4–10pm; €2/bag until 10pm) and a bar-restaurant. From here, city bus #9 runs into town every 30min (€1 from the information office, or €1.50 on board), or you can take one of the infrequent trains to Olbia's main train station in the centre. Buses also run from the Stazione Maríttima to Porto Cervo, Arzachena, Palau, Santa Teresa Gallura, Nuoro and Sássari.

Ferry companies and tickets The Stazione Maríttima holds the ticket offices for Tirrenia (☎ 892 123, ⊚ tirrenia .it) and Moby Lines (☎ 199 303 040, ⊚ moby.it); Sardinia Ferries to Livorno leave from Golfo Aranci, 15km up the coast. You can also pick up tickets (including for Sardinia Ferries from Golfo Aranci) at travel agencies in Olbia, for example Unimare, Corso Umberto 1 (☎ 0789 23 524). Book early for all departures.

Destinations Civitavécchia (Tirrenia & Moby; 1–3 daily; 5hr 15min–8hr); Genoa (Tirrenia & Moby; 3–16 weekly; 11hr–12hr 15min); Livorno (Moby; 1–2 daily; 6hr 45min–9hr); Piombino (Moby; early June to mid-Sept 2–6 weekly; 5hr 15min).

BY CAR

Drivers may have to park some distance away from their lodgings; try the large car park by the museum on the seafront, or the small car park off Via Milano near the train station.

BY TRAIN

FS trains from Sássari and Cágliari arrive at the station just off Corso Umberto, with some continuing to the Isola Bianca station for the ferry port. Most journeys to and from Cágliari, Oristano and Sássari involve a change at Ozieri-Chilivani. There are also infrequent departures to the same destinations from the Isola Bianca station. For information, call ☎ 892 021 or visit ⊚ trenitalia.it.

Destinations Cágliari (5 daily; 3hr 35min–4hr); Golfo Aranci (4–6 daily; 25min); Oristano (5 daily; 2hr 25min–2hr 50min); Sássari (6–7 daily; 1hr 45min).

BY BUS

ARST buses (☎ 800 865 042, ⊚ arst.sardegna.it) use the stops on Via Vittorio Veneto, just past the level crossing at the bottom of Corso Umberto, and most also stop at the airport and at Isola Bianca for the ferry port. Tickets are sold at Café Max at Via Vittorio Veneto 46a, from inside the

Stazione Maríttima at the port and on board the buses at the airport. Summer-only Sun Lines buses for Porto Cervo and Cannigione leave from Piazza Crispi, on the seafront, with stops at the port and airport, while Turmo buses, which run year-round services to and from Cágliari and Santa Teresa Gallura, stop outside the Municipio at the bottom of Corso Umberto; buses belonging to both companies also stop at the port and airport.

Destinations Arzachena (every 30min–1hr; 20–50min); Cágliari (Mon–Sat 1 daily; 4hr 45min); Golfo Aranci (mid-June to mid-Sept 4–7 daily; 25min); Nuoro (5–8 daily; 2hr 40min); Palau (7–15 daily; 1hr 10min); Porto Cervo (June–Sept 4–5 daily; Oct–May Mon–Sat 1 daily; 1hr 30min); Porto San Paolo (4–10 daily; 25min); Posada (5–11 daily; 1hr 20); Santa Teresa Gallura (6–12 daily; 1hr 25min–2hr 15min); San Teodoro (4–10 daily; 45min); Sássari (Mon–Sat 1 daily; 1hr 45min); Tempio Pausania (Mon–Sat 6 daily, Sun 3; 1hr 20min).

GETTING AROUND

By car There are several car rental companies at the airport, including Europcar (☎0789 69 548; ⓦeuropcar.it); Hertz (☎0789 66 024; also at Via Regina Elena 34, ☎0789 28 114; ⓦhertz.com); Maggiore (☎0789 69 457, ⓦmaggiore.it); and Pinna (☎0789 69 440, ⓦautonoleggiopinna.com). Expect to pay from around €200/week, which can rise in July and Aug.

By bike or scooter Palarent, at Via Regina Elena 119 (☎0789 24 310, ⓦpalarent.it) rents out bikes (€10/day), scooters (€30–50/day) and 700cc motorbikes (€70/day).

By bus For information on Olbia's city buses, consult ASPO at ☎0789 553 800, ⓦaspoolbia.it.

By taxi There are ranks on Corso Umberto, outside the train station (☎0789 22 718), at the port (☎0789 24 999) and at the airport (☎0789 69 150); otherwise call ☎347 361 2606 or ☎320 696 7030.

INFORMATION

Tourist office Information on the city is dispensed at the Municipio at the bottom of Corso Umberto (April & May daily 9am–7pm; June–Sept daily 9am–9pm; Oct–March Mon–Fri 9am–1pm; ☎0789 52 206, ⓦolbiaturismo.it). The office covering the whole province is at Via Nanni 47 (Mon–Fri 9am–2pm, also Tues & Thurs 3–6pm; ☎0789 557 732, ⓦolbiatempioturismo.it), and there's an information desk at the airport (daily 8am–11.30pm; ☎0789 563 444).

ACCOMMODATION

There's no shortage of **accommodation** in Olbia, though most places are quite pricey. The nearest **campsites** are north of town near the Golfo di Cugnana (see p.242) or south at Porto San Paolo (see p.240), both about a 20min drive or bus ride away.

Cavour Via Cavour 22 ☎0789 204 033, ⓦhotelcavourolbia.it. This tasteful modern renovation of a traditional building on a central alley has smart, simply furnished rooms – some quite poky – and free parking. The ambience is cool, clean and hushed. Triples and quadruples also available. **€90**

Gil's Hotel Via Galilei 16 ☎0789 58 869, ⓦgilshotel.it. Functional but pleasant modern hotel with eight spacious rooms (some with balconies), located slightly off the beaten track by Olbia's main public gardens. Breakfast is in the eponymous neighbouring restaurant, where you check in. **€90**

Hotel Martini Via d'Annunzio 21 ☎0789 26 066, ⓦhotelmartiniolbia.it. With views to the port from the back and overlooking a park at the front, this modern hotel 10min walk from the centre has bright, spacious rooms, helpful staff and a relaxing atmosphere. There's a small spa and gym, plus a bus stop for the airport and the beach at Pittulongu right outside. **€85**

★**Janas** Via Lamármora 61 ☎339 109 2836 or ☎349 872 8140, ⓦjanasaffittacamere.com. This B&B in an old townhouse has three spacious ground-floor rooms, all with private bathrooms, and one giving on to the shady garden where self-service breakfasts can be taken. Parking available. **€80**

★**Panorama** Via Mazzini 7 ☎0789 26 656, ⓦhotelpanoramaolbia.it. Classy four-star in the heart of the old town, boasting a roof terrace with sunloungers and fantastic views, plus spa facilities (€22/1hr 30min session) and a gym (free). Rooms are clean and spacious, while staff are multilingual and friendly. There's a garage (a bonus in Olbia and included in the price); breakfasts are abundant and fresh. **€129**

Porto Romano Via Nanni 2 ☎349 192 7996, ⓦbedandbreakfastportoromano.it. Friendly B&B in a central but secluded position, offering two doubles with private or en-suite bathrooms and a self-contained "bedsitter" (costing more) with cooking facilities. There's a patio with a barbecue. No credit cards. **€70**

EATING AND DRINKING

Self-caterers and picnickers will find everything they need at the Superpan **supermarket** on the seafront, Via Genova (Mon–Sat 8.30am–9.30pm, Sun 8.30am–2pm & 5–9pm).

Barbagia Via Galvani 94 ☎ 0789 51 640. With a large, beamed dining area and tables outdoors, this popular place opposite a park offers a tasty array of *antipasti*, mainly meat-based dishes and pizzas. Service is friendly and there are good-value tourist menus (€15–25). Oct–June daily except Wed 12.30–3pm & 7–11pm.

Caffè Cosimino Piazza Margherita ☎ 0789 21 001. Good for coffees, fresh *cornetti* and lunchtime snacks. It also has an impressive selection of Sardinian wines. Choose a seat on the square or inside. Daily 7am–midnight; closed Sun in winter.

De Filippi Wine Music Bistrot Via De Filippi 28 ☎ 0789 184 0784. Stylishly modern, this is a good spot for a daytime sit-down and snack, or to while away the evening over local wines and cocktails. The menu specializes in succulent steaks, but also serves healthy salads and pastas, all at very reasonable prices (€8 for a large portion of pasta). Daily 7.30am–10pm.

★**Giro Pizza** Via Fausto Noce 34 ☎ 347 134 4026. The best pizzas in town can be found at this buzzing place by San Símpicio church, with a wood-fired oven, a grooving soundtrack of jazz, blues and rock, and posters of 1960s

icons. Most pizzas are around €8, and there's a good-value €12 deal for unlimited pizza plus a drink and a pizza-dessert (a house speciality). At weekends meat and fish dishes are also available for around €12. There are some tables outside and a covered veranda too. June–Sept daily 7–11pm; Oct–May closed Mon.

Il Gámbero Via Lamármora 6 ☎ 0789 23 874. Brass pots, ceramics and hangings adorn the walls of this centrally located restaurant with a huge fireplace. They mainly serve seafood, with good *antipasti* including *affumicati di mare* (smoked tuna and swordfish). Count on €50–60 for a full meal for two including drinks. In summer, there are tables outside in the alley. June–Aug Mon 7.30–11pm, Tues–Sun 12.30–2pm & 7.30–11pm; Sept–May closed Mon

★**La Lanterna** Via Olbia 13 ☎ 0789 23 082. Tucked away in an alley off the Corso, this cellar restaurant with a/c offers superb pizzas (mostly €9) alongside an impressive menu that includes grilled mussels, *fregola sarda* (semolina pasta) and outstanding *antipasti*, all artistically presented. There's a good list of Sard wines and the home-baked bread is delicious. July–Sept daily 7–10.30pm; Oct–June closed Wed.

DIRECTORY

Hospital Via Leonardo da Vinci, Località Tannaule, on the Tempio road (☎ 0789 552 200). Call ☎ 118 for an ambulance.

Internet Log on and print out at Click, Via Porto Romano 6b (June–Sept Mon–Fri 9.30am–1.30pm & 4–8pm, Sat 9.30am–1.30pm; Oct–May closed Sat; €4/hr).

Markets General markets take place outside the central area on Piazza Crispi (Tues morning) and Via Aldo Moro (Sat morning).

Pharmacy Most pharmacies are open 9am–1pm & 4.15–7.35pm, closed on Sat afternoon and Sun, though Lupacciolu on Piazza Margherita stays open weekdays until 8.20pm in summer. Night rotas are posted on pharmacy doors or in the local newspaper.

Post office Main office at Piazza Mercato (Mon–Fri 8.20am–7.05pm, Sat 8.20am–12.35pm).

Travel agent Avitur, Corso Umberto 142b (☎ 0789 24 327); Unimare, Corso Umberto 1 (☎ 0789 23 524).

South of Olbia

The coastal stretch **south of Olbia** has rapidly grown from a wilderness of rock and scrub to become a favourite with Olbians and other holiday-makers who throng the area's beaches every summer. The cubic pink and coral-coloured constructions that have sprouted haphazardly in the last couple of decades have blighted much of the landscape, though the seaward view remains unaltered, dominated by the dramatically looming profiles of the islands of **Tavolara** and **Molara**. You can visit them from **Porto San Paolo**, a resort village 14km south of Olbia, catering like other holiday centres along this coast mainly to families. Farther south, **San Teodoro** is

OLBIA'S FESTIVALS

The Basilica di San Símplicio is the venue for Olbia's biggest **festa**, three days of processions, costumed dancing, poetry recitals, traditional games and fireworks around May 15, commemorating San Símplicio's martyrdom in the fourth century. The other big local festivals are Sant'Agostino on June 24 and Santa Lucia on the first Sunday of September, both lasting three days. Nightly free **concerts** and other events take place by the water on Molo Brin throughout the summer from late July, as well as performances on Piazza Margherita.

more of the same, a bland colony of bungalows interspersed with hotels and campsites near a wonderful beach.

Porto San Paolo and around

The biggest centre on the coast south of Olbia, **PORTO SAN PAOLO** is a modern settlement that's pretty dull for most of the year but attracts a lively crowd of Olbians and Italian holiday-makers in summer. There's a sandy **beach** here but the best ones are a short distance to either side. A couple of kilometres north, **Porto Istana** is a sandy bay with calm waters sheltered by the hulking form of Tavolara, with sunloungers to rent and a bar open in summer. From here, it's an easy excursion to **Capo Ceraso**, the southern tip of the Golfo di Olbia, where you'll find more good beaches among the thick growth of *macchia* and pink rocks. A stairway once used to reach a World War II gun emplacement leads from here to the top of **Monte Mandriolo** (126m), affording outstanding views across to Tavolara and north to Capo Figari.

Three kilometres south of Porto San Paolo, there's good swimming at **Porto Taverna**, but more seclusion another kilometre or so farther down on the curly cape known as **Capo Coda Cavallo** – "horse's tail" – which enjoys spectacular views across to Molara.

ARRIVAL AND INFORMATION   PORTO SAN PAOLO AND AROUND

By car Drivers from Olbia should take the SS125 southeast past the airport.

By bus Porto San Paolo can be reached on frequent ARST services from Olbia (4–10 daily; 25min), while Porto Istana

is the last stop on the #5 local bus route from Olbia's Via Mameli (4–5 daily; 25min).

Tourist office Viale Pietro Nenni (June–Sept daily 9am–1pm & 5–8pm; ☎ 338 160 9073).

ACCOMMODATION

Cala Cavallo Località Cala Cavallo ☎ 0784 834 156, ⓦ calacavallo.it. On the eponymous cape, this shady and well-equipped campsite has its own pool and tennis courts, as well as caravans (€55) and bungalows (€90) to rent. Closed mid-Sept to mid-May. Pitches €36

★ **Camping Tavolara** Località Porta Taverna ☎ 0789 40 166, ⓦ camping-tavolara.it. This excellent campsite, close to the beach of Porto Taverna, lies 3km south of Porto San Paolo. It's friendly and well maintained, and offers caravans to rent (from €53), use of a tennis court and a diving centre; the site is around 500m from the beach,

linked in summer by a shuttle service. Closed mid-Oct to April. Pitches €30

Castello di Tavolara Via Tavolara 2 ☎ 0789 480 012, ⓦ hotelcastelloditavolara.com. Most of the vacationing on this coast takes place in holiday apartments, but there's one good-quality hotel in Porto San Paolo that stays open all year (with prices falling sharply outside the peak months), though there's usually a minimum three-night stay in summer. Rooms are spacious and swish and have balconies; breakfasts are abundant and it's a stone's throw from the beach. €89

EATING

★ **La Conchiglia** Viale Don Sturzo 29 ☎ 0789 40 158. With plastic chairs and a bustling atmosphere, this place at the southern end of the resort on the SS125 lacks airs, but delivers huge helpings of home-made pastas (one

portion is enough for two) and tasty dishes such as *cozze alla marinara*. You'll pay €25–35 each for two courses, and pizzas are also available. Daily noon–2.30pm & 7–11pm.

Tavolara and Molara

Rising sheer above the flat coast east of Olbia, the islands of **Tavolara** and **Molara** make rewarding destinations for a day-trip from Porto San Paolo. Boat excursions combine close-up views of these tall eruptions of rock with opportunities to swim in crystal-clear waters from one of the beaches around their sides. The islands form part of a marine reserve (ⓦ amptavolara.com), with little development permitted.

Tavolara is the more impressive of the two islands: a giant limestone wedge 4km long and 1km wide, its precipitous walls towering to a height of 564m. Due to a historical anomaly, the island is said to constitute an independent kingdom (a portrait of its royal family in 1900 can be seen in the picture collection at Buckingham Palace). Its eastern flank is currently a military zone and off-limits, but its freely accessible southwestern tip at Spalmatore di Terra is inhabited and includes a couple of **restaurants**, a cemetery where Tavolara's kings are buried and a good beach. Yelkouan shearwaters, Audouin's gulls and Mediterranean shags are among the rare birds to look out for here. The island hosts an open-air **film festival** of non-mainstream Italian movies, screened on the beach during five nights in mid-July. Special boat excursions ferry ticket-holders to and from the alfresco arena. For dates and times, contact the tourist office at Olbia or Porto San Paolo, or visit ⓦ cinematavolara.it.

In contrast to calcareous Tavolara, the smaller, circular isle of Molara is composed of granite, and covered with wild olive trees. On its eastern shore, at Cala di Chiesa, are the remains of a medieval village, **Gurguray**, with the shell of a church, **San Ponziano**. Molara is a protected area with limited landings; there are no refreshments so if you do visit, bring food and drink along.

ARRIVAL AND ACTIVITIES   **TAVOLARA AND MOLARA**   **7**

By boat At Easter and from May to Sept, boats to Tavolara set off from Porto San Paolo's Pontile della Marina every 30min or hour from 9.30am until 1.30pm, with return trips from 1pm to 6.30pm (you can choose to come back at any time throughout the afternoon); return tickets are around €16. There's a less frequent service to Molara, and some operators also make a stop at Piana, a tiny rock just big enough to hold a lovely sandy beach.

Cruises and excursions There are also longer cruises around all the isles, with swimming stops, costing around €26. These currently depart daily from Porto San Paolo (May–Sept; 9.30am and – sometimes – 3pm). For more information on all excursions, contact the Cooperativa Tavolara at ☎ 339 759 0974.

San Teodoro

Fourteen kilometres south of Porto San Paolo, past the long **Stagno di San Teodoro** lagoon, used by wading flamingos and cranes, **SAN TEODORO** is another popular beach resort, its modern villas, bars and restaurants thickly planted behind the **Cala d'Ambra** beach. There's another great beach north of town on **La Cinta**, a long bar of sand separating the lagoon from the sea. **Diving** is possible at various points along this coast, and **windsurfing** is also much in evidence in summer, especially from La Cinta.

ACCOMMODATION   **SAN TEODORO**

San Teodoro Via del Tirreno ☎ 0784 865 777, ⓦ campingsanteodoro.com. One of San Teodoro's two campsites, this lies 1km north of the centre with direct access to La Cinta beach. It has plenty of shade, and bungalows sleeping four (€105) for weekly rental, but no pool or restaurant (there's a good eatery 80m away). Closed mid-Oct to April. Pitches **€32**

Golfo Aranci

The Golfo di Olbia reaches its northern extent at **GOLFO ARANCI**, a major port whose picturesque name – probably deriving from the Gallurese dialect for "Gulf of Crabs" – belies the down-to-earth reality. If you've crossed over from Livorno, this may well be your first landing in Sardinia, but otherwise there's no strong reason to venture here – it's not a particularly inspiring town, nor a great foretaste of what Sardinia has in store. Much of the long peninsula on which the town stands has been invaded by the uniform holiday villas that have become increasingly dominant along this stretch of coast, though the blandness of the architecture is compensated by the ever exuberant vegetation, with bougainvillea, tiger lily and hibiscus injecting a tropical brilliance to the granite rock. It's also a cheaper and calmer alternative to the glittery bustle of Olbia, and has a couple of good beaches as well as a nature reserve in the hills behind that is overlooked by most visitors.

The town and beaches

If Golfo Aranci has any centre, it's the port and train station, next to each other at its eastern end. Just a few metres from here is the town's only item of historical interest, the **Pozzo Sacro Milis**, a rough-hewn nuraghic sacred well with steps, whose location close to the railway tracks strips it of much atmosphere. There's a fine, sandy **beach** near the centre off Via Colombo, though the best bathing spots lie to the south, round the curve of the Golfo degli Aranci, where **Cala Sássari** includes several small sandy coves, one of which, **Sos Aranzos**, has given its name to both the gulf and the port and has beautifully limpid water. Other beaches worth seeking out include the aptly named **Cala Banana**, signposted off the Olbia road, and dune-backed **Cala Sabina**, on the northern side of the peninsula.

A *sagra di pesce*, or **fish festival**, takes place on August 14, when seafood and wine are doled out to all and sundry.

Capo Figari

Behind the town rears the immense mass of rock occupying **Capo Figari**, a protected area where thick *macchia* is interlaced with holm oaks and junipers. A few of Sardinia's long-horned **mouflons** (wild sheep) have been reintroduced here and on the offshore islet of Figarolo, whose steep slopes are visible, similarly clad in *macchia* and twisted olives.

ARRIVAL AND DEPARTURE   GOLFO ARANCI

By ferry Sardinia Ferries (☎ 199 400 500 or ☎ 0789 46 780, ⓦ sardiniaferries.com) operates crossings to and from Livorno all year (1–2 daily; 6hr 30min–11hr). For approximate costs, see Basics (see p.25); it's worth asking about any possible reductions on return crossings, such as last-minute or advance bookings. Book early for sailings in high season.

By train Golfo Aranci is connected with Olbia by infrequent trains (3–6 daily; 25min); the station is right by the port.

By bus A summer bus service links Golfo Aranci to Olbia (mid-June to mid-Sept 4–7 daily; 25min).

ACCOMMODATION AND EATING

La Lámpara Via Magellano 3 ☎ 0789 615 140, ⓦ lalamparahotel.com. Small, bright hotel, 500m from the port and just steps from the town beach. The ten rooms are modern and clean, the staff are friendly and breakfasts are big. Mid-April to Sept noon–3pm & 7–11pm. €125

La Spígola Via Colombo 19 ☎ 0789 46 286. Right on the town beach, this bar-restaurant is probably the best choice in town for home-made pasta, fresh seafood, good pizzas and wonderful sea views. First courses cost €8–12, mains €15–18. Light lunches are available too, and the owner speaks perfect English. Easter–Sept daily: bar 7am–11pm, restaurant noon–3pm & 7–11pm.

Porto Rotondo and around

Built in 1963 in the wake of the Costa Smeralda's development, **PORTO ROTONDO**'s rows of orange villas snake remorselessly over the *macchia*-covered hills, grouped more thickly around the round marina. Chic boutiques and fashion shops set the tone in central Piazzetta San Marco, from which a wide stairway leads up to the modern granite church of **San Lorenzo**. A few metres away, there's a modern open-air theatre, also granite, where entertainments are staged in summer.

But the best feature of the place is the proximity of a number of fabulous **beaches**, though these can get overwhelmed in high season. On **Punta della Volpe**, the thin headland north of Porto Rotondo, try **Spiaggia Sassi**, which has a bar, parking and sunbeds to rent, or **Cugnana**, with less in the way of facilities but more seclusion. In summer the beaches are connected by a minibus service.

ACCOMMODATION   PORTO ROTONDO AND AROUND

Camping Cugnana Località Cugnana ☎ 0789 33 184, ⓦ campingcugnana.it. Although this three-star campsite gets very crowded, it offers excellent facilities, including a generous pool. Bungalows are available (€85/night), and there's a pizzeria/restaurant and minimarket. It lies 2km from the beach at Marina di Cugnana, and a minibus shuttles campers to this and some of the Costa Smeralda's best beaches. ARST and Sun Lines buses between Olbia and Porto Cervo stop right outside. To reach it by car, backtrack some 10km from Porto Rotondo towards the SS125 and turn right onto the Porto Cervo road before reaching the highway. Closed mid-Oct to March. Pitches €24

San Pantaleo

With its backdrop of granite peaks, the village of **SAN PANTALEO**, 5km inland of the Costa Smeralda, has caught some of the airs of that fabled jetsetters' haunt but still provides a refreshing antidote to its brasher excesses. It's prettiest around its spacious, pedestrianized central piazza, where a few bars and craft shops look across to a simple granite church. The square makes a great venue for concerts and festivals throughout the summer – the village's **saint's day** is celebrated around July 26, while Thursday sees a busy **market** of crafts, clothes and trinkets.

ACCOMMODATION AND EATING   **SAN PANTALEO**   7

Café Nina Piazza Vittorio Emanuele ☎ 338 368 7288. Chic little wine bar on San Pantaleo's piazza, perfect for a beer or aperitif. Snacks are also served – a cold meat and cheese platter for two costs €10. March–Oct daily 7am– late; Nov & Dec 6pm–late.

Locanda Sant'Andrea Via Zara 36 ☎ 0789 65 205, ⓦ locandasantandrea.com. Upmarket lodging that has all the sophistication of the Costa Smeralda without its pretensions. Artistically designed, it's small – just twelve pastel-hued rooms – with a high-ceilinged, quality restaurant and a courtyard pool surrounded by bougainvillea. Closed mid-Oct to April. **€145**

The Costa Smeralda

The **Costa Smeralda** is a strictly defined 10km strip on the western shore of the Golfo di Cugnana, beginning some 12km north of Olbia. Protected by rigorous building regulations, the natural beauty of the granite littoral and the cleanliness and transparency of the sea are striking, though the coastline can hardly be described as pristine, with ribbons of red-tiled holiday chalets spreading over some areas, interspersed with a luxury golf course or two. The few centres flaunt an air of exclusivity, notably **Porto Cervo**, the only "town" on this stretch of coast, and the place to be if you want to mingle with the in-crowd. Other parts have a bland, almost suburban feel about them, however – don't expect to find anything like a genuine fishing community surviving hereabouts, nor even the lively local markets you'll see in other parts of Sardinia.

Shorn of the disorderly and spontaneous, the Costa Smeralda might lack the local touch, but this does not discourage the waves of holiday-makers who flood the **beaches** dotted along the indented coast every summer. Even with the crowds, these beaches rank among Sardinia's finest, though they sometimes require a little perseverance and a good set of car springs to reach. The best advice is to follow any dirt track – the rougher it is, the more promising – down to the sea. The most popular places are signposted, and these are the ones with bars, toilets, sunloungers and other facilities.

Porto Cervo and around

To soak up the full flavour of the Costa Smeralda, you could start at its northern end with a wander around **PORTO CERVO**, the "capital", with most of the shops and facilities. Here, the scale of the tidy, pastel-coloured architecture characteristic of the region becomes almost surreal – more virtual "Mediterranean village" than authentic resort. The main activities consist of window-shopping in the likes of Gucci, Versace, Prada and Cartier, eyeballing the incredibly grand yachts at the marina and sipping the obligatory aperitif in the **Piazzetta** – a panoramic terrace at the heart of this warren of

7

THE MAKING OF THE COSTA SMERALDA

Occupying an iconic, almost mythic role in Sardinia's international profile, the Costa Smeralda has even evolved its own legendary backstory, according to which the **Aga Khan** Prince Karim IV, Imam and spiritual leader of the Ismaili Muslims, first stumbled upon the charms of this idyllic coast in 1958, when his yacht took shelter from a storm in one of its narrow creeks. Whatever the truth of the legend, four years later the fabulously wealthy tycoon was leading a consortium of businessmen with the aim of developing this wild coastal strip. The first step was acquiring the land, and local farmers were easily persuaded to part with their largely uncultivable properties – though stories have circulated ever since of the stratagems used to dupe the locals into selling their land for a fraction of its value.

The consortium's plans were on a massive scale, limited only by the conditions imposed by the regional government. These included proper sewage treatment and disposal, restrictions on building and the insistence that the appearance of the landscape should not be unduly changed. Multistorey hotels, advertising hoardings, fast-food restaurants and even garish filling stations were banned, only local building materials could be used for new constructions, and only indigenous vegetation planted – so that pines, eucalyptus and poplars, for example, were banished in favour of oleander, mimosa, arbutus and myrtle.

By the end of the 1960s, the development included **VIP-class hotels**, a prestigious **golf course** and the **yacht marina** at Porto Cervo, and had become a byword for wealth and luxury, in turn putting Sardinia on the tourist map. The original consortium sold their stake in the Costa Smeralda in 1994 – the majority holding is currently with the **Emir of Qatar** – but the coast's cachet among the rich and famous has if anything increased, and various royals, Hollywood stars, Russian oligarchs and supermodels continue to spend leisure time here, though usually in guarded seclusion – as is the case of playboy and ex-prime minister **Silvio Berlusconi**, whose Villa Certosa here was the scene of notorious "bunga-bunga" parties, and hosted Tony and Cherie Blair, among others.

paths and passages and the place to lounge in style. A small beer at one of the bars here starts from €12, though the price includes a front-row seat for people-watching.

Steps lead down from the Piazzetta to the **Sottopiazza**, an area of posh boutiques and classy craft shops. Elsewhere, you'll find banks, phones, pharmacies, travel agents, estate agents and a supermarket.

The marina

Nearly a kilometre west of the Piazzetta, Porto Cervo's huge yacht **marina** merits a look, awash with the ostentatious baubles of the ultrarich. The marine facilities are the most expensive in Sardinia, and reputedly the best, with berths for seven hundred vessels, each with electricity and fresh water supplies. In odd-numbered years, antique sailing boats gather here during the first days of September, usually followed by a race in the Straits of Bonifacio.

Stella Maris

Via Stella Maris • Daily 9am–dusk

The marina's gleaming ranks of yachts are overlooked from a height by the **Stella Maris** church, a rough-textured, whitewashed building which houses a seventeenth-century organ and – surprisingly – a *Mater Dolorosa* by El Greco, the bequest of a Dutch aristocrat. The church was designed in 1968 by Roman architect Michele Busiri Vici, who was also responsible for the grotto-like shopping arcade in Porto Cervo's centre.

Liscia di Vacca

You'll need your own transport to get to the sequestered **beaches** around Porto Cervo, only a few of which are clearly marked. A couple of kilometres northwest of the resort, one of the best is at **Liscia di Vacca**, an exquisite bay at the end of a long, bumpy dirt road, with deckchairs to rent and bars for refreshments in season.

Cala di Volpe and around

The bay of **Cala di Volpe**, 6km south of Porto Cervo, holds a concentration of some of Italy's most select hotels as well as the eighteen-hole, 72-par **Pévero golf course**, spread out across a rolling expanse of green. It's one of Europe's most prestigious, the creation of architect Robert Trent Jones. Some of the area's most popular beaches lie within a short distance: to the northeast, **Capriccioli** and **Romazzino**, facing the offshore islands of Soffi and Mortorio, and, off Via degli Asfodeli on the road to Romazzino, the smaller **Spiagga del Príncipe**, said to be named after the Aga Khan; south of Cala di Volpe, **Liscia Ruja** is the biggest beach on the Costa Smeralda, with white sand and the full range of facilities but not too many people. In season, parking costs around €2 per hour.

ARRIVAL AND DEPARTURE   THE COSTA SMERALDA

By bus Porto Cervo is served by ARST and, in summer, Sun Lines buses.
Destinations Arzachena (Mon–Sat 3–4 daily; 40min);

Baia Sardinia (June–Sept 4 daily; 10min); Olbia (June–Sept 4 daily; 1hr 10min); Porto Rotondo (June–Sept 4 daily; 35min).

GETTING AROUND

By car You're best off having your own wheels to reach the beaches and other spots along the Costa Smeralda. You can rent a small car for around €225 a week from Europcar, Via della Marina 104, Porto Cervo (☎0789 957 085, ⓦeuropcar.it). Parking in Porto Cervo costs around €3/hr.
By bike or scooter Bikes and scooters can be rented from

Treforsail, Località Abbiadori 21 (☎0789 971 057, ⓦtreforsail.it). Bikes are €25/day, scooters €35–50/day; motor dinghies are also available from €180/day.
By taxi Porto Cervo always has taxis available outside the *Cervo Hotel* (☎347 789 0431). Try also ☎335 621 7133 or ☎335 666 1909.

ACCOMMODATION

Even three-star hotels have five-star prices on the Costa Smeralda. Cheaper alternatives lie close by, in Arzachena (see p.249), Baia Sardinia (see p.246) and San Pantaleo (see p.243). There's a fully equipped campsite at Cugnana (see p.242).

Cala di Volpe Cala di Volpe ☎0789 976 111, ⓦcaladivolpe.com. One of the Costa Smeralda's most stylish hotels, designed by celebrated architect Jacques Couelle in the 1960s and looking from the outside something like an adobe Moorish fortress. The interior is all swooping lines and grand vistas over the lawns. A magnificent pool is framed by the idyllic bay (there's another pool on the roof). From the hotel's marina, a boat whisks guests to a private beach. The food is

gourmet-class, and though the prices are daunting you'll often find big discounts online. Closed late Sept to mid-May. **€1350**
Dolce Vita Località Liscia di Vacca ☎0789 91 855, ⓦhotel-dolcevita.it. This small four-star hotel lies a kilometre or so from Porto Cervo's marina and a 20min walk from Pitrizza beach. Rooms have hints of *gallurese* decor, there's a diminutive pool area. Restaurants are also within walking distance. Closed Oct–May. **€189**

EATING, DRINKING AND NIGHTLIFE

Billionaire Club Via Rocce sul Pévero, Località Sottovento ☎0789 94 192, ⓦbillionairelife.com. If you want to mix with the glitterati, head to the cluster of classy nightclubs a couple of kilometres south of Porto Cervo. None are more ostentatious than this haunt of models, TV presenters and footballers' wives, owned by Flavio Briatore of Benetton and Formula 1 racing fame. Dress up, and expect a steep entrance fee. There are also two swanky restaurants here. June–Sept daily 10pm–late.
Hivaoa Via della Marina, Porto Cervo ☎0789 91 451. Capacious and affordable ristorante on the Marina road with three eating areas. Service is friendly and the prices are huge. The *parmigiana di melanzane* (baked aubergines) is recommended. Set-price menus are €15 and €22 for two or three courses. April to mid-Oct daily noon–midnight.

Lord Nelson Piazza della Marina, Porto Cervo Marina ☎327 718 8194. Beneath a black-and-white, Pisan-style tower on the harbourfront, this pub makes a pleasant place to spend an evening, with occasional live music Thurs–Sun plus sandwiches, burgers and a €12 "English breakfast" every morning. April–Oct daily 7am–3am.
Yachting Piazza della Marina, Porto Cervo Marina ☎0789 94 206. Given that this place decked out all in white calls itself a fashion café and occupies a fabulous location overlooking the yachts, it's a relief to find that it serves decent food at non-extortionate prices. The *pasta all'astice* (with lobster sauce) is a dream. Starters are around €15, mains about €25, and there's a €20 tourist menu. Also good for breakfast, salads, pizzas (at lunchtime too) and *gelati*. June to mid-Sept daily noon–11pm.

7

Baia Sardinia

West of Porto Cervo – just outside the controlled zone of the Costa Smeralda, though sharing its elite ethos – the headland and modern resort of **BAIA SARDINIA** has a scattering of high-class hotels discreetly hidden among the granite boulders. On the Cannigione road, the Aquadream amusement park is a hit with kids (mid-June to early Sept daily 10am–7pm; €18, children €12; ⓦaquadream.it), though the main attraction is the **beach** below the headland.

ACCOMMODATION
BAIA SARDINIA

Smeralda Località Lu Comitoni ⓣ0789 99 811, ⓦbbsmeralda.com. A kilometre outside the centre on the Porto Cervo road (ask for directions beforehand), this dainty B&B offers reasonable rates for its three spacious rooms, with the owner's art on the walls and stunning views of sea and mountain from the terrace. Breakfast is a cornucopia of home-made treats. Closed Nov–Feb. __€110__

7

Arzachena and its prehistoric sites

Outside the luxury zone but enjoying many of the Costa Smeralda's natural advantages, the **Golfo di Arzachena** is a deep, narrow bay whose western shore holds most of the tourist facilities. **ARZACHENA** itself is inland and lacks the glamour of the nearby upscale resorts, though it has some excellent eating and sleeping options; its old centre has character and it's close to two of the biggest and best-preserved nuraghic "giants' tombs" on the whole island.

At the centre of town, **Piazza Risorgimento** is the venue for nightly entertainments in summer and the centre of a **market** on Wednesday mornings. Nearby, take a look at the **Roccia Il Fungo**, or "mushroom rock" (also called *Monti Incappidatu*), one of Gallura's weathered natural sculptures, conspicuous on a rise at the end of Via Limbara, a short walk from the piazza. Fragments found here suggest that it provided shelter for Neolithic and nuraghic folk; there's no doubting its choice location, commanding extensive views up and down the coast.

A new archeological museum showing recent finds in the area is due to open on Via Mozart in 2016 – get the latest on this from Arzachena's tourist office.

Nuraghe Albucciu

Località Albucciu • Easter–Oct daily 9am–sunset; Nov–Easter book in advance • €3.50; €6 for any two of the sites or €8.50 for three • ⓣ 345 576 0538, ⓦ gesecoarzachena.it

From Arzachena, follow the SS125 2km southeast to **Nuraghe Albucciu**, nestled in an olive grove by the side of the road. It's one of Gallura's best-preserved nuraghic monuments, with one chamber, on the right of the main corridor, still roofed and intact. Near the entrance to the *nuraghe*, you can just make out a groove that was probably made by a device for sealing the door. Linked by sight to other *nuraghi* in the area, the structure is built on an almost rectangular plan, and still displays the jutting supports for the vanished wooden roof.

Tempietto Malchittu

Località Malchittu • Easter–Oct daily 9am–sunset; Nov–Easter book in advance • €3.50; €6 for any two of the sites or €8.50 for three • ⓣ 345 576 0538, ⓦ gesecoarzachena.it

Behind the ticket and tourist office outside Nuraghe Albucciu, a pleasant track (not for cars) winds north for less than 2km through fields and around hills to **Tempietto Malchittu**, dating from the first nuraghic phase (between 1500 and 1200 BC) and now overgrown

with trees and scrub. The roofless ruin was probably a place of worship and possibly a sacrificial site, its granite walls enclosing two rooms connected by a low doorway. If you want to carry on walking, follow one of the tracks that continue into the *macchia*.

Coddu Vecchju

Località Capichera • Easter–Oct daily 9am–sunset; Nov–Easter book in advance • €3.50; €6 for any two of the sites or €8.50 for three • ☎ 345 576 0538, ⓦ gesecoarzachena.it

Four and a half kilometres south of Arzachena, on the road to Sant'Antonio di Gallura, branch right onto the Luogosanto road and turn left after another 2km to reach the site of **Coddu Vecchju**, one of the most complete of Sardinia's so-called *tombe dei giganti* ("giants' tombs") consisting of carved granite slabs laid end-up in a semicircular, or bull-horn-shaped, formation. Their popular name was given by people who were clearly mystified by the enigmatic objects, but they are now known to be collective burial chambers and places of worship.

The central stele, over 4m tall, resembles an immense doorway, probably symbolizing the entry into another world. The low opening at the base, which would presumably have been sealed after burial, leads into two long chambers. Excavations here have thrown up evidence that members of the older Bonnanaro culture also used this site, and that it was later adapted by the nuraghic people.

La Prisgiona

Località Capichera • Easter–Oct daily 9am–sunset; Nov–Easter book in advance • €3.50; €6 for any two of the sites or €8.50 for three • ☎ 345 576 0538, ⓦ gesecoarzachena.it

A kilometre along the minor road past Coddu Vecchiu brings you to a monument that was possibly associated with that *tomba dei giganti*, **La Prisgiona** (also known as *Nuraghe Capichera*). Built at any time between 2000 and 1000 BC on a height overlooking the whole Arzachena plain, this trilobate (three-sided) construction has a central tower 6.5m tall, surrounded by three smaller towers and the very sparse remains of an external wall. Three niches survive in the main chamber (which is not central in respect of the tower itself), and there's a well in the space between the rampart and the wall. Dwellings that formed part of a nuraghic village have been excavated in the vicinity, with work ongoing.

Li Lolghi

Località Li Muri • Easter–Oct daily 9am–sunset; Nov–Easter book in advance • €3.50; €6 for any two of the sites or €8.50 for three • ☎ 345 576 0538, ⓦ gesecoarzachena.it

You can reach two more of Arzachena's prehistoric sites by continuing west along the Luogosanto road for nearly 3km, making a right turn and keeping right for another couple of kilometres. Just off this track on the left, the giants' tomb **Li Lolghi** has a lower central stele than Coddu Vecchju, but its inner chamber is nearly twice as long, and is considered to be the finest example of its type in Gallura. Again, the small arched doorway leads into a passage containing the two chambers where bodies were laid.

Li Muri

Località Li Muri • Easter–Oct daily 9am–sunset; Nov–Easter book in advance • €3.50; €6 for any two of the sites or €8.50 for three • ☎ 345 576 0538, ⓦ gesecoarzachena.it

From Li Lolghi it's a short distance to the oldest of Arzachena's sites, **Li Muri**, a site of wild grandeur, reached by backtracking for a couple of hundred metres to take the left-hand (west) fork off the track leading from the Luogosanto road. The track gets pretty rough, so drivers should leave their vehicles at the first suitable spot and proceed on foot, unless they have a 4WD.

The **stone circles** that make up the site constituted a third-millennium–BC necropolis once thought to belong to a so-called "Arzachena culture" – probably a variation of the Ozieri culture (3400–2700 BC). Each of the five central circles (5–8m in diameter) contained a body interred in a crouching position together with votive offerings, while smaller circles dating from a subsequent period are distinguished by a double row of stones with better-worked sides. These were probably used in funerary rites, possibly for the skinning of the corpse before burial.

ARRIVAL AND GETTING AROUND

By car Driving, you can reach Arzachena from Olbia in about 30min on the SS125.

By train Arzachena's train station is about 1km west of town, served by diesel trains operated by ARST on a slow but scenic route to Tempio Pausania, currently leaving at 10am (June–Oct 2–3 weekly; 1hr 30min). A coach service is available for the return journey. See ꝏ treninoverde.com for details.

By bus ARST services run to most places along the coast, and there are daily Turmo connections to Olbia, Palau and

ARZACHENA AND ITS PREHISTORIC SITES

Santa Teresa. In Arzachena, buses pull up on Via San Pietro, off Via Dettori (the road signposted for Luogosanto). Buy tickets at *Bar Castello*, Via Dettori 43.

Destinations Cannigione (Mon–Sat 3–9 daily; 10min); Olbia (every 30min–1hr; 20–50min); Palau (every 30min–1hr; 20min); Porto Cervo (Mon–Sat 5–8 daily; 25–40min); Santa Teresa Gallura (5–11 daily; 1hr).

By taxi If you want to take a taxi from Arzachena to any of the nuraghic sites, you'll find ranks on Via Dettori (☎ 0789 96 023) and off the central Piazza Risorgimento (☎ 0789 82 900).

7

INFORMATION

Tourist office The main information office is at Piazza Risorgimento 8 (Mon–Fri 9am–2pm & 4–7pm or 3–6pm in winter, Sat 9am–2pm; ☎ 0789 844 055); there's also an office outside town at Malchittu, between Arzachena and Cannigione (Mon–Sat 9am–2pm; ☎ 0789 83 306).

Post office Viale Costa Smeralda 159 (Mon–Fri 8.20am–7.05pm, Sat 8.20am–12.35pm); you can change cash here or at any of the banks on Viale Costa Smeralda, all with ATMs.

ACCOMMODATION

Il Vecchio Ginepro Sotgiu Pietruccia ☎ 347 388 3557, ꝏ ilvecchioginepro.it. About 1km west of the centre, reached from Via Mameli or the bypass, this traditional B&B on a farm has eight independent suites giving onto gardens, each with a fridge, and most with kitchenettes. Breakfast includes home-produced salamis and jam, goat's milk and cheese. No credit cards. **€100**

★**L'Abba Maistra** Località Nicola Calta ☎ 338 212 9548, ꝏ labbamaistra.com. Utterly tranquil *agriturismo* in a stone-walled *stazzo* (traditional *gallurese* rural dwelling), 8km west of town off the Bassacutena road. The five spacious, en-suite rooms are furnished with antiques and fridges, and there's a small pool amid the rocks. It's a little hard to find, best reached in daylight. There's currently no wi-fi. No credit cards. Closed mid-Sept to May. **€70**

Lu Pastruccialeddu Località Lu Pastruccialeddu ☎ 0789 81 777 or ☎ 340 814 6330, ꝏ pastruccialeddu .com. In granite-walled converted farm buildings, this B&B lies in open country 2km north of Arzachena (turn right at the Despar supermarket heading west out of town). The rooms, including junior suites and a family apartment, have a rustic Sardinian feel. Generous alfresco breakfasts include home-made yoghurt, as well as home-baked cakes and pies, served by the small pool. Four-night minimum stay July–Sept. Closed Nov–March. **€100**

★**Santa Lucia** Via Cágliari 11 ☎ 0789 83 012 or ☎ 338 269 3640, ꝏ bbslucia.it. This friendly B&B in a modernized townhouse lies in a quiet backstreet of Arzachena. The spacious rooms with fridges and a/c open onto a minimalist walled garden where delicious breakfasts are served, including freshly baked cakes. No credit cards. **€80**

EATING

Il Fungo Via d'Annunzio ☎ 0789 83 340. In a quiet lane off Via Ruzzitto, near the central piazza, this traditional trattoria with some seating outside serves a range of Sardinian specialities and pizzas. Service is friendly and there's occasional live music. First courses are €7–13, seconds around €14. Daily except Tues noon–3pm & 7.30pm–midnight.

Jaddhu Località Capichera ☎ 0789 80 636,

ꝏ jaddhu.com. Well off the beaten track (10min by car from Arzachena), but very close to Nuraghe La Prisgiona, this rural hotel and restaurant offers some of the best food around, which you can enjoy while admiring the views from the covered terrace. Pastas such as *malloreddus con salsiccia* (with sausage) are €13–15, mains €15–20, and there are pizzas too. June–Sept 12.30–2.30pm & 7.30–11pm.

Cannigione and around

Most tourists gravitate towards the coast, with a concentration of facilities around the small resort and yacht-stop of **CANNIGIONE**, on the western shore of the Golfo di Arzachena. It's an inviting spot to dispatch a *gelato* on a stroll by the portside and there are some decent beaches to the north, though its expensive air is borne out by the high prices. Coastal boat excursions, taking in La Maddalena archipelago (see p.252), leave from the marina in summer.

Continuing north, beyond the satellite resort of **La Conia**, the narrow coast road winds west to the **Golfo delle Saline**, a bay sheltering an exquisite, relatively undeveloped, sandy **beach**. At its far end, the headland, **Capo d'Orso**, takes its name ("Cape Bear") from a huge, strange bear-shaped rock known since ancient times and claimed to be the dwelling-place of the Laestrygonians, the mythical cannibal tribe which destroyed the fleet of Ulysses when it legendarily docked here. To reach it, you have to pass a gate and climb. At 122m high, its views are sensational, embracing the Maddalena Islands, Santa Teresa Gallura and Corsica.

ARRIVAL AND INFORMATION

CANNIGIONE AND AROUND

By bus ARST and, in summer, Sun Lines buses serve Cannigione.
Destinations Arzachena (Mon–Sat 3–7 daily; 10min); Olbia (June–Sept 4 daily; 50min); Porto Cervo (June–Sept 4 daily; 30min).

Tourist office Via Orecchioni, Cannigione (Mon–Sat 9am–2pm; ☎0789 88 229). There's also a private office at Via Nazionale 47 (April–June, Sept & Oct Mon–Sat 9am–12.30pm & 5.30–7.30pm, July & Aug also Sun 9–11am; ☎0789 88 510).

ACCOMMODATION AND EATING

Capo d'Orso Località Le Saline ☎0789 702 007, ⓦcapodorso.it. Enjoying a good location close to the eponymous headland and the beach of Le Saline, this campsite is equipped with a diving centre, boat rentals, windsurfing facilities, caravans (€55) and bungalows (€105). Closed Oct to mid-May. Pitches €27

Centro Vacanze Isuledda La Conia ☎0789 86 003, ⓦcampingisuledda.com. A couple of kilometres north of Cannigione, this family-friendly campsite is right on the shore, with excellent bathing spots, and caravans and bungalows to rent. It gets a bit overwhelmed in Aug though and there's not much shade. Sun Lines buses stop outside in summer. Closed mid-Oct to late March. Pitches €44

Hotel del Porto Via Nazionale 94 ☎0789 88 011, ⓦhoteldelporto.com. The best value of Cannigione's hotels, this place has compact rooms, some (costing extra) with balconies overlooking the marina. Rates are negotiable and plummet in winter. The hotel has a good café and restaurant open to all, the former offering a set-price menu for €14; otherwise pasta dishes cost €10–14. Daily 12.30–2.30pm & 7.30–9.30pm. €140

★**La Tavola Blu** Via Vasco da Gama 12 ☎347 121 5328. Below the church, this simple *rosticceria* has a brisk, authentic feel, offering delicious portions of fresh seafood and other hot snacks for €2–5 each (pastas are around €10). April to mid-Oct daily 9am–3pm & 5–11pm.

Palau

For years a minor port best known as the embarkation point for the Maddalena archipelago, **PALAU** has raised its profile in recent years thanks to the growth of the local holiday industry, and is now quite a lively local centre and a useful base for exploring the excellent beaches in the vicinity. It has enough bars, restaurants and all-star summer entertainments to keep you amused for an evening or two, while by day there's a choice of boat excursions for touring the coast and islands.

Fortezza di Monte Altura

Monte Altura • Tours (45min) daily: April & May 10.15am, 11.15am, 12.15pm, 3.15pm, 4.15pm & 5.15pm; June–Aug 10.15am, 11.15am, 12.15pm, 5.15pm, 6.15pm & 7.15pm; Sept to mid-Oct 10.15am, 11.15am, 3.15pm, 4.15pm & 5.15pm • €3 • ☎329 604 1373, ⓦrocciadellorso.it

Lying 3km north of town, the **Fortezza di Monte Altura** is a defensive bastion built in the nineteenth century on a rocky height above Palau. To get here, take the signposted turn-off on the right as you head towards the SS125. The winding road leads up to a set of impregnable-looking granite walls, and the tall gates from which guided tours leave. A surreal-looking flight of stone steps gives access to towers and the empty emplacements for guns installed during World War II, from where you can enjoy magnificent views over the Maddalena Islands. The fortress is the occasional venue for concerts and other performances in summer.

ARRIVAL AND DEPARTURE

PALAU

By train In summer, an infrequent Trenino Verde service operated by ARST connects Palau to Arzachena (30min) and Tempio Pausania (2hr), currently running 2–3 times weekly between late June and late Oct with a 9.30am departure. The train station is by the port at the end of the main Via Nazionale.
By bus ARST and Turmo buses stop by the port.

Destinations Arzachena (every 30min–1hr; 20min); Olbia (1–2 daily; 1hr); Santa Teresa Gallura (6–13 daily; 35–45min); Tempio Pausania (2–3 daily; 1hr 35min).
By ferry Next to train station, the Stazione Maríttima holds ticket offices for the various companies operating ferries to the Maddalena Islands (see box, p.254).

GETTING AROUND

By car Sardinya, Via Nazionale 97 (April–Oct; ☎ 0789 709 083, ⓦ autonoleggiosardinya.it) rents out cars for around

€60/day, and scooters for €30–50/day.
By taxi Call ☎ 0789 709 218 or ☎ 348 798 8281.

INFORMATION AND ACTIVITIES

Tourist office Piazza Fresi, signposted off Via Nazionale (July–Sept daily 9am–1pm & 4–8pm; Oct–June Mon, Wed & Fri 9am–1pm, Tues & Thurs 9am–1pm & 3.30–7.30pm; ☎ 0789 707 025, ⓦ palauturismo.com).
Diving Courses and packages are available at Nautilus Diving Center, Piazza Fresi 8 (☎ⓣ 0789 709 058, ⓦ divesardegna.com).

Boat tours Excursions around the Maddalena archipelago leave from the port daily between June and Sept at around 10am or 10.45am, returning between 5 & 6pm. Tours cost €30–60 and usually include swimming stops as well as lunch on board. Contact Lady Luna (☎ 339 387 7196, ⓦ giteinbarca.it) or Delfino Bianco (☎ 338 962 1717, ⓦ delfinobiancopalau.com), or just turn up at the port.

ACCOMMODATION

Baia Saraceno Località Baia Saraceno ☎ 0789 709 403, ⓦ baiasaraceno.com. The nearest campsite to Palau, this is a good option if you want to stay near the beach, located in a pinewood close to Punta Nera, less than a kilometre east (10min on foot). It's clean and quiet, with access to rocky inlets and sandy coves. Cabins (€45) and bungalows (€60) are available. Closed Nov–Feb. Pitches €30
La Fonda Via Stazione 15 ☎ 335 411 778, ⓦ bblafonda .com. This B&B run by a hospitable English lady has bright, en-suite rooms with a/c; those on the first floor have balconies and distant sea views. A small kitchen is available for preparing cold snacks. Closed Jan & Feb. No credit cards. €78

La Roccia Via dei Mille 15 ☎ 0789 709 528, ⓦ hotellaroccia.com. Named after the granite boulder that intrudes into the garden and lobby, this smart three-star hotel has friendly staff and smallish, simply decorated rooms with balconies and satellite TV. There's free parking too. Closed mid-Oct to Easter. €100
L'Orso e il Mare Vícolo Diaz 1 ☎ 331 222 2000, ⓦ orsoeilmare.com. Well-managed B&B close to the port, with three airy rooms, one (costing more) with a balcony. All have private bathrooms, a/c, fridges and TVs. Breakfast includes fresh bread and fruit salad. Closed Dec–Jan. €85

EATING

Da Robertino Via Nazionale 20 ☎ 0789 709 610. Near the port, this ristorante has an intimate interior decorated with ceramics and mementos. Portions are big and tasty but not very cheap: pasta dishes cost around €15, mains around €18, much more if you order the speciality *aragosta alla catalana* (lobster), priced by weight. There's a great array of *antipasti* too. Feb to mid–June & mid–Sept to mid–Nov Tues–Sun 1–2.30 & 7.30–10.30pm; mid–June to mid–Sept daily, same hours.

Il Ghiottone Via Don Occhioni 10 ☎ 329 129 3571. Facing the church off the main drag – you can eat on the piazzetta or on the cosy terrace upstairs – this place offers a good range of pastas, seafood and meat dishes, for example *taglioni* with spider crab, and the regional speciality *zuppa cuata*. First courses are €10–15, mains around €15. It also has a good range of pizzas. March, April, Oct & Nov Mon–Sat noon–3pm & 6.30pm–midnight; May–Sept daily, same hours.

7

Pasta & Vino Via Demartis 24 ☏ 0789 709 331. Small, elegant trattoria in a side street near the seafront with delicious seafood dishes. The spaghetti with *vongole* e *bottarga* (with clams and fish roe; €13.50) is exquisite. Main courses are €14–20, and there are tables outside. Easter–Oct Mon–Sat noon–3pm & 7–10.30pm, Sun 7–10.30pm.

Porto Pollo

Between Palau and the port of Santa Teresa Gallura, the dramatic rocky coastline is indented by a succession of lovely creeks and bays. The few small resorts get very busy in summer, but are generally deserted the rest of the time, when most hotels and campsites close.

Two or three kilometres out of Palau, **Porto Pollo** (also called Porto Puddu) is a scattered locality which has become established as Sardinia's busiest watersports centre. A slender isthmus of beach ending in a bulbous promontory, **Isola dei Gabbiani**, divides the two bays of Porto Pollo and Porto Liscia, creating a breakwater and thus ideal conditions for **windsurfing** and **kitesurfing**: downwind of the sandbank, the sea is flat; upwind, it's choppy, fast and more suited to experts. There's a whole network of surf schools and rental operations, but even if you're not a surfer, the dune-backed beaches are worth going out of your way for, not least at night when there are regular beach parties.

GETTING AROUND · PORTO POLLO

By bike or scooter Dodo's Rental (☏ 334 148 4950, ⊛ dodosrental.com) has mountain bikes for €20–30/day, scooters for €40–65/day.

ACCOMMODATION AND EATING

Isola dei Gabbiani Isola dei Gabbiani ☏ 0789 704 019, ⊛ isoladeigabbiani.it. This campsite sprawls across the "island" from which it takes its name, with splendid swimming spots along the shores, though it all gets very crowded in summer. Bungalows (€89) are available too. Closed Nov to mid-May. Pitches **€29**

Le Dune ☏ 0789 704 013, ⊛ hotelledune.it. This fortress-like three-star is the only hotel hereabouts, in a wonderful position around 200m from the sea on a height, with views across to the Maddalena Islands. The restaurant (open to all) has a menu ranging from pizzas to seafood, and enjoys the same stunning panorama. Half or full board is usually required in the functional rooms, some of which overlook the car park. April–Oct daily noon–2.30pm & 7–10.30pm. **€80** Half board per person

The Maddalena Islands

From Palau, it's a short hop across to the **Maddalena archipelago**, a cluster of seven larger islands and a sprinkling of smaller ones. The archipelago is a favourite with yachters, and hosts a number of regattas, but most people come for its glorious beaches, which are mainly small and pristine. Boats dock at the largest of the group, **La Maddalena**, holding almost all the hotels and restaurants and a small museum of naval archeology. From the main island, you can drive, bike or hike across to neighbouring **Caprera**, where Garibaldi spent the last 25 years of his life. The hero of the struggle for Italian unification is

---

WATERSPORTS IN PORTO POLLO

Among Porto Pollo's **windsurfing** and **kitesurfing** outfits, try Sporting Club Sardinia (☏ 0789 704 016, ⊛ portopollo.it) or North Kite School (☏ 347 272 2706, ⊛ northkiteschoolsardinia.com), both operating from April to October. For windsurfing, you'll pay €18–30 for the first hour for board rental, less for consecutive hours, and for tuition around €100 for four hours for group lessons, €60 per person for one hour's private lesson. For kitesurfing, it's about €40 for one hour's equipment rental, €60 for one hour's tuition. Operators have stalls on the beach near Isola dei Gabbiani, and they also rent dinghies and can arrange **sailing** and **diving** excursions.

remembered in a museum – his former home – which gives a fascinating insight into his long career on the world stage and his reclusive existence on the island.

La Maddalena is also the departure point for a range of boat tours to the other isles: **Santo Stéfano**, **Spargi**, **Budelli**, **Razzoli** and **Santa Maria**. Set amid myriad jutting rocks, they have some perfect scraps of beach to swim from, but little else besides rock and scrub.

The islands form part of Sardinia's first **national park** (wlamaddalenapark.it), whose boundaries extend south to the islands of Mortorio and Soffi off the Costa Smeralda. Accordingly, there are restrictions on sailing activities, fishing and building, and some of the smaller islands are completely off-limits. The most conspicuous **wildlife** in evidence are the gulls, cormorants and herons that perch on the innumerable granite rocks poking out of the sea; it's unlikely you'll catch sight of the extremely rare Mediterranean monk seal.

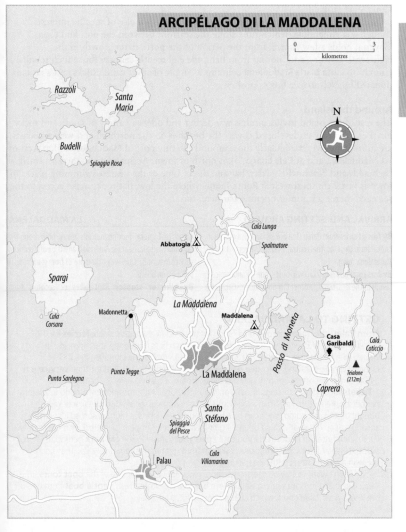

ARCIPÉLAGO DI LA MADDALENA

7

0   3
kilometres

Razzoli

Santa Maria

Budelli

Spiaggia Rosa

N

Cala Lunga

Abbatogia

Spalmatore

Spargi

La Maddalena

Cala Corsara

Madonnetta

Maddalena

Casa Garibaldi

Cala Coticcio

Passo di Moneta

Teialone (212m)

Punta Sardegna

Punta Tegge

La Maddalena

Caprera

Santo Stéfano

Spiaggia del Pesce

Cala Villamarina

Palau

La Maddalena

Just 2km from the Sardinian mainland, and measuring roughly 6km by 4km, the island of **La Maddalena** has the only town on the archipelago and some of its finest beaches, which are also the easiest to reach. The island has long played an important strategic and military role, and Mussolini was briefly imprisoned here in 1943.

La Maddalena town

Bearing the same name as the island, the port and sole town of **LA MADDALENA** is an upbeat place whose population of about 11,500 is swollen by vast numbers of (mainly Italian) tourists who make the crossing every summer. Most of the action takes place in the narrow lanes between the main square, Piazza Umberto I, and **Cala Gavetta**, a natural harbour five minutes' walk west of the ferry port. Now a marina for small boats, this was the original nucleus of the town. The main *passeggiata* takes place here, along Via Garibaldi.

Once you've given these areas the once-over, there's little else of specific interest, though Via Améndola, which runs along the seafront between the port and Cala Gavetta, holds a few *palazzi* from the period of the port's main growth in the eighteenth century, and, not far from here, the eighteenth-century (but much rebuilt) church of **Santa Maria Maddalena** contains a couple of silver candlesticks and a crucifix donated by Nelson (see box opposite).

Around the island

The rest of the island invites aimless wandering and offers a variety of sandy and rocky beaches in mostly undeveloped coves. The **beaches** on the northern and western coasts are most attractive, particularly those around the tiny port of **Madonnetta**, 5km west of La Maddalena, and at **Cala Lunga**, 5km north of town. At **Spalmatore**, there's a small, sheltered sand beach with a jetty, bar and disco. One of the nearest swimming places to town is just 2km southwest at **Punta Tegge**, where the low, flat rocks make access to the sea easy; there's a summer-opening bar here, too.

ARRIVAL AND GETTING AROUND   **LA MADDALENA**

By ferry Ferries from Palau (see box below) and excursion boats dock close to the central Piazza Umberto I in La Maddalena town.

By bus Local buses run on two routes, one ("Panoramica") taking in the beaches, the other ("Nido d'Aquila–Caprera") going to Caprera, leaving roughly every hour from the Colonna Garibaldi near Via Améndola and the port (reduced service in winter). One-way tickets are €1 from tobacconists or €1.50 on board.

By bike or scooter Rent bikes or scooters from

GETTING TO LA MADDALENA

From Palau, the main port of embarkation for the Maddalena archipelago, **ferries** for the island and port of La Maddalena leave every 15–30min (less frequently after 8pm and in winter), run by Saremar (☏ 0789 709 270, ⊛ saremar.it), Maddalena Lines (☏ 0789 739 165, ⊛ maddalenalines.it) and Delcomar (☏ 0789 727 220, ⊛ delcomar.it). A night-time **service** run by Delcomar departs roughly hourly (tickets on board). Crossing time is around 20min.

Tickets for daytime crossings are sold at Palau's Stazione Maríttima and cost around €12 return per person, €40 return for two in a medium-sized car, with significant discounts for tickets bought on the preceding day. It can be a hectic bustle for tickets in high season, so it's worth arriving half an hour early. Don't bother arguing with queue-jumpers: island residents get priority.

It's much faster for pedestrians; you could park your vehicle in the **car park** behind the ticket office at Palau (a hefty €2.50/hr); cars parked in front get fined. Alternatively, you may find a space in a nearby street with free parking.

If you don't want to stay on the archipelago, you might consider one of the **boat tours** from Palau (see p.251) or Santa Teresa Gallura (see box, p.260). Alternatively, **rent a boat** from one of the kiosks near Palau's port, which charge around €200 for a day.

NELSON IN THE MADDALENA ISLANDS

Between 1803 and 1805, the fleet of **Admiral Nelson** was a constant presence in what he called "Agincourt Sound", or the Straits of Bonifacio. It lurked in the waters around the **Maddalena archipelago** for fifteen months while Nelson stalked the French fleet during the run-up to the Battle of Trafalgar. Nelson never once set foot on shore throughout this long wait, but he sent a stream of letters to the Admiralty in London urging that steps be taken to secure Sardinia for England – it was then the only neutral shore in this part of the Mediterranean: "And I venture to predict, that if we do not…the French will." The French, docked at Toulon (nicknamed "Too-Long" by Nelson's impatient sailors), eventually fled to the West Indies before returning to meet Nelson at Trafalgar.

Megamotors, Via Améndola 2 (☎ 0789 737 606), or Nicol Sport, Via Améndola 18 (☎ 328 055 8451, ⓦ nicolsport .com), both on the seafront towards Cala Gavetta. Prices are €10–18/day for a bike, €40–60/day for a scooter (less in low season and for longer rents); you'll need ID and/or a deposit.

By taxi You'll find a rank at the port, or call ☎ 340 361 6466, ☎ 347 370 6074 or ☎ 338 262 3474.

INFORMATION AND TOURS

Tourist office The office on Via Venti Settembre, off Cala Gavetta, covers information for the whole archipelago (June–Sept daily 8.45am–8.45pm; Oct–May Mon & Wed 8.30am–1.30pm & 3.30–5.30pm, Tues, Thurs & Fri 8.30am–1.30pm; ☎ 0789 736 321, ⓦ comune.lamaddalena.ot.it).

Boat tours Various excursions around the archipelago leave daily from the port at 9.30–10.45am, most costing €25–40. The tours include several swimming stops as well as lunch on board. The Flotta del Parco is a consortium of the main operators (ⓦ flottadelparco .com).

ACCOMMODATION

Il Gabbiano Via Giulio Césare 20 ☎ 0789 722 507, ⓦ hotel-ilgabbiano.it. West of the centre beyond Cala Gavetta, this refurbished 1960s hotel enjoys a fantastic location on a point looking across to Santo Stéfano and Palau. Rooms are pretty standard (some without a/c), but all face the sea and some have balconies. **€90**

★ **La Petite Maison** Via Livenza ☎ 0789 738 432 or ☎ 340 646 3722, ⓦ lapetitmaison.net. Quirky and welcoming B&B 5min from the centre. It's run by a Dutch/Italian couple and dotted with antiques and works of art (some by the owner). Ochre- and pastel-hued rooms have private bathrooms and there's a shady courtyard garden where breakfast is taken. No credit cards. **€85**

Mongiardino Località Mongiardino ☎ 338 503 4830, ⓦ mongiardino.it. Peaceful B&B 1.5km north of the port, surrounded by gardens where breakfasts are served and which you can use for barbecues. The three spacious rooms have a/c, fridges and satellite TV. Closed Dec–Feb. **€70**

Residenza Mordini Via Príncipe Amedeo 3 ☎ 0789 737 325, ⓦ residenzamordini.it. In a renovated 1930s building close to the ferry port, this swish hotel offers well-equipped rooms with a blend of antique and modern furnishings, spa facilities and free parking. **€110**

CAMPSITES

Abbatoggia Village Località Abbatoggia ☎ 0789 738 044, ⓦ abbatoggiavillage.it. This campsite in the north of the island has a superb location right by the sea and close to three of the island's best beaches. Apart from a basic bar and pizzeria, however, facilities are spartan. Book early to rent a caravan (€60) or mobile home (€100). There's a shuttle service into town. Closed late Sept to mid-June. Pitches **€24**

Maddalena Località Moneta ☎ 0789 728 051, ⓦ campingmaddalena.it. The best-equipped of the island's campsites lies close to town and Caprera. It's sheltered and clean with friendly staff and has a great restaurant, too, but choose a pitch away from it for more peace. Chalets and bungalows are available (from €60). Closed Oct–May. Pitches **€26**

EATING

Il Ghiottone Via Oberdan 5 ☎ 0789 736 091. This central trattoria is small inside and has a small menu, but the choices are usually excellent, including *trofie casarecce mari e monti* (home-made pasta with meat and seafood) and *tagliatelle con cozze e menta* (with mussels and mint). Full meals will cost around €40/head, drinks included.

Booking essential. April–Oct daily noon–3pm & 7pm–midnight.

Osteria da Liò Via Vittorio Emanuele 4 ☎ 0789 737 507. Simple, family-run *osteria* in the centre, with some outdoor tables. The *spaghetti bottarga e vongole* (with fish roe and clams) is exceptional. You'll pay around €40 each without drinks. April–Oct Tues–Sun noon–3pm & 7.30–10.30pm.

Perla Blu Piazza Barone des Geneys ☎ 0789 735 373. It's somewhat overpriced, but this place is worth a visit for its terrace overlooking the boats on Cala Gavetta. Fresh pasta dishes are around €15, a fish steak will be about €22 and they serve pizzas too. April–Oct daily noon–11pm.

Sergeant Pepper Via G. Bruno 6 ☎ 331 509 0091. This central place off Piazza Garibaldi with a few outdoor tables is ideal for a fast and tasty pizza (€6–13) with a jug of beer. There's a good choice; the pizzas are fairly large but thin-crusted. You can't book, so you may have to wait for a table in summer. May–Sept daily noon–3pm & 7.15pm–midnight; Oct–April daily except Tues 7.15pm–midnight.

Caprera

A simple bridge built in 1891 stretches for 600m across the **Passo di Moneta** that separates La Maddalena from **Caprera**. Measuring around 7km from top to bottom, the island has been protected from development and, apart from Garibaldi's house and a couple of self-contained tourist complexes, consists primarily of woods and rocky scrub. Strike out in any direction along a network of trails to reach tranquil spots that are a welcome relief after the tourist bustle around Garibaldi's museum. Caprera's flora and fauna are among the most interesting of the islands, especially during spring when the heather, hawthorn and juniper present a multicoloured mosaic amid the pines, holm oaks and myrtles, and the birdlife includes royal seagulls, shearwaters, sparrowhawks and buzzards.

Among the small beaches around the shore, the most popular is **Cala Coticcio**, on the island's east coast (about a forty-minute walk from the bridge, less from the museum). A handful of fortifications lie dotted around, some built by the Savoy regime in the eighteenth century, and some from around the time of World War I. You can also climb a long stairway leading to the lookout tower on **Teialone**, the highest point of the Maddalena archipelago at 212m.

Compendio Garibaldino

Tues–Sun 9am–8pm (call to check in winter) • €6 • ☎ 0789 727 162, Ⓦ compendiogaribaldino.it

At the end of a tamarisk-lined road, the **Compendio Garibaldino** is in Garibaldi's old house, the elegant South American-style Casa Bianca, which has been preserved pretty much as he left it. Visitors are escorted past a collection of memorabilia which include an iconic *camicia rossa* (red shirt), the bed where he slept, a smaller one where he died, various scrolls, manifestos and pronouncements, a pair of ivory and gold binoculars

GARIBALDI ON CAPRERA

The most swashbuckling and erratic of all Italian patriots, **Giuseppe Garibaldi** (1807–82) came to live on Caprera in 1855, after a glorious and highly eventful career in arms, much of it spent in exile from Italy. It was from here that he embarked on his spectacular conquest of Sicily and Naples in 1861, accompanied by his thousand Redshirts, and it was here that he returned at the end of his campaigns, to resume a simple farming life. Having first seen the island on his flight from Rome in 1849, he subsequently bought the northern part of it for £360, no doubt attracted by its proximity to the Piemontese naval base. Increasingly marginalized by the new king of Italy, Vittorio Emanuele, and the government in Piemonte, Garibaldi eventually became something of a recluse on Caprera – while still keeping abreast of affairs, receiving numerous deputations and making regular pronouncements on issues of the day. He devoted the rest of his time to writing his memoirs and a handful of bad novels, and tending his property. His neighbour was an Englishman named Collins, with whom he had some celebrated disagreements concerning wandering herds of goats, as a result of which Garibaldi built a wall dividing their properties, which can still be seen. After Collins's death in 1864, a group of English admirers provided the money for Garibaldi to buy the rest of Caprera from his ex-neighbour's family.

given to him by the future King Edward VII and a letter from London, dated 1867, conferring on him honorary presidency of the National Reform League. A stopped clock and a wall calendar indicate the precise time and date of his death. The tour ends with Garibaldi's grave in the garden, its rough granite contrasting with the more pompous tombs of his last wife and five of his children. Garibaldi had requested to be cremated, but his corpse was embalmed on the wishes of his son Menotti. In 1932, fifty years after his death, his tomb was opened to reveal the body perfectly intact.

It's worth checking the website or calling ahead in winter, as opening hours can change.

Santo Stéfano

Halfway between La Maddalena and the coast, the island of **Santo Stéfano** was briefly captured by French forces in 1793 in an abortive attempt to take possession of Sardinia. From here, the young **Napoleon Bonaparte**, then a lieutenant-colonel in the Corsican National Guard, commanded a bombardment of La Maddalena. Part of the island is occupied by the Italian navy, and most trippers disembark on the more interesting western side at the **Spiaggia del Pesce** beach, where there are a couple of holiday enclaves, and at the southern end, **Cala Villamarina**, where traces of Neolithic life have been found.

Spargi

West of La Maddalena, **Spargi** is renowned for its sparkling beaches, the best of which – and one of the finest on the archipelago – lies on the southern littoral at **Cala Corsara**, with transparent water, though it's a regular stop for boat tours. Nearby, the wreck of a Roman vessel from the second century BC was hauled out of the sea in the 1950s.

Budelli

On **Budelli** the famous **Spiaggia Rosa** ("pink beach"), immortalized by the director Michelangelo Antonioni in his film *Il Deserto Rosso* (*Red Desert*, 1965), is now protected and out of bounds, but other beautiful beaches elsewhere around the island compensate. For physical beauty and exquisite, crystal-clear sea, try **Cavaliere** and the lagoon-like **Le Piscine Naturali**. The limpid waters also attract **scuba divers** – contact the tourist offices at Palau and La Maddalena for local dive operators.

Santa Teresa Gallura and around

On Sardinia's northern tip, the small town of **SANTA TERESA GALLURA** is the main port for ships to Corsica, whose cliffs are clearly visible just 11km away. This is no mere transit town, however. If **beaches** are your thing, Santa Teresa must rank as one of the island's most attractive holiday destinations, surrounded by scintillating stretches of sand, with exhilarating views across the Straits of Bonifacio. To cope with the demand, the town has Gallura's widest selection of hotels and restaurants, and the region's liveliest bar-culture – though life grinds to a much slower and calmer pace outside the summer months. In winter, especially, it can get very windy.

Like most of Gallura's coastal towns, Santa Teresa Gallura has a prosaic, modern look. It's arranged on a regular grid of modern streets that centre on the main **Piazza Vittorio Emanuele**, a brief walk up from Santa Teresa's beach, **Rena Bianca** – a beautiful stretch of sand, though some prefer the less congested beaches to either side of town. Jammed with yachts and blue-and-white fishing vessels, the **marina** and **port** area lie out of sight in the deep inlet of Longone (or Longosardo), reached from Via del Porto. Here you'll find kiosks selling tickets for Corsica and various boat tours (see box, p.260).

Brief history

Though there was a Roman settlement in the region, and garrisons were stationed here at different times by the Genoans and Aragonese, the present town was only founded in 1808 by order of the Savoyard king Vittorio Emanuele I, who named it after his wife Maria Teresa of Austria. Apart from a Spanish watchtower, however, few buildings date even as far back as the nineteenth century, and it owes its prevailing tone to the holiday development of the late 1950s. More recently, the growth of its yachting marina and the swelling pockets of holiday homes on the eastern side of the Longone creek have helped to make Santa Teresa one of Sardinia's most full-on holiday resorts.

Torre Spagnola

June–Sept daily 10am–1pm & 4–8pm • €2

North of Piazza Vittorio Emanuele, Via del Mare ends after a couple of hundred metres at a high bluff dominated by the **Torre Spagnola**, a well-preserved Spanish watchtower from the sixteenth century, sometimes called Torre Aragonese and officially known as Torre di Longosardo. The tower is open in summer for far-reaching views and to take in the regular exhibitions of photography, ceramics and other local craftwork. A

panoramic path leads beyond the tower and down to the waterside, and there are also steps leading west of the tower to Rena Bianca.

The beaches east of Santa Teresa

Some of Sardinia's most alluring **beaches** lie only a short ride east out of Santa Teresa, all with views over to Corsica. To reach them from town, turn off at the signposts on the main Via Nazionale or turn off the SS133bis Palau road, or use the summer bus service (see p.260). Swimmers, sailors and windsurfers should all beware of the **strong currents** coursing through the Straits of Bonifacio, particularly around the northernmost cape of Punta Falcone.

There's safe swimming 3km or so east along the coast, in the deep inlet of **Porto Quadro**. Another couple of kilometres farther east, **Punta Falcone** is the Sardinian mainland's most northerly point, sheltering to its east the biggest sandy beach along here at **La Marmorata**, an exquisite spot marred by the proximity of intrusive villa complexes. The swimming, though, is superb, with the serrated profile of the Isola di Marmorata out to sea. The next beach down, **Cala Sambuco**, is reached from the same turn-off from the SS133bis (and there are capacious parking areas here and at La Marmorata). **La Licciola** also has a scattering of holiday houses, though not enough to overwhelm this small beach.

Some 12km east of Santa Teresa, **Porto Pozzo** is a small beach and fishing settlement at the edge of the deepest of the inlets hereabouts, also called Porto Pozzo. In the season, **boat trips** depart for the islands of Spargi and Santa Maria from the quay, and you can eat at the beachside bar/pizzeria.

Capo Testa and around

Three kilometres west of Santa Teresa, **Capo Testa** is one of Sardinia's finest bathing localities, a rocky promontory at the end of a narrow isthmus, surrounded by turquoise sea. The headland has some scraps of sandy beach and even some meagre remains of the Roman settlement of **Tibula** – truncated granite columns and some fragments of stone by the waterside. Material from the nearby quarries was used both for the columns of the Pantheon in Rome and for Pisa's cathedral. Beyond, standing amid a clutter of surreal, wind-chiselled rock formations, a lighthouse casts its beam from the point.

The beaches

Among Capo Testa's **beaches**, take your pick between those facing Corsica on one side, and those with views towards the northern Sardinian coast sloping away westward on the other. The most popular ones are the **Spiaggia dei Due Mari** – situated on either side of the isthmus, facing north and south – and those actually on Capo Testa, such as **Spiaggia Rosa**. The **Spiaggia Levante** (also called Baia Santa Reparata) on the north side, and **Spiaggia Ponente** (or Cala La Colba) on the south, are the places to rent surfboards and other craft or to enrol on a diving or sailing course.

Farther afield, there are more beaches and plenty of privacy behind the thick pinewoods flanking the SS200 coastal road headed southwest. First and best of these is the extensive **Rena Maiore**, 8km due south of Santa Teresa and Capo Testa. Smaller beaches follow in quick succession farther west, all worth investigating, including a cluster around **Vignola**, about 10km west of Rena Maiore, popular with the kitesurfing crowd. The area is named after the vineyards which produce the region's most famous wine, **Vermentino di Gallura**.

ARRIVAL AND DEPARTURE	SANTA TERESA GALLURA AND AROUND

By ferry From the port on the eastern side of town, Saremar (☎ 0789 754 156, ⓦ saremar.it) and Moby Lines (April–Sept; ☎ 0789 751 449, ⓦ moby.it) operate sailings to Bonifacio in Corsica (2–7 daily; 50min; €18–25 one-way, plus €30–35/car). Look out for special discounts for booking specified return dates and for car/

7

passenger packages. Ticket offices normally open an hour prior to departure.

By bus Buses stop at Via Eleonora d'Arborea off Via Nazionale, the main road into town. Timetables and tickets for ARST buses are available from Tabacchi Fanari, Piazza Vittorio Emanuele 26. For Turmo buses (☎0789 21 487, ⓦ gruppoturmotravel.com) to Cágliari, Digitur (☎079 262 039, ⓦ digitur.it) to Castelsardo and Sardabus (ⓦ sardabus .it) to Tempio Pausania, buy tickets on board.

Destinations Arzachena (6–13 daily; 1hr); Cágliari (1 daily; 6hr); Castelsardo (2–5 daily; 1hr 20min–1hr 35min); Olbia (6–8 daily; 1hr 20min–1hr 50min); Palau (6–12 daily; 40min); Sássari (2–5 daily; 2hr 35min); Tempio Pausania (2 daily; 1hr).

GETTING AROUND

By bike, scooter or car Just Sardinia, Via Maria Teresa 58 (☎0789 754 343, ⓦ justsardinia.it), Sardinya, Via Maria Teresa 29 (☎0789 759 090, ⓦ autonoleggiosardinya.it) and Tibula Rent, at Via Mazzini 34 (☎0789 754 906) have bikes (from €10/day), scooters (from €30/day) and cars (from €65/day) to rent.

By bus From mid-June to mid-Sept, Sardabus operates 7–9 local buses daily between Santa Teresa and the beaches of Marmorata and Capo Testa (tickets on board; €3.50 return). Other buses towards Castelsardo can drop you at or near the beaches at Rena Maiore and Vignola.

By taxi There's a taxi rank near the bus station on Via Eleonora d'Arborea; call ☎0789 754 376. Just Sardinia (☎0789 754 343, ⓦ justsardinia.it) also operates a taxi service. The run to Olbia airport costs around €90.

INFORMATION AND ACTIVITIES

Tourist office Piazza Vittorio Emanuele 24 (mid-July to mid-Sept daily 9am–1pm & 4.30–8pm, Aug also 9.30–11.30pm most eves; mid-Sept to mid-July Mon–Fri 9am–1pm; ☎0789 754 127, ⓦ santateresagalluraturismo .com). There's also a seasonal kiosk at Rena Bianca beach (mid-June to mid-Sept daily 10am–noon & 4–7pm).

Diving Local diving operators include Centro Sub, Via Tibula 11 (☎338 627 0054, ⓦ marinadilongone.it) and Diving Mediterraneo, Via del Porto 16 (☎0789 759 026, ⓦ divingmediterraneo.it). Dives cost €30–40/dive, €35–50 for night dives, plus €10–15 for equipment rental.

ACCOMMODATION

Bocche di Bonifacio Località Capo Testa ☎0789 754 202, ⓦ bocchebonifacio.it. This old-school *pensione* on Capo Testa doesn't exactly ooze charm, but you can stay comfortably in its large, plain rooms just a few metres above the sands, and there's a restaurant that serves the freshest seafood. Breakfast not included. Closed mid-Oct to Easter. **€62**

Comfort Scano Inn Via Lazio 4 ☎0789 754 447, ⓦ albergoscano.it. Small and functional family-run hotel off the Capo Testa road, offering standard rooms with a/c and a decent restaurant. Slightly smarter and pricier rooms in another nearby hotel owned by the same family are available in summer. **€80**

Corallaro Rena Bianca ☎0789 755 475, ⓦ hotelcorallaro .it. Santa Teresa's classiest hotel, just back from the town beach, enjoys superb views over to the Corsican coast from its terraces. The rooms are bright and spacious, some with balconies (opt for a room at the front for the views). It also has a good restaurant, with tables by the pool. Kids are well catered for, and the staff are professional and friendly. There's usually a minimum stay of three nights. Closed Oct–May. **€190**

★ Da Cecco Via Po 3 ☎0789 754 220, ⓦ hoteldacecco .com. Great-value small hotel situated in a pink and green palazzo above the port, with friendly owners, private parking and a roof terrace. Rooms are small and don't have a/c, but some have balconies with stunning views. Closed Nov–Easter. **€80**

Domus de Janas Via Carlo Felice 20 ☎338 499 0221, ⓦ bbdomusdejanas.it. You can't get nearer the action than this B&B right next to the main piazza, which you can observe from the roof terraces – look in the other direction

---

BOAT TOURS FROM SANTA TERESA

Between Easter and September, **boat tours** from Santa Teresa around the coast and to the islands can be booked at Consorzio delle Bocche, Piazza Vittorio Emanuele 16 (☎0789 755 112, ⓦ consorziobocche.com), the Marco Polo agency (☎0789 754 942) or directly from booths at the port. The most popular excursions take in the western isles of the **Maddalena archipelago** (9.15am–5.15pm), including stops at the beaches of Santa Maria and Spargi and a stroll around the town of La Maddalena, or else follow the coast down to the **Costa Smeralda** (9am–5.30pm), with stops at Baia Sardinia and Porto Cervo; both cost around €40–50 per person, including lunch on board.

and you'll see Corsica. Rainforest showers, delicious breakfasts and use of a kitchen are further attractions. Closed Nov–March. **€90**

★ **La Chicca di Francesca** Via Basilicata 4 ☎ 347 335 0779, ⓦ lachiccadifrancesca.com. Set in a shady garden a 5–10min walk from the centre, this B&B has three rooms with balconies, parquet floors, private bathrooms and a/c. Breakfasts are a joy and include home-made cakes. The owner is very sociable and also offers apartments. No credit cards. **€75**

Marinaro Via Angioy 48 ☎ 0789 754 112, ⓦ hotel marinaro.it. Occupying a quiet spot near the town centre, this solid old building houses a bright, clean-cut hotel, with a cheerfully striped interior and a pavement café. Rooms on two floors are a decent size, some have balconies and all have good a/c. **€85**

★ **Moderno** Via Umberto 39 ☎ 0789 754 233, ⓦ modernohotel.eu. This friendly, centrally located hotel has airy rooms – including family rooms – in pale blues and greens with Sardinian motifs, spacious bathrooms and a/c. Closed Nov–March. **€90**

CAMPSITE

La Liccia SP90, Km59 ☎ 0789 755 190, ⓦ campinglaliccia.com. The nearest campsite to Santa Teresa lies 6km south, signposted off the Castelsardo road (ARST buses stop outside) and a 10min walk from a good beach. Pitches are large, terraced and shady, and you can rent caravans and bungalows (from €42). Boat excursions and bike rental are available. Closed Oct to mid-May. Pitches **€24**

SELF-CATERING

The weekly tariff for a two-bed apartment in town ranges from €300–800 in July, more at one of the bathing localities. There's normally a minimum stay of one or two weeks. The main rental agencies are Gulp Immobiliare, Via Nazionale 58 (☎ 0789 755 689, ⓦ easysardinia.net), Sardinia Holiday, Via Capo Testa 30 (☎ 0789 754 411, ⓦ sardiniaholiday.net) and Randa Tour, Via Eleonora d'Arborea (☎ 0789 754 544, ⓦ randatour.it), for apartments in town and at Capo Testa, Porto Quadro, Marmorata and Rena Maiore.

EATING

Balajana Piazza Villa Marina ☎ 0789 754 332. This pizzeria with a front terrace doles out supersize thin and crispy pizzas (€9–14) on wooden boards. If one is too much, you can order one to share with two different toppings. Service is swift and friendly, and there's a range of beers on offer too. Daily May, June & mid-Sept to Oct noon–3pm & 5–11pm; July to mid-Sept noon–11pm; Nov–April 6–10pm.

Da Thomas Via Valle d'Aosta 22 ☎ 0789 755 133. This lively ristorante with a cool white interior and a covered terrace has an enticing menu with the emphasis on fresh fish. Dishes such as *pasta allo scoglio* (with seafood) are huge, but leave room for the excellent *seadas* (cheese-filled pastries with honey). Starters are €10–15, meat and seafood dishes €15–25. Book ahead in summer, as it gets

very busy. Daily noon–3pm & 7–11pm.

Gallura Grill Via Carlo Felice 51 ☎ 347 571 4281. Grilled meats are the speciality here, from Sardinian sausages and steaks to spit-roast pork, but seafood feasts such as *grigliata di mare* are available too. Most mains are around €15. There are a few tables outside, though without much to look at. Easter–Sept daily noon–3pm & 7–11pm; April & Oct closed Wed.

Marlin Via Garibaldi 4 ☎ 0789 754 557. Seafood is the main event here – the mixed grill is a massive feast – but they also serve delicious fresh pasta and meat dishes, as well as pizzas in the evening. First courses are €12–15, mains are €14–25. March–Sept daily noon–2.30pm & 7–10.30pm; Oct–Dec closed Wed.

DRINKING AND ENTERTAINMENT

Bar Caffè Conti Via Regina Margherita 2 ☎ 0789 755 133. This comfortable bar off Piazza Vittorio Emanuele makes a cool vantage point for the comings and goings. There's a Santana soundtrack, snacks to nibble and late-night cocktails. Daily 8am–midnight.

Éstasi Località Buoncammino ☎ 393 931 7567. Seek out this secluded club when you feel like a dance under the stars, reached from a signposted turn from the SS125 3km south of town, near the church of Buoncammino. The music

is mainly house and summer chart hits, with entry costing €20–30 including a drink. The adjacent *Free Jazz Café* is an open-air piano bar for more sedate entertainment. Easter to mid-Sept Fri, Sat & other selected dates 11.30pm–late.

Groove Café Via XX Settembre. A "risto-disco-pub" on the corner of the main piazza, with *pizzette* and other snacks, nightly DJs and occasional live music. Daily 8am–2am; closed Sun in winter.

DIRECTORY

Internet Log on for free at the Mediateca Comunale, next to the tourist office on Piazza Vittorio Emanuele (Mon–Fri 9.30am–1.30pm & 5–8pm or 3.30–6.30pm in winter). The whole square is a wi-fi zone.

Laundry There are coin-op machines at Jefferson's, Via del Porto 33 (daily 8.30am–10.30pm; €5–7 for a wash, €2–5 for drying).

Pharmacy Piazza Vittoria (June–Sept Mon–Sat 9am–1pm

SUMMER EVENTS IN SANTA TERESA

There are few evenings between July and September when there isn't some organized entertainment in Santa Teresa. The main festivals include the **Sagra del Pesce**, or fish festival, with samplings, usually on a Saturday in June or July; a **sailing regatta** between Corsica and Sardinia at the end of July; a procession of fishing boats between the port and Rena Bianca beach for the Assumption at **Ferragosto** (Aug 15) and **Musica sulle Bocche**, an international jazz festival with outdoor concerts over five days around the last weekend of August (🔊 musicasullebocche.it). **Windsurfing** championships are also held in the straits most years in early summer. For more sedate entertainment, head for the **open-air Cineaerena Odeon** on Via Capo Testa (nightly screenings mid-June to Aug usually at 9.45pm).

& 4–8pm, or Sun 9am–1pm & 5–8pm; winter Mon–Sat 9am–1pm & 4.30–7.30pm).

Post office Via Eleonora d'Arborea, by the bus station (Mon–Fri 8.20am–1.35pm, Sat 8.20am–12.35pm). Cash

can be changed here.

Travel agent Viaggi Sardorama, Via Tibula 11 (☎ 0789 754 464) can arrange plane and ferry tickets, as well as excursions in the area and beyond.

Inland Gallura

Although most people are content to admire from afar the dramatic mountainscape backing onto Gallura's coast, you can't fail to be intrigued by the spiky pinnacles lying just a short way inland, where the small towns and villages retain far more of Gallura's essential character than any of the coastal resorts. Where the country is not bare and arid, it's covered with a thick mantle of holm oak and **cork oak** forest, the latter providing the area's main industry. In September and October you are sure to notice lorry loads of the silver-and-red bark being transported to processing plants in Olbia and Arbatax, and you can see at all times the lower trunks stripped to their rust-red stems.

Come in winter and you'll find the peaks snow-clad, while spring is the best time to appreciate the *macchia*-covered lower slopes, woven with cistus, gorse, juniper, heather, myrtle and a hundred other wild and pungent species, some of whose flavours find their way into the famous bitter **honey** produced in these parts and for sale in the local shops: you'll probably already have sampled it poured over *seadas*.

Gallura is one of the few areas in Sardinia where you'll see isolated farmsteads, or *stazzi*, originally founded by settlers from Corsica fleeing the strife on that island in the eighteenth century – and the *galluresi* still have a reputation for the touchy sense of honour and ancient grievances for which Corsicans are famous.

Inland Gallura's main centre, **Tempio Pausania**, has most of the region's accommodation and restaurants, making it a convenient base for excursions. The obvious destination for local outings is the nearby massif of **Monte Limbara**, holding Gallura's highest peaks, with stirring views in all directions. Northwest of Tempio, **Aggius** provides an opportunity to dig into *gallurese* culture with its pair of fascinating museums, while to the east, Gallura's cork-processing centre of **Calangianus** is a good place to purchase cork products to take home, and lies near to the village of **Luras**, site of some intriguing prehistoric dolmens. South of Monte Limbara, the museum in the village of **Berchidda** reveals insights into the world of Vermentino and other wines, while one of Sardinia's many artificial lakes, **Lago Coghinas**, makes a great area to hike around.

GETTING AROUND   **INLAND GALLURA**

Though **public transport** will get you to the towns and larger villages easily enough, you'll need your **own vehicle** to get the most out of the region.

Tempio Pausania and around

The chief town of Gallura since the Romans established camps here to control the region's inland tracts, and now joint capital of the province of Olbia-Tempio, **TEMPIO PAUSANIA** has all the slow-moving solidity of a typical mountain settlement. As you might expect at a height of 566m, it makes a cool retreat in summer, and has long views stretching out on every side – most dramatically towards the region's highest mountain, Monte Limbara (see pp.264–265).

Tempio had a greater profile in the eighteenth and nineteenth centuries, when, as well as being the administrative centre of the Gallura region, it benefited from the presence of therapeutic mineral waters. Though the springs remain, the town has been left behind as commercial activity has shifted to the coast and to Olbia. This at least has saved Tempio from the unplanned construction that has blighted much of Olbia since the 1960s, and the present-day town has a homogeneous appearance, its granite-grey centre a pleasant place for a wander. At its centre, Piazza Gallura is a good place to start, dominated by the **Municipio** and close to a harmonious ensemble of churches.

The Cattedrale

Piazza San Pietro • Daily 7.30am–noon & 3.30–7.30pm

Behind Piazza Gallura, Via Roma leads to the **Cattedrale**, originally a fifteenth-century Romanesque construction, though its present appearance owes much to a drastic nineteenth-century restoration. Only the belltower is original, and even this was modified in 1822, while the interior is mostly Baroque and devoid of much interest, though the third and fourth chapels on the left have good wooden altars.

Oratorio del Rosario

Piazza San Pietro • Daily 7.30am–noon & 3.30–6.30pm

Opposite the cathedral, with an arched Aragonese entrance, the **Oratorio del Rosario** dates from the fourteenth century but has undergone much modification since then, its austere front mixing late-Romanesque and Baroque motifs. The bare interior has a wooden altarpiece decorated with pure gold. It's thought that the church stands on the site of the Roman temple that gave its name to the town.

Oratorio di Santa Croce

Piazza San Pietro • Daily 7am–noon & 3.30–6.30pm

The trio of granite churches is completed by the **Oratorio di Santa Croce**, located behind the cathedral and joined to it at its restoration in the nineteenth century. Like the other two churches, Santa Croce is a hotchpotch of different periods, preserving a wooden altar from the early eighteenth century, originally from a Franciscan monastery in Alghero, and wood bas-reliefs on the right from the seventeenth century.

Fonti Rinaggiu

Via San Lorenzo

An easy stroll out of town will bring you to the **Fonti Rinaggiu**, a wooded spot that would make a nice venue for a picnic. The waters are prized for their diuretic qualities, and the spring is often crowded with locals filling up flagons with the stuff. It's a couple of kilometres southwest of the centre – follow signs, *Alle Terme*, up Via San Lorenzo from Largo de Gásperi.

Nuraghe Maiori

Località Conca Marina • March–Oct 9.30am–7pm; Nov–Feb call ahead • €2.50, €3 guided visit • ☎ 347 299 5933

Tempio's most compelling sight, **Nuraghe Maiori**, lies 2km north of the centre on the Palau road (SP133), signposted off to the right amid a thick cork forest. Constructed entirely of huge granite slabs, the 3000-year-old *nuraghe* has round, tholos-style chambers to right and left as you enter, and a corridor that gives access to the

7

courtyard. A colony of Lesser Horseshoe **bats** has taken up residence inside one of the chambers, which you can glimpse above with the aid of a torch provided at the ticket office (don't train the light on them, though). Usually arriving in early April, the bats give birth here in June and July, and leave in October.

From the courtyard, steps wind up to the parapet, affording glorious views of Gallura's jagged peaks, also taking in Tempio and Aggius as well as kilometres of fields and vineyards. The quirky bar-restaurant near the entrance makes a great spot for lunch or refreshments.

ARRIVAL AND INFORMATION

TEMPIO PAUSANIA

By train A few minutes south of the centre, Tempio's train station is used for the Trenino Verde summer service linking the town with Sássari, Arzachena and Palau – though there are currently no departures from here to Arzachena or Palau (train passengers arriving from the towns make the return journey by coach). At the time of writing, trains to Sássari run on Sat between late June and mid-Sept, departing at 3.30pm (2hr 45min). See ☻treninoverde.com for the latest information.

By bus ARST and Sardabus (for Aggius and Santa Teresa Gallura) buses stop at the train station and in the centre. Destinations Aggius (Mon–Sat every 30min–1hr, Sun

4–8 daily; 5–15min); Arzachena (Mon–Sat 4 daily, Sun 1 daily; 1hr 10min); Calangianus (Mon–Sat every 30min–1hr, Sun 4 daily; 25min); Olbia (Mon–Sat 6 daily, Sun 3 daily; 1hr 20min); Palau (1–2 daily; 1hr 35min); Santa Teresa Gallura (2–3 daily; 1hr 10min); Sássari (3–5 daily; 1hr 20min).

Tourist office Piazza Gallura (Mon–Fri 10am–1pm & 4–7pm, Sat 10am–1pm; ☎079 631 273, ☻comune .tempiopausania.ot.it). There's a second office in the old market building (now used for exhibitions) on nearby Piazza Mercato, but it keeps more erratic hours (☎079 639 0080, ☻visit-tempio.it).

ACCOMMODATION

Il Gallo di Gallura Corso Matteotti 28 ☎079 632 025, ☻ilgallodigallura.com. This B&B in the heart of the old centre has fully renovated rooms embellished with elegant, modern furnishings and good bathrooms. Breakfast is in the bar below. No credit cards. **€70**

Pausania Inn SS133, Km1 ☎079 634 037, ☻hotelpausaniainn.com. In tranquil rural surroundings

a kilometre north of town (on the Palau road), this modern hotel has an outdoor pool and hammocks for a siesta, and there's a top-quality but moderately priced restaurant. **€85**

Petit Largo De Gásperi ☎079 631 134, ☻petit-hotel.it. The most central of the town's hotels, this is a functional business-folks' lodge with a restaurant. Rooms are blandly modern, though some enjoy fine valley views. **€89**

EATING

Il Giardino Via Cavour 1 ☎079 671 247. Homely pizzeria/ristorante off Piazza Gallura, dating from 1926, with a pleasant ambience and outdoor seating. Choices include *scottadito di agnello* (grilled lamb chops), and there are tourist menus for €15 and €25. Mid–June to mid–Sept daily noon–2.30pm & 7–11.30pm; mid-Sept to mid-June closed Wed.

★Il Purgatorio Via Garibaldi 9 ☎079 634 394. Opposite the eponymous church near Piazza Gallura, this sober, semiformal restaurant excels in such local specialities

as hare (*lepre*) and boar (*cinghiale*) and snails (*lumache*), at around €15 a dish. Sample the mushrooms in autumn and the authentic *zuppa gallurese* at any time. Daily except Tues 12.30–2.30pm & 8–10.30pm.

La Gallurese Via Novara 2 ☎079 639 3012. This trattoria off Corso Matteotti serves typical local items such as *zuppa gallurese* (€7.50) and *cinghiale a Cannonau* (boar in red wine and olives; €12.50). There's a set-price menu for €15. Tues–Sun noon–3.30pm & 7–10.30pm; open Mon lunch in summer.

DIRECTORY

Internet There is free access at Mediateca, in the library on Piazza del Cármine (Mon–Fri 8.30am–1.45pm & 4.45–7.15pm, or 3.45–7.15pm in winter).

Pharmacy Piazza Gallura (Mon–Wed, Fri & Sat 9am–1pm & 4–8pm).

Post office Largo De Gásperi (Mon–Fri 8.20am–7.05pm, Sat 8.20am–12.35pm).

Monte Limbara and around

Though not huge by Italian standards, the **Monte Limbara** massif – beloved of hikers and free climbers – towers above the rest of Gallura. To reach the thickly wooded peak, take the signposted left turn about 8km along the main road south to Óschiri; you

---

TEMPIO'S CARNIVAL

Tempio's week-long **Carnevale** celebrations have grown hugely in recent years to become one of Sardinia's principal festivities. The pagan element is strong, featuring parades of outlandish allegorical floats, and the high points include the symbolic marriage of two puppets, Re Giorgo (King George, a sort of Carnival King) and the peasant girl Mennena, on Carnival Sunday, followed by a distribution of corn fritters (*frittelle*); on Shrove Tuesday, King George is burned in a ceremonial bonfire.

---

could park your vehicle here and walk, or else drive up along a narrow road that twists up the pine-clad flanks of the mountain. The road climbs for a long way, affording fantastic views all around, then follows a ridge before reaching a forest of TV antennas and satellite dishes. Near here is a *punto panorámico* where a statue of the Madonna and Child stands festooned with an odd miscellany of personal mementos – charms, bracelets, lighters, hairgrips, even strips of gum – donated by the faithful. Nearby, the plain church of **Santa Madonna della Neve** stands at the site of a spring.

The road passes numerous examples of the manically contorted rocks that are such a feature of the area, and within a few hundred metres of the highest summit, **Punta Balistreri** (1359m), with bracing views as far as Tavolara island (see p.240) to the east. The tourist office in Tempio Pausania can supply a very rough map of the myriad paths and tracks and a list of local operators for **guided excursions**.

7

Lago di Coghinas

The Tempio–Óschiri road continues south, descending from **Passo della Limbara** (640m); it's a scenic ride through cork forests and *macchia*, the road usually empty but for flocks of sheep. At the bottom of the valley, **Lago di Coghinas** swings into view. Dammed in 1926 to provide a reservoir and hydroelectric power, the artificial lake has a lovely shore, alternately rocky and sandy, that makes a good venue for a picnic. The scanty ruins of a medieval castle and church, a Roman fort and a *nuraghe* all lie close to each other between the lake and the village of Óschiri, 3 or 4km east (and a stop for FS **trains** between Olbia and Ozieri-Chilivani).

Berchidda

East of the Lago di Coghinas, just off the main SS199, **Berchidda** is an important producer of Vermentino wine – one of Sardinia's most renowned whites – as well as of pecorino cheese and an intriguing goat's-milk liqueur. Surprisingly, given its remoteness, the village is the venue for a distinguished jazz festival (see box below).

Museo del Vino

Via Giangiorgio Casu 5 • April–Sept Tues–Sun 10am–2pm & 4–7pm; Oct–March Tues–Sat 9am–1pm & 3–6pm, Sun 10am–1pm & 5–7pm • €3 • ☎079 705 268, ⓦmuvisardegna.it

If you've spent any time in Gallura, chances are you'll have sampled a glass of the local Vermentino with your meal, a light, dry white wine usually drunk as an *aperitivo* or to accompany seafood. At Berchidda's **Museo del Vino**, the secrets of producing this and other Sardinian wines are explained in an airy modern building, which also displays ancient presses and agricultural equipment, and allows you to sample (and buy) the end product.

BERCHIDDA'S JAZZ FESTIVAL

Over ten days in mid-August, Berchidda hosts the **Time in Jazz festival** (☎079 703 007, ⓦtimeinjazz.it), attracting musicians from around the world. It's staged mainly in the central Piazza del Pópolo, but also in such venues as the wine museum and local fields. The respected, Berchidda-born trumpeter **Paolo Fresu** is the artistic director and a regular guest. Tickets for the concerts in Piazza del Pópolo cost €18–25, while events elsewhere are normally free.

Aggius

Six kilometres northwest of Tempio, **AGGIUS** is a popular highland retreat, enlivened by its colour-washed granite houses with wrought-iron balconies. The village occupies a superb panoramic position in the midst of massive boulders and corkwoods – cork and granite are the two mainstays of the local economy, helping to account for the well-to-do appearance of the solid-looking houses.

Museo Etnográfico

Via Monti di Lizu • Feb–April & mid–Oct to Dec Tues–Sun 10am–1pm & 3.30–5.30pm; May to mid–Oct daily 10am–1pm & 3–7pm • €4 • ☎ 349 453 3208, ⓦ museodiaggius.it

As well as cork and granite, Aggius is known for its woven carpets, produced using traditional methods. You can see examples among numerous other artefacts in the imaginatively presented **Museo Etnográfico** on a backstreet signposted off the main Via Roma. Within the restored old building, each of the rooms is dedicated to an aspect of the culture and traditions of the locality, embracing everything from cork trees and cork-fashioned objects to nuptial garments, olive-pressing and cheese-making, as well as the gorgeously coloured rugs and carpets. Fascinating old photos and jars of aromatic spices from the *macchia* add to the overall experience.

Museo del Banditismo

Via Pretura • April to mid-Oct daily 10am–1pm & 4–6pm; mid-Oct to late Dec Tues–Sun 10am–1pm • €4 • ☎ 349 453 3208

Aggius holds Sardinia's only museum dedicated to criminality, or more specifically the banditry that was endemic in this corner of the island in the eighteenth and nineteenth centuries. The **Museo del Banditismo** tells the fascinating story of the individuals driven (usually by desperation) to this outlaw life, of the arms they used and the forces ranged against them. Rows of mugshots of prisoners who were often tortured before being executed cover one wall, and there's an arsenal of weaponry as well as material on the feuds (*faide* or *nimistai*) that tore local communities apart.

La Valle della Luna

Leaving Aggius northward, a left turn towards Trinità d'Agultu and Ísola Rossa soon brings you to a wilderness of rocky debris, dubbed **La Valle della Luna**. In this "lunar valley", boulders are strewn across an arena-like hillside as if flung around by a petulant giant. Many have been carted away by illegal quarriers, though plenty remain, including some said to resemble human figures – one on the left of the road is said to recall Plato's head. There's also a *nuraghe* here, **Nuraghe Izzana**, reached along a rough track on the right after the road curves to the left. The road leading northwest of here as far as the coast at Isola Rossa makes a highly scenic drive or cycle, with numerous possibilities for walks and roadside picnics. Alternatively, take the **Strada Panorámica di Aggius** signposted to the left, an even more striking and slightly shorter route to the coast.

ACCOMMODATION AND EATING AGGIUS

Il Mosto Aggius Via del Mosto 13 ☎ 079 620 303. In the centre of Aggius (on the corner of the main Via Roma), this granite-walled trattoria is a cut above most others in the area, offering honest *gallurese* cuisine at moderate prices (around €7.50 for starters, €10–20 for mains). The menu is strong on grilled meats and pecorino cheese, and there's a great range of local and international wines too. July–Sept Mon–Sat noon–3pm & 7–11pm,

---

THE BACHELORS' FEAST

On the first Sunday of October, the **Festa di li 'Agghiani** ("Bachelors' Feast") takes over the village of Aggius. Traditionally an opportunity for the young folk to meet and make merry, it's now mainly an excuse for the locals to consume a lot of *suppa cuata*, the favourite *gallurese* soup recipe.

A SARDINIAN VENDETTA

In the annals of Aggius's past, the area was the hiding place of a sinister character known as **Il Muto di Gallura** – the mute of Gallura, the last scion of a family locked in a long and deadly vendetta in the nineteenth century that claimed 72 lives and left only six survivors. Il Muto – who was born deaf and dumb – carried on the feud from his lonely eyrie, from which he descended only to dispatch his enemies. He ended his terror with the murder of the 12-year-old son of his principal antagonist, the head of the opposing family. The boy was of an unsurpassed beauty, so the story goes, and was cut down while walking through the cork forests lost in song.

Sun noon–3pm; Oct–June Mon& Wed–Sun noon–3pm & 7–11pm, Tues noon–3pm.
★ **Il Muto di Gallura** Località Fraiga ☎ 079 620 559, ⓦ mutodigallura.com. There's an outstanding *agriturismo* just outside Aggius, signposted up a dirt track to the right on the Tempio road. The old *stazzo* occupies a splendid position with mountain views from the bedroom windows; the farm includes goats, pigs and horses, and offers horseriding expeditions and tuition at all levels. Even if you don't stay, the restaurant is well worth a detour – good country cooking in an endless stream of courses; set-price meals cost €20–40 including wine (booking essential). Half board comes to €84/person, and there are discounts for stays of two days or more. Summer daily 1–2.30pm & 8–10.30pm, July & Aug closed lunchtime; winter Sat & Sun same times. **€96**

Calangianus

Seven kilometres east of Tempio, the road skirts Monte Limbara to **CALANGIANUS**, a small town surrounded by a jagged ring of peaks and, closer to hand, cork factories. This is the centre of Sardinia's biggest cork-producing area, and it's no surprise to see the local shops overflowing with the stuff, fashioned into an endless variety of unusual forms. In September, the village stages an **exhibition of cork** and its various uses.

Luras

Notable for its *logudorese* dialect – as opposed to the *gallurese* spoken elsewhere – the village of **LURAS**, 3km north of Calangianus, has a cluster of pre-nuraghic dolmens, or barrows, which date back to the third to fourth millennium BC. To reach the nearest and most impressive of these, **Dolmen Ladas**, follow the road north through the village towards Luogosanto, turn right into the last asphalted street, Via Ariosto, and follow the minor road for about 350m, following the brown signs – a couple of kilometres in all. Standing on a low hill, the dolmen measures 6m in length, the largest in Gallura. Carry on a little further along the road to see the slightly smaller **Dolmen Ciuledda**.

Sant'Antonio di Gallura and around

The tiny village of **SANT'ANTONIO DI GALLURA** lies 18km northeast of Calangianus on the SP427 and the same distance south of Arzachena), close to the **Lago di Liscia**, the artificial lake which supplies irrigation and drinking water to much of the coastal region. The neighbourhood also holds an ancient forest of wild olive trees, some reaching 14m high and 11m broad, among which is thought to be the oldest wild olive tree in Sardinia, estimated to be 2000 years old. You'll need local advice to find it, however: it's out of sight in a secluded little valley near the banks of the lake. The area is renowned for its **Nebbiolo** wines.

Nuoro and Ogliastra

ORGÒSOLO MURAL

Nuoro and Ogliastra

For the most part, the provinces of Nuoro and Ogliastra have little in common with Sardinia's modern sun-and-sand image. While many of the resorts and beaches of the east coast are as inviting as any on the island, inhospitable cliffs and mountains predominate, dotted with introverted villages and endless flocks of sheep. For many people, however, these once inaccessible tracts are the most interesting parts of the island, which have never known the heel of foreign conquerors, and whose scattered and isolated communities have retained a fierce sense of independence and loyalty to centuries-old practices.

Travelling around these provinces, don't be surprised to find a few elderly folk still unselfconsciously wearing their local costumes. However, the most practical place to view the region's huge range of costumes is the ethnographic museum in the city of **Nuoro**. Although unprepossessing, this high inland town has plenty more to discover, thanks mostly to the remarkable roster of artists and writers who lived and worked around here before achieving national fame.

8

Nuoro is a good starting point for trips into the surrounding mountains. North of town, the first obvious stop would be **Su Tempiesu**, a sacred well of the nuraghic era, splendidly sited on the side of a valley east of the village of **Orune**. West of **Bitti**, where there's a small ethnographic museum, the castle of **Burgos** occupies a lofty perch with stunning views over the Tirso valley.

South of Nuoro stretches Sardinia's **Barbagia** region, the mountainous heart of the island that encompasses its highest peaks. The name is a dialect version of Barbaria, the term given to this central core by the Romans who, like Sardinia's other conquerors, never managed to subdue it completely, foiled by the guerrilla warfare for which the mountains proved ideal. Amid forested slopes, Barbagia's population is concentrated in small, self-contained villages, interconnected by twisting mountain roads and little changed since the novelist Salvatore Satta described them as "minuscule settlements as remote from one another as are the stars". Although material conditions have improved in recent years, Barbagia is a world apart from the whitewashed luxury of the Costa Smeralda just a couple of hours' drive away.

The region is divided into different districts, of which the **Barbagia Ollolai** is the nearest to Nuoro. En route to this area, **Oliena** is the best departure point for expeditions to **Supramonte**, the dramatic massif visible from Nuoro, and, with its wide range of accommodation, is a useful base for the whole region. South of here, the village of **Orgósolo** once had one of the island's worst reputations for banditry and violence, though it is now best known for its striking murals. To the west,

Highlights

❶ Museo Etnográfico Sardo, Nuoro The island's most comprehensive collection of costumes, masks and handicrafts provides a fascinating overview of the rural culture of the interior. **See pp.276–277**

❷ Easter at Oliena Grief, joy, drama and exuberant local costumes all feature in the Easter rituals of this mountain village – and the accompanying gunfire makes earplugs essential. **See p.281**

❸ The murals of Orgósolo Sardinia has several places daubed with vibrant murals, but those at Orgósolo win hands down for their sheer inventiveness and humorous spirit. **See p.284**

❹ Láconi One of the most engaging centres of the interior, this elegant, leafy village makes a great stop for a night or two, and includes an outstanding collection of menhirs. **See pp.293–294**

❺ Hiking in the Gorropu gorge A thrilling scramble through this precipitous gorge south of Dorgali is the highlight of one of Sardinia's most satisfying walks. **See p.299**

❻ The beaches around Cala Gonone Accessible by boat, these bare patches of sand, backed by soaring cliffs, rank among the island's most memorable beaches. **See p.300**

HIGHLIGHTS ARE MARKED ON THE MAP ON P.272

NUORO & OGLIASTRA

▲ Ala dei Sardi

PROVINCIA DI OLBIA-TEMPIO

● Posada
● La Caletta
● Santa Lucia
● Siniscola

Capo Comino

● Ozieri
● Pattada
● Buddusò

PROVINCIA DI SÁSSARI

Lago di Pattada

GOCEANO

● Bultei

● Bono
● Bottida
Burgos
⚒

SS129

Monte Albo

BARONIA

● Cala Liberotto

SS129

Cedrino

● Bitti

● Orune
Su Tempiesu
⚌

Serra Orrios
⚌

● Orosei

● Lollove

① *Monte Ortobene (955m)*

● Nuoro

Grotta di Ispinigoli ◠

Spiaggia Osalla
Spiaggia Cartoe

② Su Gologone

Lago del Cedrino

● Dorgali ⑥ ● Cala Gonone

Grotta del Bue Marino ◠

● Oliena

Valle Lanaittu

Punta Corrasi (1463m) ▲

Monte Tiscali (518m) ⚌
Monte Tiscali

● Orani

● Mamoiada ▲

SUPRAMONTE

Cala Luna

Golfo di Orosei

③ Orgósolo

● Ottana

MONTES

Monte San Giovanni (1316m) ▲

⑤ *Gola di Gorropu*

Cala Sisine

Oristano

BARBAGIA OLLOLAI

● Gavoi

Funtana Bona (1052m) ▲

Genna Silana

Cala Goloritzé
Capo di Monte Santo

PROVINCIA DI NUORO

● Fonni

FLUMINEDDU

● Urzulei

SS125

ALTIPIANO SU GOLGO

● Sórgono

● Tonara

Monte Spada (1595m) ▲

● Baunei

● Désulo

Monte Bruncu Spina (1829m) ▲

SS389

● Santa Maria Navarrese

● Belvì

Punta La Mármora (1834m) ▲

● Aritzo

BARBAGIA BELVÌ

GENNARGENTU

● Arbatax
● Tortolì
● Porto Frailis

Lido Orri

● Láconi ④

SARCIDANO

● Sádali

PROVINCIA DI OGLIASTRA

● Lanusei

SS197

SS128

● Isili

Lago del Flumendosa

Cagliari

SS125

● Orroli

● Tertenia

PROVINCIA DI CÁGLIARI

● Mandas

Lago Mulargia

● Perdasdefogu

Cagliari

▲ Muravera

N

0 _____ 10
kilometres

HIGHLIGHTS

① Museo Etnográfico Sardo, Nuoro

② Easter at Oliena

③ The murals of Orgósolo

④ Láconi

⑤ Hiking in the Gorropu gorge

⑥ The beaches around Cala Gonone

Mamoiada presents one of Sardinia's most spectacular Carnival displays, while **Orani** has an absorbing museum featuring the graceful sculptures of Costantino Nivola, an eminent local artist.

Farther south, the small town of **Fonni** is one of the main gateways to the once impenetrable **Gennargentu** massif, the island's highest range, from which all of Sardinia's major rivers flow – most of them dammed to create mountain lakes. The loftiest peak, **Punta La Mármora** (1834m), can be reached on foot without too much difficulty, one of scores of treks that can be made in the area. The forested slopes of the **Barbagia Belvì**, which borders this range, shelter more close-knit communities, of which **Belvì** and **Aritzo** are the most attractive. South of here in the **Sarcidano** region, the gradients are milder, though the village of **Láconi**, surrounded by woods, still retains a fresh, mountainous feel.

The **eastern coast** preserves the rugged character of the interior, though the sheer walls rearing above the sea also leave space for some fantastic beaches. These are more popular in the northern parts, where the town of **Posada** provides a lofty vantage point from its ruined castle. South of the inland centre of **Orosei**, the swimming spots are much more inaccessible apart from those at the holiday enclave of **Cala Gonone** and around **Arbatax**, one of the few ports along this littoral, connected to the Italian mainland by ferry.

GETTING AROUND — NUORO AND OGLIASTRA

The provinces are best explored using your **own vehicle**, but it's not impossible to get around by public transport.

By train ARST-run trains (T 800 865 042, W arst.sardegna.it) connect Nuoro with Macomer, a stop on the main rail network, and in summer ARST also operates two infrequent but very scenic Trenino Verde services from Mandas (which has good transport connections with Cágliari), one line passing through Ísili, Láconi, Belvì/Aritzo and Sórgono, the other to Lanusei and Arbatax – however, it's a slow chug, best treated as a travelling experience rather than as a means of crossing the island. Check timetables at W treninoverde.com.

By bus ARST buses from Nuoro pass through most of the villages in the area at least once a day (but usually no services on Sun). For more info, call T 800 865 042, or consult W arst.sardegna.it.

8

Nuoro

"There is nothing to see in Nuoro: which to tell the truth, is always a relief. Sights are an irritating bore", wrote D.H. Lawrence, after stopping here during his Sardinian excursion of 1921. The town appeared to him "as if at the end of the world, mountains rising sombre behind". Since Lawrence's visit, an overlay of ugly apartment blocks, administrative buildings and banks has been added, but **NUORO** still preserves its end-of-the-world feel, with faded Fascist graffiti from the 1930s visible on its walls and an old-fashioned air hanging over the place. However, while it shares some of the insular and parochial qualities of Sardinia's inland villages, Nuoro occupies a unique place in the island's **cultural life**, both for its extraordinary literary fame and the artists who lived and worked here. The town's specific sights afford fascinating glimpses into the local arts scene as well as the region's rural culture, while there is no denying Nuoro's superb position, beneath the soaring peak of Monte Ortobene and opposite

ARTIGIANATO IN NUORO

Sardinia's interior is known for its **handicrafts** and other rustic artefacts – knives, carpets, musical instruments, masks and the like. Nuoro has numerous outlets where these are sold. Try Il Carro, Via Tola 21 (near the Duomo), which has shelves full of *artigianato* (folk arts and crafts). The quality is generally good, though if you're travelling through Barbagia, you can often find the same items for lower prices in the villages where they're made.

the sheer heights of Supramonte – a rather more inspiring panorama than Lawrence's brusque assessment might suggest.

Nuoro's **old quarter** is the most compelling part of town, spread around the pedestrianized axis of **Corso Garibaldi**, at its best during the buzzing *passeggiata*. Within walking distance of here, each of Nuoro's main attractions focuses on aspects of Sardinia's core identity, contrasting and complementing each other: the **Museo Etnográfico Sardo**, an engrossing overview of the island's rural culture including a colourful exhibition of local costumes; the **Museo d'Arte Provincia di Nuoro** and **Museo Tribu**, which showcase modern art, chiefly by local artists; and the **Museo Archeologico**, delving into the area's and the island's history.

Other attractions include the **Casa di Grazia Deledda**, the restored birthplace of one of the city's literary stars, offering an insight into the city's domestic life a hundred years ago, and, outside town, **Monte Ortobene** (955m), whose summit marks the end point of the procession in the annual **Sagra del Redentore** festival (see box, p.279).

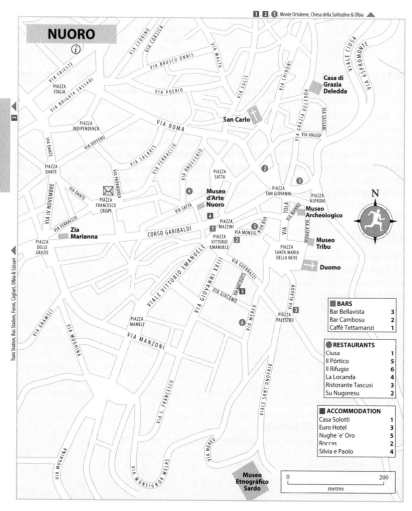

MAN (Museo d'Arte Provincia di Nuoro)

Via Satta 27 • Tues–Sun: June to mid-Oct 10am–8pm; mid-Oct to May 10am–1pm & 3–7pm • €3, €4 with Museo Tribu • ☎ 0784 252 110, ⓦ museoman.it

In a renovated nineteenth-century palazzo just off Corso Garibaldi, the **Museo d'Arte Provincia di Nuoro** is filled with the works of some of Sardinia's best-known modern artists. The ground and top floors are devoted to temporary exhibitions, while the middle two floors have a permanent display of artwork from the nineteenth, twentieth and twenty-first centuries, including moody abstracts by Mauro Manca (1913–69) and sculptures by two outstanding locals, Costantino Nivola (1911–88) and Francesco Ciusa (1883–1949). The gallery also hosts occasional poetry readings and classical and jazz concerts.

Piazza Satta

Works by Costantino Nivola – one of the local sculptors represented in the Museo d'Arte Provincia di Nuoro – can be seen in the usually deserted **Piazza Satta**, at the top of Via Satta. Here, the poet Sebastiano Satta, who was born nearby (see box, p.276), has been honoured with a cluster of menhir-like granite blocks in which small bronze figures evoking nuraghic *bronzetti* have been placed – the work of Nivola in the 1960s. The bronze statuettes depict the poet at different stages of his life.

San Carlo

Piazza San Carlo • Daily 8am–1pm & 4–7pm

Off Via Chironi, a plaque on a renovated townhouse shows it to be the birthplace of **Francesco Ciusa**. The sculptor's tomb lies opposite in the pink, rustic-looking church of **San Carlo**, which also contains a copy of Ciusa's best-known sculpture, *Madre dell'Ucciso* ("Mother of the killed man") – the original can be seen in Cágliari's Galleria Comunale d'Arte (see p.63). When the church is closed, you can obtain a key from Via Deledda 53, opposite the Casa di Grazia Deledda (see below).

Casa di Grazia Deledda

Via Deledda 42 • Tues–Sun: mid-March to Sept 9am–1pm & 3–6pm; Oct to mid-March 10am–1pm & 3–5pm • Free • ☎ 0784 258 088, ⓦ isresardegna.it

Corso Garibaldi ends at Piazza San Giovanni, from where a left turn up Via Deledda brings you to the **Casa di Grazia Deledda**, once the home of the Nobel Prize-winning author (see box, p.276), now restored and partly furnished to present an authentic example of a typical Nuorese house at the turn of the twentieth century. Much of the restoration has followed Deledda's own description of the house in her posthumous autobiographical novel *Cosima*, notably the **kitchen** with its hanging cheeses and array of brass pans. Elsewhere you'll see manuscripts, first editions, photos, letters and clippings. Upstairs, you'll find the author's **bedroom** and a film of her life. There's also a shady garden with a selection of her works to browse through (some in English).

The Duomo

Piazza Santa Maria della Neve • Daily 8am–1pm & 4–7pm

Framed by two belltowers, the orangey Neoclassical exterior of Nuoro's nineteenth-century **Duomo** often crops up on local postcards, but it lacks much presence from close up. The cool, spacious interior holds various items of religious art, including panels showing the Stations of the Cross by local twentieth-century artists Carmelo Floris and Giovanni Ciusa Romagna.

LITERARY NUORO

In Sardinia, Nuoro can boast what is almost a monopoly where **literature** is concerned, a standing discreetly advertised by the scraps of poetry and prose inscribed on the walls of the old town. The best-known Sard poet, **Sebastiano Satta** (1867–1914), was Nuorese, and his name has been given to innumerable streets and piazzas throughout the island – though he's hardly known outside Italy. In his home town, the street where he lived is named after him, as is the square at one end of it, Piazza Satta (see p.275).

In 1926, the author **Grazia Deledda** (1871–1936) became one of the six Italians to have won the Nobel Prize for Literature. It was a tribute to a steady writing career and a corpus of work based on the day-to-day trials and passions of simple folk in Nuoro and the villages around. Praised by D.H. Lawrence, she has been compared with Thomas Hardy in her style and subject matter. The house where Deledda grew up, described in her autobiographical work *Cosima*, can be seen on Via Deledda and is now a museum (see p.275); her tomb is at the bottom of Monte Ortobene, in the church of Santa Maria della Solitúdine, which also recurs in her writing. For Grazia Deledda's works in English, see Contexts (see p.319).

For the town's greatest modern writer, **Salvatore Satta** (1902–75), "Nuoro was nothing but a perch for the crows", as he wrote in his semiautobiographical masterpiece, *The Day of Judgement*. No relation to his poetic namesake Sebastiano, Satta earned his living as a jurist, which placed him at the heart of the tangled intrigues of this provincial town. His posthumously published book chronicles life in Nuoro at the turn of the twentieth century, yet much of it still rings true today, written in a dry but readable style that treads a fine line between soap opera and existential angst. A plaque at Via Angioy 1, just up from Piazza Mazzini, indicates the house where Satta wrote parts of his novel (see p.321).

8

Museo Tribu (Museo Ciusa)

Piazza Santa Maria della Neve • Tues–Sun 10am–1pm & 4.30–8.30pm • €2; €4 with MAN • ☎ 0784 253 052, Ⓦ tribunuoro.it

Next to the Duomo, the **Museo Tribu** is mainly devoted to the work of Nuoro's most celebrated artist, **Francesco Ciusa**, whose early twentieth-century sculptures invest lowly peasant figures with a heroic stature. Some of his most poignant works can be seen here, such as the powerful *L'Anfora Sarda*, showing a mother drinking from a jug while her baby breastfeeds, and *La Filatrice*, depicting a woman threading a needle. The rest of the gallery holds temporary exhibitions of pieces by other local figures in the fields of graphic art, ceramics, embroidery and jewellery.

Museo Archeologico

Piazza Asproni • Tues & Thurs 9am–1pm & 3–5pm; Wed, Fri & Sat 9am–1pm • €2 • ☎ 0784 31 688, Ⓦ museoarcheologiconuoro.beniculturali.it

In Nuoro's **Museo Archeologico**, which can be accessed from Via Mannu or Via Asproni, the simple chronological arrangement takes in everything from rocks, bones and skulls to carved vases, cooking pots and bronze spearheads. The examples of Neolithic jewellery are worth lingering over, including necklaces made from boars' teeth and amber. However, the items of nuraghic art are the most impressive: statuettes and bronze figurines of cloaked chiefs and archers, and mouflons and bulls with majestic curved horns, all probably offered as votive gifts by pilgrims to a nuraghic sanctuary, dating from the eleventh to ninth centuries BC. The well-presented museum also has stone inscriptions and amphorae from the Roman era.

Museo Etnográfico Sardo

Via Mereu 56 • Tues–Sun: mid-March to Sept 9am–1pm & 3–6pm; Oct to mid-March 10am–1pm & 3 5pm • €3 • ☎ 0784 257 035, Ⓦ isresardegna.it

At the southern edge of town, the **Museo Etnográfico Sardo** – also known as the Museo del Costume – has Sardinia's most comprehensive range of local costumes, jewellery, masks, carpets and other handicrafts, arranged in a modern purpose-built complex whose sequence of rooms, steps and courtyards is intended to evoke a Sardinian village. The most striking items on show are the **costumes**, showing an incredible diversity of pattern, design and colour, according to both their place of origin and the circumstances in which they were worn: scarves, skirts and bodices for unmarried women or widows; blouses and shawls for mourning or feasting; shirts, tunics and pantaloons for the menfolk.

Other rooms focus on Sardinia's **musical instruments**, including various drums (*tamburi*), flutes made from canes from Barbagia and La Marmilla and rudimentary clarinets (*benas*) made from oat stems. Some of these were tied together to make *launeddas*, or shepherd's pipes, said to be the island's oldest and most original instrument, made of three tubes of cane of differing lengths and diameters, and individually spaced finger-holes. Another display shows sheep- and goat-bells, the various sizes used to identify different flocks – one of the characteristic accoutrements in Barbagia's masked processions.

Elsewhere you'll see some of the various *dolci* and **breads** you may have encountered in restaurants and pastry shops throughout Sardinia (but particularly common in the Nuoro region), elaborately fashioned as birds, hearts and bows, along with the island's famous, crispy *pane carasau*. The culture of **guns** and **swords** is contrasted with wonderful examples of **lacework**, **basketwork** and **carpets**, while from every wall you'll be surveyed by dozens of solemn photos of Sardinians in every guise from days gone by.

Santa Maria della Solitúdine

Via della Solitúdine • Daily 8am–noon & 4–7pm

At the base of Monte Ortobene at the northeastern end of town, the church of **Santa Maria della Solitúdine** (known locally as the chiesa di Grazia Deledda) merits a pause. The church, an austere granite structure at the top of a flight of shallow steps, was designed in the 1950s by local artist Giovanni Ciusa Romagna on the site of an earlier church that was often mentioned in the books of Grazia Deledda (see box opposite). It contains the author's simple granite tomb.

8

Monte Ortobene

Bus #8 (not Sun) runs from Nuoro's Via Manzoni and the Duomo up to the summit of Monte Ortobene hourly between mid-June and mid-Sept (last bus down at around 8.30pm), twice daily in winter (last bus down at around 3.30pm)

On Nuoro's eastern flank, 8km outside town, the summit of **Monte Ortobene** (955m) affords awe-inspiring views over the deep valley separating Nuoro from Monte Corrasi (1463m) and the Supramonte massif. The heavily wooded slopes are a favourite destination for the townsfolk at weekends, and the **Farcana** locality (signposted off the only road leading up the mountain) has a sports complex open in July and August that includes an Olympic-size open-air pool, tennis courts and stables for riding. However, there are still plenty of areas that feel remote enough to get lost in, and the woods are perfect for picnics and walks, with paths trailing off.

Near the top of the mountain (955m), a huge bronze **statue** of the Redeemer (*Redentore*) stands poised in an attitude of swirling motion over the immense void. The figure attracts pilgrims at all times – as shown by the trinkets and other devotional gifts left here, and by Christ's polished right toe (the only part of the statue within reach) – and is the destination for the procession that weaves up from the town during Nuoro's annual Sagra del Redentore (see box, p.279). Others come for the stupendous panorama, with its dizzying views down to the valley floor.

ARRIVAL AND DEPARTURE   **NUORO**

By train ARST (☎ 800 865 042, ⓦ arst.sardegna.it) runs services from Nuoro to Macomer (Mon–Sat 6–7 daily; 1hr 10min), a stop on the main north to south line (for information on FS services, call ☎ 892 021 or visit ⓦ trenitalia.it). From Nuoro's train station it's a 15min walk to the centre of town along Via Lamármora – not much less on any of the city buses that stop on the opposite side of the road (tickets €1 from the station bar, on the right as you exit the station; valid for 1hr 30min).

By bus The bus station is on Viale Sardegna (a 10min walk south of the train station); for the centre, take bus #1 or #3 from the stop to the right as you exit (tickets from the newspaper kiosk across the road). Most bus routes within Nuoro province are operated by ARST (☎ 800 865 042, ⓦ arst.sardegna.it). The other main companies are Turmo (☎ 0789 21 487, ⓦ gruppoturmotravel.com) connecting Nuoro with Cágliari, Olbia (airport and port), Arzachena, Palau and Santa Teresa Gallura; Deplano (☎ 0784 295 030, ⓦ deplanobus.it) for Olbia airport, and Redentours (☎ 0784 30 325, ⓦ redentours.com) for Alghero's Fertilia airport.

Destinations Aritzo (1–2 daily; 1hr 50min); Baunei (Mon–Sat 1–2 daily; 2hr 5min); Belvì (1–2 daily; 1hr 50min); Bitti (Mon–Sat 4 daily, Sun 1 daily; 1hr 5min); Cágliari (4 daily; 2hr 40min–4hr 50min); Cala Gonone (Mon–Sat 6–7 daily,

Sun 3–4 daily; 1hr 10min); Dorgali (Mon–Sat 7–9 daily, Sun 3–5 daily; 45min); Fertilia airport, Alghero (2 daily; 2hr 20min); Fonni (Mon–Sat every 30min–1hr, Sun 3 daily; 40min–1hr 40min); Láconi (1 daily; 2hr 35min); Macomer (4–6 daily; 1hr–1hr 40min); Mamoiada (Mon–Sat 10 daily, Sun 4 daily; 20min); Monte Ortobene (local buses; Mon–Sat summer hourly, winter 2 daily; 20min); Olbia (2–5 daily; 2hr–2hr 40min); Olbia airport (Mon–Sat 4–11 daily, Sun 3–11 daily; 1hr 45min–2hr 40min); Oliena (Mon–Sat every 30min–1hr, Sun 5–6 daily; 20min); Orani (Mon–Sat 7–9 daily, Sun 1 daily; 30min); Orgósolo (Mon–Sat 9–10 daily, Sun 3 daily; 35min); Oristano (1 daily; 1hr 35min); Orosei (Mon–Sat 4–6 daily, Sun 2 daily; 55min); Orune (Mon–Sat 5 daily, Sun 1 daily; 40min); Posada (2–3 daily; 1hr 20min–2hr 25min); Santa Maria Navarrese (Mon–Sat 1–2 daily, Sun 1 daily; 2hr 25min); Sássari (4–5 daily; 1hr 45min–2hr 20min); Sórgono (Mon–Sat 3 daily; 1hr 40min–2hr); Tonara (1 daily; 1hr 30min).

GETTING AROUND

By car Drivers should avoid the old centre as much as possible; park your vehicle in between the blue lines, for which tickets are available from meters. For car rental, try Avis, Piazza Véneto 19 (☎ 0784 399 104, ⓦ avisautonoleggio.it) or Maggiore, Via Convento 32 (☎ 0784 30 461, ⓦ maggiore.it).

By bus ATP (☎ 0784 35 195, ⓦ atpnuoro.it) operates

Nuoro's local network. Apart from the brief ride between the stations and the centre, local buses are mainly useful for reaching Monte Ortobene (see p.277); buy tickets (€1 valid for any journeys within 1hr 30min, or €2.50 for the day) from newsagents or *tabacchini* before boarding.

By taxi There are ranks on Viale Sardegna and by the train station. Call ☎ 0784 31 411 or ☎ 335 399 174.

INFORMATION

Tourist office Piazza Italia 7 (Mon & Wed–Fri 8.30am–2pm, Tues 8.30am–2pm & 3.30–7pm; ☎ 0784 238 878), for

information on the town and province.

ACCOMMODATION

★**Casa Solotti** Monte Ortobene ☎ 0784 33 954 or ☎ 328 602 8975, ⓦ casasolotti.it. Nuoro's neighbouring mountain has an excellent, friendly B&B, with a spacious garden, assorted pets and a helpful owner who can arrange (and sometimes leads) tours to local sights, including Tíscali. There are fantastic views from most of its quiet, en-suite rooms, three of which have access to a broad roof terrace – one has cooking facilities. Breakfast may include home-made yoghurt and jams, and suppers can be arranged. Located 5km from the Grazia Deledda church, just after the Farcana turn-off, it has a bus stop right outside, and the owner will also collect guests. No credit cards. **€60**

Euro Hotel Via Trieste 62 ☎ 0784 34 071, ⓦ eurohotelnuoro.it. Combining 1930s-style furnishings with a corporate feel, the *Euro* doesn't invite a lengthy stay, though it has a quirky charm that might appeal to retro fans. It's close to the train station and a 15min walk from the old centre. Rooms have fridges and kettles, and there's parking. **€90**

Nughe 'e' Oro Via Matteotti 14 ☎ 0784 182 3255 or

☎ 340 805 2769, ⓦ nugheoro.it. On the sixth floor of a modern block near the Duomo, this B&B has bright, airy, wi-fi-enabled rooms with or without private facilities. Arty photos by the friendly host adorn the walls, while there are views over the roofs from the small terrace. Guided visits are offered to local attractions. No credit cards. **€65**

Roccas Parco Sedda Ortai, Monte Ortobene ☎ 349 578 1623, ⓦ roccas.eu. Set amid woods a short drive from Nuoro (the bus stop is 2km away), this place offers no-frills camping and, in summer, pinnettus – basic shepherd's huts (without bedding). You won't have hot water for your shower, but the compensation is fantastic views and tranquillity. There's a good restaurant too (open to all) which has meals for €40, wine included. Closed mid-Oct to mid-March. Pitches **€20**; huts **€30**

Silvia e Paolo Corso Garibaldi 58 ☎ 0784 31 280 or ☎ 328 921 7199, ⓦ silviaepaolo.it. In the heart of the old centre, this B&B with charming hosts has three modern, spotless rooms with shared or en-suite bathrooms, all overlooking the Corso. There's a spacious roof terrace too. **€55**

EATING AND DRINKING

Nuoro is surprisingly well off for **restaurants**, usually offering authentic regional fare at very reasonable prices. On some menus, or in bars, you might find traditional **pastries**, such as *s'arantzada*, a sticky local sweet made with honey and fresh oranges. This and other local specialities are also available from places on the Corso, for example Zia Marianna at no. 174. For fruit, veg and other takeaway items, there's a Saturday morning **market** on Piazza Italia, and a **supermarket** on Via Lamármora. In addition to the listings below, consider *Roccas* (see p.278), which has outdoor dining on Monte Ortobene.

RESTAURANTS

Ciusa Viale Ciusa 55 ☎ 0784 257 052. At the western end of town, this traditional restaurant with elegant, dark brown walls pulls in a well-heeled crowd for its tasty, seasonal dishes such as risotto with wine and melted sheep's cheese, meat grills and even prawn curry. Most main courses come to €16–20, and pizzas are available. Mon–Sat 1–2.30pm & 8–11pm.

★**Il Pórtico** Via Monsignor Bua 13 ☎ 0784 217 641. You'll find an innovative approach to the traditional Sard dishes on offer in this smart place with modern art on the walls – such as *lados con tonno fresco* (fresh pasta with tuna), *laganelle con cozze e zucchine* (fresh pasta with mussels and courgettes) and *spigola con crosta di patate* (sea bass in a potato crust). Leave space for the lip-smacking desserts, and there's a good wine list too. Starters are €10–12, mains around €15. Daily except Wed 12.30–2.30pm & 8–10.45pm.

★**Il Rifugio** Via Mereu 28 ☎ 0784 232 355. There's usually a full house for this consistently good ristorante/pizzeria specializing in such regional specialities as *filindeu nel brodo di pecora* (stringy pasta in a mutton broth). Most main courses cost €13–18, and service is brisk but friendly. Daily except Wed 12.45–3pm & 7.45–11.30pm.

★**La Locanda** Via Brofferio 31 ☎ 0784 31 032. There are no airs or graces in this traditional *osteria* in a large, plain room, which offers fresh pasta and authentic *nuorese* dishes at rock-bottom prices. You won't spend more than €20 including drinks, and the €9.20 fixed-price lunch menu scores highly among local workers. Mon–Sat 12.30–2.45pm & 8.30–10.30pm; closed two weeks in Aug.

Ristorante Tascusi Via Aspromonte 13 ☎ 0784 37 287. Local dishes are served in simple white rooms decorated with Sard art. The meaty menu might include *culurgiones al sugo di cinghiale* (ravioli with boar's meat sauce) and *pane frattau* (bread soaked in tomato sauce and pecorino). Pizzas are also served. All dishes are €8–12, and set-price menus are sometimes available. Aug daily 12.30–3.30pm & 7.30–11pm; Sept–July closed Sun.

Su Nugoresu Piazza San Giovanni 9 ☎ 0784 258 017. One of the rare places in Nuoro where you can dine alfresco, this trattoria on a cobbled piazza off the Corso has a wide-ranging menu that includes such concoctions as *bavette alle vongole* (pasta with clams and a creamy pistachio sauce) as well as pizzas. Most dishes are €10–15. Daily 1–3pm & 8–11pm.

BARS

Bar Bellavista Piazza Palestro ☎ 0784 35 253. This is a handy spot between the Museo Etnográfico and the cathedral for a break, not least for the *bella vista* from the panoramic covered terrace at the back, overlooking the valley. *Panini* and ice creams are available. Mon–Sat 7am–10.30pm, Sun 7am–2pm.

Bar Cambosu Via Monsignor Bua 4 ☎ 0784 31 731. On the corner of Piazza Vittorio Emanuele, this old-fashioned place has comfy chairs and lots of chat, with a separate *sala di conversazione*. A good breakfast stop. Daily 6am–9pm; closed Mon eve in winter, Sun eve in summer.

Caffè Tettamanzi Corso Garibaldi 71. Nuoro's oldest bar (from 1875) has the usual tables outside, but the mirrored interior has more character, with a painted ceiling and cherubs flitting about. It was a haunt of the author Salvatore Satta, with editions of his book *The Day of Judgement* displayed inside. Daily 6am–2am.

8

THE SAGRA DEL REDENTORE

Many costumes similar to those displayed in Nuoro's ethnographic museum are aired in the town's biggest annual festival, the **Sagra del Redentore**. Held during the last ten days of August, it involves participants from all over the island, but especially the villages of the Barbagia. The festival combines solemn religious rites with a flamboyant celebration of Sardinia's cultural heritage. The evenings are dedicated to traditional dancing and singing, enthusiastically performed in the old town's squares, while costumed parades take place during the day, culminating on the last day in a long procession out of Nuoro to the statue of the Redeemer on Monte Ortobene and the nearby church of Nostra Signora di Montenero. Together, these events constitute one of the most vibrant *feste* on the island's calendar, and accommodation at this time is at a premium.

DIRECTORY

Hospital Ospedale San Francesco, Via Mannironi, northwest of the train station (☏ 0784 240 237).

Pharmacy Gali, Corso Garibaldi 65 (Mon–Fri 8.30am–1pm & 4.30–8.30pm or 4–7.30pm in winter, Sat 8.30am–1pm; ☏ 0784 30 143). Late-closing pharmacies operate on a rota – check on any pharmacy door to see the address of the current one.

Post office Piazza Francesco Crispi (Mon–Fri 8.20am–7.05pm, Sat 8.20am–12.35pm).

North and west of Nuoro

The country **north and west of Nuoro** has a less dramatic appeal than that of the more famous Barbagia, but its scattered hamlets and high plains merit a slow exploration, preferably with your own transport. Bus connections are sporadic, and accommodation is virtually nonexistent, but much of the region can be visited on trips out of Nuoro.

Su Tempiesu

Daily 9am–sunset • €3 • ☏ 328 756 5148, ⓦ sutempiesu.it

The nondescript hill settlement of **Orune**, 13km north of Nuoro, has little intrinsic interest, but you'll need to pass this way to visit the remote site of **Su Tempiesu**, a sacred well and temple dating from nuraghic times. At the entrance to the village, take the signposted (and mostly unsurfaced) road that dips 5km east to the entrance to the site, where there's a bar selling drinks and snacks. The temple itself is hidden in the valley below the road, reached along a steeply descending path. Knowledgeable guides will explain (usually in Italian) the significance of the site, which, discovered by a farmer in 1953, constitutes Sardinia's best-preserved example of a **sacred well** from this period, and remains a good illustration of the importance of water at a time when it was often (surprisingly) in chronically short supply. Health-giving and prophetic properties were attributed to springs by the numerous cults that grew up around them, and temples were built over the outlets.

Bitti

Twelve kilometres of mountain road north of Orune, the village of **BITTI** is famed for its singing tradition; the local male group, **Tenores di Bitti**, has established an international reputation for its four-part harmonies. Other than the museums, Bitti has a couple of bars and *alimentaris*, and a bank at Via Deffenu 2.

Museo del Canto a Tenore

Via Mameli 52 • Tues & Thurs 9.30am–12.30pm, Wed & Fri–Sun 9.30am–12.30pm & 3.30–6.30pm, or 2.30–5.30pm in winter • €2.50 including Museo della Civiltà Pastorale e Contadina • ☏ 0784 414 314, ⓦ romanzesu.sardegna.it

You can find out about the famous **Tenores di Bitti** and Sardinia's polyphonic singing tradition in general at the small **Museo del Canto a Tenore**, signposted up an alley off the main Corso Vittorio Veneto (where you should park). Recordings and films give a broad overview of the different singing styles, allowing you to pinpoint the contributions of each of the components of the foursomes, and CDs are available to buy.

Museo della Civiltà Pastorale e Contadina

Via Mameli 52 • Tues & Thurs 9.30am–12.30pm, Wed & Fri–Sun 9.30am–12.30pm & 3–6pm, or 2–5.30pm Oct–March • €2.50 including Museo del Canto a Tenore • ☏ 0784 414 314, ⓦ romanzesu.sardegna.it

Ethnographic collections are not exactly rare in Sardinia, but there's always something of interest to view. Sharing a building with the Canto a Tenore museum, Bitti's **Museo della Civiltà Pastorale e Contadina** is spread out over ten rooms and devoted to the local farming and peasant culture.

Burgos

In Sássari province, some 40km west of Bitti, the village of **BURGOS** is visible from kilometres around, mainly on account of its castle, **La Reggia**, dramatically poised on a granite pinnacle high above. Although founded in the fourteenth century by Mariano IV of Arborea, the village has a predominantly modern aspect, containing not much more than a bank (in Via Marconi) and a couple of bars. However, the scenic road running 35km northwest towards Torralba (see p.226) passes through the **Foresta di Burgos**, a wooded area that's home to miniature horses, and across an evocative landscape of high, empty plains, before descending to the SS131.

La Reggia and Museo dei Castelli

Vícolo Castello • April–Sept Tues–Sun 9am–12.30pm & 2.30–6.30pm; Oct–March closes 5pm • €3 • ☎ 347 901 8930, ⓦ sareggia.it

Completed in 1133, **La Reggia** the formidably walled redoubt was strategically vital for its commanding position over the Tirso valley, at a point where the three *giudicati* (territories) of Torres, Arborea and Gallura met. It was briefly occupied by Eleonora d'Arborea (see box, p.143), and was used as a prison for various unwanted family members – guides will point out the remains of cells as well as of stables and barracks, and of an extensive space that may have been a church or central dining hall. At one end, the square tower looming over the ruins is a rather incongruous renovation from the 1950s. The same ticket admits you to the **Museo dei Castelli** (same times), below the castle entrance, where you can see temporary exhibitions and a permanent display on castles throughout Sardinia.

Oliena and around

The nearest village of any size to Nuoro, **OLIENA** is easily visible from the provincial capital, sprawled along the side of **Monte Corrasi** to the south. Rising to 1463m, this rugged limestone elevation is the highest peak of the **Supramonte massif**, famed as the haunt of **bandits** until relatively recently. Oliena itself prefers its reputation as the producer of one of the island's finest wines: **Nepente**, a variety of the prized Cannonau – a dry, almost black concoction that turns lighter and stronger over the years. Oliena is also the best base for hiking excursions in the surrounding mountainous terrain. You can gain access to Monte Corrasi from Località Maccione, a wooded area 3km south of town off the very squiggly old road to Orgósolo (see p.283).

Su Gologone

Off the Dorgali road, 6km east of Oliena, **SU GOLOGONE** makes an attractive starting point for mountain expeditions (see box, p.282). The area is named after a fast-flowing spring emerging from underground close to the church of **San Giovanni**, and there are

---

OLIENA'S FESTIVALS

The best time to visit Oliena would be during one of its annual **feast days**. The most striking are around **Easter**: on Good Friday, when a mournful procession shuffles through the streets, at the end of which the whole village pours into a pitch-black church to watch an intensely dramatic re-enactment of Christ's Deposition, and on Easter Sunday, a much more boisterous affair, when hundreds gather to witness the *Incontru*, or meeting, between the figures of the Virgin Mary and the resurrected Jesus. On this latter occasion, there's much gunfire, villagers don traditional dress (an elegant black and white or red and white costume, complete with jewellery), and there's dancing, music and free tastings in the main square. The costumes and dancing can also be viewed during the four days of revelry around **San Lussorio's day** on August 21.

usually a few locals here filling jerrycans with the therapeutic springwater. It's a good spot to picnic under the eucalyptus trees, and you can follow the course of the stream or a choice of tracks leading into the mountains. There's a hotel with a renowned restaurant here too (see opposite). ARST buses stop at the turn-off for Su Gologone.

ARRIVAL, INFORMATION AND ACTIVITIES   OLIENA AND AROUND

By bus Oliena is connected by a frequent service with Nuoro (Mon–Sat every 30mins–1hr, Sun 5–6 daily; 20min) and Dorgali (Mon–Sat 6–8 daily, Sun 3–5 daily; 25min); the last bus to Nuoro leaves at 8.10pm in summer, 8.25pm in winter (9.10pm on Sun). Dorgali-bound buses can drop you at the turn-off to Su Gologone, from where it's a brief walk to the spring.

Guided expeditions For exploring Supramonte's caves and crags, Oliena's main operators are Barbagia Insólita on Corso Vittorio Emanuele 48 (☎ 0784 286 005, ⓦ barbagiainsolita.it) and Sardegna Nascosta (☎ 0784 288 550 or ☎ 349 443 4665, ⓦ sardegnanascosta.it). **Tourist office** Corso Deledda 32, Oliena (Easter–Oct Mon–Sat 9am–1pm & 4–7pm, Oct–Easter closed Sat; ☎ 0784 286 078).

ACCOMMODATION

B&B Barbagia Corso M. Luther King 4, Oliena ☎ 0784 288 024, ⓦ cikappa.it. Friendly place on the main drag, with four colour-themed rooms with en-suite bathrooms and balconies. Breakfasts are fresh and tasty, and there's a popular restaurant run by the same management below

(see p.283). The staff can arrange expeditions of various sorts. **€70**
★**Cooperativa Turistica Enis** Località Maccione ☎ 0784 288 363, ⓦ coopenis.it. Off a steep, rough-surfaced road that corkscrews up the mountain 3km

---

8

THE WALK TO VALLE LANAITTU AND MONTE TÍSCALI

One of the most rewarding expeditions you can make on Supramonte is to **Valle Lanaittu**, a grand, secluded valley overlooked by **Monte Tíscali** (518m), which holds the remains of a nuraghic village. The best advice is to take a guide, which the tourist office in Oliena (see above) can arrange; expect to pay around €40 including lunch, sometimes with a minimum of four people. Although it's possible to reach the site unaccompanied – it's a relatively short and straightforward **hike** of four or five hours, depending on your starting point – there are some tricky sections where there's a risk of straying off the route, not least in locating the start of the ascent, and indications are few and far between. Moreover, some of the approaches are too rough for any but off-road vehicles to negotiate, meaning that you'll have a long way to walk to reach the interesting section. If you do attempt it on your own, make sure you let someone know where you're headed before leaving. Either way, you should have adequate equipment: robust walking shoes or boots, protection against the sun and at least a litre of water per person.

There are two **routes** into the Valle Lanaittu, one signposted from the **Sorgente Su Gologone**, a natural spring just by the *Su Gologone* hotel complex (see opposite) on the Oliena–Dorgali road, and the milder but longer and not so dramatic ascent that starts from the same point as the walk to the Gorropu canyon (see box, p.299), near Dorgali. The signposting is better on the latter option, which is more advisable for unaccompanied walks.

As it's well concealed behind trees, it's a bit of a shock to find the **nuraghic village of Tíscali** (daily: April–Sept 9am–7pm; Oct–March 9am–5pm; €5) in such an isolated spot, dramatically sited within a vast hollow space inside the mountain itself. Once providing a last refuge from foreign incursions during the first millennium BC, the site was inhabited well into Roman and medieval times, but was only rediscovered about a century ago, and is still under excavation. Few of the buildings have survived in a recognizable form, but it's a fascinating place nonetheless, the yellow limestone walls and stalactites giving it a weird, ghostly atmosphere. A huge hole punched through the rock where part of the roof collapsed creates a soft twilight within, and once enabled the villagers to keep an eye on any comings and goings in the valley below. There's vegetation and even trees growing inside, but the lack of ready water must have been a constant problem, probably preventing the community from ever growing very large.

From here, you can either retrace your steps back down, or – preferably with an experienced guide – you might continue along the path past Tíscali, descending into the **Flumineddu valley** to the east.

south of Oliena (signposted off the old road for Orgósolo), this hotel, campsite and restaurant complex – also known as *Monte Maccione* – is perfectly situated for mountain walks. The clean rooms, basic pitches in the woods and the restaurant (see below) all have lofty views. It's worth paying a little extra for the balcony rooms. Pitches €18; doubles

Santa Maria Corso Deledda 76, Oliena ☎ 0784 287 278 or ☎ 328 117 8551, ⊛ bbsantamaria.it. Modern B&B on Oliena's main piazza, with spacious rooms including a traditionally styled suite with its own balcony. All rooms have private bathrooms and a/c, and there's a wonderful panoramic roof terrace. The owner can offer advice on excursions. No credit cards. €60

Su Gologone Località Su Gologone ☎ 0784 287 512, ⊛ sugologone.it. Armed with your own transport and a comfortable budget, you can't do better than this luxurious complex in a rustic setting next to the spring of the same name, equipped with a swimming pool, tennis court and fitness centre. Elegantly chic, the hotel also offers a full programme of walking, horseriding and 4WD expeditions, including "lunch with the shepherds" – a hike or jeep ride which culminates in an open-air feast. The hotel lies 7km east of Oliena on the Dorgali road, handy for expeditions to Tiscali. Closed early Nov to mid-March. Per person per night half board €249

EATING

★ **Cooperativa Turistica Enis** Località Maccione ☎ 0784 288 363. The terrace restaurant at this hotel complex up a steep hill 3km south of Oliena beats all the competition for its fabulous views over the valley. Pizzas are available alongside such dishes as rabbit stew and roast sucking pig on fixed-price menus costing €22–37. Daily 12.30–3pm & 8–10.30pm; pizzeria closed Mon in summer, Mon–Fri spring and autumn, and throughout Nov–Feb.

GiKappa Via M. Luther King 4, Oliena ☎ 0784 288 024. The menu at this lively ristorante/pizzeria on the main drag specializes in land-based dishes, often incorporating wild mushrooms and boar. You can have a full meal for €25–35 or choose from one of the excellent pizzas. Daily 11am–4pm & 7pm–midnight.

Masiloghi Via Galiani 68, Oliena ☎ 0784 285 696. A 5min walk from the centre on the Dorgali road, this place is the most highly rated of Oliena's restaurants, with a semi-formal but self-consciously "rustic" ambience, plus delicious meat and seafood platters. Tasting menus are €17 and €33. You can eat on the veranda in summer. April–Oct daily noon–11pm; Nov–March closed Tues.

Su Gologone Località Su Gologone ☎ 0784 287 512, ⊛ sugologone.it. The restaurant attached to this luxury hotel 7km east of Oliena is reasonably priced but pampers diners with a succulent succession of local dishes such as ravioli with fennel, *gnocchetti* with boar-meat sauce and meat on the spit (vegetarians have a limited choice). A meal here will cost around €35–50 a head without drinks. Mid-March to early Nov daily 12.30–2.30pm & 8–10.30pm.

8

The Barbagia Ollolai

To the south and west of Oliena, the villages of the **Barbagia Ollolai** region offer contrasting glimpses into local culture and folklore: **Orgósolo** is famous for its ancient banditry and its vivid, politicized murals; the otherwise unremarkable village of **Mamoiada**, 11km west and 16km south of Nuoro, is the venue of a highly pagan Carnival, while farther west, **Orani** has a museum devoted to artist Costantino Nivola. Lacking the dramatic landscape of other parts of the Barbagia, the area is less conducive for walking, though the **Montes** region south of Orgósolo has an appealing empty grandeur that's worth experiencing.

Orgósolo and around

At the end of a straggly 18km road from Oliena, **ORGÓSOLO** is stuck with its label of **bandit capital** of Sardinia. The clans of Orgósolo, whose menfolk used to spend the greater part of the year away from home with their flocks, have always nursed an animosity towards the settled crop-farmers on the Barbagia's fringes, a tension that occasionally broke out into open warfare. On top of this, there was conflict between rival clans, which found expression in large-scale sheep-rustling and bloody **vendettas**, such as the *disamistade* (enmity) that engulfed Orgósolo at the beginning of the twentieth century. The feud arose from a dispute over the inheritance of the village's richest chieftain, Diego Moro, who died in 1903, and lasted for fourteen years,

ORGÓSOLO'S RED PRIMROSE

Orgósolo's most notorious son is **Graziano Mesina**, the so-called *Primula Rossa* ("Red Primrose"), who won local hearts in the 1960s by supposedly robbing only from the rich to give to the poor and only killing for revenge against those who had betrayed him. Roaming at will through the mountains, even granting interviews to reporters and television journalists, he was eventually captured and incarcerated in Sássari prison. Escaping in 1968, he was recaptured near Nuoro and flown by helicopter the same day to appear on television in Cágliari. In July 1992 he was dispatched to Sardinia from a mainland prison to help negotiate the release of Farouk Kassam, an 8-year-old boy held hostage for seven months in the Barbagia (see box, p.288). Mesina was eventually freed in 2004, having served a total of forty years behind bars, and returned to live with his sisters in Orgósolo. His story should have ended there, but incredibly he was arrested again in 2013, aged 71, on charges of intent to kidnap and drug-trafficking – the case is in court at time of writing.

virtually exterminating the two families involved. Between 1901 and 1954, Orgósolo (with a population of four thousand) clocked up an average of one murder every two months. In 1953 the first of the postwar **kidnappings**, which would soon become endemic in this region of Sardinia, took place near Orgósolo, and the connection was crystallized with the screening of Vittorio de Seta's film *Banditi a Orgosolo* in 1961.

The village still has an impoverished, almost abandoned air, and the locals are not always comfortable with the regular flow of camera-toting tourists, but there are signs of gentrification too, and the shops are increasingly offering crafts and souvenirs that have nothing to do with Orgósolo's nefarious past.

Orgósolo's murals

Saddled with its semi-legendary background, Orgósolo inevitably draws visitors hoping to find traces of its violent past amid the shabby collection of grey breeze-block houses, and the locals have obliged by peppering various of the village's nameplates and signs with bullet holes, and by painting a sinister scarlet and white face on a rock by the side of the main road into town.

But this is just a harbinger of things to come, for Orgósolo's narrow alleys have been daubed with a vivid array of **murals** covering whole houses and shopfronts. Most have a political element, the suppression of the many by the few or Sardinian independence, for example, while others comically depict the collision of traditional culture with the modern world. One of the most heavily painted buildings is the Municipio at the eastern end of the main Corso Repubblica, whose garish collection of cartoon figures and slogans are poignantly shot through with more bullet holes – the work of local hotheads.

Montes

Within easy reach of Orgósolo lies a tract of high country well worth exploring. Following the road through the village, a left turn takes you south out of town and steeply uphill, leading after about 5km to the high plateau of **Montes**, an empty, desolate expanse, green but rugged. It's suitable for hiking or riding and the site of a good hotel and restaurant (see below). A small road continues as far as **Funtana Bona**, at a height of 1052m, only a kilometre or two's walk from the peak of **Monte San Giovanni** (1316m), near the source of the Cedrino river.

ARRIVAL AND DEPARTURE   ORGÓSOLO AND AROUND

A regular ARST **bus** plies the route between Orgósolo and Nuoro (Mon–Sat 9–10 daily, Sun 3 daily; 35min).

ACCOMMODATION AND EATING

★**Ai Monti del Gennargentu** Località Settiles, Montes ☎0784 402 374 or ☎339 701 3183, ⓦ aimontidelgennargentu.todosmart.net. Drivers will be able to reach this remote but wonderful restaurant serving healthy mountain fare, including local *filindeu* (stringy pasta) and *porcetto arrosto* (roast pork). There are eight plain en-suite rooms, and the staff can help if you want to do any walking or riding in the area. Half board costs €65/person, otherwise meals come to around €30 for two courses. Always call ahead. It's about 3km from the SS389 Nuoro–Arbatax road, from the junction at Pratobello. May–Sept daily 12.30–2.30pm & 7.30–10.30pm. **€70**

Il Pórtico Via Giovanni XXIII ☎0784 402 929. Orgósolo isn't noted as a culinary hot spot, but this unpretentious and friendly trattoria off the main Corso Repubblica should see you right for a hearty rustic repast. The menu includes meaty local specialities such as *lados al ragù di pecora*

(pasta with mutton sauce), and pizzas are available. Fixed-price menus are €16–19. Mon–Sat noon–2.30pm & 7–10.30pm, Sun noon–2.30pm.

Sa 'e Jana Via Lussu ☎0784 402 437, ✉saejana .altervista.org. The best feature of this rather dated hotel, restaurant and pizzeria is the far-reaching views it enjoys over the valley. Half the spacious rooms have balconies – though you have to put up with kitsch murals on some of the walls. The restaurant serves local fare, reasonably priced. It's at the entrance to the village on the Mamoiada road, signposted past the graffiti-daubed school, and has parking. **€64**

Mamoiada

Like Orgósolo, the deeply traditional village of **MAMOIADA**, 11km west, has achieved its own particular fame, but in this case for its twice-yearly, highly theatrical **Carnival rituals** rather than for its murals or banditry (see box, p.286). At any other time, the village holds a couple of excellent museums that merit a look. Surprisingly, the family of Juan Perón originated in Mamoiada, and according to some the Argentine president was himself born here.

Museo delle Máschere Mediterranee

Piazza Europa • June–Sept daily 9am–1pm & 3–7pm; Oct–May closed Mon; guided tours on the hour (free) • €4 • ☎0784 569 018, ✉museodellemaschere.it

If you're not in Mamoiada for the masked festivities, the next best thing is to visit the **Museo delle Máschere Mediterranee**, housed in the *biblioteca* (library), at the bottom of the main Corso. The local masks, costumed mannequins and photos on show are augmented by examples from the Veneto and Fruili regions of Italy as well as places farther afield, from Greece to Korea. The guided commentaries (also in English) are informative, and you'll glean something of the appearance of the Carnival shenanigans from the ten-minute video, if not its spirit.

8

Museo della Cultura e del Lavoro

Via Sardegna • Tues–Sun 9am–1pm & 3–6pm • €4 • ☎0784 569 018, ✉viseras.it

Beautifully laid out, the **Museo della Cultura e del Lavoro** (Museum of Culture and Work) is well worth a visit for anyone intrigued by the region's social history, gathering costumes, artefacts and grainy photographs from Mamoiada's fairly recent but remote-seeming past. Well-informed guides explain the various displays, while a video, narrated in Sardinian but translated by the guides into Italian, French or English, supplies graphic context.

ARRIVAL AND INFORMATION   MAMOIADA

By bus Daily ARST buses connect Mamoiada with Nuoro and the villages of Barbagia.

Destinations Aritzo (1–2 daily; 1hr 20min–1hr 35min); Belvì (1–2 daily; 1hr 15min–1hr 30min); Cágliari (1 daily; 4hr 30min); Fonni (Mon–Sat 8 daily, Sun 1 daily; 20min);

Nuoro (Mon–Sat 11 daily, Sun 2 daily; 20min).

Tourist office The Pro Loco is next to the Museo della Cultura e del Lavoro on Via Sardegna (erratic hours; ☎0784 569 032, ✉mamuthonesmamoiada.it).

ACCOMMODATION AND EATING

Perda Pintà Via Nuoro 33, Località Boeli ☎0784 56 689 or ☎320 352 0920, ✉perdapinta.it. A pink villa just outside the centre on the Nuoro road houses this friendly B&B with three doubles, one with its own bathroom, and a

single room. The main point of interest, however, is the menhir, or standing stone, on display in the garden. Unearthed by chance by the owners, it's thought to be 5000 years old and is incised with odd circular symbols that may

MAMOIADA'S MAMUTHONES

The **Mamuthones of Mamoiada** are among the best known of Sardinia's traditional costumed figures, associated with the festivities around Carnival time, but with obscure roots going back several centuries. Despite their spooky, rather disturbing appearance – decked out in dark, shaggy sheepskins on which rows of jangling goat-bells are strung, and with heavy, black, oversized masks – the *Mamuthones* are symbols of abundance and good times, as manifested by the food and drink liberally dispensed during the proceedings.

The **main events** take place on Shrove Tuesday and the preceding Sunday, usually kicking off at 3pm and 3.30pm respectively. Two columns of masked *Mamuthones* stalk the main street, Corso Vittorio Emanuele, accompanied by red-jacketed **Issohadores** – or *Issokadores* – each wielding a lasso (*sa soca*). As the *Mamuthones* advance solemnly, they perform curious synchronized leaps, causing the hundreds of goat-bells tied across their backs to clang simultaneously, while the *Issohadores* twirl their lassos and ensnare victims, often from a distance of several metres, sometimes targeting spectators watching from balconies along the route. At the end of Shrove Tuesday's procession, a masked puppet known as **Juvanne Martis** is hauled on a cart through the village by participants supposedly weeping to lament the end of Carnival, though the evening sees a general carousal in Piazza Santa Croce anyway, with plates of pork and beans, traditional sweets and glasses of the local wine handed around, and dancing. There's also plenty of similarly rustic fare to eat and drink throughout the ceremonies, offered at stalls and shops around the village.

There's an alternative opportunity to view these celebrations at the **Festa di Sant'Antonio Abate**, the traditional beginning of the Carnival period, usually January 16 and 17. Then, bonfires are lit around the village and kept burning through the night, attracting groups of half-drunk festival-goers shuttling between them. Locals contend this is the best time to view the *Mamuthones*, when there are fewer distractions from the other costumed Carnival celebrations on the island, and fewer tourists.

At other times, you can view the *Mamuthones* and other local costumes at Mamoiada's Museo delle Máschere Mediterranee (see p.285).

be linked to a fertility cult. No credit cards. €60

Sa Rosada Piazza Europa ☎ 0784 56 713. The rooms of this B&B and restaurant have been preserved to an almost fanatical degree according to how they would have appeared when the house was built in the nineteenth century (the bathroom is shared). The restaurant has a limited choice of authentic local dishes, all meat, and often including *porceddu* (roast pork), but it can get pricey at around €25–35 a head. Daily except Wed noon–2.30pm & 8–11pm. €60

Gavoi

Twenty twisty kilometres southwest of Mamoiada, **GAVOI** has gained kudos in recent years as the venue for Sardinia's main **literary festival** (⊕isoladellestorie.it), held over four days in late June/early July. As well as readings and debates – some in English – there are films and alfresco music and theatre.

Orani

Sixteen kilometres north of Gavoi, the unassuming village of **ORANI** is worth a stop for the museum dedicated to its most famous son, the sculptor **Costantino Nivola** (1911–88). In fact, Nivola only spent a short part of his life here, working with his stonemason father until the age of 15 before studying in Sássari and then fleeing Fascist persecution in 1938. After spending some time in Paris, he emigrated to the US, where he forged a long association with the architect Le Corbusier and taught at Berkeley and Harvard.

Museo Nivola

Via Gonare 2 • Mon 4–9pm, Tues–Sun 10am–1pm & 4.30–8pm, or 3.30–7pm Oct–March • €5 • ☎ 0784 730 063, ⓦ museonivola.it

Most of the works in the **Museo Nivola**, located in a former public washhouse near the bottom of the village, are from the last period of Nivola's life, and reflect the artist's attitudes towards his homeland upon revisiting it after his long American exile. The small-scale and low-key bronze sculptures are beautifully displayed in simple, well-lit surroundings, both indoors and outside in the small courtyard. Many of the objects, whose sleek, minimalist lines are reminiscent of Brancusi, are clearly inspired by ancient menhirs and nuraghic *bronzetti*; other works use cement and marble, and the technique of sandcasting pioneered by Nivola.

ARRIVAL AND DEPARTURE ORANI

By bus ARST buses stopping in Piazza Italia link Orani with   Nuoro (Mon–Sat 6–7 daily, Sun 1 daily; 30min).
Fonni (Mon–Sat 5 daily, Sun 1 daily; 1hr–1hr 30min) and

The Barbagia Belvì and the Gennargentu massif

The **Barbagia Belvì** holds a significant chunk of the **Gennargentu** chain of mountains; the name means "silver gate", referring to the snow that covers them every winter – including the island's highest peaks, **Punta La Mármora** (1834m) and **Monte Bruncu Spina** (1829m). The villages hereabouts were traditionally shepherds' communities, but nowadays local people send their children to university or they go to seek work in mainland Italy and don't come back, leaving behind slowly atrophying communities whose salvation is deemed to lie in a greater awareness of their tourism potential.

Many villages have in fact succeeded in adapting to the new economic reality, serving the expanding leisure industry, even if the season is short and has only a partial impact on the local economy. Though the villages themselves are often unprepossessing and fairly uniform in appearance – **Fonni**, for example, one of the main centres on the northern outskirts of the Gennargentu range – some, such as **Aritzo** and **Belvì**, respectively Sardinia's chestnut and cherry capitals, are beautifully sited and also have good museums. But the real pleasures here are the bits between the villages: the distant views over thickly wooded slopes, where you may come across wild pigs and deer and, in the air, goshawks, sparrowhawks, peregrine falcons, griffon vultures and eagles.

The villages certainly make good bases for **walking**, best undertaken in spring and summer, and there are good, reasonably priced hotels in Aritzo, Belvì, Fonni and **Tonara**.

BANDITRY AND KIDNAPPING IN THE BARBAGIA

Until a short time ago, the villages of the Barbagia were primarily communities of shepherds, whose isolated circumstances and economic difficulties in the postwar years led to widescale emigration and, among those who stayed behind, a crime wave. Sheep-rustling and internecine feuding came to be replaced by the infinitely more lucrative practice of **kidnapping** and ransoming of wealthy industrialists or their families. This phenomenon reached epidemic proportions during 1966–68, when scores of Carabinieri were drafted into the area to comb the mountains for the hideouts, rarely with any success. The most high-profile case in recent years was that of Farouk Kassam, an 8-year-old abducted from the Costa Smeralda in 1992 and held for seven months on Monte Albo, near Sinìscola; part of his ear was severed by his kidnappers to accelerate the ransom payment. Since then, however, there has been a lull in the kidnappings, partly due to improvements in police intelligence.

By train The infrequent narrow-gauge train service – the Trenino Verde (ⓦ treninoverde.com) – running south from Sórgono is a ponderous way to reach Tonara and Belvì-Aritzo, only to be used by those with time and patience to spare.
By bus The mountain roads can be convoluted and slow,

and public transport is usually infrequent, but every village is connected to large centres by at least one bus route. Be prepared, however, for complicated short hops to travel between the villages, and also for some very early morning departures.

Fonni and around

Sixteen kilometres due south of Mamoiada, in a hilly area thick with vineyards, cork trees and oak forests, **FONNI** is, at 1000m, Sardinia's highest village. As a popular destination for skiers and walkers in the Gennargentu mountains – whose loftiest peaks, Bruncu Spina and La Mármora, are visible from the village – Fonni is also one of the Barbagia's biggest centres, a role it has occupied since the seventeenth century, when a community of Franciscans helped to make this the focus of the whole region.

Madonna dei Mártiri
Piazza dei Mártiri • Daily 7.30am–noon & 3.30–7.30pm

The church of **Madonna dei Mártiri** annexed to Fonni's Franciscan convent is still the most significant of the Barbagia's churches, both for its wealth and for its image of the Madonna, said to have been made from the crushed bones of martyrs. You can see the domed church at the highest point of the village, in the centre of a large open space off Piazza Europa, surrounded by *cumbessias*, or pilgrims' houses. Originally dating from the seventeenth century, but remodelled a hundred years later, the church is a substantial building with a peeling, salmon-coloured facade and tall, granite-grey spire. The interior is richly frescoed and painted with wooden altarpieces and pulpit; an elaborate shrine on the right as you enter holds the artless but much-venerated Madonna.

Around Fonni: the Gennargentu mountains

Fonni is well placed for exploring the heights of the Gennargentu mountains. Eight kilometres south of the village, on a signposted left turn off the Désulo road, you can follow paths that wind up to **Monte Spada** (1595m) and, to the south, **Bruncu Spina** (1829m), both of which can also be approached on a tarmacked road. It's a magnificent landscape, with bracken and other hardy shrubs taking over above the tree line, covered in snow for a good part of the year. The views from the top extend as far as Gallura and even Corsica to the north.

From Bruncu Spina, properly equipped hikers can reach the top of the island's highest peak, **Punta La Mármora** (1834m), a little way to the south, in less than three hours. You don't need to be an experienced climber to tackle either of these summits, though a guide is advisable; excursions between May and September can be organized at Fonni's hotels or from the various villages on the flanks of the mountains.

By bus Fonni is well connected to the most important Barbagia villages.
Destinations Aritzo (1–2 daily; 1hr 10min); Belvì (1–2 daily; 55min–1hr 10min); Cágliari (1 daily; 4hr 10min); Mamoiada

(Mon–Sat 9 daily, Sun 2 daily; 20min); Nuoro (Mon–Sat every 30min–1hr, Sun 4 daily; 40min); Orani (Mon–Sat 3–4 daily, Sun 1 daily; 1hr 10min); Sórgono (Mon–Sat 2 daily; 1hr–1hr 25min); Tonara (1–3 daily; 55min).

Barbagia Via Umberto 106 ☎ 0784 58 329. Unpretentious bar/ristorante/pizzeria at the southern end of town, where you can tuck into *penne al gorgonzola* or more local dishes such as *malloreddus* or *maccarrones* (both pasta dishes), or

pizzas in the evening. Starters are €4–8, mains around €8. Tues–Sun noon–3pm & 7–10pm.
Cualbu Viale del Lavoro ☎ 0784 57 054, ⓦ hotelcualbu .com. This large and fairly modern hotel has a pool, gym,

---

FONNI'S FESTIVALS

The image of Madonna dei Mártiri (see p.289) is escorted through Fonni's streets during the village's two principal **festivals**, both in June: on the Monday following the first Sunday in June and again for St John's day on June 24. Both occasions are costumed extravaganzas, with columns of immaculately turned-out women and traditionally dressed men on horseback, filing through the village.

---

garden and (occasional) disco, with standard, smallish rooms. The restaurant is fine but breakfast is a meagre affair. **€90**

★ **Sa Orte** Via Roma 14 ☎ 0784 58 020, ⓦ hotelsaorte .it. A smartly restored granite building in the cobbled heart of the village, this small hotel has fairly impersonal but well-equipped rooms (including family rooms and suites) and modern bathrooms. Breakfasts are abundant and in the restaurant (open to all) you can dine well on mainly meat dishes for around €20. Daily 8–11pm. **€80**

Belvì

As the crow flies, it's 18km south of Fonni to **BELVÌ**, a compact cluster of dwellings crowded along the side of a valley, but it's nearly twice that distance on the twisty mountain roads. The village is famed for its cherries, and once wielded a certain amount of influence locally – as reflected in the fact that it has given its name to this whole sector of the Barbagia – but it's a very low-key place now, providing useful accommodation and refreshment, and diversion in the form of its natural history museum.

Museo di Scienze Naturali

Via San Sebastiano • Daily 10am–1pm & 3–6pm, closes 5pm in winter • €3 • ☎ 339 792 0232 or ☎ 339 753 1025

An eclectic potpourri of fossils, minerals, mammals, butterflies, dragonflies, beetles and nearly four hundred stuffed birds, this private collection is crammed into a modern apartment just off Belvì's main street. The items aren't confined to the Barbagia, but include marine shells and a giant *Caretta caretta* turtle. The collection was begun in the 1970s by the entomologist Friedrich Reichsgraf Von Hartig. Always call first to make sure it's open.

ARRIVAL AND DEPARTURE   BELVÌ

By bus ARST buses stop on the main Via Roma. Destinations Aritzo (Mon–Sat 7–8 daily, Sun 1 daily; 5min); Cágliari (1–2 daily; 2hr 40min–3hr); Fonni (1–3 daily; 1hr 5min); Láconi (1–3 daily; 45min–1hr 10min); Mamoiada (1–3 daily; 1hr 25min); Nuoro (1–3 daily; 1hr 45min); Sórgono (Mon–Sat 5 daily; 40min); Tonara (Mon–Sat 6 daily, Sun 1 daily; 20min).

ACCOMMODATION AND EATING

Edera Via Roma ☎ 0784 629 825. This basic hotel with a bar-restaurant attached offers twelve very simple but comfortable en-suite rooms. Breakfast costs extra (€3 or €8). The excellent basement restaurant serves typical local cuisine, including lamb stew and wild boar, with main courses around €12 and a €15 tourist menu. The bar upstairs has delicious sausage sandwiches (€8). Daily 1–3pm & 7.30–10pm. **€60**

Aritzo

Just 3km west of Belvì, **ARITZO** is a similar huddle of grey buildings around a long main street, though it's larger and has a livelier aspect than many of the Barbagia's other villages. Corso Umberto holds everything of interest, including craft shops, a bank, the parish church and a first-class museum. The imposing crenellated structure on the left as you ascend is the neo-Gothic **Castello Arangino**, its tower and loggia lending it an old Tuscan character, though it was only built at the beginning of the twentieth century. Gaps in the buildings will allow you to appreciate the views across the valley, where the solitary **Monte Téxile** (975m) punctuates the horizon with its oddly square profile.

Museo della Montagna

Via Marconi • Tues–Sun 10am–1pm & 4–7pm, 3–6pm in winter • €3 including Sa Bovida (Prigioni Spagnoli) and Casa Devilla • ☎ 0784 627 200

Housed in the basement of a school, Aritzo's absorbing **Museo della Montagna** (signposted Museo Etnografico) is a fascinating jumble of artefacts connected with rural culture in the Gennargentu region. Between walls hung with agricultural implements and sepia photos are displayed articles for cheese- and wax-making, artisans' tools, local costumes and looms, all in fine condition. Aritzo once earned a good living selling snow for chilling drinks and preserving foodstuffs, and you can see the containers in which it was transported.

Sa Bovida

Via Scala Cárceri 6 • Call at Museo della Montagna for access • €3 including museum and Casa Devilla • ☎ 0784 627 200

With your Museo della Montagna ticket, you can take a peek in the **Sa Bovida** (also known as Prigioni Spagnoli, or Spanish prison), on an alley below the Corso. Dating back to the sixteenth century, the well-restored, schist-built structure was used as a jail until the 1940s, and manacles and other items relating to its former function are displayed. The rooms here were also used by the Inquisition in former times, and there's an exhibition of various objects used in local **"witchcraft"** practices, for which some women were charged and one was burned at the stake.

Casa Devilla

Via Caserma • Call at Museo della Montagna for access • €3 including museum and Sa Bovida • ☎ 0784 627 200

Casa Devilla, a palazzo just off the Corso with parts dating back to the seventeenth century, has been lovingly repaired, restored and furnished with items that evoke the daily life of its inhabitants. As well as heavy engraved chests and antique beds, there are also items in the cellar relating to Aritzo's chestnut industry and snow trade – the Devilla family were prominent in the latter activity – with photographs and panels. Ask at the museum for access.

8

ARRIVAL AND INFORMATION   ARITZO

By bus ARST buses stop on the main Corso Umberto.
Destinations Belvì (Mon–Sat 7–8 daily, Sun 1 daily;
5min); Cágliari (1–2 daily; 2hr 35min–3hr); Fonni (1–2
daily; 1hr 10min); Láconi (1–3 daily; 40min–1hr 5min);
Nuoro (1–2 daily; 1hr 50min); Sórgono (Mon–Sat 5

daily; 45min); Tonara (Mon–Sat 6 daily, Sun 1 daily;
25min).
Tourist office Corso Umberto 55 (Mon
9.30am–12.30pm, Tues–Sun 9.30am–12.30pm & 3.30–
6.30pm; ☎ 0784 628 205).

ACCOMMODATION AND EATING

La Baita Via Ceredi 36 ☎ 338 248 4172, ⊚ labaita
.org. Buried in greenery at the southern end of Aritzo,
this stylishly renovated villa offers B&B in three clean
and comfortable rooms sharing a bathroom. You can
breakfast on home-made cakes and jam in the garden,
from which valley views stretch out. No credit cards. **€70**
Moderno Viale Kennedy 6 ☎ 0784 629 229,

⊚ hotelmodernoaritzo.it. At the top of the Corso, this
hotel run by a young couple has seen better days, but it's
fine for a night or two, with a good restaurant open to all
and a shady garden. March–Dec daily 12.30–2.30pm &
7–9.30pm. **€60**
★ **Sa Muvara** Via Funtana Rubia ☎ 0784 629 336,
⊚ samuvarahotel.com. The smartest of the local

hotels – and one of the best in Barbagia – lies just outside the south entrance to the village. Sheltered behind trees and abundant parkland, the four-star has rooms with balconies and a good-sized pool, fitness centre and sauna; bikes are available too. The restaurant is worth sampling even if you're not staying, with tables inside and out. April–Oct daily 1–2.30pm & 7.30–10.30pm. **€140**

Tonara

Fifteen kilometres north of Aritzo, **TONARA** shares the same forested environment. Chestnuts are one of the foundations of the local economy, and the village is also famed for the manufacture of cattle bells and for its *torrone* nougat – a rich sticky feast of honey, nuts and egg whites, usually for sale in local shops and at village *feste*.

ARRIVAL AND DEPARTURE · TONARA

By bus ARST buses pull up on the main drag. Destinations Aritzo (Mon–Sat 5 daily, Sun 1 daily; 25min); Belvì (Mon–Sat 5 daily, Sun 1 daily; 20min); Cágliari (1–2 daily; 3hr–3hr 20min); Fonni (1–2 daily; 50min–1hr 5min); Láconi (1–2 daily; 1hr 5min); Mamoiada (1 daily; 1hr 10min); Nuoro (1–3 daily; 1hr 30min–2hr); Sórgono (Mon–Sat 11 daily; 20min).

ACCOMMODATION AND EATING

Il Castagneto Via Muggianeddu 2 ☎0784 610 005. On a height at the northern end of the village, this popular pizzeria enjoys wonderful views over the wooded slopes from its tables outside. Apart from pizzas, dishes include *cinghiale* (boar) and local mushrooms, all at rock-bottom prices. Easter to mid–July & mid–Sept to Oct Mon & Wed–Sun 5.30pm–midnight; mid-July to mid-Sept open daily.

★**Locanda del Muggianeddu** Via Monsignor Tore 10 ☎0784 63 885. Seven spacious en-suite rooms are available here, with wooden ceilings and schist walls. Adorned with local masks, the intimate restaurant has hearty mountain dishes including *zuppa di patate e formaggio* (potato and cheese soup) and *tagliatelle ai funghi porcini* (pasta with local mushrooms). Tues–Sun noon–2.30pm & 8–9.30pm; closed Feb. **€55**

Sa Colonia Via Muggianeddu 4 ☎392 128 2340, ⓦcampingsacolonia.it. It's unusual to find a campsite this far inland. This simple site for tents and motorhomes, signposted from the northern end of the village, is shady and clean. It has a ristorante-pizzeria and barbecue grills. Pitches **€15**

Tia Zicca Via Galusè 2 ☎0784 610 007 or ☎346 012 3114, ⓦtiazicca.it. In the upper and older part of the villlage, this simple, welcoming B&B has two en-suite rooms, a garden and a terrace with breathtaking views where breakfast can be served. No credit cards. Closed Nov & Jan. **€55**

D.H. LAWRENCE IN SARDINIA

"Comes over one an absolute necessity to move," begins *Sea and Sardinia*, the travelogue by **D.H. Lawrence**, written in response to a restless desire to take a break from Sicily, where he was then living with his wife Frieda. Disembarking in Sardinia in January 1921, the couple made the briefest tour of the island, just six days, for most of which they were in trains and buses, having decided to travel the hardest route – straight up through the interior from Cágliari on the painfully slow narrow-gauge railway. At Sórgono, the Lawrences changed onto a bus to Nuoro and proceeded to Olbia, whence they returned by ferry to the mainland.

It was Sardinia's inland villages that left the deepest impression, however. **Sórgono** – which at first appeared like "some little town in the English West Country" – possessed just one hotel, the *Risveglio*, where the only bedroom available contained "a large bed, thin and flat with a grey-white counterpane, like a large, poor, marble-slabbed tomb in the room's sordid emptiness; one dilapidated chair on which stood the miserablest weed of a candle I have ever seen: a broken wash-saucer in a wire ring: and for the rest, an expanse of wooden floor as dirty-grey-black as it could be, and an expanse of wall charted with the bloody deaths of mosquitoes." A stroll through the village did not improve his mood: "A dreary hole! A cold, hopeless, lifeless, Saturday-afternoon-weary village, rather sordid, with nothing to say for itself."

Despite the ill humour that characterizes much of the book, it's a good read: a close-up description of travelling on the cheap interspersed with observations on the state of the world in the wake of World War I. For more on the book, see Contexts (see p.319).

Láconi

On the southern fringes of the Barbagia, the **Sarcidano** region is a quickly changing landscape of verdant hills and desolate limestone plateaux. There's ample evidence here of Sardinia's prehistory, starting with a fascinating collection of menhirs in the museum at **LÁCONI**. The village is a pleasurable place to explore, with a surprising number of attractions and a fresh, woodsy feel.

Menhir Museum

Piazza Marconi • Tues–Sun: April–Sept 10am–1pm & 3.30–7pm; Oct–March 10am–1pm & 3–6pm • €5 including guided tour • ☎ 0782 693 238, ⓦ menhirmuseum.it

Not the least of Láconi's attractions is the elegant Neoclassical **Palazzo Aymerich** across from the town hall off the main Corso Garibaldi. Designed in 1846 by one of Sardinia's most eminent architects, Gaetano Cima (1805–78), it was the last home of the local *marchese*, and now holds the fascinating **Menhir Museum**, primarily dedicated to Sardinia's extraordinary menhirs (prehistoric standing stones), an unusual concentration of which has been found in this area. Most of the bigger examples of these megaliths, which are mainly of trachyte stone and reach up to 7m in height, have been left in their original sites, as seen in photographs displayed here, but the museum has a fine selection of smaller pieces, grouped according to the genre they represent. The majority date back to the **Neolithic cultures** of Ozieri and Arzachena in the second half of the fourth millennium BC, and are a principal source of information for this obscure era, particularly regarding its divinities. The museum also displays Neolithic ceramics and obsidian arrowheads.

8

Male and female menhirs

The earliest menhirs have few, if any, characteristic marks, though later ones bear primitive facial characteristics, mainly noses and eyes. These more interesting "anthropomorphic" menhirs may be male or female in form, and are especially common around Láconi; the "males" are distinguished by the horn-shaped tridents embossed on one side, perhaps indicating membership of a warrior class, while "feminine" menhirs have a smaller and less defined form, with disc-shaped breasts. One, in Sala 2, shows a grooved circle below the "neck", perhaps representing a hair arrangement. Others are "asexual", though still retaining the facial features.

Casa Natale di Sant'Ignazio

Via Sant'Ignazio • Always open • Free • ☎ 0782 869 027

From Corso Garibaldi, the cobbled Via Sant'Ignazio leads to the **Casa Natale di Sant'Ignazio**, family home of one of Sardinia's most revered saints (see box, p.294). You need to go round to the back to appreciate how the dwelling must have originally appeared in the eighteenth century – the rough stonework here is quite unlike the spruced-up exterior of the front. The house itself is little more than a bare room with a typical wood-beamed and bamboo-covered ceiling, and there are benches for prayer and meditation facing a shrine festooned with rosaries.

Sant'Ignazio

Via Sant'Ambrogio • Daily 9.30am–9pm

Behind the Casa Natale, walk up Via Don Minzoni and turn left at the little remembrance park to reach the church dedicated to **Sant'Ignazio**, conspicuous by its metal dome and square, pointy campanile. The bronze sculpted doors, carved in the 1980s, depict miracles and scenes from the saint's life, the first chapel on the left was where he received his baptism, and the second one, richly mosaicked, holds his reliquaries.

SANT'IGNAZIO DA LÁCONI

Born Vincenzo Peis, and apparently called "Il Santarello" even in his youth because of his extreme piety, Sardinia's most popular "modern" saint, **Sant'Ignazio da Láconi**, became a lay Capuchin monk in 1721. He spent the next sixty years practising penitence, humility and charity; as an inscription in his birthplace relates, "*Conobbe le cose occulte, penetrò il segreto dei cuori, ed ebbe il dono dei miracoli*" ("he knew occult things, he penetrated the secrets of the heart, and he had the gift of miracles"). Though born in Láconi, he lived for most of his life in Cágliari, where he is said to have performed various miracles, dying there in 1781 and spawning an enthusiastic cult. Beatified in 1940, he was canonized in 1951.

Parco Aymerich di Láconi

Via del Parco • Daily 8am–1hr before sunset • Free

Below the church of Sant'Ignazio, the terraced **Parco Aymerich di Láconi** makes an ideal place to take a breather or have a picnic. Once over a bridge that crosses a pretty stream, you'll find a marvellous shady retreat full of surprises: springs, grottoes, waterfalls, a pond with goldfish and much bigger, darker fish lurking, great overhanging rocks, rare orchids and beautifully crafted rustic benches.

Castello Aymerich

Buried within the park's thick groves is the **Castello Aymerich**, a ruined redoubt, parts of which go back to 1051. The building sports some engaging details, such as the small carving of a castle above the arched gateway, and windows with an ace of spades motif. In front of the roofless hall there's a terrace with fine views over the valleys and countless paths curving round the hill.

8

ARRIVAL AND DEPARTURE

LÁCONI

By train Láconi is a stop on the narrow-gauge Trenino Verde, with services running from mid-June to mid-Sept once a week on Sun only on Sun only. The station is a 10min walk west of town.
Destinations Belvì-Aritzo (1hr 35min); Ísili (1hr); Mandas (1hr 15min); Sórgono (2hr 20min).
By bus ARST buses stop right by the museum on Corso Garibaldi.

Destinations Aritzo (1–3 daily; 40min–1hr 5min); Belvì (1–3 daily; 40min–1hr 10min); Cágliari (2–4 daily; 2–4hr); Ísili (Mon–Sat 5–6 daily, Sun 2 daily; 20–35min); Mandas (2 daily; 50min); Nuoro (1 daily; 2hr 35min); Oristano (Mon–Sat 5 daily; 1hr 40min–2hr); Sórgono (1–3 daily; 55min–1hr 25min); Tonara (1–2 daily; 1hr 5min).

ACCOMMODATION AND EATING

★ **Antico Borgo** Via Sant'Ambrogio 5 ☎ 0782 869 047, ⊕ anticoborgoweb.it. Láconi has a first-rate place to stay in the form of this B&B, in an old house situated below the church, beautifully renovated and furnished. Each of the attic rooms has its own bathroom, and the hosts are genial. No credit cards. **€70**

Sardegna Corso Garibaldi 97 ☎ 0782 869 033, ⊕ albergosardegna.it. This *pensione* enjoys fantastic

mountain views from half of the rooms, which are mostly spacious (some have balconies). The simple restaurant has a fairly limited menu of local favourites, including home-made *ravioli di formaggio e spinaci* (with cheese and spinach) and lamb with artichokes – you'll pay €15–25 for two courses, and there's a set menu for €17. April–Sept daily 12.30–3pm & 7.30–9.30pm; Oct–March call ahead. **€75**

The eastern coast

Nuoro province's **eastern seaboard** is highly developed around the resorts of **Posada** and **Orosei**, but further south it preserves its rugged beauty, virtually untouched apart from the isolated **Cala Gonone**. Farther down, the province of Ogliastra shares the same terrain of mountains and sea, with pockets of holiday activity on the coast at **Santa Maria Navarrese** and around the port of **Arbatax**, while a foray 20km west of here will give you a taste of the mountains at the village of **Lanusei**.

The **beaches** along this coast are some of Sardinia's wildest, including some extremely swim-worthy stretches around **Cala Liberotto**. The coast around Cala Gonone is also studded with isolated sandy coves, most of them inaccessible by road, and there are more beaches to the south around Santa Maria Navarrese and Arbatax.

GETTING AROUND   THE EASTERN COAST

By car The SS125 runs parallel to the eastern coast, taking in some magnificent scenery en route to Arbatax and beyond. You'll need your wits about you on some stretches, though traffic tends to be light in these parts.

By train Arbatax and Tortolì (the provincial capital) are on the narrow-gauge Trenino Verde line (see p.304) that operates in summer only, following an inland route to Mandas, which has frequent connections with Cágliari. With the current timetables, however, the full journey from the coast to Cágliari would spread over two days.

By bus Daily buses connect Cágliari and Nuoro with Tortolì, some of them also going on to Santa Maria Navarrese and Arbatax.

Posada

Northeast of Nuoro, the SS131dir highway follows the course of two river valleys, passing close to the inland town of **Siniscola**, the main centre of the rich agricultural land around here. The main road reaches the coast at **POSADA**, sited on a rise a little way inland, near the mouth of the river of the same name. Once a power base for the surrounding districts, the town was prey to repeated attacks by seaborne raiders during the Middle Ages, and now only the ruins of its once impregnable castle – still commanding impressive views for kilometres around – attest to its former importance.

8

Castello della Fava

Via Eleonora d'Arborea • Daily: April–Sept 9am–dusk, July & Aug closes 10pm; Oct–March 9am–1pm • €3 • ☎ 347 480 1421

Reached by a brief climb up some steps above Piazza Eleonora d'Arborea in Posada's old town (drivers should leave their vehicles in the square or lower down), little survives of the **Castello della Fava** beyond a single oblong upright tower ringed by broken-down walls. Visitors must climb up four levels of wooden steps and iron rungs to reach the trapdoor at the top, but they're rewarded by a sweeping panorama that takes in the citrus groves clustered around the coast and on the banks of the Posada river, the lagoons stretching south to the resort of La Caletta (see p.296) and Barbagia's inland peaks. Call ahead in winter to confirm the *castello* is open.

ARRIVAL AND DEPARTURE   POSADA

By bus ARST buses pull up in Via Véneto, in the lower town.

Destinations La Caletta (Mon–Sat 9 daily, Sun 4–8 daily; 15min); Nuoro (Mon–Sat 7–8 daily, Sun 4–7 daily; 1hr 20min); Olbia (Mon–Sat 9–10 daily, Sun 6–9 daily; 1hr 20min); Orosei (1–2 daily; 1hr 10min).

THE TALE OF THE BEAN

The Castello della Fava may owe its strange name – "**Bean Castle**" – to a colourful story. According to medieval legend, when besieged here by Turkish raiders, the *giudice* of Gallura took a homing pigeon, attached to it a message addressed to a fictitious army of rescuers, and forced the garrison's last remaining broad beans down its gullet. As planned, the Turks intercepted the bird, read the message and found the beans, concluding that not only was there an army on the way, but that the besieged Sards had plenty of provisions (enough to waste on pigeons, anyway) – and promptly withdrew. Scholars, however, are more in favour of an alternative explanation: *fava* may be a corruption of the Sard word *faedda*, meaning speak or voice – hence "the tower that sounds the alarm" when enemies are spotted.

ACCOMMODATION

Il Castello Via Nazionale 3 ☎ 349 146 8768, ✉ renaton@ gmail.com. This *affittacámere* (no breakfast served) has three small en-suite rooms with Sard furnishings, wrought-iron beds and panoramic verandas, with use of a kitchen. German and English are spoken by the owner. A three-night minimum is usually requested but it's worth asking about shorter stays. Closed mid-Oct to April. No credit cards. **€50**

Sa Rocca Piazza Eleonora d'Arborea ☎ 0784 854 139,

🖥 hotelsarocca.it. Right below the castle in the old centre, this small three-star hotel/restaurant offers slightly outdated but functional rooms, some with great views. Breakfast costs €3–7/person extra. There are more striking views from the restaurant, which serves good pasta and seafood dishes at higher-than-average prices (starters are around €11, mains around €14). Pizzas are available in the evening. Easter–Oct daily 12.30–3pm & 8–10.30pm. **€65**

The coast to Orosei

South of Posada, the coast is dotted with small holiday centres – **La Caletta**, **Santa Lucia** and **Cala Liberotto** – none of them with much in the way of character or even shops, but with a plentiful supply of bars, pizzerias and hotels, while the long tracts of pinewoods shelter a scattering of villas and **campsites**. The big draw, of course, is the almost unbroken line of **beaches**, from which sailing and windsurfing are available in summer. It's one of Sardinia's most enticing stretches, the fine white sands often backed by dunes and pinewoods, and overlooked by ruined Spanish watchtowers. Twelve kilometres north of Cala Liberotto, Sardinia's easternmost point, **Capo Comino**, is a wild and desolate spot of jagged rocks and abundant *macchia*.

Orosei

South of Cala Liberotto, the SS125 tracks away from the sea for 12km before crossing the Cedrino river, thick with reeds, to the town of **OROSEI**, the main centre of the **Baronia** region. Though it now stands 3km from the coast in a flat and fertile zone planted with vines and citrus groves, medieval accounts of Turkish raids suggest that Orosei was a significant harbour before the silting up of the river pushed back the shore. The town certainly shows signs of a prosperous past, in the many fine Spanish *palazzi* scattered around its interesting old quarter, and in its splendid ecclesiastical architecture, much of it constructed in the local grey-black basalt.

Piazza del Pópolo

A stroll through the old town's streets will at some point take in Orosei's central **Piazza del Pópolo**, the focus of a group of medieval buildings including the church of **San Giácomo**, whose cluster of tiled cupolas and campanile is fronted by a plain white Neoclassical facade at the top of a flight of steps.

Piazza Sas Ánimas and around

From Piazza del Pópolo, take a right turn from Via Nazionale to reach **Piazza Sas Ánimas**, holding the sorely neglected remains of a fourteenth-century castle that was later used as a gaol – hence its name **Castello Prigione Vecchia** (or Sa Prejone Vezza); it's usually open to the public on summer evenings (June–Sept Tues–Sat 8–11pm). Next to it stands the pretty **Chiesa delle Ánime**, constructed in 1718 of rough brick and stonework with a tiled cupola and a handsome portal.

A brief walk from here (and well signposted) lie two more churches worth a glance: **San Gavino**, on the eastern edge of town, and the ruin of **San Sebastiano**, in a cobbled alley draped with bougainvillea on the western side.

Sant'Antonio

Piazza Sant'Antonio • Daily 8am–noon & 4–7pm

Foremost among the monuments in the rest of the town are the church and towers of **Sant'Antonio**, entered through an ogival arch at the bottom of Via Caduti in Guerra.

The church precincts include a cobbled space surrounded by *muristenes*, temporary pilgrims' dwellings (known as *cumbessias* elsewhere in Sardinia), in the centre of which stands a Pisan tower converted into a private residence.

ARRIVAL AND INFORMATION OROSEI

By bus Orosei has daily ARST-run bus connections with Nuoro and some other centres, plus a summer service along the coast operated by Deplano.
Destinations Dorgali (1–3 daily; 30min); Nuoro (Mon–Sat 7–9 daily, Sun 1–2 daily; 1hr); Olbia (2 daily; 2hr 35min); Posada (2 daily; 1hr 20min).

Tourist office The Pro Loco is on Piazza del Pópolo (Easter–Sept Mon–Sat 9am–1pm & 4–8pm; ☎ 0784 999 242, ⓦ oroseiturismo.it). There's also a tourist desk in the town hall in Via Santa Veronica (Mon 9am–2pm & 3.30–6.30pm, Tues–Fri 9am–2pm). Pick up walking itineraries of the old quarter or ask about guided tours at either.

ACCOMMODATION AND EATING

Cala Ginepro Viale Cala Ginepro ☎ 0784 91 017, ⓦ campingcalaginepro.net. Most of the local campsites are north of Orosei, including this well-organized place, right on the sea with its own private beach. You can rent caravans (€41), two-bed *"tuculs"* (cabins, €53) and four-person bungalows (€105). Closed Nov–March. Pitches €36.50

★**Mannois** Via Angioy 32 ☎ 0784 991 040, ⓦ mannois .it. This boutique-style *albergo diffuso* has rooms spread between different buildings in Orosei's historic centre. It's all immaculately designed, and the main building has a courtyard garden where guests take breakfast. There's a

good rooftop restaurant too, a bus service to a private beach and free bikes for guests. €120

Su Barchile Via Mannu ☎ 0784 98 879, ⓦ subarchile.it. Family-run three-star with comfortable rooms, plus home-made pastries and jam for breakfast. The long-established and highly regarded restaurant (open to all) offers a small but delectable menu of Sard specialities such as *makkarrones de busa* and *porcetto* cooked in myrtle, plus a formidable array of seafood dishes as well as pizzas (including gluten-free), and it has a rooftop terrace. Most dishes cost €11–14. Easter–Oct daily 12.30–3pm & 7.30–10.30pm; Oct–Easter closed Mon. €90

Dorgali and around

Centre of a region renowned for its **Cannonau** wines, the small inland town of **DORGALI** has also established a reputation for its craftwork. Apart from a couple of significant attractions in the neighbourhood, the **handicrafts shops** are the main reason to stop here, though you could also visit the town's small **archeological museum**.

Museo Archeologico

Via Lamármora • Daily 9.30am–1pm & 3.30–6pm, or 4–7pm June–Aug • €3 • ☎ 349 442 5552

Below the school on the corner of Via Vittorio Emanuele, Dorgali's **Museo Archeologico** has a low-key collection of relics and minerals unearthed in the area, displayed in three rooms. Finds from the Neolithic age are contained in the first of these; the second shows nuraghic items, many of them found at the site of Serra Orrios (see p.298); the third concentrates on the Punic, Roman and medieval periods, including a good collection of coins, and amphoras and anchors retrieved from the sea.

The Grotta di Ispinígoli

SS125, 5km north of Dorgali • Daily: April, May & Oct 10am–1pm & 3–6pm; June & Sept 10am–6pm; July & Aug 10am–7pm; Nov–March tours at noon & 3pm; last tour 1hr before closing • €7.50 • ☎ 0784 96 243 (Pro Loco, Dorgali)

The **Grotta di Ispinígoli**, signposted off the main road between Dorgali and Orosei, is a deep cave containing a mind-bending collection of stalagmites and stalactites, dominated by one 38m column that appears to hold the whole lot up. Traces of some distant human presence have been found within – jewels, amphorae and bones, probably dating from Phoenician times. The local name for the cave, Abisso delle Vérgini ("Abyss of the Virgins"), probably owes more to popular imagination than to fact, but it is likely that such an impressive natural phenomenon would have attracted some kind of religious ritual. The 50min **tours** inside the grotto leave daily on the hour (in winter twice daily).

8

Serra Orrios

Off SS129, 10km northwest of Dorgali • Daily: April–June & Sept 9am–1pm & 3–6pm; July & Aug 9am–1pm & 4–8pm; Oct–March
9am–1pm & 2–5pm; last tour 1hr before closing • €6 • ☎ 338 834 1618

Though lacking a *nuraghe* as such, the nuraghic site of **Serra Orrios** makes a fascinating
stop, vividly illustrating how a typical community of that era was organized. The
remains of the village lie on a small plain surrounded by olive trees and overlooked by
the peaks of Monte Albo to the north, located within a long, walled enclosure at the
end of a 600m track through an olive grove.

Entered through a lintelled portal, the extensive **site** consists chiefly of the closely
packed circular walls of the seventy-odd village buildings, about 2m high and separated
by paths. Among them are two rectangular temples labelled "Tempietto A" and
"Tempietto B", the first of which lies within a round walled area and is thought to have
been used by visiting pilgrims. Tempietto B was probably the villagers' centre of
worship – a long building surrounded by a wall, with a doorway at one end topped by
a curved slab and a low bench running along the inside. All in all, it's an attractive site
to wander around; guides provide a commentary in Italian or English, but are mainly
there to keep you off the walls. Before setting off, it's worth examining the diagram
near the entrance showing how the village must once have appeared. There's a bar and
paninoteca on the site.

The Flumineddu valley

South of Dorgali lies the **Flumineddu valley**, one of Sardinia's last truly untouched
tracts. The SS125 affords bird's-eye views of this majestic mountain landscape, largely
devoid of human life, at the bottom of which lies the Gorropu canyon (see box
opposite). The SS125 continues into the neighbouring Codula di Luna valley at the
Genna Silana pass (1017m), a departure point for walking expeditions in the area.

8

ARRIVAL, INFORMATION AND ACTIVITIES   **DORGALI AND AROUND**

By bus All services to and from Dorgali are operated by
ARST, apart from a daily summer service to Olbia, Cala
Gonone and places between run by Deplano.
Destinations Baunei (1–2 daily; 1hr 15min); Cala
Gonone (Mon–Sat 7–14 daily, Sun 4–11 daily; 20min); Nuoro
(Mon–Sat 7–9 daily, Sun 3–5 daily; 45min); Oliena (Mon–
Sat 7–9 daily, Sun 3–5 daily; 25min); Orosei (Mon–Sat 2–3
daily, Sun 1 daily; 25min).
Excursions One of the best local outfits for trekking and

tours around the local archeological sites is Ghivine, Via
Lamármora 31 (☎349 442 5552 or ☎338 834 1618,
ⓦghivine.com), staffed by friendly young guides and
specializing in walking, caving and climbing trips, with
accommodation options. Dorgali's Pro Loco has a complete
list of excursion companies.
Tourist office Pro Loco Via Lamármora 108 (Mon–Fri
9am–1pm & 4–7pm; ☎0784 96 243, ⓦdorgali.it).

ACCOMMODATION AND EATING

S'Adde Via Concordia 38 ☎0784 94 412, ⓦhotelsadde
.it. Fairly basic lodging, very central but in a peaceful spot
signposted above Via Lamármora. The en-suite rooms
come with a/c, and some have fridges. The restaurant is
worth visiting for its homely and cheap country dishes
(starters are €8–10, mains €8–16), including gluten-free
options. Aug & Sept daily 12.30–2pm & 7.30–11pm; Oct
–July closed Mon. **€70**
★**Sant'Elene** Località Sant'Elene ☎0784 94 572,
ⓦalbergosantelene.net. Set on a quiet and secluded

hillside 3km south of town (and invisible until you reach
it), this classic mountain hotel has good-sized rooms –
though few with views. It's a good choice for anyone
tackling the Gola di Gorropu, located close to the start of
the route. There's a great restaurant here, too, where you
can dine on authentic Sardinian specialities and enjoy
the grand panorama from its veranda. A three-course
meal should cost €20–30. The hotel is also signposted
off the SS125. Daily 12.30–3pm & 7–10.30pm; may
close Mon. **€70**

Cala Gonone and around

A couple of kilometres south out of Dorgali, a left turn from the SS125 brings you
into a tunnel through the mountain wall, from which the road corkscrews down

A HIKE IN THE GOLA DI GORROPU

The **Gola di Gorropu** (Gorropu, or Gorruppu, canyon), one of the deepest and most spectacular in southern Europe, with walls reaching over 200m high, can be walked for much of its length between April and October. If you're considering it, however, you should find out the state of the **Flumineddu river** which bores through it; large sections of the gorge may be flooded, requiring specialist skills and even dinghies to negotiate. When conditions are good, there's little possibility of losing the way, but the walk can also be undertaken accompanied by a guide. The entire excursion will take a minimum of three hours, its length depending on how far up the gorge you want – or are able – to reach.

Unless you're with a guide, you'll need your own transport to get to the **start of the trail**, which can be approached from **Dorgali**. From the Circonvallazione that bypasses the town to the west, take the side road signposted for the *Sant'Elene* hotel (southwards). Past the hotel, take the left-hand turn, slightly descending, then take the middle road at the subsequent three-way fork. About 5km from Dorgali, you'll pass the Chiesa di Buoncammino on your right. After a farther 4km, the unsurfaced road becomes increasingly bumpy before crossing the Flumineddu river. Take the left turn, signposted Gorropu, and you'll soon come to the **car park** and seasonal **ticket office** (tickets are €5), beyond which you must proceed on foot.

This point can also be reached from Campo Base Gorropu, a visitor centre 12km south of the Cala Gonone turning on the SS125, though this involves a very steep descent on foot taking around one and a half hours. Alternatively, you might choose to make use of a jeep service (April to mid-Nov €10 one-way; ☎389 420 8595).

Following the **track** southwards, parallel to the river, take the left-hand fork after a few minutes, which dips before beginning a gentle ascent. Passing in and out of woods, and alongside copious growths of lentisk, myrtle, wild cyclamen and other plants of the *macchia*, the path – occasionally indicated by green arrows – follows the course of the river on its left. About one and a half hours after setting out, you'll finally descend to the **river**. This idyllic spot, with glades of oleander shading the rocky pools on all sides and the sheer walls of the gorge rising dramatically above, makes a good place for a pause. There's usually water here, even in high summer, and in winter it can be torrential.

To enter the *gola*, remain on the right side of the river, keeping as high as possible. The path will eventually become clear and once you're in the canyon there's no straying from the route, with high rock walls on either side. Much of the time it's simply a matter of negotiating the boulders, usually not unduly difficult, though some parts are challenging and demand concentration. Where **rockfalls** have blocked the way, look out for lengths of rope secured to the rock, which you can use to haul yourself up; these are occasionally marked with green paint.

How far you go, of course, depends on your perseverance and stamina. The total walkable length is about 8km, though you'd need **equipment** and a **guide** to go so far, and with expert help you could even reach the village of Urzulei and beyond. Even for shorter distances, some form of head protection is advisable. The biggest danger is of slipping on the smooth surfaces of the rocks – particularly when these are wet – so don't attempt the walk in shoes lacking a secure grip and ankle support.

8

through groves of cork to an azure bay. Beautifully sited at the base of the 900m-high mountains, **CALA GONONE** was once a tiny settlement huddled around a harbour, until recently accessible only by boat. Now hotels and villas dominate the scene, though these have not entirely spoilt the sense of isolation, even in summer, when the place positively hums. Abundant activities are offered, most popular of which are the numerous boat excursions to the various secluded coves up and down the coast.

The port and town beach

Cala Gonone's sheltered **port** is crowded with pleasure craft, with kiosks on the quay hawking boat tours to the beaches (see box, p.300) and dinghy rentals. Backed by a busy beach promenade, a curve of sand extends south from here, culminating in a full-sized **beach** at the end of Lungomare Palmasera.

Beaches out of town

The town beach is convenient and will do for a dip, but it's a poor substitute for the beaches farther afield, most easily reached on boat tours from the port. However, **south of Cala Gonone**, you can also reach one of the best beaches on foot from Cala Fuili, the rocky cove at the southern end of Viale del Bue Marino. From here, a rough track leads parallel to the sea for nearly 4km to **Cala Luna**. It's fairly level, but very stony, so you need more than sandals (and there's no water along the way, so carry at least a litre). The path is signposted with painted green arrows and white arrows chiselled into the rock. The walk might take one and a half to two hours – if you don't feel like returning on foot, jump on one of the boats shuttling back to the port (frequent in summer; €9).

North of town, a car or bike would do for the pair of idyllic swimming places at **Spiaggia Cartoe** and **Spiaggia Osalla**, reachable from the narrow road dug out of the mountains that eventually connects up with the SS125 (and also from Orosei). Osalla is about twenty minutes by car, Cartoe a little less.

Nuraghe Mannu

Località Nuraghe Mannu • Daily: March & Oct 10am–1pm & 3–6pm; April 9am–noon & 3–6pm; May & June 9am–noon & 4–7pm; July & Aug 9am–noon & 5–8pm; Sept 9am–noon & 4–6pm; last entry 1hr before closing • €3

Signposted left off the main road leading up to the SS125, **Nuraghe Mannu** lies at the end of a 3km rocky track (not recommended for laden cars). On a ledge over the bay, with a ravine on one side, it's a marvellous site, one of Sardinia's few nuraghic structures to be built right by the sea, and affording magnificent views. The topless main tower has steps off to one side, and niches in the central chamber. All around lie the traces of dwellings, some paved, and mostly dating from much later times – there's evidence that the site was occupied as recently as the Middle Ages.

Acquario

Via la Favorita • March Sat & Sun 10am–6pm; April–July & Sept daily 10am–6pm; Aug daily 10am–8pm; Oct Tues–Sun 10am–6pm; last entry 1hr before closing • €10 • ☎0784 920 052, ⓦ acquariocalagonone.it

A kilometre south of the centre, Cala Gonone's modern, well-designed **Acquario** is probably not what you came here to see, but it makes a good, family-friendly change

---

BOAT TRIPS FROM CALA GONONE

From Cala Gonone's port, numerous operators offer a range of **boat trips** to the truly spectacular swimming spots dotted along the cliffy coast hereabouts. Between April and October, the most popular trips ply between the town and the remote inlets of **Cala Luna** and **Cala Sisine**, respectively 6km and 11km to the south. Return tickets for these cost €20–35, and departures are frequent. There are plenty of even more secluded beaches to visit, while other cruises explore some of the area's deep grottoes. The most famous of these is the **Grotta del Bue Marino** (€20 return, including the entrance charge of €8), which counts among Sardinia's most spectacular caves. The luminescent gallery is filled with remarkable natural sculptures resembling organ pipes, wedding cakes and even human heads – one of them is known as "Dante" for its fondly imagined likeness of the poet. The grotto is also famous as it was the final refuge in Italian waters of the Mediterranean monk seal, or "sea ox" (*bue marino*); the last of these creatures disappeared some years ago. **Night visits** are also occasionally available.

A **mini-cruise** of the coast – typically heading south for around two hours as far as Arco di Goloritzè or Spiaggia Aguglia for diving and swimming, then returning with stops at Cala Mariolu, Cala Biriola, Cala Sisine, Cala Luna and Grotta del Bue Marino – can also be booked from the quayside agencies, for around €36. Boats depart from 9am, returning at around 6pm. Note that food and refreshments are not available at the remoter beaches, so you should carry your own water at least. General **information** on all of these can be obtained from the Nuovo Consorzio Trasporti Maríttimi at the port (☎0784 93 305, ⓦ calagononecrociere.it). For longer trips, book the day before, and take a sunhat and water.

from the beach. In 24 tanks, the aquarium concentrates on sea life – fauna and flora – from the Golfo di Orosei, but includes a few tropical species too. You'll see dogfish sharks, as well as some of the fish (snapper, grouper and mullet) you might find on a local menu. Feeding time is at 3pm.

ARRIVAL AND DEPARTURE   CALA GONONE

By bus ARST buses pull up above the centre on Viale Bue Marino – handy for those with hotels nearby or camping – and again nearer the port on Via Cala Luna. Seasonal Deplano buses connecting Cala Gonone with Dorgali and Olbia airport also stop on Viale Bue Marino.

Destinations Dorgali (Mon–Sat 7–14 daily, Sun 4–11 daily; 20min); Nuoro (Mon–Sat 5–7 daily, Sun 2–4 daily; 1hr 10min); Olbia airport (June–Sept 4 daily; 2hr 15min); Oliena (Mon–Sat 5–7 daily, Sun 2–4 daily; 50min).

INFORMATION AND ACTIVITIES

Tourist office Viale Bue Marino, opposite bus stop (daily: April & Oct 9am–1pm; May–Sept 9am–1pm & 3–7pm; ☎0784 93 696, ⓦdorgali.it). See also ⓦcalagonone.com.
Bike and boat rental Bikes, scooters, kayaks and dinghies can be rented from Prima Sardegna, Lungomare Palmasera 32 (☎0784 93 367, ⓦprimasardegna.com); bikes are around €24/24hr, scooters €48/24hr and single kayaks €30/24hr. Kiosks at the port also offer boat rental (see the renting consortium's website ⓦcalagononenoleggio.com): a simple motor-driven dinghy (*gommone*) in high season costs around €120/day; fuel costs an extra €30–40.

Diving Argonauta Diving Club, Via dei Lecci 10 (☎0784 93 046, ⓦargonauta.it) and Dimensione Mare, Via Colombo 8 (☎338 825 1040, ⓦdimensionemarediving .com) arrange dives and snorkelling tours for all abilities, with equipment to rent. Two dives including all the gear will cost around €90.
Excursions Prima Sardegna (see above) offers a drop-off/pick-up service for hikers, and also – together with Dolmen, Via Vasco da Gama 18 (☎347 669 8192, ⓦsardegnadascoprire.it) and Centro Escursioni in Sardegna, Viale Colombo (☎349 672 7750, ⓦescursioniinsardegna.com) – organizes walking, biking, 4WD and boat excursions.

ACCOMMODATION

Cala Luna Lungomare Palmasera ☎0784 93 133, ⓦhotelcalaluna.net. At the southern end of the seaside strip, this bougainvillea-covered holiday hotel has direct access to the beach, modern art on the walls and a great roof terrace, where the restaurant is located. The comfortable rooms have satellite TV, and some (costing €10–20 extra) have balconies overlooking the sea. Closed Nov–March. **€115**
★**Hotel Pop** Piazza del Porto ☎0784 93 185, ⓦhotelpop.it. Right in front of the port, this hotel, open all year, has clean rooms of varying sizes with a/c and small balconies (most rooms have sea views). There's a lively restaurant *Al Porto* (see p.302), staff are friendly, and they offer good deals for boat excursions. **€98**
Ichnos Via delle Conchiglie 5 ☎328 001 4014, ⓦbbichnos.com. Unspectacular but central and good-value B&B just 30m from the lungomare. The three rooms are very simple and a bit dark, but they have a/c and separate entrances from the shady patio where breakfast is served. Closed Nov–March. No credit cards. **€70**
La Favorita Lungomare Palmasera 30 ☎0784 93 169, ⓦlafavoritahotel.com. On the seafront, this budget two-star hotel offers great value, with functional, spacious rooms – some of them with small balconies – though the cheapest ones have no a/c or sea view. It has an excellent restaurant too. Closed Nov to late April. **€60**
★**L'Oasi** Via Lorca ☎0784 93 111, ⓦloasihotel.it. This

small, modern *pensione* occupies a lofty site above the town, with breathtaking views and an air of pampered seclusion. Spacious rooms, landscaped gardens and fine dining are added advantages. Make sure you get a sea-facing room. The port is just 5min down along a steep short cut (15min on the return climb). Closed Nov–Easter. **€105**
Miramare Piazza Giardini 12 ☎0784 93 140, ⓦhtlmiramare.it. Central, modern hotel, offering mainly spacious rooms, the best having large sea-facing balconies. There's a sun terrace with a great view and a pizzeria/restaurant with outdoor seating. Service is professional and friendly. Closed mid-Oct to March. **€105**
Piccolo Viale Colombo 32 ☎0784 93 235, ⓦpiccolohotelcalagonone.it. The resort's cheapest hotel is centrally located about 50m from the port. Rooms are fairly basic, all with small en-suite bathrooms, and some have balconies and sea views. Closed Nov–Easter. **€60**

CAMPSITE

Camping Cala Gonone Via Collodi ☎0784 93 476, ⓦcalagononecamping.com. This campsite lies in the pinewoods above the resort, a brief walk from the bus stop and tourist office, and 300m up from the seafront. Chalets (€70) can be rented, and a pool and tennis court are available in summer, but it can get very crowded. Closed Dec–March. Pitches **€30**

8

EATING AND DRINKING

Al Porto Piazza del Porto ☎ 0784 93 185. This restaurant attached to the *Hotel Pop* has all-day service, tables outside and various good-value set-price menus including for vegetarians and children. À la carte, first courses cost around €14 (try the *ravioli di mare*), second courses about €18. It gets packed out in summer. Daily noon–11pm.

Bue Marino Via Vespucci 8 ☎ 0784 920 078. On a hotel rooftop above the port, you can soak up the wonderful view while enjoying fresh fish and meat dishes (around €14 for firsts, €15–18 for mains), pizzas and a good wine list. The restaurant also has an off-street terrace which serves snacks at lunchtime and cocktails in the evening – all very romantic. April to mid-Oct daily 12.30–2.30pm & 6.30–11pm.

Il Cormorano Via Vespucci ☎ 0784 93 601. Easy-going trattoria opposite the port with tasty dishes, moderate prices and a terrace for dining alfresco. Sample the *tagliolini della casa* – fresh pasta with artichokes, tomatoes, shrimps and *calamari* – or one of the various salads on offer. The tourist menu is €24, otherwise starters are €8–14, mains €14–18. April, May & Oct Tues–Sun noon–2.30pm & 6.30–11pm; June–Sept daily.

★ **Il Pescatore** Via Acquadolce 7 ☎ 0784 93 174. Gourmet seafood parlour on the seafront, a bit pricey but worth it for the lobster pasta, linguine and clams, and grilled fish platters. You should book ahead or arrive early for one of the tables overlooking the sea, otherwise there's usually plenty of space available inside. Tourist menus are €28 and €30; à la carte reckon on €45–60 for a full meal. April–Oct daily noon–3pm & 7.30–11pm.

La Poltrona Località Iscrittiorè ☎ 0784 93 414 or ☎ 328 278 9578. This place specializes in "zero-kilometre" ingredients (ie strictly local and seasonal), but its marvellous terrace and wonderful views also pull in the punters. The pizzas, fresh pasta and meat and fish dishes are all first class – expect to pay €25–35 for a full meal. It's on the main road 2km from the port, by the Centro Sportivo – call ahead to arrange a lift. April–Dec daily 6.30–11pm, also 12.30–3pm Sat & Sun & daily in July & Aug .

★ **Nuraghe Mannu** Lungomare Palmasera 34 ☎ 0784 93 264 or ☎ 328 868 5824, ⓦ agriturismonuraghemannu.com. Aim for the *nuraghe* of the same name, then keep going along a dirt track to find this *agriturismo* high above the coast, with wonderful views from its outdoor tables. The set-price meals (€25 or €15 for guests) include multiple servings of *antipasti*, fresh pasta and local meats. Always call ahead. Rooms cost €68 and camping pitches €24. No credit cards. April to mid-Oct daily noon–2.30pm & 7.30–10.30pm.

Roadhouse Blues Lungomare Palmasera 28 ☎ 0784 93 187. Overlooking the sea, this bar-restaurant has a rock'n'roll theme, with "Led Zeppelin" and "Hendrix" among the pizzas listed (around €8). The menu extends from burgers to red snapper Sardinian style, and cocktails and beers are served until late. March–mid-Nov daily 7am–midnight.

Su Recreu Piazza Andrea Doria ☎ 0784 93 135. Up from the port, this café-bar serves the town's best ice cream as well as smoothies, sandwiches, salads and grills till late (tourist menus are €20). There's live salsa music on summer evenings from 9.30pm. Mid-March to early Nov daily 11am–late.

DIRECTORY

Internet *Iris Café*, Viale Colombo, has free wi-fi and a terminal for €2.50/30min (March–Oct daily 7am–midnight, closes 2am in summer).

Laundry Via Cala Luna (always open); €5/wash (soap included) and €5/drying.

Pharmacy Viale Colombo 36 (June–Sept daily 9am–1pm & 4.30–8pm; Oct–May closed Sun).

Post office Via Cala Luna (Mon–Fri 8.20am–1.45pm, Sat 8.20am–12.45pm).

Supermarket Zizzone/ISA, Via Vasco de Gama (Mon–Sat 7.30am–1pm & 4.30–8pm, Sun 8am–1pm).

Baunei

The mountain route following the SS125 south is undeniably exhilarating but can be exhausting too. But the village of **BAUNEI**, 48km south of the Cala Gonone turn-off, provides welcome bars for refreshment, with tables perched right on the edge of the valley. A typical village of the area, but one overlooked by most tourists passing through, Baunei makes a useful base for excursions to the **Altipiano Su Golgo**, a wild, rocky and highly scenic terrain to the north that offers superb hiking and climbing opportunities as well as holding nuraghic remains. Reached by a steep descent from Su Golgo (or by boat), the beach at **Cala Goloritzè** is dominated by a dramatic pinnacle of rock ("Aguglia") and has a natural arch. To explore the area, follow the signs to Golgo and Supramonte di Baunei off the main road through the village; guide services are recommended.

ARRIVAL AND ACTIVITIES
BAUNEI

By bus Baunei is a stop on all bus routes between Tortolì and Dorgali.

Destinations Dorgali (1–2 daily; 1hr 15min); Nuoro (Mon–Sat 1 daily; 2hr); Santa Maria Navarrese (Mon–Sat every 30min–1hr, Sun 5 daily; 20min); Tortolì (Mon–Sat 1 daily; 35min).

Excursions Cooperativa Goloritzè (☎368 702 8980, ⩎coopgoloritze.com) leads guided walks and 4WD excursions in the area. In summer you can also board a tourist train that gives you a taster of Su Golgo, departing from Baunei (☎389 064 3429, ⩎treninosupramonte.it; prices vary, around €20 for over 3hr).

ACCOMMODATION

★**Dommu Agostina** Via SS Mártiri 19 ☎327 334 3346, ⩎dommuagostina.it. This B&B lies both in the centre of the village (near the church) and on its edge, grappled onto the steep side of the valley and enjoying unforgettable vistas across to the sea. The renovated house has four simply but tastefully designed rooms (one with bunks) with modern bathrooms. Breakfast on the terrace is a real treat. No credit cards. Closed Nov–March. **€80**

Santa Maria Navarrese

A turning off the SS125 some 5km south of Baunei descends sharply to the sea and the minor resort of **SANTA MARIA NAVARRESE**. A calm, picturesque place for ten months of the year, backed by greenery and set against a mountain backdrop, it gets extremely busy in high summer when the nearby beaches draw thousands of visitors. The main **beach** is right in front of the town, facing two isles punctuating the horizon, with umbrellas and deckchairs available for around €12 per day. Many, however, prefer the broader expanses south of town, backed by pines and embellished by reddish granite outcrops, for example **Lido delle Rose**.

From the bijou **port** north of the centre, at the end of Via Lungomare, boat **excursions** around the Golfo di Orosei depart in summer (€35–45/person).

ARRIVAL AND INFORMATION
SANTA MARIA NAVARRESE

By bus Santa Maria has frequent ARST connections with Tortolì, the main transport hub for the region.

Destinations Baunei (Mon–Sat every 30min–1hr, Sun 4 daily; 20min); Dorgali (1–2 daily; 1hr 35min); Nuoro (Mon–Sat 1 daily; 2hr 25min); Tortolì (Mon–Sat every 30min–1hr, Sun 6 daily; 15min).

Tourist office Piazza Principessa di Navarra has a Pro Loco in the Comune (May–Sept Mon–Sat 8am–2pm & 3–6pm; ☎348 253 3222, ⩎turismo.ogliastra.it). In summer, the office transfers to a kiosk on the seafront, in front of the piazza (July–Sept daily 9am–10pm).

ACCOMMODATION AND EATING

Il Pozzo Viale Plammas ☎0782 615 039. You'll find a good range of pizzas here, as well as a regular seafood menu that includes such local dishes as fish ravioli (€9) and *seppie arrosto* (roast cuttlefish, €11). In summer, you can eat on the veranda across the road. Easter–Nov daily noon–3pm & 6.30–11pm; Nov–Easter closed Mon.

Nicoletta Via Lungomare 1 ☎0782 614 045, ⩎hotelnicoletta.info. Stylish and select hotel in the resort's centre, close to the beach. There are antique trimmings in its bright, clean rooms, and breakfast can be taken on a patio. Closed Nov–April. **€110**

★**Ostello Bellavista** Via Pedralonga ☎0782 614 039, ⩎ostelloinogliastra.com. Though it's officially a hostel, this is more like an informal lodge, where each of the clean white doubles has a bathroom and a sea view (rooms with balconies cost €6–12 extra). Its biggest selling point is its wonderful position, elevated above Santa Maria's port. Buffet breakfasts are good and evening meals are available for €18. **€74**

Arbatax and around

Other than its docks from which ferries ply to and from Genoa and Civitavecchia, **ARBATAX** amounts to little more than a few bars and restaurants, though it can boast some of the striking red-tinted rocks for which the area is famous in a cove just south of the port. The town is also within reach of some alluring **beaches**, the best ones south of the centre in the **Porto Frailis** district, home to a cluster of hotels and restaurants, and there's another series of broad sand and rock beaches at **Lido Orri**, 4km farther down, accessible from the SS125. At both, all the usual facilities are available in summer – bars, deckchairs and watersports – while **boat tours** depart from Arbatax's quayside for the premier beaches of the Golfo di Orosei to the north, including the sublime sandy cove of **Cala Mariolu** and the Grotta del Bue Marino (see box, p.300).

Five kilometres inland, at the end of the long Via Virgilio, the unremarkable town of **TORTOLÌ** is one of the two capitals of Ogliastra province (along with Lanusei), worth a stop mainly for its bus connections, banks and shops.

ARRIVAL AND DEPARTURE

By ferry Tirrenia (☎ 892 123, ⓦ tirrenia.it) runs a regular ferry service to the mainland from Arbatax, sometimes via Cágliari or Olbia. The Tirrenia office is near the port at Via Venezia 10 (☎ 0782 667 067). A general travel agent operates out of the same office.

Destinations Civitavecchia (2 weekly; 10hr); Genoa (late July to early Sept 2 weekly; 17hr 30min).

By train Between mid-June and mid-Sept, the narrow-gauge Trenino Verde line follows a scenic inland route to Lanusei and Mandas, leaving Arbatax at 8am (daily except Tues); the full journey from the coast to Mandas takes 12hr, including a break of 6hr 40min at Sádali – but note that there are no onward connections from Mandas to Cagliari on the same day. Arbatax Statzione is by the port, where the agency InfoPoint Arbatax on Via Lungomare (☎ 339

ARBATAX AND AROUND

899 2939, ⓦ infopointsardegna.it) offers a day package consisting of a return journey to Sádali, lunch, a walk around the old centre and rural excursions to the Is Janas grottoes and local charcoal pits (€60).

Destinations Lanusei (1hr 20min); Sádali (3hr 35min); Tortolì (10min).

By bus Buses to Santa Maria Navarrese, Cágliari and Nuoro leave from Tortolì, connected to Arbatax by local buses (see below).

Destinations from Tortolì Arbatax (every 30min–1hr; 10–25min); Cágliari (2–4 daily; 3hr 10min); Dorgali (1–2 daily; 1hr 50min); Lanusei (Mon–Sat 7–9 daily, Sun 3 daily; 40min); Nuoro (1–2 daily; 2hr–2hr 40min); Santa Maria Navarrese (Mon–Sat every 30min–1hr, Sun 5 daily; 15min).

GETTING AROUND

By car Local rental companies include Europcar at Via Tirso 37, Tortolì (☎ 0782 620 090, ⓦ europcar.it).

By bus Without your own vehicle, you can make use of the hourly local bus service (☎ 0782 623 622, ⓦ puscedduviaggi.it) that links Arbatax, Tortolì and Porto Frailis (not Sun). Between mid-June and mid-Sept there's

also a daily service connecting all three places with Lido Orrì. Buses stop almost opposite the Tirrenia office on the road to the port (one-way tickets €1 from the nearby bar), and at the port. The last service is at 9pm (midnight June–Sept).

ACCOMMODATION

Entula Via Sindaco Lorrai 2, Porto Frailis ☎ 0782 667 811 or ☎ 329 348 1855, ⓦ entula.com. Modern B&B 600m from the beach and close to good restaurants, with spacious a/c rooms and a grassy garden. Apartments are also available. No credit cards. Closed Dec & Jan. €55

Telis Porto Frailis ☎ 0782 667 140, ⓦ www .campingtelis.com. Close to the beach and shaded by eucalyptus and mimosa trees, this campsite has efficient,

modern facilities (including two pools). It also offers bungalows (€106) and caravans (€96) to rent. Pitches €35

Vecchio Mulino Via Parigi, Porto Frailis ☎ 0782 664 041, ⓦ hotelilvecchiomulino.it. This small hotel set amid trees and plants has a calm, rustic feel, solidly furnished rooms and good breakfasts. Family rooms are also available. It's off Viale Europa, about a kilometre from the beach. €90

EATING

Il Faro Porto Frailis ☎ 0782 667 499. There are a few restaurants in Arbatax itself, but you're better off heading to this place by the beach, offering a good choice of grilled fish and a lively atmosphere. Two courses will cost €20–30. May–Sept daily 12.30–2.30pm & 7.30–10.30pm; Oct–April Tues–Sun 12.30–2.15pm & 7.15–10pm.

La Baia Via dei Portoghesi, Porto Frailis ☎ 0782 667

808. In a backstreet a few minutes from the beach, this trattoria has three dining areas including a terrace, but still gets very crowded. The menu features delicious *antipasti*, including *polpette di pesce* (fish balls), and crusty pizzas in two sizes. Starters cost €9–12, mains €12–15. April–Oct daily 12.30–3pm & 7.30–11pm; Nov–March Sat & Sun noon–2.30pm & 7.30–10.30pm.

Lanusei and around

To sample the more traditional culture of the mountainous interior of Ogliastra province, it's only necessary to take a 25-minute drive or bus ride west out of Tortolì up the squiggly SS198 to **LANUSEI**, an attractive mountain village (590m) with a lively old centre. There are good walks in the area, the woods, rivers and lakes offering a cool respite from the coastal heat. Six kilometres west on the SS198, the **Parco Archeologico Selene** holds the remains of a nuraghic village and burial site amid a thick forest of holm oaks and chestnuts at an altitude of 960m.

ARRIVAL AND DEPARTURE   LANUSEI

By train Lanusei is a stop on the summer-only Arbatax–Sádali line, the station only minutes away from the centre. All services run once daily except Tues from mid-June to mid-Sept only.
Destinations Arbatax (1hr 5min); Sádali (2hr 15min);

Tortolì (55min).
By bus by ARST buses connect the village with Nuoro (1 daily; 1hr 15min) and Tortolì (Mon–Sat 8–9 daily, Sun 3 daily; 40min). There's a stop in Piazza Marcia.

ACCOMMODATION AND EATING

Da Giancarlo Via dei Ciclamini 34 ☎ 0782 40 428. Although it can be hard to find (take the Arzana road north and look for signs), this simple place makes a welcome stop for a lunch or dinner of typical Ogliastra dishes. Set-price menus are €25 (seafood) and €20 (meat), and there are pizzas in the evening. Tues–Sun noon–3pm & 7–11pm.

★ **La Nuova Luna** Via Indipendenza ☎ 0782 41 051, ⓦ lanuovaluna.it. On a narrow lane off the main Via Umberto I, this excellent hostel has beds in modern, clean rooms, and a large common area with a gigantic fireplace. There's a bar, kitchen and washing machines, and the friendly staff have heaps of information on the area. Oct–March groups only. Dorms €15, doubles €35

8

ROMAN REMAINS, NORA

Contexts

History

Sardinia's position at the centre of the Mediterranean has ensured that for most of its history it has been subject both to the great power struggles which convulsed this inland sea and prey to pirates for whom the island's exposed shores were an irresistible target. Only in remote prehistory did the island appear to enjoy relative freedom from external interference.

Prehistoric times

No one can say where the first Sards came from, though rival legends suggest they were the followers of Sardus, son of Heracles, or the descendants of the Libyan Shardana people. The earliest phase of the island's development is also the most intriguing, with mysterious remnants still dotting the landscape. Though recent discoveries indicate the presence of communities in the Paleolithic era, the first traces of human settlement go back to before 6000 BC, when a hunting and pastoral society lived in grottoes, creating tools, weapons of flint and obsidian, and crudely decorated ceramic bowls.

The Bonu Ighinu, Ozieri and Bonnanaro cultures

In the fourth millennium BC, a more advanced culture appeared, called **Bonu Ighinu** after the grotto 11km northwest of Bonorva where their most significant remains have been found. The people of this society seem to have inhabited villages of huts and practised more advanced systems of agriculture. Finds show that they had trading links with Corsica, southern Italy and the south of France, while statuettes suggest a cult based on a mother goddess.

Between around 3400 and 2700 BC, Sardinia's **Ozieri culture** achieved dominance in the island (also called the San Michele culture, after the grotto of San Michele at Ozieri, its first important settlement). This was a significantly advanced society of hunters, shepherds and farmers, who worked copper as well as flint, obsidian and ceramics. Their cult of the dead was also much developed; bodies were interred in caves cut into rock that were often decorated and came to be called *domus de janas* ("fairy houses") by later generations. The earliest remains at one of Sardinia's most important sites, the sanctuary of Monte d'Accoddi, near Porto Torres, can be attributed to the Ozieri culture in around 3000 BC.

The **Bonnanaro culture**, which held sway during the first centuries of the second millennium, seems to have attained a lower level of artistic achievement, and has left few surviving fragments.

The nuraghic culture

Sardinia's Bonnanaro culture was overshadowed by the emerging **nuraghic culture**, which has yielded the most ubiquitous and imposing remains of any of Sardinia's historical phases, and which survived until the third century BC or later. The first

3400–2700 BC	1800–900 BC	900–800 BC
The Ozieri (or San Michele) culture holds sway, responsible for the first development of the sanctuary of Monte d'Accoddi.	Sardinia's nuraghic culture flourishes, leaving a legacy of around seven thousand stone towers scattered around the island.	Phoenicians begin trading in Sardinia, establishing colonies and exploiting mineral reserves.

nuraghic phase, between about 1800 and 1500 BC, overlapped in many respects with the preceding cultures, including the use of *domus de janas* and menhirs. The second, lasting until around 1200 BC, saw the development of the **nuraghic towers** and the *tombe dei giganti* – "giants' tombs", or collective burial chambers. During the third phase (1200–900 BC), the nuraghic towers became elaborate complexes sheltering sizeable villages, such as those at Su Nuraxi and Santu Antine, while **sacred wells** indicate the existence of a water cult.

The nuraghic culture reached its apogee between the twelfth and eighth centuries BC, cultivating at home and trading abroad. This was also the last time that the island was free of outside interference. Everything changed, however, when Sardinia became embroiled in the commercial and military rivalries of other Mediterranean powers. The last nuraghic phase is characterized by an increasing engagement with these external forces, even as the indigenous people were producing sophisticated *bronzetti*, bronze statuettes that have provided invaluable insights into **nuraghic society**, suggesting a tribal and highly stratified social organization comprising an aristocracy, priests, warriors, artisans, shepherds and farmers. These and other artefacts reveal the extent of the mercantile network of which Sardinia formed a part, encompassing Italy, North Africa and Spain.

Phoenicians and Carthaginians

From the eastern Mediterranean, **Phoenicians** first began trading in Sardinia around 900 BC, and soon established peaceful commercial bases at Cágliari (Karalis); Bythia and Nora, southwest of Cágliari; Monte Sirai and Sant'Antíoco (Sulki, or Sulcis), farther west; and Tharros, near Oristano. The Phoenicians were also attracted by the island's mineral resources – as was every subsequent group of invaders and settlers.

From the sixth century BC, the main protagonists were the much more warlike **Carthaginians**, whose capital, Carthage, was across the Mediterranean near present-day Tunis, and for whom the island was of crucial strategic importance in their rivalry with the Greek cities of Italy. Intent on drawing Sardinia into their sphere of influence, the Carthaginians took over and expanded the main Phoenician settlements, and almost all traces of the Phoenician presence were eradicated.

The Romans

Carthaginian expansion in Sardinia was arrested by the need to confront the growing power of **Rome**, which in 259 BC turned against Sardinia itself. The Sards – now in league with Carthage – struggled fiercely against the new aggressors, at first with some success, but the inevitable defeat occurred in 232 BC, followed five years later by the establishment of the Roman *provincia* of Sardinia and Corsica.

Resistance continued, however, and towards the end of the **Second Punic War** between Rome and Carthage (218–202 BC), a concerted attempt to shake off the Roman yoke was organized under **Ampsicora**, a Sard of Carthaginian culture who suffered a crushing defeat at Cornus, north of Oristano, in 216 BC. Other revolts followed, including one in 177 BC when twelve thousand of the islanders were slaughtered and many more sent away as slaves to the mainland. The survivors of these rebellions, and

600–500 BC	**227 BC**
The Carthaginians establish a military presence in Sardinia, taking over the Phoenician settlements.	Having overcome the combined Sard and Carthaginian forces, the Romans establish the *provincia* of Sardinia and Corsica.

others who refused to bow to the Romans, fled into the impenetrable central and eastern mountains of the interior, where they retained their independence in an area called Barbaria by the Romans, and known today as Barbagia.

Under **Roman occupation**, Sardinia was bled of its resources – minerals and agricultural produce mainly, especially grain – and heavily taxed, without any great benefit to its people. Although the island was rewarded for supporting Julius Caesar in Rome's civil war of 49–45 BC, little was done over seven centuries to instil Roman values or develop the island.

The attitude of the Romans towards the island was summed up in the use they found for it as a **place of exile** for "undesirable elements", including four thousand Jews sent by Emperor Tiberius, and early Christian subversives, who helped to spread the gospel. Apart from some impressive ruins at Nora and Tharros, there are few **Roman remains** on the island. The most notable are at Porto Torres, seat of an important colony (Turris Libyssonis); the baths at Fordongianus (Forum Traiani), east of Oristano; the Tempio di Antas in the Iglesiente, which shows the integration of Roman and Sardinian cults; and the amphitheatre at Cágliari. Rome's most lasting contribution was perhaps the strong Latin element that can still be heard in the Sard dialect today.

Byzantine rule and the Giudicati

With the eclipse of the Roman Empire in the fifth century AD, Sardinia became vulnerable to barbarian raids and plundering that reached far inland. For a short period the island was held by the Vandals, then after 534 AD, by the **Byzantines**. It was too remote an outpost of Byzantium to benefit greatly, though the island was given some protection from the incursions of Goths and Lombards.

One survival of Byzantine rule was the division of the island into **giudicati**, a system which was to endure right through the Middle Ages. There were four main *giudicati*: Cágliari, Arborea (around Oristano), Torres in the northwest and Gallura in the northeast, each a small kingdom with an elected king – originally a judge, or *giudice*. In practice, however, these were the preserve of local oligarchies, and the island was left to its own devices, increasingly prey to raids from the new **Muslim** empires of North Africa and Spain, which were to continue sporadically from the eighth century for over a thousand years. Fear of death or slavery at the hands of the corsairs was a fact of life in Sardinia throughout this period, and had the long-term effect of depopulating the island's coasts. Another reason for the move inland was the increasing prevalence of **malaria** on the coasts and lowlands, the result of neglected irrigation works, deforestation and the silting-up of rivers. The combination of marauders and malaria led to the gradual abandonment of much crop cultivation in the lowlands in favour of sheep and livestock farming in the safe highland pastures of the interior.

Pisa and Genoa in Sardinia

The Arab threat was not confined to local attacks: larger forces occupied Cágliari in 720 AD and further inroads were made in 752. In 1015 a substantial force from the Arab emirate in Spain landed and threatened to take over the entire island; the pope encouraged the Italian mercantile republics of **Pisa** and **Genoa** to intervene, and

450–534 AD	1015
Following the Roman withdrawal, Sardinia is prey to raids by Vandals and other marauders, and a Byzantine administration is established in Cágliari.	Arab forces attempt to occupy Sardinia, leading to the intervention of the republics of Pisa and Genoa.

together they succeeded in ousting the invading army. The Pisans and Genoans themselves, however, proved harder to dislodge, and from this time on Sardinia was increasingly open to trading and political links with mainland Italy.

The influence of **monastic orders** from Italy and Provence also grew during this period; granted special privileges on the island, they played an important part in restoring decayed irrigation works and industries such as salt extraction. They also influenced artistic and architectural currents: the Benedictine Vittorini, for example, were as instrumental in diffusing Romanesque building styles in the south of Sardinia as the Tuscans and Lombards were in the island's north.

By lending their support in the various conflicts between the *giudicati*, the rival cities of Pisa and Genoa began to take an increasingly active role. The driving forces were **individual families** rather than the cities themselves: the Visconti in Logudoro; the della Gherardesca in Iglésias; the Malaspina in Bosa; and the Doria dynasty with a power base in Castelsardo. In the northern *giudicato* of Torres, the influence of **Pisan merchants** can be seen in a string of churches such as San Gavino in Porto Torres, Santa Trinità di Saccárgia and San Pietro di Sorres (both southeast of Sássari). Farther south, Pisan power centred on Cágliari, where the defences built around that city's citadel still stand, but by the end of the thirteenth century, the balance had swung entirely in the favour of Genoa.

The struggle against Aragon

Around the turn of the fourteenth century, a new player appeared on the scene: the Iberian kingdom of **Aragon**, which had recently taken possession of Sicily. In 1297, Pope Boniface VIII managed to persuade James II to give up the Aragonese claim to Sicily in return for rights over the newly created kingdom of Sardinia and Corsica. The title was a mere formality, however, since Aragon was very far from asserting any control over the island, and the struggle to do so lasted more than a century. The campaign proved easier in the south of the island, with Cágliari taken from the Pisans in 1326; in the north, the biggest obstacle was the Doria family – of whom the king of Aragon was nominally feudal overlord – and there was continual fighting between Aragonese forces and an alliance of Sards, Genoans and the mixed-blood aristocracy.

The islanders' cause was led by the *giudicato* of Arborea, and championed in particular by **Eleonora d'Arborea** (see box, p.143), a warrior queen who granted Sardinia its first written code of laws which remained in force for the next four centuries. Eleonora succeeded in stemming the Aragonese advance, but after her death in 1404 Sardinian resistance crumbled. Following a decisive victory at Sanluri in 1409, the Aragonese finally triumphed.

The Spanish in power

Following the unification of the kingdoms of Aragon and Castile in 1479, Sardinia became a colony of a united Spain. Although this was an unusually peaceful period in the island's history, the three centuries of **Spanish rule** in Sardinia were not accompanied by any significant improvement in the lot of most Sards, and there were few attempts to develop or even maintain the infrastructure. Government was

1326	1392	1410–78
The Aragonese prise Cágliari from the Pisans, a significant step in Spanish efforts to conquer Sardinia.	Eleonora d'Arborea institutes the Carta de Logu, which forms the basis of Sardinia's laws until 1817.	Consolidation of the Aragonese conquest – Sardinia becomes a peripheral part of the Spanish empire.

entrusted to viceroys uninterested in the island's welfare, trading links with the Italian mainland were cut, and Spain's shift of focus to its profitable Atlantic empire left Sardinia on the margins.

The Spanish introduced a **feudal system** under which the land was parcelled up and distributed among Catalan-Aragonese nobles who enjoyed absolute powers within their domains. However, these men rarely lived on the island, and day-to-day governance was left in the hands of local officials. Spanish influence was strongest in the cities, which absorbed elements of Catalan Gothic and later Baroque architecture. On the coasts, the most visible contribution was the series of defensive towers that still line Sardinia's shores, providing at least some warning of attacks from North African corsairs, who remained a constant threat. The Spanish king (and Holy Roman Emperor) **Charles V** attempted to end these destructive assaults by assembling huge fleets in 1535 and 1541, with which he hoped to extirpate the raiders from their lairs in Tunis and Algiers. But these armadas had only short-term success, and Charles and his successor Philip II were too preoccupied with their far-flung empire to devote much time to the island's welfare.

Throughout this period, Sardinia was hard hit by the malaria rife in all but the highest points of the island. In addition to this, plague swept the island in the 1650s, killing up to 25 percent of the population, while the famine of 1680–81 is thought to have accounted for around eighty thousand deaths. More positively, universities were founded in Cágliari in 1626 and Sássari in 1634, encouraging the growth of a professional class.

The Kingdom of Sardinia

As Spain's power declined, events elsewhere in Europe began to impinge on Sardinia. During the War of the Spanish Succession in 1701–13, Cágliari was bombarded by an English fleet in 1708 and briefly occupied. The ensuing negotiations led to the island being ceded first to Austria, then, in 1718, to the Piemontese **House of Savoy**, a duchy on the French-Italian border. The united possessions of Vittorio Amedeo II of Savoy became the new **Kingdom of Sardinia**.

Social unrest

Although Sardinia's Savoy period is associated with the beginnings of reconstruction, reforms did not take place quickly enough to stem the simmering discontent engendered by high expectations. The frustration manifested itself in a variety of forms during the **eighteenth century**. *Banditismo* – the factional fighting, clan warfare, robbery and kidnapping that had always existed in the rural interior – assumed chronic proportions, while the forced adoption of Italian as the language of government alienated an aristocracy for whom Spanish was the mother tongue.

For the majority of Sardinia's population, the chief problems included the low level of **education**, with schools dominated by the Church and illiteracy almost universal; the island's continued vulnerability to seaborne attacks; and Sardinia's very sparse population. The government attempted to solve the last of these by a poorly organized and ultimately unsuccessful attempt to introduce **foreign colonies** to the island. The most deep-rooted cause of Sard hostility to the new ruling elite, however, was the continuing existence of the feudal system.

1626–34	1718	1794–96
Universities are founded in Cágliari and Sássari.	Following the War of the Spanish Succession, the island is ceded to the Piemontese House of Savoy and becomes part of the Kingdom of Sardinia.	Revolts in Cágliari provoke uprisings across the island against the Savoy regime.

Matters came to a head in the wake of the **French Revolution**, when the general turmoil prevailing in Europe exposed the drawbacks inherent in the island's links to the Piedmont regime. The House of Savoy's quarrels became Sardinia's, and in 1793 French troops succeeded in occupying the island of San Pietro, while another force which included the young **Napoleon Bonaparte** was repulsed at La Maddalena, as was a fleet which bombarded Cágliari. Though the Savoy king rewarded his Piemontese officials for their part in the rout, the role of the islanders was unacknowledged. What rankled even more was the refusal of the royal court to respond to a delegation from Sardinia bearing the *Cinque Domande*, or "Five Demands", which called for a full constitutional reform, including the restoration of ancient privileges and the regular convocation of an island parliament.

Between 1794 and 1796 an **insurrection** in Cágliari forced the viceroy and his entourage to take flight, and full-scale revolts subsequently broke out all over Sardinia, which ended with Sássari being taken by the rebels. At their head was **Giovanni Maria Angioy**, an aristocrat whose anti-feudal stance made him popular among the peasants, but whose increasingly radical demands for a Sardinian republic alienated the more moderate elements. In 1796 Angioy was driven out of Sardinia and died in exile in Paris, leaving behind a name that has been given to streets and squares throughout the island. His followers were savagely persecuted by the Piemontese.

The beginnings of reform

The most noteworthy Savoyard kings in the **nineteenth century** were Carlo Felice (1821–31), who did much to modernize the island's infrastructure, not least by building the Carlo Felice highway – today the SS131 – that runs the length of the island from Cágliari to Porto Torres, and Carlo Alberto (1831–49), responsible for the final **abolition of the feudal system** in 1836–43. Although this led to a bitter conflict over the introduction of enclosures to demarcate private land in the mountains – thereby restricting the ancient liberty of shepherds to wander freely in search of fresh pasturage – it was an essential prelude to rural reform.

Unified Italy

The Kingdom of Sardinia came to an end in 1861, when Vittorio Emanuele II, son of Carlo Alberto, became king (1861–78) of the newly unified Italy. The island had played a significant role in the Risorgimento (the struggle for nationhood) by providing a base from which **Giuseppe Garibaldi** embarked on both his major expeditions.

NELSON'S FINEST ISLAND

During the fifteen months he spent hovering around the coasts of Sardinia in his pursuit of the French fleet – an operation that culminated in the Battle of Trafalgar in 1805 – **Admiral Horatio Nelson** expressed an interest in the island as a potential base. "God knows," he wrote in his dispatches home, "if we could possess one island, Sardinia, we should want neither Malta, nor any other: this which is the finest island in the Mediterranean, possesses harbours fit for arsenals, and of a capacity to hold our navy, within 24 hours' sail of Toulon…"

1836–43	1861	1921
Abolition of the feudal system, leading to wide-ranging rural reforms.	Sardinia joins the new Kingdom of Italy.	The Partito Sardo d'Azione is founded to campaign for regional autonomy.

Sardinia's problems entered a new phase. Adjusting to its role as part of a modern nation state became the central theme of the next century or so – some would argue up to and including the present. Matters weren't helped by the fact that colonial attitudes towards the island persisted, while its natural resources were ruthlessly plundered (accounting for much of the deforestation still evident today) and wages remained low. Agriculture also suffered, leading to soaring unemployment, which in turn fuelled widespread banditry. There was little money available to tackle the root causes of the problem, and although there was a degree of political reform, by the end of the nineteenth century voting rights were still only available to less than five percent of the island's population.

Nonetheless, Sardinia contributed notably to both world wars, with the Sássari Brigade in particular achieving lasting distinction during **World War I**, albeit at a heavy cost. The experience of war radicalized many Sards, and elections based on universal suffrage in 1920 and 1921 saw the creation of the **Partito Sardo d'Azione**, or Sardinian Action Party, whose manifesto demanded autonomy.

Fascism and World War II

Ironically, Sardinia had to wait for a ruthless centralizing dictatorship before real changes began to make themselves felt. **Benito Mussolini**, the Italian Fascist leader who came to power in 1922, saw the backward island as fertile ground for his social and economic experiments, particularly in the context of his drive for Italian self-sufficiency. In the 1920s and 1930s the Fascist government initiated a series of schemes which led to genuine improvements: the island's many rivers were harnessed and dammed to provide irrigation and power, land was drained and made fertile, agricultural colonies were set up, and the new towns of Carbónia, Arborea and Fertilia were founded – though the industrial projects were mostly failures. The island suffered badly during **World War II**: in 1943 Cágliari endured some of the heaviest bombing of all Italian cities, with 75 percent of its houses destroyed. Traumatized, the island awoke to a postwar era in which nothing seemed to have changed – once more, it felt itself to be a second-class member of the Italian state, subject to a remote bureaucracy and irrelevant legislation. As before, attempts to force the island to integrate into the new centralized, bureaucratic Italy gave rise to a host of resentments.

An attempt to offset this was made in 1948, when the *regione* of Sardinia was granted **autonomy**, allowing the regional government direct control over such fields as transport, tourism, police, industry and agriculture. Two years later, the central government's fund to speed up the development of the South of Italy, the Cassa per il Mezzogiorno, was extended to Sardinia, and the island began to receive hefty injections of capital investment. Perhaps more significantly, through the intervention of the US Rockefeller Foundation, Sardinia was saturated with enough **DDT** in the years immediately following World War II to rid it once and for all of malaria.

Sardinia today

The success of this combined effort to haul Sardinia up from a peripheral, third-world status is apparent everywhere, and some areas of Sardinian life are as streamlined and

1928	1943	1948
Arborea is built as part of Mussolini's regeneration programme, followed ten years later by Carbónia.	Cágliari suffers intense bombardment during World War II.	Sardinia is granted regional autonomy.

sophisticated as anywhere on the mainland. Visitors to the island today will recognize a piece of Italy – the same shops, cars and language – to the extent that it is growing ever harder to distinguish "the real Sardinia" underneath the Italian gloss.

However, the island's transformation would have taken a different course were it not for two initiatives that had lasting effects on its economy and infrastucture. In 1962, the Italian parliament finally authorized a **programme of industrialization**, which led to the introduction of heavy-duty petrochemical plants completely at odds with the island's traditional activities. In the same year, a consortium of investors led by the Aga Khan began to develop the **Costa Smeralda** as an elite jet-setters' enclave, opening up the tourist industry and giving Sardinia a new role which has been largely embraced by the locals, bringing a degree of wealth to a substantial section of the population.

The awakening of the island's tourist potential has gone hand in hand with a new appreciation of Sardinia's **traditional culture**, a re-evaluation of its language and folklore and a corresponding pride in Sard identity. On the minus side, the island has suffered the usual pitfalls of tourist economies everywhere – namely, poorly regulated construction and the degradation of the natural environment in pursuit of short-term profit.

Still, with its relatively prosperous population of 1.66 million, Sardinia today seems comfortable enough with its modern role. Despite a simmering resentment towards the centralized bureaucracy and the Italian state in general, overall there is satisfaction with the island's place within Italy and the European Union, while the main party campaigning in the long term for complete independence, the Partito Sardo d'Azione, is too marginal to exert much influence except at a local level.

Sardinia's modern profile is represented by such individuals as **Renato Soru**, born in Sanluri in 1957, founder and chairman of Milan-based internet service provider Tiscali, and president of the *Regione di Sardegna* 2004–2009 at the head of a centre-left coalition. The image of Sardinia as a playboy's playground, on the other hand, is illustrated by the antics of **Silvio Berlusconi**, ex-prime minister of Italy, famous for the lavish entertainments he hosted in his sumptuous villas on the Costa Smeralda. The shameless devotion to *la dolce vita* embodied by this millionaire's resort appeared ever more incongruous in the context of the dire financial plight that has gripped Italy – and Europe – since 2009, which has resulted in a significant drop in tourist revenue for the islanders.

Soru was replaced as regional president in 2009 by Ugo Cappellacci of Berlusconi's Forza Italia party, who was in turn ousted by the economist Francesco Pigliaru, of the centre-left Partito Democratico in 2014.

1962	**2008**	**2013**
A consortium led by the Aga Khan begins to develop what would become known as the Costa Smeralda, opening up the island to tourism.	US naval base on La Maddalena archipelago closes after 35 years.	Serious floods in Olbia, following a cyclone; state of emergency declared.

Sardinian wildlife

In common with all islands, Sardinia has that element of uniqueness that arises from isolation, in which plants and animals evolve differently from those on the mainland. Many species are found only here, or are shared with neighbouring Corsica, while the proximity of Africa gives the local fauna and flora a distinct, almost tropical character. In addition, Sardinia's location on a key bird-migration route between Africa and Europe accounts for the seasonal visitations of a number of bird species.

Sardinia's **island ecology** also means that a number of species present on the mainland are absent here – notably poisonous snakes, but also wolves, otters and moles. Those species which are present display a brilliant diversity, linked to the range of different terrains – mountain, forest, plain and coast – that exist within a relatively limited area, and to the typically Mediterranean climate, which keeps rainfall between 600mm (24 inches) on the plains to 990mm (39 inches) in the mountains.

Habitats

Sardinia boasts a significant proportion of Italy's **lagoons** and **wetlands**, as well as extensive areas of **maquis** (Mediterranean scrub), remnant **forests**, hot **plains** and high **mountains**. The overwhelming presence of mountains accounts for the island's numerous **rivers**, of which the Tirso and Flumendosa are the most important.

Lagoons

In ornithological terms, the **lagoons** (*stagni*) and wetlands are perhaps the most important feature of the island. Sardinia still has 130 square kilometres of protected lagoons, constituting 25 percent of all the lagoons located within Italy. Those in Sardinia are internationally designated both for their importance during migration time and for the presence of rare breeding birds.

The richest *stagni* are to be found in the vicinity of Oristano and Cágliari, where it is common to spot flocks of pink **flamingos**; they have long used both of these areas as a stop-off on their migrations between Africa and the Camargue region of France, though they have also started nesting and breeding in some lagoon areas on the island. The range of wetland species here is remarkable – most notably **black-winged stilt** (the "cavalier of Italy", named for its extraordinary leggy appearance), spoonbill, crane, avocet, cattle egret, tern, cormorant, glossy ibis, white-headed duck, osprey, pratincole, purple gallinule, ferruginous duck, marsh harrier and Andouin's gull.

In winter, there are large numbers of **ducks** and **cormorants**, their V-shaped skeins a prominent feature in the skies, not to mention numerous waders and wheeling flocks of **lapwings**. The spring and autumn migrations see significant numbers of passage

---

WHEN TO WATCH WILDLIFE

Timing is essential for wildlife watchers in Sardinia. A visit in **spring** or **autumn** is best for viewing bird migrations and the flowering of plants and shrubs, many of which bloom first in spring and again in autumn, after the summer drought. In **winter**, there's less to see in higher terrain but the lowlands, particularly around lagoons, still shelter a range of waders and other aquatic birdlife.

birds, and this is a good time to see the **curlew sandpiper**, **Caspian tern**, **short-toed eagle** and **red-footed falcon**.

The area around Oristano has the island's best-protected lagoons, not least those on the Sinis peninsula, where the flatlands around the lakeside town of Cabras have the Pauli e Sali reserve, sheltering reeds and a wide range of waterfowl. The nearby Stagno di Sale Porcus is the place to see wintering flocks of the **European crane**. Another general feature of these wetlands are the reed beds, home to **great reed**, **fan-tailed** and **Cetti's warbler**s and hunted over by the fast, acrobatic **hobby**.

Coastal zones

In coastal areas, **Aleppo**, **dwarf** and **maritime palms** lend a tropical feel, while the long **sand dunes** on the west coast of the provinces of Carbónia-Iglésias, Medio-Campidano and Oristano create a more arid environment, notably around Piscinas and Is Arenas. **Turtles** use these and other remote beaches to lay eggs.

Sardinia's eastern coast is mainly cliffy and undeveloped, the mountains ending in a sheer rocky wall of limestone. Capo di Monte Santu, at the southern end of the Gulf of Orosei, hosts a significant colony of the highly unusual **Eleonora's falcon**, a "semi-colonial" nesting falcon named after Sardinia's medieval warrior queen who decreed that she alone was permitted to hunt with it. Only found in the Mediterranean, this large migratory falcon is one of Europe's rarest and most enigmatic raptors, with long, thin, speedily vibrating wings, and is most often seen in autumn, since the species breeds late to feed its young on autumn-passage birds, catching its prey on the wing. The best place to spot this bird, however, is on the east coast of the island of San Pietro (most commonly around Capo Sándalo).

The Gulf of Orosei is also important as the last home of the monk or **Mediterranean seal** (in Italian *bue marino*, or "sea ox"). Sadly, it's either already extinct or facing extinction, with at best only a handful of individuals remaining scattered in the coves and grottoes of this rocky coast.

Off the Stintino peninsula in the northwest, the island of Asinara, now a national park, is most famous for the unique and diminutive **albino ass**. Some of these tiny creatures can also be found south of the peninsula on the massive cliffs of Capo Caccia, where they share the Prigionette reserve with **wild boars** as well as **griffon vultures** – Italy's largest colony of these immense creatures is to be found here and a few kilometres further south on the desolate Alghero–Bosa coast. A short distance north of Alghero, Sardinia's only natural lake, Lago di Baratz, has a species of **freshwater tortoise** and a system of pine-covered dunes and maritime *macchia*.

Plains and plateaus

Sardinia's **plains** are among the flatlands being agriculturally "improved" across much of Europe, but here they still shelter a range of flora and fauna. The island's most extensive plain is in the Campidano region, between Cágliari and Oristano, home to the **little bustard**, a turkey-like creature that was once much hunted by aristocratic falcons. The whole bustard family is endangered in much of Europe, but Sardinia is one of the few places where this particular member is expanding and flourishing in the mosaics of pasture particularly favoured by this species. The plains are also a rich habitat for **Barbary partridge**, **bunting** and **woodchat shrike**, while the vividly colourful exotics – **roller**, **hoopoe** and **bee-eater** – are all found here. Springtime is the best time to visit, when the *macchia* and grasslands are a riot of colour.

East of Campidano, La Marmilla is characterized by odd-looking, bare hummocks and a series of high tablelands virtually empty of human developments, where **asphodel**, euphorbia, poppies, lavender, buttercups and daisies form a brilliant tapestry. The largest of these high basalt **plateaus** is the Giara di Gésturi, holding a concentration of the island's most interesting plants, including a number of rare species of **orchid**. Sheltering a range of wildlife including hares, boars and foxes, the plateau is also the principal habitat of Sardinia's famous *cavallini* – miniature **wild horses** whose origins are shrouded in mystery and which are notoriously difficult to spot.

The macchia

Sardinia's rocky slopes are everywhere covered with a thick layer of Mediterranean **maquis** (in Italian, *macchia*). This invasive scrub flourishes after fire or the felling of forests and also colonizes abandoned cultivated land. Tangled, heavily scented and richly colourful, *macchia* includes **juniper**, **lentisk**, **myrtle** and **arbutus** (strawberry tree); **heather** and the yellow-flowering **broom** and **gorse** are also common, as are the pink and white petals of the **cistus** family. Leaves here are often thick and gummy to help prevent water loss, and the shrubs are intermingled with herbs, flowers and orchids in more open patches.

Near the coast, the *macchia* has a more typically maritime selection of plants, while in the drier areas it is interspersed with **prickly pear** cactus (introduced from Mexico by the Spanish), the fruit of which ("Indian fig") is considered a delicacy. The typical **warblers** here – Sardinian, Marmora's, subalpine, spectacled and Dartford – are all of interest to those more familiar with northern European species. At night one can hear the calls of the **Scops owl** and the echoing, warm, low churring of the **nightjar** intermingling with the cicadas.

Mountain and woodland areas

As the altitude increases, the shrub layer gives way to taller **woodland** where trees such as cork and holm oak start to appear. Here, the richly lyrical **blackcap** and the **Orphean warbler** become more predominant as the thickening canopy shades out the *macchia*. Traditional olive groves and fruit orchards are very important for a number of bird species, the most important of which is the rare **wryneck**. Alder and the pink blossom

---

A CHECKLIST OF SARDINIAN WILDLIFE SITES

Alghero–Bosa coast Home to Italy's largest colony of griffon vultures. See p.189.

Cágliari's lagoons and saltpans Sardinia's largest wetland area (the Molentargius and Santa Gilla water systems in particular) is home to flamingos, shelducks, grebes and many species of gulls and terns. See p.71.

Capo Figari Mouflons have been reintroduced on this cape and on the offshore islet of Figarolo. See p.242.

Caprera Dense *macchia* and woods, where sea and land birds nest. See pp.256–257.

Foresta di Minniminni and Monte dei Sette Fratelli Rugged terrain sheltering deer, boar, wildcat and various birds of prey. See pp.132–133.

Gennargentu This thickly forested central mountain range has boar and, more visibly, wild pigs. See pp.288–292.

Giara di Gésturi A high basalt plateau famous as the island's main habitat of the miniature wild horses (*cavallini*); it's also a good place to see rare species of orchid. See p.125.

Monte Arcosu The Sardinian stag (*cervo sardo*) and other forest fauna, as well as a range of predatory birds, can be spotted here. See p.83.

Piscinas High dune system where esparto grasses and even wild lilies take root in the sands. See p.108.

Le Prigionette This reserve has wild boar and griffon vultures, though these are more common farther south, on the Alghero–Bosa coast. See p.186.

San Pietro The island's western cliffs are the habitat for rare sea birds and falcons. See p.99.

Sinis The dunes, marshes and lagoons here shelter reeds and a huge range of aquatic birdlife, including the European crane. See pp.150–156.

Supramonte Wild goats clamber the slopes of this desolate massif, and eagles and other raptors circle above. See pp.281–283.

Tavolara The sheer cliffs of this island shelter peregrine falcons and Yelkouan shearwaters, Audouin's gulls and Mediterranean shags, among other rare birds. See p.240.

of oleander may mark the line of watercourses, often totally dried out in summer, while on the more established streams the semiaquatic **dipper** can sometimes be seen. Woodland is also one of the favoured habitats of the **Barbary partridge** – apart from Gibraltar, Sardinia is the only place in Europe where this species can be found. Outside reserves like Le Prigionette, however, you'll be lucky to glimpse one, just as you'll need luck and patience to spot the rare **Sardinian salamander**.

Sardinia has the highest level of **forest** cover of all the Italian regions. **Cork oak** trees stretch from Gallura to the northern Barbagia (the central zone of mountains), providing one of Europe's main sources of cork – the plantations are particularly thick around the village of Calangianus. The **holm oak** is another tree ubiquitous on the island: the Gennargentu mountains and the Abbasanta plateau near Oristano hold the remnants of a holm oak forest that once covered much of Sardinia, and at Sas Badas and Su Lidone on the Supramonte massif are remains of an ancient forest that has never been felled, its gnarled specimens numbering among the last remaining examples in Europe. The island even has a **petrified forest** near Soddi on the shore of Lake Lago Omodeo, the result of a primeval volcanic eruption.

Higher up in the mountains, where the chiming of sheep- and goat-bells is a constant accompaniment, the species in the tree line change, with the appearance of **bay oaks** and **maples** whose red leaves provide a blaze of colour in autumn, and scattered clumps of **holly** and **yew** – residual vegetation from a cooler era. The **jay** is common here, while **goshawks** and **peregrine falcons** prey on the **wood pigeons**; rarer species include **golden eagles**. Towards the summits of the mountains, the forests largely disappear and are replaced by grassland and scattered **junipers** beautifully contorted by the mistral wind.

Many species of rare and unique mountain plants are to be found in the Gennargentu, but pride of place goes to the **peony** whose blooming announces the arrival of spring. A notable mammal to be found in this terrain is the **Sardinian stag**, a few hundred of which have survived here and in the forests around Cágliari, for example Monte Arcosu, in the mountains of Sulcis – also the place to see **martens**, **wildcats** and **boar**.

Mouflons, or long-horned wild sheep, are now found only in the mountains of Sardinia, and on Corsica and Cyprus. You'll have to penetrate quite far into the deep and rugged valleys to glimpse examples of this extraordinary animal, perched on high ledges with enormous, regally curved horns. Lower down, the groves of hazel, almond, walnut and chestnut carpeting the slopes of the interior are grazed by both wild *cinghiali* (boar) and the more domesticated pig – which in many cases has interbred with its wild cousin. Although Sardinia's wild boar are hunted for both sport and their meat, numbers have not declined significantly in recent years.

Sardinians are unreconstructed **hunters**, and will shoot at anything that moves. It is not uncommon to come across heavily armed hunting parties trailing through the *macchia*, though European public opinion is having an impact on reducing the destructive effects of this "sport", and the provision of protected areas is increasing.

Books

Surprisingly little has been written about Sardinia, though the island has provided the inspiration for a small number of outstanding works. Titles marked ★ are particularly recommended.

TRAVEL, MUSIC AND FOOD

★Malachi Bogdanov *Sardinia Baby!* Highly readable and entertaining account of living and working in Sássari by this theatre director, with thoughtful insights into the island's culture not to mention some great recipes for Sard specialities.

★D.H. Lawrence *Sea and Sardinia*. Lawrence's six-day journey through Sardinia in 1921 did not give the island much of a chance, and his account bristles with impatience and irritation. Travelling up from Cágliari to Nuoro and Olbia in the company of the "Queen Bee" (Frieda Lawrence), his highly personal travelogue alternates between disgust and rapture, though it sparkles with closely observed cameos.

Bernard Lortat-Jacob *Sardinian Chronicles*. Examines the music of the island through twelve vignettes of locals who continue to practise the tradition of choral singing. CD included.

Giovanni Pilu and Roberta Muir *A Sardinian Cookbook*. All your favourite Sard dishes are included in this lavishly illustrated culinary compendium, from *pane carasau* to *seadas*, via *porcetto arrosto* and *zuppa gallurese*.

Amelie Posse-Brázdová *Sardinian Sideshow*. Translated from the Swedish in 1932, this light-hearted memoir relates the experiences of the protagonist and her Middle-European companions in exile during World War I in Alghero. Illuminating mainly for its descriptions of the island in the days before package tourism.

★Alan Ross *The Bandit on the Billiard Table*. Well-written account of a journey through Sardinia in the 1950s, full of sympathetic descriptions of people and places; informative and readable, if a little old-fashioned.

WALKING, CYCLING AND DIVING

Paddy Dillon *Walking in Sardinia: 50 Walks in Sardinia's Mountains*. This Cicerone guide ignores large areas of the island, but has excellent info on walks in the Ogliastra region, Supramonte and the Gennargenu range. There's lots of practical material on transport and the language, too.

Peter Herold, Amos Cardia and Davide Deidda *Mountain Bike Sardinia*. Seventy rides in the south and centre of the island, with clear overviews, detailed descriptions, maps and photos – it's well produced, but pricey.

★Walter Iwersen and Elisabeth van de Wetering *Sardinia* (Rother Walking Guides). This excellent recent update is the best hiking guide to the island, with 63 walks lucidly described, each with a colour map (1:25,000, 1:50,000 or 1:75,000), photographs and downloadable GPS coordinates.

Egidio Trainito *Sardinia Diving Guide*. Lavishly illustrated guide outlining Sardinia's principal underwater ecosystems and describing 31 dives, with details of marine life and wrecks. Maps and diagrams show the sites, while photos help to identify fish and other sea life. Its shortcomings include poor translation, some serious omissions regarding dive centres and background, and unhelpful artwork.

HISTORY AND ARCHEOLOGY

★Rainer Pauli *Sardegna*. Digestible survey of Sardinia's archeological and historical sites, and an excellent handbook for anyone keen to deepen their knowledge of the island. It has not yet appeared in an English version, though copious photos, drawings and diagrams aid understanding.

Robert H. Tykot and Tamsey Andrews *Sardinia in the Mediterranean: A Footprint in the Sea*. Comprehensive (and very expensive) study of Sardinian archeology that covers Paleolithic and Neolithic cultures and nuraghic, Phoenician, Punic, Greek and Roman settlements on the island.

Gary S. Webster *A Prehistory of Sardinia, 2300–500 BC*. Heavyweight academic tome bringing together all the research on Sardinian prehistory, with particular attention given to nuraghic society.

SARDINIAN LITERATURE

Sergio Atzeni *Bakunin's Son*. The portrait of a man conveyed through interviews with those who knew him. Though there is a disjointed and unfinished feel about the book, it develops into an engaging multilayered narrative. Atzeni drowned while swimming in 1995, and the book, published in 1991, was adapted as a film in 1997.

★Grazia Deledda *After the Divorce, Cosima, Elias Portolu, La Madre* and *Canne al Vento*. Grazia Deledda's Sardinia is a raw place of instinct and passion, which she evokes in her simple, unsentimental tales set around her

SARDINIAN FILMS

Sardinia has no distinctive **film-making** tradition, although a few directors have taken advantage of its landscape. The following list highlights the most notable films associated with the island.

6 Desires: D.H. Lawrence and Sardinia (written and directed by Mark Cousins, 2014). This experimental, low-tech film retracing Lawrence's 1921 journey dwells on the Sardinian landscape and explores the complexities of Lawrence himself – who is voiced by Jarvis Cocker and rather awkwardly addressed as Bert.

Banditi a Orgosolo (*Bandits of Orgosolo*, directed by Vittorio de Seta, 1961). This film capitalized on the publicity given to kidnapping and violence as practised by the outlaws living in the hills around the village of Orgósolo, outside Nuoro. The first feature film of this Sicilian-born director, made with minimal technical and financial resources, it was enthusiastically received at the 1961 Venice Film Festival, but has disappeared almost without trace now.

Disamistade (*Enmity*, directed by Gianfranco Cabiddu, 1988). Focusing on the conflicts between old ways and modern life, this tells the story of a young man in the 1950s who returns to the island and is forced to conform to traditional practices which have become alien to him.

Il Deserto Rosso (*Red Desert*, directed by Michelangelo Antonioni, 1965). Filmed on Budelli – one of the Maddalena Islands – and responsible for propelling its *spiaggia rosa* or "pink beach" to instant fame, the movie has since sunk into obscurity.

Il Figlio di Bakunìn (*Bakunin's Son*, directed by Gianfranco Cabiddu, 1997). This film by *Disamistade*'s director is based on the book *Bakunin's Son* by Sergio Atzeni (see p.319). Set in a mining community, it describes the plight of a shoemaker's son in the context of Sardinia's postwar history. Both films had a limited release.

Padre Padrone (directed by Paolo and Vittorio Taviani, 1977). This is the most famous film to come out of Sardinia, and the island's rugged mountain backdrops are used to full effect. All the same, the film, which was based on the autobiography of the writer Gavino Ledda (see below), was hated by Sards for giving a negative portrayal of the island, even if its main theme is chiefly an exploration of a boy's relationship with his tyrannical father. The cruelty and bleak poverty of the shepherds' society is overplayed, but it's a strongly atmospheric piece, the first film to win both the Palme d'Or and International Critics' Prize at Cannes, and for years *de rigueur* viewing at Communist Party gatherings. Roberto Rossellini, head of the Cannes jury, declared that the film "embodies everything which is most impressive, vigorous and coherent, and most daring, socially and artistically, in the Italian cinema".

The Mandrake Root (directed by Malachi Bogdanov, 2008). Comedy drama, the first feature film of this theatre director, taking Machiavelli's sixteenth-century play *La Mandragola*, set in Florence, and transposing it to Sássari. Low-budget, it's a deft, witty, undemanding entertainment that's worth seeking out.

hometown of Nuoro. In *After the Divorce* (1902), she writes of the grim sense of exclusion from the tribal mores prevailing in the village of Orlei, where the main protagonist is driven to betray her husband who has been convicted of murder. *Cosima* is an autobiographical novel published posthumously, vividly evoking the struggles of a Nuorese girl with literary aspirations. *Elias Portolu* (1900) relates the moral and social dilemmas of a convict returned to his rigid shepherds' society. *La Madre* (1920) deals with the frustrated love of a village priest and the efforts of his mother to dissuade him from giving up his vocation in order to follow his passion. *Canne al Vento* (1913), translated as *Reeds in the Wind*, tells of the decline of three noble spinster sisters, the guilt-ridden, unpaid servant who looks after them and the local characters who inhabit this densely superstitious society. Deledda's writing is full of what D.H. Lawrence called "uncontaminated human instinct" and "the indescribable

tang of the people of the island, not yet absorbed into the world". She won the Nobel Prize for Literature in 1926. Interested readers should search for the biography written by one of her translators, Martha King: *Grazia Deledda, A Legendary Life*.

Giuseppe Dessì *Il Disertore*. Published in 1961, "The Deserter" narrates the tale of a young Sardinian shepherd who is sent to fight in World War I. He flees from the front after killing his captain in a fit of rage and returns to Sardinia. Other works by Dessi include *Paese d'Ombre* ("Land of Shadows"), published in 1972 and winner of the Strega Prize that year.

Gavino Ledda *Padre Padrone*. Though best known outside Italy as a film (see box above), this autobiographical novel from 1975 is the most famous literary work to have come out of Sardinia in recent times. Dragged out of school to tend sheep, Ledda (b.1938) was illiterate until the age of 20, when he entered the army and started on a journey of self-education. *Padre Padrone*, the story of his turbulent upbringing in the mountains and eventual rebellion against his sadistic father, was followed by other books, but none enjoyed the same success.

Emilio Lussu *Marcia su Roma e dintorni*. First published in 1933, "March on Rome" is an autobiographical account by a leading Sardinian republican politician of resistance to Fascism in Sardinia between 1918 and 1930, narrated with humour and evocative descriptions of the island.

★**Salvatore Satta** *The Day of Judgement*. A respected jurist, Salvatore Satta wrote this classic over several years, though it was not published until after his death in 1975. Like Deledda's work, it is set in Nuoro, peopled by a procession of theatrical characters who seem to inhabit a bleak dreamscape of a long-dead past. The book lacks much in the way of narrative, but powerfully evokes a lost world, set in the remotest recesses of Sardinia's impoverished interior.

Flavio Soriga *Diavoli di Nuraiò, Neropioggia* and *Sardinia Blues*. First published in 2000, Soriga represents a new generation of Sard writers, his stories and novels (so far untranslated into English) peopled by intellectuals, tourists, druggies, bohemians and aristocrats – a refreshing antidote to the world described in Sardinia's established literary canon. Seek out too his "counterguide" to the island of Sardinia, *Sardinia Blues*.

SARDINIAN MUSIC AND DANCE

Music and dance are taken extremely seriously in Sardinia. You're bound to encounter both at any of the numerous festivals taking place in the island throughout the year, as well as at concerts and recitals in squares, parks and even archeological sites. It comes in a diversity of forms, though the island is probably best known for unaccompanied harmony singing. Most singing groups fall into one of two camps: the **coros** (choral), usually dedicated to liturgical song, with any number of participants, and the **tenores**, four-part male groups singing mainly secular material. The latter groups in particular have made quite an impact internationally in recent years, the most famous being **Tenores di Bitti** (see p.280). The four voices of a *tenores* group are said to imitate the typical sounds of the rural shepherds' society: "bassu" (bass, from the cow), "contra" (contralto, from the sheep), "mesu oche" (*mezza voce*, from the sound of the wind) and "oche" (*voce*, the human voice). Almost all vocal groups are male, though it is possible to hear women's voices in groups such as **Actores Alidos**, creating quite a different sound.

Festivals are also a good place to see **traditional instruments** being played, for example the *launeddas*, a simple, polyphonic triple pipe made from reed. **Efisio Melis** and **Antonio Lara** established themselves in the 1930s as the greatest players in this genre. You'll also see the more versatile accordion, or *organetto*, whose most famous living exponent is **Totore Chessa**, a light-fingered virtuoso.

There's no specific Sardinian rock music scene – radio and TV are dominated by mainstream Italian chart music, with a smattering of British and American hits. Local singer **Elena Ledda** has dabbled in pop while retaining specifically Sard elements in her music, especially in more recent recordings. The island has a higher profile in the field of jazz, reflected in the number of jazz festivals taking place, usually in summer. One of the best is at Berchidda, west of Olbia, in which the trumpeter **Paolo Fresu** is closely involved. Fresu has long been known on the Italian and European jazz circuit, though without accentuating the Sard connection in his work. **Antonello Salis** is another musician with an international reputation – an idiosyncratic pianist and accordionist who has worked with Billy Cobham, Pat Metheny and others.

Accordion, drum, tambourine, guitar and *launeddas* are the usual accompaniments to Sardinian **dancing**, a curiously twitchy spectacle in which the feet perform a constant fast rhythm while the rest of the body remains still. The group of men and women might have to sustain the synchronized movement for a long time, exercising flawless control during the elaborate sequences – definitely worth catching if you get the chance, at many of the island's festivals.

AN INTRODUCTION TO SARDINIA'S MUSIC – SOME SAMPLE RECORDINGS

Actores Alidos *Canti delle Donne Sarde* (2005)
Totore Chessa *Organittos* (2000)
Paolo Fresu *Sonos e Memoria* (2001)
Paolo Fresu & Ralph Towner *Chiaroscuro* (2009)
Elena Ledda *Amargura* (2005)
Efisio Melis and Antonio Lara *Launeddas* (2001)

Antonello Salis *Pianosolo* (2006)
Tenores di Bitti *S'Amore e Mama* (1996)
Various artists *Antologia della Musica Sarda Antica e Moderna* (2003)
Various artists *Music of Sardinia* (2005)

Italian

The ability to speak European languages other than Italian is increasingly widespread in Sardinia. You'll often find the staff in museums, tourist offices and hotels, as well as guides, able to communicate in English, and students in particular are frequently willing to show off their knowledge. Outside the tourist areas, however, few people know more than some simple words and phrases – more often than not culled from pop songs or computer programs.

Anyone interested in Sardinia and the Sards will find their experience greatly enriched by learning a few basic phrases of **Italian**. Even if only a very superficial knowledge from a phrasebook is gained, just the ability to ask for a glass of water will make you feel less helpless. In any case, it's one of the easiest European languages to learn, especially if you already have a smattering of French or Spanish, which are grammatically similar. Keep your ears open on buses and trains, pick up a local newspaper and tune into a bit of TV or radio in your hotel room – and you'll be surprised how much you subconsciously absorb. When speaking, enunciate everything with maximum clarity, as mumbled or fumbled pronunciation often leads to misunderstanding.

All Italian words are **stressed** on the penultimate syllable unless an **accent** denotes otherwise, although in practice accents are often left out. Thus, Cágliari and Sássari are pronounced with the accent on the first syllable. Note that the ending -ia or -ie counts as two syllables, hence *trattoria* is stressed on the i. We've put accents in, throughout the text and below, wherever it isn't immediately obvious how a word should be pronounced: for example, in *Maríttima*, the accent is on the first i; conversely *Olbia* should theoretically have an accent on the o. Other words where we've omitted accents are common ones (like *Isola*, stressed on the I), some names (*Domenico*, *Vittorio*), and words that are stressed similarly in English, such as *archeologico* and *Repubblica*.

Lastly, it's pleasantly surprising how much can be communicated by the use of **body language** alone – gestures, gesticulations, facial expressions and miming – an art at which Italians are supremely adept.

Pronunciation

The rules of **pronunciation** are easy, since every word is spoken exactly as it's written: you articulate each syllable of every word – the louder and clearer the better. Double consonants – two s's or two p's, for example – are individually articulated, ie pronounced more forcefully than if they are single. The letter "h" is not aspirated at all, as in "hour". The only difficulties you're likely to encounter are the few consonants that change their pronunciation according to the letters following:

LINGUISTIC ETIQUETTE

To avoid making unnecessary gaffes, it's worth noting some elementary guidelines. When **speaking to strangers**, the third person is the polite form (ie *Lei* instead of *Tu* for "you"); using the second person may be taken as a mark of disrespect or ignorance. Likewise, "ciao" is only used informally to acquaintances; to others use *buongiorno* or *buona sera* for "hello"; you may also hear *salve*, a less formal greeting. When saying "goodbye", use *arrivederci* or (more formally) *arrivederla*. It's also worth remembering that Italians use "please" and "thank you" far less frequently than we do: it's all implied in the tone, though if you're in doubt, err on the polite side.

PHRASEBOOKS AND DICTIONARIES

The best **phrasebooks** are the Rough Guides' own *Italian Phrasebook* (£5.99) and *Italian Audio Phrasebook & Dictionary* (ebook £3.99), both of which have large but accessible vocabularies, detailed menu readers and useful dialogues. Collins also publishes a comprehensive series: its *Gem* or *Pocket* dictionaries are fine for travelling purposes, while its *Concise* dictionary is adequate for most language needs.

c before **a**, **o** or **u** is hard, as in **c**at; before **e** or **i** it is pronounced as in **ch**urch, while **ch** before the same vowels is hard.

The same goes for **g** – soft before **e** and **i**, as in **g**entle; hard when followed by **a**, **o** or **u**, or by an **h**, as in **g**arlic.

gn has the ni sound of o**ni**on.

gl in Italian is softened to something like li in English, as in vermi**li**on.

sci or **sce** are pronounced as in **sh**eet and **sh**elter respectively.

The Sard dialect

Italy has been a separate state for only a little over 150 years, and each of the regions of Italy speaks its own **local dialect** which has only very recently taken second place to "standard" Italian. But in informal family or social circles, it's often still the dialect that is instinctively spoken.

In Sardinia, isolated in the middle of the Mediterranean, the parlance is distinct enough to be classified as a separate language, while every area of the island, almost every village, has its own **dialect** or at least variation – as you might expect in a place that is both mountainous and, from ancient times, poorly integrated. These local strains will incorporate a concoction of ingredients according to each area's particular historical circumstances. Thus on the isle of San Pietro off the southwest coast of Sardinia, a strong **Genoan** dialect is spoken, owing to its settlement by a colony of Ligurians, invited by King Carlo Emanuele III in 1737. At around the same time there was a wave of immigration from Corsica into the northern region of Gallura, which still retains a dialect close to that spoken in the southern parts of Sardinia's sister island. And the people of Alghero still speak a variety of **Spanish Catalan** – over six hundred years after the Aragonese king made the town his main base in northern Sardinia and flooded it with Catalonians. Visitors there will find Catalan street names in the old quarter, though it's often difficult to distinguish in speech.

The influence of **Spanish** permeates all the island's various dialects – hardly surprising in a place that was a Spanish colony for three centuries. The evidence is also on maps, where you will see examples like *riu* used for a river, where the Italian would be *fiume*.

SOME SARDINIAN DIALECT WORDS

abba	water
bruncu	peak, protuberance or promontory
cala	inlet, beach
domus de janas	"fairy houses" – the name given to prehistoric burial chambers
flumineddu	river
genna	gate
giara	plateau
mannu	big
pranu	plain
riu	river
sa (pl. sas)	the (feminine)
scala	steep path
serra	chain of mountains
su (pl. sos)	the (masculine)

Sard dialects also have large infusions of **Latin**, a residue of the much older Roman occupation. "House", for example, in Italian *casa*, is called *domus* in areas of Sardinia, the same as Latin. The words for "the" in northern Sardinia – *su* and *sa* in the singular, *sos* and *sas* in the plural – are derived from the Latin noun-endings. In the south of the island, "the" is *is*, from the Latin *ipse*. Again, you'll find copious examples on the maps. The region which has the greatest preponderance of Latin in its dialect is Logudoro, in the island's northwestern quarter; its inhabitants boast of speaking the purest form of *sardo*, which in effect means the form least corrupted by later influences.

Added to the innate **insularity** of islanders, Sards have a particular reputation for being *isolani*, meaning that they are not only insular but a closed and introspective people, with little interest in anything beyond immediate concerns. Whether or not this is still true today, the trait has influenced – and been influenced by – the local variations in speech. Within the artificially imposed provincial boundaries, Sardinia is a conglomerate of diverse regions – Campidano, Arborea, Logudoro, Gallura, the Iglesiente and Barbagia, to name but the principal ones – each with distinct traditions and a fierce awareness of their differences from one another. The use of dialect became not just a colloquial mode of speech, but also a symbol of **local solidarity**, enabling Sards to identify each other according to the particular area of the island they inhabit, just by listening.

The result of this linguistic confusion is that Italian has become the best means for people of different areas of the island to communicate effectively, and it has been learned, as a foreign language is learned, to perfection. Indeed, it is claimed that Sards speak the most correct form of Italian anywhere. Television, of course, has also played its part in diffusing standard Italian.

To get a taste of *la limba sarda* (the Sardinian language) in its written form, take a look at ⓦditzionariu.org.

BASIC ITALIAN TERMS AND PHRASES

NUMBERS

one	uno	forty	quaranta
two	due	forty-one	quarantuno
three	tre	fifty	cinquanta
four	quattro	sixty	sessanta
five	cinque	seventy	settanta
six	sei	eighty	ottanta
seven	sette	ninety	novanta
eight	otto	one hundred	cento
nine	nove	one hundred and one	centouno
ten	dieci	two hundred	duecento
eleven	undici	one thousand	mille
twelve	dodici	two thousand	duemila
thirteen	tredici	three thousand	tremila
fourteen	quattordici	one million	un milione
fifteen	quindici		
sixteen	sedici	**DAYS AND MONTHS**	
seventeen	diciasette	Monday	lunedì
eighteen	diciotto	Tuesday	martedì
nineteen	dicianove	Wednesday	mercoledì
twenty	venti	Thursday	giovedì
twenty-one	ventuno	Friday	venerdì
twenty-two	ventidue	Saturday	sábato
thirty	trenta	Sunday	domenica
thirty-one	trentuno	January	gennaio
thirty-two	trentadue	February	febbraio

March	marzo	hot/cold	caldo/freddo
April	aprile	near/far	vicino/lontano
May	maggio	vacant/occupied	líbero/occupato
June	giugno	quickly/slowly	velocemente/lentamente
July	luglio	slowly/quietly	piano
August	agosto	with/without	con/senza
September	settembre	more/less	più/meno
October	ottobre	enough, no more	basta
November	novembre	Mr…	Signor…
December	dicembre	Mrs…	Signora…
		Miss…	Signorina… (il signore, la signora, la signorina when speaking about someone else)

USEFUL PHRASES

Good morning	Buongiorno		
Good afternoon/evening	Buona sera		
Good night	Buona notte	first name	primo nome
Hello/Goodbye	Ciao (informal; when speaking to strangers use the phrases above)	surname	cognome

ACCOMMODATION

Goodbye	Arrivederci (formal)	hotel	albergo
Yes	Sì	Is there a hotel nearby?	C'è un albergo qui vicino?
No	No	Do you have a room…?	Ha una cámera…?
Please	Per favore		
Thank you (very much)	Grázie (molte/mille grazie)	for one/two/ three people	per una persona, due/ tre persone
You're welcome	Prego	for one/two/ three nights	per una notte, due/ tre notti
Alright/That's OK	Va bene	for one/two weeks	per una settimana/ due settimane
How are you? (informal/formal)	Come stai/sta?		
I'm fine	Bene	with a double bed	con un letto matrimoniale
Do you speak English?	Parla inglese?	with a shower/bath	con una doccia/un bagno
I don't understand	Non capisco	with a balcony	con una terrazza
I haven't understood	Non ho capito	with air conditioning	con aria condizionata
I don't know	Non lo so	hot/cold water	acqua calda/fredda
Excuse me/Sorry	Scusa (informal)	How much is it?	Quanto costa?
Excuse me/Sorry	Scusi/mi scusi (formal)	It's expensive	È caro
Excuse me	Permesso (in a crowd)	Is breakfast included?	È compresa la prima colazione?
I'm sorry	Mi dispiace		
I'm here on holiday	Sono qui in vacanza	Do you have anything cheaper?	Ha niente che costa di meno?
I live in…	Abito a…		
today	oggi	full/half board	pensione completa/ mezza pensione
tomorrow	domani		
day after tomorrow	dopodomani	Can I see the room?	Posso vedere la cámera?
yesterday	ieri	I'll take it	La prendo
now	adesso	I'd like to book a room	Vorrei prenotare una cámera
later	più tardi		
Wait a minute!	Aspetta!	I have a booking	Ho una prenotazione
in the morning	di mattina	Can we camp here?	Possiamo fare il campeggio qui?
in the afternoon	nel pomeriggio		
in the evening	di sera	Is there a campsite nearby?	C'è un camping qui vicino?
here/there	qui/lì		
good/bad	buono/cattivo	tent	tenda
big/small	grande/píccolo	cabin	cabina
cheap/expensive	económico/caro	youth hostel	ostello per la gioventù
early/late	presto/ritardo		

QUESTIONS AND DIRECTIONS

Where? (Where is/are…?)	Dove? (Dov'è/Dove sono?)
When?	Quando?
What? (What is it?)	Cosa? (Cos'è?)
How much/many?	Quanto/Quanti?
Why?	Perché?
It is/There is	È/c'è (È/c'è…?)
(Is it?/Is there…?)	
What time is it?	Che ora è/Che ore sono?
How do I get to…?	Come arrivo a…?
How far is it to…?	Quant'è lontano a…?
Can you give	Mi può dare un
me a lift to…?	passaggio a…?
Can you tell me	Può dirmi quando
when to get off?	devo scéndere?
What time does it open?	A che ora apre?
What time does it close?	A che ora chiude?
How much does it	Quanto costa?
cost (…do they cost?)	(Quanto costano?)
What is it called in Italian?	Come si chiama in
	italiano?
left/right	sinistra/destra
Go straight ahead	Sempre diritto
Turn to the right/left	Gira a destra/sinistra

TRANSPORT

aeroplane	aereo
local bus	autobus
long-distance bus	pullman
train	treno
car	mácchina
taxi	taxi
bicycle	bicicletta
ferry	traghetto
ship	nave
hitchhiking	autostop
on foot	a piedi
bus station	autostazione
railway station	stazione ferroviaria
ferry terminal	stazione maríttima
port	porto
a ticket to…	un biglietto a…
one-way/return	solo andata/andata e
	ritorno
Can I book a seat?	Posso prenotare un
	posto?
What time does it leave?	A che ora parte?
When is the next bus/	Quando parte il próssimo
train/ferry to…?	pullman/treno
	/traghetto per…?

Where does it leave from?	Da dove parte?
Which platform?	Da quale binario parte?
Do I have to change?	Devo cambiare?
How many kilometres is it?	Quanti chilómetri sono?
How long does it take?	Quanto ci vuole?
What number bus	Que número di
is it to…?	autobus per…?
Where's the road to…?	Dov'è la strada a…?
Next stop, please	La próssima fermata,
	per favore

DRIVING

parking	parcheggio
no parking	divieto di sosta/sosta
	vietata
one-way street	senso único
no entry	senso vietato
slow down	rallentare
road closed/out of order	strada chiusa/guasta
no through road	vietato il tránsito
no overtaking	vietato il sorpasso
crossroads	incrocio
speed limit	límite di velocità
traffic light	semáforo

SOME SIGNS

entrance/exit	entrata/uscita
free entrance	ingresso líbero
gentlemen/ladies	signori/signore
wc	gabinetto, bagno
vacant/engaged	líbero/occupato
open/closed	aperto/chiuso
arrivals/departures	arrivi/partenze
closed for restoration	chiuso per restauro
closed for holidays	chiuso per ferie
pull/push	tirare/spíngere
out of order	guasto
drinking water	acqua potábile
to let	affítasi
platform	binario
cash desk	cassa
go/walk	avanti
stop/halt	alt
customs	dogana
do not touch	non toccare
danger	perícolo
beware	attenzione
first aid	pronto soccorso
ring the bell	suonare il campanello
no smoking	vietato fumare

ITALIAN FOOD TERMS

BASICS AND SNACKS

aceto	vinegar
aglio	garlic
biscotti	biscuits
burro	butter
caramelle	sweets
cioccolato	chocolate
focaccia	oven-baked bread snack
formaggio	cheese
frittata	omelette
gelato	ice cream
grissini	bread sticks
maionese	mayonnaise
marmellata	jam
olio	oil
olive	olives
pane	bread
pane integrale	wholemeal bread
panino	bread roll/sandwich
patatine	crisps/potato chips
patatine fritte	chips
pepe	pepper
piadina	flatbread, usually stuffed with cheese or cold cuts
pizzetta	slice of pizza to take away
riso	rice
sale	salt
uova	eggs
yogurt	yoghurt
zúcchero	sugar
zuppa	soup

ANTIPASTI AND STARTERS

antipasto misto	mixed cold meats, seafood and cheese (plus a mix of other things in this list)
caponata	mixed aubergine, olives, tomatoes
caprese	tomato and mozzarella cheese salad
insalata di mare	seafood salad (usually squid, octopus and prawn)
insalata di riso	rice salad
melanzane alla parmigiana	fried aubergine in tomato sauce with parmesan cheese
mortadella	salami-type cured meat with white nuggets of fat; in Sardinia, often with pistachios
pancetta	bacon

peperonata	grilled green, red or yellow peppers stewed in olive oil
pomodori ripieni	stuffed tomatoes
prosciutto	ham
salame	salami
salmone/tonno/ pesce spada affumicato	smoked salmon/tuna/ swordfish

PIZZAS

biancaneve	"snow white" mozzarella and oregano
calzone	folded pizza with cheese, ham and tomato
capricciosa	literally "capricious"; topped with whatever they've got in the kitchen, usually including baby artichoke, ham and egg
cardinale	ham and olives
diávolo	spicy, with hot salami or Italian sausage
frutti di mare	seafood; usually mussels, prawns, squid and clams
funghi	mushrooms; tinned, sliced button mushrooms unless it specifies fresh mushrooms, either funghi freschi or porcini
margherita	cheese and tomato
marinara	tomato and garlic
napoletana	tomato, anchovy and olive oil (often mozzarella, too)
quattro formaggi	"four cheeses", usually mozzarella, fontina, gorgonzola and gruyère
quattro stagioni	"four seasons"; the toppings split into four separate sections, usually including ham, peppers, onion, mushrooms, artichokes, olives, egg, etc.
romana	anchovy and olives

THE FIRST COURSE (IL PRIMO)

SOUPS

brodo	clear broth
minestra	any light soup

minestrone	thick vegetable soup	pomodoro	tomato sauce
pasta e fagioli	pasta soup with beans	puttanesca	"whorish"; tomato,
pastina in brodo	pasta pieces in		anchovy, olive oil
	clear broth		and oregano
stracciatella	broth with egg	ragù	meat sauce
		vongole (veraci)	clam and tomato sauce
PASTA			(fresh clams in shells,
cannelloni	large tubes of pasta,		usually served with oil
	stuffed		and herbs)
farfalle	literally "bow"-shaped		
	pasta; the word also		
	means "butterflies"	**THE SECOND COURSE (IL SECONDO):**	
fettuccine	narrow pasta ribbons	**MEAT (CARNE)**	
gnocchi	small potato and dough	agnello	lamb
	dumplings	ásino	ass, donkey
lasagne	lasagne	bistecca	steak
maccheroni	macaroni (tubular pasta)	capretto	young goat
pappardelle	pasta ribbons	cavallo	horse
pasta al forno	pasta baked with minced	cervello	brain
	meat, eggs, tomato	cinghiale	wild boar
	and cheese	coniglio	rabbit
penne	smaller version of *rigatoni*	costolette/cotolette	cutlets/chops
ravioli	ravioli	fegatini	chicken livers
rigatoni	large, grooved tubular	fégato	liver
	pasta	involtini	anything sliced, rolled
risotto	cooked rice dish,		and stuffed
	with sauce	lepre	hare
spaghetti	spaghetti	lingua	tongue
spaghettini	thin spaghetti	lumache	snails
tagliatelle	pasta ribbons, another	maiale	pork
	word for *fettuccine*	manzo	beef
tortellini	small rings of pasta,	montone	mutton
	stuffed with meat	monzette	snails
	or cheese	ossobuco	shin of veal
vermicelli	very thin spaghetti	pollo	chicken
	(literally "little worms")	polpette	meatballs
		rognoni	kidneys
		salsiccia	sausage
THE SAUCE (SALSA)		saltimbocca	veal with ham
aglio e olio	tossed in garlic and olive	scaloppina	escalope (of veal)
(e peperoncino)	oil (and hot chillies)	spezzatino	stew
amatriciana	cubed pork and tomato	tacchino	turkey
	sauce (originally	trippa	tripe
	from Rome)	vitello	veal
arrabbiata	tomato sauce spiced		
	with chillies	**FISH (PESCE) AND SHELLFISH**	
bolognese	meat sauce	**(CROSTACEI)**	
burro e salvia	butter and sage	Note that *surgelati* or *congelati* written on the menu next to	
carbonara	cream, ham and	a dish means "frozen" – it often applies to tuna, swordfish,	
	beaten egg	squid and prawns.	
frutta di mare	seafood		
funghi	mushroom	acciughe	anchovies
panna	cream	anguilla	eel
pesto	ground basil, pine nut,	aragosta	lobster
	garlic and pecorino sauce	arselle	clams

baccalà	dried salted cod
bottarga	salted and dried eggs of mullet and tuna
calamari	squid
céfalo	grey mullet
cozze	mussels
dáttile	razor clams
déntice	dentex (like sea bass)
gamberetti	shrimps
gámberi	prawns
granchio	crab
merluzzo	cod
múggine	mullet
orata	gilthead
óstriche	oysters
pesce spade	swordfish
polpo/pólipo	octopus
ricci di mare	sea urchins
ricciola	amberjack
rospo	monkfish
sampiero	John Dory
sárago	bream
sarde	sardines
seppie	cuttlefish
sgombro	mackerel
sógliola	sole
spígola	sea bass
tonno	tuna
triglie	red mullet
trota	trout
vongole	clams

VEGETABLES (CONTORNI) AND SALAD (INSALATA)

aspáragi	asparagus
basílico	basil
bróccoli	broccoli
cápperi	capers
carciofi	artichokes
carciofini	artichoke hearts
carotte	carrots
cavolfiori	cauliflower
cávolo	cabbage
ceci	chickpeas
cetriolo	cucumber
cipolla	onion
fagioli	beans
fagiolini	green beans
finocchio	fennel
funghi	mushrooms
insalata verde/mista	green salad/mixed salad
melanzane	aubergine/eggplant
orígano	oregano
patate	potatoes

peperoni	peppers
piselli	peas
pomodori	tomatoes
radicchio	red chicory
spinaci	spinach
zucca	pumpkin
zucchini	courgettes

DESSERTS (DOLCI)

amaretti	macaroons
gelato	ice cream
macedonia	fruit salad
torta	cake, tart
zabaglione	dessert made with eggs, sugar and Marsala wine
zuppa inglese	trifle

CHEESE

caciocavallo	a type of dried, mature mozzarella cheese
dolce sardo	dry, hard shepherds' cheese, often going into sandwiches
fiore sardo	sheep's cheese frequently used in cooking
fontina	mild northern Italian cheese used in cooking and in rolls
gorgonzola	soft, strong, blue-veined cheese
grana	hard cheese often used instead of *parmigiano* on pastas and soups
mozzarella	soft white cheese, traditionally made from buffalo's milk
parmigiano	parmesan cheese
pecorino	sheep's cheese, either *romano* or *sardo*, both from Sardinia
provolone	cheese with grooved rind, either mild or strong
ricotta	soft white cheese made from ewe's milk, used in sweet or savoury dishes

FRUIT AND NUTS

albicocche	apricots
ananas	pineapple
anguria/coccómero	watermelon
arance	oranges
banane	bananas

cacchi	persimmons
ciliegie	cherries
fichi	figs
fichi d'India	prickly pears
frágole	strawberries
limone	lemon
mándorle	almonds
mele	apples
melone	melon
néspole	medlars
pere	pears
pesche	peaches
pignoli	pine nuts
pistacchio	pistachio nut
prugne	plums
uva	grapes

COOKING TERMS AND USEFUL WORDS

affumicato	smoked
arrosto	roast
ben cotto	well done
bollito/lesso	boiled
alla brace	barbecued
brasato	cooked in wine
cotto	cooked (not raw)
crudo	raw
al dente	firm, not overcooked
ai ferri	grilled without oil
al forno	baked
fritto	fried
grattugiato	grated
alla griglia	grilled
al marsala	cooked with Marsala wine
milanese	fried in egg and breadcrumbs
pizzaiola	cooked with tomato sauce
ripieno	stuffed
sangue	rare
allo spiedo	on the spit
stracotto	braised, stewed
surgelato	frozen
in úmido	stewed
al vapore	steamed

SARDINIAN SPECIALITIES: STARTERS, BREADS AND CHEESES

| sa burrida | dogfish boiled and marinated in garlic, parsley, walnuts and vinegar |
| culurgiones | ravioli stuffed with potato, cheese, garlic and mint |

fainè	chickpea pizza to a Genoan recipe served plain, or with onion, sausage or anchovy (not usually available in summer)
sa frégula	couscous-type semolina pasta, either in a meat stock or dry with mussels or clams
lados	fresh pasta discs, speciality of Barbagia and Gallura, traditionally prepared on November 2, the Day of the Dead
malloreddus	gnocchetti, or pasta shaped in little shells, with various toppings, for example, *alla campidanese*, a spicy sausage sauce
pane carasau	crisp wafer bread, often served with olive oil and salt to add flavour
pane frattau	*carasau* bread soaked in tomato sauce with pecorino and an egg, typically from Mamoiada
spianadas	soft round bread from the Logudoro district, often served with sausages
zuppa/suppa cuata	bread, cheese and tomato soup

SARDINIAN SPECIALITIES: MAIN COURSES

aragosta catalana	lobster in sauce as served in Alghero
cashcà	couscous-type wheat semolina steamed with meat, vegetables or fish as prepared in Carloforte on San Pietro
sa córdula	roasted or barbecued sheep's entrails
cuscus	a version of North African couscous, a speciality of the island of San Pietro, usually served with a fish and vegetable sauce

fritto di pesce	as above but also with other fried fish, like sardines and whitebait
fritto misto	a standard seafood dish; deep-fried prawns and calamari rings in batter
giogghe	snails boiled and then fried with garlic, parsley and paprika
gran premio	horsemeat steak
grigliata di pesce	a mixed fish grill, usually quite substantial and expensive
sa merca	salted mullet from the Cabras lagoon, cooked in herbs
monzette	small snails roasted with salt, a speciality of Sássari; the rarer *giogghe* are boiled, then fried slowly with garlic, parsley and paprika
panadas	pastry rolls filled with meat, fish and vegetables, or all three, originating in Assémini, near Cágliari
pécora in capotta	mutton boiled with vegetables, garlic and rosemary, typical of the Nuoro area
porceddu/porcheddu	young pig roasted whole on a spit with myrtle leaves
stufato di capretto	chunks of kid casseroled with wine, artichokes and saffron
zuppa di pesce	a big dish of mixed fish in rich wine-based soup
zuppa gallurese	"Galluran soup" made from layers of bread and fresh cheese, soaked with meat broth and baked in the oven until golden and fluffy

SWEETS AND DESSERTS

aranciatte/aranzada	very sweet confection, available from Nuoro, made with almonds, oranges and honey
pardulas/casadinas	cheese-based pastries flavoured with saffron, vanilla and the peel of citrus fruit
seadas/sebadas	fried ricotta-filled pastry bubbles soaked in honey
torrone	crystallized almonds and honey, the best from the Barbagia villages of Tonara and Aritzo

DRINKS

acqua minerale	mineral water
aranciata	orangeade
bicchiere	glass
birra	beer
bottiglia	bottle
caffè	coffee
cioccolata calda	hot chocolate
ghiaccio	ice
granita	iced coffee/fruit drink
latte	milk
limonata	lemonade
selz	soda water
spremuta	fresh fruit juice
spumante	sparkling wine
succo di frutta	concentrated fruit juice, sometimes sugared
tè	tea
tónico	tonic water
vino	wine
rosso	red
bianco	white
rosato	rosé
secco	dry
dolce	sweet
caraffa	caraffe, usually a litre
litro	litre
mezzo	half litre
quarto	quarter litre
Salute!	Cheers!

Glossary

affittacámere literally rooms to rent, in practice a slightly larger B&B

agriturismo rural B&B, usually with restaurant

albergo diffuso hotel with rooms in different buildings

anfiteatro amphitheatre

artigianato handicrafts, made by an *artigiano* ("artisan")

autostazione bus station

belvedere lookout point

cappella chapel

castello castle

cattedrale cathedral
centro centre
chiesa church (*chiesa matrice/madre*, main "mother" church)
comune an administrative area; also, the local council or the town hall
corso avenue/boulevard
duomo cathedral
entrata entrance
festa festival (plural *feste*)
fiume river
giudicato medieval administrative territory headed by a *giudice* (literally, a judge)
golfo gulf
lago lake
largo square (like piazza)
lungomare seafront promenade or road
macchia *maquis*, or Mediterranean scrub
mare sea
mercato market
mezzo veloce/unità veloce high-speed ferry
municipio town hall
palazzo palace, mansion or block (of flats)
parco park

passeggiata the customary early evening walk
piano a plain (also "slowly", "gently")
piazza square
pineta pinewood
Pro Loco a local tourist office, usually run by the town hall and with limited hours
sagra festival or special feast, usually an agricultural or religious event
santuario sanctuary
spiaggia beach
stazione station (train station, *stazione ferroviaria*; bus station, autostazione; ferry terminal, *stazione maríttima*)
strada road/street
tabacchino tobacconist's shop, often selling newspapers, stamps and bus tickets too
teatro theatre
tempio temple
torre tower
traghetto ferry
uscita exit
via road (always used with name; as Via Roma)
zona zone

ART, ARCHITECTURE AND ARCHEOLOGY

apse domed recess at the altar end of a church
architrave the lowest part of the entablature
atrium forecourt, usually of a Roman house
campanile belltower
capital top of a column
Catalan-Gothic hybrid form of architecture, mixing elements from fifteenth-century Spanish and Northern European building styles
cavea the seating section in a theatre
cella sanctuary of a temple
cupola dome
decumanus the main street in a Roman town
entablature the part of the building above the capital on a classical building
ex-voto decorated tablet or other small item designed as thanksgiving to a saint or deity
hypogeum underground vault, often used as an early Christian church
loggia roofed gallery or balcony

menhir standing stone, often tapering towards the top, and sometimes showing rudimentary human characteristics (a "statue-menhir")
nave central space in a church, usually flanked by aisles
polyptych painting or carving on several joined wooden panels
portico the covered entrance to a building
Punic Carthaginian/Phoenician
putti cherubs (singular *putto*), as portrayed in paintings and sculpture
retablo painted wood panel, usually in a church
stele (plural *stelae*) inscribed stone slab
thermae baths, usually elaborate buildings in Roman villas
tholos a dome- or beehive-shaped structure, usually associated with the Greek Mycenaean period
triptych painting or carving on three joined wooden panels

ACRONYMS

ACI Italian Automobile Club
CAI Club Alpino Italiano (Italian climbing club)
FS Italian state railways, now also called Trenitalia
IVA Imposta Valore Aggiunto (VAT)
PD Partito Democrático

PSd'Az Partito Sardo d'Azione (Sardinian Action Party)
RAI the Italian state TV and radio network
SP Strada Provinciale (a minor road, eg SP70)
SS Strada Statale (a main highway, eg SS195)

Small print and index

Rough Guide credits

Editor: Lucy Cowie
Layout: Ankur Guha
Cartography: Deshpal Dabas
Picture editor: Michelle Bhatia
Proofreader: Samantha Cook
Managing editor: Monica Woods
Assistant editor: Divya Grace Mathew

Production: Jimmy Lao
Cover photo research: Michelle Bhatia, Nicole Newman
Editorial assistant: Freya Godfrey
Senior DTP coordinator: Dan May
Programme manager: Gareth Lowe
Publisher: Keith Drew
Publishing director: Georgina Dee

Publishing information

This sixth edition published June 2016 by
Rough Guides Ltd,
80 Strand, London WC2R 0RL
11, Community Centre, Panchsheel Park,
New Delhi 110017, India
Distributed by Penguin Random House
Penguin Books Ltd, 80 Strand, London WC2R 0RL
Penguin Group (USA), 345 Hudson Street, NY 10014, USA
Penguin Group (Australia), 250 Camberwell Road,
Camberwell, Victoria 3124, Australia
Penguin Group (NZ), 67 Apollo Drive, Mairangi Bay,
Auckland 1310, New Zealand
Penguin Group (South Africa), Block D, Rosebank Office
Park, 181 Jan Smuts Avenue, Parktown North, Gauteng,
South Africa 2193
Rough Guides is represented in Canada by DK Canada, 320
Front Street West, Suite 1400, Toronto, Ontario M5V 3B6
Printed in Singapore
© Robert Andrews, 2016
Maps © Rough Guides

344pp includes index
A catalogue record for this book is available from the
British Library
ISBN: 978-0-24123-867-7
The publishers and authors have done their best to ensure
the accuracy and currency of all the information in **The
Rough Guide to Sardinia**, however, they can accept
no responsibility for any loss, injury, or inconvenience
sustained by any traveller as a result of information or
advice contained in the guide.
1 3 5 7 9 8 6 4 2

MIX
Paper from
responsible sources
FSC www.fsc.org FSC™ C018179

Help us update

We've gone to a lot of effort to ensure that the sixth
edition of **The Rough Guide to Sardinia** is accurate
and up-to-date. However, things change – places get
"discovered", opening hours are notoriously fickle,
restaurants and rooms raise prices or lower standards. If
you feel we've got it wrong or left something out, we'd like
to know, and if you can remember the address, the price,
the hours, the phone number, so much the better.

Please send your comments with the subject line
"**Rough Guide Sardinia Update**" to mail@uk.roughguides
.com. We'll credit all contributions and send a copy of the
next edition (or any other Rough Guide if you prefer) for
the very best emails.

Find more travel information, connect with fellow
travellers and plan your trip on Ⓦ roughguides.com.

ABOUT THE AUTHOR

Robert Andrews has been visiting and working in Sardinia for twenty years, writing on the island for various publications and escorting individuals and groups on activity breaks and culture tours. He has also written on Sicily, Calabria and Basilicata, as well as his home city of Bristol and England's West Country.

Acknowledgements

Mille grazie to Lucy Cowie for her perceptive and scrupulous editing, to Monica Woods for expertly steering the project through the straits, and to Michelle Bhatia for picking the right pics. Huge thanks are also due to Mario Zizi of Casa Solotti (Nuoro) for his constant kindness, to Luigi, Miranda and Luca Palmas of *AeR Bundes Jack* (Cagliari) for friendly welcomes, to the helpful and efficient staff at the tourist offices of Cagliari, Nuoro, Cala Gonone, Olbia and Alghero, to the extensive and extremely useful advice of Nicola Baccetti, and to QBC for staunch support and inspirations.

Readers' updates

Thanks to all the readers who have taken the time to write in with comments and suggestions (and apologies if we've inadvertently omitted or misspelt anyone's name):

Nicola Baccetti, Dick Capel Davies, Joe Chapman, Davina Hagan, Nick Hooper, Peter Howlett, Kate Ostrowska

Photo credits

Index

Maps are marked in grey

F

U

V

W

Y

Z

Map symbols

The symbols below are used on maps throughout the book

▬ ▪ ▪	International boundary	▬▬	Wall	♟	Castle	⤴	Bridge
▬ ▪ ▪	Provincial boundary	✈	Airport	⛲	Campsite	▲	Mountain peak
▬ ▬ ▬	Chapter division boundary	★	Bus stop	Ⅲ	Archeological site	⌃⌄	Mountain range
▨▨▨	Superstradas	@	Internet café/access	▟	Tower	♦	Church (regional map)
═══	Pedestrianized road	ⓘ	Information office	♜	Fortress	⛪	Church (town map)
───	Road	P	Parking	🏛	Monument	▨	Building
▥▥▥	Steps	✚	Hospital	♇	Museum	▢	Park
- - - -	Path	✉	Post office	∿	Spring/spa	▢	Beach
▬▬	Railway	♦	Point of interest	◠	Cave	⊞	Cemetery
─ ─	Ferry route	∴	Ruin	⊠	Gate		

Listings key

■ Accommodation

● Restaurant

■ Bar/café/venue

● Shop